"This text provides helpful context for the roles that all professionals play on a project, and its strength is that it engages with a global audience in its use of case studies and other examples."

- **Jaclyn Masters**, *Principal Lawyer Level Crossing Removal Project, Victoria*

"The book achieves the aim of assisting engineers to understand better the role of contracts in their work and their necessary interaction with lawyers and by developing a greater awareness among lawyers of engineers' roles in the successful execution of construction projects."

- **John Sharkey AM**, *Commercial Arbitrator*

"This book is that rare thing in an engineer's or construction lawyer's bookshelf. While it is undoubtedly a useful legal reference in any dispute, the perspective and material it contains are also both interesting and enjoyable to read."

- **Toby Shnookal QC**, *Arbitrator, Expert Determiner, Mediator, Facilitator, Adjudicator, Expert Determination Chambers*

"This is a book that is not only informative but is also well sourced, comprehensive and consistently easy to read. The case studies are particularly interesting and provide a useful insight into the rights and wrongs on engineering and construction contracts."

- **Steven Goldstein**, *Barrister, Arbitrator, Expert Determiner, Mediator, Dispute Board Member*

CONTRACTS FOR CONSTRUCTION AND ENGINEERING PROJECTS

Contracts for Construction and Engineering Projects provides unique and invaluable guidance on the role of contracts in construction and engineering projects. The work explores various aspects of the intersection of contracts and construction projects involving the work of engineers and other professionals engaged in construction, whether as project managers, designers, constructors, contract administrators, schedulers, claims consultants, forensic engineers or expert witnesses.

Compiling papers written and edited by the author, refined and expanded with additional chapters in this new edition, this book draws together a lifetime of lessons learned in these fields and covers the topics a practising professional might encounter in construction and engineering projects, developed in bite-sized chunks.

The chapters are divided into five key parts:

1. The engineer and the contract
2. The project and the contract
3. Avoidance and resolution of disputes
4. Forensic engineers and expert witnesses, and
5. International construction contracts.

The inclusion of numerous case studies to illustrate the importance of getting the contract right before it is entered into – and the consequences that may ensue if this is not done – makes this book essential reading for professionals practising in any area of design, construction, contract administration, preparation of claims or expert evidence, as well as construction lawyers who interact with construction professionals.

Donald Charrett practises in construction law as an arbitrator, mediator, dispute board member and expert. Prior to becoming a lawyer, he worked as a consulting engineer for over 30 years. He has published widely on legal and engineering subjects, including as the author/joint author/editor of six books on construction law.

PRACTICAL LEGAL GUIDES FOR CONSTRUCTION AND TECHNOLOGY PROJECTS

Series Editor: Donald Charrett

The books in this series provide lawyers and construction professionals with the relevant knowledge, resources and practical guidance to understand the contemporary construction industry and the law necessary to achieve successful outcomes for construction projects. The topics covered include front-end issues such as project procurement, the production, negotiation and administration of contracts, and the avoidance of disputes, as well as backend issues such as taking part in, managing or resolving disputes. The series aims to keep abreast of the technologies that have increasing impact in changing traditional ways of working, contracting and resolving disputes.

FIDIC Contracts in Asia Pacific
A Practical Guide to Application
Donald Charrett

Contracts for Construction and Engineering Projects
Second Edition
Donald Charrett

For more information, please visit: www.routledge.com/Practical-Legal-Guides-for-Construction-and-Technology-Projects/book-series/PLGCTP

CONTRACTS FOR CONSTRUCTION AND ENGINEERING PROJECTS

DONALD CHARRETT

SECOND EDITION

informa law
from Routledge

Cover image: © Donald Charrett

Second edition published 2022
by Informa Law from Routledge
2 Park Square, Milton Park, Abingdon, Oxon, OX14 4RN

and by Informa Law from Routledge
605 Third Avenue, New York, NY 10158

Informa Law from Routledge is an imprint of the Taylor & Francis Group, an informa business

First edition published by Informa Law from Routledge 2019

British Library Cataloguing-in-Publication Data
A catalogue record for this book is available from the British Library

Library of Congress Cataloging-in-Publication Data
Names: Charrett, D. E. (Donald Eric), author.
Title: Contracts for construction and engineering projects / Donald Charrett.
Description: Second edition. | Abingdon, Oxon [UK]; New York, NY: Routledge, 2022. |
Series: Practical legal guides for construction and technology projects |
Includes bibliographical references and index.
Identifiers: LCCN 2021030899 (print) | LCCN 2021030900 (ebook) |
ISBN 9781032073835 (hardback) | ISBN 9781032074344 (paperback) |
ISBN 9781003206897 (ebook)
Subjects: LCSH: Construction contracts. | Engineering contracts. |
Construction industry–Law and legislation. | Dispute resolution (Law)
Classification: LCC K891.B8 C43 2022 (print) | LCC K891.B8 (ebook) |
DDC 343.07/8624–dc23
LC record available at https://lccn.loc.gov/2021030899
LC ebook record available at https://lccn.loc.gov/2021030900

ISBN: 978-1-032-07383-5 (hbk)
ISBN: 978-1-032-07434-4 (pbk)
ISBN: 978-1-003-20689-7 (ebk)

DOI: 10.4324/9781003206897

Typeset in Times New Roman
by Deanta Global Publishing Services, Chennai, India

This book is dedicated with grateful thanks to my wife, Jeyami, without whose continued understanding of and tolerance for the time-consuming demands entailed by my writing activities, this book would not have been possible.

CONTENTS

ILLUSTRATIONS

TABLES

ACKNOWLEDGEMENTS

DONALD CHARRETT

I would like to thank the many colleagues who have contributed to this book, and to those who have inspired me in my writing endeavours. The kind reviews of the first edition encouraged me to add six chapters of new material for this second edition. I am grateful to those reviewers whose quotes appear below.

To Dan Washington, the late Professor Andrew Potts, and Philip Loots who co-authored the papers in Chapters 6, 10, 13 and 31, thank you for your contributions and the additional perspectives you added.

Thank you to Sir Rupert Jackson who wrote the Foreword to this second edition, and to Justice John Digby of the Supreme Court of Victoria for writing the Foreword to the first edition.

Over the past ten years or so I have attended a number of international conferences on contracts, construction law, Dispute Boards and arbitration in a number of countries, and I have gained immeasurably from the discussions with many friends and colleagues. They are far too numerous to mention, but I would like to acknowledge their contribution to the international perspective I have gained, that hopefully, is reflected in this book.

Many friends and colleagues, too numerous to mention, have made positive suggestions and have had a significant influence on my writings. I would particularly like to acknowledge the input from Wayne Jocic of Melbourne University, whose constructive suggestions have added further value to this second edition. To those I have not named, thank you for your ideas, your input and your feedback.

Publication of this book would not have been possible without the professional expertise and hard work of Routledge staff. Guy Loft and Julia Pollacco have been very supportive and ably project managed the production of the second edition. I would also like to thank Elizabeth Fitzgerald for the demanding job of copy editing over thirty papers written for different audiences and different journals into a cohesive whole. However, any shortcomings in the book are my sole responsibility.

April 2021
Melbourne, Australia

FOREWORD TO THE SECOND EDITION

SIR RUPERT JACKSON

This second edition of Dr Donald Charrett's book, under the new title *Contracts for Engineering and Construction Projects*, is most welcome. In addition to updating the existing chapters, Dr Charrett has added six new chapters on insurance for construction projects, the "story" of Sydney Opera House, *Lex Constructionis*, the new (2017) FIDIC conditions, construction disputes after COVID-19 and the impact of COVID 19 on construction contracts.

Having visited Sydney Opera House and enjoyed a wonderful Mahler concert there, I went straight to that chapter first. It is a gripping read. Jørn Utzon developed the design concept in the 1950s. In 1958, preliminary construction work started and Ove Arup came on board. Design work for the shells and other unique features would have taken approximately 100 million hours if done manually, but sadly that amount of time was not available in the human lifespan. So, Arup had to access the most powerful computers then available and write their own software-programs. Owing to a fees dispute, Utzon dropped out in 1966. The replacement architect, Peter Hall, re-designed the interior of the building. The result of massive endeavours by builders, designers and many others was a world-famous opera house, opened by the Queen in 1973. It must be admitted that there was a hefty cost overrun. The original estimate was Aus$7 million. The final cost was Aus$100 million.

The chapter entitled '*Lex Constructionis* – or my country's rules?' is also of particular interest. It is based on Dr Charrett's Zoom lecture on this topic (which I attended remotely) in September 2020. The theme of this chapter is that universal principles of construction law are emerging. They should be developed and applied as *lex constructionis*, a similar concept to the long-recognised *lex mercatoria*. The observations in this chapter are pertinent and accord entirely with my own experiences from conducting international construction arbitrations.

The chapter on the new FIDIC conditions concentrates on the provisions concerning DABs and DAABs. These are now a significant feature of the construction landscape. The two COVID-related chapters are of immediate relevance and will, no doubt, be much cited. The insurance chapter is important because, as the author observes, insurance arrangements can have the effect of provoking or complicating disputes. I recall grappling with some of those problems 24 years ago in *Hopewell Project Management Ltd v Ewbank Preece Ltd* [1998] I Lloyd's Rep 448 – but without the assistance of Dr Charrett's excellent book. The author makes some interesting and innovative proposals for reducing the scope for disputes. He rightly commends the Heathrow Terminal 5 approach of taking out project-wide insurance covering the whole supply chain.

I warmly commend this book for three reasons. First, it contains much helpful legal information. Second, it contains much original thinking and stimulating ideas – for example, the suggested 20 principles of *lex constructionis*. Third, the book is highly readable – the best example being the Sydney Opera House chapter. But even that chapter contains some wisdom. The author points out that the saga of the cost overrun "provides a salutary lesson on the consequences of 'fast track' construction, that is, commencing construction before the design is finalised". No doubt readers can recall other projects where the same thing has happened, but perhaps not to quite such a dramatic extent or involving such a colourful story.

This book will be widely read and is destined to go into a third edition. I wish it every success.

9 April 2021
4 New Square, Lincoln's Inn

FOREWORD TO THE FIRST EDITION

JUSTICE G JOHN DIGBY

Dr Donald Charrett's substantial, and partly collaborative work, *The Application of Contracts in Engineering and Construction Projects* will in due course, I predict, form part of the reference library of most project managers and contract administrators, professional advisers to construction and engineering clients and academics interested in that discipline.

This most informative and comprehensive book amply reflects that the author has been able to draw on both his past experience as a practising consultant design engineer, and Director of a consulting engineering practice, and also upon his extensive experience as a barrister and arbitrator practising in the engineering and construction field.

It is notable that this work traverses most of the key areas of interest to construction and engineering lawyers, engineers and contract administrators, and many others, in an especially helpful fashion in that the chapters of this text which address those areas, deal not only with the legal framework within which they are to be considered, but also outline, often step by step, how ubiquitous issues may be managed via contractual mechanisms.

Dr Charrett's text also treats a number of interesting topics which are not usually discussed, such as "the evolution of the role of the engineer", "managing design risk" and "the engagement of Forensic Engineers" and "getting the most out of expert witnesses".

As well as shedding light on various aspects of the intersection of construction and engineering contracts and the legal framework within which the engineers and lawyers advising their clients in this area must work, Dr Charrett's work, although expressly not intended to be a legal textbook as such, addresses key legal concepts and principles and on many occasions unpacks leading cases in areas of ongoing interest in the construction and engineering project design and delivery context , such as delay/time, costs , design and build quality and intellectual property. The work is also richly cross-referenced to relevant articles, cases, decisions, papers and other helpful reference materials.

A most attractive and valuable point of distinction of Dr Charrett's work, *The Application of Contracts to Engineering and Construction Projects*, is the author's systematic and successful elucidation of the core concepts, legal questions, and activities and steps which often need to be addressed by designers and project engineers, contract supervisors, administrators and project managers, and also by their legal advisers.

The usual consultants and advisers to construction and engineering clients will be very thankful to Dr Donald Charrett for the extensive and valuable work that he, and on some chapters those who have collaborated with him in producing parts of this fine text, has done to provide them with a practical compendium volume dealing with the areas referred.

In summary, this work is a fine example of a well-balanced practical aid and learned reference in relation to the legal, engineering and practical considerations associated with a number of the most important and common issues encountered by those dealing with the design and delivery of construction and engineering projects and the professional advisers to them.

This is a most commendable work.

February 2018
Judges' Chambers
Supreme Court
Melbourne, Australia

ABOUT THE AUTHOR

DR DONALD CHARRETT

Dr Donald Charrett BE (Hons), LLB (Hons), M Const Law, PhD, Prof Cert Arb, Dip International Arbitration, FIE Aust, FCI Arb

Dr Charrett is a barrister, arbitrator, mediator, expert and dispute board member practising in technology, engineering and construction (TEC) disputes. Prior to joining the Victorian Bar, he worked as a solicitor at a large Australian law firm. His construction law briefs have included litigation, mediation, expert determination, facilitation of experts' conferences, arbitration and membership of dispute boards. He is a member of the FIDIC President's List of Adjudicators and a Fellow of the Chartered Institute of Arbitrators. He was named as Best Construction Law Practitioner, Australia 2016 by *Business Worldwide Magazine*. In 2019 and 2020, Who's Who Legal included him on their list of Thought Leaders – Construction, saying "Donald Charrett is looked on with enormous favour by sources for his vast experience in construction and engineering disputes".

Prior to becoming a lawyer, he worked as an engineer for over 30 years, including 12 years as a director of a consulting engineering firm. Dr Charrett's engineering experience included computer applications, structural design, managing engineering projects, acting as an expert witness, and management roles in contract negotiation and administration, insurance, international joint ventures and corporate restructuring. From 2012 to 2014, he was non-executive chairman of consulting engineering company AMOG.

Dr Charrett has published widely on legal and engineering subjects, and presented conference papers, workshops and training courses in Australia and internationally. He is a Senior Fellow at the University of Melbourne, teaching a Master of Construction Law subject on international construction law.

His legal publications include articles on expert evidence, FIDIC contracts, dispute boards, dispute avoidance and resolution, contract risk, forensic engineering, contractual lessons from past projects, design and construct contracts, *quantum meruit*, solidary liability, construction insurance, professional indemnity insurance and reinsurance. He is the author of *The Application of Contracts in Engineering and Construction Contracts* (2018), joint author of *The Application of Contracts in Developing Oil and Gas Projects* (2019) and the editor of *FIDIC Contracts in Asia Pacific: A Practical Guide to Application* (2021), *The International Application of FIDIC Contracts: A Practical Guide* (2020), and *Global Challenges Shared Solutions* (2013).

Dr Charrett is the editor of the Routledge series *Practical Legal Guides for Construction and Technology Projects.*

CONTRIBUTORS

Philip Loots has practised internationally exclusively as a construction lawyer for more than 50 years. He is a recognised authority on construction law, having practised as a partner in a large law firm, acted as general counsel for construction companies and employers and as a statutory adjudicator. Philip has considerable practical experience in developing and delivering megaprojects, including infrastructure, marine construction and dredging.

The late Professor **Andrew Potts** was the founder and Chief Executive Officer of the AMOG Group of Companies. Professor Potts had extensive experience in the offshore energy sector, in particular the analysis and design of fixed and floating structures. Throughout his career, Professor Potts was engaged in the provision of expert advice for numerous legal cases.

Dan Washington is an engineer and currently an Executive Director of the AMOG Group of Companies. Dan has worked in a range of commercial, technical and executive roles within the AMOG Group. Dan's experience covers a range of industry sectors, including defence and offshore energy.

TABLE OF CASES

TABLE OF LEGISLATION

CHAPTER 1

Overview

1.1 Introduction

The theme of this book is that contracts are at the heart of the work of engineers and other construction professionals and should guide and inform their work on engineering and construction projects. The contents explore various aspects of the intersection of contracts and construction law with the work of engineers and other professionals involved in construction, whether as project managers, designers, constructors, contract administrators, schedulers, claims consultants, forensic engineers or expert witnesses. It is aimed at professionals practising in any area of design, construction, contract administration, preparation of claims or expert evidence, as well as construction lawyers who interact with construction professionals in drawing up contracts or resolving disputes. It includes discussion and case studies on issues relevant to construction contracts globally, with particular relevance to common law jurisdictions.

Contracts are the bedrock of commercial relationships around the world. They are fundamental to the implementation of any engineering or construction project and are important for many reasons. First, a contract defines the legal relationships that apply to the commercial interactions that occur whenever a professional carries out work on a project. Second, a contract defines the rights and obligations that are created when parties enter into a contract. Third, a contract provides the legal avenue for enforcing each party's rights and obligations. Fourth, each party to a contract accepts risks, explicitly or implicitly, by entering into the contract, and the risk "allocation" in a contract can mean the difference between a successful and an unsuccessful project. Fifth, a comprehensive construction contract is also a contract management manual, by clearly defining the scope of work, each parties' rights and obligations, and the notification and approval processes required for appropriately managing those rights and obligations. Sixth, a thoughtfully written contract will promote important socially desirable objects, such as protection of the environment, avoidance of corruption, elimination of worker exploitation and advancing health and safety. Seventh, a well-written contract will specify clear, structured procedures for dealing with risks when they materialise, in a way that minimises the likelihood of disputes. Finally, if disputes do occur, a well-written construction contract provides for their resolution in the timeliest and most cost-effective manner.

This book is not intended to be a legal textbook for professionals administering engineering and construction contracts. For that, the reader is referred to *Contracts for Infrastructure Projects: An International Guide* by Loots and Charrett. This book does, however, seek to explain and illustrate the myriad ways in which contracts are at the heart

 DOI: 10.4324/9781003206897-1

of the work of engineers and other construction professionals, no matter what aspect of design, construction or dispute resolution they are involved in. It uses many case studies to illustrate the importance of getting the contract right before it is entered into, and the consequences that may ensue if that is not done, or if the work is not executed in accordance with the requirements of the contract.

A recurring theme in this book is that every engineering or construction project involves an interaction between time, cost and quality. A successful project is one that fulfils its stakeholders' expectations, and, inter alia, requires all three elements to be achieved to the satisfaction of the contracting parties. The relevant contracts play a central part in this, by defining what is expected of all parties. Ultimately, project success will only be fully realised if contract success is achieved by the fulfilment of the parties' expectations in respect of time, cost and quality. Fulfilment of the necessary "technical" quality in the sense of the required functional performance of a facility is not sufficient to guarantee a successful project. Performance within the required time and within cost expectations is also necessary for successful contract and project performance.

The book comprises edited versions of papers written by the author (or, in the case of four of the papers, co-written with others), that have been published in various engineering and construction law journals. The kind permission of my co-authors and the publishers of those journals to reproduce the papers in this book is gratefully acknowledged. These papers were written at different times and for different audiences, and there is therefore some unavoidable repetition. However, this also means that each chapter is self-contained in relation to its theme.

Although written on a variety of topics, the common theme of the papers in this book is the significance and importance of the contract in relation to the work of the engineer and other construction professionals. My interest in this subject originally derived from my work as a consulting engineer and a director of a medium-sized Australian consulting engineering practice engaged in design of major infrastructure, and facilities for the mining and offshore oil and gas industries. In later years, my role included many commercial aspects involving contracts, such as contract review, professional indemnity insurance, international joint ventures, company restructuring and involvement with major legal disputes. That interest in contracts was subsequently given a sound academic basis when I left the engineering profession to obtain a Bachelor of Laws and a Master of Construction Law at Melbourne University. As a barrister and solicitor admitted to the Supreme Court of Victoria, I practised as a solicitor at a major Australian law firm for a few years and, since 2004, I have been a barrister at the Victorian Bar, practising in construction law as counsel, arbitrator, mediator, Supreme Court referee and Dispute Board member. My perspective as a lawyer involved in construction disputes has inevitably been influenced by my years as a consulting engineer, and the experience gained from being a participant, and not just an observer, of the operation of construction contracts.

Terms with a specific meaning are in bold where they are first used or defined; many are capitalised. These terms are listed and defined in the Glossary at the end of the book. Notwithstanding the disparate sources of the chapters, usage of defined terms is generally consistent throughout the book, although some of the defined terms are specific to one chapter.

In this book, the **Contract** means the construction contract being referred to. The **parties** to it are the **Employer** (the party for whom the work is done), and the **Contractor** (the party who carries out the work). A **construction contract** is any contract where one person (including a corporation) agrees for valuable consideration to carry out construction of a physical structure (including building or engineering works) for another. A third-party **Engineer** frequently administers a construction contract. The **works** refers to the work, materials and plant which the Contractor is or may be required to carry out and complete or provide under the Contract, and includes variations, rectification of defects, temporary works and equipment. A **design contract** is a contract for the preparation of a design to be constructed under a construction contract.

The book is in five parts:

- Part 1: The engineer and the contract
- Part 2: The project and the contract
- Part 3: Avoidance and resolution of disputes
- Part 4: Forensic engineers and expert witnesses
- Part 5: International construction contracts.

1.2 Part 1: The engineer and the contract

This part explores a number of the ways in which an engineer has a role in the execution of a contract. That role takes many different forms: in the execution and management of the works under a construction contract; in striking the appropriate balance between the competing demands of time, cost and quality; in managing contractual risks; and, at the heart of an engineer's design role, in the design contracts that s/he enters into. On a particular project, e.g. a building project, the "engineer" may in fact be an architect or other construction professional.

Chapter 2 discusses the various roles of an engineer in the promotion, execution and management of the works, and in the administration of a construction contract as the Engineer (in this book the term "engineer" has its ordinary meaning as a person who undertakes any engineering function, whereas the term "Engineer" is used for the person who administers a construction contract). The Engineer's role as administrator and supervisor of the Contract has evolved over the years from a position essentially independent of both parties, to one that is now generally the agent of the Employer. However, even in contracts in which the Engineer is the Employer's agent in all matters, s/he nevertheless has to act fairly in the execution of certain certifying functions. The changed role of the Engineer is reflected in the separation of the various roles of the engineer, widespread use of design and construct and EPC contracts, the development of new forms of contracts such as alliances, and new forms of dispute resolution and avoidance such as Dispute Boards.

Chapter 3 is a discussion of the three elements that form part of every construction project, every construction contract and every design contract: time, cost and quality. There is an inherent tension in satisfying expectations of all three elements in equal measure. The history of many major projects shows that management of project costs within expectations can be difficult, as can the delivery of a project on time to the required quality. Failure, as a difference between expected and observed performance, applies to any of the elements of time, cost or quality, and may lead to a dispute. The importance of aligning expectations with what the Contract requires is discussed as an important aspect of dispute avoidance.

Chapter 4 considers the objectives and expectations of the parties in construction contracts, and how these relate to successful and unsuccessful contracts. Risk, in the sense of a chance of not achieving the contractual objectives, is central to the terms and operation of a contract. The scope of a contract involves not only a definition of the extent of the obligations of each contractual party, but also considerations of time, cost and quality of contractual performance. Each of these characteristics entails risks that the contractual objectives will not be achieved. However, it is suggested that risk of non-performance can be reduced by clear definition of scope, on the assumption that the clearer the objective definition of the contractual scope, the closer the parties' subjective expectations will be aligned with the contractual objectives. The extent to which a contract recognises and "allocates" risks, and the parties' understanding of and management of risks may be a major factor in whether the Contract ultimately results in a dispute. The Abrahamson Principles are widely known as the basis of "fair" risk allocation. The central theme of this chapter is that contracts have a central role to play in risk minimisation by:

- Selection of the appropriate form and terms of the contract
- "Allocation" of risks to the contractual party best able to control them, and
- Promoting the cooperative management of risks by the formal execution and reporting requirements of the Contract.

A different aspect of risk is considered in Chapter 5 – design risk. This chapter looks at the nature of design and its influence on a constructed facility. As an intellectual exercise, design "deliverables" are intellectual property. Identified design risks discussed are scope, time, cost, design quality, intellectual property, interfaces and designer's insolvency, as well as client risks identified by the International Federation of Consulting Engineers (**FIDIC**). Who should bear these risks and management of risks by the Employer and the designer are discussed.

Contracts for design services are discussed in Chapter 6, jointly authored by Dan Washington. Procurement of design is considered, taking into account the allocation of risk. Contract terms addressing risk transference are reviewed and illustrated by examples of risk transfer in design contracts that, in the authors' view, are inappropriate. The chapter emphasises that design contracts involve activities that are conceptually different to construction and require different types of contracts.

Chapter 7 considers several engineering concepts that are important for understanding the art and science of engineering, and the contractual obligations of designers and design and construct contractors. The application of design Standards, and the concepts of reliability, limit state design and robustness are important aspects of structural design. The chapter explains the difference between design life and service life, an issue that may be important in the context of design and construct contracts. The "default" legal obligation to prepare a design with due skill and care is contrasted with the common contractual obligation for a constructed facility to be fit for purpose. These issues are illustrated by reference to recent case law.

Chapter 8 continues the theme of the tension between a design prepared with due skill, care and diligence, and a design that is fit for purpose. This issue was at the heart of the UK case of *MT Højgaard v E.ON Climate and Renewables UK Robin Rigg East Ltd.* This important case commenced in the Technology and Construction Court, was overturned in the Court of Appeal, and the first instance judgment was restored by the Supreme Court. The differences of opinion on the meaning of the terms of the contract for the design and construction of a wind farm off the coast of Scotland by nine senior and experienced judges, highlights many of the difficulties faced by engineers and other professionals who are daily involved in understanding and administering contracts. Construction contracts for major facilities are voluminous, complex, many-authored and sometimes opaque. Experienced personnel can reasonably differ on the meaning of a construction contract, even learned judges!

Design and construct contracts are considered in Chapter 9. Such contracts differ from construct-only contracts that were more commonly used in the past, in that the designer is engaged by the Contractor, not the Employer. This chapter addresses one of the issues peculiar to design and construct contracts – which party bears the risk that the final as-constructed cost exceeds the estimated cost of the preliminary design on which the successful tender was based. This requires scrutiny of the contractual relationships between the Contractor and its designer, and the different ways in which these are implemented. The principles involved in such final design cost risk are illustrated by reference to the limited case law that has dealt with this issue.

Engineers typically design facilities by reference to published Standards, which are generally considered to represent the "state of the art" of the competent and skilful practitioner. Chapter 10, co-authored by the late Prof Andrew Potts, addresses the question as to whether engineers can rely on such Standards to discharge their duty of exercising due skill, care and diligence in design. The process of writing Australian Standards is reviewed, noting the broad spectrum of stakeholder interests involved to incorporate the current "state-of-the-art" – the art and science that would be applied by competent and experienced practitioners involved in the relevant practice of engineering, not necessarily the science of engineering as known to academics researching at the cutting edge of known technology. The statutory and contractual significance of Standards are discussed, as well as the designer's duty of care under the common law and statute. The engineer's obligation to comply with a Standard is considered, and whether that is sufficient to discharge his or her duty. A case study is presented in which an engineer was found liable in negligence, notwithstanding that its design complied with the current Standard.

1.3 Part 2: The project and the contract

Part 2 is focussed on the application of construction contracts and their importance to the successful execution of construction projects. Such contracts may be in a standard form intended to be used for a wide variety of projects and locations, which may be heavily amended to alter the "balanced" risk allocation. Problems arising from inappropriate contractual conditions are highlighted by a number of case studies of the issues arising in unsuccessful projects and failures.

Chapter 11 discusses standard form contracts, and contrasts these with "bespoke" contracts – unique contracts written for a specific "one-off" project. The many advantages of using a standard form contract over a bespoke contract are outlined, including predictability, economics and reduced disputes. The use of standard form contracts by oil companies for projects in the UK Continental Shelf is a notable case study that attests to their commercial advantages.

The impact of the COVID-19 pandemic in 2020 on construction contracts is considered in Chapter 12. Construction projects were significantly delayed, postponed or terminated as a result of COVID-19; those that continued were subject to increased costs as a result of the health measures required to keep workers safe. The chapter discusses the measures that governments took to ameliorate the impacts of COVID-19 on the execution of construction projects and the operation of construction contracts. The rights arising under common law and civil law for the time and cost impacts are discussed. Examples of general legislation providing relief for hardship or *force majeure* are given, as well as specific legislation providing contractual relief. The types of claims arising under FIDIC contracts are reviewed. Examples are provided of measures passed by governments to provide economic relief to assist Contractors.

Megaprojects, those with a cost in excess of $1b, are considered in Chapter 13, co-authored by Philip Loots. Notwithstanding the obvious commercial importance of such projects, their widespread application and the resources applied to them, their track record of success is significantly worse than projects of smaller value. International and Australian literature that has surveyed the outcomes of megaprojects and the factors, contractual and otherwise, found to be significant to their lack of success is reviewed, and supplemented with the authors' own observations.

Chapter 14 considers the procurement, design and construction of the Sydney Opera House from a construction law perspective. The procurement was the result of the winning entry in a world-wide architectural competition. The original concept design of a thin concrete shell was not feasible and after years of design work using thousands of hours of computer time, the final design incorporated a complex space frame of massive prestressed concrete ribs. The originally constructed podium required substantial additional piling for the increased weights. The contract for construction of the concrete superstructure was a "cost plus" contract. Design and construction involved many cutting-edge innovations. Due to differences of opinion between the architect and the government, the architect resigned before the final stage of design was completed. The interior and glass walls were designed by a different architect. The government ultimately commissioned the original architect to formulate the "Utzon Design Principles", which were the basis for a substantial refurbishment, and will be the basis of future conservation of this World Heritage-listed building. The chapter is illustrated with photographs of the construction and the completed building.

Chapter 15 is a case study of the procurement of two high-profile public buildings – the Australian Parliament House, opened in 1988, and the Scottish Parliament House, opened in 2004. These two buildings had many features in common, including their procurement under a construction management form of contract. The chapter identifies some of the time, cost and quality issues discussed in the previous chapters that were relevant to the outcome – final cost substantially above the initial budget and, in the case of Scottish Parliament House, delivery of the completed building years late.

The procurement of two high-profile Australian bridges under design-construct contracts is discussed in Chapter 16. These bridges present a contrast: the procurement of Sydney Harbour Bridge by a design-construct contract was criticised at the time as inappropriate, but undoubtedly resulted in a project that was successful by any measure. By contrast, Kings Bridge in Melbourne collapsed less than a year after its opening to traffic. Whilst the collapse had "technical" causes, the Royal Commission into the collapse considered that the procurement by a design and construct contract was a contributing factor to the failure.

Chapter 17 looks in some detail at the judgment in a dispute over a design and construct contract for construction of a road in Tasmania. The case did not involve any new or unusual issues of law and did not involve any dispute over the quality of the final product. It is, however, of interest as a detailed discussion of how many detailed and voluminous documents constituting the contract interacted and created particular challenges for the Contractor. The extensive environmental documents incorporated in the contract, and the obligations they imposed on the Contractor, were not atypical for modern design and construct contracts. The discussion of the case highlights the issues involved in design and construct contractors determining the real contractual obligations from a complex set of contractual documents in the limited time available for preparation of a tender. The hearing time, 80 days in the Supreme Court, is a salutary reminder of the costs involved in formal dispute resolution.

The contractual lessons to be learned from the 2010 and 2011 Canterbury earthquakes in Christchurch New Zealand are considered in Chapters 18 and 19. A Royal Commission was appointed to inquire into the buildings that collapsed and caused fatalities. Its Terms of Reference included making recommendations on the adequacy of legal and best practice requirements for building design, construction and maintenance related to managing the risks of building failures caused by earthquakes. The Royal Commission report, in seven volumes, contains a wealth of information of interest to engineers and construction lawyers. Chapter 18 reviews the best practice processes adopted by the Royal Commission to gather and assess expert evidence. The chapter considers design standards and risk, and the issue of an engineer's duty to warn of known structural inadequacies in the light of legal and ethical constraints. Chapter 19 considers some different aspects of the Royal Commission Report, and explains certain technical matters that are relevant to an understanding of the construction law issues, such as safety assessments and the assessment of existing buildings to modern standards.

Chapter 20 is on the lessons to be learned from construction failures. The theme of this chapter is that the lessons to be learned from construction failures are not confined to the technical quality of the engineering and construction, but include the contractual, organisational and managerial aspects of project execution. Unlike most construction disputes which, at their heart, are about money and who pays how much to whom, most of the public inquiries considered here had the further dimension that the construction failure resulted in significant (and sometimes substantial) loss of life. This should be a salutary reminder to construction law practitioners that the engineer's "art of directing the great sources of power in nature for the use and convenience of man"[1] in every project carries

1 The objects of the Institution of Civil Engineers, as recited in the 1828 Royal Charter, were:

> The general advancement of mechanical science, and more particularly for promoting the acquisition of that species of knowledge which constitutes the profession of a civil engineer; being the art of directing the great sources of power in nature for the use and convenience of man, as the means of production and of traffic in states, both for external and internal trade, as applied in the construction of roads, bridges, aqueducts, canals, river navigation, and docks, for internal intercourse and exchange; and in the construction of ports, harbours, moles, breakwaters, and light-houses, and in the art of navigation by artificial power, for the purposes of commerce; and in the construction and adaptation of machinery, and in the drainage of cities and towns.

with it attendant execution risks which, if they materialise, can involve significant injury and loss of life.

Engineering failures of two well-known bridges are considered in Chapters 21 and 22. Historically, failures have played an important role in advancing engineering knowledge and providing lessons for the future. Many engineering failures have been followed by a public enquiry, such as a Royal Commission, with terms of reference intended to determine the causes of failure and how such failures can be avoided in the future. The reports of public inquiries have a number of advantages over case law on failures, even though they may not be as well-known after the passage of time. These chapters comprise case studies of the failures of two bridges during their construction, drawn from the reports of the resulting Royal Commissions. Although both failures occurred a considerable time ago, the author believes they contain timeless lessons for the successful management of contracts and project execution which are still relevant today.

Chapter 21 reviews the procurement of Quebec Bridge by a design and construct contract, over 100 years ago. This bridge collapsed during construction with tragic loss of life. The collapse had clear "technical" causes, but the Royal Commission report identified a number of contractual issues of time, cost and quality that were contributing factors in the collapse.

West Gate Bridge in Melbourne was procured in the 1960s in the "traditional" way by the Employer engaging consultants to prepare the design for construction by the construction Contractor. However, the bridge collapsed during construction, with substantial loss of life. The Royal Commission into the collapse identified the "technical" causes and highlighted those contractual matters which were contributing factors. Chapter 22 reviews the contractual issues highlighted by the Royal Commission, as well as by an English enquiry into the collapse of the Milford Haven Bridge. It is suggested that that some of these issues had been identified 60 years earlier in the Quebec Bridge Royal Commission report.

Insurance is a widely used risk management tool to transfer to a third party specific risks that a contracting party is liable for. In practice, insurance does not always result in payment following the occurrence of an insured event. Instead of preventing disputes as to who is liable for the financial consequences of a risk event, in many situations the insurance itself provokes or complicates disputes. Chapter 23 discusses why insurance is important for construction contracts. It reviews the current insurance landscape for design and construction risks in Victorian construction projects. A number of problems that arise from the conventional approach to insurance for construction projects are identified. Different approaches to project insurance used in a large project and a civil law jurisdiction are discussed. The benefits that could flow from adopting these different approaches to make insurance more fit for the purpose for which it is intended are outlined.

1.4 Part 3: Avoidance and resolution of disputes

Construction contracts have a high incidence of disputes around the world. Such disputes are frequently complex, time-consuming and expensive to run, and the magnitude of contract damages in some cases can result in the liquidation of major companies. Part 3 addresses disputes from two perspectives: avoidance of disputes if possible, and efficient resolution of disputes that have not been avoided. Several of the chapters in this section look at different aspects of Dispute Boards – a type of tribunal that can wear the two hats of dispute avoidance and dispute resolution.

Chapter 24 is on the avoidance of disputes by Contractors in design and construct contracts. It focuses on the obligations assumed under a contract in the context of the doctrine of freedom of contract and stresses the importance of getting the contract right before it is entered into. It is therefore essential to understand the legal effect of the proposed terms for a contract in order to prepare the tender, and to understand the risks and formulate the appropriate strategies for managing those risks during execution of the work. Some suggestions are made that may assist design and construct contractors to avoid contractual disputes resulting from issues arising before entering into the Contract, as well as during its execution.

Three "evaluative" methods of alternative dispute resolution (**ADR**) are discussed in Chapter 25: adjudication, expert determination and Dispute Boards. Each of these ADR methods seeks to provide the parties with a determination of their rights according to the contract and the law, prepared by an independent and impartial third party with relevant legal and technical skills, and based on the facts. The important role of Dispute Boards in dispute avoidance is also discussed.

Dispute Boards have been used for over 30 years in the United States and internationally on major projects and have proven to be very effective both in dispute avoidance, and where disputes are unavoidable, in reducing the cost and time of their resolution. The efficacy of a Dispute Board derives from its ability to assist the project parties to determine solutions to problems before they become disputes, often by suggesting "non-contractual" means of resolving issues. If it must assume a dispute resolution role, a Dispute Board can conduct a hearing and assess the evidence and submissions and provide a determination on the merits of a dispute in much less time and at lower cost than could be achieved by other alternatives such as arbitration. Some aspects of Dispute Boards are considered in Chapter 26. These include the contractual requirements of a contract clause, procedural rules and a tripartite agreement between the contracting parties and the Dispute Board members, as well as the costs of Dispute Boards. The history of Dispute Boards in Australia to 2016, and their benefits and reasons for success, are briefly reviewed.

The use of Dispute Boards under FIDIC contracts is discussed in Chapter 27, both standing and *ad hoc*. Whilst the 1999 First Editions of the Yellow and Silver Books only provided for an *ad hoc* Dispute Board, implemented after a dispute has arisen, the 2017 Second Editions provide for a standing Dispute Avoidance/Adjudication Board, in which the Board's dispute avoidance role is emphasised. The question of whether a Dispute Board decision is a pre-requisite to referring a dispute to arbitration is considered in the light of published court and arbitration cases. The controversial issue of a provisionally binding Dispute Board decision is considered by reviewing the long-running saga of the *PT Perusahaan Gas Negara (Persero) TBK (PGN) and CRW Joint Operation (CRW)* cases in the Singapore High Court and Court of Appeal.

Chapter 28 discusses the changes between the 1999 and 2017 FIDIC contracts relating to Dispute Boards. The essential differences between claims and disputes are clearly distinguished by separating them into two clauses. Other significant changes include more prescription in the 2017 editions, changes in terminology, use of standing Dispute Avoidance and Adjudication Boards for the Red, Yellow and Silver Books, more detailed Procedural Rules and Dispute Avoidance and Adjudication Agreement and a greater focus on dispute avoidance. The chapter concludes with suggestions for administration of claims and techniques for a DAAB to use in its dispute avoidance role.

Chapter 29 discusses the challenges of using different methods of dispute resolution for international construction disputes in the post COVID-19 environment. Protagonists have the choice of "jaw-jaw" methods involving discussion, negotiation and compromise (such as mediation) or "war-war" adversarial methods in which an independent Neutral will determine legal rights in a winner takes all process, typically arbitration.

Chapter 30 raises the question of whether there is a "best" method of resolution for construction disputes, or whether such a search is illusory. There is now a wide range of dispute resolution techniques, each of which has its protagonists who sell its benefits and virtues. It is suggested that other things being equal, the appropriate dispute resolution technique will generally be chosen to achieve the most appropriate proportionality of speed, economy and justice for the specific circumstances that the individual disputant judges to be efficacious. However, particular features required, such as confidentiality, the ability to choose an appropriate technically qualified Neutral, or the requirement for a legally binding precedent, may in fact determine the "best" method of dispute resolution. To the extent that disputing parties may have very different perspectives, the search for the "best" method for a particular dispute may be elusive. The fundamental thesis of this chapter is that there is no one "best" method of dispute resolution, either for a particular type of dispute, or from a particular protagonist's point of view. To that extent, the search for the "best" method is illusory.

1.5 Part 4: Forensic engineers and expert witnesses

Part 4 deals with the roles that engineers (and other construction professionals) fulfil in the determination of the causes of "failure" of constructed facilities, and in acting as an expert witness in judicial or quasi-judicial proceedings. A forensic engineer applies the art and science of engineering in the jurisprudence system. Forensic engineering may include investigation of the physical causes of accidents and other sources of claims and litigation, preparation of engineering reports and rendering advisory opinions to assist the resolution of disputes. A forensic engineer may act as an expert witness by giving evidence of his or her opinion in a dispute resolution process, based on specialised knowledge acquired from training, study or experience.

Chapter 31, co-authored by the late Prof Andrew Potts, relates to the engagement of forensic engineers: what corporate counsel (and forensic engineers) need to know about engaging forensic engineers. This chapter provides guidance for corporate (and other) counsel who must engage the services of a forensic engineer. Faced with such a need for the first time, counsel may be bewildered by the range of expertise available and may not be clear on the most suitable procedures for finding and engaging the most appropriate forensic engineer for the task in hand. The chapter suggests procedures for finding, engaging and managing a forensic engineer who is appropriately qualified, and who will deliver value for money with appropriate predictability and accountability. A forensic engineer who understands counsel's requirements will be in a much better position to deliver the required services in a way that satisfies counsel's needs.

Chapter 32 comprises guidance for engineers or other professionals who are engaged as experts in connection with arbitration or litigation. It distinguishes between a "clean" expert who may have to give evidence in a hearing and must therefore be separated from the details of the legal conduct of the case, and a "dirty" expert who is engaged to assist the legal team directly. Guidelines are provided for the preparation of expert reports and giving evidence in a hearing.

The important issue of expert witnesses is addressed in detail in Chapter 33, which considers when to brief an expert, what ethical considerations apply to the legal team and the expert, dealing with adverse opinion and court rules on expert evidence. Suggestions are given on how lawyers can work effectively with experts. A number of issues arising from expert conferences and conclaves, and expert evidence in court, are discussed in light of a large class action case in the Victorian Supreme Court. In the course of *Matthews v SPI Electricity*, 15 rulings were made by judges on various aspects of the expert evidence process. These rulings are summarised, as they are invaluable for their articulation of the relevant principles, and their application to the complexities in this case "to facilitate the just, efficient, timely and cost-effective resolution of the real issues in dispute".

The final aspect of expert evidence considered is court Rules in Chapter 34. The differences between the eight Australian State and Territory Supreme Courts and Federal Courts, Singapore and UK evidence law, and their rules for expert evidence are reviewed and tabulated. Specific provisions are considered in detail, and the differences between jurisdictions highlighted. Recommendations for the content of expert reports are provided, which the author believes would satisfy the requirements of superior courts in most common law jurisdictions.

1.6 Part 5: International construction contracts

Part 5 considers two aspects of international construction contracts. The first of these is whether there are universally accepted principles of construction law. The second explores the extent to which the UNIDROIT Principles may provide a truly international body of contract law that could be applied to resolve construction law disputes, independent of the law of any particular State.

Chapter 35 looks at a cross-jurisdictional issue: is there a *lex constructionis*? As there are differences in terminology and in legal principles between legal systems and even between jurisdictions within a legal system, it can be difficult to discern even broad principles of a common construction law. Each jurisdiction has laws that impact on contracts for construction work: for the governing law of the contract, for the site of the construction work, or for the seat of dispute resolution. Nevertheless, the principles of freedom of contract and *pacta sunt servanda* form the basis of construction law around the world and form the basis of a thriving international construction industry. Construction contracts can be executed in the knowledge that, notwithstanding local law differences, there are appropriate methods of dispute resolution, broad agreement on what constitutes a just outcome in most situations and international norms that ensure remedies can be realised. Three issues are discussed that can promote greater uniformity in the international practice of construction law: the use of FIDIC contracts, international commercial arbitration and the modern statements of the *lex mercatoria*. A list of twenty principles of *lex constructionis* is proposed.

Chapter 36 discusses the application of the UNIDROIT Principles to construction contracts. These principles have been articulated by a learned body of lawyers from around the world to distil the basic principles of contract law that are recognised by most legal systems, civil law, socialist law and common law. There is considerable jurisprudence on the application of the UNIDROIT Principles from the courts of various countries, as well as in many arbitration awards. Aspects of this jurisprudence on the various applications of the UNIDROIT Principles are discussed, noting the limitations that may apply where disputes are resolved in court. Such limitations do not apply to international arbitration of construction disputes, and it is suggested that the UNIDROIT Principles could be applied to make such dispute resolution truly independent of any national law. Suggestions are made as to how the Principles may have application to resolve some of the issues that often arise in construction disputes.

Chapter 37 contains commentary on the importance of the construction industry in the world economy, and in the context of improving living standards in less developed countries. The basics of a construction contract are reviewed, and their role as a contract management manual discussed. Some challenges arising from rule of law issues are outlined, and how they may be counteracted by the use of international arbitration. Appropriate application of contracts is suggested to be instrumental in achieving successful projects. The engineers' and lawyers' roles in the application of contracts to construction projects are emphasised in a brief review of the five parts of the book.

PART 1

THE ENGINEER AND THE CONTRACT

CHAPTER 2

The evolution of the role of the engineer[1]

2.1 Introduction

Engineers have an essential role in any construction project. The extent of that role differs from project to project, and over time. In the past, the engineer in charge of a construction project often had a multi-faceted role as promoter, designer, project manager, contract administrator, certifier, adjudicator and sometimes even arbitrator.

A number of those functions were fulfilled as "the Engineer" under a construction contract, in which the engineer, although engaged by the Employer, was expected to act independently of both contract parties in his/her administration of the contract. That role is largely defunct under many modern construction contracts (e.g. FIDIC, NEC), as the authors of many standard form construction contracts have perceived that it is no longer possible for one individual/entity to satisfactorily discharge the manifold responsibilities implicit in the traditional independent Engineer (or Architect) role.

This chapter discusses the evolution of the role of the engineer, and its modern fragmentation into different roles with different functions. It is suggested that definition and proper execution of these functions are as important to the successful outcome of projects as ever. Splitting the roles between different people is not necessarily an improvement because of the increased number of interfaces, higher cost and longer time to resolve issues.

2.2 The civil engineer

The historical definition of civil engineering in the first (and subsequent) Royal Charter(s) of Institution of Civil Engineers (**ICE**) is: "The general advancement of mechanical science" and "the art of directing the great sources of power in nature for the use and convenience of man".[2] If "man" is taken in the modern context as encompassing all members of the human species, this definition is as apt today as it was in 1828 when the ICE was granted its first Royal Charter. It encapsulates the essence of what civil engineering is, and it is suggested, articulates a powerful driver of why many people become civil (and other) engineers – the opportunity to use both art and science to do something creative that is

1 This chapter is an edited, expanded and updated version of the paper "The Engineer is dead. Long live the engineer!" which was awarded the Society of Construction Law Hong Kong essay prize for 2010. It was subsequently published as: Donald Charrett, "The Engineer is dead. Long live the engineer!" (2010) 134 *Australian Construction Law Newsletter* 20.

2 The full definition is in footnote 1 in Chapter 1 (this volume).

 DOI: 10.4324/9781003206897-3

needed by humanity. A modern statement on the ongoing importance of the role of civil engineers to the community is that:

> Civil engineers are creative people who solve problems. They come up with lots of ideas and then turn them into real things for people around the world to use. They design the transport systems to keep big cities on the move. They create easy-to-build schools so children in faraway places have somewhere to learn. They use the sun and wind's energy to make electricity for our homes.[3]

The following quotations encapsulate the appeal of engineering as a creative and fulfilling profession:

> Engineering is a great profession. There is the satisfaction of watching a figment of the imagination emerge through the aid of science to a plan on paper. Then it moves to realisation in stone or metal or energy. Then it brings homes to men or women. Then it elevates the standard of living and adds to the comforts of life. This is the engineer's high privilege.[4]

> Engineering is not merely knowing and being knowledgeable, like a walking encyclopedia; engineering is not merely analysis; engineering is not merely the possession of the capacity to get elegant solutions to non-existent engineering problems; engineering is practising the art of the organized forcing of technological change … Engineers operate at the interface between science and society.[5]

Civil engineers have made and continue to make an essential contribution to humanity – without the water supplies, sewerage systems, roads, bridges etc., civilisation as we know it could not exist, nor could a large number of the planet's current population. One of the reasons that the Roman empire lasted for so long was because it had brilliant civil engineers who were able to design and build the durable and high-quality infrastructure needed by a city of over a million people, and by an empire that extended from England to Asia Minor. Another reason for the longevity of the Roman Empire was its advanced rule of law that not only provided the foundations for a stable civil society at the time, but also formed the basis of much modern law around the world, including the contract law which is fundamental to most if not all engineering projects.

Whilst there may have been only two types of engineer at the time of the Roman empire (civil and military), the engineering profession evolved over the nineteenth and twentieth centuries to include other main branches of engineering that are recognised as distinct today: mechanical, electrical and chemical. Within each of these branches of engineering there are further specialisations, e.g. civil engineering encompasses geotechnical, structural, traffic, hydraulic, ocean engineering etc. Many engineering projects such as chemical processing or oil and gas facilities involve design and construction input from engineers from all the different branches and specialisations. All but the simplest buildings require not only architects, but also civil, geotechnical, structural, mechanical and electrical engineers. Thus, references in this book to an engineer in the context of a construction project are not confined to civil engineers, although civil engineers may still be the most numerous in many projects.

3 www.ice.org.uk/careers-and-professional-development/what-is-civil-engineering/what-do-civil-engineers-do (accessed 4 June 2016).

4 Herbert Hoover, US mining engineer and politician (1874–1964) www.quotationspage.com/quote/27227.html (accessed 16 January 2018).

5 Dean Gordon Brown (1907–1996) www.quotationspage.com/quote/27227.html (accessed 16 January 2018).

It should also be noted that modern building and environmental regulations have become so complex that there are now specialist professions, distinct from engineering, that have the role of ensuring and certifying that statutory requirements have been complied with, e.g. building surveyors and environmental auditors. In earlier, simpler times, these roles, to the extent that they existed at all, were fulfilled by engineers.

2.3 What is the role of the engineer?

There are a number of roles fulfilled by an engineer in connection with a major construction project. The role of a particular engineer may include one or more of the following:

1. Promoting the functional and technical aspects of the project to potential project sponsors/financiers/regulatory authorities.
2. Advising the Employer at the concept stage of a project on possible options for project delivery, including suitable design and construction concepts, cost estimates and project procurement options (including appropriate forms of contract).
3. Calling tenders on behalf of the Employer.
4. Assessment of Contractors' proposals and advising the Employer on the most appropriate company to be contracted to execute the works.
5. Preparation of preliminary designs to refine concepts and enable more realistic cost estimates to be determined.
6. Preparation of design documentation in sufficient detail to enable contractors to determine appropriate construction methods and prepare accurate tenders for the construction costs.
7. Project managing the project on behalf of the Employer, including monitoring progress, and reporting on the Contractor's achievement of contractual time, cost and quality obligations.
8. Preparation of "for construction" drawings and documentation.
9. Technical review and inspection of the Contractor's work, including assessment as to whether the Contractor's fabrication and erection methods will have any adverse impact on the suitability of the as constructed design to fulfil its purpose in accordance with the design assumptions.
10. Administering the construction contract on behalf of the Employer, including an assessment of the Contractor's compliance with the contractual requirements, and taking proactive steps to foresee and manage risks so that the Contractor achieves the requirements of the Contract.
11. Issuing instructions to the Contractor on behalf of the Employer, particularly with respect to variations.
12. Assessing the Contractor's claims for time and money and certifying the Contractor's progress to enable the Employer to make progress payments as required by the construction contract.
13. Adjudication of contractual disputes between the Contractor and Employer.

In this book, the term **engineer** is used for the person/entity providing one or more "engineering" (including project management) services in relation to one or more aspects of a construction project, such obligations being defined under the engineer's contract with the Employer. The term **Engineer** is used for the person(s)/entity who fulfils the contract administration role of the Engineer (referred to in some contracts as the Architect or Superintendent) under a construction contract.

England's most famous engineer (and on one assessment its second most famous person),[6] IK Brunel, epitomised the traditional nineteenth-century engineer and Engineer. He nurtured a wide range of ground-breaking and visionary projects from conception through design to execution by Contractors whose contracts he administered and adjudicated upon. However, as discussed below, as Engineer he was not necessarily independent and impartial.

It is apparent that 1–6 above are functions carried out before the construction contract between Employer and Contractor (the Contract) is entered into. Functions 7, 8 and 9 are essentially separate to any role involving the administration of the Contract. In carrying out these functions, the engineer is undoubtedly acting as the agent of the Employer, even if not in a strict legal sense. Functions 10–12 are those involved in contract administration (as Engineer), whereas 13 is a dispute resolution role. These functions comprising the role of the engineer are categorised in Table 2.1.

Modern contracts generally do not assign the adjudication of disputes to the Engineer, recognising that many disputes arise from the Contractor's rejection of the Engineer's determination. As noted in ¶Section 2.6 below, it is not consonant with natural justice for the Engineer to judge the legitimacy of his/her own actions. The other roles in Table 2.1 may be performed by one individual or organisation, as in the case of FIDIC contracts, or by more than one person in the case of NEC contracts. The NEC Engineering and Construction Contract (**ECC**) identifies four individuals/organisations that carry out the functions in Table 2.1:

- The Project Manager, who carries out functions 1–7 and 10–12
- The Supervisor, who carries out some of functions 10 and 11
- The Designers, who carry out functions 5, 6, 8 and 9
- The Adjudicator, who carries out function 13.

2.4 The project manager

Engineering, particularly civil engineering, has always involved the delivery and management of projects. In other words, civil engineers have always been project managers. Successful projects require high quality project management, as well as high quality engineering design, but outstanding project management and engineering design skills are not necessarily found in the one person.

For some decades now, project management has been seen as a distinct profession, separate from engineering. The Australian Institute of Project Management, founded in 1976, is a professional organisation which aims to "improve the knowledge, skills and competence of project managers and related project personnel, all of whom play a key part in the achievement of business objectives – not just project objectives".[7]

6 In 2002, BBC television gave its viewers an opportunity to vote on who was the Greatest Briton. Isambard Kingdom Brunel came second only to Winston Churchill, and was the only engineer in the top ten (Andrew Kelly and Melanie Kelly (eds), *Brunel in love with the impossible* (2006) 17).

7 www.aipm.com.au/about-us (accessed 10 April 2021).

TABLE 2.1 Functions carried out by an engineer

	Agent of Employer		*The Engineer*		
			Contract Administrator		
	Project Manager	*Designer*	*Agent of Employer*	*Certifier*	*Adjudicator*
Pre-construction	1. Promoting the functional and technical aspects of the project to potential project sponsors/financiers/regulatory authorities. 2. Advising the Employer at the concept stage of a project on possible options for project delivery, including suitable design and construction concepts, cost estimates and project procurement options (including appropriate forms of contract). 3. Calling tenders on behalf of the Employer. 4. Assessment of Contractors' proposals and advising the Employer on the most appropriate Contractor to be contracted to execute the works.	5. Preparation of preliminary designs to refine concepts and enable more realistic cost estimates to be determined. 6. Preparation of design documentation in sufficient detail to enable Contractors to determine appropriate construction methods and prepare accurate tenders for the construction costs.			
Construction	7. Project managing the project on behalf of the Employer, including monitoring progress, and reporting on the Contractor's achievement of contractual time, cost and quality obligations.	8. Preparation of "for construction" drawings and documentation. 9. Technical review and inspection of the Contractor's work, including assessment as to whether the Contractor's fabrication and erection methods will have any adverse impact on the suitability of the as constructed design to fulfil its purpose in accordance with the design assumptions.	10. Administering the construction contract on behalf of the Employer, including an assessment of the Contractor's compliance with the contractual requirements, and taking proactive steps to foresee and manage risks so that the Contractor achieves the requirements of the contract. 11. Issuing instructions to the Contractor on behalf of the Employer, particularly with respect to quality and variations.	12. Assessing the Contractor's claims for time and money and certifying the Contractor's progress to enable the Employer to make progress payments as required by the construction contract.	13. Adjudication of contractual disputes between the Contractor and Employer.

In this book, a distinction is made between the skills of specialist project managers and those of engineers, not because project management and engineering are necessarily different professions, but because, in the author's experience, engineers and project managers generally have a different approach to the achievement of project expectations. Trained and experienced engineers tend to have predominant skills as either project managers or engineers, but rarely in both. It is suggested that the distinction between project managers and engineers is in the emphasis each put on the "elements" that are fundamental to every project: time, cost and quality. For a project manager, the order of precedence is: first and foremost, time, followed by cost (which is frequently intimately connected with time through the cliché "time is money"), with quality conditioned by the requirements of time and cost. Thus, the project manager's focus is centred on the perceived requirements of the Employer: delivering a project on time within the budget cost, and to the required level of quality that the Employer is prepared to pay for. As noted in Section 2.3 above, the NEC ECC explicitly assigns the project management function to the Project Manager: "His role within the ECC is to manage the contract for the *Employer* with the intention of achieving the *Employer's* objectives for the completed project."[8]

2.5 The engineer

The project manager's approach to the elements of a project can be contrasted with the engineer's approach – quality is the overriding criterion, because the engineer focuses on the requirements of the project itself, and this demands his/her highest loyalty, sometimes more than to the Employer who is paying the bills. The engineer's *raison d'être* is quality: the engineer knows that, in many projects, without the required quality, the project could fail catastrophically, perhaps with substantial loss of life. Some obvious examples of such civil engineering structures are long span bridges and large dams. Without a single-minded focus on the overriding requirement of the engineering quality required for such projects, they would not function successfully. The engineer's second priority is cost: engineers are well aware of the constraints on project costs. At least at the conceptual and feasibility stages, if the estimated project costs are unaffordable, the project will not be built. Time is generally the third priority for the engineer, as ultimately the time required is controlled by the project quality and cost.

In the author's view, this distinction between project managers and engineers explains the apparent ascendancy in the project delivery hierarchy of those professionals labelled project managers over those content to be called engineers (and over architects, who in the recent past were not only the primary consultants on building projects, but were also the project managers of the building process). The project manager is focused on what the Employer wants: his/her project on time and on budget, and with appropriate quality so as to fulfil the purpose for which it was created. The Employer reasonably expects that the project will function as it should, as this is what it is paying the engineers for. There may however be a perception that, left to their own devices (i.e. without "control" by a project manager), the engineers might be too focused on the quality of the engineering required for the project, and not sufficiently concerned with completing the project on time and on budget. It is suggested that it is because the project manager has promised to deliver the

8 *NEC3 Engineering and Construction Contract Guidance Notes* (Thomas Telford Ltd, 2013) 10.

Employer what it wants that project management has been marketed and sold as a distinct profession, and perhaps at a premium to the price for the engineering itself.

The success of some of the world's seminal engineering projects can be attributed to a brilliant engineer who combined in one person all the necessary attributes of the project manager (who balanced the often conflicting demands of time, cost and quality), with those of the engineer (who was focused on the technical quality of the engineering required to achieve the project objectives).

The BBC show "Seven Wonders of the Industrial World" and the book of the same name identified a number of projects in which there was one individual project manager/engineer whose single-minded vision was the driver, not only to create the project, but to carry through the engineering of the design and project management of the construction to ensure that the vision became reality. Projects that qualified as one of those Seven Wonders because of the vision and persistence of one project manager/engineer were:

- Bell Rock Lighthouse Scotland (1806–1811): Robert Stevenson
- London Sewers (1856–1870): Joseph Bazalgette
- Brooklyn Bridge (1867–1883): John Roebling and subsequently his son Washington Roebling
- Great Eastern ship (1854–1860): Isambard Kingdom Brunel.

The challenge for the project manager is to deliver a project that is on time and on budget whilst maintaining the necessary quality. The challenge for the engineer is to deliver the quality that is sufficient for the project to function in accordance with expectations, whilst maintaining the project on time and on budget.

2.6 The engineer's historical role

The role of the engineer in any construction project is determined by the terms of the relevant contracts. As between Employer and Contractor, the terms of the construction contract are determinative. As between Employer and engineer, the terms of the engineer's retainer (contract) are determinative. Thus, after the construction contract is executed, the engineer's contract may cover functions 7–13 above, whereas the Engineer's role under the construction contract will be confined to the contract administration and dispute resolution functions 10–13 only. Any conflict between the Engineer's role as defined in the two contracts (i.e. the Contract and the Engineer's contract with the Employer) will almost inevitably give rise to difficulties.

A properly drawn up construction contract will define the contract administration role(s) of the Engineer somewhere on a spectrum between acting as agent of the Employer in all matters, and acting independently of the Employer in relation to matters of time cost and quality under the contract. The following two cases illustrate each end of the spectrum.

In *Ranger v Great Western Railway Co*[9] the Engineer (Brunel) was, in effect, the alter ego of the Employer:

9 (1854) 5 HLC 72, 10 ER 824.

> But here the whole tenor of the contract shows it was never intended that the engineer should be indifferent between the parties. When it is stipulated that certain questions shall be decided by the engineer appointed by the Company, that is, in fact, a stipulation that they shall be decided by the Company. It is obvious that there never was any intention of leaving to third persons the decisions of questions arising during the progress of the works. The Company reserved the decision to itself, acting however, as from the nature of things it must act, by an agent, and that agent was, for this purpose, the engineer. His decisions were, in fact, those of the Company. The contract did not hold out, or pretend to hold out, to the Appellant [Contractor], that he was look to the engineer in any other character than as the impersonation of the Company: in fact, the contract treats his act and the acts of the Company, for many purposes, as equivalent, or rather identical. I am therefore of opinion that the principle on which the doctrine as to a judge rests, wholly fails in its application to this case. The Company's engineer was not intended to be an impartial judge, but the organ of one of the contracting parties. The Respondents [Company] stipulated that the engineer for the time being, whoever he might be, should be the person to decide disputes pending the progress of the works, and the Appellant [Contractor], by assenting to that stipulation, put it out of his power to object on the ground of what has been called the unindifferency of the person on whose decision he agreed to be bound.[10]

By contrast, in *In re De Morgan, Snell & Co and Rio De Janeiro Flour Milling Co*,[11] the chief engineer and the resident engineer (appointed by the chief engineer) were found to be independent of the Employer:

> I am clear that the resident engineer is not the servant of the company; that he stands in a position quite distinct from and different from that of a servant; that he is a person who has been selected by the chief engineer, and the chief engineer himself has been selected by the contracting parties, and in the event of any vacancy in the chief engineer's office it is to be filled up by consent, or by an independent appointment, and in the event of any vacancy in the resident engineers appointment that is to be filled up by the chief engineer. So that the appointment of the resident engineer is not the appointment of the company, and he is not in any sense a servant of the company. He stands in a position of much greater independence. He is a person who owes duties alike to the company and to the contractor; he is a person who is bound to be independent alike of the one and the other; he is a person who is bound to act impartially between the two contracting parties; therefore there is an entire misapprehension of the true view of the position of the resident engineer in the view which was taken by the arbitrator. …
>
> … a misconception of the position of the engineer, analogous to the misconception that the arbitrator entertained with regard to the position of the resident engineer. He has not perceived the position which the chief engineer, as well as the resident engineer, may maintain. He is, in fact, not a servant of the company, but a person who has to do his duty between the two contracting parties.[12]

In contracts where the Engineer had autocratic control over the work and the power to issue final and binding determinations, he was generally regarded as independent of both contracting parties:

> The engineer is not, with reference to any difficulties that arise under a contract of this sort, the agent of his employers. He was not the agent of his employers in this case. He occupied a position of quasi-arbitrator, and even if he honestly made mistakes in the course of the discharge of his duty, it is perfectly clear that neither party to the contract could complain of that. It was his duty to do his best to act fairly between the parties, and as long as he acted in good faith his decision, in a case of this sort, would be final, and for any blunder, if any blunders

10 [1854] 10 ER 824, 831.
11 *Hudson's Building Contracts* (4th edn, 1891) Vol II 185.
12 Ibid 201–202.

> were proved, neither party could claim that he had done wrong or made the other contracting party responsible.[13]

In that case, the Engineer had a unilateral right to approve work and make a final adjudication on disputes, contained in the following clause of the contract:

> It is to be distinctly understood that the specification is to receive its strict literal interpretation, and that the works are in all respects to be carried out in accordance with it and the drawings, to the satisfaction of the engineer: but it is hereby provided that in case any dispute, question or difference arises as to the value of any particular work not clearly stated in the bill or schedules, or with regard to any other matter or thing connected with the contract, such dispute, question or difference shall be decided by the engineer, whose decision and award shall be final and binding upon all parties.[14]

Such a contract clause effectively made the Engineer the judge in his own cause, since any dispute on the meaning of any of the contract documents would relate to documents prepared by the Engineer, such as the drawings and specification. It is unsurprising that the courts would see the potential for conflict of interest and apply very strict standards of behaviour to an Engineer with such power.[15] In *Mackintosh v Great Western Railway Company*, the contractual implications of an Engineer (Brunel) who did not act impartially were put forcefully by Lord Cranworth:

> To apply these observations [in *Ranger v Great Western Railway Co* [1854] 10 ER 824, 831 on the duties of the engineer] on a question as to the consequences of an erroneous or unjust certificate would be absurd. If the engineer is to be considered as the mere organ of the employer, as a partisan and not an impartial judge – as one who had a right, as he had an absolute power, to make his measurements partial, and in such a way as to serve the interests of the employer whose organ he was – the whole scope and purpose of the contract is violated.[16]

It is worth noting that Brunel, whilst unquestionably a brilliant engineer, had severe shortcomings as the Engineer, well-illustrated by the case of *Mackintosh v Great Western Railway Co*, finally resolved in 1864, after Brunel's death in 1859. Mackintosh was the Contractor who took over several contracts when William Ranger became bankrupt after Brunel (the organ of the Employer) withheld payments. Mackintosh experienced the Engineer at his worst: Brunel imposed his own interpretations on the wording of contracts, always to the Contractor's detriment; he insisted on quality in excess of that required by the Contract; he failed to ensure that the site was made available to the Contractor on time, and withheld payments time and again on a variety of pretexts. Mackintosh's case dragged through the courts for over 20 years before the House of Lords finally awarded the Contractor £100,000 with 20 years' accrued interest and all costs.[17]

---

13 *Bottoms v York Corporation* (1892) in *Hudson's Building Contracts* (4th edn) Vol II 208, 215.

14 Ibid 211.

15 *Page v Llandaff and Dinas Powis Rural District Council* (1901) in *Hudson's Building Contracts* (4th edn) Vol II 316, 318.

16 (1865) 10 ER 881, 888.

17 Steven Brindle, *Brunel the man who built the world* (2005) 237–238.

2.7 The engineer as agent of the employer[18]

In the absence of clear words in the Contract to the contrary, the Engineer is required to discharge his/her decision-making functions fairly, impartially and honestly (and arguably, reasonably), even if directly employed by the Employer. This position was summed up by McFarlan J in the case of *Perini Corporation v Commonwealth of Australia*[19] as follows:

> the cases make plain that throughout the period of performance of all these duties, the senior officer [Engineer] remains an employee of the government or semi-government body [Employer], but that in addition and while he continues as such an employee he becomes vested with duties which oblige him to act fairly and justly and with skill to both parties to the contract.[20]

Thus, whilst the Engineer is the agent of the Employer in many of his/her roles, s/he remains obliged to act in respect of decision-making functions in a manner which is independent, impartial, fair and honest. Judges have used a variety of other words to express the obligations of the Engineer or Superintendent, including: "independence and impartiality",[21] "act in a fair and unbiased manner" and "reach such decisions fairly, holding the balance between his client and the contractor";[22] "he must be fair and he must be honest" and "impartially and fairly";[23] "honestly and impartially";[24] "fairly, impartially and in accordance with the powers given to him by the conditions"[25] and "to hold the balance fairly as between employer and contractor".[26]

The requirement of impartiality in the Engineer's decision-making functions would require very plain words in the Contract to negate it. For example, even in the case of an Engineer's contract that specifically provided that the Engineer was the agent of the Employer in "all matters relating to the design and construction of the project", the court found that in exercising his certifying functions under the Contract, the Engineer was required to act honestly and impartially and was not acting as the Employer's agent in the strict legal sense.[27] The court also found, controversially,[28] that the Engineer's (Superintendent's) power to extend time was capable of being exercised in the interests both of the Employer and the Contractor (even after the Contract had come to an end), and the Engineer was obliged to act honestly and impartially in deciding whether to exercise this power.[29]

The distinction between the obligations of the Engineer as the Employer's agent and that of the "traditional" independent Engineer in respect of the decision-making functions

18 This section is an edited extract from Philip Loots and Donald Charrett, *Practical Guide to Engineering and Construction Contracts* (2009) ¶7.1.

19 *Perini Corporation v Commonwealth of Australia* [1969] 2 NSWLR 530.

20 Ibid 536.

21 *Dixon v South Australian Railways Commissioner* [1923] HCA 45, (1923) 34 CLR 71 per Isaacs J.

22 *Sutcliffe v Thackrah* [1974] AC 727, 737 per Lord Reid.

23 Ibid 740, 741 per Lord Morris.

24 *Peninsula Balmain Pty Ltd v Abigroup Contractors Pty Ltd* [2002] NSWCA 211, (2002) 18 BCL 322.

25 *Cantrell v Wright and Fuller Ltd* [2003] EWHC 1545 (TCC), (2003) 91 Con LR 97.

26 *Scheldebouw BV v St James Homes (Grosvenor Dock) Ltd* [2006] EWHC 89, [24] per Jackson J.

27 *Peninsula Balmain Pty Ltd v Abigroup Contractors Pty Ltd* [2002] NSWCA 211, (2002) 18 BCL 322, 338 per Hodgson JA.

28 Adrian Baron, "The superintendent's discretion to extend time: a long story must be told to satisfy 'the earnest inquirer'" (2007) 23 *BCL* 410.

29 Above n 24, 343.

may be more apparent than real. Arguably, in cases where the contract specifically makes the Engineer the agent of the Employer, s/he may only be required to act honestly, not necessarily fairly or reasonably. However, even in cases that have considered the Engineer's role as the Employer's agent, the courts have used very similar words to those that have been applied to the obligations of the Engineer. In a contract in which there was no Engineer, the court found that the power of the Employer to value variations "in its sole discretion" was to be exercised "honestly, bona fide, and reasonably".[30] In the *Peninsula Balmain Pty Ltd v Abigroup Contractors Pty Ltd* case, Hodgson JA found that the Project Manager, acting as agent of the Employer, was still required to exercise its certifying functions honestly and impartially. And in a case where the Employer's Representative took the place of the Engineer in the ICE Conditions of Contract, the court nevertheless found that the Employer was bound to act honestly, fairly and reasonably in arriving at its judgment, even where no such obligation was expressed in the contract.[31]

2.8 Modern contractual provisions on the engineer

The FIDIC Contracts[32] are typical of the modern contractual approach to the Engineer's role. The FIDIC Contracts' provision that the Engineer "shall be deemed to act for the Employer" unless otherwise stated is explicit acknowledgement of the role of the Engineer as agent of the Employer. Of the many references to the Engineer's function, the only vestige of the traditional explicitly stated even handed role as between Employer and Contractor is the requirement that "When carrying out his/her duties under this Sub-Clause [Agreement or Determination] the Engineer shall act neutrally between the Parties and shall not be deemed to act for the Employer."[33]

The standard form contract for civil engineering government work in Hong Kong makes it clear that the Engineer is the agent of the Employer in all matters, who is subject to the directions of the Employer:

(a) The Engineer shall carry out the duties and may exercise the powers specified in or necessarily to be implied from the Contract.
(b) Before carrying out any such duty or exercising any such power, the Engineer may be required under the terms of his appointment by the Employer to obtain confirmation that the Employer has no objection to the Engineer's proposed course of action and, in the event of an objection, to act in accordance with the Employer's direction. If the Engineer is subject to any such requirements, particulars thereof shall be set out in the Appendix to the Form of Tender.[34]

30 *WMC Resources Ltd v Leighton Contractors Pty Ltd* [1999] WASCA 10, (2000) 16 BCL 53, 62 per Ipp J.

31 *Balfour Beatty Civil Engineering Ltd v Docklands Light Railway Ltd* (1996) 78 BLR 42.

32 FIDIC Conditions of Contract for Construction (2nd edn, 2017) and FIDIC Conditions of Contract for Plant and Design Build (2nd edn, 2017), Clause 3.2.

33 FIDIC Conditions of Contract for Construction (2nd edn, 2017) and FIDIC Conditions of Contract for Plant and Design Build (2nd edn, 2017), Clause 3.7.

34 General Conditions of Contract for Civil Engineering Works 1999 (Government of Hong Kong SAR), and General Conditions of Term Contracts for Civil Engineering Works 2002 (Government of Hong Kong SAR) Clause 2.1. See also similar provisions in the General Conditions of Contract for Mechanical & Engineering Works 1999, General Conditions of Contract for Building Works 1999 and the General Conditions of Contract for Design and Build Contracts 1999 in respect of the Engineer/Architect/Survey/Supervising Officer.

Some standard form contracts still do not explicitly state whether the Engineer retains his/her traditional "independent" role or acts as agent of the Employer. For example, current Australian standards include the following provision:

> The *Principal* shall ensure that at all times there is a *Superintendent*, and that the *Superintendent* fulfils all aspects of the role and functions reasonably and in good faith.[35]

"Superintendent" is the term widely used for the Engineer in Australia. A contract still used by some local and State Governments in Australia contains the following "neutral" definition of the role of the Superintendent:

> The work under the Contract shall be executed in accordance with the Contract and in accordance with any directions of the Superintendent pursuant to the provisions of the Contract.[36]

It is interesting to note that, in this form of contract, the Superintendent retains his/her "traditional" role of first tier dispute adjudicator, to make the first decision on any dispute or difference raised by the Contractor.[37] By contrast, the FIDIC contracts now provide for the first tier of dispute adjudication to be by means of an independent Dispute Avoidance/Adjudication Board.[38]

2.9 The decline of the engineer's role

Signs of the decline of the traditional engineer's role have been apparent for a considerable time. It is suggested that the following are some of the harbingers of this decline:

- The rise of project management as a "new" profession, distinct from engineering.
- The fragmentation of the engineer's design role into a number of "packages", procured separately.
- Selection of engineers based on competitive fee bidding, in a competitive culture that finds it difficult to distinguish price from value.
- Reduced engineer's fees as a consequence of competitive bidding, leading to reduced scope of work in the assessment of alternative concepts, less checking and reduced professional skills.
- Increasing use of sophisticated computer programs for analysis, design and drafting, leading to a perception that engineering is being de-skilled.
- The rise in the influence of banks over project funding, and their desire for "certainty" in project costs.
- The declining influence of engineers at the highest levels of government and private enterprise (at least in Western countries), and the increasing influence of accountants and financiers.
- A rise in litigation against engineers for alleged negligence, both in respect of their design role and their contract administration role.

---

35 General conditions of contract (AS4000–1997), Clause 20; General conditions of contract for design and construct (AS4902–2000), Clause 20.

36 National Public Works Contract 1981 (**NPWC3**), Clause 23.

37 NPWC3, Clause 45.

38 FIDIC Conditions of Contract for Construction (2nd edn, 2017) and FIDIC Conditions of Contract for Plant and Design Build (2nd edn, 2017), Clause 21.4.

- Reduced input from the design engineers at the fabrication/construction stage, often as a consequence of design and construct procurement in which the Contractor client wishes to minimise the cost of external consultants.
- Changes in forms of contract which make the Engineer the Employer's agent in all matters.
- The rise of alternative forms of project procurement that do not require an Engineer in the traditional sense, e.g. construction management.

Whether there is substance in many of these factors is very arguable. However, the continuing importance of an appropriate role for engineers in project delivery is unarguable.

The consequences of inadequate involvement of the design engineers at the fabrication/construction stage in design and construct contracts are illustrated by the disastrous outcomes arising from the failure of the Quebec Bridge during construction in 1907 (see Chapter 21), and the failure in service of Kings Bridge in Melbourne in 1965 (see Section 16.3), where the consulting engineers had a very limited role during fabrication and erection. These projects can be contrasted with the successful outcome of Sydney Harbour Bridge in 1932, where the design consulting engineer had an ongoing role in relation to fabrication and erection (see Section 16.2).

The collapse in service of the New World hotel in Singapore in 1986 is a further graphic example of the impact of poor engineering, inadequate checking and a disconnect between the design and construction.[39] Following this tragedy, which killed 33 people and injured many more, the Singapore Government legislated to ensure that building designs were independently checked and every project has an engineer of record who has responsibility not only to ensure that the design is correct, but that the works are built in accordance with the design.

The collapse of the Heathrow Express tunnel at Heathrow airport in 1994 was directly linked to inappropriate contractual arrangements which precluded the design engineers from carrying out their appropriate functions. The cost of the failure of a project with a tender price of £60m was £440m, with the Contractor and specialist design consultant fined substantial sums for breaches of health and safety legislation.[40] Although the failure clearly had immediate "technical" causes, Muir Wood identified a number of contractual issues as the underlying causes of the collapse.[41]

Both the Institution of Civil Engineers and the Federation of International Consulting Engineers have apparently been overwhelmed by the realities of the current competitive and cost-conscious environment, and the sometimes irresistible pressures on an employed engineer, and have conceded the demise of the independent Engineer. This is not to say that the new "Engineer" does not have obligations to exercise her/his contract administration obligations in a reasonable and fair manner; however, it is clear that the wording in many current standard form contracts puts the Engineer unequivocally in the position of representing the Employer.

39 AM Netto and A Christudason, "Who pays?: Culpability of experts for building failures in Singapore" in Proceedings of the second international conference on forensic engineering organised by the Institution of Civil Engineers and held in London, UK, on 12–13 November 2001, 127.

40 Philip Loots and Donald Charrett, *Practical Guide to Engineering and Construction Contracts* (2009) 344–346.

41 Alan Muir Wood, *Tunnelling Management by Design* (2000) 285–288.

In government and aid-funded major infrastructure projects around the world, the procurement authority is generally a government department. In many countries, the majority of civil engineers have traditionally been employed by government, with limited capability available in the private sector. In these circumstances, it is unsurprising that the Engineer administering a major construction contract has usually been a government employee, responsible not only for ensuring that the project is built on time and to the required quality, but also within the budget and available finance. For a government employee, future career promotion, continuing employment and even a retirement pension might well be contingent on the successful delivery of projects within budget. In such circumstances, it is perhaps asking too much of human nature to expect an engineer to fearlessly assert his/her independence as the Engineer holding the balance between his/her own employer and the Contractor, and rule against the Employer in a disputed claim under the Contract.

2.10 Long live the engineer!

The morphing of the traditional independent Engineer into the Engineer as agent of the Employer is not yet universal, as there are still some standard form contracts in use which retain the Engineer's traditional even-handed role between Employer and Contractor in respect of certification of contractual entitlement. However, it is suggested that these are now in the minority. There are pragmatic reasons to recognise the reality that it may be very difficult for the engineer who faithfully looks after the Employer's interests in project management and in design to "change hats" and act independently of the Employer's interests when it comes to administering the Contract. However, as the cases show, even as agent of the Employer, the Engineer must still act fairly in making decisions and giving determinations. Such a role still requires real professionalism by the engineer.

The possibility or even the perception of the Engineer's bias to the Employer's interests in contractual decisions and determinations requires that the Contractor should have an avenue to appeal decisions of the Engineer believed to be wrong. Historically, the Contractor has ultimately been able to challenge the Engineer's decisions in arbitration, although this has become more time consuming and expensive than in the past. The recent rise of the use of Dispute Boards in major projects has proved to be an effective way of avoiding disputes or, if a dispute is unavoidable, by providing for a quick adjudication by experienced independent engineers, knowledgeable in both the relevant type of construction, and the specific project. Similarly, the widespread use of adjudication to provide a quick and economical method of dispute resolution, even if only provisionally binding, can be a cost-effective and speedy mechanism for the application of independent engineering judgment to the facts of a contractual dispute. The NEC ECC contract provides for an Adjudicator to give a speedy and binding decision on a dispute, before it can be referred to arbitration or litigation. It should be recognised, however, that both Dispute Boards and adjudication involve more time and cost than the determinations of an independent Engineer, and frequently involve lawyers and other professionals such as "claims engineers" at a much earlier stage than previously. Adjudication and Dispute Boards are discussed in more detail in Chapters 25–27 below.

The emphasis in many modern construction contracts is on promoting cooperation between the contracting parties, with the contract terms structured to promote effective management of the work. The NEC ECC is perhaps the best example of this type of contract, which requires the Employer, the Contractor, the Project Manager and Supervisor to act "in a spirit of mutual trust and cooperation". Alliancing contracts take such cooperative working to a new level, by aligning the contractual objectives of all parties, and rendering the independence of the Engineer moot.

Finally, the technical challenges posed by modern construction contracts require engineering skills of the highest order in design as well as in construction. The lessons from past project failures discussed in later chapters emphasise the importance of retaining appropriate engineering input at all stages of a project, and ensuring that the contractual arrangements promote and do not inhibit or prevent appropriate communication of that input to all relevant contracting parties.

CHAPTER 3

Time, cost and quality – the engineer's eternal challenge[1]

3.1 Time, cost and quality

Every contract must define the extent of each party's obligations. A construction contract must define what work the Contractor will carry out, and how much the Employer will pay for that work. The scope of obligations is thus at the heart of a construction contract. But scope involves far more than a definition of the extent of the work to be done.

3.1.1 Quality

Is the work required to last (durability)? What maintenance is required to ensure it continues to operate correctly? Are there any special requirements necessary to operate correctly? These are all questions relating to the required quality of the work and must be defined as part of the definition of the scope of work. An Employer may desire the highest quality, but must be aware that this comes at a price. We would all like to drive a car with Rolls Royce quality, but most of us have to settle for quality we can afford, perhaps a Toyota. A good working definition of **quality** is *the attributes the client is prepared to pay for*, i.e. the quality required of an engineering project is ultimately determined by the Employer.

This definition also illustrates the interconnection between quality and cost: higher quality almost invariably means higher cost. High quality, involving more extensive and/or costly work may require more time to execute. Thus, definition of the required quality is intrinsic to the definition of the scope of the work to be done. Construction contracts frequently define the required quality in detailed terms, as well as the **quality assurance** processes the Contractor or designer is required to comply with to provide assurance that the contractual quality is achieved, e.g. quality assurance procedures to ISO 9000. (Based on a number of disputes involving defects on projects with independently certified quality assurance (**QA**) procedures, this writer questions the extent to which formal QA procedures ultimately "assure" quality. Perhaps the focus should be more on rigorous quality control (**QC**) procedures).

The quality "attributes" that a client is prepared to pay for include not only those that are mandated by legislation such as the minimum standards of occupational health and

1 This chapter is based on a presentation given by the writer at the First Society of Construction Law Australia conference in Perth, June 2010: "Is contractual risk a zero-sum game?".

DOI: 10.4324/9781003206897-4

safety and environmental protection, but also those that the client considers essential to comply with its own culture. In the modern world, such "cultural issues" might include the requirement for diversity in the construction workforce, enhanced employee benefits and protections, community benefits or minimising the carbon footprint. For example, the MDB Harmonised Edition of the FIDIC Conditions of Contract for Construction contains 11 sub-clauses on the Contractor's obligations for cultural issues, in addition to those in the FIDIC Red Book (Conditions of Contract for Construction). The issues that the Multilateral Development Banks (**MDBs**) consider essential contract obligations in aid-funded projects would be subject to legislation or other norms in many advanced economies, and include obligations in respect of the supply of suitable food and adequate water, constraints on the supply of alcohol, guns and ammunition, respect for local religious and other customs, and prohibition of forced or compulsory labour or harmful child labour.

As used here, "quality" is a comprehensive term that includes not only the physical standard of materials and construction, but also all of the "soft" attributes involved in the performance and outcome of the construction that are included in the scope of work. Thus, whilst the important issues of safety and environmental protection are frequently considered as separate issues to quality, for the purposes of this book they are considered to be an integral component of "quality".

3.1.2 Time

A second area that must be defined relates to the time in which the work has to be completed. Is there an externally defined date by which the facilities must be available? For example, a stadium for the Olympic Games, the opening date of which was set eight years previously. Is the work required to be completed before other works can be commenced? For example, foundations for a large machine to be installed. Are there some parts of the facilities required to be completed before others (stages)? Can the work physically be carried out in the required time frame?

Thus, the time in which the works have to be executed is an essential part of the definition of the scope of the work. It is clearly related to the cost of the works: executing works in a shorter time than the optimal, based on normal availability of resources, involves additional cost. As does **fast track construction** – starting construction before the design is complete.

A good illustration of the sorts of additional costs that can arise from fast track construction is the podium of the Sydney Opera House. For political reasons, it was imperative to start construction of the podium (base) level works at the earliest opportunity. Thus, the contract was let for piling and foundation works on the assumption that the superstructure (sails) of the Opera House would be thin shell concrete. The architectural design competition was won on the basis of sketches before any structural engineering had been carried out to determine the form of its construction. After extensive engineering calculations, it was found that the structure could not be made from thin shell concrete 100–200 mm thick as originally envisaged, but required a series of complex and massive prestressed concrete ribs, metres deep. Inevitably the weight of the superstructure was considerably in excess of the original estimate on which the initial foundation design had been prepared and constructed, and a large number of additional piles had to be installed through the already completed substructure.[2] Such rework inevitably involved more cost and complexity than the cost of installing the final completed substructure design without rework. In that case, the total construction time may have been longer than the time to finalise the design and carry out the foundation work once. Such rework required because construction was commenced before design was sufficiently advanced is not consistent with the modern QA exhortation: "do it right the first time".

In addition to this interrelationship between time and cost, as noted previously the time required for project execution may be related to the quality required.

3.1.3 Cost

The cost of a project is intimately connected with the extent of the work required, and the quality and the time in which the works must be completed. It may also be dependent on other issues in the contract dealing with the way in which the work must be done. Thus, issues of time, cost and quality are interrelated and are central to the definition of the scope of the works.

3.1.4 Historical perspective

Issues of scope, cost and quality in constructed works were legislated in Mesopotamia in 1950BC in the following extracts from the Code of Hammurabi:[3]

> **228** If a builder build a house for some one and complete it, he shall give him a fee of two shekels in money for each sar of surface.
> **229** If a builder build a house for some one, and does not construct it properly, and the house which he built fall in and kill its owner, then that builder shall be put to death.
> **230** If it kill the son of the owner the son of that builder shall be put to death.
> **231** If it kill a slave of the owner, then he shall pay slave for slave to the owner of the house.
> **232** If it ruin goods, he shall make compensation for all that has been ruined, and inasmuch as he did not construct properly this house which he built and it fell, he shall re-erect the house from his own means.
> **233** If a builder build a house for some one, even though he has not yet completed it; if then the walls seem toppling, the builder must make the walls solid from his own means.

These laws cover issues of reasonable payment for work done, compensation for consequential loss, rectification of defects and compliance with reasonable standards of workmanship, issues that are still with us today. Whilst the Code's remedies for these issues are not inconsistent with modern standards, the legal consequences of fatalities caused by defective construction would undoubtedly be struck down as penalties in many jurisdictions today!

---

2 See Chapter 14 below for more details on the design and construction of the Sydney Opera House.

3 http://avalon.law.yale.edu/ancient/hamframe.asp (accessed 4 June 2016).

A thousand years later, Vitruvius (a construction, civil, military, mechanical, chemical and materials engineer, architect, urban planner and construction manager), highlighted the challenges inherent in estimating the cost of construction before the scope has been fully defined. Writing in 1BC, he referred approvingly to an ancient law in Ephesus:

> When an architect accepts the charge of a public work, he has to promise what the cost of it will be. His estimate is handed to the magistrate, and his property is pledged as security until the work is done. When it is finished, if the outlay agrees with his statement, he is complimented by decrees and marks of honour. If no more than a fourth has to be added to his estimate, it is furnished by the treasury and no penalty is inflicted. But when more than one fourth has to be spent in addition on the work, the money required to finish it is taken from his property.[4]

3.2 Tension in contracting parties' expectations

Every written construction contract has detailed provisions that endeavour to document the agreement of the parties on these issues. Because of their central importance, a party that perceives a shortfall in one or more of his/her expectations of time, cost or quality in the execution of project is likely to consider that to be a "failure", and this may be the trigger for a dispute. Every construction contract dispute involves arguments over one or more of scope of work, time, cost or quality, and who bears liability for the risks that have materialised.

Given that a construction contract is between parties with different objectives and expectations, often irreconcilable, it is submitted that there is an inherent tension in the fulfilment of both parties' expectations with respect to time, cost and quality, irrespective of what the contract provisions are. The expectations of both parties frequently cannot be fulfilled in full measure with respect to all of time, cost and quality. Sometimes that shortfall is a consequence of unrealistic expectations, or it may result from the inherent difficulty of simultaneously satisfying the interconnected, demanding and often conflicting criteria in which the fulfilment of one may be to the detriment of one or both of the others.

The procurement of Scottish Parliament House discussed in Section 15.4 highlights the consequences of ignoring the interrelatedness of time, cost and quality; a focus exclusively on quality, without regard to the time and cost implications, resulted in substantial time and cost overruns.

3.3 Graphical representations

The interrelationship between the expectations for time, cost and quality can be represented graphically by means of a triangle, with time, cost and quality at the vertices, or along the sides. Many writers on project management have referred to such a triangle, or variants of it. Included among the many appellations of such a scope triangle are: the Barnes triangle (named after Martin Barnes, an early writer on it), the iron triangle, the golden triangle, the titanium triangle, the devil's triangle, the infernal project triangle, the magic triangle, the triangle of trauma and the cost quality trade-off triangle. A Google search on "time, cost and quality" will reveal a number of papers and books

4 Morris Hicky Morgan (translator), *Vitruvius: the ten books on architecture* (1960) 281.

which have been written on the representational value of the triangle in relation to project management.

The use of the triangle as a visual aid has been expressed as follows:

> The triangle is representative of the way a real project works. The three sides of the triangle are mutually dependent on each other, just as the three factors of a project are mutually dependent on each other as well. A change on one side of the triangle will affect at least one of the other sides.[5]

In the representation used in this book, the area of the triangle represents the scope of the project, and the orientation represents the priority of each of the three factors: the higher up the page the side of the triangle, the higher the priority given to that factor. The symbolism of a triangle emphasises that one factor can be given priority over the other two, or two factors can be given equal priority. However, all three factors cannot have the same priority: a cheap, quick and high-quality project is an oxymoron.

In addition to its application to project management, the iron triangle is useful to illustrate certain concepts in relation to contracts and disputes. Figure 3.1 illustrates a typical situation facing a contractor preparing a tender.

In this ideal situation, the contractual scope of time, cost and quality which the Contractor must price is precisely defined. Ideally, the Contractor would plan its performance to just match the contractual scope, and this would be the basis of its tender. However, planning execution of a complex project is not such an exact science, and there are risks, which, if they materialise, would result in the contract scope exceeding the planned performance. Accordingly, the prudent Contractor will provide a contingency to allow for those risks that it anticipates might occur, so that the performance it provides for in its tender exceeds the contract scope. In the example shown, the Contractor has

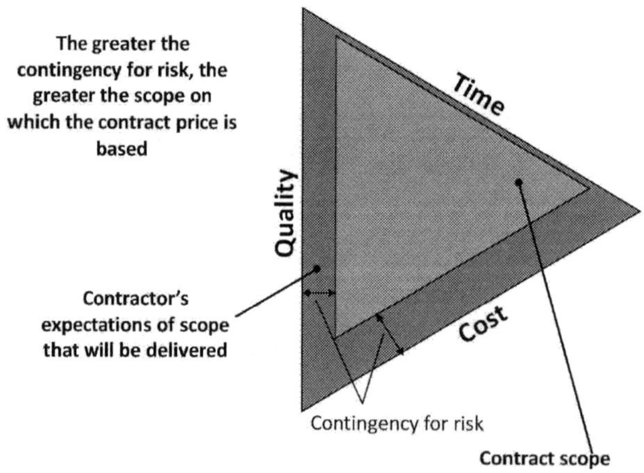

FIGURE 3.1 Contractor's considerations in preparing a tender

5 Rick A Morris, Brette McWhorter Sember, *Project management that works* (1999) 66.

provided contingency for cost and quality. The greater the perceived risks, the greater the contingency allowance, and the more the tendered scope exceeds the contract scope.

The iron triangle can also be used to illustrate the difference between a successful project and an unsuccessful project. Using the definition of an unsuccessful project as one that has failed because there is an unacceptable difference between expected and actual performance, Figure 3.2 illustrates an unsuccessful project.

In an unsuccessful project, the scope expectations exceed the project scope delivered. In the diagram shown, the cost expectations have exceeded the cost actually delivered, i.e. a cost overrun. The principle applies equally to both the Employer and the Contractor. If the Contractor's performance did not match its own expectations on cost, it will regard the project as unsuccessful, even if the contractual scope has been delivered.

Conversely, a successful project is one in which the project scope delivered exceeds the scope expectations, as shown in Figure 3.3.

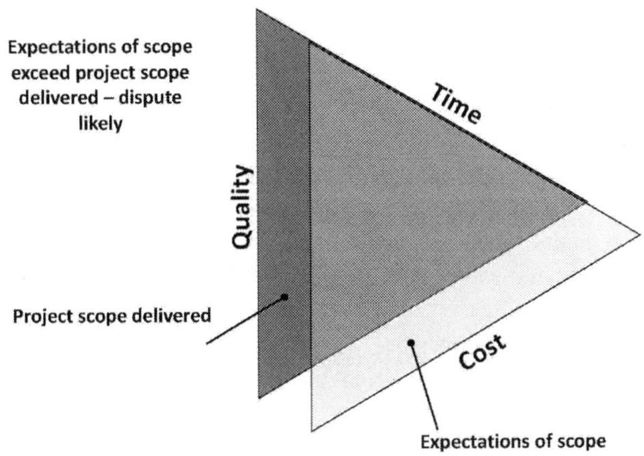

FIGURE 3.2 Unsuccessful project execution

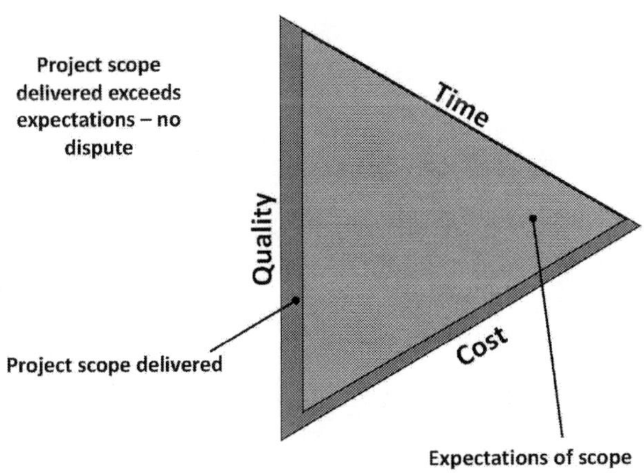

FIGURE 3.3 Successful project execution

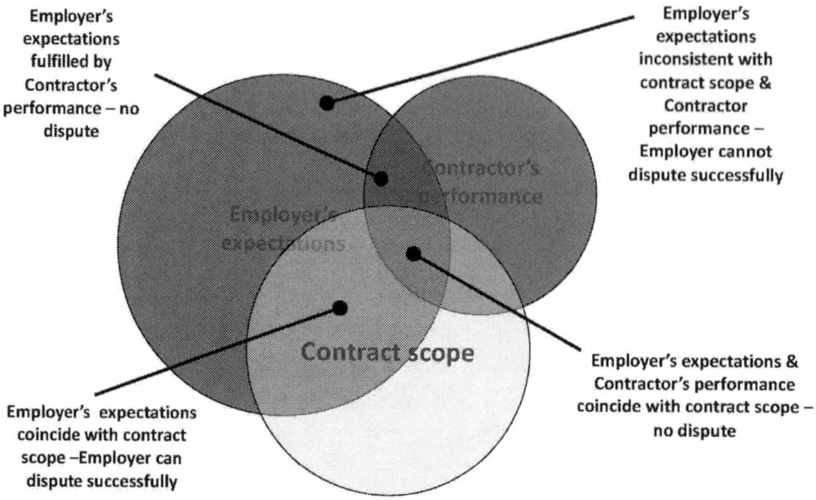

FIGURE 3.4 Scope: expectations and performance

It is suggested that disputes typically arise from unfulfilled expectations, and those expectations may, or may not, be consistent with the contract scope. However, a dispute founded on unfulfilled subjective expectations is unlikely to be successfully prosecuted, unless those subjective expectations are consistent with the (objective) contract scope.

These principles are illustrated in Figure 3.4, in which for simplicity the expectations or performance of scope relevant to the Employer are illustrated by circles instead of triangles. The size of the circle represents the magnitude of the scope (time, cost and quality). The scope required by the contract is the objective benchmark against which subjective expectations or performance are measured. To the extent that the Contractor's performance coincides with the requirements of the contract and the Employer's expectations, there will be no dispute. To the extent that the Employer's expectations coincide with the contract scope but these are not matched by the Contractor's performance, the Employer can successfully dispute the Contractor's breach of contract. The Employer's expectations may not coincide with either the Contractor's performance or the contract scope; whilst this might not prevent the Employer raising a dispute in respect of its unfulfilled expectations, such a dispute is unlikely to be successful. The same type of diagram would apply equally if the words "Employer" and "Contractor" were interchanged.

In Figure 3.4, the Employer's subjective expectations of scope are greater than the (objective) contractual scope, and do not coincide with the detailed provisions of the contract. The Contractor's performance is less than required by the contract scope, and does not coincide with the detailed provisions of the contract.

3.4 Project costs

However, it is worth reflecting that, without visionary engineers for whom the time and cost aspects are subordinate to the quality of the project, many important projects might never be commenced. The following quote encapsulates a problem on costing major projects which is endemic:

> Brunel was adept at persuading his project sponsors of the infrastructure legacy they were funding, even if he was less clear about the eventual outturn costs.
>
> Perhaps if he had been, some of his lasting achievements might never have seen the light of day. Major construction projects are frequently under costed, but once started, are notoriously difficult to stop. And it is no less true today. Witness the Scottish Parliament Building, the Channel Tunnel (at the third attempt), the new Wembley Stadium, and the Millennium Dome. Other spectacular examples of cost underestimation were the Sydney Opera House (actual costs approximately 15 times higher than projected), the supersonic Concorde aeroplane (costs 12 times higher than predicted), the Suez Canal (completed in 1869 with actual costs 20 times higher than the earliest estimated costs and three times higher than the cost estimate for the year before construction began).[6]

A recent example highlighting the difficulty of managing the cost of major engineering projects is the new eastern spans of the San Francisco Oakland Bay Bridge, the largest public infrastructure contract in California's history. The Richter 7.1 magnitude Loma Prieta earthquake of 1989 caused a 15 m span of the upper deck of the 3.1 km long truss and cantilever bridge to collapse. Subsequent analysis revealed that structure needed to be able to resist 0.25 g horizontal accelerations to be able to survive an 8.5 magnitude earthquake, instead of the 0.1 g it was designed for in the 1930s. Initial estimates of the cost of a simple new bridge were only several hundred million dollars more than the cost of retrofitting the structure with the required strengthening. A new bridge was ultimately chosen, with a "signature span" comprising self-anchored suspension spans of 180 m and 385 m. The 1997 estimate was $1.1 b (for a simple viaduct) and a March 2003 estimate of $2.6 b included a tower supported span. The final cost on its opening in 2013 after 12 years of construction was estimated to be $6.4 b.[7]

The problems of managing the costs of major infrastructure projects within budget are pervasive over time, geography and type of project. In a study of cost overruns in transportation infrastructure projects originally published by the World Bank, Flyvbjerg reported that nine out of ten projects had cost overruns, and overruns were found in the 20 countries and five continents covered by the study. He noted that comparative research showed that the findings in respect of transportation projects were also applicable to a wide range of other project types.[8]

Chapter 13 highlights the challenges in achieving successful megaprojects. On one estimate, 65% of projects with a value of over $1 b are failures, including where the actual final cost exceeds the cost estimate made at the project sanction stage by more than 25%, or where a project spends more than 25% greater than other projects with similar scopes. In the face of such widespread cost overruns, Loots and Charrett have opined that price as the determining factor in construction procurement decisions is wrong, and that a resourced schedule should take the place of price as the primary comparator.[9]

---

6 www.ice.org.uk (accessed May 2007).

7 http://en.wikipedia.org/wiki/San_Francisco-Oakland_Bay_Bridge (accessed May 2007).

8 Bent Flyvbjerg, "Policy and Planning for Large Infrastructure Projects: Problems, Causes, Cures" (2007) 34 *Environment and Planning B: Planning and Design* 578–597 http://flyvbjerg.plan.aau.dk/Publications2007/EPB31PRINT.pdf (accessed 28 August 2009).

9 Philip Loots and Donald Charrett, "Reconsidering Procurement Criteria and Procedures for Major Infrastructure Projects" (2017) 1 *International Construction Law Review* 70.

3.5 Design

In the past, the "traditional" method of procurement of construction projects was design-bid-build: the Employer engaged the designer to prepare the design and prepare documents on which contractors submitted competitive bids, and the Contract was awarded to the lowest bidder who then built the facility. Most non-residential construction projects in the United States are still procured by the design-bid-build method of delivery.[10]

However, procurement by design and construct contracts has become widely used over the past 30 years. In design and construct contracts, the designer is engaged by the Contractor, not the Employer. In this author's experience, some design and construct contractors procure design by competitive bidding and selection of the lowest bid, without due regard to the importance of the quality of the design and its impact on constructability and project costs. Some of the problems that can arise from inappropriate procurement of design are outlined in the following:

> One problem noted by many practising professionals is the loss of control by the designer over execution of the design. This loss of control is the result of an undue emphasis on reduction of construction time and construction cost. Non-traditional "fast-track" approaches have been introduced, with new opportunities for misunderstood communications and unclear lines of responsibility. Designers have always had to compete against the costs of time, but the unprecedented era of double-digit inflation in the 1970s placed new pressures on design and construction schedules. Society began to define the "best" project as the one that could be completed in the shortest time, for the least initial cost. The "psychology of the low bid" became fully entrenched in the construction industry. Competitive bidding for design services and the ethical conflicts of design/build package services have become potential contributors to escalating failure rates.[11]

The disproportionate influence of design on construction and life cycle costs is discussed in Section 5.2, and the author's views on the appropriate management of design risk are outlined in Section 5.6.

3.6 Failure

The definition of failure of engineered facilities accepted by the Technical Council on Forensic Engineering of the American Society of Civil Engineers is: "an unacceptable difference between expected and observed performance".[12] In this context "performance" generally refers to "engineering" performance. However, it is a definition of broad application, and if "performance" encompasses not just "engineering performance" (or quality), but also time and cost, this is a comprehensive definition of the "failure" that underlies every construction dispute: one party is unsatisfied with the outcome of one or more of time, cost or quality on a construction project. A dispute arises from a failure when one party is unable to resolve the unacceptable difference between expected and observed performance with the other party (or parties) assumed responsible, without resorting to

10 Amicus Curiae Brief of Construction Industry Trade Associations in Support of Petition for Review, No 927448 Supreme Court of the State of Washington, 1 www.courts.wa.gov/content/petitions/92744-8%20Amicus%20Brief%20Construction%20Industry%20Trade.pdf (accessed 16 January 2018).

11 Kenneth L Carper, "Learning from Failures" in Kenneth L Carper (ed), *Forensic Engineering* (2nd edn, 2001) 15, 30.

12 G A Leonards "Investigation of Structural Failures" (1982) No GT2 (February) *Journal of the Geotechnical Engineering Division (ASCE)* 108

formal independent adjudication (e.g. by a court of law or an arbitrator), or an alternative dispute resolution mechanism (e.g. mediation or expert determination).

Thus, any unacceptable difference between observed and expected performance in respect of any one or more of time, cost, or quality is a recipe for a dispute that will distract an engineer from the creative aspects of his or her project work. As is illustrated by the examples in Chapters 20–22, engineering failures also have much wider consequences, including:

- Loss of life
- Substantial monetary loss (including legal fees)
- Prosecution of engineers responsible for negligent work, and
- Loss of the right to practise as an engineer.

3.7 Disputes arise from unfulfilled expectations

The premise that disputes arise from unfulfilled expectations is relevant to the significance of the pre-contract stages leading up to entry into a contract, as well as execution of the contract work itself. The contract is, of course, the document formalising the agreement between the parties, in a form that is legally enforceable. It is the point at which the parties' expectations should be aligned with what the contract can deliver. This may involve a party lowering its expectations to the time, cost and quality scope defined by the contract, or by enlarging the contractual scope to match the time, cost and quality expectations. This applies equally to the Employer and the Contractor. In this writer's experience, it is a recipe for a dispute if an Employer insists on contract terms in respect of time, cost or quality that the Contractor cannot deliver, likewise if the Contractor agrees to contractual terms in respect of time, cost or quality with which it cannot or does not intend to comply. This is illustrated graphically in Figure 3.4.

Thus, the tension that exists between time, cost and quality, and the expectations of each party should be resolved to the extent possible before the contract is executed. This puts a heavy onus on lawyers advising their clients as to the contract terms – the defined contract scope, including time, cost and quality, should be aligned with the client's expectations. Further, those expectations should be cognisant of the almost inevitable tension between time, cost and quality. Employers should be encouraged to have realistic expectations as to what is achievable commercially and in practice, recognising that contractors are commercial organisations that must make a profit if they are to stay in business. The Employer should recognise the difficulty of maximising time, cost and quality expectations in equal measure, and decide which of them is the most important, as that is likely to be a large factor in selecting the appropriate procurement strategy and contract. For example, an expectation of Rolls Royce quality is fundamentally inconsistent with minimum project cost and time.

No doubt there are many reasons for successful projects, just as there are many reasons for unsuccessful projects. However, it is suggested that the following are some of the significant issues in many successful projects:

- The Employer realistically determines its time, cost and quality priorities.
- The project procurement method selected is appropriate to the Employer's priorities/acceptance of risks.
- The form and terms of the contract are consistent with the contract parties' expectations.
- The risks are allocated to the party best able to manage them.
- The parties execute the agreed contract before the work is started.
- The execution of the work is managed in accordance with the requirements of the contract.
- The risks are appropriately managed.
- Any disputes are managed in such a way as to maintain working relationships and avoid interference with the ongoing execution of the work.

CHAPTER 4

Risk and construction contracts[1]

4.1 Introduction

Contract risks refer to the chance that contractual objectives will not be fulfilled. The contract defines who bears the liability for the contract risks, and the form and/or terms of the contract can increase or decrease those risks from the norm. That is, use of the appropriate form or terms of a construction contract can play a major role in minimising the risk that the contractual objectives will not be fulfilled. The obverse is that use of an inappropriate form or terms of a construction contract can significantly increase the risk that the contractual objectives will not be fulfilled:

> The contract is the vehicle for risk allocation. Whether the contract is for construction, construction engineering and inspection, design, design-build, or some other aspect of highway construction management, it defines the roles and responsibilities for risks. Risk allocation in any contract affects cost, time, quality, and the potential for disputes, delays, and claims. In fact, contractual misallocation of risk has been found to be a leading cause of construction disputes in the United States.[2]

Many contracts, particularly bespoke contracts, are based on the philosophy of transferring as much risk to the Contractor as possible without any consideration of whether that increases or decreases the overall contract risk.[3]

This chapter considers the nature and cause of the risks involved in construction contracts and the parties' objectives. It is suggested that contract risk can be minimised by selecting the appropriate form of contract as that which gives primacy to achievement of the Employer's most important objective(s). Further, for any type of contract, contract risk is minimised by following well-established principles of balanced risk allocation.

1 This chapter is an edited and updated version of the published paper Donald Charrett, "Is Contractual Risk a Zero-sum Game in Construction Contracts" (2010) 38 *BDPS News* 12. It is reproduced by kind permission of the Building Dispute Practitioner's Society.

2 US Department of Transportation Federal Highway Administration, *Risk Assessment and Allocation for Highway Construction Management* (2006) 31 https://international.fhwa.dot.gov/pubs/pl06032/guide_to_risk_assessment_allocation_for_highway.pdf (accessed 10 April 2021).

3 Christopher Kerin, "Risky business: risk management cruises into the 21st century" (2008) 24 *Building and Construction Law* 94, 116.

 DOI: 10.4324/9781003206897-5

4.2 The contract and expectations

The following is a simplistic definition which emphasises the reciprocal relationships in a contract: a **contract** is a legally binding agreement in which each party accepts obligations in exchange for rights granted by the other party in order to achieve the contract objective. It is suggested that one of the most important functions of a contract is to define the rights and obligations of the parties pursuant to the contract objective, in a legally binding form. Each of the key terms "obligations", "rights" and "contract objective" are discussed below in the context of construction contracts.

For example, in a conventional construct-only contract the Contractor accepts the obligation to construct a facility of the specified quality in the time provided for in the contract (plus a number of ancillary obligations related to the manner or quality of performance), in exchange for the right to be paid by the Employer the amount(s) of money at the time(s) provided for in the Contract. The Employer accepts the obligation to pay the Contractor the amount(s) of money at the time(s) provided for in the Contract in exchange for the right to receive a facility of the specified quality at the time provided for in the Contract.

As a consensual agreement in which each party voluntarily accepts obligations in exchange for rights in order to achieve something, a contract has an objective, and the contracting parties have expectations of their rights and obligations. Those expectations, to the extent that they are objectively based on the terms of the contract, are the **contractual expectations**. It is these expectations that are legally enforceable and sustain a claim for damages for breach of contract if they are not fulfilled. In the well-known formulation, damages are the amount of money that will put the non-defaulting party in the position it would have been in if its contractual expectations had been fulfilled and the contract not breached.[4]

Looked at from a slightly different perspective, a contract could also be said to define the scope of each party's obligations and rights in pursuance of the contract objective. As usually applied in construction contracts, the overarching meaning of scope is the extent of the work. At a more detailed level however, the scope of each party's obligations and rights under a construction contract not only includes their extent, but also their characteristics. These characteristics can be conveniently summarised under the headings of time, cost, quality.

There are potentially different scopes (or at least perceptions) of time, cost and quality associated with any contract:

- The expectations of the Employer
- The expectations of the Contractor
- The scope of what is achievable
- The scope defined in the Contract, i.e. the objective scope of time cost and quality which are legally enforceable, and
- The scope of what is actually delivered.

4 *Robinson v Harman* (1848) 1 Ex 850, 855, (1848) 154 ER 363, 365.

Any difference between the Employer's and Contractor's expectations of scope and the scope actually delivered will lead to unfulfilled expectations and potential dispute. Whether such a dispute can be successful will depend on the contractual scope, and the extent to which it coincides with a party's expectations of the scope. An incorrect perception of unfulfilled contract scope may not prevent a dispute, but it is unlikely to result in a satisfactory outcome. Ultimately, in any formal resolution of a dispute, the determinative factor is whether there is a difference between the scope of what was actually delivered (performance) and the scope defined in the contract (contractual expectations), not the subjective expectation of one of the parties. To the extent possible, a contract should therefore align the Employer's and Contractor's subjective expectations with the contractual expectations.

These principles are illustrated in Figure 3.4 (Scope: expectations and performance) in Section 3.3.

The more unambiguous and detailed the scope definition in the Contract, the more likely it is that the Employer's and Contractor's expectations will be aligned with the Contract scope, and the fewer the unknown risks there will be for both Employer and Contractor. Of course, it is possible that the scope of what is achievable does not coincide with the scope defined in the Contract, but absent an appropriate contractual term modifying the common law obligations to achieve the contract objective, this will not relieve the relevant party (usually the Contractor) from the consequences of its breach of contract in not delivering the contractual scope.[5]

4.3 Objectives and expectations

The contract objective is achievement of the outcome that is the subject of the contract, the reason for its existence. In the case of a construction contract, this is construction of the relevant facility. In unusual situations, a contract might explicitly state the contract objective.[6] It can always be objectively determined by construction of the terms of the contract.

In the absence of mutual abandonment by the parties, the contract objective must be achieved for the contract to be satisfactorily completed, and therefore for the parties' expectations to be fulfilled. If the contract objective is not achieved, a defaulting party may have a legal liability for "causing" the shortfall between the contract objective and the scope of what was achieved. The consequences of not achieving the contract objective in a construction contract can be very significant, as indicated by the following judicial statement on damages for defective work:

> Where the contract breaker has entirely failed to achieve the contract objective it may not be difficult to conclude that the loss is the necessary cost of achieving that objective. Thus if a building is constructed so defectively that it is of no use for its designed purpose the owner may have little difficulty in establishing that his loss is the necessary cost of reconstructing.[7]

---

5 *Thorn v London County Council* (1876) 1 App Cas 120, 128 and 135.

6 e.g. the contract referred to in *Thiess Services Pty Ltd v Mirvac Queensland Pty Ltd* [2005] QSC 364; (2006) 22 *BCL* 218.

7 *Ruxley Electronics Ltd v Forsyth* [1996] AC 344, 358 per Lord Jauncey of Tullichettle.

4.4 Contractual success and failure

As outlined in Section 3.5, a useful definition of failure is "an unacceptable difference between expected and observed performance".[8] Using the converse of this definition, it is suggested that an objectively **successful contract** is one in which the contractual expectations are fulfilled by the actual performance of the contractual obligations, and there are no issues arising between the contracting parties that have to be resolved judicially by an independent tribunal, external to the contracting parties. Thus, the absence of disputes is a useful indicator of success and vice versa, and this is consistent with the industry focus on minimising or eliminating disputes.[9]

The definition of contractual expectations should theoretically be straightforward, since they can be determined by clear and unambiguous definition of the scope of the Contract. Scope is about those things that the parties know about. These are the contract objective and the extent of obligations accepted by each party: the agreed quality of the constructed facility, the time at which the contract objective is to be achieved and the cost and timing of payments. In addition, there are likely to be constraints on the manner of performance of obligations, such as complying with all statutory requirements, ensuring the health and safety of project participants and third parties, and protection of the environment. As noted in Section 3.1.1, "quality" is a comprehensive term used in this book to include not only the physical standard of materials and construction, but also all of the "soft" attributes involved in the performance and outcome of the construction that are included in the scope of work.

Using Donald Rumsfeld's famous trichology of terms,[10] a properly defined contractual scope will include all of the "known knowns", those things that the parties have knowledge of which will need to be addressed during performance of the contract. In addition, the contractual scope will normally also include provision for the "known unknowns", those things which the parties suspect may, but not necessarily will, impact on the performance of the contract. For obvious reasons, the contractual scope will not explicitly address the "unknown unknowns". Nevertheless, if one of these "unknown unknowns" materialises, the parties' rights and liabilities will be determined by the terms of the contract.

4.5 Risk

Risk is "the chance of something happening that will have an impact on objectives".[11] The "something happening" will be referred to in this book as a **risk event**, i.e. an event that, if it occurs, has an impact on fulfilment of the contractual objectives. Common usage of

8 G A Leonards "Investigation of Structural Failures" (1982) No GT2 (February) *Journal of the Geotechnical Engineering Division (ASCE)* 108.

9 e.g. NPWC/NBCC Joint Working Party, "No Dispute Strategies for Improvement in the Australian Building and Construction Industry" (May 1990); Sir Michael Latham, "Constructing the Team" (July 1994) Final Report; Sir John Egan, "Rethinking Construction" (1998).

10 The former US Secretary of Defense Donald Rumsfeld presented his trichology at a Defense Department Briefing on 12 February 2002:

> Reports that say that something hasn't happened are always interesting to me, because as we know, there are "known knowns"; there are things we know we know. We also know there are "known unknowns"; that is to say we know there are some things we do not know. But there are also "unknown unknowns" – the ones we don't know we don't know. (http://en.wikipedia.org/wiki/Unknown_unknown (accessed 10 April 2021)).

11 AS/NZS 4360:2004 Risk Management.

the term "risk" in relation to construction contracts is usually focused on adverse risks, i.e. those that have an adverse impact on attainment of the contract objective. However, it should be noted that the definition of risk above includes risk events that can either have an adverse or positive effect on the attainment of objectives.

Risk relating to "known knowns" is essentially project execution risk, i.e. the chance that defined project obligations in respect of time, cost or quality will not be fulfilled. In a well-written contract the consequences of the relevant identified risk events happening are usually adequately defined. Contracts frequently also make explicit provision for the obligations and rights arising from "known unknown" risks, since there is at least a suspicion that these may occur. A typical example of a "known unknown" risk event is latent ground conditions. Whilst the parties may have a suspicion that rock could be encountered during excavation for the foundations, it is not known if it will be nor, if it is, the extent or exact character of the rock. Nevertheless, the parties can define the obligations and rights of each of them in the event that rock is encountered. The unknown aspect of the latent conditions does not prevent appropriate definition of the scope of each party's relevant obligations and rights. Appropriate contractual provisions can be made for such latent conditions because they are foreseeable, even if the exact way and extent that they ultimately materialise is not actually foreseen.

"Unknown unknowns" relate to unforeseen risks that the parties have neither knowledge nor suspicion of. The "unknown unknown" risk events may be the most problematic if they happen, since the contract may not have made explicit provision for the rights and obligations arising. Each party may have different perceptions of the contractual consequences of such an event. An example of an "unknown unknown" risk event was the unacceptable vibration of the London Millennium Footbridge over the Thames which occurred immediately on its opening in 2000. The very unusual phenomenon of lateral vibrations under pedestrian traffic was not anticipated by the designers, and accordingly no provision had been made in the original design to control it.[12]

A risk, being the chance of a risk event happening, either materialises or it does not. If a contractual risk event does not happen, neither party assumes obligations nor gains rights in respect of the non-event. If a contractual risk event does happen, contractual action will need to be taken because the event impacts on the attainment of the contract objective. Contractual action in this sense will involve the exercise of (additional) obligations to deal with the impact of the risk event to mitigate its effect on attainment of the contract objective. The additional obligations arising result in a concomitant accrual of the obverse rights by the other party.

4.6 The relationship between contract "success" and risk

It is a widely held view that disputes in construction contracts are inevitable. Anecdotal experience behind the formation of so many enquiries into disputes in the construction industry[13] and the limited available statistics indicate a significant probability for the

12 P Dallard and others, "The London Millennium Footbridge" (2001) Vol 79 No 22 *The Structural Engineer* 17, 21.

13 e.g. Fourteen reports on construction since 1944 are listed in Peter Fenn, "Why construction contracts go wrong (or an aetiological approach to construction disputes)" (Paper given at a meeting of the Society of Construction Law, Derbyshire, 5 March 2002).

occurrence of a dispute in a construction contract.[14] Clearly a dispute is not inevitable in any one contract, as many contracts of various types are successful. However, the chance or probability of success is less than one because, demonstrably, some contracts end up in dispute.

To determine whether the form and/or terms of a construction contract reduces contractual risk, it would be necessary to have meaningful statistics of the probability of success for different types of contract, based on appropriate sample sizes. A specific form of contract which demonstrated greater "success" than the norm for all construction contracts would then indicate a higher probability of achieving the contract objective for that form of contract. The wide variety of different contractual approaches, different contract forms and the permutations and combinations resulting from individual contract clauses in different factual situations make this a formidable, if not impossible, challenge.

It follows that the success of an individual project (indicated by no disputes) could result from any one or more of, inter alia:

- A chance outcome of probability because risks did not materialise
- The form and/or terms of the contract which minimised contractual risk, or
- Successful risk management during execution of the project ensured that the risks that materialised did not impact the contract objective.

The latter two bullet points may well be interrelated, as the form and/or terms of the contract may encourage or promote successful risk management during the execution of the project itself.

Because of the intervention of probabilities, the success or lack of it in an individual contract cannot prove or disprove whether contractual risk is reduced or increased. However, one useful assessment that can be made is whether the form/terms of a contract in the particular circumstances contain provisions that are generally regarded as reducing the likelihood of disputes.

4.7 "Allocation" of risk

Davenport has suggested that it is misleading to refer to contracts as "allocating" risk, as contracts allocate obligations.[15] A risk, being the chance of an event happening, is not "allocated" to either party by the contract. It may exist separate and independent of the obligations and rights of the parties, or the risk event may be under the "control" of one of the parties. To use the example of extreme weather conditions, neither party "controls" the risk in the sense of having any responsibility for the risk event happening, namely the occurrence of extreme weather conditions different from those expected by both parties. However, the risk that the equipment used will not be capable of constructing the facility

14 e.g. according to one survey, more than one-third of the owners of major new construction projects in the United States are involved in arbitration or litigation of construction contract claims: B Bramble and M Callahan, *Construction Delay Claims* (3rd edn, 2000) 16–6.

15 Report by NPWC/NBCC Joint Working Party, "No Dispute Strategies for improvement in the Australian building and construction industry" (May 1990) 7.

is under the control of the Contractor who has the obligation to provide appropriate equipment to undertake the work.

Whether or not one of the parties has "control" over a risk event, it is the obligations and rights arising as a consequence of the risk event happening that is "allocated" by the contract. Thus, in respect of latent ground conditions, in addition to the Contractor's obligation to carry out the additional work, the contract may give it the right to both an extension of time (**EOT**) and additional compensation for the unforeseen additional work, whilst simultaneously placing an obligation on the Employer to grant an extension of time and pay the additional cost.

4.7.1 Abrahamson Principles of balanced risk allocation

The **Abrahamson Principles**, well known to construction lawyers, are widely regarded as the basis of "balanced" or "fair" or "efficient" risk allocation. These principles dictate that a party to a contract should bear a risk where:

1. It is in his control, i.e. if it comes about it will be due to wilful misconduct or lack of reasonable efficiency or care; or
2. He can transfer the risk by insurance and allow for the premium in settling his charges to the other party (or to his other customers) or spread it directly in his prices, and it is most economically beneficial and practicable for the risk to be dealt with in that way; or;
3. The preponderant economic benefit of running the risk accrues to him; or
4. To place the risk on him is in the interests of efficiency (which includes planning, incentive, innovation) and the long-term health of the construction industry on which that depends; or
5. If the risk eventuates, the loss falls on him in the first instance and it is not practicable, or there is no reason under the above four principles to cause expense and uncertainty, and possibly make mistakes, in trying to transfer the loss to another.[16]

Many standard form contracts are based on the explicitly stated principle of balanced or fair risk allocation, e.g. the Australian Standard 4000 series,[17] the US ConsensusDocs,[18] the UK New Engineering Contract,[19] the European Engineering Industries Association,[20] the International Chamber of Commerce,[21] the Baltic and International Marine Council[22] and contracts for the UK offshore oil and gas industry.[23] The principle of balanced or fair risk

16 Max W Abrahamson, "Risk Management" (1983) *International Construction Law Review* 241, 244.

17 "Standard Conditions of Contract" (2001) 4 *BDPS News* 1, 4.

18 https://www.consensusdocs.org/faqs/ (accessed 10 April 2021).

19 Brian Eggleston, *The New Engineering Contract A Commentary* (1996) 7.

20 Orgalime, *Turnkey Contract for Industrial Works*.

21 International Chamber of Commerce Model Turnkey Contract for Major Projects (2007). www.iccbooks.com/Product/ProductInfo.aspx?id=488 (accessed 14 June 2016).

22 www.bimco.org/Corporate%20Area/About/BIMCO_a_century_of_service.aspx (accessed 25 November 2008).

23 Leading Oil and Gas Industry Competitiveness (LOGIC) www.logic-oil.com (accessed 10 April 2021).

allocation is also espoused by government procurement agencies in the UK,[24] Australia[25] and the United States.[26] Many writers suggest that adherence to the principle of balanced risk allocation enhances the prospect of successful contracts, by encouraging contractual performance that minimises adverse outcomes and thereby reduces disputation.[27]

4.7.2 Inappropriate allocation of risks

Conversely, many contracts inappropriately allocate risks:

> One of the worst kept secrets in the construction industry is that the provision of design and construction services is egocentric and inefficient. Risk assessment is a dark art. Risk allocation is an exercise in economic Darwinism. Traditional contracts rigidly delineate responsibilities with much elaboration on the consequences of failure. These contracting approaches reinforce self-protective behaviour and instil mistrust. Moreover, while many risks can be identified and evaluated such that the effort to do so is well spent, often the unknowable remains material to the success of the enterprise. Nevertheless, traditional construction contracting improperly presumes a high degree of clairvoyance when allocating risk. More often than not risk flows down the contracting tiers to those least able to bear or control the risk. Not surprisingly, classical contracts combined with traditional delivery methods often produce sub-optimal results.[28]

Following significant criticism of the procurement of Sydney's light rail, in 2018 the NSW Government published "A ten-point commitment to the construction sector" in which it recognised

> that not all risks are capable of being fully assessed, priced, managed or absorbed by the private sector, and that such risks must be managed collaboratively – including risks related to utilities, planning approvals and latent conditions. As a matter of principle, risks should be managed by the party best able to manage them, and should be shared where necessary.[29]

Significantly the NSW Government accepts that obtaining value for money does not mean obtaining the lowest price for every project; a broader, longer-term view about the need to drive quality, innovation and cost-effectiveness is necessary for a thriving and sustainable construction sector.

---

24 "The governing principle is that risk should be allocated to whichever party from the public or private sector is best placed to manage it. The optimal allocation of risk, rather than maximising risk transfer, is the objective, and is vital to ensuring that the best solution is found." HM Treasury, *The Green Book Appraisal and Evaluation in Central Government* http://greenbook.treasury.gov.uk/annex04.htm (accessed 26 August 2008).

25 "Both the government and the private party should seek to ensure that cost and adequate risk transfer are balanced as far as possible to achieve the best value for money on a particular project." Department of Treasury and Finance Victorian Government, *Partnerships Victoria Updated Standard Commercial Principles* (2008) 99.

26 "A fundamental tenet of risk management is to allocate the risks to the party best able to manage them. The party assuming the risk should be able to best evaluate, control, bear the risk of, and benefit from its assumption." US Department of Transportation Federal Highway Administration, *Risk Assessment and Allocation for Highway Construction Management* (2006) 31 https://international.fhwa.dot.gov/pubs/pl06032/guide_to_risk_assessment_allocation_for_highway.pdf (accessed 10 April 2021).

27 NPWC/NBCC Joint Working Party, "No Dispute Strategies for Improvement in the Australian Building and Construction Industry" (May 1990) 6–7; Sir Michael Latham, 'Constructing the Team' (July 1994) Final Report 37.

28 Patrick J O'Connor Jr, "Integrated Project Delivery: Collaboration through New Contract Forms" (2009), www.faegre.com/webfiles/AGC-IPD%20Paper.pdf (accessed 14 June 2016).

29 https://www.infrastructure.nsw.gov.au/media/1649/10-point-commitment-to-the-construction-industry-final-002.pdf (accessed 10 April 2021).

4.7.3 The consequences of inappropriate risk allocation

A consequence of inappropriately allocating excessive risk to the Contractor is that it can actually increase the Employer's risks. The Japan International Cooperation Agency (**JICA**) commissioned the Association of Japanese Consulting Engineers to prepare a "Check List for One Sided Contracts" to be used for the preparation of reasonable bidding documents. JICA noted that if modifications for a particular project alter the originally contemplated risk distribution in a FIDIC Red Book Contract to a large extent and the risks allocated to the Contractor become excessively high, the following problems may occur:

- Higher bid price.
- Bid failure and disruption of project implementation.
- Non-participation in the bid by conscientious and capable contractors.
- Contract awarded to a bidder who failed to, or was not capable of, estimating the risks properly.
- Poor construction quality and delay to the progress of the work due to lack of risk contingency.
- Undermining the relationship of mutual trust and respect between the Employer and the Contractor.
- Repetition of groundless claims from the Contractor,
- Frequent disputes between the Employer and the Contractor.
- In an extreme case, termination of the contract.[30]

4.8 Risk management

"Risk management" is a widely used term which means different things to different people. Consistent with international standards, Australian Standard AS4360:2004 states that risk management is a holistic management process involving: identification, analysis, evaluation, treatment, communication and monitoring of risks. Treatment involves ways of dealing with identified risks in various ways in order to change them, and the term is synonymous with "control" in the Abrahamson sense. The term "risk management" is often used in the more restricted sense of risk treatment or control. Avoidance, abatement (minimisation) or transfer of a risk are specific methods of risk treatment.

The Abrahamson Principles are predicated on the concept of which party "controls" a risk. A neutral risk is one which neither party "controls". It is suggested that "control" by a party in respect of non-neutral risks means that the party can influence at least one of:

- The likelihood of the risk event happening
- The nature of the risk event, or
- The consequences if the risk event happens.

30 Check List for One Sided Contracts (Japan International Cooperation Agency, 2011), 1 https://www.jica.go.jp/activities/schemes/finance_co/procedure/guideline/pdf/check_e.pdf (accessed 12 April 2021).

4.9 Scope and risk

As noted above, a contract defines the scope of each party's rights and obligations in pursuit of the contract objective. Each such obligation carries with it the risk of non-performance and the obverse risk of the other party not receiving its corresponding right. Many clauses in construction contracts are terms that are designed to "encourage" performance of the contractual obligations, by use of either the "carrot" or the "stick". A bonus/penalty clause for early/late completion is an example of both approaches. Whatever method is adopted, the aim of such provisions is to reduce the risk of non-performance of contractual obligations. Of course, the ultimate stick is the legal sanction of damages for breach of contract to "encourage" performance of contractual obligations.

It is suggested that the better the definition of the scope of contractual obligations, the smaller the risk of non-performance of those obligations. The more "known knowns" there are, the fewer the "known unknowns" and "unknown unknowns", and the smaller the ambit of the risks. Ambiguity of contract terms is the antithesis of a clear definition of contract scope, since each party may have a different view of its rights and obligations arising from such terms. Such ambiguity must increase the risk of non-performance and the likelihood of subsequent disputes.

4.10 Risk events

True "unknown unknowns" form an important class of risks and risk events, as by definition they are not foreseeable, or at least were not foreseen by either contractual party. Contractually, the occurrence of an "unknown unknown" risk event can have the following consequences:

(a) One party has a contractual liability arising from the happening of the risk event, because dealing with the event is within that party's contractual obligations.
(b) The event is a *force majeure* event that triggers the relevant contractual provisions excusing performance.
(c) The contract is frustrated.

As an example of (a), in a contract with no *force majeure* or unforeseeable events clause, a severe earthquake in an area classified as not subject to significant earthquakes might cause collapse of a partly constructed structure, leaving the Contractor with expensive reinstatement work to complete at its own cost (which event it may or may not have insured for).

The determination of which category an "unknown unknown" risk falls into depends on construction of the terms of the contract. The consequences of risk events (a) and (b) are determined in accordance with the provisions of the contract. A *force majeure* clause is a contractual mechanism to prevent an "unknown unknown" risk event outside the control of either party triggering termination of the contract because of frustration.

However, a type (c) risk event is one in which the law steps in to determine the outcome by terminating the contract. Frustration occurs

> whenever the law recognizes that without default of either party a contractual obligation has become incapable of being performed because the circumstances in which performance is

> called for would render it a thing radically different from that which was undertaken by the contract.[31]

That is, the contract does not allocate the consequences of the risk event happening to either party.

It is submitted that the more work done to convert "unknown unknowns" into "known unknowns", or to convert "known unknowns" into "known knowns", the better the project scope will be defined, and the fewer and smaller the risks will be. In other words, careful attention to the contractual terms that define the obligations of each party and the scope of time, cost and quality will reduce contractual risk.

4.11 The choice of contract type

For the purposes of this book, the term "construction contract" is confined to contracts in which construction of a physical structure is undertaken, thereby excluding e.g. design contracts etc. Even with this limited definition, there are a number of more or less distinct species of construction contract, as a perusal of the list of standard forms published by organisations such as the Joint Contracts Tribunal, Australian Standards and ConsensusDocs (US) will confirm.

Although there are various ways of distinguishing one type of contract from another, what is significant for present purposes is the extent to which each contract party, Employer or Contractor, assumes contractual risk. Considering contractual risk as the aggregation of time, cost, quality (and perhaps design) issues, the following hierarchy lists "adversarial" contracts in increasing order of Employer risk and decreasing order of Contractor risk:

- EPC/turnkey
- Design and construct
- "Traditional" (design-bid-build)
- Management contracting/project management
- Construction management.

An **EPC contract** (engineer, procure and construct contract) is a construction contract (also referred to as a **turnkey contract**) in which the Contractor takes total responsibility for the engineering (design), procurement and construction, and provides a fully equipped facility ready for operation (at the "turn of the key").

At the opposite end of the Contractor risk spectrum is an **EPCM contract**: a typical form of construction management contract in which the Contractor, as Construction Manager, designs, procures and manages the construction as agent of the Employer.

Within any one of these contract categories there can be a spectrum of risk allocation, e.g. the lump sum, measurement or "cost plus" variants of a traditional construct-only contract. These types of contracts are termed "adversarial" because of the way in which the legal rights and obligations of each party are formalised in the traditional way by means of the contract. Typically, assuming more risk also means more control over the

31 *Davis Contractors Ltd v Fareham Urban District Council* [1956] AC 696, 723.

relevant risk events. By contrast, the risk allocation in modern collaborative contracting arrangements such as alliancing or partnering explicitly seeks to manage execution of the contract cooperatively to share risks and rewards on an equitable basis, and eschew disputes between parties.

It is submitted that, in practice, an Employer procuring a project must make a trade-off between its desires in respect of time, cost and quality. A quick, cheap and high-quality project is an oxymoron. It is therefore suggested that parties need to understand what each type of contract can and cannot achieve in respect of time, cost and quality, and who takes the risks. Thus, the biggest contribution to minimising risks is by selection of the most appropriate form of contract that increases the likelihood of achieving the most important outcome(s). The differences between the different types of contract are essentially in who manages and controls particular risks. The following discussion of the characteristics and risk allocation of different types of contract illustrates the importance of selecting the appropriate procurement strategy and form of contract consistent with the Employer's priorities.

Construction management/EPCM is an appropriate form of contract for an Employer who wants to have ultimate control of the quality of construction, whilst endeavouring to minimise the overall elapsed time. By directly contracting the designers and trade subcontractors, coordinated by a Construction Manager, the Employer retains "control" over the designers and quality desired to be built into the project, as well as over the construction. If required, a construction managed project can be "fast tracked", in which construction starts before the design is completed. There is, however, a cost penalty in starting construction before design is completed, both for the design stage and the construction, which may not be able to be competitively bid. Furthermore, because open-ended commitments to construction contractors and subcontractors may need to be made to achieve the target completion date, the ultimate cost may not be known before completion of the work. The Employer minimises its quality risk by appropriate selection and management of its designers and Construction Manager; however, it will generally assume both time and cost risk.

Parliament House in Canberra is an example of a large complex building (actually a number of buildings) procured by construction management. One of the main drivers of this form of procurement was the opening date for the building, fixed in the late 1970s to be in Australia's bicentennial year 1988. Maintaining the highest standards of quality to produce a durable building designed to last 200 years was of equal importance to delivering the building on time. Whilst there was a rigorous cost control programme, and there were many legitimate reasons for cost increases, the ultimate cost escalated substantially over the initial budget. A part of the substantial cost of this building was undoubtedly the result of the fast track construction, and the construction management form of procurement. This project is discussed in detail in Section 15.3. See also Section 3.1.2 for an example of the consequences of fast track construction on the Sydney Opera House.

An Employer focus exclusively on quality in a construction management contract results in significant time and cost risks – the final cost will not be known until near the end of the project, and the completion date may be much later than anticipated. This is exactly what happened at the new Scottish Parliament House – the Employer's single-minded focus on delivering an outstanding architectural building design produced by a signature architect resulted in massive time and budget overruns (see Section 15.4). By contrast, the Australian Parliament House Construction Authority appears to have managed both quality and time within the Employer's expectations (see Section 15.3).

If the Employer's primary focus is on achieving high quality with minimal cost risks, the traditional design-bid-build contract may provide the best option. The Employer directly engages the designers and has maximum control over the quality to be achieved, both in design and construction. The design can be finalised to the Employer's satisfaction before it is put out to competitive bid by competent acceptable contractors. Assuming an appropriate remuneration structure, the designers have no conflict of interest in designing to the quality desired by the Employer. Engagement of the designers to supervise the construction work provides the best opportunity to "keep the Contractor honest" and ensure that the contractual quality is achieved. Costs can be managed by the appropriate fee arrangement with the designers, and competitive bidding on a completed design to select the construction Contractor. Time during the design stage is more difficult to manage, as there may not be effective controls to ensure that the designers perform within the desired timeframe (see Section 6.3.1). The appropriate use of liquidated damages encourages the Contractor to manage the construction time within the contractual expectations, subject to a "penalty" for late completion. Successful design-bid-build with minimal variations requires that the design be completed before bids are sought for construction, and accordingly this contractual approach generally cannot deliver a project in the minimum feasible time.

Design-construct is an appropriate contractual approach for an Employer who requires a project completed in minimum time for a defined price with minimal cost risks. The Contractor assumes responsibility for design, thereby eliminating one source of potential disputes between Employer and Contractor – the risk of late delivery of or errors in design to the required documentation quality. Subject to adequately specifying the required quality in the design brief, the Employer knows the ultimate design and construction cost at the time that the design and construct contract is entered into. However, as the design is the responsibility of the Contractor, the Employer will have limited opportunity to influence or control the resulting quality after the Contract is entered into. As with other forms of contract, there are risks that, if they materialise will increase the ultimate cost; however, the extent of risks assumed by the Employer in a design and construct contract is considerably less than in a design-bid-build contract. Sydney Harbour Bridge was a successful project delivered by design and construct in which the Employer meticulously specified the required quality in the tender documentation; this is discussed in detail in Section 16.2.

In reality, every successful project does reconcile the tensions between achieving the required time, cost and quality. Clearly there are successful projects delivered by every form of project procurement, be it construction management, design-bid-build, design and construct or the many other methods of procurement beyond the spectrum of these three, such as partnering/alliancing at one end or turnkey/PPP at the other end.

It is apparent from this brief summary of the different types of construction contract that there are "horses for courses". An Employer that requires time and price certainty is ill-advised to adopt Construction Management, amply demonstrated by the time and cost overruns on Scottish Parliament House.[32] An Employer that requires the shortest possible

32 Scotland, *A Report by the Rt Hon Lord Fraser of Carmyllie QC, The Holyrood Inquiry*, SP Paper No 205 (2004).

construction time will need to select an alternative to traditional contracting, perhaps design and construct. However, it may not have the same level of control over the quality of the finished facility as it would under the traditional design-bid-build procurement. Thus, it is suggested that irrespective of the specific terms of the contract, if the type of contract is inappropriate for the Employer's most important criteria for success, the risks of not achieving its objectives will be higher than necessary.

4.12 Risk and contract forms

In a 1996 paper, Fenn and others reported the results of a significant survey of users of Standard Form Contracts.[33] This survey endeavoured to determine users' perceptions of the influence of the form of contract on the incidence of disputes. The survey reports on the perceived expectancy of disputes of users of 14 different standard form contracts. The contracts were various standard forms published by Institution of Chemical Engineers (**IChemE**), Joint Contracts Tribunal (including design and build), ICE (including design and build) and the UK Government (GC Wks 1). The statistical results presented were derived from a total of 1,873 uses of Standard Form contracts. In addition, there were 117 uses of a one-off or bespoke contract reported. It was found that there were significant differences between some contract forms in the expectation of disputes. In particular, the NEC, IChemE and JCT 81 Design and Build forms were found to have a significantly lower expectation of disputes than the JCT 80, ICE (Fifth Edition, 1973) and GC Wks 1. It is interesting to note that the bespoke contracts had the highest expectation of disputes, followed closely by GC Wks 1. It is submitted that this data suggests that, as some contract forms are perceived to result in a higher incidence of disputes than others, the use of some contract forms involve higher risk than others.

Risk is an explicit consideration in the NEC suite of contracts. Transparent allocation and reduction of risk is a stated aim of the drafting of each of the different forms.[34] The most significant contribution of the NEC contracts to contractual risk reduction may be in the specific obligation to establish and maintain a risk register. Good risk management practice is thereby promoted by the requirements of the contract itself. The experience of the widespread use of NEC contracts over the period of more than 20 years since the First Edition appears to confirm its success. Lloyd reported that up to 2008 there was only one significant judicial decision involving NEC contracts.[35] This does seem to indicate that in comparison to other standard form and bespoke contracts over the same period, NEC contracts resulted in fewer disputes and therefore reduced contractual risk.

4.13 Conclusion

Every contract has risks that the contract objective will not be achieved because of a shortfall in one or more of the contractual expectations of time, cost and quality. Notwithstanding the well-documented history of problems with many construction contracts, some projects are successful because there is no shortfall between contractual

33 Peter Fenn, David Lowe and Christopher Speck, "Conflict and dispute in construction" (1997) 15 *Construction Management and Economics* 513.

34 Brian Eggleston, *The New Engineering Contract A Commentary* (1996) 7.

35 Humphrey Lloyd, "Thoughts on NEC3" (2008) 25 *International Construction Law Review* 468, 470.

expectations and performance. Whilst such outcomes can be a statistical outcome of probability in that risks did not materialise or impact achievement of the contract objective, it is suggested that risk management at both pre- and post-contract stages is a central feature of many successful projects.

This chapter has suggested that the contract has a central role to play in risk minimisation. First, the selection of the appropriate form of contract gives priority to the most important aspects of delivery of the Employer's project. Second, the terms of the contract can have a positive effect in minimising contract risk by "allocating" risks to the party best able to "control" them. Third, the contract can promote the cooperative management of risks by its formal execution and reporting requirements, rather than leaving them as the individual responsibility of one party to deal with during execution of the project. Risks that have been understood, analysed and evaluated can often be treated (controlled) to reduce the likelihood of occurrence, the nature of the risk or the impact of occurrence. Such "contractual" risk management, it is submitted, can reduce the overall contractual risk. If, however, risks are ignored or inappropriately "controlled", there will be an increased risk that the contract objective will not be achieved.

CHAPTER 5

Managing design risk[1]

5.1 Introduction

Every construction project has a substantial element of design in it, whether the Employer or the Contractor engages the designer. In percentage terms, the cost of design is generally a small part of the overall cost of a construction project, and a very small part of the overall cost of a project considered over its life cycle. However, as it is the design that defines not only the form and nature of the construction, but also the characteristics of the constructed facility that determine the ongoing operating and maintenance costs over its entire life, its importance is substantially greater than the proportion of its percentage cost of the project.

The Employer in a construction project has a real interest in ensuring that design risks are appropriately managed to ensure, to the greatest extent possible, that the final constructed facility will fulfil its expectations. Equally, the designer has its own commercial interest in managing the design appropriately so that its own commercial and other objectives are fulfilled. This chapter explores the ways in which design risks can be managed by the Employer, as well as by the designer. It looks at the nature of design in the context of construction projects, and who typically carries it out, and then identifies what are the significant design risks. Those risks are looked at from the perspective of who should bear them, contrasted with the situation of who typically bears those design risks. A number of common issues in mismanaging design risk are reviewed, followed by some suggestions as to good practice in minimising design risk. The fundamental thesis of this chapter is that, because of the fundamental importance of design to the functionality and overall cost of a constructed facility, the quality of design is of overarching importance in construction contracts. The corollary of this is that sufficient time and cost need to be devoted to the design to ensure that the appropriate quality is achieved.

5.2 What is design?

Some appropriate dictionary definitions of design are: "to intend for a definite purpose" or "to form or conceive in the mind; contrive; plan".[2] Another which encapsulates the

1 This chapter is an edited version of papers published in: Donald Charrett, "Managing Design Risk" (2012) 142 *Australian Construction Law Newsletter* 6; Donald Charrett "Managing Design Contracts" (2012) 15(10) *Inhouse Counsel* 317.

2 The Macquarie Dictionary.

DOI: 10.4324/9781003206897-6

essence of design in a construction context is: "formulation of an idea and turning it into a practical reality".[3]

For the purposes of this book, **design** of a facility is taken to include all plans, drawings, sketches, instructions, and descriptions that determine the way the facility (or parts of it) is (are) to be constructed. Design includes the writing or selection of specifications, as well as the production of plans and drawings and any element of choice on the part of the designer, such as requirements as to materials or working methods. Many modern construction projects typically involve a significant element of computer software, the writing of which is an important design task.

The design of a facility involves all the large and small decisions required, inter alia, to determine its form, how its elements work individually and in combination to fulfil their functional requirements, what materials will be used in construction, how these are connected, how the facility is to be constructed, and how it should be operated. Decisions made during the design of the facility will dictate how it will need to be maintained to retain its functionality, what the operating costs will be and the ultimate design life. In the context of a specific construction project, "design" may also include the selection of appropriate equipment or even an entire manufacturing process to be incorporated in the facility; the original design of such equipment or process has been prepared previously, and that design IP is already embedded in the equipment or process.

Design is typically the province of the "designer", frequently a different organisation to the Employer or the Contractor. Nevertheless, as the above definition of design indicates, the Contractor itself may be the "designer" of specific elements. Thus, in a design-construct contract where the Contractor engaged another organisation to carry out the design of sewerage lagoons, the Contractor was responsible for the design of the anchorage of the waterproof membrane:

> In this case, [the designer's] design made it clear that the installation of the [membrane] was a matter for [the Contractor] to attend to, in accordance with the manufacturer's installation guidelines. It is clear that the "for construction" design drawings did not specify any detail for stabilizing or securing the [membrane] at the top of the embankments.[4]
>
> I conclude that the failure to install the [membrane] using an anchor trench was a departure from [the designer's] design that was not approved by [the designer]. It was a departure for which, relevantly, [the Contractor] bore sole responsibility.[5]

5.2.1 Intellectual property

It is clear from these definitions that an essential distinction between the design task and the construction task is that the former exclusively involves the production of intellectual property (**IP**), whereas the latter involves the assembly of components of real property into a constructed facility on the land. In legal terms, a contract for design is a contract for services (typically considered to be professional services) whereas a contract for construction is a contract for goods and services, the services in this case being the labour applied

3 *The New Penguin Dictionary of Civil Engineering* (2005).
4 *CH2M Hill v New South Wales* [2012] NSWSC 963, (2014) 30 BCL 35, [192].
5 *CH2M Hill v New South Wales* [2012] NSWSC 963, (2014) 30 BCL 35, [228].

to the goods to construct the facility, as well as the IP required for whatever design the contractor must supply.

5.2.2 The influence of design on a facility

The design of a facility has a pervading influence, not only on the cost of construction but, perhaps even more importantly, on the operating and maintenance costs throughout its life. Indeed, it is the design that ultimately determines the effective life of a facility, and the requirements for repairs, renovation or refurbishment during its life. In many if not most construction projects, there is a well-known trade-off between the capital cost of construction, and the ongoing maintenance and operating costs throughout the operating life of the facility. Cheaper construction costs, achieved by the selection of less durable materials or less robust equipment, often lead to significantly higher maintenance and operating costs. This issue was brought into sharp focus during the construction of the Channel Tunnel: the consortium of civil engineering contractors who constructed the infrastructure and procured the equipment had a real contractual interest in minimising the construction costs, whereas the operating entity's interest was in minimising the life cycle costs, including the costs of operation and maintenance over many decades. The contractual arrangements did not adequately address those conflicts of interest – there was an ambiguous optimisation clause, which required the best balance that could be achieved between capital costs and operating, costs. Inevitably, this resulted in expensive and complex disputes.[6]

5.2.3 The 1:10:100 "rule"

The significance of design cost in relation to a project is succinctly encapsulated in the 1:10:100 "rule":

> Over one typical "life cycle" of a facility, for every one dollar $1 spent on design, at least ten dollars $10 are spent on construction and at least one hundred dollars $100 are spent on OM&R [operation, maintenance and repairs/refurbishment].[7]

Thus, whilst design may represent of the order of 10% of the construction cost, it is typically only of the order of 1% of the total life cycle costs of a facility. Considering the importance of the design function in making the fundamental decisions which will determine not only the constructed cost but also the total life cycle cost, it is clearly of the utmost importance to obtain the best (most appropriate?) design. These relative cost figures indicate that, in the overall picture, the cost of design itself is of far less significance than the quality of the design that determines the life cycle costs of the project.

The following highlights the fallacy of least construction cost necessarily being the most economical:

> True economy in engineering consists in always designing and building structures, machines and other constructions so that, while they will perform satisfactorily in every way for the

6 Alan Muir Wood, *Civil Engineering in Context* (2000) at 174; Terry Gourvish, *The Official History of Britain and the Channel Tunnel* (2006) at 352–356.

7 www.barchanfoundation.com/index.php?option=com_content&view=article&id=47:life-cycle-methods-will-remain-after-the-gfc&catid=3:public-content&Itemid=9 (accessed 14 June 2016).

> functions for which they are required, the sum of their first cost and the equivalent capitalised cost for their maintenance, operation and repairs shall be a minimum. The ordinary notion that the structure or machine that is least in first cost must be the most economical is a fallacy. In fact, in many cases just the opposite is true, the structure or machine involving the largest first cost being often the cheapest.[8]

Although this statement was made over 100 years ago, it is equally true in the 21st century, articulated in the following:

> Price and cost are two different things. Price is meaningless; you can have a higher price at the start, but it may serve to lower costs over the lifetime of a construction. When working on price only, it is more than certain that the product, whether it is a road, or a building, or a whole infrastructure, will not be designed the optimum way.[9]

5.2.4 Quality-based procurement

The European Union recognises that best value public procurement is not achieved by solely focussing on lowest cost. Directive 2014/24/EU requires public contracts to be based on the most economically advantageous tender (**MEAT**), which requires the use of a cost-effectiveness approach, such as life cycle costing. Criteria for determination of the MEAT may include aspects such as quality, including technical merit, aesthetic and functional characteristics, accessibility, design for all users, social, environmental and innovative characteristics and trading and its conditions.[10]

The European Federation of Engineering Consultancy Associations (**EFCA**) has published a document on how to derive MEAT criteria for procurement of consulting services, in its efforts to encourage clients to use criteria other than, or in addition to, price in awarding contracts for design services.[11] The quality criteria recommended by EFCA are: functionality, availability, aesthetics, sustainability (of the product), sustainability (of the process), life cycle costs, risk management and environment.

FIDIC has long championed the use of Quality Based Selection (**QBS**) as the primary method for the procurement of engineering services. QBS is the means of procuring the most appropriate, experienced and reputable professionals to produce the designs that satisfy the client's needs. In respect of using the lowest price to procure professional services (including design), FIDIC cautions:

> FIDIC acknowledges that many Client organisations see competition based on price as being fundamental to maintaining integrity and probity. While this may be true in respect of product supply against a specification, it is rarely an effective approach when procuring professional services. Professional services are provided from knowledge and experience bases built up over many years, from many highly qualified people and from thousands of projects. The intrinsic value of these intellectual assets is not reflected in the fees

8 JAL Waddell, "The Relations of Civil Engineering to Other branches of Science" in JAL Waddell and JL Harrington (eds), *Addresses to Engineering Students* (1911) 266.

9 Kevin Rudden, EFCA President in EFCA, *How to Derive MEAT Criteria* (EFCA, 2019) 5.

10 Directive 2014/24/EU of the European Parliament and of the Council of 26 November 2014 on public procurement Article 67.

11 EFCA, *How to Derive MEAT Criteria* (EFCA, 2019).

professionals charge their clients, but in the qualifications and quality of the services offered and delivered by the Consultant.[12]

5.3 Who carries out design?

As noted above, design is an intellectual exercise. It is based on the knowledge, experience and skill of the practitioners who carry out the design. All these three elements are fundamental to the production of designs that are suitable for their purpose. Knowledge is usually gained initially from tertiary education, supplemented by the lifelong learning that is the hallmark of a true professional. Self-evidently, experience is gained from having worked on other projects. The skill arises from the synthesis of the knowledge and experience in a relevant way to the project at hand. It is the quality of this exercise of intellect that ultimately determines the quality of the design. Neither knowledge nor experience alone or in combination is adequate; skill is necessary to produce an appropriate design.

The employer who wishes to build a facility engages a designer to produce the required IP for initial construction, and (possibly) also for the subsequent operation and maintenance (the term "employer" is used in this chapter to refer to the entity that engages the designer, irrespective of whether the employer is an owner or a design and construct or EPC Contractor). To produce the project IP the designer must draw on his/her own IP in the form of his/her knowledge, experience and skill (**personal IP**). Typically, an employer will seek to engage the designer who has what is perceived to be the most appropriate personal IP for the project, taking into account such other factors as time and cost. Other things being equal, experience in similar projects is a significant aspect of the required personal IP. An employer would generally prefer to engage a designer who has relevant experience of similar projects over one who, although otherwise apparently equal, has no such experience.

In much of the world, independent professionals in the form of consulting engineers or architects carry out the majority of design. Construction contractors, even major international contractors, do not normally have a large in-house staff of designers for the permanent works, although they may well have in-house designers with particular expertise in the design of the temporary works needed during construction. The barriers to entry for new consultants are few, and there is a wide spectrum of sizes of consulting firms. Statistics on the size of consulting engineering firms in Australia show that the industry was predominantly composed of small-scale firms of one to ten people; in 2006 only 6% of total establishments employed more than 20 people, and only 0.3% employed more than 200 people.[13] Thus, notwithstanding the size and capacity of the largest consulting engineers, in Australia at least, small firms of fewer than 20 people carry out the majority of consulting engineering.

Consulting engineering and architectural practice is based on "peopleware", and not on significant capital assets. It is often said that a consulting engineer's assets go home every night. The consequence of this is that the bottom line of a consulting engineer's balance sheet is typically comprised of mainly intangible assets that retain their value only whilst the organisation is an ongoing entity, able to continue to win consulting assignments in a

12 FIDIC, *Selection of Consultants* (FIDIC, 3rd edn, 2019) 8 https://fidic.org/sites/default/files/selection%20of%20consultants%20guide_2019.pdf (accessed 11 April 2021).

13 Anthony Kelly, *Ibis World Industry Report L7823 Engineering Consultancy Services in Australia* (June 2011) 25.

competitive marketplace. One need only reflect on the rapid collapse of Arthur Andersen in 2002 to realise how a consultant's ability to continue in business is dependent on its reputation, and how ephemeral are the intangible assets of even a large consulting organisation.

It is suggested that employers should be very cautious in assessing the financial ability of a consulting engineer to meet contractual obligations based on the balance sheet value of the business. In the event of a major claim against a consulting engineer, the only predictable financial resources available may be the proceeds of professional indemnity insurance. The balance sheet is almost certain to substantially overestimate the value of the business in the event of insolvency, as the intangible assets are unlikely to be realised.

5.4 What are the design risks?

It is suggested that, similar to the risks in a construct-only contract, design risks can simplistically be considered under the headings of scope, time, cost and quality.

5.4.1 Scope

The extent of the works to be designed, i.e. the scope of the design, is likely to be the biggest single determinant of the cost of design. In a competitive environment where the cost of the design services is a significant factor in selecting a designer, a consulting engineer/architect will minimise fees by tailoring the scope of the design services to deliver precisely what is required by the contract and no more.

For the employer, the scope risks are that the designer has not allowed in the design price for completing the scope required by the employer. For the designer, the scope risks are that it will be required under the design contract to carry out a greater scope than it will be paid for.

5.4.2 Time

The time taken to prepare the design as well as its cost are usually at the forefront of the employer's considerations in selecting a designer. Most construction projects have significant time constraints, as well as a limited budget. The inherent time risk for the employer is that the design will not be completed on time, thereby delaying construction with an inevitable increase in cost. This risk is particularly acute once a contractor has been appointed and has been given possession of the site; any delay in completing the design which delays construction may have significant cost consequences, out of proportion to the cost of the design delay itself.

The designer's time risk is that it will not complete the design within the time required under the design contract, thereby exposing it to claims for financial loss by the employer. Parliament House Scotland is a well-known example of substantial time and cost overruns in the construction of a seminal building, significantly contributed to by the time and cost overruns of the design, coupled with "fast track" construction and a construction management form of contract[14] (see Section 15.4).

14 Scotland, *A Report by the Rt Hon Lord Fraser of Carmyllie QC, The Holyrood Inquiry*, SP Paper No 205 (2004) 136.

5.4.3 Cost

The risk inherent in the cost of design for the employer is that it will not get the value it is expecting; that may be a consequence of the employer's unreasonable expectations not supported by the provisions of the design contract, or the designer not delivering the value required by the contract.

In a competitive environment for consulting services, competition is likely to have a levelling effect on the cost of design. Although there will be a range of skills and experience among the available designers competent to prepare the design for a particular facility, their basic capabilities are likely to be substantially similar. The employment cost of professionals (the greatest single cost factor) will be based on the prevailing marketplace, and typical overhead costs including office accommodation are likely to be comparable. Designer's fee rates will therefore generally fall within a limited range; however consultants with greater skill and experience may have higher employment costs and may also be able to command a premium for their skill. Higher quality design may therefore entail higher cost.

Conversely, a substantially lower cost design for a defined scope of work may be based on under bidding ("buying the job"), or a lack of appreciation of the work necessary to complete a competent design. The designer who understands least what is required to complete the design to the employer's requirements may submit the minimum tendered cost for design.

Whether low design costs result from buying the job or underestimation of the design task, the result is likely to be that the designer faces the prospect of a significant financial loss in completing its design scope. A fixed lump sum contract for design may be legally effective in forcing the designer to complete the design for the agreed price, but where the designer is in a serious loss-making situation because it has under bid or underestimated, the quality of the end product may suffer from lack of resources: inadequate checking to correct mistakes, failure to coordinate designs between different disciplines, or inadequate consideration of what the appropriate design solution should be, to name just a few possibilities. The inevitable result, it is submitted, is that the quality of the design will suffer.

The cost risks for the designer are that it will not be adequately paid for the design it is obliged to carry out under the design contract. This may result from the designer's own underestimation of the design task, an inadequate understanding of its obligations under the design contract, a failure to recognise and claim for scope changes as variations, incompetent personnel who do not possess the appropriate skills, or inadequate supervision and coordination of the design team.

5.4.4 Design quality

It is submitted that, because of the role of the design in determining the aesthetic, functional and economic characteristics of the completed project, the quality of the design is of overarching importance, not only to the employer for whom the design is prepared, but also for the designer in terms of its ongoing reputation and potential liability. The quality risks for both employer and designer are therefore paramount.

The design quality risks for the employer are that the design will not be of the appropriate quality to satisfy its manifold requirements, including aesthetics, functionality, maintainability, operability, economic performance and design life. The design quality risks for the designer include the possibility of liability for damages for poor quality design, and reputational risks that could have severe long-term effects on its ability to win future work in the marketplace.

5.4.5 IP risk

There is a further risk that needs careful consideration in a design contract: IP risk. The employer's IP risk is that it may suffer delay or additional cost in construction, operation, maintenance, repair or renovation of the facility because of an aspect of IP embedded in the design which it does not have legal title to. One of the designer's IP risks is that, for IP it created for a specific project, it may not retain the right to use that IP in future projects, thereby foregoing future opportunities. Another designer's IP risk is that, in the absence of an appropriate agreement with a subcontractor, it may not have the IP rights in designs prepared by the subcontractor which the designer is contractually required to transfer to the employer.

5.4.6 Interface risk

The interface risk is that the facility will not be constructed strictly in accordance with the design.

5.4.7 Insolvency

In addition to the "execution" risks identified above, there is also the risk of the designer's insolvency. Whilst that may normally be a remote risk, if it eventuates it will inevitably have severe consequences for the employer (as well as for the designer itself!). Those consequences for the employer include inevitable delays in appointing another designer and the time taken for that designer to come up to speed, as well as the additional costs for the new designer completing another's unfinished work, and possibly rectifying defects in that work. There may also be issues in using the original designer's IP.

5.4.8 FIDIC-identified risks

FIDIC have identified the following areas of risk for consulting engineers in all professional services appointments:

(i) The client
(ii) The fee
(iii) The scope of services
(iv) Resources
(v) Professional services agreement.[15]

The client (employer) risk for the designer is summed up as follows: "If a client fails to perform the project will fail, leading to the risk of non-payment, dispute and counterclaims.

15 FIDIC, *Five key areas of risk in consultants' appointments A short guide* (2009).

This is not in the interests of either the project or any party interested in the project's success".[16] Management of these identified design risks by the employer and the designer is covered in the following sections.

5.5 Who should bear the design risks?

As noted in Section 4.7, it is generally accepted that the party that can best manage or transfer a risk should be the one to bear that risk under the contract, often referred to as "fair" risk allocation. This is a good principle to determine the desirable contractual allocation of risk, but it is frequently not followed in practice. In this writer's experience, designers are frequently expected to assume risks under a design contract over which they have no control, and have no way of managing.

Furthermore, the principle does not adequately address those risks that are created by the terms of the design contract itself. For example, the imposition of onerous requirements such as inadequate fees or time to prepare the design, or specifying performance requirements that are impossible to achieve in practice. Whilst it could be argued that the rational designer would not or should not enter into such a contract, in the commercial world an employer may have an overwhelming advantage in bargaining power because of its size, and the likelihood that another designer may well accept such onerous terms.

For those risks that relate to the designer's performance of its obligations under the design contract, i.e. to produce the agreed scope of design deliverables on time, for the contract price and to the specified quality, the designer undoubtedly is best placed to, should and usually does manage those risks. However, there are other risks that the employer is in a better position to manage, and which accordingly should be assumed by the employer.

The primary risk that the employer can and should manage is the scope risk. It is the employer that knows what is required of the project, not only its functional and aesthetic requirements, but also what it is prepared to pay for future operations and maintenance. It is the party that must make the decisions on procurement in terms of the contractual arrangements, the form of contract and the time within which the project must be completed.

Although many design contracts are "bespoke", purpose written for the particular contract by lawyers acting for the employer, in this writer's view there is considerable merit in using standard form design contracts which have evolved through the input of personnel experienced in the industry. Such standard form contracts have what is generally perceived as a fair risk allocation, in which the party best able to control and manage risk is the one that assumes that risk under the contract. Two examples of such standard form contracts are the FIDIC Client/Consultant Model Services Agreement (Fifth Edition, 2017) (**White Book**), and Australian Standard AS4122. It is submitted that these standard form contracts are a good guide to balanced risk allocation, with due regard to the legitimate interests of both employer and designer.

16 Ibid.

5.6 Managing design risk by the employer

5.6.1 Design interface with construction

For a particular project, one of the important factors in managing design risk is to ensure the appropriate interface between designer and constructor. This interface can occur in a variety of ways contractually, e.g.:

- In a traditional "construct-only" construction contract or under other contractual mechanisms such as construction management/EPCM or project management, the designer and constructor are separately engaged by the employer.
- The designer is engaged by the constructor in a design and build or EPC project delivery.
- The design team is assembled from individuals employed by various organisations comprising an alliance.

5.6.2 Designer's contract

The selection of the form of contract for the design services is likely to be made as part of the employer's overall procurement strategy. Consideration of the best method of procuring the design within the constraints of a specific project is usually a significant factor in that procurement strategy. In some cases, there may be no choice of designer, such as a situation where proprietary technology or IP must be used, or there is only one designer who is appropriately qualified.

It is suggested that where an employer wishes to have maximum control over the design, this can best be achieved via a contractual mechanism in which the designer is directly contracted to the employer. Inevitably, where the contractor under a design-build or EPC contract engages the designer, the employer has less control over the design, and arguably its quality. However, such a contract may achieve completion of the project earlier than under a traditional construct only contract, because of the ability to "fast track" by overlapping design and construction. A properly managed alliance gives perhaps the greatest control to the employer in regard to quality, as sourcing the individual members of the design team is not confined to a specific design organisation.

5.6.3 Scope risks

The employer can manage its scope risks by careful attention to the details of the design contract before it is entered into, and appropriate supervision of the designer during preparation of the design. This includes ensuring that the full scope of the required design is fully and unambiguously defined in the design contract, and that there is a proper mechanism for the issuing and approval of scope variations before they have been implemented. During the design, the employer should monitor completion of the contractually defined deliverables, and insist on compliance with contractual procedures for scope variations.

As with time and quality, the scope of the design task cannot be divorced from a consideration of its cost. Where the scope is clear and well defined, a fixed price will provide certainty for the employer, and leave the risk of managing the design within the price with the designer.

Conversely, where the scope is not well defined, where research or innovation may be necessary, where there are complex requirements that require considerable investigation and consideration of a range of alternatives, it may be impossible to pre-estimate the amount of effort needed. In these situations, a fixed price for design is inappropriate, and a more appropriate fee arrangement is likely to be based on payment for the amount of design work necessary for the actual scope of work. With the use of appropriate reporting procedures by the designer, the employer can be kept appraised of its financial commitment for the design work carried out, as well as the projected design expenditure over the coming period. In this way, the employer can limit its commitment for design fees by managing the scope of the design.

Bearing in mind the 1:10:100 "rule" referred to in Section 5.2.3, the most effective way of an employer ensuring that the life cycle costs of the project are minimised may well be to have a greater, rather than a lesser, scope for the design concept work; the more design work that is done at the conceptual stage in determining the most appropriate form of the project, the more likely it is that adequate consideration will have been given to all the critical issues that will ultimately determine the life cycle cost of the project.

5.6.4 Time risks

There are limits to the extent to which the employer can manage the time risks. The normal contractual mechanisms of requiring a programme of works which must be kept up to date and regularly reported on (similar to that used in a construction contract) will at least give the employer early warning of time problems. In the event of schedule slippage, the employer can implement appropriate contractual mechanisms such as requiring acceleration or a "show cause" notice, if these are provided for in the design contract. Milestone payment mechanisms may also provide a powerful financial incentive for a designer to perform to an agreed timetable.

5.6.5 Quality risks

Managing the quality risks of design is perhaps the most challenging of all for the employer. Typically, the employer engages the designer because it does not have the appropriate design skills itself. It may not have sufficient technical skills to adequately address the quality of the design being prepared. It is suggested that an employer can nevertheless minimise its design risks by:

- Careful selection of the designer, based on its proven knowledge, experience and skill, and an assessment of its capability to design the particular facility to the required quality within the defined time.
- Requiring the designer to have adequate internal procedures for checking the quality of the design against the contractual requirements.
- Auditing the designer's internal procedures to ensure that the design checking has been carried out in accordance with the defined procedures.
- Appointing a checking or "proof engineer" where independent assurance of design quality is deemed to be appropriate.

5.6.6 *Managing cost*

It should be noted that each of these actions might have cost consequences for the employer. It is specifically not suggested that the cost of design should be a primary basis for the selection of designer, as this is likely to run counter to the selection of the designer who will produce the required design quality. A consultant with a sophisticated quality assurance system, particularly one certified to the requirements of ISO 9000, will inevitably have a higher cost structure than one that relies on *ad hoc* checking. Similarly, the cost structure of a single person design company will be much less than that of a company employing tens or hundreds of qualified people; it would be naïve to assume that such disparate organisations were in any way comparable in their ability to produce quality checked designs.

Auditing of the designer's internal quality procedures, and appointing a proof engineer, have an obvious cost for the employer. However, they will significantly decrease the risks that the design is not of the required quality. Bearing in mind the 1:10:100 "rule", the additional cost spent during the design phase is "insurance" that the life cycle costs will be minimised because the design has been prepared to the appropriate quality.

5.6.7 *IP risks*

The employer can manage its IP risks by appropriate warranties, indemnities and undertakings in the design contract. It will require an indemnity from the designer for any breach of any other party's IP by the designer. As the entity paying for the design, the employer would normally expect to receive as part of that design all of the IP required to construct, operate, maintain, renovate, alter or demolish the facility as it sees fit, without payment of additional cost over that agreed to in the design contract. It is submitted that, in the majority of construction contracts, the employer can manage those IP risks appropriately by ensuring that it has a royalty free, irrevocable licence to use the IP in connection with the facility for any purpose during its life; it would not normally be necessary to require a complete assignment of all IP by the designer to the employer.

The issue of moral rights in connection with the design may need separate consideration in respect to designs in which aesthetics play a large part, such as seminal buildings. A world-leading designer may be reluctant to surrender some of its legally protected moral rights, such as for attribution of authorship or right of integrity; in such cases a mutually acceptable sharing of IP risk will need to be negotiated.

5.6.8 *Interface risks*

Another aspect of managing the risk of design services is in the extent to which the designer's scope includes an involvement during construction. Appropriate management of interface risks generally requires that the designer's scope include inspections during construction to ensure that the design intent is met.

Traditionally, the full design services of a consulting engineer included inspections during construction to ensure that the design intent was met. Many employers still recognise that this is an important function in ensuring quality of the finally constructed design. Where the designer is engaged directly by the employer this is unproblematic. However, in a design and construct contract where the designer's scope is fixed by the contractor, it may be necessary to include a contractual requirement for some form of formal designer's certification, to ensure that the contractor maintains adequate designer involvement during the construction phase. This is particularly important in those situations in which the erection itself is a critical design condition, such as the erection of long span bridges.

This issue was emphasised by the Committee of Inquiry into the failure of the Milford Haven Bridge in 1971, which noted in its final recommendations on contractual procedures: "The Engineer should carefully watch the progress of construction to ensure compliance with the agreed erection method; he should scrutinise the Contractor's site staff and where necessary exercise his powers under the contract."[17] Although that recommendation was made over 40 years ago, it is submitted that it as pertinent today as when it was made. For further details of the Committee of Inquiry's report, see Section 22.3.

5.6.9 Insolvency risk

There are limits to the ability of an employer to manage the risk of a designer's insolvency, as this may be triggered by events over which the employer has no influence. An employer should carry out appropriate due diligence on the designer's **PI insurance** (Professional Indemnity insurance) and financial strength before the design contract is entered into. A financially strong designer that maintains its commercial viability and PI insurance is likely to be in the best position to satisfy any liability for damages.

However, as outlined above, the balance sheet assets of most consulting engineers are confined to intangible assets that will quickly dissipate in the event of insolvency. Their ability to meet a claim for damages is often confined to the PI insurance they carry. It is submitted that it is ultimately not in the employer's interest to insist on contractual terms which might have the effect of jeopardising the coverage or existence of the designer's PI insurance. Further, whilst properly drawn up contractual warranties are undoubtedly legally enforceable, to the extent that they are not supported by the terms of an appropriate insurance policy, the designer may have inadequate financial resources to meet any liability for damages. PI Insurance is discussed in more detail in Section 23.3.1

5.7 Managing design risk by the designer

The threshold issue for the designer's risk management is due diligence on the employer, to ensure it is competent to procure the project and pay for it. No matter how attractive the project, a designer takes on unquantifiable and unmanageable risk if it cannot be reasonably sure that the employer has the ability to complete the project and pay the designer's fees when they fall due.

Once satisfied of the employer's bona fides, the designer should ensure that the conditions of the design contract:

- Define the scope of the design required clearly and unambiguously, both in relation to the extent of the work, as well as the quality standards it must comply with.

17 Great Britain, Department of the Environment, Committee on Steel Box Girder Bridges, *Inquiry into the Basis of Design and Method of Erection of Steel-Box Girder Bridges: Report of the Committee* (1973) 25.

- Provides for adequate payment for the required scope of work.
- Provides sufficient time for completing the scope of work to the required quality, including the necessary checking.
- Does not require the designer to undertake contractual risks over which it has no control and cannot obtain insurance for.
- Does not contain terms that might impact its ability to carry out similar work in the future.

Many designers will see this as a counsel of perfection, unachievable in the real commercial world where typically the employer has considerably greater bargaining power, and the option of choosing another designer who may not object to one-sided contract terms. Nevertheless, each of these issues involves real financial risk to a designer and is ignored at its peril. They cover managing the FIDIC risks (ii), (iii) and (v) above.

The first three bullet points above have already been discussed and are sufficiently obvious that they are likely to be at the forefront of a designer's mind in negotiating a design contract. In relation to contractual risks over which they have no control and cannot contain insurance for, designers may be requested under a proposed contract to:

- Take responsibility for information provided by others and which cannot be verified
- Provide a fitness for purpose warranty
- Provide an unqualified warranty to maintain PI insurance for an extended period of time, perhaps up to 12 years, or
- Provide PI insurance of an unlimited amount.

The best way of the designer to manage the risks arising from such onerous terms is to ensure that it does not commit to them in the design contract. Designers in the common law world are aware that their PI insurance is generally confined to covering their liability for a failure to take reasonable care (and in Australia for misleading or deceptive conduct in breach of the *Australian Consumer Law*), and do not cover breaches of contractual warranties which do not involve a failure to take reasonable care. Thus, any liability for breaches of such contractual warranties must be met from the designer's own financial resources, and not from PI insurance. To the extent that the designer cannot negotiate such terms out of the design contract, it takes on an uninsurable financial risk that, if it eventuated, could have severe commercial consequences.

Designers are well aware that PI insurance is expensive, it is generally issued on an annual basis, it responds only to claims or alerts made during the policy year, and is for an agreed and limited amount. The ability to obtain PI insurance in subsequent years depends upon such insurance being available on reasonable commercial terms, the designer not being refused insurance because of a poor claims history, and ongoing operations of the designer which generate sufficient revenue to pay the insurance premiums on an annual basis. An unqualified warranty to maintain such insurance for a number of years in the future entails a commercial risk for the designer. The most that should reasonably be expected from a designer is that it will make best endeavours to maintain insurance for the required period, provided it is available on commercial terms.

Once committed to the terms of a design contract, a designer best manages its execution risks by fulfilling its obligations in accordance with the requirements of the design contract. This usually entails proper internal management of the design teams: adequate resourcing at the "coalface", proper planning, supervision and coordination, reporting to the employer on a regular basis, appropriate checking and quality assurance, and provision of the required deliverables on time – all issues related to managing the resources risk (iv) in Section 5.4.8 above identified by FIDIC. These are all issues that are very familiar to every competent designer; in any organisation with a quality system certified to ISO 9000 there are usually detailed procedures that define a systematic and auditable process for delivering a quality product. An employer should be able to rely on a designer complying with its procedures. Any departure from them entails increased risk for the designer.

5.8 Conclusion

This chapter has endeavoured to identify the major design risks in a construction project, generally under the headings of scope, time, cost and quality. The fundamental importance of design in achieving a project that satisfies the manifold requirements of aesthetics, functionality, constructability, operability, maintainability and economic performance over its life cycle has been emphasised.

The 1:10:100 "rule" brings into sharp focus the impact that design decisions made at the earliest stage of a project have on the ultimate outcome over its life. The corollary to this "rule" is that the most effective investment in ensuring project success is that made to obtain the most appropriate design. A "better" design, even if it costs more to produce, can reap substantial financial returns over a long period of time in the form of lower operating or maintenance costs, or a reduced requirement for upgrading or refurbishment.

The employer can manage its design risks by appropriate selection of the most appropriate designer, agreeing to reasonable and equitable terms in the design contract which protect the employer's interests without an unreasonable or unrealistic shifting of risks to the designer, and by agreeing to reasonable remuneration and time to perform an agreed scope of work to the required quality. In addition to auditing of the designer's compliance with the requirements of the contract, in appropriate cases it may be appropriate to engage an independent "proof engineer" to ensure the quality of the design. The employer's best risk management will be to have an unrelenting focus on the quality of the design, and provide an appropriate contractual setting in which this has the best opportunity of being achieved.

The designer can best manage its design risks by appropriate due diligence on the employer, by not agreeing to contractual terms which place unmanageable and uninsurable risks on it, by ensuring that it will be adequately remunerated for a clear and unambiguously defined scope of work it is required to execute, and by executing that scope of work in accordance with the contractual requirements. Managing risks during execution of the design requires that adequate attention be given to resources, not only those at the "coalface" but also those required for supervision, coordination and checking. Quality certified design organisations generally have sophisticated procedures intended to achieve designs to the appropriate quality, delivered on time with an acceptable financial outcome. A designer ignores those procedures at its risk.

CHAPTER 6

Contracts for design services[1]

Dr Donald Charrett & Dan Washington

6.1 Introduction

In the construction industry, contracts for design services are frequently viewed as another "trade" subcontract, and are prepared accordingly. This chapter notes the key aspects of design contracts that distinguish them from trade contracts. It highlights several types of what the writers consider inappropriate risk transfer in design contracts, and suggests that an employer's risks can be more appropriately managed to obtain the best value from the designer's services.

6.2 Procurement of design

Broadly, there are three ways in which an employer can procure the design for a project:

- Directly, by the employer engaging the designer itself, or
- Via the construction contractor in a design and construct or EPC contract, in which the Contractor typically engages one or more consulting engineers (and in building projects, an architect) to prepare the design, or
- In an alliance team in which the Employer, Contractor and designers enter into a collaborative contract.

The issue of which method of procurement of design is most appropriate for a particular project is of fundamental importance to an employer. A long-term employer who is going to operate a facility may be looking to procure the most appropriate design for minimising the ultimate life cycle costs and maximising functionality. Such an employer can achieve maximum control over the design by engaging the designer directly (the "traditional" design-bid-build). A design and construct contract may be appropriate for an employer who does not have the appropriate resources to engage and manage the designer directly, or who seeks a "fast track" project execution. In such a contract, the designer's employer (i.e. the Contractor) controls the design, and is likely to be focused on minimising the construction costs, consistent with satisfying its contractual obligations to the ultimate client. Ensuring that due account is taken of the owner's interests in minimising life cycle

1 This chapter is an edited version of the paper published in: Donald Charrett and Dan Washington, "Contracts for Design Services" (2012) 15(9) *Inhouse Counsel* 293.

 DOI: 10.4324/9781003206897-7

costs in a design and construct contract therefore requires very careful attention to the specification of the Employer's requirements in the Contract.

For a major project that an owner has decided to procure via a design and construct contract, it will contract with a contractor to manage the delivery of the project. The owner typically does this for two reasons:

- To acquire access to the resources (specialist and generalist) required to deliver the project. Few if any organisations employ the in-house resources as permanent staff required to deliver a major project; hence the acquisition of additional resources is typically sought from others via a contractual arrangement.
- To transfer the delivery risk of a project to another organisation. Conceptually, to enhance the prospect of a successful project, this should be an organisation that is better equipped to manage the delivery risk.

As noted in the previous chapter, even the largest construction contractors typically do not have in-house design resources with the complete range of skills needed for the final design of a major project, and almost invariably engage consulting engineers and architects for the permanent design.

In contracting other organisations to assist it, the Contractor also seeks access to resources and to transfer risk. As it will typically require a number of subcontractors and suppliers to deliver a project, it is important that the Contractor transfer appropriate types and amounts of risk to each of its subcontractors and suppliers. Ideally, this risk should be transferred to the organisation best able to manage it. Arguably, from an equity perspective, risk should also be transferred in proportion to the reward being derived by the organisation agreeing to take on that risk.

As discussed in Section 4.7, one of the major functions of any contract, and a construction contract in particular, is the allocation of rights and responsibilities between the contracting parties. This is commonly, if somewhat inaccurately, referred to as allocation of risk. The common law provides a "default" allocation of risk in a construction contract, and any modification of that default position is achieved via the terms and conditions of the contract. This chapter focuses on the transference of risk to design consultants and the appropriateness or otherwise of commercial terms and conditions used in effecting this transfer, together with some short comments on general contract terms that, in the writers' view and experience, are inappropriate for design contracts.

6.3 Contract terms and conditions addressing risk transference

Absent specific contractual provisions to the contrary, the common law will imply a term into a design contract that the design services will be provided with due skill, care and diligence. In contrast to the construction Contractor, the design contractor does not implicitly warrant that the object of the contract (i.e. the design) will be fit for purpose. Whilst contracting parties still sometimes rely on the common law and do not have a written design contract for small projects, major projects almost always have a written design contract, sometimes as detailed in its general conditions as the construction contract itself.

A number of model contracts and guidelines exist to inform the engagement of designers. General conditions of design contracts include:

- FIDIC White Book (Client/Consultant Model Services Agreement) (Fifth Edition, 2017)
- General Conditions of Contract for Consultants AS 4122–2010
- ACE Professional Services Agreement Advisory, Investigatory and other Services 2019 Edition
- Consult Australia Contract (March 2010).

Guidelines on the application of design contracts include:

- FIDIC Guidelines for the Selection of Consultants 2003
- FIDIC Client/Consultant Model Services (1998 White Book) Guide (Second Edition, 2001)
- ACE Professional Appointments Contracts – good practice
- Consult Australia Guide to Contract Terms (March 2011).

Such model contracts and guidelines have typically been developed to address what their authors consider to be an appropriate balance between transfer of risk and accrual of commercial reward for the conduct of design activities. Unfortunately, such model contracts and guidelines are not widely used for the engagement of design consultants. It appears to the writers that many of the terms and conditions used to engage design consultants have been generated with the view to transferring as much risk as possible from the designer's employer, to the designer. Often such transference of contract risk is, in the writers' view, inappropriate and counterproductive. This view is shared by others, for example the Parliament House Construction Authority, responsible for procurement of the Australian Parliament House in Canberra:[2] "The Authority believes that agreements – particularly with consultants – are only successful if they are fair to both sides.[3]

The following are some typical examples of clauses in design and construct contracts that seek to transfer risk from the employer (the Contractor) to the designer, together with a short discussion of their likely effect.

6.3.1 Responsibility for delays – liquidated damages

It is common for the Contractor to seek to pass down head contract risk for delays to a designer through the imposition of liquidated damages. Typically, such clauses will take the form of:

> In the event that the Subcontractor fails to complete the works by the due date, Liquidated Damages shall be paid to the Contractor at the rate of X% of the value of the service order, per day of delay, up to a maximum of Y%.

2 The procurement of the Australian Parliament House is discussed in Section 15.3.

3 Parliament House Construction Authority, Commonwealth, *Project Parliament: the Management Experience* (1990) 171.

There are two major issues with the imposition of liquidated damages on designers: the first is a risk issue, the second a practicality.

The first issue with imposing liquidated damages on a designer is associated with the nature of design risk. As noted above, engineering design represents only a small fraction of the overall project budget; however, a significant design failure can result in very substantial rectification costs, or even result in a total loss scenario. As such, the magnitude of the design risk is proportional to the total project cost, rather than to the fees paid for the design activity.

It is well known that errors in design become more expensive to fix as a project progresses and the design is constructed.

The nature of design risk makes it important, from a risk-reduction perspective, to get the design right: to "measure twice and cut once". Extra time spent on design to fix problems before construction reduces project risk. This is at odds with the disincentive of a liquidated damages clause. The imposition of liquidated damages clauses on a designer will focus the management of the design organisation on getting the design finished by the due date at all costs. This increases the risk that there will be latent design defects that will not surface until later in the project, typically with very expensive rectification costs.

The second issue with liquidated damages clauses is a practical one. The design activity requires a significant amount of input from a range of stakeholders in order to be successful. Such input typically includes input from:

- The Employer on requirements and desired outcomes
- The fabricator on constructability in order to minimise the cost of fabrication
- The installation contractor in order to minimise the cost of installation
- Specialist consultants in areas such as geotechnical engineering, meteorology, oceanography, etc.

The implications of this requirement for input and review from a range of stakeholders is that it can be difficult to pin down responsibility for a design delay, in particular when the delay is due to input provided by a party external to the designer over whom the designer has no control. Whilst the imposition of responsibility and thus liability for payment of liquidated damages may be forced on the designer via carefully worded contractual conditions, such application of liquidated damages in cases where the designer has relied on input from other parties may be inequitable and strongly resisted.

It should also be noted that any payment of liquidated damages must come from the design contractor's own financial resources. As a contractually imposed liability, the designer's professional indemnity insurance will generally not respond in the absence of negligence. A demand for payment of significant liquidated damages may therefore trigger potentially expensive and inevitably disruptive litigation or arbitration.

6.3.2 Responsibility for design data

It is not uncommon for contract terms and conditions to require the designer to take responsibility for the accuracy of client-supplied data. Typically, such clauses take the form:

> The Service Provider agrees that it has satisfied itself as to the accuracy of any information given to it and accepts full responsibility for any use by it of such information including, without limitation, responsibility for any conclusions drawn by it from such information.

The issue with such clauses is that the development of a design requires input from a range of parties and often relies on the data supplied by such other parties that has taken considerable time and cost to assemble. Often geotechnical, meteorological or oceanographic data is supplied by the Employer and, as such, should be able to be relied upon by the designer. The equitable alternative would be to pay the designer to undertake its own surveys and investigations to establish the requisite input engineering data, or to properly verify the data supplied to it. This is not something that is typically allowed for in a project budget.

6.3.3 Generally inappropriate contract clauses: Destruction of confidential information

It is very common for design contracts to contain a clause requiring the return or destruction of confidential information (which is generally defined to include most if not all the project-related documentation) upon completion of a project. The issue with such clauses is that a designer will almost invariably be required to maintain a copy of such documentation for both quality assurance (as part of an ISO 9001 system) and insurance purposes. Accordingly, it is recommended that clauses associated with the destruction of confidential information be accompanied by a sub-clause to the effect of:

> Notwithstanding Clause XX, the Design Contractor may retain one copy of the Confidential Information for quality management system and insurance record purposes. The retained copy shall be subject to the confidentiality provisions of this Agreement.

6.4 Conclusion

Design, being the provision of services and the delivery of IP, is a conceptually different activity to construction. Although its cost is a small proportion of the overall life cycle cost of a project (perhaps only of the order of 1%), it is of overwhelming importance in determining the construction cost as well as the operation, maintenance and refurbishment costs of the constructed facility, as well as its functionality.

Accordingly, different considerations apply to the procurement of a designer from a construction Contractor (or subcontractor). Contractual terms should be conducive to obtaining the quality of design required by the employer as its first priority. As an intellectual exercise, the preparation of design requires adequate time, and this will in turn have a strong influence on its price. Contractual terms that provide a disincentive for a designer to spend appropriate time in preparing the design and checking it properly before construction starts are not in the interests of the Employer in obtaining a project that fulfils its requirements. Competitive bidding for design services was found to be a contributing factor in the collapse of the Burnaby supermarket parking deck in British Colombia in 1988 (see Section 20.12). The Commission of Inquiry into the collapse of the De la Concorde overpass in Quebec in 2006 recommended that design engineers be selected based on competency and past performance, with cost only considered for those firms meeting the competence criteria (see Section 20.13).

A designer's PI Insurance will typically not respond to the materialisation of contractually assumed risks that go beyond the common law requirement of due skill and care in preparing a design. Accordingly, compensation for breach of such contract terms, or liquidated damages for late performance, will be sourced from the designer's assets, which may be limited.

The importance of the appropriate contractual relationship between designer and Employer is highlighted by the following:

> All good engineering, introducing innovation to the benefit of the project and its Owner, must entail periodical mistakes, usually insignificant in relation to the project overall. If however, each such instance is to provoke intervention of the law, the Engineer and the entire project will tend to be conservative in intention and expensive in out-turn. The consequence has been increased costs, reduced innovation, increased confrontation. This adversary situation has for many years attracted comment in the USA and more recent steps for improvement. As a consequence, it is noticeable that, in the USA, there is a greater chasm between "design" and "construction" than in Europe or Japan, leading to greater conservatism and legal intervention. Most innovation in tunnelling has either come from overseas or from the manufacturers.[4]

4 Alan Muir Wood, *Tunnelling Management by Design* (2000) 264.

CHAPTER 7

Design life or service life

What is the difference?[1]

7.1 Introduction

Many construction law cases involve an intersection of legal and technical issues related to a constructed facility, such as defects, fitness for purpose, durability, strength, serviceability, maintainability or operability. The common denominator of these issues is the design of the facility.

The design of a constructed facility involves all the large and small decisions required to determine its form, how its elements work individually and in combination to fulfil their functional requirements, what materials will be used in construction, how these are connected, how the facility is to be constructed, and how it should be maintained and operated. It is the design that determines not only the form and nature of the construction, but also the economic characteristics of the constructed facility such as its durability, the ongoing operating and maintenance costs and ultimately its commercial life.

This chapter discusses a number of aspects of structural design to explain the difference between design life and service life, an issue that may be important in the context of design and construct contracts. The "default" legal obligation to prepare a design with due skill and care is contrasted with the common contractual obligation for a constructed facility to be fit for purpose. These issues are illustrated by reference to recent case law.

7.2 Design of constructed facilities

Those responsible for the design of constructed facilities are constrained by, inter alia, the laws of physics, the known, available and usable mathematics, and the known "state of the art" of the relevant technology. Notwithstanding the continual advances in technology and the "state of the art", the design and engineering of facilities "for the use and convenience of man"[2] will continue to create new frontiers, and reveal hitherto unknown gaps in our knowledge. In this book "**state of the art**" refers to the art and science that would be applied by competent and experienced practitioners involved in the relevant practice of engineering, not necessarily the science of engineering as known to academics researching at the cutting edge of known technology.

1 This chapter is an edited and updated version of: Donald Charrett, "Design Life or Service Life. What is the Difference?", first published in (2017) *International Construction Law Review* 16, published by Informa Law, London.

2 The 1828 Royal Charter Institution of Civil Engineers defined civil engineering as the "art of directing the great sources of power in nature for the use and convenience of man".

 DOI: 10.4324/9781003206897-8

Notwithstanding the availability of cheap and extremely powerful computing facilities, and the evolution of new technologies such as artificial intelligence, in this writer's view the design of facilities will (at least for the foreseeable future), rely on the skill and professionalism (including both art and science) of engineers and other professional practitioners. We can reasonably expect and require that those professionals be trained, skilled, experienced and up to date with "the state of the art" as defined above. Does that mean that they can "guarantee" a specific outcome in respect of the facilities they design? Specifically, can a designer, using up-to-date and "state of the art" knowledge, guarantee that a facility will have a specific service life in every situation?

All **facilities** the subject of construction law (buildings, infrastructure, structures and equipment for the extraction of natural resources or for the processing of natural resources into manufactured products etc.) are designed on the basis of certain assumptions, to perform specific functions over a service life (which may be implicit). The required functions, service life and assumptions made for the design of a facility will be referred to as the **design parameters**. A facility as a whole, and its individual components, must be designed individually and collectively so as to comply with the design parameters.

Whilst certain parameters may be precisely known or are able to be calculated, many parameters can only be estimated on the basis of mathematical calculations, statistical measurement, experiment or engineering experience. For example, the required functionality may be capable of precise definition (e.g. a power station required to generate 500MW of power at a 90% availability for a service life of 30 years), whereas other parameters fundamental to the design may have to be determined by experiment, e.g. the practically achievable thermal efficiency of the coal fuelling the power station. Important design parameters arising from the forces of nature, such as wind loading, earthquake loading or the maximum anticipated flood level, are generally determined on the basis of professional consensus based on experience at the relevant location and statistical analysis of the available records.

The Structural Engineers Association of Southern California defines structural engineering as

> the science and art of designing and making, with economy and elegance, buildings, bridges, frameworks and other similar structures so that they can safely resist the forces to which they may be subjected.[3]

7.3 The art and science of engineering

All branches of engineering involve both "art" and "science". Our understanding of physics and chemistry, and our ability to apply mathematics to their application in practical situations, is the "science" of engineering. That science, aided by the enormous computational power of computers, is always evolving and developing to open up new frontiers in engineering. However, the "art" of engineering remains – the ability to know what and how much science to apply to a given engineering problem, in the face of an ever-expanding knowledge base. An important parameter in that decision is (usually) the requirement to prepare, at a reasonable cost, a design that represents value for money. This

3 https://seaosc.org/Structures (accessed 11 April 2021).

may implicitly limit the extent to which sophisticated and expensive computer analyses are warranted.

Some areas of engineering are more amenable than others to the rigorous application of physics, chemistry and mathematics. For example, the design of a jet engine to operate flawlessly over a required number of hours before maintenance has a much higher confidence level than determining the actual loads a bridge may be subjected to during its intended service life.

The focus in this chapter is on what may be termed civil engineering facilities (roads, bridges, building structures, wharfs, tunnels etc.), rather than mechanical, electrical or electronic components. Each civil engineering facility is unique – at least to the extent that every structure is attached to a different part of the earth's surface, and subject to the environmental conditions unique to that location. Different functional requirements are also common, even between apparently similar facilities. In addition, major elements of a civil engineering structure must be built on site. On the other hand, mechanical, electrical and electronic components are generally produced to comply with well-defined input and output parameters, in quantity and in factory-controlled conditions. The production in quantity enables incremental refinement and evolution over a long period of time. For example, modern day turbines have a higher efficiency and reliability than those designed 20 years ago.

The design of civil engineering structures involves a number of design parameters that are typically not known with precision. Some of the most important of these parameters are the properties of naturally occurring materials, the environmental conditions that a structure may be subjected to during its life, and the loads it must withstand in service or under extreme events.

In a case involving the failure of the structure supporting a wind turbine offshore, Jackson LJ made the following pertinent comments about the random nature of environmental loads:

> J101 *[DNV international standard for the design of offshore wind turbines]* is, as Mr Streatfeild-James submits, stochastic. Weather conditions at sea and the forces which will be imposed upon offshore structures cannot be predicted with certainty. The authors of J101 prescribed what needed to be done in order to create a structure which has a sufficiently high probability of functioning for 20 years. Paragraph F301 in section 2 provides a good illustration. In ULS *[ultimate limit state]* design the designer is required to assume a characteristic combined load which is likely to occur once in 50 years. In any given year the chance of that load being imposed upon the structure is only 2%. Nevertheless this is not a matter about which there can be certainty. It is possible, although unlikely, that that combined load effect will be exceeded in year 1, again in year 2 and so forth. The authors of J101 regarded paragraph F301 as appropriate for a structure with design life of 20 years. No-one suggests that that provision would achieve a structure with a guaranteed life of 20 years.[4]

7.4 Standards

Civil engineers use a variety of tools to cope with these ill-defined parameters, to design structures that, in the main, safely and satisfactorily perform their required function over their service life. Codes of Practice, or Standards, are an important part of the civil

4 *Mt Højgaard A/S v E.ON Climate and Renewables UK Robin Rigg East Ltd* [2015] EWCA Civ 407 [93].

engineer's armoury. A Standard is generally the consensus view of skilled practitioners working in the specific field of the Standard, as to what constitutes current good practice, i.e. the "state of the art" of the competent practitioner. The detailed and formal processes involved in writing or amending Standards means that they do not represent the state of the science or technology the most knowledgeable academics or practitioners might employ. However, Standards are of great assistance to the ordinary practitioner in defining what standard the ordinarily diligent and competent practitioner should achieve, or what parameters should be used in design. They are not meant to be a straitjacket, and diligent and competent engineers may choose not to follow all the requirements of a Standard if they have a sound, rational engineering alternative. However, an engineer's use of an alternative approach that resulted in a lesser strength than that defined in the relevant applicable Standard could be very difficult to justify legally in a failure situation, on the basis that the Standard represents a widely accepted consensus view within the profession of the "state of the art" that an ordinarily diligent and competent practitioner should apply.

Standards are frequently cited in construction contracts, both in general terms, and specifically in a detailed list of Standards to be followed. For example, the FIDIC Yellow Book requires that:

> The Contractor's Documents, the execution of the Works and the completed Works (including defects remedied by the Contractor) shall comply with the Country's technical standards, building, construction and environmental Laws, Laws applicable to the product being produced from the Works and other standards specified in the Employer's Requirements, applicable to the Works, or defined by applicable Laws.[5]

The Technical Requirements that typically comprise one of the contract documents in a design and construct contract usually specifically define the Standards that must be complied with. Such Technical Requirements are normally prepared by engineers who are skilled and experienced in the particular type of facility. In this writer's view, such engineers should be selective and focussed in the Standards that they list. It is less than helpful to have Standards from different jurisdictions listed if the specified requirement is to satisfy the highest standard from those different Standards. Such an approach does not take due account of the different bases on which the Standards were prepared, nor of the possible jurisdictional differences. It is an unnecessary fetter on the designer and may lead to confusion and unnecessary extra cost in design and checking, without necessarily resulting in a superior product.

It is significant that modern standards are based on a recognition that design parameters are inherently variable, and cannot be predicted with certainty:

> Recently revised national and international standards for structural design are systematically based on probabilistic concepts, mathematical statistics and on the theory of structural reliability. The International Standard ISO 2394:1998 and EN 1990:2002, based on materials of JCSS [Joint Committee on Structural Safety], play a key role to constitute a common basis for defining design rules relevant to the construction and use of the wide majority of buildings in civil engineering works (ISO 13822:2001, ISO 22111:2007).[6]

5 International Federation of Consulting Engineers, *Conditions of Contract for Plant: and Design Build* (2nd edn, 2017), sub-clause 5.4.

6 M Holicky and JV Reteif, "Probabilistic basis of present codes of practice" in Zingoni (ed), *Advances and Trends in Engineering, Mechanics and Computation* (2010), 101.

7.5 Reliability

Reliability is the probability that a system will perform its intended function for a specific period of time under a given set of conditions. Reliability is also the probability that unsatisfactory performance or failure will not occur.

Structural reliability is an overall concept covering structural actions, response and resistance, workmanship and quality control, all of which are mutually dependent. Structural reliability is quantified in a **structural reliability index**. The calculation of this index depends upon the mean values and coefficients of variation of actions and resistance. The calculations also assume that the levels of workmanship and quality control are maintained in accordance with current standards, and are appropriately accounted for in the resistance model. It is applicable to the design of structural elements. "The reliability index could be thought of as a form of safety factor that includes the uncertainties in the determination of the actions and resistances."[7]

The Australian National Construction Code states that the structural performance requirements are verified for the design of structural components and connections when the calculated annual structural reliability index, for each action, is not less than specified values. For a building or structure of normal importance (importance level 2), the minimum annual structural reliability index is required to be:

- 3.8 for permanent and imposed actions, and
- 3.4 for wind, earthquake and snow actions.[8]

These target structural reliability indices have been set as the averages of the reliability indices found in current design Standards for steel, concrete and timber.

There is a mathematical relationship between the structural reliability index and the probability of failure. Applying this mathematical relationship shows that the assumed annual probability of failure of primary structural components of structures of importance level 2 in Australia is:

- .00007 for permanent and imposed actions, and
- .0003 for wind, earthquake and snow actions.

The mathematical model for the reliability index takes actions and resistances and represents these as random variables in probabilistic models. That is, actions and resistances are assumed to have a range of possible values that can be represented by distribution curves, in this case assumed to be lognormal distributions.

To calculate the reliability index, a resistance model must be created and used with models for the various actions to which the component or connection will be subjected. The models for actions represent typical characteristics of the actions as related to Australian conditions, but not specific to a particular location or a type of occupancy.[9]

7 *Australian Building Codes Board, Structural Reliability Handbook* (2015), 7.

8 *Australian Building Codes Board, National Construction Code 2016* Volume 1 Building Code of Australia Class 2 to Class 9 Buildings, s BV1.

9 Australian Building Codes Board, *Structural Reliability Verification Method* (2019), 11 https://www.abcb.gov.au/Resources/Publications/Education-Training/Structural-Reliability (accessed 11 April 2021).

As the resistance is a random variable, the resistance model must account for all sources of uncertainties in the determination of the resistance of a structural component or connection. The starting point is to determine the standard specified resistance. This is usually established by identifying the main parameters that affect the behaviour of the component, and constructing appropriate structural models to account for their effects. It must be formulated using five percentile characteristic material properties.[10]

The calculated resistance is related to the standard specified resistance (which is a deterministic value) by a number of factors. These factors account for the uncertainties in the assessment of the resistance, and are random values that are assumed to be statistically independent. The sources of uncertainties must include, but are not limited to, the following:

- Variability in mechanical properties of the materials (usually obtained from test data used for quality control of the material manufacturing process)
- Variation in dimensions as the result of fabrication or construction processes (usually obtained from the established allowable tolerance and measurement of the dimensions of the component)
- Uncertainties in the structural modelling of the component (usually obtained from the test research data used in the construction of the structural model).[11]

This method of calculating the structural reliability index provides a scientific way of establishing the appropriate design parameters for new or innovative structural products for which there are no standard specifications or deemed to satisfy provisions. As the target values for the structural reliability index are set at the average values of those found in current practice using steel, concrete, timber, the public can have confidence that rational criteria are being applied to justify acceptance of new or innovative products, and that their probability of failure is no greater than the traditional and widely used products.

The use of structural reliability as a verification method is provided for in the Australian National Construction Code,[12] and is the basis for structural design in many international Standards.[13]

7.6 Limit state design

Modern structures in many countries are designed using the current state of the art such that they are expected to withstand certain defined limit states. The **ultimate limit state (ULS)** is the limit state of a structure at incipient collapse or other similar forms of structural failure. The **serviceability limit state (SLS)** is the state of a structure that corresponds to conditions beyond which specified service criteria are no longer met. These

10 Ibid.

11 Ibid.

12 *Australian Building Codes Board, National Construction Code 2016* Volume 1 Building Code of Australia Class 2 to Class 9 Buildings, sBV1; *Australian Building Codes Board, National Construction Code 2016* Volume 2 Building Code of Australia Class 1 and Class 10 Buildings, s V2.1.1.

13 e.g. EN-1990:2002+A1 Eurocode – Basis of Design is the basis of structural Standards in Europe.

criteria are based on the intended use and may include limits on deformation, vibratory response, degradation or other physical aspects.[14]

The procedure for ULS design of a structure involves the following steps:

- Determine the importance level for the structure and the associated annual probability of exceedance for the applied environmental loads (wind, snow, ice and earthquake).
- Determine the ultimate permanent and imposed loads.
- Determine the ultimate environmental loads.
- Determine the ultimate values of any other applied loads such as liquid pressure, ground water, rain water ponding or earth pressure.
- Determine combinations of actions.
- Analyse the structure and its parts for the relevant combinations of actions.
- Design and detail the structure for robustness and earthquake.
- Determine the design resistance of the structural elements (the physically distinguishable parts of the structure, such as walls, columns, beams and connections) using the applicable Standards.
- Confirm that the design resistance exceeds the appropriate action effects.[15]

The basis of ULS is a recognition that the design parameters are inherently variable, and that the values adopted for design of the ultimate strength of a structure may be exceeded. It is generally obvious that the construction cost of a structure designed for higher loads or more conservative assumptions of material strength will be more than for a structure designed for lower loads or less conservative assumptions. That is, there is a trade-off between increased safety (a lower probability of failure) and cost.

This trade-off is brought into sharp focus in respect of strengthening of masonry buildings in New Zealand to resist earthquake loads. It is well known that such buildings are subject to catastrophic collapse in earthquakes, and that strengthening them to enhance earthquake resistance is expensive and may not prevent failure in extreme events. Where such buildings are required to be strengthened (e.g. where the occupancy class has changed), the regulations only require strengthening to 34% of the current earthquake design loads. Presumably this 34% limitation was selected on the basis of the unacceptable community cost of adopting a higher figure. As was known, such strengthening was inadequate to prevent collapse in a "design" earthquake. The 2010 and 2011 Canterbury earthquakes in fact imposed loads of the order of or higher than those specified by the Standard, with tragic consequences.[16] Some of the lessons learnt from the Royal Commission on the Canterbury earthquakes are outlined in Chapters 18 and 19.

Thus, implicit in the setting of design loads in Standards is a recognition of the cost implications. The consensus procedure involved in writing Standards suggests that design parameters are set at values that involve an acceptable level of risk at a cost the community is prepared to accept (at least in the view of the Standard writers). But it is important to

14 Australian Standard AS1170.0:2002 Structural design actions Part 0: General Principles.
15 Australian Standard AS1170.0:2002 Structural design actions Part 0: General Principles, s 2.2.
16 See Chapters 18 and 19.

recognise the obverse of the acceptable level of risk – there is a probability (small, but not zero), that a properly designed structure will fail, perhaps because of a combination of loads exceeding the design value and the materials not reaching their expected strength.

The ULS design process makes such probabilities overt. Design loads are set with an annual probability of exceedance, selected with regard to the importance of the structure, the type of load and the design working life. Thus, an ordinary structure with a design working life of 50 years whose failure has medium consequences for loss of human life, is required to be designed for an annual probability of exceedance of 1/500 for wind and earthquake loads. However, a structure with post-disaster functions with a design working life of 100 years, is required to be designed for an annual probability of exceedance of 1/2,500 for wind and earthquake loads.[17]

The procedure for SLS design of a structure involves the following steps:

- Determine the type of serviceability conditions to be considered for the whole structure and its individual elements.
- Determine the serviceability load event and serviceability limits for the design serviceability condition being considered.
- Determine the permanent loads and serviceability imposed loads.
- Determine serviceability loads for wind, snow and ice.
- Determine the serviceability values of any other applied loads such as liquid pressure, ground water, rain water ponding or earth pressure.
- Determine applicable combinations of actions.
- Analyse the serviceability response of the structure and its parts for the relevant combinations of actions for each serviceability condition.
- Determine the serviceability response.
- Confirm that the serviceability response does not exceed the appropriate limiting values for each of the serviceability conditions identified.[18]

The significance of SLS and ULS design are illustrated by their application in the design of buildings in New Zealand to resist earthquakes:

> The SLS involves designing the building so it remains fit for use in the event of an earthquake with a magnitude of shaking that may be expected to occur once or twice during the design life of the building. If damaged in such an event it should be repairable at low cost.
>
> For the ULS the design criteria have been developed to ensure that life is protected in the event of a major earthquake. This is achieved by requiring the building to have suitable levels of strength, stiffness and ductility to survive a major earthquake without collapsing as a result of structural failure. For commercial buildings of normal importance this major earthquake is assumed to have a return period of 500 years. Post disaster structures, structures that are designed to contain significant numbers of people, and school buildings are designed for earthquake actions with return periods of 2500 and 1000 year respectively (assuming a building life of 50 years). Satisfying the design criteria for the ULS should enable building to be repaired after earthquakes that are more intense than those envisaged for the SLS. However the ULS design criteria do not imply that repairs are possible after a ULS earthquake.[19]

17 Australian Standard AS1170.0:2002 Structural design actions Part 0: General Principles, s 2.2.
18 Australian Standard AS1170.0:2002 Structural design actions Part 0: General Principles, s 2.3.
19 NZ, *Canterbury Earthquakes Royal Commission, Final Report* Volume 1 (2012) 54.

Thus, for New Zealand commercial buildings of normal importance with a design life of 50 years, the annual probability of exceedance for earthquake ULS is 0.2% (1/500), whereas the annual probability of exceedance for earthquake SLS is 4% (1/25).

7.7 Robustness

Structures are designed to withstand normal loads and actions over their service life. This includes design so that facilities remain operational under operating or serviceability loads (SLS design), and so that the structure does not fail under loads less than the ultimate design loads (ULS design).

However, abnormal events can occur that are unexpected and unpredictable, such as fire, explosion, impact, consequences of human errors or loads in excess of the design loads. The consequences of such events were drawn to the attention of structural engineers by the partial collapse of the 22-storey Ronan Point apartment building in East London in 1968. Following a gas explosion, one corner of the building collapsed, killing four people.

The subsequent inquiry noted the importance of guarding against progressive collapse in the following terms:

> The extent of the collapse subsequent to the explosion was inherent in the design of the building. The collapse has exposed a weakness in the design. It is a weakness against which it never occurred to the designers of this building that they should guard. They designed a building which they considered safe for all normal uses; they did not take into account the abnormal. They never addressed their minds to the question of what would happen if for any reason one or more of the load bearing members should fail. … The designers of Ronan Point were not alone in the attitude they adopted; it is significant that we have not been referred to any English publication which has drawn attention to the need to think of tall system buildings as civil engineering structures requiring alternate paths to support the load in the event of the failure of a load bearing member. It appears to us that there has been a blind spot among many of those concerned with this type of construction and it would be wrong to place the blame for the failure to appreciate the risk of progressive collapse upon the shoulders of the designers of this building alone. They fell victims, along with others, to the belief that if the building complied with existing building regulations and Codes of Practice it must be deemed to be safe. Experience has shown otherwise.[20]

The progressive collapse of Ronan Point focussed structural engineer's attention on the importance of designing robustness into a structure, so that it has capacity to withstand abnormal loads. Further details on the collapse of Ronan Point and the subsequent inquiry are in Section 20.8.

In the years since the collapse of Ronan Point, the importance of such design has been re-emphasised by terrorist attacks, which have resulted in the collapse of major buildings such as the World Trade Center in 2001[21] and the Federal Building in Oklahoma in 1995. In the Oklahoma Federal Building, whilst only 4% of the building was destroyed by the bomb blast, a further 38% was subsequently destroyed by progressive collapse.[22] NIST

20 Ibid 4.

21 https://www.nist.gov/topics/disaster-failure-studies/world-trade-center-disaster-study (accessed 11 April 2021).

22 www.bfrl.nist.gov/861/861pubs/collapse/workshop/5.WorkshopSlides(Murrah%20Bldg).pdf (accessed 15 May 2016).

concluded that although the building frame was adequately designed in accordance with the prevailing Standard, it could not sustain the level of ductility required to redistribute the loads with three columns missing in the first storey.[23]

Thus, in addition to the requirements for ULS and SLS design of a structure, it is now a requirement that the design exhibit **structural robustness**: the ability of a structure to withstand events like explosion, fire, impact or consequences of human errors, without being damaged to an extent disproportionate to the original cause.[24] Robustness is achieved by detailing structures such that all parts of the structure are tied together both in the horizontal and the vertical planes so that the structure can withstand an abnormal event without being damaged by an event disproportionate to that event.[25]

In a 2016 addition to the Australian National Construction Code, compliance with the structural performance requirements for a building or structure is verified for structural robustness by:

(a) assessment of the structure such that upon the notional removal in isolation of –
  (i) any supporting column; or
  (ii) any beam supporting one or more columns; or
  (iii) any segment of a load-bearing wall of length equal to the height of the wall,

the building remains stable and the resulting collapse does not extend further than the immediate adjacent storeys; and

(b) demonstrating that if a supporting structural component is relied upon to carry more than 25% of the total structure a systematic risk assessment of the building is undertaken and critical high risk components are identified and designed to cope with the identified hazards or protective measures chosen to minimise the risk.[26]

Other design aspects that can enhance a structure's robustness are redundancy and ductility. **Redundancy** is achieved by having multiple load paths that can transmit forces to the ground where they are resisted. Thus, if one load path is destroyed, e.g. by failure of one load-carrying member, the forces in that member can be conveyed to the ground by an alternate load path. The importance of redundancy was highlighted by the behaviour of the Hotel Grand Chancellor in the Christchurch earthquake. This building suffered complete failure of a shear wall during the 2011 earthquake. Although that failure came close to causing a catastrophic collapse of the 27-storey building, there was sufficient redundancy and resilience within the overall structure to redistribute load from the failing element and to halt the collapse.[27]

Ductile behaviour (**ductility**) of a member or connection is the ability to deform without losing strength above the point where the member or connection is unable to sustain increased load. Brittle behaviour is the opposite to ductile behaviour – a member fails in a brittle manner when it fails completely and is unable to sustain any load once its

23 https://www.nist.gov/el/oklahoma-city-bombing-1995 (accessed 14 April 2021).

24 Australian Standard AS1170.0:2002 Structural design actions Part 0: General Principles, s 1.4.21.

25 Australian Standard AS1170.0:2002 Structural design actions Part 0: General Principles, s 6.1.

26 *Australian Building Codes Board, National Construction Code* Volume 1 Building Code of Australia Class 2 to Class 9 Buildings (2016) 75.

27 NZ, *Canterbury Earthquakes Royal Commission, Final Report* Volume 2 (2012) s 3.

maximum load strength is reached. Unreinforced concrete and cast iron fail in a brittle manner under tension, and are therefore unsuitable for use in applications such as beams where they are required to withstand tension.

Ductile behaviour is particularly important in structures that are required to withstand earthquake loads. The modern approach to earthquake-resistant design is to build ductility into the structure so that it has the capacity to undergo repeated deformation whilst dissipating substantial energy through the deformations of the structure. Steel and properly designed reinforced concrete are inherently ductile materials; unreinforced masonry (brick and stone) is not. A well-designed ductile structure to modern standards will be able to withstand moderate earthquakes without significant structural damage, and a severe earthquake even greater than the "design earthquake" with substantial damage, but without collapsing. Such a damaged building may need to be demolished after the earthquake, but it will have performed its most important function of protecting the lives of its occupants:

> Protection against collapse in most modern buildings is provided by ensuring that in the event of a major earthquake the structure will behave in a ductile manner. This involves cracking of concrete and yielding of reinforcement in reinforced concrete buildings and yielding of structural steel members in steel buildings. This causes damage to structural elements as well as damage to non-structural elements such as the linings in the building. A consequence of this is that protection against collapse and protection of life may be at the expense of the building, which may have to be demolished after the earthquake.[28]

The Canterbury Royal Commission identified a number of major advantages of designing a structure so that it behaves in a ductile manner in a major earthquake:

1. Lower strengths are required, reducing the construction cost.
2. There is more freedom in the architecture of the building, enabling greater clear floor spans to be used with smaller beams, increased spacing of columns, etc.
3. A ductile building is tough in an earthquake and can generally withstand earthquakes considerably greater than design level (ULS) without collapse.
4. A ductile structure generally gives warning well before collapse occurs by opening up wide cracks in reinforced concrete structures and sustaining high displacements in steel and concrete members.
5. Non-ductile buildings give no warning of collapse and generally have less reserve capacity to sustain earthquakes greater than design level without collapse.[29]

7.8 Service life

In this book, the **service life** of a facility is defined as the period of time that it is in functional operation.

The service life of a facility is of fundamental importance to the long-term owner of that facility, since it is required to deliver an economic return over the service life. Further, the facility may have to be replaced when it is no longer functional. Long-term facility owners are usually interested in long service lives, subject always to the economics of

28 NZ, *Canterbury Earthquakes Royal Commission, Final Report* Volume 1 (2012) 55.
29 NZ, *Canterbury Earthquakes Royal Commission, Final Report* Volume 1 (2012) 58.

procurement and available funding. A rational decision of the required service life would be based on a determination based on the minimum net present value:

> Fenwick and Rotolone (2003) explored the economics of service life for civil infrastructure from a long term asset owner's perspective. They adopted the AASHTO (2006) definition of service life as the period of time that the structure is expected to be in operation, and considered a simple example of a culvert, exploring service lives between 30 and 300 years. For almost all cases over a range of feasible interest rates, a service life of 300 years before replacement proved to be the most economical outcome on a net present value basis.[30]

The determination of the optimum service life of a facility also needs to consider the operational costs:

> In targeting a service life performance for a structure, the asset owner needs to be aware not only of the initial cost of creating the structure, but its service life and the long term cost of maintaining and repairing it over that service life, and finally its replacement cost.[31]

Facilities designed today typically have an **expected service life**, although only time will tell whether a particular facility ultimately achieves its expected service life. Standards are often explicitly or implicitly based on an expected service life. It is doubtful that the issue of expected service life was overtly considered or addressed in the past. For example, did the designers or funders of the Brooklyn Bridge over the East River in New York contemplate or require that this bridge would be carrying traffic over 130 years after it was opened?

The **required service life** of a facility is the service life desired by the owner. It is one of the objectives of the design process, and will usually coincide with the design life:

> A service life performance must be formulated into specific design criteria to provide the designer with objectives for the design which are then encapsulated in specification requirements that must be met by the builder during the construction. The codes usually define a design life that implies a particular service life regarded by society as acceptable. For example, AS5100 (2004)[32] adopts a design life of 100 years. BS5400.1 (1988)[33] assumes a design life of 120 years and AASHTO[34] (2006) is based on a design life of 75 years. It is usual to simply apply these codes and standards that imply a particular assumption of service life performance. These are based on current materials and technologies and perhaps inhibit achieving very long service lives through the use of new materials or combinations of materials and new technologies.[35]
>
> *[citations added]*

30 John Connal and Marita Berndt, "Sustainable Bridges – 300 Year Design Life for Second Gateway Bridge" www.outokumpu.com/SiteCollectionDocuments/Research-paper-Susstainable%20Bridges.pdf (accessed 13 August 2015).

31 John Connal and Marita Berndt, "Sustainable Bridges – 300 Year Design Life for Second Gateway Bridge" www.outokumpu.com/SiteCollectionDocuments/Research-paper-Susstainable%20Bridges.pdf (accessed 13 August 2015).

32 Australian Standard for Bridge Design.

33 British Standard code of practice for the design and construction of steel, concrete and composite bridges – General Statement.

34 American Association of State Highway and Transportation Officials.

35 John Connal and Marita Berndt, "Sustainable Bridges – 300 Year Design Life for Second Gateway Bridge" www.outokumpu.com/SiteCollectionDocuments/Research-paper-Susstainable%20Bridges.pdf (accessed 13 August 2015).

However, the required service life is ultimately the choice (explicit or implicit) of the sponsor (or funder) of a project. A service life in excess of the norm can be required by an explicit specification of design life in the relevant contract. For example, the second Gateway Bridge over the Brisbane River in Brisbane, Australia was required to have a design life of 300 years, a world first and far in excess of the typical 50–100-year design life of infrastructure in Australia. This far-sighted decision was taken by Queensland Motorways in the knowledge that the long-term benefits would far outweigh the immediate cost. In the event, the actual premium was small. Using existing, known technology, the required changes to "normal" design and construction involved minor design and construction changes such as: the use of galvanised reinforcement in some areas, increased cover to reinforcement, design of the concrete mix, and an unrelenting focus on the constructed quality of the concrete, focussing on the well-known issues of the three C's: cover, compaction and curing.

7.9 Design life

For the purposes of this book, **design life** of a facility can be defined as the expected service life that results from the design process. Australian Standard AS1170.0:2002[36] defines **design working life** as:

> Duration of the period during which a structural element, when designed, is assumed to perform for its intended purpose with expected maintenance but without major structural repair being necessary.
>
> NOTE: In the context of this Standard, the design working life is a 'reference period' usually stated in years. It is a concept that can be used to select the probability of exceedance of different actions [sets of concentrated or distributed forces acting on a structure (direct action) or deformation imposed on a structure or constrained within (indirect action)].

The following example is the specified requirement in a design specification for the design life of sewerage lagoons:

> All equipment shall be designed and constructed to have a working life of at least 15 years, working 24 hours a day, 365 days per year. Valves and pipework shall be designed and constructed of materials that shall have a design life of 30 years. Structures such as concrete and steel shall be designed and constructed of materials that have a design life of 50 years and be maintenance free for 50 years.[37]

As indicated above, the design life is an outcome of the design process that takes into account a range of relevant factors such as prevailing environmental conditions, durability, operational parameters and material behaviour. The design life for normal structures in Australia is generally taken as 50 years.

The following summarises the process adopted to achieve a design life of 300 years for the Second Gateway Bridge over the Brisbane River:

> The durability design process for extended life requires the specific analysis of the environmental conditions in which the structure is placed, the strategic use of a range of materials and an understanding of the means by which they deteriorate and the rate of that deterioration.
>
> …

36 Structural design actions Part 0: General Principles.

37 *CH2M Hill v New South Wales* [2012] NSWSC 963, (2014) 30 BCL 35, [99].

> The process takes a first-principles and deterministic approach to modelling the environmental influences and material performance, but rather than just adopting mean values of the governing parameters, it overlays an understanding or assumption of their variation using known or assumed coefficients of variation to account for the stochastic nature of the deterioration process.
>
> ...
>
> The project scope and technical requirements (PSTR) for the bridge specified that the durability be applied diligently and continuously throughout the process of design, construction and throughout the maintenance period, and that the Second Gateway Bridge have a design life of 300 years, with some replaceable sub-items having design lives ranging from 20 years (wearing course) to 100 years (bearings). Design life was defined as the period assumed in design for which the structure or structural element is required to perform its intended purpose without replacement or major structural repairs.[38]

7.10 A case study on design life and service life

The distinction between design life and service life was brought into sharp focus in the case of *Mt Højgaard A/S v E.ON Climate and Renewables UK Robin Rigg East Ltd.* The project was a design and construct contract for a wind farm offshore of Scotland, the contractor being Mt Højgaard A/S and the Employer E.ON Climate and Renewables UK Robin Rigg East Limited.

The litigation in this case arose from the failure of the grouted connections between piled foundations and the towers supporting the wind turbines. The grouted connections were designed to accepted international Standards and verified by the independent certifying authority of Det Norske Veritas (**DNV**). There was no negligence in the design of the grouted connections.

The Technical Requirements (**TR**) that formed part of the contract stated that "The design of the foundations shall ensure a lifetime of 20 years in every respect without planned replacement." At first instance, the judge found this was a contractual obligation and that the Contractor was liable for the financial consequences of a failure to achieve the required 20-year service life, evidenced by the failure of the grouted connections before 20 years had elapsed.[39]

The grouted connections were designed for a design life of 20 years in accordance with the prevailing "state of the art" as detailed in the specified international standard. However, there was a serious (and unknown at the time) error in the DNV Standard for the design of the grouted connections.

In addition to the requirement for the facility to be designed for a life of 20 years, the judge found that the specified service life of 20 years was also a contractual obligation. Thus, even though the connection had a design life of 20 years in accordance with the "state of the art" (the accepted DNV Standard), failure to achieve the required service life was found to be a breach of contract.

On appeal, the Court of Appeal had a different view on the contractual obligations in relation to the design:

38 John Connal and Marita Berndt, "Sustainable Bridges – 300 Year Design Life for Second Gateway Bridge" www.outokumpu.com/SiteCollectionDocuments/Research-paper-Susstainable%20Bridges.pdf (accessed 13 August 2015).

39 *MT Højgaard a/s v E.ON Climate and Renewables UK Robin Rigg East Ltd* [2014] EWHC 1088 (TCC).

89. The starting point must be consideration of TR paragraph 3.2.2.2 (2). ['The design of the foundations shall ensure a lifetime of 20 years in every aspect without planned replacement. The choice of structure, materials, corrosion protection system operation and inspection programme shall be made accordingly.'] This is the provision which was critical to the judge's decision.

90. That paragraph undoubtedly says that the foundation design shall ensure a lifetime of 20 years. At first sight, such a provision, if incorporated into the contract, is a warranty that the foundations will function for 20 years.

91. On the other hand, all of the other provisions in the TR are directed towards a design life. If a structure has a design life of 20 years, that does not mean that inevitably it will function for 20 years, although it probably will. As noted in Part 2 above, the TR contain many references to the requirement for the foundations to have a design life of 20 years. See, for example, TR paragraphs 1.6 and 3.2.6.

[1.6 The Wind Farms are to be designed, constructed and operated to provide the lowest lifetime cost option capable of meeting the full requirements of this Specification. Maximum output with minimum maintenance and maximum availability to generate are the prime requirements of the scheme.

...

The Works, together with the interfaces detailed in Section 8, shall be designed to withstand the full range of operational and environmental conditions with minimal maintenance. The Works elements shall be designed for a minimum site specific 'design life' of twenty (20) years without major retrofits or refurbishments; all elements shall be designed to operate safely and reliably in the environmental conditions that exist on the site for at least this lifetime.]

[3.2.6 All parts of the Works, except wear parts and consumables shall be designed for a minimum service life of 20 years. ...]

...

98. In fact the obligations imposed by clause 8 are the opposite of requiring an absolute warranty of quality. What they require is due care, professional skill, adherence to good industry practice, compliance with the Employer's Requirements and so forth.

...

101. Clause 8.1 (x) requires that the works as a whole shall be 'fit for purpose'. Those words are qualified, however, by the phrase 'as determined in accordance with the Specification using Good Industry Practice'.[40]

Jackson LJ clearly articulated the distinction between design life and service life: "If a structure has a design life of 20 years, that does not mean that inevitably it will function for 20 years, although it probably will."[41] These two judgments of judges experienced in construction law highlights the difficulties faced by designers in construing their contractual obligations. One judge determined that achievement of a specified service life was a contractual obligation, and failure to achieve that (without negligence), was a breach of contract. Conversely, the Court of Appeal found, based on a detailed legal construction of the terms of the contract, that the Technical Requirements (fourth in the hierarchy of contract documents) did not warrant that the foundations would have a service life of 20 years. The Court of Appeal found that the obligations imposed by the conditions of contract were the opposite of requiring an absolute warranty of quality: due care, professional skill, adherence to good industry practice, compliance with the Employer's Requirements etc.

40 *Mt Højgaard A/S v E.ON Climate and Renewables UK Robin Rigg East Ltd* [2015] EWCA Civ 407.
41 *Mt Højgaard A/S v E.ON Climate and Renewables UK Robin Rigg East Ltd* [2015] EWCA Civ 407, [88].

However, designers cannot draw much comfort from the Court of Appeal's decision:

- It was derived from a close legal analysis of the specific words of "contractual documents of multiple authorship, which contain much loose wording", construing their meaning in accordance with conventional legal analysis.
- It differed from the conclusion of the judge at first instance, illustrating that the correct legal analysis was not obvious.
- It highlighted that, if a contract is worded with sufficient clarity, it can impose a double obligation on the contractor:
    - to comply with particular specifications and standards, and
    - to achieve a particular result.

In a salutary reminder to designers and contractors of the importance of understanding the contractual obligations they undertake, Jackson LJ noted:

> It is not unknown for construction contracts to require the contractor (a) to comply with particular specifications and standards and (b) to achieve a particular result. Such a contract, if worded with sufficient clarity, may impose a double obligation upon the contractor. He must as a minimum comply with the relevant specifications and standards. He must also take such further steps as are necessary to ensure that he achieves the specified result. In other words he must ensure that the finished structure conforms with that which he has warranted. As Mr Marrin points out, the design and build agreement in *Independent Broadcasting Authority v EMI Electronics Ltd* (1980) 14 BLR 1 was a contract of that character.[42]

7.11 Fitness for purpose

The common law duty of care owed by a professional to exercise the due skill and care of an ordinarily competent member of the profession (also implied into contracts for design) is not a guarantee of success:

> if you employ (an architect) about a novel thing, about which he has little experience, if it has not had the test of experience, failure may be consistent with skill. The history of all great improvements shows failure of those who embark in them.[43]

In other words, a designer is not automatically providing a warranty that the design will be fit for purpose. However, the situation may be different in the case of a design and construct contract:

> But, in the absence of a clear, contractual indication to the contrary, I see no reason why one who in the course of his business contracts to design, supply, and erect a television aerial mast is not under an obligation to ensure that it is reasonably fit for the purpose which he knows it is intended to be used.[44]

Arguably, fitness for purpose is an implied term of a design and construct contract, absent clear words to the contrary. In the *Mt Højgaard* Court of Appeal case discussed above, Jackson LJ found sufficiently clear words in the contract to define the designer's obligation

42 *Mt Højgaard A/S v E.ON Climate and Renewables UK Robin Rigg East Ltd* [2015] EWCA Civ 407, [79].

43 *Turner v Garland and Christopher, Hudson's Building Contracts* (4th edn, 1853) Vol II 1.

44 *Independent Broadcasting Authority v EMI Electronics Ltd and BICC Construction Ltd* (1980) 14 BLR 1, 47 per Lord Scarman.

as the exercise of due skill and care, and not fitness for purpose. The issue will always ultimately depend on construction of the contract, as highlighted by Jackson LJ's careful analysis in the *Mt Højgaard* case.

Notwithstanding that the terms of a contract may impose the additional requirement that a design must be fit for purpose, judges will circumscribe that obligation by requiring that the purpose must be made known to the contractor, and "fit for purpose" will be limited to reasonably fit for purpose having regard to reasonably expected conditions. Further, fit for purpose obligations may not apply to the extent that the Employer has not relied on the Contractor's expertise.

The following statements indicate the limitations on the fitness for purpose of the design for lagoons at a sewerage treatment plant. In this case, the designer accepted that there would be at least an implied term of the design contract that the design to be provided pursuant to it would be fit for the purposes that it was required to serve, as those purposes had been made known to the designer.

> I repeat that [the designer] was not obliged to provide a design that took account of, and guarded against, all possibilities of harm, no matter how remote. Its obligation was to provide what might be summarized as cost effective solutions that would achieve the design objectives – including of course, a 50 year maintenance free service life for the lagoons. As [the lead designer] in effect said, that requires an assessment of the remoteness of the risk.[45]

> It cannot be suggested that [the designers] were obliged to provide a design that guarded against every risk, no matter how remote the risk and how expensive the prevention of its guard. Its obligations included the provision of 'effective, efficient and economical solutions to satisfy the performance objectives and other requirements set out in the Brief'. In pursuit of that obligation, [the designer] was obliged 'to provide details of alternative proposals that satisfied these objectives and requirements'. (In each case, the quotation comes from cl 8.1 of the general conditions forming part of the design contract.)[46]

7.12 Conclusion

This chapter has endeavoured to explain some of the engineering issues involved in the design of civil engineering structures. Notwithstanding the known "state of the art", the knowledge of the behaviour of materials and the enormous computational power available to designers, there is still considerable art complementing the science in structural design. The application of that art and science means that properly designed structures to modern standards usually perform their function as intended over their working life.

However, modern ULS design explicitly recognises that there is a probability (albeit small) that a design prepared with due skill and care may fail during its service life. That is, the actual service life does not achieve the design life.

In such a situation, the legal consequences will usually depend on the terms of the contract. Absent a contractual term that the designer warrants that the design will be fit for purpose, the common law limits the designer's liability to any failure to exercise due skill and care. However, it is clear that in an appropriately worded contract, the designer may warrant that the design will be fit for purpose and the service life will be achieved. In such

45 *CH2M Hill v New South Wales* [2012] NSWSC 963, (2014) 30 BCL 35, [330].

46 *CH2M Hill v New South Wales* [2012] NSWSC 963, (2014) 30 BCL 35, [319].

a case, the designer will be liable for the consequences of breach of contract if the service life is not achieved, irrespective of any fault on the part of the designer.

It is common for construction contracts to consist of a large number of complex legal and technical documents, authored by a number of lawyers and engineers. As the *Højgaard* case illustrated, construing the terms of a such a construction contract where there are conflicting requirements may not be an easy task, and the outcome may not be obvious even to experienced lawyers.

This chapter was written before the Supreme Court considered the appeal from the Court of Appeal's decision. The following chapter contains an analysis of all three judgments in this important case.

CHAPTER 8

Fit for purpose or due skill and care?[1]

8.1 Introduction

This chapter reviews the outcome of a recent case in England which considered the contractual obligations of a design and construct contractor who was required not only to exercise due skill and care in performing the design, but also to warrant that the design would be fit for purpose.

The case is significant because the issues were addressed by learned judges in three courts: it was initially decided in the Technology and Construction Court, reversed in the Court of Appeal, and the first instance judge's decision was reinstated by the Supreme Court.

Ultimately, as is frequently the case, the outcome depended on construction of the documents comprising the contract. Not unusually for a construction contract, the contractual documents were of multiple authorship and contained much loose wording – an ideal environment for competing interpretations of the meaning of the contract.

What is of particular interest in this case is that the three learned judges of the Court of Appeal, construing the same documents, considering the same case law and, applying the same tools of construction, came to the opposite conclusion to the five judges of the Supreme Court and the judge at first instance. This highlights the difficulties faced by parties considering entering into a construction contract comprising an intersecting web of legal and "technical" documents – even skilled and experienced practitioners may come to differing conclusions as to how the documents would be construed by the fictitious "reasonable" person in possession of the relevant background information.

8.2 Technology and Construction Court

The case, *MT Højgaard a/s v E.ON Climate and Renewables UK Robin Rigg East Ltd*,[2] arose from the structural failure of wind turbine towers within two years after they were installed in Solway Firth in Scotland by MT Højgaard a/s (**MT Højgaard** or Contractor) for E.ON Climate and Renewables UK Robin Rigg East Ltd (**E.ON** or Employer).

The foundation for each wind turbine consisted of a single driven pile of slightly over 4 m in diameter. The tower supporting a wind turbine was connected to its foundation by

1 Chapter 8 is an edited version of an article first published by Thomson Reuters in *Building and Construction Law* and should be cited as (2018) 33 BCL 271. For all subscription inquiries please phone, from Australia: 1300 304 195, from overseas: +61 2 8587 7980 or online at legal.thomsonreuters.com.au/search.

2 [2014] EWHC 1088 (TCC).

 DOI: 10.4324/9781003206897-9

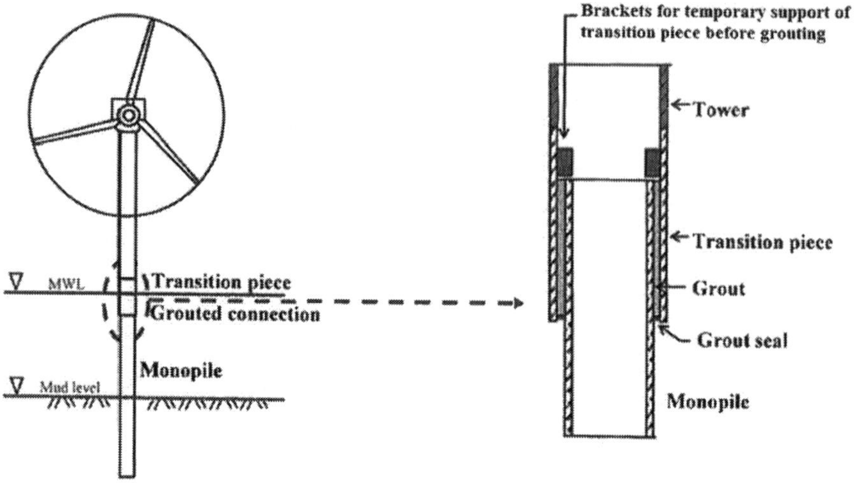

FIGURE 8.1 Details of grouted connection between monopile and tower. Appendix to *MT Højgaard A/S v E.ON Climate and Renewables UK Robin Rigg East Ltd* [2015] EWCA Civ 407 Crown Copyright

means of an 8 m long sleeve over the pile, the gap between pile and sleeve being filled with a sand–cement mixture called grout. Such a grouted connection transfers loads between the tower and the pile by friction. Figure 8.1 shows a diagram of the grouted connection between monopile and tower.

The Contractor's designer (Rambøll Danmark a/s) designed the grouted connection in accordance with the requirements of Det Norske Veritas (DNV) Standard DNV-OS-J101 (**J101**). At the time the Robin Rigg wind farm was designed, this Standard represented the "state-of-the-art" for the design of grouted connections for offshore wind turbines.

The Employer's Requirements formed part of the contract and contained the following Key Functional Requirement:

> The Works elements shall be designed for a minimum site specific 'design life' of twenty (20) years without major retrofits or refurbishments; all elements shall be designed to operate safely and reliably in the environmental conditions that exist on the site for at least this lifetime.

The Technical Requirements (TR) for the Design Basis (Wind Turbine Foundations) in the Employer's Requirements contained the following provision:

> **3.2.2.2 Detailed Design Stage**
> The detailed design of the foundation structures shall be according to the method of design by direct simulation of the combined load effect of simultaneous load processes (ref: DNV-OS-J101). Such a method is referred to throughout this document as an 'integrated analysis'.
>
> The design of the foundations shall ensure a lifetime of 20 years in every aspect without planned replacement. The choice of structure, materials, corrosion protection system operation and inspection programme shall be made accordingly.

Clause 8.1 General Obligations of the Conditions of Contract contained the following provision:

> The Contractor shall, in accordance with this Agreement, design, manufacture, test, deliver and install and complete the Works:
>
> (i) with due care and diligence expected of appropriately qualified and experienced designers, engineers and constructors (as the case may be).
>
> ...
>
> (iv) in a professional manner ... in accordance with ... Good Industry Practice
>
> ...
>
> (viii) so that the Works, when completed, comply with the requirements of the Agreement.
>
> ...
>
> (x) so that each item of Plant and the Works as a whole shall be fit for its purpose as determined in accordance with the Specification using Good Industry Practice.

The Conditions of Contract contained the following definitions:

> 'Fit for Purpose' means fitness for the purpose in accordance with, and as may properly be inferred from, the Employer's Requirements.
>
> "Good Industry Practice" means in relation to any particular undertaking or task ... those standards, practices, methods and procedures ... to be performed with the exercise of skill, diligence, prudence and foresight that can ordinarily be expected from a fully skilled contractor who is engaged in a similar type of undertaking or task in similar circumstances consistent with recognised international standards.

Thus, the contract contained the following explicit requirements in respect of the design of the grouted connections:

(1) The design was to be prepared with due skill and care, in a professional manner and in accordance with good industry practice.
(2) The design was to be prepared by the method of integrated analysis in accordance with J101.
(3) The Works would be fit for purpose in accordance with the Employer's Requirements.
(4) A minimum site-specific "design life" of 20 years.
(5) A lifetime of 20 years without planned replacement.

In the event, the grouted connections failed within two years, and the towers started slipping down the piles. The remedial work cost €26.25 m, and the court case was brought to determine whether the Contractor or the Employer was liable for this cost.

In the Technology and Construction Court, Edwards-Stuart J determined that the designers had exercised due skill and care, and had prepared the design in accordance with the requirements of J101. However, unknown to DNV and the designers at the time, there was an error in one of the parameters in a formula in J101 that meant the strength of the grouted connection was seriously overestimated. Notwithstanding that the designers had not been negligent, and that they had carried out the design of the grouted connections in accordance with the requirements of J101, the failure of these connections showed that they clearly did not have a service life of 20 years.

Edwards-Stuart J thus had to resolve which of the contractual requirements was determinative: a design prepared with due skill and care in accordance with the requirements of J101, or a design that "ensured" a service life of 20 years.

His Honour referred to several cases in which a contractor was required to follow plans and specifications and provide a constructed facility that was fit for a specific purpose. In such cases, the obligation to provide a fit for purpose facility overrode the requirement to follow the plans and specifications:

> If, for the purpose of this case, one treats J101 as 'an owner's specification', then these decisions are authority for the proposition that the existence of an express warranty of fitness for purpose by the contractor can trump the obligation to comply with the specification even though that specification may contain an error.[3]

In determining that, in this case, the Contractor was liable for the remedial costs, his Honour applied well-established principles to construe the terms of the contract as a whole. He did not consider that, where the Contractor has a design obligation, there was any incompatibility between a term that the completed work be fit for purpose and the "lesser obligation" that the design be prepared with due skill and diligence.[4] Of particular importance in this case was the contractual provision that the structures were to have a "minimum" service life of 20 years. In his Honour's judgment:

> MTH warranted that the foundations would have a service life of 20 years and E.ON is entitled to rely on that warranty notwithstanding that MTH was required to design the grouted connections in accordance with J101. Since those connections failed within 2–3 years, MTH was in breach of that obligation.[5]

8.3 Court of Appeal

MT Højgaard appealed Edwards-Stuart J's decision on liability, and E.ON cross-appealed Edwards-Stuart J's finding that MT Højgaard had not breached two provisions of the contract. The judgment of the Court of Appeal was delivered by Jackson LJ, with whom Patten LJ agreed.[6] Underhill LJ delivered a separate judgment in which he agreed with Jackson LJ's judgment on liability, and provided separate reasons in respect of the finding on E.ON's cross-appeal.

Jackson LJ reviewed the case law referred to in the trial below and accepted that a construction contract may require the Contractor to comply with particular specifications and standards and also to achieve a particular result. The issue in the appeal was whether the contract between E.ON and MT Højgaard was a contract of that character.[7]

In contrast to Edwards-Stuart J's view that there was no inconsistency between the contractual requirements to exercise due skill and care and ensure a life of 20 years, Jackson LJ considered that the contractual provisions were inconsistent:

> TR paragraphs 3.2.2.2 (2) and 3b.5.1 are inconsistent with the remainder of the TR and J101. They are too slender a thread upon which to hang a finding that MTH gave a warranty of 20 years life for the foundations. If TR paragraph 3.2.2.2 (2) and paragraph 3b.5.1 do not have

3 *MT Højgaard a/s v E.ON Climate and Renewables UK Robin Rigg East Ltd* [2014] EWHC 1088 (TCC) [74].
4 *MT Højgaard a/s v E.ON Climate and Renewables UK Robin Rigg East Ltd* [2014] EWHC 1088 (TCC) [77].
5 *MT Højgaard a/s v E.ON Climate and Renewables UK Robin Rigg East Ltd* [2014] EWHC 1088 (TCC) [80].
6 *MT Højgaard a/s v E.ON Climate and Renewables UK Robin Rigg East Ltd* [2015] EWCA Civ 407.
7 *MT Højgaard a/s v E.ON Climate and Renewables UK Robin Rigg East Ltd* [2015] EWCA Civ 407, [79].

> that effect, then without them clause 8.1 of the conditions cannot avail E.ON. Clause 8.1 does not contain any warranty that the foundations will have a 20 year life.[8]

His Lordship reached this conclusion after a detailed examination of "contractual documents of multiple authorship, which contain much loose wording".[9] He applied well-established principles of contractual interpretation, noting that, in complex documents of the kind in issue, there are bound to be ambiguities, infelicities and inconsistencies. In this case he considered there was an inconsistency between provisions in the conditions of contract and those in the Technical Requirements, a document lower in the contractual hierarchy. This inconsistency was resolved as follows:

> When there is tension between different provisions within contractual documents, the guidance given by Lord Mance in *Re Sigma Corp (in administrative receivership)* [2009] UKSC 2; [2010] 1 All ER 571 at [12] is of assistance. He said that the resolution of a construction issue is an iterative process. It involves checking each of the rival meanings against the other provisions of the document and investigating its commercial consequences.[10]

TR para 3.2.2.2 was critical to Edwards-Stuart J's finding that MTH provided a 20-year service life warranty. However, Jackson LJ recognised a contractual difference between service life and design life in the following terms:

> On the other hand, all of the other provisions in the TR are directed towards a design life. If a structure has a design life of 20 years, that does not mean that inevitably it will function for 20 years, although it probably will. As noted in Part 2 above, the TR contain many references to the requirement for the foundations to have a design life of 20 years. See, for example, TR paragraphs 1.6 and 3.2.6.[11]

Jackson LJ discussed the probabilistic nature of design, and the basis of J101 to create a sufficiently high probability of achieving a service life of 20 years, although "No-one suggests that that provision would achieve a structure with a guaranteed life of 20 years."[12] J101 is intended to provide "an internationally acceptable level of safety" in which the annual probability of failure is to be in the range of 10^{-5}–10^{-4}.[13]

His Lordship's view was that a reasonable person in the position of E.ON and MTH would have known that the normal standard required in the construction of offshore wind farms was compliance with J101 and that such compliance was expected, but not absolutely guaranteed, to produce a life of 20 years. Importantly, he considered that it was not clear how a contractor, complying with J101 and the Technical Requirements, could in fact achieve a guaranteed operational life of 20 years. Such a warranty would involve additional cost that would need to be included in the tender, and the need for such allowance clearly flagged in the contract documents.[14]

Jackson LJ also upheld E.ON's cross-appeal and found that MT Højgaard breached the contract in that it did not carry out testing to justify the omission of shear keys, as was required by J101 and the Contract. These provisions required that the Contractor had to do

8 *MT Højgaard a/s v E.ON Climate and Renewables UK Robin Rigg East Ltd* [2015] EWCA Civ 407, [105].

9 *MT Højgaard a/s v E.ON Climate and Renewables UK Robin Rigg East Ltd* [2015] EWCA Civ 407, [71].

10 *MT Højgaard a/s v E.ON Climate and Renewables UK Robin Rigg East Ltd* [2015] EWCA Civ 407, [83].

11 *MT Højgaard a/s v E.ON Climate and Renewables UK Robin Rigg East Ltd* [2015] EWCA Civ 407, [91].

12 *MT Højgaard a/s v E.ON Climate and Renewables UK Robin Rigg East Ltd* [2015] EWCA Civ 407, [93].

13 For a discussion of modern design principles, see Charrett, "Design Life or Service Life – What Is the Difference?" (2017) 1 *International Construction Law Review* 16.

14 *MT Højgaard a/s v E.ON Climate and Renewables UK Robin Rigg East Ltd* [2015] EWCA Civ 407, [105].

something more than rely on calculations in accordance with J101; he had to demonstrate with "test data" that the grouted connection had sufficient axial capacity. Although the failure to provide such test data was a breach of contract, Jackson LJ accepted that, on the basis of the evidence and the balance of probabilities, such testing would not necessarily have detected the inadequate axial load capacity. Accordingly, he awarded only nominal damages in respect of these breaches.[15]

8.4 Supreme Court

E.ON appealed the Court of Appeal's decision to the Supreme Court. Lord Neuberger delivered a judgment with which Lords Mance, Clarke, Sumption and Hodge agreed.[16]

8.4.1 No inconsistency between a lifetime of 20 years and complying with J101

The central issue in this appeal was the enforceability of para 3.2.2.2(ii) according to its terms. His Lordship found, using ordinary principles of construction, that the requirement to ensure a lifetime of 20 years in accordance with para 3.2.2.2(ii) was not inconsistent with the requirement that the structures be designed in accordance with J101.

In addition to the case law relied on in the courts below, Lord Neuberger referred to English case law going back over 100 years as support for the primacy of a contractual requirement to construct a work capable of carrying out a specified duty; such a duty may entail that more is required than compliance with the specification.[17]

Acknowledging that each case must turn on its own facts, his Lordship noted:

> However, in many contracts, the proper analysis may well be that the contractor has to improve on any aspects of the prescribed design which would otherwise lead to the product falling short of the prescribed criteria, and in other contracts, the correct view could be that the requirements of the prescribed criteria only apply to aspects of the design which are not prescribed.
>
> In those circumstances, in my judgment, where two provisions of Section 3 impose different or inconsistent standards or requirements, rather than concluding that they are inconsistent, the correct analysis by virtue of para 3.1(i) is that the more rigorous or demanding of the two standards or requirements must prevail, as the less rigorous can properly be treated as a minimum requirement. Further, if there is an inconsistency between a design requirement and the required criteria, it appears to me that the effect of para 3.1(ii) would be to make it clear that, although it may have complied with the design requirement, MTH would be liable for the failure to comply with the required criteria, as it was MTH's duty to identify the need to improve on the design accordingly.[18]

This puts a heavy onus on a designer where a fitness for purpose obligation is imposed by a contract. In such a case, following international standards or the current state-of-the-art will not avail a designer where a standard or the current state-of-the-art is inadequate.[19]

15 *MT Højgaard a/s v E.ON Climate and Renewables UK Robin Rigg East Ltd* [2015] EWCA Civ 407, [115]–[129].

16 *MT Højgaard a/s v E.ON Climate and Renewables UK Robin Rigg East Ltd* [2017] UKSC 59.

17 *MT Højgaard a/s v E.ON Climate and Renewables Robin Rigg East Ltd* [2017] UKSC 59, [38]–[43].

18 *MT Højgaard a/s v E.ON Climate and Renewables Robin Rigg East Ltd* [2017] UKSC 59, [44]–[45].

19 For a case in which a designer was found liable for not following the provisions of an unpublished draft Standard, see Section 10.8.

The higher fitness for purpose standard will apply, notwithstanding that a designer may have no way of determining those inadequacies.

8.4.2 Design life and service life

Lord Neuberger canvassed the previously accepted meaning of para 3.2.2.2(ii) of the TR that this was a 20-year warranty of service life. However, he went on as follows:

> It appears to me that there is a powerful case for saying that, rather than warranting that the foundations would have a lifetime of 20 years, para 3.2.2.2(ii) amounted to an agreement that the design of the foundations was such that they would have a lifetime of 20 years. In other words, read together with clauses 30 and 42.3 of the Contract, para 3.2.2.2(ii) did not guarantee that the foundations would last 20 years without replacement, but that they had been designed to last 20 years without replacement.[20]

Thus, as had been assumed in the Court of Appeal, Lord Neuberger suggested that para 3.2.2.2(ii) could be interpreted as specifying a design life of 20 years, rather than a service life of 20 years.

The relevant facts in this case were that the grouted connections failed within the 24-month Defects Liability Period. His Lordship found it unnecessary to decide whether para 3.2.2.2(ii) was a warranty that the foundations would have a lifetime of 20 years (i.e. a service life of 20 years), or a contractual term that the foundations were to be designed to have such a lifetime (i.e. a design life of 20 years), although he was inclined to favour the latter meaning.

His Lordship stated, without analysis: "However, it is clear that, if para 3.2.2.2(ii) is an effective term of the Contract, it was breached by MTH whichever meaning it has, and therefore the issue need not be resolved."[21] He acknowledged that: "J101, while concerned with making recommendations and requirements linked to the intended life of a structure to which it applies, makes it clear that there is a risk, which it quantifies, of that life being shortened."[22] This seems to be a recognition that, although a structure might be designed to have a service life of 20 years, it might not in fact achieve that. As his Lordship found it unnecessary to decide whether the contractual provision in TR para 3.2.2.2 was a requirement for a design life of 20 years or a service life of 20 years, it appears that he considered that the failure demonstrated that the structures had neither a service life of 20 years, nor a design life of 20 years.

This raises the question as to what is meant by the term "design life". In the previous chapter, this was defined as follows: "design life can be defined as the expected service life that results from the design process".

On this definition, by following the "state-of-the-art" design procedure in J101, the structures were designed for a life of 20 years according to then-current practice. The designers expected a service life of 20 years because they followed the recognised international standard.

In this case, because of the error in J101, the structure did not function for 20 years, and clearly did not have a service life of 20 years, although it had a design life of 20 years

20 *MT Højgaard a/s v E.ON Climate and Renewables Robin Rigg East Ltd* [2017] UKSC 59, [30].
21 *MT Højgaard a/s v E.ON Climate and Renewables Robin Rigg East Ltd* [2017] UKSC 59, [32].
22 *MT Højgaard a/s v E.ON Climate and Renewables Robin Rigg East Ltd* [2017] UKSC 59, [31].

according to the then-prevailing standard. As noted above, Lord Neuberger apparently took the view that the structures did not have a design life of 20 years. While that is now known with the benefit of hindsight, it was not known at the time the design was carried out. The designer no doubt believed that, by following J101, the structures had a design life of 20 years, as did DNV, which issued the Foundation Design Evaluation Conformity Statement.

8.4.3 Satisfying J101 was a minimum requirement

Paragraph 3.1(ii) of the TR provided that: "It shall be the responsibility of [MTH] to identify any areas where the works need to be designed to any additional or more rigorous requirements or parameters." His Lordship stated:

> Furthermore, para 3.1(ii) [of the TR] makes it clear that MTH should have identified that there was a need for a "more rigorous" requirement than δ being "taken as 0.00037Rp" to ensure that the design was satisfactory, or at least complied with para 3.2.2.2(iii).

From a contractual perspective (which of course was the basis on which the case was decided), para 3.1(ii) of the TR undoubtedly put the onus on MTH to determine whether more rigorous requirements than J101 were required to ensure compliance with all the requirements of the Contract. However, from a practical perspective, how was MTH to determine what "more rigorous" requirements than J101 were necessary? J101 was the product of DNV, an internationally recognised standards organisation that was also the Certifying Authority for MTH's design. DNV in fact provided the required Foundation Design Evaluation Conformity Statement that would normally provide comfort to a designer that it had complied with the necessary requirements. DNV was unaware at the time of the error in J101, as surely would have been the users of this Standard. As noted above, Jackson LJ squarely raised this issue in the Court of Appeal, in support of his view that the need for such additional work should have been clearly flagged so that appropriate allowance could be included in the tender price.

One of the notable issues in this judgment is its lack of commentary on the error in the DNV J101 Standard for the design of grouted pile connections. While Lord Neuberger stressed those aspects of the Technical Requirements that stated that compliance with the specified requirements (including the erroneous DNV Standard) were *minimum* requirements, there was no discussion as to what investigations may have been appropriate or necessary to determine whether or not additional measures over and above the Standard were required.

The writer's view on the use of Standards by ordinarily competent designers is summarised as follows:

> Australian Standards are published documents that set out specifications and procedures with the aim of ensuring that products, services and systems are safe, reliable and consistently perform the way they were intended to. They establish a common language which defines quality and safety criteria acceptable to a broad range of interested parties.
>
> ...
>
> In essence, by documenting norms in a common language, Standards enable the community and industry to seek and contract for goods and services on a level playing field. They specify minimum acceptable requirements pertaining to the majority of transactions that were anticipated in conceiving and scoping the particular Standard.

> ...
> Professionals generally accept that appropriate procedures have been applied in the drafting, review and adoption of a Standard, so that it represents the 'state-of-the-art'. On what informed or qualified basis would the regular practitioner be aware of the specific basis of each provision of the Standards, background research and deliberations of the Technical Committee and its individual members? In the writer's view, it is commercially impractical and contrary to the professional objective of Standards for a user to review the project specific circumstances to assess the applicability and adequacy of each and every provision of a contractually specified Standard.[23]

8.5 Conclusion

This case is an important reminder for contractors and designers entering into complex construction contracts for the need to understand and allow for the contractual obligations they are undertaking.

The principle of freedom of contract means that parties are free to agree to anything that is not against the law or public policy, irrespective of whether that is in accord with common norms or is objectively "reasonable". The words of the contract, construed in accordance with well-known principles that require all the documents comprising the contract to be considered as a whole, and generally given their ordinary meaning, will usually determine the outcome of a dispute – particularly in a case such as *MT Højgaard a/s v E.ON Climate and Renewables UK Robin Rigg East Ltd*, where the contract remedies were stated to be exclusive of any other remedy (save in the case of misconduct).

The obverse of freedom of contract is the principle of *pacta sunt servanda*: parties will be held to the bargain they have agreed to. In the event of a contractual dispute, the role of a court is essentially to determine what the parties have objectively agreed to, and to apply the appropriate remedies.

There is a particular caveat for designers highlighted by this case. Applying due skill and care and the state of the art as understood by the profession may not be sufficient to avoid liability where there is also a contractual obligation for the design to be fit for purpose. The obligation in each case will depend on the specific terms of the relevant contract, but it is clear from this case and others that, in a carefully worded contract, a fit for purpose obligation may trump the normal professional exercise of due skill and care. This is of particular concern to designers (and it is suggested, should also be of concern to Employers) faced with a contractual liability which, in the absence of negligence, would not normally be covered by Professional Indemnity insurance.

The judgment of the Supreme Court does, however, highlight the fact that contractual terms can be a shield as well as a sword. In the contract between MT Højgaard and E.ON, the Contractor was obliged to rectify any defects that occurred within 24 months after the Works were handed over, and any claim after that time was barred. Lord Neuberger considered that, because the contractual remedies were intended to operate as an exclusive regime, E.ON only had two years to detect any defects, irrespective of whether the warranty was for a design life or a service life of 20 years. If the defect had been discovered

23 See Section 10.2.4.

more than two years after the Works were handed over, MT Højgaard would not have been liable for the rectification costs.

This case also highlights that, notwithstanding the well-established canons of contractual construction, this is not a trivial exercise for a complex and detailed construction contract, and skilled and experienced judges can have different views on the objective meaning of such a contract.

CHAPTER 9

Design and construct contracts and final design cost risk[1]

9.1 Introduction

This chapter considers the critical issues in final design cost risk in design and construct contracts where there is a single independent design subcontractor with responsibility for tender and final design. The factors that influence final design cost risk are identified from several cases that have been before Australian courts, and the difficulties usually faced by a Contractor in passing risk to a designer assessed by considerations of tender and final design contracts. Suggestions are made as to what actions a Contractor could take to manage the identified risks better.

9.2 Design and construct contracts

In the "traditional" method of project delivery, the Employer employed its in-house designers or contracted design consultants for the preparation of the design of the project. The Employer subsequently called for tenders from contractors, often on a lump sum price basis, on essentially complete design documentation prepared by the Employer's designers. The risks of increased construction costs arising from design changes or late delivery of final design documentation was therefore carried by the Employer, unless negligence of the designer could be proved.

Design and construct contracts have become a popular method of project delivery in Australia and other countries over recent years. The essence of a design and construct contract is that the Contractor undertakes the responsibility and liability for the final design and documentation, as well as the construction.[2] There are no doubt many reasons for Employers' preference for design and construct, including the following:

- The substantial reduction of in-house engineering capability, consequent on privatisation of the engineering function of many Government departments

1 This chapter is an edited version of the published paper Donald Charrett, 'Design and construct contracts and final design cost risk' (2003) 13 *BDPS News* 10; (2003) 91 *Australian Construction Law Newsletter* 5. It is reproduced by kind permission of the Building Dispute Practitioner's Society.

2 In 'Contracts for Industrial Projects' (1984) 1 *International Construction Law Review* 322, 324, Ian Duncan Wallace QC defined "turnkey" as follows:a contract where the essential design emanates from, or is supplied by, the contractor and not the owner, so that the legal responsibility for the design, suitability and performance of the work after completion will be made to rest … with the contractor … 'Turnkey' is treated as merely signifying the design responsibility as the contractor's.

 DOI: 10.4324/9781003206897-10

- Design and construct reduces the number of contracts to deliver a project, thereby reducing the extent of the Employer's contract management
- Risks associated with the design (time, cost and quality) are assumed by the Contractor, not the Employer
- The potential for a significant saving in the overall time required to deliver the project, as the contract can be awarded and construction started before the design is complete.

9.2.1 Tender design

The extent of tender documentation for a design and construct contract varies considerably from one contract to another. At one extreme, the Employer specifies only the functional and performance requirements and leaves the form of the design to be determined by the tenderers. In these cases, a tenderer has to undertake substantial conceptual and preliminary design work in order to have sufficient information to cost and prepare a tender. In other cases, the Employer's design is substantially complete, leaving little scope for tenderers to make significant changes.

In all these cases, the common feature is that the design is not fully detailed, leaving scope for the tenderers, to a greater or lesser degree, to input their own design ideas, materials and construction methods in an endeavour to reduce costs in a competitive environment. As a design prepared for a design and construct tender is "preliminary" and not complete, it is almost inevitable that there will be items not shown on the tender drawings, either in terms of extent, quality or complexity. It is only when the drawings have been completed for a project that the design is fully detailed, showing all items comprehensively. The skill in tendering design and construct contracts is in the extrapolation from incomplete documentation to cost the entire project. This extrapolation includes the undocumented components, and judging what allowances must be made to cover the cost of the undocumented and unknown components, and any design changes that might ultimately be necessary in developing the preliminary tender design into the final "for construction" design.

As Australian contractors do not have any substantial "in house" design capacity, they normally engage consulting engineers, architects and other consultants to prepare preliminary designs sufficient for the contractor to price a major design and construct contract tender. The cost of preparing this preliminary design is additional to the normal contractor's/subcontractor's costs to price the work to be constructed, thus the total costs of tendering are significantly greater for a design and construct tender than for a tender to construct the same project to an Employer-supplied design.

Irrespective of the contractual relationship between the designers and the contractor during the tender, and who is taking the cost risk of the design if the tender is unsuccessful, there are significant commercial pressures to minimise the extent of preliminary design and hence tender costs. However, the less design that is done at this preliminary stage, the greater the pricing risk that the tender will have inadequate cost provision for construction of those design elements that were incompletely considered during tender design. There is also the risk that if inadequate design and investigation is carried out during the tender stage, the concept design on which the tender is based may not be appropriate for the project, and will have to be changed during final design with consequent substantial unforeseen cost increases.

9.2.2 Final design cost risk

Given the significant risk that the Contractor's cost of the final constructed design could be substantially greater than the tendered price based on the preliminary design, the question arises as to whether the contractual arrangements commonly used for design and construct satisfy the Abrahamson Principles, that is, are the risks borne by the party best able to manage them? Most of the Contractor's risk of increased cost, referred to herein as **final design cost risk**, is specific to design and construct contracts, as the most significant component arises from the incompleteness of the design which is priced for tender, and this aspect does not usually exist in construct-only contracts. Any excess cost of construction arising from materialisation of final design cost risk will be referred to herein as **unforeseen final cost**. Whilst final design cost risk would exist even if the contractor's designer was in-house, the contractor needs to manage this risk more carefully where the designer is a consultant with its own commercial imperatives.

9.3 Potential factors in final design cost risk

One of the features of design and construct contracts is that, as the Contract is almost invariably executed before the design is completed, the Employer knows precisely (more or less) the cost, but neither the Employer nor the Contractor know with any precision what will be provided for that price.[3] This can be seen in an acute form in one reported case where, in a contract for $2m for the sale of land and design and construction of a transport depot, there was no specification, and only five basic plans of which the judge commented that "a stranger to the transaction would be unlikely to be able to envisage the completed project".[4]

Although project delivery via design and construct projects is not new, it has only recently been widely used in Australia. Accordingly, relevant case law that has directly considered the issue of unforeseen final cost does not appear to have been judicially adjudicated. In one significant case, the Contractor's claims for unforeseen final cost from its design subcontractor were central to the dispute, and are discussed in the case report,[5] but ultimately the claims were not judicially decided.

Table 9.1 summarises the potential factors in unforeseen final design cost risk from a distillation of the reported cases and the writer's experience as an engineer and lawyer, and consideration of the responsibilities of and relationships between the parties associated with a contractor preparing a design and construct tender.

The reference to "causally responsible party" in the above table does not necessarily import legal responsibility, and this is discussed below. Although the factors listed under "Contractor" include those caused by trade subcontractors, they can be all managed and resolved by the Contractor using the normal techniques and procedures of the construction industry. Attention is focussed herein on those factors listed under "designer", as these are specific to design and construct contracts and are the most difficult for a Contractor to manage.

3 RAIA Practice Division The Package Deal RAIA Practice Note PN13 February 1972 cited in *Lolita v Mohyla Construction in Australia: Law and Project Delivery* (1996) 151.

4 *McPhee & Son (Aust) Pty Ltd v Technopolis Pty Ltd* (1997) 13 BCL 189, 193.

5 *John Holland Construction & Engineering Pty Ltd v Kvaerner RJ Brown Pty Ltd* (1997) 13 BCL 262.

TABLE 9.1 Potential factors in final design cost risk

DESIGN PHASE	*CAUSALLY RESPONSIBLE PARTY*	
	DESIGNER	*CONTRACTOR*
Tender design	TD1. Tender design does not identify full extent of final design (insufficient precision on which to base an accurate tender): – required elements not shown in tender design (scope) – underestimate of sizes, quality or quantity of elements in final design (extent) – underestimate of complexity (concept) TD2. Designer did not warn Contractor of design risk TD3. Designer did not warn Contractor of pricing risk TD4. Misstatements as to accuracy or suitability of tender design TD5. Misstatements on designer's procedures, skill, expertise, resources and experience	TC1. Work shown on preliminary drawings under-priced by Contractor/ trade subcontractors TC2. Inadequate contingency allowance for finalising design TC3. Errors in preparing bid by Contractor/trade subcontractors
Final design	FD1. Design changes from tender design: – additional elements not shown in tender design (scope) – increased sizes, quality or quantity of elements from tender design (extent) – additional complexity from tender design (change of concept) FD2. Design not suitable for Contractor's project strategy FD3. Final design exceeds contractual performance requirements FD4. Final design does not satisfy contractual performance requirements FD5. Design changes that impacted procurement or construction FD6. Late delivery of design information	FC1. Contractor's/ trade subcontractor's inefficiencies in procurement or construction result in constructed costs being greater than priced for at tender stage FC2. Inefficient contract administration FC3. Non-recoverable costs arising from Employer's acts

9.4 Relevant cases

9.4.1 Leighton Contractors Pty Ltd v Kinhill Engineers Pty Ltd[6]

One of the potential advantages of design and construct is that, as the designers are engaged by and contractually liable to the Contractor, the resulting design will be more appropriate to the Contractor's requirements regarding proposed methods of construction, schedule, preferred materials etc. A Contractor is likely to take the view that a designer who did not deliver a design to those requirements would be in breach of its obligations. This issue arose in a design and construct project for a Melbourne office building, where the Contractor claimed that the structural engineer's negligence had increased the cost of the project. In this case, the engineer was contracted to the Contractor after work on site had commenced, so there was no issue of any cost differences between the tender and final design. However, the Contractor's final project cost was greater than the contract price, and it claimed that the engineer breached its structural engineering contract in that it "failed to design a car park layout that satisfied the requirements of a suitable project design strategy" and should have adopted another design.[7] The Contractor asserted that the engineer's breach was the negligent failure to provide an efficient, effective and economical design, and one that would permit adherence to the Contractor's work programme.[8]

The whole dispute was referred to a referee who opined that there was no negligence in the design as alleged, and there was no causal connection with any loss, even though a better engineering solution was now recognised.[9] Giles J accepted that a failure to offer a design could be a negligent breach of contract, even if the design offered was not negligently executed; however, on the facts of this case, there was no proven duty of the engineer to offer alternatives.[10] It appears that the engineer's performance was assessed against the usual implied duty of a professional to exercise reasonable care and skill in the provision of its services. Apparently, neither the referee nor Giles J was convinced that, absent specific contractual terms, there was any higher duty on the engineer that its design should be fit for the Contractor's purpose, particularly as none of the issues subsequently complained of was drawn to the engineer's attention.[11]

The case highlights one of the practical difficulties confronting a design and construct contractor that has suffered a loss arising from building a design prepared by an independent consultant. It is more difficult to prove breach of contract where the standard of performance is based on the provision of reasonable care and skill rather than the production of a design to suit the contractor's requirements, particularly where the contractor does not communicate those requirements. Furthermore, there is the additional substantial hurdle of proving that the loss suffered is causally related to the designer's breach of contract or duty of care.

6 (1996) 12 BCL 415.
7 Ibid 426.
8 Ibid 419.
9 Ibid 419 and 424.
10 Ibid 426.
11 Ibid 421.

9.4.2 *John Holland Construction & Engineering Pty Ltd v Kvaerner RJ Brown Pty Ltd*[12]

This case involved a design and construct contractor's claim for damages, against its design consulting engineer in relation to the lump sum turnkey contract for the process skids for a floating production storage offloading facility. For preparation of its tender, the contractor entered into a consultancy agreement with the Employer, and the design engineer entered into a "Pre-Bid Agreement" with the contractor and agreed to carry out the specialist design and engineering services that the contractor was bidding to provide to the Employer. The tender deliverables prepared by the engineer were alleged to be most of the documents used by the contractor in preparing its lump sum bid.

After the Contractor had been awarded the contract, the engineer entered into a "Design Agreement" in which it undertook to complete the engineering and detailed design for the project. Following project completion, the Contractor instituted proceedings, claiming extra costs from the engineer that the Contractor alleged it had incurred in executing its contract with the Employer, above the cost estimates on which it had based its tendered lump sum price. The Contractor claimed damages for breach of contract in either or both the Pre-Bid and Design Agreements. In addition, the Contractor made alternative claims for breaches of duty of care under both agreements, as well as claims under the *Trade Practices Act* (now *Australian Consumer Law*) and for negligent misstatement that, during the bid preparation and during final design, the engineer made representations to the Contractor that were misleading and deceptive.[13] These alleged representations included that the engineer would provide the information necessary for the preparation of an accurate tender, and if the tender were accepted, the engineer would deliver design engineering that would not increase the cost of the project to the contractor from the tender price.

The case reported was an application by the engineer to strike out substantial parts of the Contractor's statement of claim. One of the main objections was that the claims were pleaded as global claims, in that there was no attempt to attribute any specific loss to a specific breach of contract, but a composite loss was claimed as a result of all the alleged breaches. Byrne J concluded that the form of a number of the global claims made was bad, as the causal nexus between the alleged wrongful acts and omissions of the engineer and the damages for extra costs incurred and claimed by the Contractor was not apparent. The Contractor was required to make substantial changes to its pleading to establish the nexus between alleged wrongful acts and omissions and the losses claimed. It was also required to amend its form of pleading for breaches of duty of care to show in what respect there was a departure from the duty of care, what loss was suffered and how that loss was caused by the breach.

The fundamental questions in this case were whether the designer had any liability and, if so, on what basis and to what extent, for the Contractor's cost overrun. These questions were ultimately not publicly argued or considered judicially as the case settled before a final hearing. The case does however highlight some of the pleading difficulties faced by a contractor who wishes to recover unforeseen final cost. Byrne J suggested that it is easier to prove that a contract has not been performed than that it was done so negligently, and that, where the claims for damage for negligence are based on the same acts or omissions

12 *John Holland Construction & Engineering Pty Ltd v Kvaerner RJ Brown Pty Ltd* (1997) 13 BCL 262.
13 Ibid 264.

as for breach of contract, it is unlikely that there will be any benefits from pursuing those claims in tort. However, the most significant issue is that of proving the causation of losses suffered from any contractual or other breaches. Thus, even where the Contractor has suffered a financial loss and could prove breach of contract or breach of a relevant duty of care, putting the claim forward as a global claim may not be acceptable and may be risky for the Contractor. It must be able to prove how those losses flow directly from the relevant breaches.

The issues raised in these cases are considered below in the context of contracts for preliminary and final design in design and construct contracts.

9.5 Design subcontracts

There are several aspects of design, particularly preliminary tender design, that have a significant influence on the contractual relationship between Contractor and designer. Most obviously, the designer's role is to prepare the design for the whole project, which takes the form of intellectual property in drawings, specifications etc., and relevant subsets of these are required prior to procurement or construction. Second, a design subcontractor is required to start the task of design during the tender period and, if the tender is successful, the preliminary design will form the basis on which the final contract design will be prepared. Thus, during the tender period a designer must carry out a proportion of the work of final design that will only be required if the contractor is successful in its tender. In principle, the extent of this work must not only determine the appropriate conceptual design, but must develop that design to a sufficient extent to define the scope and quality of the final design in enough detail to provide the contractor with adequate drawings, specifications etc. that will enable the contractor to prepare an accurate price to deliver the entire project within the contractual time.

In addition, the extent of preliminary design, and the related matters of its cost and which party bears that cost, are critically important elements in the relationship between the designer and contractor during the tender period. In the common situation where the Employer pays no or token fees for tender design, the significance of this cost is that one or both of contractor and designer takes the risk of paying for the costs of the preliminary design if the contractor's tender is unsuccessful. At one extreme, the contractor could pay normal full design fees and thereby assume the risk, or at the other extreme, the designer could prepare the tender design "on spec" with no remuneration unless the tender was ultimately successful. There is also the common compromise whereby both designer and contractor assume some cost risk, in which the contractor pays the designer reduced fees for the tender design work, and the designer only makes up the shortfall from its full design fees if the tender is successful.

It is suggested that this extent of payment and consequent tender design cost risk assumption will have a fundamental influence on the informal, as well as the formal contractual relationship between designer and contractor for the tender design period. If the contractor pays full design fees, the tender design subcontract may be no different to the normal style of contract for design between a designer and an employer, in which the designer is commissioned to carry out a defined scope of work under defined contractual terms. In this situation, there is no further obligation on either side whether or not the contractor is successful in winning the design and construct contract. However, if the designer has prepared the tender design on spec, it will only recover its tender design costs if the contractor wins the contract and then pays the designer.

In considering a designer's obligations with regard to final design cost risk, the contractual arrangements between contractor and designer need to be considered separately for the two phases of the work: tender design and final design. There may be two separate contracts covering these phases, or alternatively a single contract with two phases, the commission for the final design phase being contingent on the fulfilment of the condition precedent of the contractor being awarded the design and construct contract.

Even where both phases are covered by one contract, the nature of the designer's work required by the contractor in the tender design phase is different to that for the final design phase. The tender design ideally requires preparation of the appropriate concept design and documentation of the project defined by the tender documents, to an extent just sufficient for the contractor to be able to prepare an accurate price for construction of the complete project, with the extent and quality of work defined to within an accuracy acceptable to the contractor. Final design, on the other hand, requires complete documentation of the project whose requirements are defined in the head contract documents, to an extent and to a quality sufficient for the Contractor to procure the materials and construct the project within the contractual time. In both design phases, the designer must have due regard to construction in the most expeditious way appropriate to the Contractor's preferred methods of working, and the most suitable economical materials that satisfy the specified quality and functional requirements.

9.6 Design for tender

It is trite to observe that final design cost risk arises because the tender design is incomplete, and this is a result of neither the contractor nor the designer normally being prepared to fund the significant costs of completing the design and documentation during the tender period. Even if adequate time was available during the tender phase for preparation of a complete design (which would very unusual), the costs of complete design are too high to risk in a competitive tendering situation. Furthermore, it is suggested that there is no necessary correlation between the extent of design carried out and likely success in winning the tender. The Employer's selection of the winning tender for a design and construct project may be based on various factors, such as the price, completion date, quality, functionality, or the life cycle costs of the design offered. Lowest price could result from a contractor's keenness of pricing, natural efficiencies or an innovative concept design that permitted speedy construction or fewer construction resources. It could also result from an underestimation of the scope of work required by the Contract.

There are thus many potential reasons for success, some of which will not be related to the quantity of tender design work carried out. Whilst the quality of the tender design may be crucial to success, it is not cost-effective for a contractor to commission any more tender design than is necessary for the purposes of the tender. The contractor's aims for the tender design include winning the tender at minimum cost, whilst maintaining the final design cost risk at an acceptable level.

During the tender stage, issues that are relevant to final design cost risk that the contractor has some control over, or choice of, include selection of the designer, the designer's scope of work during the tender period, and the terms of the designer's subcontract for both tender and final design phases. One way in which the contractor may endeavour to minimise final design cost risk is to have it assumed by the designer under the terms of the design subcontract. In any tender design subcontract, the designer's liability in preparing the preliminary design will prima facie be governed by the terms of that contract, although there may also be potential liability in tort and, in Australia, for misleading or deceptive conduct under the *Australian Consumer Law* (previously the *Trade Practices Act*). This chapter is confined to consideration of contractual issues, notwithstanding the importance of negligence and misleading or deceptive conduct in assessing liability for losses arising from the materialisation of final design cost risk.

There are two aspects of any design contract that are relevant to the extent of the designer's liability. The first of these is the scope of the work to be carried out by the designer, and the second is the contract terms, express or implied, that govern the performance of the work.

9.6.1 Scope of work

There is a tension between the formal nature of a written contract (assuming one has been prepared and executed), including the procedures to amend it, and the dynamic nature of the relationship between contractor and designer during the tender period. At the start of the design, particularly if conceptual design is required, neither party will necessarily have any clear idea of what form the project will take, and how much preliminary design will be necessary for the contractor to cost it. There is thus likely to be substantial interaction between contractor and designer as the tender design is developed, and this is typically at a professional level between project personnel, rather than on a formal contractual basis.

It can therefore be very difficult to define with any precision in the design subcontract what the exact scope of work is or will be, as it may change as the tender design develops. The actual scope of work is also likely to be influenced by the agreed remuneration to the designer. If it is a fixed sum, there is an inevitable internal pressure on the designer to minimise the amount of design work executed (consistent with its contractual obligations) to minimise its cost risk if its contractor client does not win the tender. Conversely, the contractor's interest is in maximising the amount of design work done to minimise its final design cost risk if the contract is won. If, however, full fees are to be paid, it is in the designer's interest to maximise to the greatest extent the scope of tender design to minimise any final design cost risk that they might bear, whilst the contractor's interest is in minimising the cost of tender design (consistent with an acceptable final design cost risk) to minimise its costs in the event that the tender is unsuccessful.

It is suggested that the specific definition of the scope of work will be fundamental to the designer's liability. The following issues, amongst others, may be relevant to that liability:

- Whether the scope is defined in terms that import specific performance by the designer, such as the preparation of the preliminary design sufficient to cost the final design to within ±x% accuracy
- Whether and to what degree the extent of preliminary design is directed by the contractor or is to be determined by the designer

- Whether the contractor constrains the amount of design work by a cap on fees where these are to be paid on a reimbursable basis
- Whether the contractor directs the designer to focus on specific areas of the design.

The significance of these matters can only be determined in the context of a specific case, and in the light of the other contractual terms.

9.6.2 Tender design subcontract terms

A design subcontract for design and construct contracts can be bespoke, written specifically for the requirements of the particular project,[14] or it may be based on a standard form contract such as those published by Consult Australia,[15] the Standards Association of Australia[16] or FIDIC.[17] The contract/subcontract between a design and construct contractor and designer is no different in principle to any other design contract between employer and designer. In traditional design contracts, absent specific terms to the contrary, there is an implied term that the design will be performed to a reasonable standard of professional competence by the exercise of due care, skill and diligence usual amongst designers.[18] This is the requirement defined in terms in the FIDIC White Book:

> Notwithstanding any term or condition to the contrary in the Agreement or any related document or any legal requirement of the Country or any other relevant jurisdiction (including, for the avoidance of doubt, the jurisdiction of the place of establishment of the Consultant), in the performance of the Services the Consultant shall have no other responsibility than to exercise the reasonable skill, care and diligence to be expected from a consultant experienced in the provision of such services for projects of similar size, nature and complexity.[19]

There is generally no implied term in a design contract/subcontract that the final design will be fit for purpose. This is in contrast to the requirement in a construct-only contract, in which there is normally an implied term that both the workmanship and materials will be reasonably fit for the purpose for which they are required.[20] The "normal" obligation of the designer has been stated as follows: "The law does not usually imply a warranty that he will achieve the desired result, but only a term that he will use reasonable care and skill."[21] It is submitted that this duty to exercise reasonable care in performing the tender design may be a very different obligation from that which the contractor desires, namely the obligation to prepare a tender design fit for the contractor's purpose of using it as the basis of an accurate cost estimate to base the tender on.

If the designer's contractual obligation is explicitly or implicitly confined to the exercise of the degree of skill, care and diligence expected of a reasonable professional, then

14 Philip Loots & Donald Charrett, *Practical Guide to Engineering and Construction Contracts* (CCH Australia, 2009) 31.

15 Consult Australia Contract (November 2011).

16 e.g. Standards Australia, AS4122–2000 General conditions of engagement of consultants.

17 FIDIC Clients/Consultants Model Services Agreement (5th edn, 2017) (White Book).

18 *Voli v Inglewood Shire Council* (1962–1963) 110 CLR 74, 84; *Orlit Pty Ltd v J F & P Consulting Pty Ltd* (1995) 11 BCL 260, 263.

19 FIDIC Clients/Consultants Model Services Agreement (5th edn, 2017) sub-clause 3.3.1.

20 I N Duncan Wallace, *Hudson's Building and Engineering Contracts* (11th edn, 1995) 519.

21 *Greaves & Co (Contractors) Ltd v Baynham Meikle & Partners* [1975] 1 WLR 1095, 1100 per Denning MR.

the central issue in claiming damages for breach of the tender design (phase) contract would not be whether the final construction cost was greater than a reasonable costing of the tender design prepared by the designer. It would be whether, in preparing that tender design, the designer had breached his/her contractual obligations of exercising due skill care and diligence. Whilst each case would turn on its own facts, it is submitted that there could be situations where, in the applicable circumstances, the designer had discharged its professional obligations, yet the contractor still lost money because the tender design did not reveal the full extent, complexity or quality of the final design.

As an example of the distinction between the exercise of due skill, care and diligence and a fit for purpose design, in the case of *Manufacturers Mutual Insurance Ltd v The Queensland Government Railways*,[22] a railway bridge collapsed in an unprecedented flood because the piers had insufficient strength to withstand the forces they were subjected to. The High Court held that, although the design was not negligent, it was "faulty" as the existing engineering knowledge was inadequate, and accordingly the insurance exclusion for faulty design operated to deny indemnity for the loss. It appears that this is a case in which the design was executed with professional skill, yet the owner suffered loss because the design was not fit for its purpose. The *MT Højgaard a/s v E.ON Climate and Renewables UK Robin Rigg East Ltd* case discussed in Chapters 7 and 8 is a more recent example of a design that was not prepared negligently, nevertheless it was "faulty" because of an error in the relevant DNV standard.

In tender design, the agreed scope of work for the preliminary design and a limited budget of hours will arguably shape the outcome that would be expected from a reasonably competent designer. In this situation, the product of the designer's reasonable skill, care and diligence within the agreed parameters might not reveal the actual scope, extent or complexity of all the design elements. There is thus no necessary correlation between the exercise of the designer's professional obligations and the contractor's desired outcome, a fit for purpose tender design.

9.6.3 Fitness for purpose

Notwithstanding the general implied professional responsibility referred to above, there have been some circumstances in which a court has imposed on a designer the more onerous duty of preparing a design fit for its purpose. In the limited number of design and construct cases where a fit for purpose obligation on the designer has been indicated, it is submitted that there have been special circumstances, such as reliance,[23] common intention[24] or joint venture[25] before such a term has been construed or implied. In the absence of such special circumstances or an explicit contractual obligation between designer and contractor, the normal obligation for a professional to use due skill and care applies, notwithstanding that a higher obligation of fitness for purpose may apply under the contractor's contract with the Employer.[26]

22 (1968) 118 CLR 314.

23 *Viking Grain Storage Ltd v T H White Installations Ltd and Another* (1985) 33 BLR 103, 117; *Independent Broadcasting Authority v EMI Electronics Ltd and BICC Construction Ltd* (1980) 14 BLR 9, 47.

24 *Greaves v Baynham Meikle* above n 122, 1100.

25 *Consultants Group International v John Worman Ltd* (1985) 9 Con LR 46, 59.

26 *George Hawkins v Chrysler (UK) Ltd* (1986) 38 BLR 36, 51.

The presence of a fitness for purpose term in the head contract between Employer and Contractor, explicit or implicit,[27] may, however, be directly relevant to the design subcontract. In managing its risks on a contract, a head Contractor will frequently let contracts to its subcontractors, including design subcontractors, on a "back-to-back" basis, i.e. the terms of the subcontracts purport to import the terms of the head contract between the Contractor and the Employer. This is sometimes done by including the head contract as a subcontract document, to be applied by replacing "Principal" or "Employer" with "Contractor" and "Contractor" with "Subcontractor', perhaps qualified by words to the effect of "as appropriate to the circumstances". Where such back-to-back provisions are effective, if there is an explicit or implied term of fitness for purpose in the head contract, prima facie that will apply also to the design subcontract, and the designer may then have a contractual obligation to prepare a design fit for the Employer's purpose.

Even where the design is required to be fit for the Employer's purpose, this does not necessarily mean that a term can be implied that the design is to be fit for the Contractor's purpose. In Australia, any implication of contractual terms must fulfil the criteria laid down by the Privy Council[28] and endorsed by the High Court.[29] It is submitted that implying a term in the design subcontract to the effect that the designer will produce a tender design fit for the Contractor's purpose would not pass at least two of the required conditions. It is difficult to see that such a term is required for business efficacy, as many design contracts are performed without a fitness for purpose obligation. Second, such a term is not "so obvious that it goes without saying"; it is extremely unlikely that the designer and the Contractor, with their different risk reward considerations, would have both agreed the term was obvious at the time that the design subcontract was entered into. If the foregoing analysis is correct then, notwithstanding the possibility that the designer might be required to produce a final design fit for the Employer's purpose (which is probably the Contractor's contractual obligation), there would be no term of fitness for the Contractor's purpose in a design subcontract, unless it was explicitly stated. In the absence of such a term, any designer's liability for unforeseen final cost arising from the tender design would require proof of the designer's negligence in carrying out the tender design.

9.6.4 Explicit subcontract term for fitness for purpose

A fit for purpose tender design can be imposed as a contractual requirement on the designer by a specific term of the subcontract and, if such a clause is appropriately worded to define the Contractor's purpose (e.g. preparation of a tender design which, when priced, would represent the construction cost achievable by a competent and diligent contractor within ±x%), it is submitted that this would be effective in passing at least some of the final design cost risk from the Contractor to the designer.

There may be practical difficulties in finding a designer willing to enter into a contract with such a clause, because of the financial risks involved. It is usually a contractual requirement for designers on major projects to demonstrate professional indemnity

27 e.g. *McKone v Johnson* [1966] 2 NSWLR 471, 472–473 cited in J R Cooke, *Architects, Engineers and the Law* (2nd edn, 1997) 73.

28 *BP Refinery (Westernport) Pty Ltd v Shire of Hastings* (1977) 180 CLR 266.

29 *Secured Income Real Estate (Aust) Ltd v St Martins Investments Pty Ltd* (1979) 144 CLR 596; *Codelfa Constructions Pty Ltd v State Rail Authority of New South Wales* (1982) 149 CLR 337, 41 ALR 367.

insurance cover of at least $10m. This insurance cover typically indemnifies consultants up to the insured limit against claims above the value of its deductible arising from its negligence, and in Australia usually claims made under the *Australian Consumer Law* (previously the *Trade Practices Act*). However, professional indemnity insurance usually does not indemnify consultants for breach of a contractual condition of fitness for purpose in the absence of any negligence or breach of the *Australian Consumer Law*. In these circumstances, any liability would have to be funded from the designer's own financial resources. Professional indemnity insurance is discussed in Section 23.3.1.

9.6.5 Summary for tender design subcontract

The designer would assume liability for unforeseen final cost if there was a term in the design subcontract that explicitly stated this, although a prudent designer might not agree to it. The same result may be achieved by a "fit for purpose" term, if the Contractor clearly made known the purpose for which the tender design was required, including, it is submitted, the required accuracy of the tender design. However, this could be problematic if the defined scope of work was insufficient for the required accuracy.

In the absence of an explicit fit-for-purpose contractual term, it is unlikely, given the authorities of case law, that such a term would be implied in lieu of the normal term that the work be executed using the skill care and diligence of the normally competent professional carrying out the scope of work defined in the subcontract. In this case, a designer would only be contractually liable for unforeseen final cost if it had been negligent in preparing the tender design, which in this context could include items TD1–TD5 in Table 9.1. To succeed against the designer, the contractor would have to prove breach of the implicit or explicit standard of care term of the subcontract, and that the breach caused the contractor's unforeseen final cost.

The nature of the designer's work during final design is significantly different to that during tender design, and accordingly there are different considerations relating to final design cost risk.

9.7 Final design

For the terms applicable to the final design, the full extent of the designer's liability is determined by construing the terms of the design contract/subcontract. As for the tender design, in the absence of express terms extending or diminishing the "normal" design responsibility, it is likely that there will be an implied term that the designer is to apply due skill, care and diligence in preparing the final design. The designer's responsibility may also extend to requiring that the final design be fit for the Employer's purpose, if that can be discerned from the contractual performance specification.

The Contractor has the full design and construct liability to the Employer and will therefore have the contractual responsibility of delivering a project that satisfies the performance specifications by the time the Contract reaches practical completion. The circumstances considered here are those in which the constructed project is in fact fit for the Employer's purpose, and there is no loss suffered by the Employer, whereas the Contractor has suffered a financial loss that it perceives has arisen solely from unforeseen final cost. From the Contractor's perspective, the final design is not fit for the Contractor's purpose, since satisfaction of the Employer's performance requirements is only part of the Contractor's purpose. The Contractor also has the aim or purpose of constructing the project for a cost that does not exceed that allowed for in preparing the tender.

In this postulated scenario, there may be a tension in endeavouring to hold the designer liable for unforeseen final cost arising from its work during the final design phase, where that final design is no more than required to satisfy the Employer's performance requirements.

9.7.1 Scope of work

In contrast to preliminary design during the tender phase, the scope of the designer's final design is generally well defined. The starting point is the preliminary tender design, and the finishing point is the design for construction by the Contractor in accordance with the Employer's performance specification.

This scope of work differs from the designer's traditional scope for an owner Employer in one important respect. In an owner–designer relationship, the designer, within the parameters of its brief and its design contract, will have due regard to the owner's long-term interests, and will endeavour to fulfil the owner's perceived (even if unstated) criteria as comprehensively as possible, even if this involves convincing the owner client to spend more money to achieve a higher quality or functionality than originally specified. In contrast, in design and construct, the designer can best fulfil its contractor client's requirements by providing a final design that just satisfies the contractually specified performance requirements and no more. Any enhanced quality or functionality over that contractually specified may be desired and appreciated by the Employer owner but, unless the Contractor is interested in and prepared to negotiate a variation with the Employer for the additional cost, it will not be consistent with the Contractor's objectives of constructing the project for the minimum cost. A designer who ignores the difference between an owner's long-term interests and its Contractor client's more limited contractual obligations does so at the risk of the Contractor seeking to recover any loss through legal action against the designer, as occurred in the *Leighton Contractors Pty Ltd v Kinhill Engineers Pty Ltd* case discussed in Section 9.4.1.

This scope of final design as required by the Contractor may be explicitly and unequivocally defined in the design subcontract, or it may be a term that could reasonably be implied in all the circumstances of the design and construct project, and the reliance of the Contractor on the designer to carry out all the design work required under the head contract. Construction of the general terms of the design subcontract may also be relevant in defining the scope of the final design.

9.7.2 Final design subcontract terms

As with the tender design stage, the most significant subcontract term relevant to liability for unforeseen final cost is whether, explicitly or implicitly, the designer is required to carry out the design with reasonable skill care and diligence, or whether there is an obligation that the design be fit for purpose. Some of the factors identified in Table 9.1 for the designer being causally responsible for unforeseen final cost could be the result of a lack of the designer's required skill care and diligence. Specifically, preparing a final design that did not meet the contractual requirements (FD4), design changes that impacted on procurement or construction (FD5) or late delivery of design information (FD6) may result from a breach of the required professional standard and thus lead to legal liability for breach of the subcontract. It is suggested that factors FD1–FD3 in Table 9.1 would normally only result in the designer being liable if the design was required to be fit for the Contractor's purpose.

The combination of the known Employer's requirements, the Contractor having a contractual fit-for-purpose liability to the Employer, the Contractor's reliance on the designer and the accepted inter-relationships between contractors and subcontractors in the construction industry, would provide arguments to imply a term of fitness for the Employer's purpose in the design subcontract. The same reasons against implying a term that the final design be fit for the Contractor's purpose apply as discussed above in the context of the tender design. In addition, there is the further reason that, if changes resulting in increased cost are found necessary to the tender design to satisfy the contractual performance requirements, the express term of the design subcontract that the final design satisfy the performance requirements may also be inconsistent with an implied term that the final design be fit for the Contractor's purpose by not exceeding the Contractor's tender pricing.

It would of course be possible to have an explicit contractual term that required the designer to accept liability for any unforeseen final cost and, as discussed under tender design, such a term could be effective if the designer agreed to it.

9.7.3 Summary for final design subcontract

Where a designer made changes in scope, extent or complexity to the tender design arising from its incomplete nature, and to no greater extent than required by the contractual scope of work, it is difficult to see how this alone could be viewed as a breach of the required skill, care and diligence. It is submitted that, in the absence of an explicit term that the design be fit for the Contractor's purpose or that the designer accepts liability for unforeseen final cost, the Contractor would need to prove that the designer had been negligent for the designer to be liable for unforeseen final cost.

In addition to an action for breach of the design subcontract, a Contractor could seek to recover unforeseen final cost from a designer by an action in tort for negligence or negligent misstatement or, in Australia, for misleading or deceptive conduct under the *Australian Consumer Law*.

9.8 Possible mechanisms for a contractor to minimise final design cost risk

Whilst a contractor may have a better chance of winning a design and construct tender on the basis of a preliminary design that seriously underestimated the complexity and cost of the final project, such a contract is doomed to lose money from its award. Any remedy the Contractor may have against its designer to recover the resulting unforeseen final costs may not provide adequate recompense for all the costs of the inevitable dispute and inadequate cash flow arising. Accordingly, it is suggested that the Contractor's real interests lie in minimising the final design cost risk, rather than maximising the recovery of unforeseen final cost if it occurs.

The distinctly different role traditionally undertaken, and limited responsibility assumed, by designers compared with trade subcontractors in the Australian building industry has made it difficult for a Contractor to pass on final design cost risk to its designers. It is suggested that the single most compelling reason for this difficulty is that the rational self-interest of designers militates against their acceptance of a significantly greater risk reward ratio in design and construct projects than they have traditionally accepted. When combined with the likelihood that the professional indemnity insurance normally carried by a designer may not cover claims made for breach of contract in the absence of negligence, it is understandable that a designer may be reluctant to undertake commissions where its liability goes further than the traditional exercise of due skill care and diligence and extends to the provision of fit-for-purpose design. Notwithstanding these practical difficulties, the following actions are suggested as possible ways in which a contractor could reduce its final design cost risk, and maximise its opportunities for passing at least some risk to the designer. To the extent that these actions are achievable, their effectiveness may ultimately lie in changing designer's behaviour so that the risk and magnitude of unforeseen final cost is reduced to a manageable and acceptable level.

The first and probably most important action a contractor can take is to select the most appropriate designer, using a process that considers the designer's relevant technical expertise, experience and competence, available resources, and the financial strength of the design firm. Other actions the contractor can take to manage design quality risks are discussed in Section 5.6.5 above. The terms of the agreement between designer and contractor for the preparation of the preliminary tender design are crucial to transfer of risk. As none of the standard form contracts for the engagement of designers are well suited to the specific needs of contractor clients in design and construct projects, it would be advisable for a contractor to prepare a project-specific agreement, with particular attention to the following aspects:

- Clear definition of the required scope of work for the preliminary and final design phases
- A statement of the way in which the contractor would use the preliminary design in the tender e.g. nomination of the percentage contingency that would be applied to the cost determined from a takeoff from the preliminary design
- A requirement that the preliminary design be fit for the contractor's purpose of preparing the tender, and form the basis for preparation of the final design that will not exceed the cost allowed for in the tender
- A designer's warranty that the preliminary design was prepared in accordance with the specified design criteria and contractor's requirements.

Notwithstanding the time constraints built into all design and construct tenders, it is imperative that the contractor execute such an agreement before the end of the tender period. In the absence of agreement on specific terms, is unlikely that any court would imply such turns into the contract between contractor and designer.

The fee arrangements for both tender and final design are also important elements in striking the appropriate balance between carrot and stick. It is suggested that the contractor's aims of winning the tender and completing the project at a profit will be best protected by endeavouring to align the designer's interests with those of the contractor. This could be approached by a partnering or alliance arrangement but could also be addressed within the normal contractor–subcontractor relationship. For the tender design phase, alignment of designer's and contractor's aims requires the magnitude of the design fee to be an appropriate balance between encouraging the designer to undertake the optimum amount of work to prepare a design to the required accuracy and ensuring that sufficient financial reward for the tender design effort accrues only in the event that the contractor wins the tender. In straightforward projects where the required amount of tender design is not extensive, an appropriate tender design fee may be zero; in other cases, where considerable work is required, payment of costs incurred may be more appropriate.

The appropriate fee for final design needs to consider not only any shortfall in design fees for the tender stage, but also the risk aspects inherent in any explicit or implicit passing or sharing of final design cost risk. It is possible that a designer may accept the opportunity to earn higher fees than its normal fees as the quid pro quo for acceptance of some or all of the final design cost risk. It is suggested that appropriately structuring the final design fee may be the most effective practical way of managing final design cost risk once the designer has been selected. A fee arrangement that gives the designer an appropriate financial reward related to the extent to which unforeseen final costs are negative, or financial pain if the unforeseen final costs exceed the contingency allowance, could align the designer's and contractor's aims within the existing structural constraints of the construction industry. Pragmatic considerations might require acceptance of the reality that the designer may not have the financial resources to sustain the entire unforeseen final costs that could arise, and this could be achieved by capping the gain/pain aspects of the final design fee.

9.9 Conclusion

The existence of final design cost risk arises from the separation of traditional design and construction roles, and the limited responsibilities normally accepted by designers. Actions for breach of contract or in negligence are available to a contractor to recover unforeseen final cost from a designer who has breached the reasonable standards of skill, care and diligence in the preparation of a tender design and the resulting final design. However, they may prove ineffective due to the difficulties of proving negligence or causation of damage resulting from the breaches. An explicit fit-for-purpose term of the design subcontract would provide considerably greater scope for recovery. Actions for misleading and deceptive conduct under the *Australian Consumer Law* may also offer the possibility of recovering unforeseen final cost in circumstances where there was no negligence.

A contractor can take steps to minimise final design cost risk by selection of an appropriate designer, by careful structuring of the scope and terms of the design subcontract, and by implementing a fee arrangement that aligns the designer's aims with those of the contractor. There may be substantial practical impediments that prevent a designer from accepting the full risk as a condition of its design subcontract; however, even a limited passing of risk to the designer may be effective in lowering the magnitude of final design cost risk.

CHAPTER 10

The duty of care in design – can engineers rely on codes of practice?[1]

Dr Donald Charrett & Professor Andrew Potts

10.1 Introduction

As discussed in Chapter 8, contracts for engineering design normally include the obligation that the services will be performed with the reasonable skill, care and diligence that would be applied by a normally skilled member of the profession in similar circumstances. The profession makes considerable use of Codes of Practice, or "Standards", which codify current design practice. The prevailing view of the design profession is that such Standards represent the "state of the art" that they are expected to apply. But does compliance with the current applicable Standard mean that the designer has discharged his/her contractual duty of care? Might something more be required? Does the designer need to anticipate how the design Standards may evolve? This chapter addresses these questions in the light of a case in which the judge's findings on the applicable standard of care in relation to the use of current design Standards may be surprising to many designers.

10.2 Codes of practice and standards

10.2.1 What is a Standard?

Standards can be guidance documents including the following types of documents:

- Australian Standards
- International Standards and Joint Standards
- Codes of Practice
- Specifications
- Handbooks
- Guidelines.

The following definitions from a UK publication define the different meanings ascribed by engineers to "Standards" and "Codes of Practice":

> **Standards** "set out certain tests, dimensions, tolerances and qualities for a product or process. Historically in certain areas, e.g. structures, they have set out prescribed methods for specific

1 This paper is an edited and updated version of a paper presented by Donald Charrett and Andrew Potts at the Third Society of Construction Law of Australia conference, Sydney August 2013, and subsequently published as Donald Charrett and Andrew Potts, "The Duty of Care in Design – Can Engineers Rely on Codes of Practice?" (2013) 152 *Australian Construction Law Newsletter* 6.

DOI: 10.4324/9781003206897-11

calculations and even prescribe permissible stresses. More recently these kinds of standards have become normative".[2]

Codes of Practice "are not standards but do set out the standard to be followed. The specific requirements in a code of practice must be followed either for best practice or because the document has a legal status. For example specific partial factors of safety are stated in structural codes. Requirements for tying together tall buildings, to ensure robustness and prevent progressive collapse are set out in the UK Building Regulations. The ways of complying are set out in codes that are deemed to satisfy that part of the Building Regulations."[3]

In the context of the engineer's duty of care and for the purposes of this chapter, there is no significant difference between Standards and Codes of Practice (**Codes**), and the terms are used interchangeably.

10.2.2 Process for issue of an Australian Standard

Australian Standards are issued by Standards Australia, an independent company whose principal activity is the development of Australian Standards. Whilst Standards Australia is an independent company, it is acknowledged by the Australian Government (via a memorandum of understanding) as Australia's peak non-government Standards-writing body and the Australian representative on the International Organisation for Standardisation (**ISO**).

In developing a Standard, Standards Australia uses a process based on transparency, consensus and balance of representation.

Consensus means

> General agreement, characterised by the absence of sustained opposition to substantial issues by any important part of the concerned interests and by a process that involves seeking to take into account the views of all parties concerned and to reconcile any conflicting arguments.[4]

Notwithstanding the requirement for general agreement, consensus need not imply unanimity within the broad spectrum of stakeholders brought together as the Standard Committee to draft the final Standard.

Transparency means

> that information on current work programs and proposals is available to all interested parties. Transparency also includes the concepts of openness, participation on a non-discriminatory basis, impartiality and a balanced participation in the Standards development process by interests that will be significantly affected by the Standard.[5]

Transparency is intended to avoid the potential for skewing the provisions of a Standard towards particular commercial interests. However, where there are few, or only a single, Australian manufacturer, it is often difficult to separate implicit commercial interests from provisions that appropriately cover the spectrum of Australian manufactured products. Thus, if these Australian manufactured products do not represent world's best practice, then the Standard may reinforce inferior standards. However, the movement towards bringing national standards in line with other major trading nations, and the associated

2 David Blockley, *The New Dictionary of Civil Engineering* (Penguin Books Ltd, 2005) 462.
3 Ibid 463.
4 Standards Australia, 'Standards Development – SG-001: Preparing Standards' [5].
5 Ibid.

drive towards greater commonality with ISO Standards, works against such parochial practices.

Balance of representation:

> The membership of a Standards Australia Committee is formally balanced as part of the constitution of the Committee to represent the broadest possible spectrum of stakeholder interests.[6]

In reality, participation on all Standards Australia Committees is voluntary in nature, as participants are not remunerated for their efforts by Standards Australia. Participation typically requires time given by employers, so membership on a Technical Committee may often be additional to normal work duties, and/or done in personal time as an extra curricula activity. Consequently, the best qualified persons or leading practitioners are not always available for such sustained participation.

Thus, the balance achieved in the "spectrum of stakeholder interests" can be subjective and, once established, can by its own make-up be self-perpetuating in the interests and expertise being represented.

The entire process of writing Standards is itself formalised and documented in a series of Australian Standards:

- SG-001 Preparing Standards
- SG-002 Structure and Operation of Standardisation Committees
- SG-003 Standards and Other Publications
- SG-004 Roles and Responsibilities in Standardisation
- SG-005 Technical Governance and Advisory Structures for the Standards Development Process
- SG-006 Rules for the Structure of Australian Standards
- SG-007 Adoption of International Standards
- SG-009 Preparation of Standards for Legislative Adoption
- SG-015 Australian Involvement in International Standardisation
- SG-017 Drafting of Standards Referenced Under OH&S Legislation
- SG-018 Standards Referenced by Water Utilities
- SG-020 Participation by Consumers in Standardisation.[7]

10.2.3 Interested parties

The content of a Standard is the responsibility of a Technical Committee. The basis for the composition of a Technical Committee is to ensure balanced participation by those interests that are significantly affected by the resulting Standard. Individual members of a Technical Committee are selected by Nominating Organisations that may include, but are not restricted to, government bodies, industry associations, community-based and consumer organisations, employee organisations and professional, technical or trade associations.

6 www.standards.org.au (accessed August 2013).

7 www.standards.org.au/StandardsDevelopment/Developing_Standards/Pages/Standardisation-Guides.aspx (accessed 18 January 2018).

For example, the following 17 interested parties represented on Committee BD-025 that was responsible for AS2870–2011 Residential slabs and footings, shows a wide range of representation:

- Australian Building Code Board.
- Australian Chamber of Commerce and Industry.
- Australian Geomechanics Society.
- Australian Institute of Building Surveyors.
- Cement Concrete and Aggregates Australia.
- Concrete Masonry Association of Australia.
- Construction Industry Advisory Council.
- Engineers Australia.
- Foundations and Footings Society of Australia.
- Housing Industry Association.
- Master Builders Australia.
- National Timber Development Council.
- Plastics and Chemicals Industries Association.
- Steel Reinforcement Institute of Australia.
- Think Brick Australia.
- University of Newcastle.
- University of South Australia.

The diversity of the interested parties being represented meets the charter "to represent the broadest possible spectrum of stakeholder interests", but does not necessarily have influence over the personnel being nominated in terms of qualifications, expertise, currency of research or industry practice, etc. Indeed, without in any way casting aspersions on the example Committee cited above, it is readily apparent that whilst there are numerous "industry sector interest groups" represented, it is not apparent whether their nominees are representing current "state-of-the-art" products and practices, or leading-edge technology and practices that may arise from within each sectoral interest. Is the "industry sector interest group" nominating an employee whose regular responsibilities involve commercial, promotional or technical support, or seeking interested, available and qualified personnel from within its sector? If the latter, what selection criteria are adopted – the nominees of its major corporate supporters, from its semi-retired members, or driven individuals with particular pet interests?

10.2.4 Outcome of standard development process

Australian Standards are published documents that set out specifications and procedures with the aim of ensuring that products, services and systems are safe, reliable and consistently perform the way they were intended to. They establish a common language that defines quality and safety criteria acceptable to a broad range of interested parties.

All Australian Standards are expected to deliver a net benefit to the Australian community, taking into consideration:

- Public health and safety
- Social and community impact
- Environmental impact
- Competition
- Economic impact.[8]

These are an appropriate set of expectations to strive for in terms of net benefit to the community at large. However, it is submitted that Standards should not introduce or engender provisions that have implicit or explicit negative impacts on the status quo of the above-listed community considerations. Nor are, nor should, Standards be a channel for back-door social engineering.

In essence, by documenting norms in a common language, Standards enable the community and industry to seek and contract for goods and services on a level playing field. They specify minimum acceptable requirements pertaining to the majority of transactions that were anticipated in conceiving and scoping the particular Standard. The minimum acceptable requirements may address safety, quality and reliability, with implications for environmental impact and public health and safety considerations. The ability to contract for goods and services on a level playing field of minimum acceptable requirements is good for competition within the marketplace, with implications for society at large through ensuing economic benefits.

However, establishing such norms as the basis for putting out to tender and contracting for goods and services also sets the technical basis for which these goods or services are priced and the commercial terms of offer. The upside of Standards is that the common forms of transaction for normal goods or services do not require a critical evaluation of the specific circumstances in order to establish alternate applications or project specific requirements or basis of design. This efficiency streamlines the process of scoping the goods and services sought and being offered, enables proceduralisation and standardisation of their delivery, and removes uncertainty in the technical requirements for delivery and acceptance criteria.

The downside can arise on the infrequent occasions when the Standards, or particular elements of a Standard, may not be adequate or are inappropriate for the circumstances in question. If not recognised and accepted upfront by either the employer or the tenderer, the request for tender may be an inadequate or unsound basis upon which to price and apply regular terms of offer. Thereafter, once the scope and commercial terms of contract are agreed, the momentum of the works will overwhelm the unnatural tendency to query the adequacy or applicability of the industry accepted Standard which is applied in most regularly contracted goods or services.

Professionals generally accept that appropriate procedures have been applied in the drafting, review and adoption of a Standard, so that it represents the "state-of-the-art". On what informed or qualified basis would the regular practitioner be aware of the specific basis of each provision of the Standards, background research and deliberations of the Technical Committee and its individual members? In the writers' view, it is commercially

8 Standards Australia, Standardisation Guide 001: Preparing Standards [7.1.2] www.standards.org.au/StandardsDevelopment/Developing_Standards/Documents/SG-001%20Preparing%20Standards.pdf (accessed 18 January 2018).

impractical and contrary to the professional objective of Standards for a user to review the project-specific circumstances to assess the applicability and adequacy of each and every provision of a contractually specified Standard.

10.3 Statutory significance of codes and standards

As issued by Standards Australia, a private non-government organisation, Australian Standards have no intrinsic statutory significance. Certain individual Standards achieve statutory force when they are incorporated into legislation. Many Standards are never incorporated into legislation, and thus have no statutory significance.

Typically, Standards are incorporated indirectly via subordinate legislation, as illustrated by the following Victorian example in the context of domestic housing.

The *Building Act 1993* (Vic) lists as one of its main purposes: "to regulate building work and building standards". The *Building Act* empowers the Governor in Council to make Regulations for or with respect to, inter alia: "building permits, occupancy permits and temporary approvals, including the duration of permits and approvals and the matters to be complied with by the relevant building surveyor before a permit or approval can be issued".[9]

The *Building Regulations 2018* (Vic) includes amongst its objectives: "to provide for matters relating to the accreditation of building products, construction methods, designs, components and systems connected with building work".[10]

The Building Code of Australia (**BCA**) forms part of the National Construction Code (**NCC**), which is Australia's primary set of technical and design construction provisions for buildings. The BCA is incorporated in the *Building Act 1993* (Vic) via Reg 10 of the *Building Regulations 2018* (Vic): "The BCA is adopted by and forms part of the Regulations as modified by these Regulations."

The BCA does not contain details of every design and construction requirement for a building, but references other documents such as Australian Standards. Schedule 4 in Volume 1 lists 122 Australian Standards as referenced documents.

When an engineering failure is investigated by a government body, it will first seek to verify that the design, operation or equipment complies with the prevailing Australian Standard, or another recognised international Standard, if there is no appropriate Australian Standard. Notices of failure to comply and rectification, fines, shut-down notices, or progression to litigation, often result from an identified failure to meet recognised Standards. In the writers' experience in litigation, the prevailing Standard is frequently used as the fundamental measuring stick of engineering adequacy. Often this is done on the advice of inspectors or practitioners, who may have little knowledge as to the background and basis of development of the Standards they are citing, the operating paradigm for which they were conceived, or indeed the suitability of all the Code provisions to the circumstances to which they are being applied.

In these circumstances, Standards are implicitly assumed as embodying the "state-of-the-art", where non-compliance is, prima facie, a fundamental breach of the duty of care by the professional practitioner. As in Section 7.2, "state-of-the-art" refers to the art and science that would be applied by competent and experienced practitioners involved in the

9 S 261(1)(a).
10 R101.

relevant practice of engineering, not necessarily the science of engineering as known to academics researching at the cutting edge of known technology.

10.4 Contractual significance of codes and standards

Many contracts specify that particular applicable Codes and Standards form part of the Contract.

For example, the Second Editions of the FIDIC Conditions of Contract for Plant and Design Build (**Yellow Book**) and Conditions of Contract for EPC/Turnkey Projects (**Silver Book**) provide as follows:

> **5.3 Contractor's Undertaking**
> The Contractor undertakes that the design, the Contractor's Documents, the execution of the Works and the completed Works will be in accordance with:
>
> (a) the Laws of the Country; and
> (b) the documents forming the Contract, as altered or modified by Variations.
>
> **5.4 Technical Standards and Regulations**
> The Contractor's documents, the execution of the Works and the completed Works (including defects remedied by the Contractor) shall comply with the Country's technical standards, building, construction and environmental Laws, Laws applicable to the product being produced from the Works, and other standards specified in the Employer's Requirements, applicable to the Works, or defined by applicable laws.
>
> ...
>
> "Employer's Requirements" means the document entitled employer's requirements, as included in the Contract, and any additions and modifications to such document in accordance with the Contract. Such document describes the purpose(s) for which the Works are intended, and specifies Key Personnel (if any), the scope and/or design and/or other performance technical and evaluation criteria, for the Works.

In addition to these overarching requirements in the FIDIC General Conditions, it is common for Employers to specifically nominate an extensive list of Standards and Codes of Practice in the Particular Conditions that the designer is required to comply with. In these circumstances, compliance with Standards is a contractual obligation, in addition to obligations that might arise from a duty of care.

10.5 Duty of care in design

10.5.1 Common law

There are many judicial statements on the standard of the common law duty of care that a professional person must comply with, e.g.:

> Where you get a situation which involves the use of some special skill or competence ... the test is the standard of the ordinary skilled man exercising and professing to have that special skill. A man need not possess the highest expert skill ... it is sufficient if he exercises the ordinary skill of the ordinary competent man exercising that particular art.[11]

11 *Bolam v Friern Hospital Management Committee* [1957] 1 WR 582, HL, 586 per McNair J.

And in somewhat more detail:

> a professional man should command the corpus of knowledge which forms part of the professional equipment of the ordinary member of the profession. He should not lag behind other assiduous and intelligent members of his profession in knowledge of new advances, discoveries and developments in his field. He should have such awareness as an ordinarily competent practitioner would have of the deficiencies in his knowledge and the limitations in his skills. He should be alert to the hazards and risks inherent in any profession or task he undertakes to the extent that other ordinarily competent members of his profession would be alert. He must bring to any professional task he undertakes no less expertise, skill and care than other ordinarily competent professional would bring, but need bring no more. The standard is that of the reasonably average. The law does not require of a professional man that he be a paragon, combining the properties of polymath and prophet.[12]

The message in these statements to designers is clear: be up to date with the knowledge of the profession in your area of expertise and know your limitations!

10.5.2 Statutory modification of the common law

The Parliaments of the Australian States and Territories have legislated significant statutory modifications to the common law of negligence since the turn of the century. Some of these statutory modifications are directly applicable to an engineer's duty of care.

For example, the *Wrongs Act 1958* (Vic) contains the following relevant sections:

> **59 Standard of Care for Professionals**
>
> (1) A professional is not negligent in providing a professional service if it is established that the professional acted in a manner that (at the time the service was provided) was widely accepted in Australia by a significant number of respected practitioners in the field (peer professional opinion) as competent professional practice in the circumstances.
> (2) However, peer professional opinion cannot be relied on for the purposes of this section if the Court determines that the opinion is unreasonable.
> (3) The fact that there are differing peer professional opinions widely accepted in Australia by a significant number of respected practitioners in the field concerning a matter does not prevent any one or more (or all) of those opinions being relied on for the purposes of this section.
> (4) Peer professional opinion does not have to be universally accepted to be considered widely accepted.
> (5) If, under this section, a Court determines peer professional opinion to be unreasonable, it must specify in writing the reasons for that determination.
>
> **60 Duty to Warn of Risk**
>
> Section 59 does not apply to a liability arising in connection with the giving of (or the failure to give) a warning or other information in respect of a risk or other matter to a person if the giving of the warning or information is associated with the provision by a professional of a professional service.

12 *Eckersley v Binney & Partners* (1988) 18 Con LR 1.

Section 60 thus contains an important carve-out from the "peer professional opinion standard" – it does not apply in relation to the duty to warn of a risk. That duty is somewhat unhelpfully articulated as follows:

50 Duty to Warn of Risk – Reasonable Care

> A person (the defendant) who owes a duty of care to another person (the plaintiff) to give a warning or other information to the plaintiff in respect of a risk or other matter, satisfies that duty of care if the defendant takes reasonable care in giving that warning or other information.

Arguably, this is a subjective standard that does not provide the same measure of predictability that s 59 provides in relation to the "peer professional opinion standard".

There are three potential sources for requiring a duty of care in design:

- An implied or express term in the designer's contract of engagement that the design will be prepared with reasonable skill, care and diligence
- A tortious duty of care under the common law that is generally co-extensive with the contractual obligation to exercise due care in preparing the design
- Statutory provisions on duty of care that codify and perhaps limit common law rules.

In a case where s 59(2) of the *Wrongs Act 1958* (Vic) applied, Judge Woodward held that peer professional opinion of building surveyors that the use of aluminium composite cladding on buildings complied with the deemed to comply provisions of the BCA was unreasonable. Accordingly, the peer professional opinion defence of the building surveyor failed, and he was found to have been negligent in certifying the use of aluminium composite cladding on the Lacrosse building in Melbourne.[13]

10.6 Is there an obligation for an engineer to comply with a code or standard?

It is suggested that there are three possible sources of such an obligation:

- A mandatory statutory requirement, such as incorporation of a Standard in legislation, e.g. the *Building Act 1993* (Vic) cites the *Building Regulations 2006* (Vic), which cites the BCA which cites specific Standards
- A mandatory express provision of the Contract to comply with a Standard, e.g. FIDIC Silver Book, and/or
- A duty of care arising from either or both a contractual or tortuous duty to exercise reasonable skill, care and diligence in carrying out engineering.

The statutory or contractual obligations to comply are known and unexceptional. However, the issue of compliance arising from an engineer's duty of care is less clear. It is contended that in most cases compliance satisfies the "peer professional opinion standard".

13 *Owners Corporation No 1 of PS613436T v LU Simon Builders Pty Ltd (Building and Property* [2019] VCAT 286 [357]–[397].

Arguably, a Standard documents the "state-of-the-art" of the ordinarily competent professional, whereby:

- It is the product of a formal, structured process.
- The Technical Committee responsible is deemed competent in the relevant fields.
- A broad and disparate spectrum of interested parties are represented on the Technical Committee.
- The published Standard is the result of consensus between the Technical Committee members.
- A broad range of community interests are considered in establishing the appropriate balance between conflicting requirements.
- Amendments can be made, and communicated to the profession, if there are advances in the "state-of-the-art" or deficiencies or errors in the Standard identified after publication.

It should be borne in mind that Standards prescribe minimum requirements. Hence, any non-compliance with minimum specified criteria would need to satisfy the "reasonable professional" test: would the non-compliance be "widely accepted in Australia by a significant number of respected practitioners in the field (peer professional opinion) as competent professional practice in the circumstance"?

An engineer's conscious decision not to follow the requirements of a Standard may create additional risks for their employer. This is equally applicable to a conscious decision to substantially exceed a Standard's minimum requirements just as it is not to achieve them. There are cases in which an engineer has been found to be negligent in preparing a costly design that substantially exceeded a Standard's requirements. Thus, there are risks and potential consequences if a Standard is not complied with. A prudent engineer electing not to comply with a Standard would therefore be well advised to warn their employer of the risks and ensure that the employer acquiesced in the decision.

It should also be noted that the provisions of Standards and Codes of Practice are not suited to "mix and match" clauses from different documents. Like a contract, a Standard should be construed as a whole document in which the individual provisions are integrated into an overarching conceptual framework. For example, the limit state design of steel structures in accordance with AS4100 Steel Structures Code should be carried out for loads derived from AS1170 Structural Design Actions. It could be quite unsafe to design a structure to AS4100 for loads derived from a Standard that was based on inconsistent assumptions in respect of partial factors for material strength.

10.7 Is compliance with a Code or Standard sufficient?

The writers' proposition is as follows: in respect of conventional infrastructure, a Standard represents the "state-of-the-art" endorsed by the profession, and compliance with it is consistent with acting "in a manner that (at the time the service was provided) was widely accepted in Australia by a significant number of respected practitioners in the field (peer professional opinion) as competent professional practice in the circumstances".

In other words, compliance with a Standard in the design of conventional infrastructure is an exercise of "the ordinary skill of the ordinary competent man exercising that particular art". It is not suggested that this proposition would be valid in respect of major hazard facilities, or structures involving new or untested concepts.

Highly skilled practitioners, or academics specialising in a particular field, may consider that the provisions of a Standard are inadequate, or are not "state of the art" in the context of "leading edge". The writers suggest that that does not immediately translate to the "state-of-the-art" of the ordinarily competent practitioner.

Standards are living documents, regularly updated either by specific amendments to particular provisions (which can occur when a significant deficiency becomes known), or by a general revision to incorporate advances in the "state of the art". A major revision of a Standard may require the profession to undertake retraining to adopt new approaches. The profession usually accepts such revised Standards as an evolution of the "state of the art" of the ordinarily competent practitioner. However, before a Standard is formally revised and re-issued, there may have been a number of draft revisions in progress at various times, and circulated for comment. Such draft revisions typically receive wide exposure in the technical community as part of the transparent and consensual process of Standard preparation, but they are by no measure adopted prior to the "official" revision.

Does the provision of a draft revised Standard issued for review immediately translate to the "state-of-the-art" of the ordinarily competent practitioner? The writers submit that it does not; by their nature, "draft" revisions are circulated for comment and review, and the finally adopted provisions in the revised Standard may bear little relation to the draft provisions, or the inclusion of subtle changes in a draft may significantly alter its interpretation and application to particular circumstances.

The situation may be different if it was universally accepted in the profession that certain provisions of a Standard were deficient. In that case, the ordinarily competent practitioner would be aware of the deficiencies and, in the exercise of her/his duty of care, would make appropriate provision in the design (note: a clear distinction is made between the profession adopting Amendments or Warning Notices pertaining to an existing Code or Standard, as opposed to observing the provisions of an incomplete or unadopted draft version of a Code or Standard that has been distributed for comment).

However, if the inadequacy of certain provisions of a Standard was controversial, s 59(3) of the *Wrongs Act 1958* (Vic) (or equivalent in other States) could provide a defence supporting compliance:

> The fact that there are differing peer professional opinions widely accepted in Australia by a significant number of respected practitioners in the field concerning a matter does not prevent any one or more (or all) of those opinions being relied on for the purposes of this section.

Whilst compliance with a current Standard should, in the writers' view, be sufficient to discharge the engineer's duty of care, that does not necessarily apply to compliance with the requirements of the designer's contract. As discussed in Chapters 7 and 8 above, in the case of *MT Højgaard a/s v E.ON Climate and Renewables UK Robin Rigg East Ltd*, the grouted connections between the pile substructures and the towers supporting wind turbines failed because of a serious (but unknown) error in the DNV international Standard for the design of such connections. The judge at first instance and the Supreme Court found that the design and construct contractor had breached the contract because the wind turbines did not have the contractually specified service life of 20 years, even though the Standard had been complied with and there was no negligence by the designer. In the Court of Appeal, Jackson LJ stressed that the outcome depended on the proper construction of the contract, and that a sufficiently clearly worded contract could require a designer, in addition to exercising due skill and care, to also warrant that its design was fit for purpose.[14]

10.8 A case study

10.8.1 BHP Coal Pty Ltd v O & K Orenstein & Koppel AG

Some of the issues discussed above in relation to an engineer's duty of care in respect of compliance with Standards and Codes were highlighted in *BHP Coal Pty Ltd v O & K Orenstein & Koppel AG*[15] (***Goonyella* case**). This case concerned the total collapse of a Bucket Wheel Excavator (**BWE**) at the Goonyella mine in Central Queensland.

Design, supply and installation of the BWE took place between 1978 and 1981. In November/December 1984 grounding of the bucket wheel due to misoperation of the BWE caused buckling damage to the rear tower flanges. The owner arranged for an engineer from O & K Orenstein & Koppel AG (**O&K**) (the designer and supplier of the BWE) to inspect the damage and prepare an on-site emergency repair proposal. The repair of the buckling and addition of eight stiffeners was executed by a third party under the supervision of an O&K supervisor, who was primarily there for stabilisation of the balanced machine before and after the repair works.

Sometime after the repair was completed, fatigue cracks in the steel columns started to propagate from the repair welds at the ends of the added stiffeners.

Between 1985 and 1999 TKEA carried out bi-annual inspections of the BWE structure, with the final inspection in March 1999. In March 2000 the BWE collapsed. There was a Mine Warden's Court Inquiry into the collapse in 2002 and, in 2003, BHP initiated legal proceedings against O&K and TKEA.

The court hearing occupied a total of 120 sitting days between April 2007 and February 2008.

In his judgment, McMurdo J found that, in respect of the design of the repair stiffeners, O&K had breached its duty of care and had engaged in misleading or deceptive conduct in breach of the *Trade Practices Act* (now *Australian Consumer Law*). He also found that, in respect of the inspection of the BWE after the repair work had been completed, TKEA had breached its contract, breached its duty of care and had engaged in misleading or deceptive conduct in breach of the *Trade Practices Act*. The misleading and deceptive conduct ruling will not be discussed further herein, as it is not germane to the theme of this chapter, which is covered by the other part of the ruling.

The negligence case against O&K ultimately hinged on the judge's findings in respect of detailed aspects of the design of the welding of the repair strengthening stiffeners, and the location of the fatigue cracks that ultimately propagated to an extent that was sufficient to cause complete collapse of the BWE. The upper stiffener terminations terminated in an area with bending stresses higher than further up the tower. The design of these upper stiffener terminations was awkward and increased the local stress. The judge found that if the engineer had made proper fatigue stress calculations he would have identified that the

14 See Section 7.10.

15 [2008] QSC 141.

upper stiffener terminations were in a critical spot. Further, if the engineer had identified the problems caused by the chosen details, he could have extended the stiffeners to the end of the tower or designed a better detail that would not have been as susceptible to fatigue.

The Contract for construction of the BWE required it to be constructed according to the operative German Standard specific to BWEs at the time, BG60. This was still the operative standard for BWEs used by O&K in 1984, although a draft revision had been circulated for discussion within the drafting Committee in 1984. ISO 5049 was an alternative international standard applicable to mining machinery (including BWEs, though this was not its predominant area of focus) that resulted in lower fatigue strengths of welded joints than BG60. The welded detail of the upper stiffener termination implemented (F_I) had adequate fatigue strength according to BG60, but not according to ISO 5049. ISO 5049 was developed for application to the design of bulk-ore handling machinery, such as stackers, reclaimers, bucket-wheel reclaimers and shiploaders, where the load duty handling excavated material in stockyards and the like is more consistent than bucket-wheel excavators digging hard material directly from the earth. As such, the fatigue load duty provisions of ISO 5049 was aligned to a more uniform load duty spectrum, which was not the case for fatigue load duty provisions in the design Codes that were mostly in use for BWEs (including BG60 and its successor BG86).

McMurdo J considered the following issues relevant to his conclusion that BG60 was unreliable as a standard with which to design the F_I welded detail (the writers' comments on these issues are in square brackets).

- BG60 was "being challenged by some and officially reviewed" in 1984 and was replaced by BG86 in 1986. [It should be noted that the fatigue provisions of the 1984 Draft were more onerous than BG60 and were not adopted in the final Standard BG86. The welded repair details complied with the requirements of BG60 and BG86 but would have failed the 1984 Draft.]
- BG60 did not take dynamic loads into account, although this was not necessarily a prevalent professional opinion in 1984. [BG60 did not include a specific dynamic load factor on the statically determined loads in its load case combinations, as did BG86, but BG86 was actually calibrated against BG60 to produce similar design outcomes.]
- O&K knew that ISO 5049 specified lower allowable fatigue stresses; "ISO 5049 should have alerted an engineer to the risk of using only BG60". [Although ISO 5049 includes BWEs in its scope, it was not in general use by the industry for the design of BWEs as was BG60, where there are significant differences in load duties between the two Codes. Also, ISO 5049's fatigue S-N curve for the F_I category was significantly more conservative than BG60 and BG86.]

McMurdo J expressed his findings on this Standard issue as follows:

> But I do not accept that a reasonable engineer would have been obliged to give up a long-standing code (BG60), if otherwise considered to be reliable merely because some engineers, however eminent, were publishing an opinion suggesting otherwise. ...[16]

16 Ibid [157].

> ... I am not satisfied that such an engineer would have thought that BG60 overstated the fatigue strength of an F_I detail. ...
>
> However, any reasonable engineer in his position should have doubted the reliability of BG60. After all there was a review of BG60 which had been put in place by the relevant West German authority. The review committee had been constituted, made up of leading engineers from the major manufacturers and academics. ... All of that amounted to more than a professional opinion being ventilated occasionally in published journals or seminars. ... In the midst of that review the reasonable engineer in [the designer's] position could not have said to himself at the same time that BG60 was reliable.
>
> ... Because BG60 was unreliable, that margin for error should not have been accepted as reasonable. ...[17]

10.8.2 Comments on practical design engineering aspects of judgment

Merely because a Standard is under review by an eminent Committee, which, as part of its remit, is to update/modernise the Code, with respect it does not follow that "a reasonable engineer should have doubted the reliability of BG60". The ultimate "official" revision, BG86, was in fact calibrated to BG60 because that had been found to produce reliable designs that had adequate fatigue service lives.

If no notices of warning or amendments to the Standard had been issued, even during the Standard review phase, what if any basis was there for the conclusion that "a reasonable engineer should have doubted the reliability of BG60"? Indeed, many Standards are subject to regular periodic review (with draft revisions in the public domain) – does this automatically oblige the design engineer to consider the current, unamended version as suspect and potentially "unreliable"?

What would have been the legal standing of the design engineer in adopting the provisions of an interim draft Standard that was still subject to considerable deliberation by the Committee? In the case of the fatigue provisions of the 1984 Draft, these were ultimately rejected by the Committee in the final issue of BG86. Arguably, design of an entire machine to the 1984 draft provisions would have ultimately proved to have been unnecessarily conservative and added unwarranted cost.

Design Codes are intended to be inherently conservative in their provisions, as they are intended to apply to the majority of applicable systems for which they have been developed. Factors of safety are applied to and allowable stresses are used in conjunction with conservatively compounded design loads. In the case of fatigue, the design load combinations are used in conjunction with lower bound S-N curves used for design purposes.

When in design is it appropriate to apply even more conservative factors of safety over and above accepted and current codified values in Standards? Such additional conservatism has commercial and feasibility implications for the employer to whom the engineer owes a duty of care. Thus, if there was no valid basis to conclude that "BG60 was unreliable", why then should the codified "margin for error ... not have been accepted as reasonable"?

Even if there was some concern as to the adequacy of the codified factors of safety, what would be an acceptable technical basis for employing higher values? Would it be +5%, +10%, +25%, ...? If the Standard is unreliable but you can't put your finger on it, what

17 Ibid [160]–[162].

is a "reasonable" fix?). If a designer arbitrarily adopted, say an additional 10% margin for safety, to cover some unquantifiable reservations, and then the structure still failed at some time in the future, would the Court view this as the prudent act of a reasonable engineer, or an ill-fated guess in the absence of a more technically supported engineering design decision?

At the heart of engineering design Codes, there is an intent to provide inherent conservatism, not to sail close to the wind and thereby court regular failure. This enables engineers to make safe design decisions with a degree of comfort that they do not in most circumstances need to question the basis and applicability of the Codes they are relying upon. The professional training of engineers, whilst not eliminating the prospect of Codes being limited, or occasionally in error, is largely skewed towards engineers practising their profession by following the provisions of the many Codes that apply to their sector. Most engineers are "Code practitioners" not "Code questioners". If Codes have required constant questioning, then the engineering profession has over the years progressively amended and improved the deficient elements of such Codes. This has involved drawing on the expertise and experience from other countries with similar Codes, and this has reduced the instances where Codes need to be questioned. The profession would have a fundamental problem were there a Court-implied requirement that on all occasions the "Code practitioners" should become "Code questioners".

10.9 Conclusion

The genesis of Standards, the common law and relevant statutory provisions suggest that engineers should generally be able to rely on current relevant Standards and Codes of Practice when designing conventional infrastructure.

It would be chaotic for the majority of the engineering profession undertaking design on a daily basis if they were not able to rely upon current Codes and Standards. There is neither the time nor the fees for designers to undertake a critical review of the provisions of design Codes and Standards for conventional and well-understood infrastructure for which they have been written.

If in hindsight courts judge that the conservatism in design Codes and Standards is inadequate, this brings into question the "professional consensus" underlying their development and status within the engineering profession and as the basis of construction contracts. It provides no guidance to the practising professional as to what is an acceptable degree of conservatism.

The judgment in the *Goonyella* case contains some surprising and salutary warnings for practising engineers:

- There may be an obligation to question, monitor and understand the reliability of current Codes in light of "potential" amendments.
- There may be an obligation to consider other Standards than those specified in the contract and, if more, conservative apply such provisions.

PART 2

THE PROJECT AND THE CONTRACT

CHAPTER 11

Standard form contracts[1]

11.1 Introduction

Parties entering into a contract for the construction of a major facility can use general conditions in one of: (a) a standard form contract (such as the FIDIC "rainbow suite" or an NEC contract), (b) a standard form with some terms modified, or (c) a "bespoke" contract which has been written specifically for the particular features of the construction project at hand.

One writer expresses the significance of standard form contracts in the following terms: "The construction project, with its linked set of construction contracts between many participants and its complexity could not survive today without standard construction contracts."[2] It is usually the owner or Employer who invites tenders for construction, and it is normal for such an Employer to select the conditions of contract it proposes to use for the construction contract.[3] Many Employers in Australia, perhaps the majority in respect of major resource projects, put forward bespoke contracts prepared by one of the major law firms experienced in construction contracting.[4] It is suggested that such a preference for a bespoke contract is based on a view that none of the applicable standard form contracts adequately looks after the Employer's interests, and that the usual risk allocation between Contractor and Employer embodied in standard form contracts is unsatisfactory from the Employer's perspective. It is submitted that a substantial driver of an Employer's desire for a bespoke contract is a perception that such a contract can shift more risk to the Contractor than would be the case under most standard form contracts.

The thesis of this chapter is that, whilst such risk "reallocation" may have superficial attractions, the use of bespoke contracts with unbalanced risk allocation in preference to standard form (perhaps modified) contracts, generates other risks and costs for the Employer.

1 This is an edited and updated version of the paper published in: Donald Charrett, "The Importance of Standard Form Contracts" (2012) 24(7) *Australian Construction Law Bulletin* 106.

2 Justin Sweet, 'Standard Construction Contracts in the USA' [2011] *ICLR* 101.

3 A survey on the use of standard form contracts in 379 projects in Australia found that the Employer or the Employer's lawyer were responsible for choosing the standard form contract in over 80% of cases. Professor John Sharkey, Matthew Bell and others, *Standard Forms of Contract in the Australian Construction Industry* (University of Melbourne, 2014) 5.

4 A survey on the use of standard form contracts in 379 projects in Australia found that only 28% of projects with a value of over AUD500 m used standard contract forms, with the lowest use being in the mining and resources infrastructure sector. Professor John Sharkey, Matthew Bell and others, *Standard Forms of Contract in the Australian Construction Industry* (University of Melbourne, 2014) 4.

 DOI: 10.4324/9781003206897-13

11.2 Appropriate contract terms

The answer to the question "What are the most desirable conditions of contract?" for a particular project no doubt depends on whom the question is addressed to, in the context of the particular project. In the absence of the constraints of what can realistically be achieved in the marketplace, it is suggested that typical contracting parties on either side of the table might respond along the lines of:

- Employer: conditions that deliver a complete project of the highest quality for the lowest contract price, to be completed in the shortest time with all unforeseen risks the responsibility of the Contractor.
- Contractor: conditions that unambiguously define the required scope and quality of the work for the highest contract price, to be completed within a time that is sufficient to carry out the work with available resources and allowing for contingencies, with unforeseen risks the responsibility of the Employer.

Clearly, any such putative objectives of the parties are incompatible, and are unlikely to be attainable in any contract that both parties would be prepared to enter into. The more reasonable and constructive question to ask is: "What are the most appropriate conditions of contract that are most conducive to a successful project?" In common with many other commentators, this author suggests that part of the answer to that question is the use of the Abrahamson principles of balanced risk allocation, in which each risk is allocated to the party best able to manage it. In many instances, these can be achieved in a (modified) standard form contract, of a type appropriately selected for the desired form of project delivery (e.g. construction only, design and construct, management contracting, etc.).

As discussed in Section 4.7, the Abrahamson Principles of balanced risk allocation,[5] well known to construction lawyers, are widely regarded as the basis of "balanced" or "fair" or "efficient" risk allocation. Many standard form contracts are based on the explicitly stated principle of balanced or fair risk allocation, e.g. FIDIC contracts,[6] the UK New Engineering Contract,[7] the Australian Standard 4000 series,[8] the US ConsensusDocs,[9] the European Engineering Industries Association,[10] the International Chamber of Commerce,[11] the Baltic and International Marine Council[12] and contracts for the UK offshore oil and gas industry.[13] The principle is also espoused by government procurement

5 Max W Abrahamson, "Risk Management" (1983) *International Construction Law Review* 241, 244.
6 https://fidic.org/bookshop (accessed 26 April 2021).
7 Brian Eggleston, *The New Engineering Contract A Commentary* (Blackwell Science, 1996) 7.
8 "Standard Conditions of Contract" (2001) 4 *BDPS News* 1, 4.
9 https://www.consensusdocs.org/faqs/ (accessed 10 April 2021).
10 Orgalime, *Turnkey Contract for Industrial Works*.
11 International Chamber of Commerce Model Turnkey Contract for Major Projects (2007).
12 https://www.bimco.org/contracts-and-clauses/bimco-contracts (accessed 26 April 2021).
13 Leading Oil and Gas Industry Competitiveness (LOGIC) www.logic.com (accessed August 2008).

agencies in the UK,[14] Australia[15] and the United States.[16] Many writers suggest that adherence to the principle of balanced risk allocation enhances the prospect of successful contracts, by encouraging contractual performance that minimises adverse outcomes and thereby reduces disputation.[17]

It has been suggested that the traditional approach to construction contracts leads to aggressive and adversarial relationships that result from the type of contract the client puts in place.[18] The more recent approaches of partnering and alliancing that originated in the oil and gas industry, focus on contractual conditions which encourage cooperation and alignment of the Employer's and Contractor's objectives, through mechanisms such as gain and pain share and incentivisation to change traditional adversarial behaviours. However, traditional forms of construction contracts are still appropriate for many projects, and it is in these projects that the use of standard form contracts may be the most appropriate.

11.3 Standard contract forms and "bespoke" contracts

11.3.1 Standard form contracts

Typically, a standard form contract is the result of a collaborative effort of a number of people with a range of perspectives on how such contracts have operated in the past, and how they should operate in the future. Most such standard form contracts are the result of an evolutionary process, in which successive editions take account of previous operational experience and the difficulties of interpretation or implementation that have been identified by courts in the published case law, or by changes in relevant legislation. The process for issue of an Australian Standard form contract is outlined in Section 10.2.2.

Part of the evolution of standard form contracts over the last 20 or 30 years has been the recognition that different types of construction contracts have distinctly different requirements, and that standard form contracts should be prepared accordingly. The range of procurement options now in use for major projects demands a greater variety of contractual provisions than are provided by a single standard form contract. Whereas in the past a single standard form contract was widely used for construction work, project experience has demonstrated the pitfalls of using a standard form contract in circumstances for which

14 "The governing principle is that risk should be allocated to whichever party from the public or private sector is best placed to manage it. The optimal allocation of risk, rather than maximising risk transfer, is the objective, and is vital to ensuring that the best solution is found." HM Treasury, *The Green Book Appraisal and Evaluation in Central Government* http://greenbook.treasury.gov.uk/annex04.htm (accessed 26 August 2008).

15 "Both the government and the private party should seek to ensure that cost and adequate risk transfer are balanced as far as possible to achieve the best value for money on a particular project." *Department of Treasury and Finance Victorian Government, Partnerships Victoria Updated Standard Commercial Principles* (2008) 99.

16 "A fundamental tenet of risk management is to allocate the risks to the party best able to manage them. The party assuming the risk should be able to best evaluate, control, bear the risk of, and benefit from its assumption." US Department of Transportation Federal Highway Administration, *Risk Assessment and Allocation for Highway Construction Management* (2006) 31 https://international.fhwa.dot.gov/pubs/pl06032/guide_to_risk_assessment_allocation_for_highway.pdf (accessed 10 April 2021)

17 NPWC/NBCC Joint Working Party, "No Dispute Strategies for Improvement in the Australian Building and Construction Industry" (May 1990) 6–7; Sir Michael Latham, 'Constructing the Team' (July 1994) Final Report 37.

18 Sharon Doherty, *Heathrow's Terminal 5 History in the Making* (2008) 33.

it was not designed.[19] Both FIDIC and the ICE publish standard form contracts intended for use for international construction contracts.

11.3.1.1 FIDIC contracts

The Fédération Internationale des Ingénieurs-Conseils (**FIDIC**) (known by its English name of the International Federation of Consulting Engineers) publishes standard form Conditions of Contract that are used in many countries and are probably the most widely used for international construction contracts in the world. FIDIC publishes the construction contracts in Table 11.1 and the subcontracts in Table 11.2.[20]

TABLE 11.1 FIDIC standard forms of construction contract between Employer and Contractor

1977 Red Book	Conditions of Contract for Works of Civil Engineering Construction – Third Edition 1977
1987 Red Book	Conditions of Contract for Works of Civil Engineering Construction Fourth Edition 1987
1987 Yellow Book	Conditions of Contract for Electrical and Mechanical Works – Third Edition 1987
1995 Orange Book	Conditions of Contract for Design-Build and Turnkey – First Edition 1995
1999 Red Book	Conditions of Contract for Construction – First Edition 1999
1999 Yellow Book	Conditions of Contract for Plant and Design-Build – First Edition 1999
1999 Silver Book	Conditions of Contract for EPC/Turnkey Projects – First Edition 1999
2017 Red Book	Conditions of Contract for Construction – Second Edition 2017
2017 Yellow Book	Conditions of Contract for Plant and Design-Build – Second Edition 2017
2017 Silver Book	Conditions of Contract for EPC/Turnkey Projects – Second Edition 2017
Green Book	Short Form of Contract – First Edition 1999
Pink Book	Conditions of Contract for Construction – Multilateral Development Bank Harmonised Edition for Building and Engineering Works Designed by the Employer – Version 1: 2005, Version 2: 2006, Version 3: 2010
Gold Book	Conditions of Contract for Design, Build and Operate Projects – First Edition 2008
Blue-Green Book	Form of Contract for Dredging and Reclamation Works – First Edition 2006, Second Edition 2016
Emerald Book	Conditions of Contract for Underground Works First Edition 2019

TABLE 11.2 FIDIC standard forms of subcontract between Contractor and Subcontractor

Conditions of Subcontract for Work of Civil Engineering Construction – First Edition 1994
Conditions of Subcontract for Construction – First Edition 2011
Conditions of Subcontract for Plant and Design (Yellow Book 1999) – First Edition 2019

19 Philip Loots and Donald Charrett, *Practical Guide to Engineering and Construction Contracts* (2009) 31–32.

20 These FIDIC contracts were listed on the FIDIC website (https://www.fidic.org/bookshop) on 12 April 2021.

The Red Book, Yellow Book and Silver Book are commonly referred to as the rainbow suite. There are differences between the standard forms in the rainbow suite in who carries out the design (Employer or Contractor), who administers the contract (Engineer or Employer's Representative), the form of Dispute Board (standing or *ad hoc*, DAB or DAAB), and how the Contractor is paid (remeasurement of lump sum). These differences are summarised for the 1999 and 2017 rainbow suite in Table 11.3.

The FIDIC contracts have evolved through a number of editions since the first Conditions of Contract for Construction were published in 1957, becoming significantly longer and more prescriptive. Table 11.4 compares some features of the 2017, 1999 and 1987 Red Books.

As can be seen from Table 11.4, the 2017 Red Book is over 50% longer than the 1999 Red Book. A significant reason for this is the much greater level of prescription and deeming provisions in the 2017 edition. The 2017 edition is arguably more even-handed between Employer and Contractor than the 1999 edition. Significant changes between these two editions are as follows.

The Employer and Contractor have reciprocal rights: e.g. sub-clauses 1.12, 1.13, 6.3, 8.4, 13.6, 15.2 ⇔ 16.2, 20.
Sub-clause 1.15: Carve-outs from limitation of liability have been expanded.
Sub-clauses 2.3 ⇔ 6.9: Removal of personnel engaged in corrupt practices.
Sub-clause 4.8: Health and safety obligations have been expanded.
Sub-clausc 4.9: Quality assurance provisions have been expanded.
Sub-clause 4.18: Requirement for the Contractor to comply with the environmental impact assessment.
Sub-clause 4.15: The Contractor is entitled to an EOT and Cost for changes to the access route.
Sub-clause 6.12: New provision for Key Personnel.
Sub-clause 8.3: Enhanced programme requirements.
Sub-clause 8.4: New provision for advance warning applies to Employer and Contractor.

TABLE 11.3 Differences between 1999 and 2017 FIDIC standard forms of contract between Employer and Contractor

<table>
<tr><th>Red Book First Edition 1999</th><th>Red Book Second Edition 2017</th><th>Yellow Book First Edition 1999</th><th>Yellow Book Second Edition 2017</th><th>Silver Book First Edition 1999</th><th>Silver Book Second Edition 2017</th></tr>
<tr><td colspan="2">Design by Employer</td><td colspan="4">Design by Contractor</td></tr>
<tr><td colspan="4">Contract administered by Engineer</td><td colspan="2">Contract administered by Employer's Representative</td></tr>
<tr><td>Standing DAB</td><td>Standing DAAB</td><td>Ad hoc DAB</td><td>Standing DAAB</td><td>Ad hoc DAB</td><td>Standing DAAB</td></tr>
<tr><td colspan="2">Contractor paid on remeasurement basis</td><td colspan="4">Contractor paid on lump sum basis</td></tr>
</table>

TABLE 11.4 Comparison of 2017, 1999 and 1987 Red Books

	2017 Conditions of Contract for Construction	*1999 Conditions of Contract for Construction*	*1987 Conditions of Contract for Works of Civil Engineering Construction*
General Conditions	128 pages	74 pages	45 pages
Guidance for the Preparation of Particular Conditions	65 pages	29 pages	27 pages
General Conditions of DAAB/DAB Agreement	12 clauses – 9 pages	9 clauses – 4 pages	11 clauses – 4 pages
DAAB/DAB Procedural Rules	11 Rules – 6½ pages	9 Rules – 1½ pages	7 Rules – 1½ pages
Definitions	88	60	32
Claims	Clause 20 – 4½ pages (Employer & Contractor)	**2.5** Employer's Claims – ½ page **20.1** Contractor's Claims – 1 page	53. Contractor's Claims – 1 page
Engineer's Agreement or Determination	**3.7** – 2 pages	**3.5** – 2 paragraphs	**2.6** – 1 paragraph
Deeming provisions	7 Definitions 51 Sub-Clauses	0 Definitions 26 Sub-Clauses	
Omission Variation	Permissible with Parties' agreement	Not permitted if work to be carried out by others	Not permitted if work to be carried out by others

Sub-clause 8.5 Concurrent delay: The Contractor's entitlement is assessed in accordance with the Special Provisions.

Sub-clause 8.8: The cap on delay damages does not apply to fraud, deliberate default, reckless misconduct or gross negligence.

Sub-clause 11.10: The Contractor is not liable for defects or damage occurring more than 2 years after the expiry of the Defects Notification Period.

Sub-clauses 15.2, 16.2: New triggers for termination, e.g. failure to comply with a final and binding Engineer's determination, failure to comply with any DAAB decision.

Sub-clause 15.5 Termination for Employer's convenience: The Contractor is paid for loss of profit and other losses and damage suffered, not subject to the exclusion in sub-clause 1.15.

Sub-clause 16.2: The Contractor can terminate if a Notice of Commencement Date is not received within 84 days of receiving the Letter of Acceptance.

Sub-clause 17.4: The Contractor's indemnities have been expanded to include any design by the Contractor or lack of fitness for purpose.

Sub-clause 17.5: The Employer's indemnities have been expanded to include damage to property arising from any Employer's risk events.

Clause 19 Insurance (previously clause 18) has been rewritten. There are new provisions for the Contractor to maintain PI insurance for design and it is required to provide Goods insurance.

More time limits for the Engineer, Contractor and Employer are specified and failure to comply with them results in sanctions.

There are additional time-bars, but some may be waived.

There is more prescription, particularly in relation to the Engineer's role and the Claims procedure. These involve enhanced contract management procedures.

The previous clause 20 [Claims, Disputes and Arbitration] has been separated into clause 20 [Employer's and Contractor's Claims] and clause 21 [Disputes and Arbitration] to clearly distinguish Claims from Disputes.

The Dispute Adjudication Board (DAB) has been renamed the Dispute Avoidance/ Adjudication Board (DAAB) to emphasise that the Dispute Board's role has been explicitly expanded to include dispute avoidance. The DAAB in the 2017 Yellow and Silver Books is a standing Dispute Board.

There are new provisions to promote the Parties' collaboration in sub-clause 3.6 [Meetings], sub-clause 8.4 [Advance Warning] and sub-clause 21.3 [Avoidance of Disputes].

There is improved clarity and certainty for the agreement/determination by the Employer's Representative in sub-clause 3.5, and for Tests on Completion in clause 9.

These significant changes generally also apply to the Yellow and Silver Books. There is improved clarity and certainty in those books in respect of design and review in sub-clause 5.1, and Contractor's documents in sub-clause 5.2.

One of the advantages of using a FIDIC standard form contract is the wealth of information available in books and articles that provide detailed guidance.[21] The recent book by Corbett & Co on the 2017 editions is a massive 807 pages.[22] The short introduction outlines the best features of the 2017 editions that resolved issues with the 1999 forms, as well as other features of interest. However, the author also highlights those features he considers are ill considered or poorly drafted, in particular the length of about 50,000 words he considers is far too long and "the draft needed vigorous editing".[23] The book contains a review of the origin of each clause, highlighting new features or changes from the 1999 editions with references to relevant predecessors, followed by a detailed discussion on each clause. The enhanced contract administration requirements and the prescriptive nature of the 2017 editions is emphasised by the 135 draft Notices in the Appendix for use by the Engineer, Employer or Contractor.

21 Published books on the 1999 editions include: Raveed Khalani & Mahdi Saadat Fard, *FIDIC Plant and Design-Build Forms of Contract Illustrated* (Wiley, 2015); Jeremy Glover & Simon Hughes, *Understanding the FIDIC red book: a clause-by-clause commentary* (Sweet & Maxwell, 3rd edn, 2011); Axel-Volkmar Jaeger & Götz-Sebastian Hök, *FIDIC – A Guide for Practitioners* (Springer, 2010); Ellis Baker, Ben Mellors, Scott Chalmers & Anthony Lavers, *FIDIC Contracts: Law and Practice* (Informa Law, 2009); Brian Totterdill, *FIDIC users' guide: A practical guide to the 1999 red and yellow books* (Thomas Telford, 2006); Robert Knutson (ed), *FIDIC An Analysis of International Contracts* (Kluwer Law International, 2005); Nael G Bunni, *The FIDIC Forms of Contract* (Blackwell, 2005).

22 Corbett & Co, *FIDIC 2017* (Corbett & Co, 2020).

23 Ibid, vi.

11.3.1.2 NEC contracts

The Institution of Civil Engineers publishes the NEC standard form contracts in Table 11.5.

11.3.2 Standard contract forms with modifications

One of the potential drawbacks to the use of standard form contracts is that, because of the variety of interest groups involved in their production, the ultimate form of the terms as published may represent a compromise between conflicting interests which may not be totally acceptable to anyone. The inevitable result is modifications to the standard

TABLE 11.5 NEC standard form contracts

NEC3[a]	**NEC4**[b]
Adjudicator's Contract (AC)	
	Alliance Contract
	Design Build and Operate Contract
	Dispute Resolution Service Contract
Engineering and Construction Contract (ECC)	Engineering and Construction Contract
Engineering and Construction Contract Option A: priced contract with activity schedule	Engineering and Construction Contract Option A: priced contract with activity schedule
Engineering and Construction Contract Option B: priced contract with bill of quantities	Engineering and Construction Contract Option B: priced contract with bill of quantities
Engineering and Construction Contract Option C: target contract with activity schedule	Engineering and Construction Contract Option C: target contract with activity schedule
Engineering and Construction Contract Option D: target contract with bill of quantities	Engineering and Construction Contract Option D: target contract with bill of quantities
Engineering and Construction Contract Option E: cost reimbursable contract	Engineering and Construction Contract Option E: cost reimbursable contract
Engineering and Construction Contract Option F: management contract	Engineering and Construction Contract Option F: management contract
Engineering and Construction Short Contract (ECSC)	Engineering and Construction Short Contract
Engineering and Construction Short Subcontract (ECSS)	
Engineering and Construction Subcontract (ECS)	
Framework Contract (FC)	
Framework Contract Guidance Notes and Flow Charts	
Professional Services Contract (PSC)	
Professional Services Short Contract (PSSC)	
Supply Contract (SC)	
Supply Short Contract (SSC)	
Term Service Contract (TSC)	
Term Service Short Contract (TSSC)	

[a] https://www.neccontract.com/NEC3-Products/NEC3-Contracts/NEC3-All-Contracts-Associated-Documents (accessed 12 April 2021).

[b] https://www.neccontract.com/NEC4-Products/NEC4-Contracts/NEC4-All-Contracts-Associated-Documents (accessed 12 April 2021).

terms that must be negotiated between the contracting parties prior to entry into the contract. The ambit of such modifications will generally depend on the extent to which the contracting parties are not prepared to accept the allocation of risk provided for in the standard terms. To the extent that each such proposed modification of a standard form contract requires careful assessment of the potential cost and risk by each contracting party, there may be little difference from the process involved in negotiating a bespoke contract. However, provided the cumulative effect of such nonstandard terms is not such as to change the entire character of the standard form of contract, the departures from the norm can be readily identified and assessed.[24]

Another reason for modification of standard form contracts intended for international use is that some provisions may be incompatible with mandatory law in a particular jurisdiction. The minimal extent of such modifications for the FIDIC rainbow suite for a number of jurisdictions is outlined in Tables 35.1, 35.2 and 35.3 in Section 35.7.

The substantial extent of amendments to standard form contracts in Australia was revealed in a 2014 survey: 75% across almost all contract values, contracting sectors and standard forms. The extent of amendment was particularly high for high contract values: 94% for AUD50 m–100 m, 97% for AUD100 m–500 m and 100% for contract values greater than AUD500 m.[25] Part of the reason for the extensive amendments may be that many of the Australian standard form contracts have not been amended for over 20 years, and do not have appropriate clauses for more recent developments such as GST and *Security of Payment* legislation.

11.3.3 Bespoke contracts

Bespoke contracts for large construction projects are very common in Australia, frequently drawn up by solicitors who are very experienced in construction law and usually acting for the Employer. Accordingly, it can be expected that bespoke construction contracts included in tender documents will be more "Employer-friendly", and the risk allocation may be significantly different to the standard form construction contracts. A prudent tenderer faced with a proposed bespoke contract will ensure that the terms are very carefully and thoroughly scrutinised by an experienced construction lawyer to determine the impact of the risk allocation and other contract terms, and to propose acceptable alternatives if necessary. Such a process is invariably expensive, as it requires high calibre legal resources to go through each clause and consider its likely operation in the light of the contract as a whole, existing case law and the usual allocation of risks as between Contractor and Employer. Even if major issues such as price and timing of a tender are acceptable, the importance of, and time and energy involved in negotiating, a substantial number of significant changes to a proposed contract should not be underestimated.[26]

One of the risks of a bespoke contract is that the risk allocation may not be transparent, and the contracting parties may have differing views of how the contract terms operate. In theory this should not occur, as the words of a contract are to be construed in accordance with their plain and ordinary meaning. However, construction contracts usually comprise

24 Brian Eggleston, *The New Engineering Contract A Commentary* (1996), 34.

25 Professor John Sharkey, Matthew Bell and others, *Standard Forms of Contract in the Australian Construction Industry* (University of Melbourne, 2014) 5.

26 Brian Eggleston, *The New Engineering Contract A Commentary* (1996), 35.

a number of legal and technical documents that must be construed together as a single instrument, and it is not unknown for this extensive documentation to have inconsistencies or ambiguities. See Chapters 7 and 8 for a discussion of the *MT Højgaard a/s v E.ON Climate and Renewables UK Robin Rigg East Ltd* cases in which "The court is confronted in this case with contractual documents of multiple authorship, which contains much loose wording."[27]

It is submitted that ambiguities and inconsistencies are more likely to occur in a bespoke contract than a standard form contract, because the evolutionary and consultative process of creating a standard form contract involves detailed consideration of their provisions by a number of skilled practitioners with a range of skills and perspectives. Inevitably, more man-hours are invested in the production of a standard form contract than a bespoke contract, which, it is submitted, reduces the likelihood of creating discrepancies or ambiguities.

Hibberd identified the reasons for making amendments to standard forms as being commercial pressures and the desire to change the risk profile: "The dumping and hedging of risk to reflect the commercial muscle of the parties and the emergence of risks becomes all too clear in the tension between the supply and demand sides of the industry."[28] It is submitted that these are also the reasons for the selection of a bespoke contract in circumstances where, prima facie, a standard form contract could be adopted.

In a 1996 paper, Fenn and others reported the results of a significant survey of nearly 2,000 uses of Standard Form Contracts and bespoke contracts.[29] This survey found that there were significant differences between some standard contract forms in the perceived expectancy of disputes. One of the standard contract forms found to have a low level of disputes was the NEC suite of contracts, in which transparent allocation and reduction of risk is a stated aim of the drafting. The study also found that bespoke contracts had the highest expectation of disputes, followed closely by a government form.

11.4 Advantages of standard form contracts

It is suggested that the advantages of using a standard form contract that aims to be even-handed as between the contracting parties, in preference to a bespoke contract, may include the following:

- More certainty in the meaning of contract terms, because the way in which standard contract terms operate in practice are widely understood.
- Reduced transaction costs of entering into a contract because of the parties' familiarity with the contract wording. Tenderers have to spend considerable time and expense in analysing "one-off" contract conditions in bespoke contracts, pricing the increased risks and negotiating acceptable contract conditions. Those

27 *Mt Højgaard A/S v E.ON Climate and Renewables UK Robin Rigg East Ltd* [2015] EWCA Civ 407.

28 Professor Peter Hibberd, "The place of standard forms of building contract in the 21st century" (Paper based on a talk given at a Society of Construction Law conference in Wakefield on 11 March 2004, November 2004), 3.

29 Peter Fenn, David Lowe and Christopher Speck, "Conflict and dispute in construction" (1997) 15 *Construction Management and Economics* 513.

transaction costs are likely to be paid by Employers, either through increased tender prices of the contract being bid, or in increased prices for future contracts.

- Reduced tender prices for a widely understood regime of risk allocation and contract administration. Tenderers may put a higher price on the unfamiliar risks in a bespoke contract than they would in respect of the more familiar standard form contracts.
- Reduced contracting costs resulting from familiarity with the form of the contract. Increased project execution costs for the use of a bespoke contract are likely to result from the additional work required by contract administration personnel to train for and administer unfamiliar contract terms.
- Reduced disputation because of familiarity with the risk allocation in a standard form contract. Unfamiliar risks in a bespoke contract may be underpriced, leading to an under-bid project in which the Contractor may endeavour to recover costs in any legitimately arguable way.
- Reduced risk of Contractor default – the contract price in a bespoke contract may not adequately provide for the unfamiliar risks the Contractor assumes.
- Potentially more bidding competition – some possible bidders may not be prepared to contract on the basis of a bespoke contract perceived to be too one-sided.
- The benefits of precedent – the wide usage of standard form contracts means that over time these are subject to judicial analysis and interpretation as to the meaning of the words used in specific clauses. Such judicial precedents for the meaning of the contract provisions in published case law[30] would normally provide a persuasive precedent for other judges to follow in respect of the same wording. They do not of course constitute legal authority, since every contract must be considered as a whole, and the terms of a standard contract must be construed in relation to their use in the particular circumstances.

The positive impact of judicial consideration of standard contract terms was summed up by Lord Hoffmann as follows:

> The evolution of standard forms is often the result of interaction between the draftsman and the courts and the efforts of the draftsman cannot be properly understood without reference to the meaning which the judges have given to the language used by his predecessors.[31]

A compelling case for the use of standard form contracts in a more efficient approach to contracting in the oil and gas industry for the UK continental shelf (**UKCS**) has been made as follows:

> Invitations to Tender issued by UKCS operators in the past typically contained individual specific contract terms and conditions. More often than not these terms would differ from the form previously seen by contractors thus necessitating a fresh review on each and every occasion. A variety of contracts, legal and project/operational personnel will typically be involved in this process. The contract form issued by the operator would normally be drafted in the operator's favour, anticipating, and receiving, lengthy qualifications by tenderers. Tenderers

30 e.g. Dorter and Sharkey, *Building and Construction Contracts in Australia* (looseleaf) 411–417 comprises a Table of References to a number of the standard forms used in Australia with reference to applicable reported cases where appropriate.

31 *Beaufort Development (NI) Ltd v Gilbert Ash NI Ltd* (1998) 59 Con LR 66 per Lord Hoffmann.

in turn would demand more concessions than they would expect the operator to agree to as 'negotiation' was expected. Often lengthy discussion followed, involving many individuals, before an agreed position was reached.

The above process, on an industry wide basis, taking into account the number of operators, contractors and suppliers involved in the whole range of exploration, development and production activities covered, has a very significant resource and cost impact.

What does this process achieve? For many who have worked with this arrangement over many years the belief is that that it achieved very little. Risk is not managed or allocated where it can most appropriately be borne, rather it is pushed from one party to another depending on prevailing market conditions. Additional insurance costs can result and contract costs may be increased due to uncertainties and/or contingencies being added. Ultimately, however, the contracts that are signed by different operators and contractors often end up being remarkably alike.[32]

11.5 Conclusion

It is noteworthy that the large UK oil and gas industry promotes the economic advantages arising from a standard approach to contracting, whereas the Australian oil and gas and other resource industries still seem to be wedded to the approach of bespoke contracts (generally written on behalf of the Employer), with contract conditions peculiar to each Employer and each project. It is suggested that the use of bespoke contracts in Australia ultimately achieves very little other than adding unnecessary costs and uncertainty to the contracting process.

Any apparent advantage that may appear to be achieved by the use of contracts that alter the traditional "balance" between Employer and Contractor by transferring risk to the Contractor is likely to be illusory, because of higher costs either on the current or future contracts. A rational Contractor will increase its tender price by an appropriate contingency sum if it understands that a particular contract requires it to accept risks that it cannot properly manage. An irrational Contractor that does not price those risks, or a Contractor that does not understand such risks, will under-price its tender. This may appear to give an advantage to the Employer, but is likely to result in increased disputation under the contract, and higher costs on future similar contracts, arising from the collective understanding of the performance of contracts within the construction industry. In an extreme case, under-pricing of risk by a Contractor could lead to its insolvency, and consequent termination of the contract before completion, a distinctly unpalatable risk for any Employer!

32 Standard Contract for the UK Offshore Oil and Gas Industry General Conditions of Contract for Construction Part 2 Guidance Notes, Edition 2 October 2003, published by LOGIC (Leading Oil and Gas Industry Competitiveness), 1.

CHAPTER 12

The impact of COVID-19 on construction contracts

12.1 Government responses to COVID-19

The worldwide advent of the COVID-19 pandemic in 2020 had tragic impacts on the lives of many people and had a substantial impact on economic life around the world, including the construction industry. Governments responded with legislation that implemented unprecedented policies in containment and border closure, economic assistance and health measures. The Blavatnik School of Government at the University of Oxford collected data from 186 countries and regions on the policies governments implemented to respond to the pandemic and presented their findings in the Coronavirus Government Response Tracker (**Response Tracker**).[1] The dataset in the Response Tracker contains 19 indicators and a miscellaneous notes field organised into four groups:

- Containment and closure policies
- Economic policies
- Health system policies
- Miscellaneous policies.

In addition to the 19 individual policy indicators, the Response Tracker calculates several indices to give an overall impression of government activity. The **Stringency Index** provides a single index combining all of the eight containment and closure policies, thereby providing one comparative measure of the impact of the pandemic on economic life.[2] The eight containment and closure policies recorded numerical measures for the following:

- C1 – closings of schools and universities
- C2 – closing of workplaces
- C3 – cancelling public events
- C4 – limits on gatherings
- C5 – closing of public transport

1 Thomas Hale and others, 'Oxford COVID-19 Government Response Tracker' (2020) *Blavatnik School of Government* https://www.bsg.ox.ac.uk/research/research-projects/coronavirus-government-response-tracker #data (accessed 24 February 2021).

2 https://github.com/OxCGRT/covid-policy-tracker/blob/master/documentation/index_methodology.md (accessed 24 February 2021).

 DOI: 10.4324/9781003206897-14

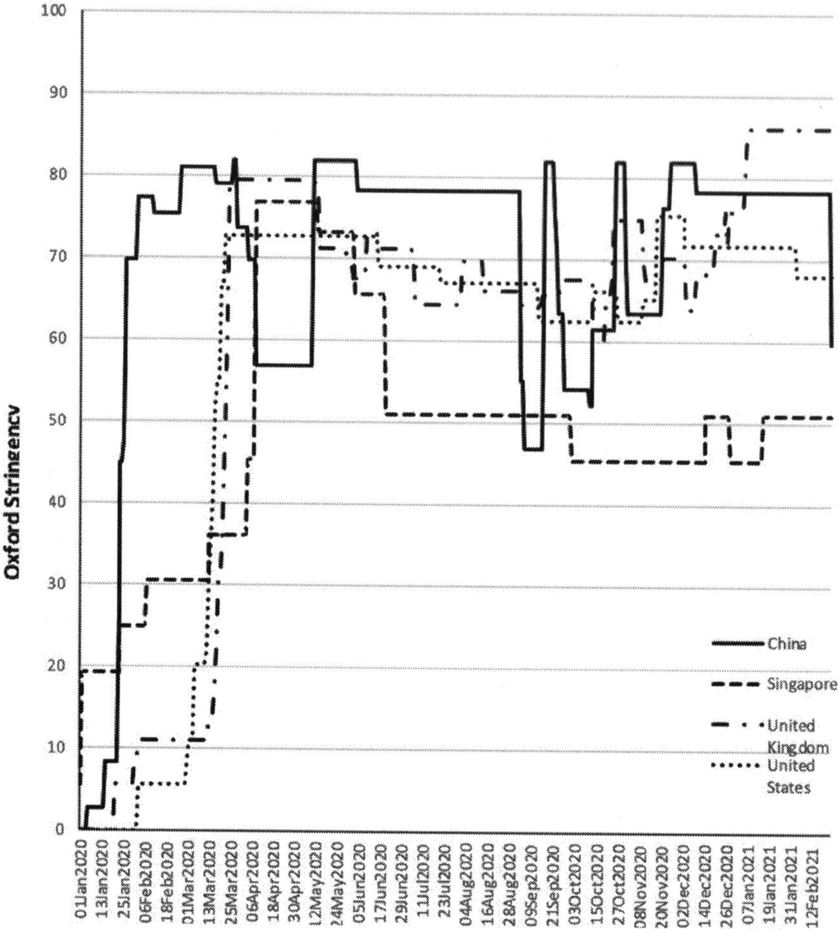

FIGURE 12.1 Oxford Stringency Index

- C6 – orders to "shelter in place" and otherwise confine to the home
- C7 – restrictions on internal movement between cities/regions
- C8 – restrictions on international travel for foreign travelers.[3]

These indices have been plotted in Figure 12.1 for four countries (China, Singapore, United Kingdom and the USA) for the period 1 January 2020 to 22 February 2021.

The graph in Figure 12.1 shows the speed with which these governments reacted to the pandemic in January, February and March 2020, and the strength of the policies they adopted over the following months. Singapore stepped up the level of its stringency until late April, after which it was significantly reduced, and remained at a much lower level. The graphs for China, the USA and the UK demonstrate reductions in stringency followed

3 https://github.com/OxCGRT/covid-policy-tracker/blob/master/documentation/codebook.md (accessed 24 February 2021).

by subsequent increases as a result of second and third waves that required the reintroduction of greater stringency. The level of stringency was 51 in Singapore, 60 in China, 68 in the USA and 86 in the UK on 22 February 2021, indicating the persistent impact of significant government containment measures into the second year of the pandemic.

12.2 The impact of COVID-19 on construction

The general measures governments took to control the spread of COVID-19 inevitably impacted construction. Construction projects were significantly delayed, postponed or terminated as a result of COVID-19; those that continued were subject to increased costs as a result of the health measures required to keep workers safe. The closure of borders, shutdown of businesses, restrictions on movement, physical distancing, wearing masks, stringent cleaning and disinfection and increased use of personal protective equipment (**PPE**) all impacted construction projects, resulting in increased costs and delays. The CEO of one of Australia's major construction companies estimated the cost of the extra burden of COVID measures such as temperature checking equipment, on-site COVID-19 marshals and providing extra space for distancing to be between 0.5% and 1% of the project cost.[4] Contractors will inevitably seek costs and EOTs from these impacts and a substantial number of claims can therefore be expected. At the time of writing (September 2021), the COVID-19 pandemic is far from over, and there is already anecdotal evidence of claims on many construction projects, including an increase of spurious claims.[5] Some of those claims will no doubt be rejected and result in disputes, discussed in more detail in Chapter 29.

The unprecedented array of legislation to deal with the health and economic impacts of COVID-19 significantly constrained freedom of contract in many situations, not least of which were those laws and regulations that impacted construction projects and construction contracts. The legislative interventions that are relevant to construction were measures that constrained:

- The execution of construction projects
- The operation of construction contracts
- Resolution of disputes arising out of COVID-19.

In some jurisdictions, the government passed legislation to ameliorate specific impacts of the pandemic on the construction industry; in other jurisdictions the government passed legislation to provide economic support to impacted individuals and businesses more generally.

12.3 Execution of construction projects impacted by COVID-19

Where contracts were entered into after the outbreak of the pandemic, the parties were in a position to negotiate appropriate conditions of contract that allowed for the impact of

4 'Builders count the cost of COVID compliance', *The Australian Financial Review* (Sydney, Australia), 22 January 2021, 31.

5 HKA, 'CRUX Insight Engineering and Construction A Regional Analysis of Causation Lessons Learned from Claims and Disputes' (October 2020) 3 https://www.hka.com/2020-crux-insight/ (accessed 5 April 2021).

carrying out construction in a COVID-19 affected environment. However, for those contracts entered into before the outbreak of the pandemic, the time and cost consequences of the applicable mandatory government measures were determined by the provisions of the contract and the applicable law.

The following are some examples of the COVID-19 specific mandatory requirements introduced by governments (**COVID-19 requirements**) in various jurisdictions that impacted the time and cost of executing construction projects.

Restrictions on travel – countries and regions closed their borders to non-residents, e.g. Australia closed its borders to non-residents and banned most international travel by residents; most Australian States closed their borders to residents of other States for months.

Shut down of construction sites – some countries shut down construction sites after the onset of infection, e.g. Singapore issued an advisory that all building works as defined in the *Building Control Act* were required to cease with effect from 7 April 2020 to 4 May 2020; Malaysia only permitted "essential services" to operate in the period from 18 March to 31 March. The Philippines only permitted construction of essential facilities (healthcare facilities and isolation quarantine facilities) and priority projects under the Build Build Build Infrastructure Program to continue during the period of enhanced community quarantine from 16 March 2020. Small-scale construction activities intended for private and personal use were permitted during the subsequent period of modified enhanced community quarantine.

Constraints on working on construction sites – e.g. following a more severe second wave of infections in Victoria in July 2020, the operation of construction projects was significantly restricted by limiting the number of personnel on construction sites.

Increased hours of working – e.g. New South Wales permitted construction sites to operate on weekends and public holidays irrespective of what consents might otherwise allow.

Physical distancing was the primary method of protection mandated in many countries, requiring all persons outside their homes (and including construction sites) to be separated by a distance of 1.0, 1.5, 1.8 or 2 metres.

Additional OHS precautions – many jurisdictions required additional health precautions to be implemented, e.g. wearing of face masks outside the home; Singapore issued an advisory on supporting mental well-being of workers under COVID-19 work arrangements; the Philippines required temperature checks prior to entering workplaces.[6]

Stringent cleaning protocols were required, including frequent hand-washing and sanitising by regularly and frequently disinfecting contact surfaces in an endeavour to prevent infection, and deep cleaning of premises where infection had occurred.

Enhanced documentation of employees – e.g. Singapore required mandatory daily declarations and updating by employers of work permits in the construction sector on stay-home notices; Victoria mandated enhanced record-keeping to ensure that persons who had been in close contact with an infected person could be identified, advised and tested.

6 Philippines Department of Public Works and Highways (DPWH) Department Order No. 39, series of 2020, dated 19 May 2020.

Isolation of infected personnel – personnel diagnosed with COVID-19 were required to isolate from others, typically for a period of 14 days.

Quarantine – many countries required incoming travellers (including returning residents) to be quarantined for 14 days. Some countries required particular areas of high risk to be quarantined from outside contact, e.g. Singapore issued an advisory requiring foreign employees in the construction sector to be quarantined in their accommodation from 20 April to 4 May.

Labour laws – some constraints on the employment of labour were temporarily put in abeyance, e.g. in Singapore, employers were permitted to introduce flexible work schedules to use unused working hours to offset overtime hours; in the Philippines, reduction of work-hours and/or work-days per week, rotation of workers and forced leave were permitted.

Labour payments – some countries introduced new requirements to protect the income of infected persons, e.g. in Indonesia the salary of a documented infected worker was required to be paid in full for up to 14 days, a worker categorised as a suspect COVID-19 infection and quarantined/isolated was required to be paid in full during the quarantine/isolation period and a worker unable to work due to COVID-19 illness was required to be paid wages in accordance with applicable laws.

FIDIC published a Guidance Memorandum 'On-site working and project team organisation' in May 2020.[7] That Memorandum discussed the following project execution issues, addressing the identified risks and the measures recommended to mitigate them:

- Loss of communication channels
- Over-delivery or inclusion of non-essential tasks
- Problems with PPE and/or specific equipment
- Contact with contaminated persons
- Direct and indirect contact
- Personnel transport/office housing
- Site inductions and hazard identification
- Personal hygiene/equipment cleaning (tidying up)
- Emergency attendance and response at site
- Important things to remember.

Commissioned research for Loughborough University reported in August 2020 on the impacts of COVID-19 on six projects. The Loughborough Report noted a number of rapid and effective responses: changes to site layouts and working practices; more time spent planning activities; smaller groups and trades working in sequence resulting in improved housekeeping and productivity; changes to induction processes and welfare and hygiene arrangements resulting in improved safety, well-being and motivation; substantial cost, productivity and flexibility benefits from working at home for those able to do so. Other impacts reported included a high demand on many management and supervisory staff with adverse impacts on some, increased demands on the supply chain and increased

7 https://fidic.org/sites/default/files/FIDIC%20Guidance%20Memorandum_RLQC.pdf (accessed 15 April 2021).

expectations on supervisors for worker engagement, briefing, induction and increased communication between trades to facilitate safe working.[8]

12.4 Operation of construction contracts

As noted above, where a contract was entered into before the outbreak of the pandemic, the time and cost consequences of the applicable mandatory government measures are determined by the provisions of the contract and the applicable law. In common law jurisdictions and in the absence of specific COVID-19 legislation, the contract itself will generally determine whether or not the Contractor is entitled to additional payment and/or time to comply with the applicable COVID-19 requirements.

There is no general common law provision to relieve parties from hardships that arise from unforeseen circumstances not contemplated by the contract. That is, any provisions dealing with *force majeure* must be provided by the terms of the contract itself. It is only in situations where performance of the contract becomes impossible through circumstances not contemplated by the contract that the common law provides the remedy of frustration. However, it is unlikely that the impact of COVID-19 on a construction contract would amount to frustration of the contract. Whilst the cost and time delays may be substantial and make operation of the contract significantly more onerous for the Contractor, they are unlikely to reach the high bar of the impossibility of performance that constitutes frustration.[9]

The General Conditions of FIDIC contracts illustrate the types of contractual provisions that may determine the allocation of time and cost impacts arising from COVID-19 between the Contractor and the Employer:

- Unforeseeable shortages in the availability of personnel or Goods (or Employer-Supplied Materials, if any) caused by epidemic or governmental actions
- Delays caused by authorities
- Adjustments for changes in laws
- *Force majeure* or Exceptional Events
- Delay, impediment or prevention caused by or attributable to the Employer, or the Employer's personnel.

The applicability of any of these contractual provisions will of course depend on the relevant facts and the specific terms of the Contract. Possible scenarios that could trigger claims under these provisions are discussed in Section 12.6.

12.5 General legislation relevant to impacts arising from COVID-19

Whilst *force majeure* is not a term of art in common law jurisdictions, there are specific *force majeure* provisions in many *Civil Law Codes* where good faith is a fundamental

8 Wendy Jones, Vivien Chow, Alistair Gibb, 'COVID-19 and construction: Early lessons for a new normal?' (August 2020) 2 https://www.balfourbeatty.com/media/318555/covid19-and-construction-early-lessons-for-a-new-normal.pdf (accessed 5 April 2021).

9 See Section 4.10.

TABLE 12.1 *Force majeure* provisions in Asia Pacific jurisdictions

Australia	*Common law*	*No statutory recognition.*
China	Civil law	Article 180 of the PRC *General Rules on the Civil Law* and article 117 of the *PRC Contract Law.*
Hong Kong	Common law	No statutory recognition.
Indonesia	Civil law	Articles 1244 and 1245 of the Indonesian *Civil Code.*
Japan	Civil law	Some statutory recognition in article 419-3 of the Japanese *Civil Code.*
Malaysia	Common law	*Civil Law Act 1956.*
Philippines	Mixed civil law and common law	Article 1174 of the *Civil Code.*
Singapore	Common law	No statutory recognition.
Taiwan	Civil law	Taiwan *Civil Code.*
Thailand	Civil law	Section 8 of the *Civil and Commercial Code.*
Vietnam	Civil law	Article 156.1 of Vietnam *Civil Code.*

principle of contract law. Good faith is the bedrock principle on which various "hardship" provisions are founded. However, there is no uniformity as to what events will constitute *force majeure*, as these can differ significantly between jurisdictions.

Baker McKenzie published a *force majeure* tracker in May 2020 that identified *force majeure* provisions in 11 jurisdictions in Asia Pacific.[10] Table 12.1 lists the *force majeure* provisions recognised in statute identified in the tracker.

The Baker McKenzie *force majeure* tracker also contains, for each of the 11 jurisdictions, details of *force majeure* pursuant to contract, the formalities to invoke *force majeure*, whether there is any obligation to mitigate, and the outcome of invoking *force majeure*.[11]

12.5.1 UAE

Article 273 of the *UAE Civil Code* is barely distinguishable from common law frustration, as it depends on impossibility of performance, and has the consequence that the contract is brought to an end:

> (1) In contracts binding on both parties, if force majeure supervenes which makes the performance of the contract impossible, the corresponding obligation shall cease, and the contract shall be automatically cancelled.
>
> (2) In the case of partial impossibility, that part of the contract which is impossible shall be extinguished, and the same shall apply to temporary impossibility in continuing contracts, and in those two cases it shall be permissible for the obligor to cancel the contract provided that the obligee is so aware.

10 https://www.bakermckenzie.com/-/media/files/insight/publications/2020/04/force-majeure-comparative-table-040520.pdf (accessed 2 September 2020).

11 Ibid.

12.5.2 France

The consequences of *force majeure* are different in other civil law jurisdictions. For example, in France, a Contractor may be entitled to be indemnified above a certain threshold as a consequence of ***sujétions imprévues*** – technical difficulties of an unforeseeable nature and of sufficient magnitude to fundamentally affect the Contractor's performance. The threshold may be informed by the caselaw in a particular circumstance. Whilst the solution will take into consideration the intention of the parties and their agreed risk allocation, the administrative courts are free to decide a right of indemnification of the Contractor for *sujétions imprévues* notwithstanding any contract clause to the contrary.[12]

12.5.3 Philippines

Article 1174 of the Philippines *Civil Code* provides:

> Except in cases expressly specified by the law, or when it is otherwise declared by stipulation, or when the nature of the obligation requires the assumption of risk, no person shall be responsible for those events which could not be foreseen or which, though foreseen, were inevitable.

Arguably, this Article could apply as a defence to breach of contract as a consequence of failure to perform contractual obligations arising from the impact of COVID-19, e.g. failure to complete the works by the contractually specified date for completion.

12.5.4 UNIDROIT Principles

The UNIDROIT Principles of International Commercial Contracts[13] include similar provisions using the terminology of "hardship". Article 6.2.3 defines "hardship" as follows:

> There is hardship where the occurrence of events fundamentally alters the equilibrium of the contract either because the cost of a party's performance has increased or because the value of the performance a party receives has diminished, and
>
> (a) the events occur or become known to the disadvantaged party after the conclusion of the contract;
> (b) the events could not reasonably have been taken into account by the disadvantaged party at the time of the conclusion of the contract;
> (c) the events are beyond the control of the disadvantaged party; and
> (d) the risk of the events was not assumed by the disadvantaged party.

The effects of hardship can be ameliorated by a court (or an arbitral tribunal) as provided for in Art 6.2.3 of the UNIDROIT Principles:

> (1) In case of hardship the disadvantaged party is entitled to request renegotiations. The request shall be made without undue delay and shall indicate the grounds on which it is based.

12 Mark Frilet, 'France' in Robert Knutson (ed), *FIDIC An Analysis of International Construction Contracts* (Wolters Kluwer Law International, 2005) 79, 83.

13 Discussed in Chapter 36.

(2) The request for renegotiation does not in itself entitle the disadvantaged party to withhold performance.
(3) Upon failure to reach agreement within a reasonable time either party may resort to the court.
(4) If the court finds hardship it may, if reasonable,
    (a) terminate the contract at a date and on terms to be fixed, or
    (b) adapt the contract with a view to restoring its equilibrium.

12.5.5 Other remedies

In France, ***imprévision*** provides that the Contractor has the right to indemnification when there is a major change in economic factors existing at the time of contracting and which destroys the contractual equilibrium:

> The *imprevision* theory is based on the *rebus sic stantibus* principle, which is the venerable principle limiting the 'sanctity of contract' theory (*pacta sunt servanda*). The Contractor has the right to indemnification when there is a major change in economic factors existing at the time of contracting and which destroys the contractual equilibrium (*bouleversement de l'économie du contrat*). It is not the magnitude of the event by itself which is sufficient to trigger the right of indemnification but its major impact on the Contractor's obligations. [14]

12.6 Specific legislation relevant to impacts arising from COVID-19

The following are examples of specific legislation promulgated in 2020 to ameliorate the impact of COVID-19 on construction contracts.

12.6.1 The Philippines

The Philippines Department of Labor and Employment issued Labor Advisory No 18 of 2020 applying to all Employers, including Contractors and subcontractors in the private sector that specified:

> The employer shall shoulder the cost of COVID-19 prevention and control measures such as but not limited to the following: testing, disinfection facilities, hand sanitisers, personal protective equipment (PPEs i.e. face mask), proper orientation and training of workers including IEC materials on COVID-19 prevention and control.[15]

12.6.2 Singapore

Singapore acted early to provide significant relief for the impacts of the pandemic in the *COVID-19 (Temporary Measures) Act 2020 (the **Act**)*, passed on 7 April 2020. Part 2 of the *Act* contained a number of measures for temporary relief for inability to perform an

14 Above, n8.
15 Guidelines on the Cost of COVID-19 Prevention and Control Measures, 18 May 2020 https://www.dole.gov.ph/news/labor-advisory-no-18-series-of-2020-guidelines-on-the-cost-of-covid-19-prevention-and-control-measures/ (accessed 6 August 2020).

obligation in a scheduled contract after 1 February 2020 caused by a COVID-19 event. The *Act* defines a COVID-19 event as:

(a) the COVID–19 epidemic or pandemic; or
(b) the operation of or compliance with any law of Singapore or another country or territory, or an order or direction of the Government or any statutory body, or of the government or other public authority of another country or territory, being any law, order or direction that is made by reason of or in connection with COVID–19.

The *Act* provides for a prescribed period of six months. A construction contract is a scheduled contract. The *Act* provides that where a party (**A**) to a scheduled contract is unable to perform a contractual obligation caused to a material extent by a COVID-19 event and has served a notification for relief with the other party or parties to the contract (**B**), then despite any law or anything in the contract, B may not take any of the following actions for the specified period:

(a) the commencement or continuation of an action in a court against *A* or *A*'s guarantor or surety;
(b) the commencement or continuation of arbitral proceedings under the *Arbitration Act* (Cap. 10) against *A* or *A*'s guarantor or surety;
(c) the enforcement of any security over any immovable property;
(d) the enforcement of any security over any movable property used for the purpose of a trade, business or profession;
(e) the making of an application under section 210(1) of the *Companies Act (Cap. 50)* for a meeting of creditors to be summoned to approve a compromise or an arrangement in relation to A or A's guarantor or surety;
(f) the making of an application for a judicial management order in relation to A or A's guarantor or surety;
(g) the making of an application for the winding up of A or A's guarantor or surety;
(h) the making of a bankruptcy application against A or A's guarantor or surety;
(i) the appointment of a receiver or manager over any property or undertaking of A or A's guarantor or surety;
(j) the commencement or levying of execution, distress or other legal process against any property of A or A's guarantor or surety, except with the leave of the court and subject to such terms as the court imposes;
(k) the repossession of any goods under any chattels leasing agreement, hire–purchase agreement or retention of title agreement, being goods used for the purpose of a trade, business or profession;
(l) the termination of a scheduled contract (being a lease or licence of immovable property) where the subject inability is the non–payment of rent or other moneys;
(m) the exercise of a right of re-entry or forfeiture under a scheduled contract (being a lease or licence of immovable property), or the exercise of any other right that has a similar outcome;
(n) the enforcement against A or A's guarantor or surety of a judgment of a court, an award made by an arbitral tribunal in arbitral proceedings conducted under the Arbitration Act, or a determination by an adjudicator under the Building and Construction Industry Security of Payment Act; and
(o) such other action as may be prescribed.[16]

16 *COVID-19 (Temporary Measures) Act 2020* (Singapore) s 5(3).

Any applicable *force majeure* clause in the Contract and the *Frustrated Contracts Act* (Singapore) will prevail over the provisions of the *Act*.[17]

Section 6 of the *Act* provides for additional relief for inability to perform an obligation in a construction or supply contract as a consequence of a COVID-19 event:

- Subject to specified conditions, the term of a performance bond is to be extended to a date seven days after the end of the prescribed period
- B may not make a call on the performance bond for the specified period
- For the purposes of calculating liquidated damages payable under the Contract after 1 February 2020 and before the expiry of the prescribed period, any period for which the inability exists is to be disregarded in determining the period of delay
- The inability to perform an obligation in the Contract to a material extent caused by a COVID–19 event is a defense to a claim for a breach of contract for the period after 1 February 2020 and before the expiry of the prescribed period.

The *Act* provides for an assessor to determine whether a party falls within s 5 of the *Act* – i.e. whether their non-performance was in fact due to a COVID-19 event. The assessor "must seek to achieve an outcome that is just and equitable in the circumstances of the case" and may take into account the ability and financial capacity of a party to perform its obligations. This includes requiring a party to the contract to do anything or pay any sum of money to discharge any obligations under the contract and requiring a party to a contract to pay reasonable costs incurred by another party in the performance of the contract. With leave of the court, judgment may be entered in the terms of the assessor's determination. Each party must bear its own costs for proceedings before an assessor, and they are not entitled to legal representation except with the assessor's permission.[18]

The measures in the *Act* were only temporary and only froze legal rights and obligations in place while it was in force, allowing proceedings to be commenced, if necessary, after the prescribed period.

12.7 Economic measures

In addition to the measures outlined above that directly impacted the execution of construction projects and the operation of construction contracts, governments provided financial assistance to individuals and businesses that indirectly assisted the construction industry. For example, in Australia, the government made a AUD1,500 (USD1,150) per fortnight Jobkeeper payment for a period of six months for each employee in an enterprise that had suffered a 30% (50% for large organisations) reduction in turnover as a result of COVID-19. This was extended at lower rates for a further six months.

The Hong Kong government introduced an Anti-epidemic Fund to implement targeted measures to support the construction industry, paying eligible consultants, contractors and subcontractors HKD50,000 (USD6,500) each and eligible construction workers HKD1,500 (USD200) each in the first round, with further payments to construction

17 Ibid, s 5(13).
18 Ibid, Part 2 Division 4.

workers, contractors and suppliers in the second round. Hong Kong also introduced the Employment Support Scheme of HKD81 billion (USD10 billion) to provide time-limited financial support to employers to retain their employees; the first tranche of the scheme provided wage subsidies for three months from June to August 2020.

The Philippines Government:

- Provided an emergency subsidy to around 18 m low-income households (minimum of PHP5,000.00 (USD100) and maximum of PHP8,000.00 (USD165))
- Provided health workers with a special risk allowance, in addition to the regular hazard pay given to health workers under the *Magna Carta of Public Health Workers* under R.A. No. 7305
- Directed the Philippine Health Insurance Corp to shoulder all medical expenses of public and private health workers exposed to COVID-19
- Provided compensation of PHP100,000.00 (USD2,000) to public and private healthcare workers who contracted severe COVID-19 while in the line of duty, and PHP1 m (USD20,000) to public and private healthcare workers who died while fighting the COVID-19 pandemic. [19]

12.8 Claims arising from COVID-19 under FIDIC Contracts

Early in the pandemic (April 2020) FIDIC issued the 'FIDIC COVID-19 Guidance Memorandum to Users of FIDIC Standard Forms of Works Contract'.[20] That Memorandum contains an outline of the provisions in FIDIC's standard forms of contract for works relevant to likely scenarios arising as a consequence of COVID-19:

> FIDIC's core purpose of drafting this Guidance Memorandum is to help Parties to a FIDIC contract to consider mutually satisfactory solutions and avoid disputes arising between them. COVID-19 pandemic is a unique broad scale and extraordinary event which should be recognized as such.

The Guidance Memorandum does not refer to any specific legal system or jurisdiction and cautions that the legal interpretation of the contract will depend upon matters such as the precise wording of the various documents in the Contract and the governing law. The Memorandum takes the approach of outlining a number of possible scenarios and suggests likely relevant responses by reference to relevant provisions of FIDIC contracts.

FIDIC's list of scenarios identifies the following circumstances that are expected to give rise to claims unique to the impact of COVID-19:

1. The local authorities/government do not promulgate any new piece of legislation or regulation banning construction activity or works on Site. However, the Contractor is facing difficulties in mobilizing personnel, who fear for their safety, and in obtaining Goods due to issues in the supply chain.
2. The Contractor is under the same circumstances as scenario No. 1 above. However, instead of facing difficulties in mobilizing personnel or obtaining

19 *Bayanihan to Heal as One Act* R. A. 11469 effective on 25 March 2020, s 4(c) (d) (e).

20 https://fidic.org/sites/default/files/COVID%2019%20Guidance%20Memorandum%20-%20PDF.pdf (accessed 15 March 2021).

Goods, the Contractor is suffering delays caused by the authorities (for example making repeated health and safety inspections on the Site).

3. The local authorities or government have promulgated changes to the Laws restricting construction activities and works on the Site. The Contractor is still able to proceed with the Works, however it is suffering delay and or incurring additional Cost as a result of those changes.
4. The local authorities/government have issued an order(s)/decree(s) preventing construction activities (including lockdown, curfew, inaccessible quarantined areas, etc), and execution of the Works on Site has now become impossible. Consequently, the Contractor and/or the Employer is prevented from performing obligations under the Contract.
5. Under scenario No. 4 above, can the Contractor subject this scenario to Clause 17 [Risk and Responsibility/Care of the Works and Indemnities]? Under Clause 17 the Contractor is entitled to a financial compensation in addition to an EOT, rather than only an EOT, when a natural *Force Majeure* or Exceptional Event occurs.
6. Under scenarios Nos. 1, 2, or 3, above, can the Employer or the Contractor resort to Clause 19 [Force Majeure], Clause 18 [Exceptional Events], or Clause 18 [Exceptional Risks] (in the relevant FIDIC contract as the case may be), to address such scenarios?
7. There has been no change in Laws of the Country nor real impact on the availability of personnel or on the supply chain so far. However, the personnel of the Employer (including the Engineer or the Employer's Representative, as the case may be) are, as a precaution, working remotely and hence are most of the time away from Site. As a consequence, the Contractor suffers delay and/or incurred additional Cost due to slow decision making. [21]

12.9 Dispute resolution

The spread of COVID-19 prompted government, judicial and other bodies around the globe to adopt measures responding to the need for greater flexibility and remote connectivity on the operation of courts and dispute resolution practice. The IBA documented the impact of COVID-19 on court operations and litigation practice in 37 countries.[22] The Chartered Institute of Arbitrators issued guidance for remote proceedings,[23] as did other arbitral institutions such as HKIAC[24] and AAA-ICDR.[25] The Dispute Resolution Board

21 Ibid.

22 'The Impact of COVID-19 on Court Operations and Litigation Practice' (June 2020), *International Bar Association* https://www.ibanet.org/Covid-19/Home.aspx (accessed 25 February 2021).

23 'Guidance Note on Remote Dispute Resolution Proceedings' (2020) *Chartered Institute of Arbitrators* https://www.ciarb.org/media/9013/remote-hearings-guidance-note_final_140420.pdf (accessed 25 February 2021).

24 'HKIAC Guidelines for Virtual Hearings' (2020) *HKIAC*.

25 'AAA-ICDR Virtual Hearing Guide for Arbitrators and Parties' (2020) *AAA-ICDR* https://go.adr.org/rs/294-SFS-516/images/AAA268_AAA%20Virtual%20Hearing%20Guide%20for%20Arbitrators%20and%20Parties.pdf (accessed 25 February 2021).

Foundation recognised the restrictions on in-person meetings during the pandemic and published best practice guidelines and a checklist for virtual Dispute Board proceedings.[26]

The use of different methods of dispute resolution for international construction disputes in the post-COVID-19 environment is discussed in more detail in Chapter 29.

26 'Best Practice Guidelines for Virtual Dispute Board Proceedings' (2020) *Dispute Resolution Board Foundation* http://www.disputeboard.org/wp-content/uploads/2020/07/Best-Practice-Guidelines-for-Virtual-Dispute-Board-Proceedings-5-August-2020.pdf (accessed 25 February 2021); 'Checklist for Dispute Board Members in Preparation for Virtual Dispute Board Proceedings' (2020) *Dispute Resolution Board Foundation* http://www.disputeboard.org/wp-content/uploads/2020/07/DRBF-Checklist-for-Virtual-DB-Proceedings-5-August-2020.pdf (accessed 25 February 2021)..

CHAPTER 13

Challenges in achieving successful megaprojects[1]

Dr Donald Charrett and Philip Loots

13.1 Introduction

Megaprojects are increasingly common around the world. For the purposes of this chapter a megaproject is a project with a capital cost in excess of USD1 b. Megaprojects are large-scale projects involving substantial capital expenditure and cash flow, and a correspondingly large design, procurement and construction workforce that must be appropriately managed. Further, the scale and number of interfaces in a megaproject necessarily imply a level of complexity greater than in smaller projects.

The financial significance of megaprojects to their owners is self-evident – they consume large amounts of capital that is invested for anticipated future income streams (in the case of private enterprises), or for the provision of efficient public infrastructure (in the case of government enterprises). Whether publicly or privately funded, project sponsors are looking for efficient deployment of capital to produce successful projects.

Notwithstanding the importance of megaprojects to their sponsoring organisations, and to the Contractors who build them, there are well-documented examples of unsuccessful megaprojects that have destroyed billions of dollars of capital.[2] The scale of such capital destruction in some cases has resulted in the insolvency of the sponsoring company or the Contractor. In a 2014 study of oil and gas megaprojects, Ernst & Young noted:

> Our comprehensive research into the performance of 365 megaprojects shows that despite the importance of project performance as it relates to enterprise value and share price, a high percentage of projects fail to deliver on time or meet approved budgets. While our research is a detailed review of current industry performance, longer-term industry outlooks suggest that project delivery success is actually decreasing, especially in certain segments of the industry, such as deepwater, where complexity is considerably higher.[3]

Detailed studies of construction projects around the world have revealed a disturbing fact: the success rate of megaprojects is less than the success rate of smaller projects. These studies have identified a number of factors that have contributed to the lack of megaproject success. This chapter discusses the findings of recent research in the hope that lessons can

1 This article was first published in *Construction Law International*, Vol 10 No 2, June 2015, and is reproduced by kind permission of the International Bar Association, London, UK. © International Bar Association.

2 For example, Merrow refers to the failure of BHP's Hot Briquetted Iron Project in 1999 that contributed to the company losing more than half of its market value, as well as unsuccessful projects conducted by Shell and BP that resulted in substantial capital losses: Edward W Merrow, *Industrial Megaprojects* (2011), 12.

3 Ernst & Young, *Spotlight on oil and gas megaprojects* (2014) 2.

 DOI: 10.4324/9781003206897-15

be learned from past unsuccessful projects to ensure that future megaprojects will have a higher likelihood of success.

13.2 Project success and failure

The authors have previously discussed examples of unsuccessful projects, where that term was applied to projects that did not fulfil their expectations, or more specifically, where there was an unacceptable difference between expected and observed performance.[4] This definition includes unacceptable shortcomings in the execution time, cost or quality of a project. In this context, quality encompasses not only the quality of construction in respect of materials and workmanship, but also the design and whether the completed project fulfils the expectations for functionality and performance.

Merrow assessed the success or failure of 318 industrial megaprojects (projects that make a product for sale with a total capital cost of more than USD1 b), based on a detailed analysis of their performance. In his assessment of these megaprojects, Merrow used measurable criteria to assess project success or failure. He characterises an industrial project as a failure if it exceeds one or more of the following cost, time and quality thresholds:

- Actual final cost exceeds the cost estimate made at the project sanction stage by more than 25%
- Project spends more than 25% greater than other projects with similar scopes
- The execution schedule slips more than 25% from the schedule forecast at project sanction
- The project execution schedule is greater than 50% more than the length of execution relative to similar projects
- There is significantly reduced production relative to that planned into the second year after mechanical completion.[5]

The reported outcome of this assessment is quite surprising. Only 35% of the megaprojects were successful, and these tended to be genuinely excellent projects on the time, cost and quality criteria. However, the 65% of megaprojects that were considered to be failures:

- Averaged 40% cost overrun whilst being very expensive in absolute terms
- Slipped their execution schedule by an average of 28% whilst being 15% slower than a competitive schedule, and
- Averaged only 65% of planned production in the first year.

The 140 projects in the oil and gas production sector (41% of the projects assessed) fared the worst of all. Of these megaprojects, 78% were assessed as failures: cost overruns averaged 33%, cost competitiveness was almost 40% more than the industry average,

4 Philip Loots and Donald Charrett, *Practical Guide to Engineering and Construction Contracts* (2009), 333–358.

5 Edward W Merrow, *Industrial Megaprojects* (2011), 37–38.

and nearly two-thirds suffered severe operability problems. Minerals megaprojects failed around 70% of the time, and had poor operability and cost growth.[6]

A survey of Australian construction projects in 2006 provided data on time and cost outcome of projects, based on quantitative research. Only 56% of all projects surveyed were completed on time; 66% of projects in the A$20–50m range were completed on time, whereas only 50% of projects valued at over A$500m were completed on time.[7] The 2006 survey revealed that 38% of projects were completed over budget. D&C contracts performed better than construct-only projects in this regard: 33% of D&C projects exceeded their budget, by an average of 15%, whereas 46% of construct-only projects exceeded their budget, by an average of 19%.[8]

13.3 Australian research

A major Australian law firm collaborated with the Australian Constructors Association in 2006, 2008, 2011 and 2014 (and with Infrastructure Partnerships Australia in 2006, 2008 and 2011) to carry out surveys of the Australian construction industry that were reported in four "Scope for Improvement Reports" (**SfIR**).[9] These surveys involved more than 120 respondents, representing the spectrum of participants in Australian construction and infrastructure projects: public and private sector Employers, Contractors, consultants, financiers and industry bodies.

The SfIR are valuable not only for their identification of issues that have contributed to unsuccessful projects, but for their constructive suggestions as to how these issues can be addressed to achieve more successful projects in the future. The timeframe spanned by these reports covered the build up to and execution of an unprecedented number and scale of megaprojects in the Australian resources industry. For example, there were seven LNG plants with a total capital value of over A$200b under construction in early 2015.

The 2006 Report identified five "pressure points" – issues that inhibit project delivery and create stress on a project or its participants. The 2014 Report also identified five pressure points, three of which were in the 2006 Report:

- A shortage of skilled resources
- Inadequate scoping, and
- Poor risk allocation.

Two new pressure points were identified in 2014: productivity and costs of tendering. These issues, and the shortage of skilled resources, are specific to Australian conditions, and may be related to the unprecedented demands on the construction industry arising from the boom conditions. Productivity and the shortage of appropriately skilled resources

6 Edward W Merrow, *Industrial Megaprojects* (2011), 48–49.

7 Blake Dawson Waldron Lawyers, *Scope for Improvement: A Survey of Pressure Points in Australian Construction and Infrastructure Projects* (2006), 24.

8 Ibid 24–26.

9 Blake Dawson Waldron Lawyers, *Scope for Improvement: A Survey of Pressure Points in Australian Construction and Infrastructure Projects* (2006); Blake Dawson, *Scope for Improvement 2008: A Report on Scoping Practices in Australian and Infrastructure Projects* (2008); Blake Dawson, *Scope for Improvement 2011: Project Risk – Getting the Right Balance and Outcomes* (2011); Ashurst Australia, *Scope for Improvement 2014: Project Pressure Points – Where Industry Stands* (2014).

may impact the competitiveness of Australian megaprojects with those in alternative locations. However, they are external to any particular project; as longer-term issues, they need to be addressed on an industry-wide basis.

13.4 International research

Merrow identified seven key mistakes that companies make in developing and executing megaprojects:

- Project sponsors endeavouring to retain all the benefits of a project without adequate regard to the legitimate interests of other stakeholders
- An aggressive project schedule that does not pay sufficient attention to project requirements
- Project development carried out without alignment with the underlying business deal
- Insufficient time and money invested in investigating the project's viability and feasibility prior to the final investment decision to sanction the project
- Reducing cost estimates to satisfy investment criteria
- Transfer of cost and schedule risk to Contractors, and
- Terminating project managers of projects which overrun their budgets.[10]

13.5 What can be done to improve megaproject outcomes?

The various studies referred to have identified a number of issues that need to be addressed to improve project outcomes. This chapter focuses on just two: scoping and risk allocation, issues that are within the control of the Employer. These issues were addressed in detail in the 2008 and 2011 SfIR respectively.

13.5.1 Project scoping

Scoping is the process of determining the contractual expression of an owner's project requirements. It involves the identification of the fundamental objectives of the project; development of the project requirements in the form of functional and performance outcomes and/or specific technical requirements to achieve those objectives; selection of the most appropriate contractual model and risk profile; and translation of these requirements into appropriate contractual scope documents for the project.[11]

Merrow uses the term "**front end loading**" for the period in which the scope and execution detail of a project are defined before a final investment decision is made. He notes that adequate front end loading is expensive (3–5% of project cost), but is essential to successful projects as it drives cost and schedule predictability, and minimises operational problems. The writers concur with Merrow, who considers that scope development, the

10 Edward W Merrow, *Industrial Megaprojects* (2011), 2–8.

11 Ashurst Australia, *Scope for Improvement 2014: Project Pressure Points – Where Industry Stands* (2014), 31.

second of the three phases of front end loading, is the most important stage in any project's development.[12]

Preparation of the project scope is based, implicitly and explicitly, on the required "quality", which includes performance, functionality, durability, maintainability and operability. Selection of the appropriate quality will often involve a trade-off in determining the appropriate balance between schedule, cost and quality. A clear, well-defined project scope is necessary to produce a realistic cost estimate. It follows that cost estimates produced prior to project scoping will be unreliable. Further, if the scope subsequently changes, the costs will inevitably change.

The same applies in relation to the project schedule – a reliable schedule can only be prepared when the project scope has been defined. Subsequent significant changes in scope indicate that the project schedule will need to be reassessed in the light of those changes, which may impact the time in which the scope can practicably be executed.

Thus, in one sense, quality is an input into the scoping exercise, and cost and schedule are outputs from the process. However, as is well known, there can be a complex trade-off between time, cost and quality in a project. Merrow presents a graph showing how changes in a project's internal rate of return are related to changes in operability ("quality"), capital cost and schedule. This graph shows, for a target 15% real return on investment and constant market factors, that operability and capital costs have a far greater impact on internal rate of return than schedule. For example, a 30% growth in capital cost results in investment returns of less than 10%, below a typical company's cost of capital. However, it would take more than a 5% schedule improvement for every 1% of additional cost for the return to be investment neutral.[13] Sometimes the additional cost of acceleration is necessary to address the bigger risk of failure to honour product sales contracts because of delayed completion.

Merrow emphasises that the targets for cost, schedule and quality must be established at the point when they are at least feasible in principle and will result in a valuable outcome for the project. He identifies three misguided trade-offs that frequently result in project failure:

- Quality is sacrificed for low cost
- Cost is sacrificed for fast schedules; and
- Quality is sacrificed for fast schedules.[14]

The 2006 SfIR highlighted that poor scoping at the outset of a project almost inevitably resulted in cost overruns, delayed completion and disputes. The 2008 SfIR identified a number of factors that result in poor scoping of Australian construction and infrastructure projects:

- Lack of experienced and sufficiently competent personnel.
- Insufficient time to prepare the scope documents.

12 Edward W Merrow, *Industrial Megaprojects* (2011), 101.
13 Ibid 108.
14 Ibid 110.

- Inadequate definition of project objectives by the Employer, resulting in subsequent changes to the scope.
- Corrections to scope documents.
- Lack of consultation with end users.
- Insufficient site information.[15]

The 2008 SfIR identified 16 practical steps for successful scoping, consistent with many of the front-end loading issues identified by Merrow, including:

- Clearly identify project objectives.
- Bring together all relevant stakeholders and end users for the project.
- Set realistic timeframes and budgets.
- Interface the proposed project with related projects and existing infrastructure.
- Manage the interplay between project scoping and the statutory environmental and planning approval process.
- Clearly describe the project objective and requirements once identified.
- Choose the right approach for scope description.
- Choose the right contract delivery model.[16]

The consequences of inadequate scoping of a project before a construction contract is entered into are well known. Changes to scope during construction are inevitably disruptive, time-consuming and costly to implement via variations. Further, they frequently lead to disputes that are a distraction to the parties' project delivery aspirations, are time-consuming and expensive to resolve, and adversely impact their working relationship.

These consequences were revealed in the 2008 SfIR: 61% of respondents said that inadequate scope documents resulted in a cost overrun, with more than half of those overruns costing more than 10% of the value of the project and a third more than 20%. For megaprojects with a value of over A$1b, approximately one-quarter experienced a cost overrun of more than 20% of project value because of inadequacies in scope documents.

Loots & Charrett have suggested that the use of "price" as the determining factor in construction procurement decisions is wrong, and that it should at least be replaced with a resourced schedule as the dominant parameter in bid evaluation.[17] Bid evaluation based predominantly on a resourced construction schedule will materially improve the prospects of completion on time and on budget. As noted by Merrow, resource loading the schedule evaluates whether the project is actually feasible as planned and whether the contractor tendering to execute the project actually understands the job.[18]

15 Blake Dawson, *Scope for Improvement 2008: A Report on Scoping Practices in Australian and Infrastructure Projects* (2008), 7–8.

16 Ibid 8–9.

17 Philip Loots and Donald Charrett, "Reconsidering Project Procurement Criteria and Procedures for Major Infrastructure Projects" (2017) 1 *International Construction Law Review* 70.

18 Edward W Merrow, *Industrial Megaprojects* (2011), 319, 320.

13.5.2 Risk

The definition of risk in Australian Standard AS4360:2004 is "the chance of something happening that will have an impact on objectives". Whilst that definition includes positive as well as negative impacts, consideration of risk in construction contracts usually refers to adverse impacts. A variety of risks are inherent in any construction project, and they need to be identified, allocated and managed.

It is a widely accepted principle that in a construction contract, each risk should be allocated to that party in the best position to manage and control it (the Abrahamson Principles). It is also generally accepted that for each risk assumed by the Contractor in a construction contract, a rational Contractor will include the "price" of that risk in its tender price. The price that a Contractor puts on a particular risk will however vary with market circumstances. In the authors' view, under certain market conditions, not all Contractors can be expected to be "rational", so bid evaluation procedures should make appropriate allowances for this.

Risks need to be identified before they can be allocated or managed, and the time to do that is during the scoping process. One of the potential consequences of applying inadequate time and resources to the preparation of a project scope is that significant risks may not be identified. The 2011 SfIR stated that in nearly 30% of projects, key risks were first identified only after contract signing.

The allocation of risks between Employer and Contractor is an area of significant contention. As the party generally preparing the tender and contract documents, the Employer is normally the one that determines the allocation of risks in the construction contract. For a variety of reasons, Employers are increasingly reluctant to assume many risks that, traditionally, have been their responsibility. Many Contractors feel that they are inappropriately forced to assume many risks that they are unable to control or manage. Further, the competitive tendering environment means that they are unable to appropriately price these risks. Allocation of risks is discussed in Section 4.7.

Respondents in the 2011 SfIR identified the following key risks as commonly allocated in an inappropriate manner:

- Time for completion/delay
- Design
- Scope inadequacies, and
- Site conditions.

Various consequences may arise from the inappropriate allocation of risks, and these will vary depending on the economic and individual circumstances. In a sellers' market, a Contractor will put a high price on risks to ensure that its profit margin is preserved in the event that the risks eventuate. To the extent that risks do not eventuate, the Employer has paid a high "insurance" price that results in a windfall profit to the Contractor, an outcome that may be acceptable to the Employer. Conversely, in a buyers' market where the Contractor has not adequately priced the risks (because of competition for contracts or because the risks have not been identified), the Employer makes a windfall gain by not paying for the real cost of the risks. However, that windfall gain comes with a new set of risks for both Employer and Contractor, arising from the Contractor being unable or unwilling to perform its contractual obligations.

Where unpriced (or inadequately priced) risks eventuate, the Contractor may suffer substantial delay and/or monetary loss that put quality, schedule and completion at risk. Such circumstances will inevitably result in additional claims that have to be managed, and may also trigger a formal dispute. In a worst-case scenario, where the Contractor has insufficient balance sheet strength to absorb the loss, the Employer may be forced to terminate the contract. The consequences of inappropriate risk allocation are discussed in Section 4.7.3.

Management of risks during the execution of a project is an ongoing exercise. There are a variety of appropriate project and contract management tools that need to be applied. Many provisions in modern construction contracts are written to ensure that risks are appropriately managed when they do eventuate. Early warnings, strict time limits on notification of events or circumstances, risk registers, timely processing of claims and formal monthly reports are just some of the tools currently used. The formal procedures for contract administration in many modern construction contracts define a process for good risk and project management. Complying with them is not only required as a matter of law, it will also minimise the adverse consequences arising from the materialisation of risks.

13.6 Conclusion

Various studies have shown that, notwithstanding their high cost and importance, megaprojects have a poor track record of performance, not only in absolute terms, but also with respect to projects of lesser value. The evidence shows that, when properly executed, megaprojects can be an outstanding success. However, the substantial number of megaprojects that have failed on time, cost and quality criteria suggest that we should be learning their lessons so that future megaprojects will be more successful.

This chapter has touched on two important issues that are important for the success of any project, but are critical to the success of megaprojects.

The proper definition of the scope is the essential foundation of a megaproject. Without it, the Employer will not have defined its fundamental project objectives, nor will it have incorporated its requirements in appropriate contractual form. Inadequately prepared scope is likely to lead to expensive and time-consuming variations, delay, claims and possible disputes. Proper scoping requires adequate and appropriately skilled resources, and sufficient time to comprehensively identify all the relevant issues.

Project risks are those issues that have the potential to adversely impact the anticipated project outcomes. They need to be identified at the earliest stage during scoping, appropriately allocated to one of the contracting parties (preferably the one best placed to manage and control them), and then managed appropriately with adequate resources during project execution. Adherence to the formal contract requirements for notification of issues, regular reporting and claims procedures are generally fundamental to successfully managing those risks that, inevitably, materialise during the execution of any megaproject.

CHAPTER 14

Sydney Opera House – quality, quality, quality![1]

14.1 Introduction

The Sydney Opera House is undoubtedly Australia's most iconic building, and one of the most recognised buildings in the world. Frank Gehry said of this building that it "changed the image of an entire country".[2]

The Sydney Opera House was included on the UNESCO World Heritage List under the World Heritage Convention in 2007, placing it alongside the Taj Mahal, the ancient pyramids of Egypt and the great Wall of China as one of the most outstanding places on earth. The UNESCO report said: "Sydney Opera House stands by itself as one of the indisputable masterpieces of human creativity, not only in the 20th century but in the history of humankind".[3]

The history of the procurement, design and construction of this building is a rich tapestry of events, containing many issues of interest to construction lawyers more than half a century on. Of the triad of issues that make up every construction project – time, cost and quality – the Sydney Opera House demonstrated both the consequences of focusing almost exclusively on quality (initially), and subsequently of elevating the requirements of time and cost over quality.

14.2 Procurement

The concept of a Sydney Opera House was promoted by influential people from the late 1940s, but it took a visionary Premier of New South Wales to turn the concept into reality. In 1955, the government announced that Bennelong Point was the site for the new Opera House. At that time, it was occupied by a tram shed built at the turn of the 20th century.

After taking advice from the Royal Australian Institute of Architects, a worldwide architectural competition was held in 1956. The winning entry was designed by Danish architect Jørn Utzon, who was appointed the architect for the project.

The Sydney Opera House was procured in three stages:

1 This article was first published in [2017] *Construction Law International* 12 No 3, September 2017, and is reproduced by kind permission of the International Bar Association, London, UK. © International Bar Association.

2 https://www.sydneyoperahouse.com/our-story.html (accessed 15 March 2021).

3 https://www.sydneyoperahouse.com (accessed 15 March 2021).

DOI: 10.4324/9781003206897-16

- Stage 1: foundations, substructure and podium
- Stage 2: the "shells" enclosing the performance halls and restaurant
- Stage 3: the interiors.

The initial 1957 estimate for construction of the Sydney Opera House was AUD7 million and about five years, based on the estimate of a quantity surveyor who had no experience with this type of construction. To be fair, no one had any experience with this type of construction, because nothing like this had ever been built before. However, this initial estimate was the source of ongoing public and political controversy, as the cost and time of construction continued to expand.

The building was funded by the Sydney Opera House lottery, established in 1957 before any construction had commenced, and the income from this lottery eventually paid for the entire cost of the building.[4]

Following a change of government in 1965, the incoming Minister for Works sought to exercise more government control, purportedly to better manage the cost and time of construction. In the event, Utzon resigned, and the design and construction of Stage 3 was carried out under another architect. The result was that the interiors of the Sydney Opera House were not completed in accordance with Utzon's design concept.

14.3 Design concept

In November 1954, the "father" of the Opera House, Premier Joe Cahill, appointed a small working committee to progress the project and make recommendations to the government. In February 1956, the 25-page competition booklet was released to the world's architects, who were required to register their interest by mid-March. Eight hundred and eighty-one competitors registered, representing 45 countries. By the closing date of 3 December 1956, 222 entries had been received from 28 countries, including 65 from Australia and 51 from England.

The judging panel comprised four architects: two Australian architects and two world renowned architects from overseas – one with a modern outlook and one with a conservative outlook. Judging took place over ten days, and winning entry number 218 was announced on 29 January 1957. Jørn Utzon's prize was AUD10,000.

The Sydney Morning Herald's headline was "Dane's Controversial Design Wins Opera House Contest". According to that newspaper, the chairman of the judging panel stated that quantitative (sic) surveyors had examined the plans of the ten leading entries and the winning entry was by far the cheapest to build. The two international judges said that although the drawings of the winning design were simple to the point of being diagrammatic, "we are convinced that they present a concept of an Opera House which is capable of being one of the great buildings of the world. Because of its very originality, it is clearly a controversial design. We are, however, absolutely convinced about its merits."

Utzon's simple prize-winning drawings "emphasise the contrast of a solid base, terraced with the stepped auditorium levels carried across the width of the platform to create

4 Daryl Dellora, *Utzon and the Sydney Opera House* (Penguin Books Australia, 2013).

a sculptured terrain, and floating shell roofs which step up to accommodate the volumes within them".[5]

His conception was of the roof "shells" as clouds that appear to float above the platform without touching it. In the competition drawings, the concrete shells were a mere 100 mm thick. In the postwar period when building materials were in short supply, thin concrete shell structures became very popular. Their economy derives from resisting external forces by compression within the thickness of the shell; however, they are unable to resist bending arising from discontinuities of shape.

Utzon's sketches

> showed roof shapes which were lyrical and beautiful. It was a sculptural building, elegant in appearance from every aspect, sheer joy to behold. The roof shapes were described at the time as poetry, shapes the like of which had never been built before. They broke all the engineering rules of shell design.[6]

Significantly, the sketches were free-form, and not based on any geometrical construct. There had been no engineering input prior to the announcement of the winning shell design. It is apparent that the judge's comment that Utzon's design would be the cheapest to build was based on the concept of thin concrete shells.

14.4 Structural design

The architect and engineers worked together to derive mathematically definable shapes for the shells that were then capable of being analysed. The mathematical calculations involved in analysing the stresses and deflections in just one defined geometrical shape of "shell" were complicated and time-consuming.

Over the period from 1958 to 1963 the original freehand drawn single skin reinforced concrete shells went through 11 iterations before the final design was complete with all working drawings. These iterations included consideration of parabolic, circular and ellipsoidal schemes, before the final spherical scheme was adopted. The late 1961 conceptual breakthrough that made analysis and construction of the shells feasible and efficient was Utzon's idea of making each member a segment of a sphere of 75 m radius. The ribs that make up each main shell all radiate from a point or pole near the support of the shell. They have varying cross-sections along their length, but the cross-sections of all ribs at the same arc length from the pole are the same. This enabled considerable economies in construction.

Figure 14.1 shows a small bronze sculpture placed in the forecourt of the Sydney Opera House to illustrate the simple geometry of the final spherical scheme. The plaque on this sculpture contains the following quote from Jørn Utzon explaining the 1961 conceptual breakthrough:

> I call this my 'key to the shells' because it solves all the problems of construction by opening up for mass production, precision in manufacture and simple erection and with this geometrical system I attain full harmony between all the shapes in this fantastic complex.

---

5 On the history of the design, see Anne Watson (ed), *Building a Masterpiece: The Sydney Opera House* (Lund Humphries, 2006) 71.

6 Ibid, 105.

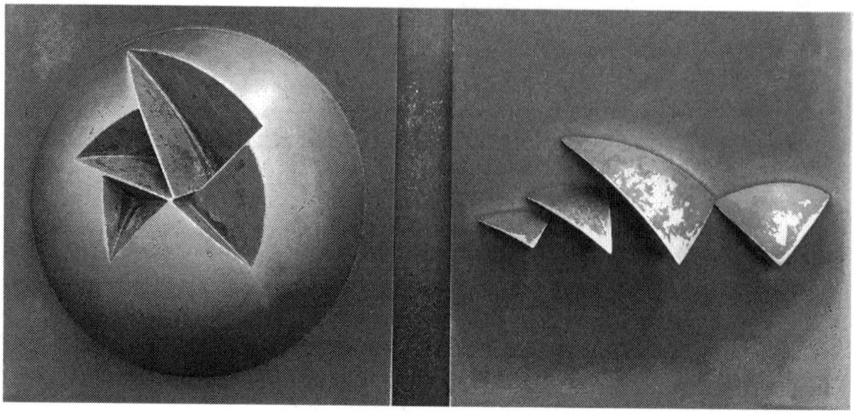

FIGURE 14.1 Model showing how the different size shells all have the same radius ribs

Structural concepts investigated included single skin reinforced concrete shells with ribs, double skin reinforced concrete shells with two-way ribs and steel spaceframe with reinforced concrete skin, before finally settling on precast concrete ribs and partial in-situ concrete.

Given the complex geometry, there were no analytical precedents to follow, and no routine calculation methods available. The complexity forced the design team to source large-scale computing power.

In 1958, computers were in their infancy; they were very large, very expensive, and did not have user-friendly interfaces. At that stage there was still a choice between analogue computers and digital computers for carrying out mathematical computations. The use of computers in engineering design offices was unknown, and slide rules were used for most mathematical calculations.

The structural engineers, Ove Arup & Partners, obtained access to the most powerful computers available, at enormous cost. As there was no application software available, the engineers had to write their own software programs from scratch. This entailed considerable risks, such as whether the answers were correct or the algorithms for the basic geometric functions correctly coded for all extremes of data. Whilst the computer performed complex mathematical calculations in a fraction of the time that humans would have taken, the engineers had the responsibility of ensuring that the resulting designs were consistent with their estimates of construction material performance and equation solution. The Arup engineers had a maxim that is equally applicable today: "if you don't know the order of magnitude of the answer, don't use the computer".[7] In other words, computer output should be consistent with what is expected, not implicitly believed and retrospectively justified.

In addition to the calculations for the shells, computers were extensively used for the analysis of the complex prestressed concrete podium beams. These beams were shaped and folded like the hulls of boats, had a kink along their length and spanned approximately

7 Ibid, 89.

50 m. The complex calculations for these beams ensured that their cross-sections were an optimum design, with material where it was most needed.

The complex glass façade infills to the shells also required considerable computation to determine the length of every supporting member, the angle of cut of each piece of glass at its ends, the position of the bolts, the shape of each connection to the shell rib and the size and shape of every sheet of glass, as well as the forces on them.

Arup staff estimated that by 1967, they had used 2,000 computer hours, work which would have taken an estimated 100 million hours if done manually. The central role of computers in the design of the Sydney Opera House was summed up by the following statement from Ove Arup and Jack Zunz, a partner responsible for the Sydney Opera House project:

> With hindsight, it is felt that the shells would probably not have been built without the use of computers. We could not have produced the mass of information, let alone the analytical work, necessary to erect the building in the time available.[8]

In addition to the extensive use of computers for calculation, two physical models were tested. A wooden model was tested for wind pressure distribution in the wind tunnels at Southampton University and the National Physical Laboratory London. And a 1:60 Perspex roof model was tested at Southampton University. That model was loaded with weights and the stresses measured by means of strain gauges recorded at an electrical console. The testing took nine months and required a computer to analyse the output from the large number of strain gauges.

14.5 Construction

Political imperatives dictated that construction at Bennelong Point should start as early as possible, before a forthcoming State election. The tram sheds were demolished in 1958, and construction of Stage 1 (foundations and podium) by Civil & Civic contractors commenced in March 1959. Included within the Stage 1 works were approximately 1,000 rooms, including theatres, stage areas and public lobbies below the podium level.

Ove Arup & Partners were only engaged in November 1958 and had limited time to carry out the structural design of the foundations and podium to support the as-yet-undefined shells. Accordingly, the initial foundation design was based on estimates of dead load for thin concrete shells, of the order of 100 mm thick.

However, the Opera House shells as ultimately designed were not concrete shells millimetres thick, but massive concrete space frame structures with arch ribs metres thick. The substantially greater weight of concrete structure required a redesign of the already constructed substructure, necessitating driving additional piles at considerable expense. There were also many other design changes as the functions of the building developed while construction was being carried out. A salutary lesson on the consequences of "fast track" construction, that is, commencing construction before the design is finalised!

In 1963, MR Hornibrook was awarded the contract for Stage 2 – construction of the shells. This contract was let on a cost reimbursement plus fee basis, eminently sensible given the unique nature of the construction task, and the many unknowns. The Contractor

8 Ibid, 85.

was involved early so that it could influence the design, and it worked closely with the engineers to develop the construction strategy.

The Stage 2 Contractor had to devise a practical and economical method of constructing the roof. The ribs comprising each shell were made up of a number of precast concrete segments, epoxy-glued and post-tensioned together. A total of 2,194 segments were cast in steel forms on site. As each of the segments had the same curvature based on the spherical geometry, the same moulds could be used for segments ranging from the T-shaped sections 1,200 mm deep and 400 mm wide near the springing, to a Y-shaped section 2,033 mm deep by 3,660 mm wide at the top of the longest rib. Each of these segments had to be lifted by a large crane and temporarily supported prior to completion of an arch. The Contractor devised a travelling erection arch that enabled scaffolding to be dispensed with. This comprised a steel lattice truss, curved to the same shape as the roof ribs, and able to telescope and twist to accommodate the ribs of varying length and each half arch lying in a different plane. Design development and testing of this erection arch took 18 months.

Figures 14.2–14.7 show the stages of construction in 1964 and 1965. Figures 14.3 and 14.4 show the in-situ concrete ribs for the start of the roof shell construction have been placed on the podium structure. Figure 14.5 shows the substantial podium structure supporting the shell roofs, viewed from the west. Figures 14.6 and 14.7 show the partially constructed shells in 1965. The structure of the ribs can be seen, subsequently covered by the roof tiles.

The concept and shape of the glass walls changed after Utzon's departure in 1965. Laminated glass was used, though it had never been used before in such sizes. Because of the long delivery time of cut glass from the manufacturer in France, a glass factory was

FIGURE 14.2 Construction of the Sydney Opera House in 1965, with the podium beams in the foreground

FIGURE 14.3 Construction of the Sydney Opera House in 1964, taken from Sydney Harbour Bridge

FIGURE 14.4 The in-situ concrete ribs that subsequently supported the precast concrete ribs for the roof shells

FIGURE 14.5 The podium structure with the first in-situ concrete ribs constructed

FIGURE 14.6 Construction of the shells of Sydney Opera House in 1965, viewed from the west

FIGURE 14.7 Construction of the shells of Sydney Opera House in 1965, viewed from the north

established on site. Slightly oversized rectangular sheets of glass were supplied, and then cut to size on site.

Figure 14.8 shows a part of the complex glass wall at the northern end of the main hall, enclosing a promenade with magnificent views of Sydney Harbour and the Harbour Bridge.

14.6 Issues with time and cost

As noted above, the original cost estimate was AUD7 million, and a five-year construction period, based on a quantity surveyor's estimate. At that stage, the roof concept was for thin concrete shells.

Construction of Stage 1 commenced in March 1959. The time and cost of this construction stage was undoubtedly increased by the additional piling required after the actual dead load of the final design was determined. In 1962, a new estimate put the cost of the Opera House at AUD27.5 million. Following the change of government in 1965, the new Minister for Works advised a cost estimate of AUD49.4 million and a completion date of 1969. By 1968, the Minister announced an estimated cost of AUD85 million and opening in 1972. When Queen Elizabeth II opened the Opera House on 20 October 1973, the final cost had reached AUD100 million.

FIGURE 14.8 The glass wall at the northern end of the main hall

14.7 Change of architect and its consequences

The change of government in 1965 resulted in a new Minister of Works with oversight of the Opera House project. There had been considerable media attention and public controversy over the escalating costs. The new Minister was determined to find a solution to the cost escalation, and apparently had very different ideas on how the Opera House was to be completed. Working relations with the architect broke down.

In the face of very large unpaid fees, Utzon wrote to the Minister on 28 February 1966 stating that he had been forced to leave the job. Instead of negotiating an appropriate resolution, the Minister immediately accepted the resignation, and issued a press statement to that effect. Utzon left Australia within a few weeks, never to return. It is interesting to speculate on what the outcome might have been if Utzon had had access to rapid adjudication of his fee disputes, as would now be available under security of payment legislation.

In the event, in 1968 Utzon initiated proceedings in the Supreme Court, seeking AUD350,000 for outstanding fees. This action was settled in 1974 for AUD46,000. The government and Utzon agreed that neither party was at fault, and that there would be no further claims. The settlement amount brought the total fees earned by Utzon in relation to the architectural work to AUD1,250,000.[9]

Professional and public opinion was mobilised to try to have Utzon reinstated. Despite a vigorous public campaign conducted over nearly two years, supported by many leading architects, the Minister was unrelenting. A new architect was appointed, Peter Hall, who until recently had been with the Public Works Department.

Although it has since transpired that Utzon and Hall did have discussions, the new architect essentially started with a clean sheet of paper and designed the interiors of the theatres and the glass walls (Stage 3) from scratch. Thus, neither the interiors nor the glass walls are Utzon's concept or designs. All the conceptual work that Utzon had carried out, and his holistic design of exteriors and interiors of the Opera House, came to nothing.

14.8 Refurbishment

In 1999, the New South Wales government effected a reconciliation with Utzon and engaged him as design consultant on the Opera House upgrade program. In 2002, Utzon produced the "Utzon Design Principles" as a permanent reference for the long-term management and conservation of the building. A conservation management plan incorporating the Utzon Design Principles has been developed that will guide any future adaptation of the Opera House.

The NSW Government committed AUD200 million for the Opera House Renewal project, which includes:

- Concert hall upgrades to improve acoustics, accessibility, stage and backstage areas, and replace worn-out theatre systems
- A new creative learning centre to give children and young people a space to experiment and learn
- Entry and foyer upgrades to transform the area under the monumental steps into a vibrant, welcoming, car-free entrance and meeting place, and
- A new function centre to celebrate significant events and mark important occasions for community and government events.

Including several upgrades to the Joan Sutherland Theatre, a total of AUD273 million was allocated for the first stage of the Renewal. One of its important themes is to respect the heritage and integrity of the building in accordance with the Utzon Design Principles, the Conservation Management Plan and consultation with the Eminent Architects Panel and Conservation Council.

9 'Utzon's opera house claim settled', *The Canberra Times* (23 June 1970).

14.9 Conclusion

Sydney Opera House is not only notable for its unique and world-renowned sculptural architecture, its design and construction were at the cutting edge of available technology. In the words of the engineers, "it was undoubtedly the first computer-design and building of significant scale which could not have been built without the use of computers".

Because of its unique shape, none of the traditional details of building or bridge construction applied, and all had to be researched and developed from first principles. Its many "firsts" included:

- Factory manufacture and erection of large precast concrete units
- Pre-calculation of all dimensions down to the positions of the last bolt and hole
- Epoxy jointing of matched concrete segments
- Development of cement grouts based on investigations using radioactive trace elements, and
- Large-scale use of walls and roofs with laminated glass.

The architect's and engineers' relentless focus on the quality of the building achieved the World Heritage icon that we know today, and which will be enjoyed by others for hundreds of years. The change of focus to "controlling" time and cost ultimately did no such thing, and the change of Architect for Stage 3 resulted in interiors and glass walls that are substantially different from Utzon's holistic design concepts.

FIGURE 14.9 The western side of the Opera House in 2017

FIGURE 14.10 The eastern side of the Opera House showing the shells over the two main halls

The international architectural profession recognised Utzon's brilliant design and execution of the Opera House by bestowing on him the world's top architectural award, the Pritzker Prize, in 2003.

Figures 14.9 and 14.10 show the completed Opera House from two different angles that illustrate the striking shapes of the roof "shells".

CHAPTER 15

Managing time, cost and quality – a tale of two buildings[1]

15.1 Introduction

Successful project management of the delivery of a building involves managing the three elements of time, cost and quality to the satisfaction of the Employer. Conversely, a perceived shortcoming in one or more of those elements in the procurement of a building project will be seen by the Employer as a "failure" – "an unacceptable difference between expected and observed performance".[2] That is, an Employer may perceive the outcome of a building project to be a failure if the project cost more than anticipated, took longer to complete than anticipated or the final quality fell below expectations.

Engineering or building failures in the more generally accepted sense of structural failure capture the public's attention, particularly when they result in significant loss of life. However, "failures" in the broader sense as defined above are also newsworthy, particularly if they involve publicly funded buildings or infrastructure. Cost overruns and late delivery of public infrastructure are virtually certain to be subject to public scrutiny. Such public attention can in turn capture the attention of politicians who can be subjected to considerable political pressure to "do something". That "something" not infrequently takes the form of a public enquiry or investigation, sometimes a Royal Commission. Further, substantial Government expenditure is usually subject to scrutiny by an independent Auditor.

The theme of this chapter is the lessons that can be learned from the delivery of two seminal building projects – the Australian Parliament House in Canberra (**APH**), and the Scottish Parliament House in Edinburgh (**SPH**). Whilst these projects were completed at different times (1988 and 2004 respectively), and in different countries, it will be seen that there are many common factors, including the method of project delivery. APH received significant adverse comments on the cost and time management of the construction by the Auditor General, who published a critical "Efficiency Audit".[3] After completion of the building, the Parliament House Construction Authority (**PHCA**) prepared its own publication documenting the history of the project and the lessons learned, and rebutting the

1 This chapter is an edited version of the paper published in: Donald Charrett, 'Managing time, cost and quality – a tale of two buildings' (2007) 28 *BDPS News* 10. It is reproduced by permission of the Building Dispute Practitioner's Society.

2 G A Leonards, 'Investigation of Structural Failures' (1982) No GT2 (February) *Journal of the Geotechnical Engineering Division (ASCE)* 108.

3 Commonwealth, *Parliament House Construction Authority: construction project management*, Parl Paper No 147 (1987).

DOI: 10.4324/9781003206897-17

Auditor General's criticisms.[4] There was, however, no independent public enquiry as such into the procurement of APH. The procurement of SPH was also the subject of examination by the Scottish Auditor General on two occasions, in 2000 when construction was at an early stage,[5] and in 2004 near the end of the project.[6] Further, no doubt as a consequence of the publicity given to the substantial time and cost overruns of SPH, there was a public enquiry into all aspects of the procurement of SPH conducted by Lord Fraser, building on the Auditor General's findings.[7] The sources of the following comments on these two high-profile public buildings was derived from these public documents.

It should be emphasised that neither of these two buildings could be considered a "failure" in the traditional sense, nor is it suggested that there was any shortfall in the expected quality of either building. These buildings are both architectural award-winning very high-quality nationally symbolic buildings, providing an environment for the complex workings of democratic parliaments, accessible by the people. It is however arguable that the substantial cost overrun for SPH constituted a "failure" in that there was an unacceptable difference between the budget cost and the final as constructed cost, as well as an unacceptable difference between the scheduled date for completion and the actual date of completion. Whether or not the final cost and time of delivery of APH constituted a "failure" depends on whether the view of the Auditor General or the PHCA is accepted.

15.2 Similarities in delivery of the Australian Parliament House and the Scottish Parliament House

Clearly, no two buildings on different sites, let alone in different countries, with different functional requirements and constructed at different times, can be directly comparable. However, the following factors relevant to the project delivery method and its implementation were similar for these two buildings:

- Construction of a long-lasting Parliament building as a National Symbol.
- Procurement and project management by civil servants responsible to the Government and Parliament.
- Architect selected after an international design competition.
- Emphasis on very high building quality, both as a functioning, long-lasting durable building, and as a showcase for local craftspeople, artisans and artists.
- Procurement and construction by a Construction Manager who managed the construction by letting and administering a large number of trade subcontracts.
- A very tight construction programme that could only be achieved through fast track construction in which construction was commenced before the design was complete.

4 Parliament House Construction Authority, Commonwealth, *Project Parliament: the Management Experience* (1990).

5 Auditor General, Scotland, *The new Scottish Parliament building An examination of the management of the Holyrood project* (2000).

6 Audit Scotland, *Management of the Holyrood building project* (2004).

7 Scotland, *A Report by the Rt Hon Lord Fraser of Carmyllie QC, The Holyrood Inquiry*, SP Paper No 205 (2004).

- Changed user requirements, including significant increase in space after the design had been commenced.
- Considerable public scrutiny of achievement of time, cost and quality targets.
- Architect's pursuit of excellence, notwithstanding the (largely unsuccessful) Project Manager's attempts to impose budgetary constraints.

15.3 Australian Parliament House

15.3.1 Procurement

An international design competition was held in 1979 to select the design for Australia's new Parliament House. Key aspects of the competition brief were:

- Budget cost $151m in May 1978 prices.
- Building to be opened on Australia Day 1988.
- Usable area of 60,300 m^2 for 188 Parliamentarians, 124 Representatives and 64 Senators.
- High-quality materials and finishes.
- National symbol.
- Building to last 200 years.

No doubt mindful of the possible time and cost consequences of innovative structural design (e.g. Sydney Opera House,[8] 1976 Montréal Olympic Stadium), an early decision was taken that the structure was to be conventional, using existing technology. Nevertheless, there were substantial challenges "which derived from the building's massive size, extensive range of facilities, number of advanced electronic systems, tight program, shortage of resources, extensive approval process and quality standards".[9] The site for the building covers 32 ha, and the building itself an area 300 m long by 300 m wide.

The Australian Government formed the Parliament House Construction Authority as the government body with overall responsibility to project manage the delivery of the project. The PHCA provided overall direction to the project, and was responsible to the Parliament and the Cabinet through the Minister for the Capital Territory. A Cabinet Committee and a Joint Standing Committee of Parliament provided the PHCA with user requirements.

The PHCA made an early decision that the project would have to be "fast tracked" by commencing construction before design was completed, in order to meet the opening date, set by Parliament. As a consequence of fast tracking, the construction was procured by construction management, in which a joint venture of John Holland and Concrete Constructions managed a large number of trade subcontracts. The architect was the Principal Consultant engaged by PHCA, and the engineering consultants (structural, mechanical, electrical etc.) were secondary consultants, technically responsible to the

8 See Section 14.6.

9 Parliament House Construction Authority, Commonwealth, *Response to the Order to the General's efficiency audit report on the new Parliament House project/Parliament House Construction Authority* (1987) 88.

architect. The cost consultant (quantity surveyor) was directly responsible to PHCA, as was the Construction Manager.

PHCA explained its choice of procurement method as follows:

> In simple terms, the task was to design and build the country's largest piece of public architecture, designed to last more than 200 years, to exceptional levels of quality and finish. ... Time constraints meant that bold planning decisions were needed in the early stages to achieve this completion target. The most significant of these was the adoption of a fast track approach, which enabled construction to begin while planning was still in progress. The Parliament House Construction Authority (PHCA) believes that the building could not have been completed on time if traditional methods had been employed.[10]

The original building budget of $151 m was prepared by the National Capital Development Commission (**NCDC**) based on a conceptual notional design with a usable floor area of 58,000 m^2 and a gross area of 80,000 m^2. The winning architectural design had a usable area of 69,057 m^2, which the PHCA estimated added an additional $33 m to the budget. The PHCA also estimated that the winner's design involved an additional $36 m for underground car parking, circulation, plant rooms, site works, landscaping, energy-saving devices and increased standards and finishes that were not provided for in the competition brief budget. Significantly, not only did the winner's design include a larger usable area than provided for in the competition brief, but the efficiency factor (usable area divided by gross area) was 53.5%, considerably less than the 72.5% assumed by the NCDC in its conceptual design. After the winning design had been selected in 1980, the approved budget was revised from $151 m to $220 m in May 1978 prices, the basis on which the PHCA was required to report to the Parliament. The budget approved by Parliament contained neither contingencies, nor any provision for cost escalation arising from inflation.[11] As the PHCA noted: "The building budget for the new Parliament House was destined to be controversial because of misunderstandings of its base cost and the effects of additions, variations and other factors which were not part of the original calculation."[12]

15.3.2 *Project performance*

In the event, APH was opened in May 1988 (not 26 January as originally planned), and the actual final cost was $1,076 m. The Auditor General conducted an "Efficiency Audit" of the design and construction of APH in 1987 during the last stages of construction. His report was critical of virtually every aspect of PHCA's management of time, cost and quality, and he considered that the requirements of Parliament in respect to time and cost had not been met. He noted that: "Many of the difficulties arose from the fast track system which the Authority adopted to try to meet the target date for completion." The Auditor General considered that PHCA's deficiencies in managing the architect and the construction manager and the multitude of contractors on the project added to the costs of the project. He identified that some of these problems arose from the particular terms of the standard form contracts with the architect and the construction manager which had not

10 Parliament House Construction Authority, Commonwealth, *Project Parliament: the Management Experience* (1990) vii.

11 Parliament House Construction Authority, Commonwealth, *Project Parliament: the Management Experience* (1990) 21–23.

12 Ibid 21.

been appropriately prepared to protect the Commonwealth from cost and time overruns.[13] In respect of the architect's time and cost performance he noted: "The Architect continually has been late with design documentation work for a large part of the project and has made costly changes to work after the tender date",[14] and in respect of quality: "the Architect's pursuit of excellence appears to have had detrimental cost and time effects on the project".[15]

PHCA objected to the Auditor General's Report in an Appendix,[16] and rebutted the criticisms in a published response to the Auditor General's Report,[17] and in a subsequent comprehensive report prepared after the building had been completed.[18] PHCA claimed that APH was completed within the budget approved by Parliament and on time, noting that a strike closed the site for 14 weeks in 1984 and budget cuts caused delays and imposed cost penalties. In a detailed analysis of the cost revisions to the budget of $220 million that occurred over the life of the project, PHCA identified the major contributors to the increase to be:

- Escalation in building costs from inflation of May 1978 prices, accounting for $487 m, 45.3% of the final cost.
- Non-building items – $82 m (7.6%).
- Extensions to the House of Representatives and Senate wings to provide for an increase in the size of Parliament to 226, comprising an additional 23 Representatives and 12 Senators – $41 m (3.8%).
- Changed user requirements, including dining facilities, relocated and additional security areas, enlarged underground eastern car park, landscaping, additional minister's suites and cost of not using rainforest timber – $77 m (7.2%).
- Items that would normally come from a contingency allowance – $87 m (8.1%).
- Insolvencies, exchange rate variations, government fees etc. – $82 m (7.6%).

The PHCA reviewed the operation of the fast track design and construction method and considered that, "despite its drawbacks, fast track will provide the building some 2–3 years earlier and at a significantly lower completed cost than the conventional construction method".[19] In respect of the criticism of the Architect's "pursuit of excellence", PHCA noted:

> A proper balance has been achieved between the many conflicting criteria including cost, time, quality and symbolism. There will be instances where the pursuit of one of the criterium

13 Commonwealth, *Parliament House Construction Authority: construction project management*, Parl Paper No 147 (1987) 65.

14 Ibid 26.

15 Ibid 68.

16 Commonwealth, *Parliament House Construction Authority: construction project management*, Parl Paper No 147 (1987) Appendix B.

17 Parliament House Construction Authority, Commonwealth, *Response to the Order to the General's efficiency audit report on the new Parliament House project/Parliament House Construction Authority* (1987).

18 Parliament House Construction Authority, Commonwealth, *Project Parliament: the Management Experience* (1990).

19 Parliament House Construction Authority, Commonwealth, *Response to the Order to the General's efficiency audit report on the new Parliament House project/Parliament House Construction Authority* (1987) 84.

> will to some extent have a detrimental effect on other criteria. The Authority is proud of the role it has played in balancing the competing criteria.[20]

The report prepared by PHCA is a comprehensive analysis of the impact of the myriad of issues that contributed to the project delivery. Clearly this report, written from the perspective of a Government Authority that had been heavily criticised by the Auditor General, cannot be viewed as an independent assessment of its own performance. Whilst it may not have the persuasiveness of the report of an independent Public Enquiry, it nevertheless provides a useful summary of the entire project, prepared by the one body that was involved in all aspects of the project delivery. As such, it is an invaluable resource on the procurement of one of Australia's two most important buildings of the twentieth century. In a final chapter, the PHCA provides conclusions and recommendations under a number of headings, including a discussion of the following topics which have a wider application than to APH or government projects alone, and are of interest to anyone involved in project procurement and contract management:

- Project implementation: the cost of time lost.
- Design competition.
- The budget.
- The fast track method.
- Project management by the Principal (Employer).
- Organisational arrangements.
- Project planning – design, construction, design consultants' agreements.
- Construction management agreement and experience.
- Method of contracting.
- General conditions of contract.
- The Superintendent.
- Selection of consultants.
- Project insurances.
- Workers compensation insurance.
- Quality assurance.
- Legal advice and arbitration.

15.3.3 Contributing factors to project performance

The following specific conclusions and recommendations identified by PHCA are still relevant today. They are of particular interest in a broader context, and as will be seen from what follows, are of particular relevance to the procurement of SPH:

> An earlier decision to commence, given the target end date, would have enabled considerable cost savings. ... The Authority believes that clients should be made aware of the value of potential savings through the earliest possible decision to begin their projects. Implementation is greatly assisted through the maximisation of time for preplanning, efficiently establishing the operational organisation and utilising the most economical form of project delivery.[21]

---

20 Ibid 91.

21 Parliament House Construction Authority, Commonwealth, *Project Parliament: the Management Experience* (1990) 165.

The design competition for the Parliament House was well managed and produced an outstanding piece of public architecture. But it was deficient in failing to finalise the terms of agreement for the Architect in time to include them in the conditions. The Authority believes that projects should endeavour to achieve this if they rely on a competition for their design.[22]

Political considerations have an inevitable bearing on the conduct of some public projects. ... The Authority believes that, although its role is not to question such matters, the consequences have to be accepted and there are lessons to be learned.[23]

The Authority would not have adopted the fast track method of delivery if there had been more time available to complete the project ... Nevertheless, fast tracking also yielded a number of specific benefits.[24]

Coordination problems experienced would have been more severe if the designers had been operating from different cities and if the Architect had not been given responsibility for the engineering consultants.[25]

... the Authority believes that a specialist Project Planner (PP) should be employed as a consultant on major and complex projects to ensure that independent and professional expertise is readily available.[26]

The Authority believes that agreements – particularly with consultants – are only successful if they are fair to both sides.[27]

Large numbers of variations are inevitable on projects such as the Parliament House. The reasons include design alterations ranging from user changes, improvements in previously designed sections, coordination problems, consultant errors, principal-generated scope changes and non-availability of materials.[28]

The PHCA strongly recommends the formulation of an industry approved standard form of agreement for the engagement of a CM [Construction Manager] as an agent.[29] [Author's note: Standards Association Australia has since produced AS 4916–2002 Construction management – General conditions and AS 4917–2003 Construction management trade contract – General conditions as part of a suite of contracts based on AS4000–1997.]

The decision of the Authority to construct the building on a trade basis was justified by the experiences, especially in the early part of the program. This enabled the achievement, using the fast track system, of greater speed and flexibility than with other methods.[30]

Traditional forms of contract are not specifically designed for, nor – at least in an unamended form – suited to fast tracking or to projects where a CM is employed rather than a main Contractor.[31]

In the case of the Parliament House project the PHCA chose to nominate the Construction Director [as Superintendent] with largely satisfactory results. ... Perhaps the most satisfactory solution, at least on major projects where there is sufficient demand for the full-time services of a superintendent, would be to devise a method for appointing a qualified nominee acceptable to all parties or at least perceived as the most independent choice.[32]

The PHCA always recognized that the project had to achieve high standards of quality and durability. This presented no problems as far as the design consultants were concerned but difficulties were anticipated in obtaining the specified standards in the field. ... In anticipation of the need to introduce a refined quality assurance program, the PHCA, following a detailed study, adopted a system similar to that used in Canada. Many of the philosophies adopted

---

22 Ibid 166.
23 Ibid 167.
24 Ibid 168.
25 Ibid 169.
26 Ibid 170.
27 Ibid 171.
28 Ibid.
29 Ibid 172.
30 Ibid 173.
31 Ibid.
32 Ibid 174.

can now be found in the new Australian Standard for Quality in Buildings (AS2900). ... The Authority strongly recommends quality assurance programs for all major projects, particularly when the achievement of standards above the norm is a requirement.[33]

Major projects require expert legal advice and inevitably need to resolve disputes through the arbitration process. The new Parliament House was no exception. The Authority believes it successfully managed this aspect, despite the lack of a standard form contract for a fast track CM-type project. While strongly recommending a study of its experiences, detailed in Chapter 21, the Authority would like to emphasise the following points:

- In the absence of a suitable form of contract, it is not satisfactory to try to amend an unsuitable form. It is preferable to word a new contract carefully, specifically tailored to the structure and requirements of the particular fast track project.
- At an early stage, select and engage the best available firm of solicitors specialising in the building and construction industry.
- Establish a comprehensive information management capability to provide an effective project database. Access to such information is essential when a contract enters the arbitration process.[34]

15.4 New Scottish Parliament House

When the Blair Labour Government came to power in 1997, one of its early commitments was to legislate for the devolution of power over Scottish affairs to a Scottish Parliament. That Parliament needed a Parliament house, and planning for it started in 1997, even before the *Scotland Act 1998* was passed. The man who was to become Scotland's Chief Minister took a proactive role in driving the project from its inception, and he recognised the architectural importance of the building as a national symbol, as well as the need to secure a workable, durable building that would last for a long time. Indeed, he is quoted as having said that "he had a mandate to act as the most important patron of the architecture of government for 300 years".[35]

The White Paper to the passing of the *Scotland Act 1998* identified the following essential features of the building, which were later incorporated into the user brief on which the design competition was based:

10.2 The building the Scottish Parliament occupies must be of such a quality, durability and civic importance as to reflect the Parliament's status and operational needs; it must be secure but also accessible to all including people with special needs; it must promote modern and efficient ways of working and good environmental practice.

10.3 It will be an important symbol for Scotland. It should pay tribute to the country's past achievements and signal its future aspirations. It must be flexible enough to accommodate changes over time in operational requirements. Quality and value for money are also key considerations.

33 Ibid 177.

34 Ibid.

35 Scotland, *A Report by the Rt Hon Lord Fraser of Carmyllie QC, The Holyrood Inquiry*, SP Paper No 205 (2004) 55.

10.4 The accommodation must allow Scottish Parliamentarians and their staff to work efficiently harnessing the best of modern technology. People must be able to see and meet their elected representatives and to watch the Scottish Parliament in operation. Provision needs to be made to permit easy reporting and broadcasting of Parliamentary proceedings so that people throughout Scotland can be aware of its work and decisions.[36]

Following the selection of the four-acre site at Holyrood, adjacent to the Royal Palace of Holyrood House in January 1998, an international competition was held to select a designer. The brief for this design competition included:

- Budget cost £50 m at March 1998 prices.
- Building to be opened in July 2001.
- Gross area of 21,000 m^2.
- High-quality materials and finishes.
- National symbol.
- Building fabric to last at least 100 years.[37]

The winning entry was the concept design put forward by a "signature" Spanish Architect, Enric Miralles.[38] The Chief Minister was keen to have a Scottish Architect, and the architectural brief was subsequently awarded to a specifically incorporated joint venture comprising Miralles' firm and a Scottish firm of Architects. The Miralles' design was a striking and very complex collection of buildings with high-quality materials and some unusual design and construction features, including:

- Exposed laminated oak roof beams in the debating chamber, connected by 110 uniquely specified stainless-steel nodes
- Themed irregular window and construction forms
- Distinctive curved ceilings of the committee rooms and vaulted concrete ceilings of the public area below the debating chamber.

Project management was carried out by a team including civil servants and private sector appointees on secondment to the team. The organisation and senior personnel underwent a number of changes, including a change of client from the Secretary of State for Scotland to the Scottish Parliamentary Corporate Body, comprising the Presiding Officer and four members of Parliament. From the acceptance of schematic design in June 2000, the project management team was headed by a Project Director/Sponsor, accountable to the Scottish Parliament through the Clerk who was the Principal Accountable Officer.[39]

---

36 United Kingdom, Scotland's Parliament, *White Paper presented by Secretary of State to Scotland* (1997) 10.7 www.scotland.gov.uk/government/devolution/scpa-13.asp (accessed 2007).

37 Audit Scotland, *Management of the Holyrood building project* (2004) 14.

38 "A signature architect is [a] high profile individual who is very clearly identified personally with a building and its design. The top (household) names in architecture can be regarded as signature architects." (Audit Scotland, *Management of the Holyrood building project* (2004) 77).

39 Auditor General, Scotland, *The new Scottish Parliament building An examination of the management of the Holyrood project* (2000) 4.

The design team, headed by the architect, was responsible to the Project Team, as was the cost consultant.

Because of the perceived importance of having the new Parliament House functioning as soon as possible, an early decision was made to "fast track" the project to enable construction to commence before design had been completed. The Project Team decided to procure the construction by engaging a construction manager (Bovis Lend Lease) to manage construction to be carried out by a number of individual trade subcontractors, with the design, tendering and construction overlapping. Each of the works package contracts was let by the Project Team. This method of project procurement appears to have been selected by the responsible civil servants without a clear understanding of the time and cost risks entailed, and without preparation of a comprehensive procurement strategy document. Furthermore, it was selected without properly informing the politicians responsible for the project that construction management meant the final cost could not be fixed before the project was complete, and of the substantially higher risk adopted by the Employer in that mode of project delivery. It appears that the requirement to deliver a landmark, high-quality project at the earliest possible time was the ultimate driver of the decision to adopt construction management, notwithstanding the cost risk, or perhaps because it was not fully understood.[40]

In his report on the procurement of SPH, Lord Fraser opined that this was inappropriate:

> In my view at relatively early stages a number of decisions were taken which were fundamentally wrong or wholly misleading. It is the consequences of those decisions which have caused the massive increase in costs and delays.[41]

The first published cost estimates of building SPH were £10–40 m,[42] although these figures were not rationally based on a notional building or a specific site, and a minimum of £24.5 m had been identified previously.[43] The £40 m figure could never have been a realistic estimate for anything other than the most basic of new Parliament buildings, and there was no clear understanding whether that was the total cost including professional fees or only a construction cost.[44]

The assessment of the space requirements for the new Parliament by civil servants was originally 20,740 m^2 of gross area. This was costed for budget purposes at £50 m for the basic building cost (excluding fees, VAT and acquisition costs) of a notional design of a single building on the Holyrood site. Additional non-building costs for site acquisition (£5 m), construction contingency (£5 m), fees (£10 m), furniture and fit out (£8 m) and VAT (£13 m) brought the total estimated project cost to £90 m. This was based on an anticipated 129 Members of Parliament.

40 Scotland, *A Report by the Rt Hon Lord Fraser of Carmyllie QC, The Holyrood Inquiry*, SP Paper No 205 (2004) 86.

41 Scotland, *A Report by the Rt Hon Lord Fraser of Carmyllie QC, The Holyrood Inquiry*, SP Paper No 205 (2004) 8.

42 United Kingdom, Scotland's Parliament, *White Paper presented by Secretary of State to Scotland* (1997) 10.7 www.scotland.gov.uk/government/devolution/scpa-13.asp (accessed 2007).

43 Scotland, *A Report by the Rt Hon Lord Fraser of Carmyllie QC, The Holyrood Inquiry*, SP Paper No 205 (2004) 21.

44 Ibid 27; Auditor General, Scotland, *The new Scottish Parliament building An examination of the management of the Holyrood project* (2000) 21.

The winning Miralles concept design had a gross area of 27,610 m^2, which was estimated to cost £62.6 m. Following design development to produce a scheme design that was accepted in June 2000, the architect reported that the gross area had increased to 30,600 m^2. The additional area resulted from:

- Additional provision of 3,000 m^2 net usable space requested by the Employer and project management
- Additional 6,300 m^2 balance area because the original brief assumed an efficiency factor of 87%, whereas only 68% of the gross area of the scheme design was net usable space;
- 2,500 m^2 additional net space because of architectural changes accepted by the Employer,
- Reduction in area of car parking of 1,900 m^2 for 65 instead of 130 spaces.

Subsequently the cost consultant and construction manager independently measured the gross area of the scheme design which revealed an additional 2,200 m^2 and 2,400 m^2 over the 30,600 m^2 which the architect had reported, and the Employer had approved.[45] The reason for this area increase was never satisfactorily explained by the architect but meant that the gross area was actually approximately 33,000 m^2.

By June 2000, the estimated construction cost had increased to £108 m (based on March 1998 prices), with the increase in gross area accounting for about half of the increase, with the other half arising from an increase in unit costs due to the nature and high-quality of the design for the building, delays to the design and progress of the works and other risk factors which had crystallised.[46] Some of the additional non-building costs had also increased: construction contingency (to £11 m), fees (to £26 m), furniture and fit out (to £17 m) and VAT (to £28m) bringing the total estimated project cost to £209m including landscaping of £14m.[47]

In October 2000, a risk workshop identified risks with a total estimated risk cost of £51m, substantially higher than the £11m contingency provision at that stage. 70% of that identified risk was for items that were categorised as "highly likely" with at least a 95% probability of occurring. Furthermore, it did not account for the monetary value attached to risks to the time schedule. The £11m contingency provision was required to meet construction inflation (estimated to be £11–13m), as well as all the other significant construction risks. By the middle of 2001 it was apparent that the building could not be delivered for the then £195m total budget approved, and Parliament passed a motion which effectively removed the previous overall budget constraint and did not set an upper limit.[48]

In June 2004, the Auditor General reported a total forecast cost of £431 m for the project,[49] comprised of:

45 Audit Scotland, *Management of the Holyrood building project* (2004) 21.

46 Auditor General, Scotland, *The new Scottish Parliament building An examination of the management of the Holyrood project* (2000) 23–24.

47 Ibid 25.

48 Audit Scotland, *Management of the Holyrood building project* (2004) 21–24.

49 Ibid 18.

- Construction: £241 m.
- Construction risk contingency: £28 m.
- Programme contingency: £10 m.
- Fees and site organisation: £68 m.
- VAT on construction: £42 m.
- Fit out: £20 m.
- Landscaping: £18 m.
- Site, demolition and archaeology: £6 m.

The increase in construction cost from the approved budget of £108 m in 2000 to £273 m (including risk) in 2004 was estimated to arise from the following:[50]

- Inflation from published indices: £19 m
- Design development: £1 m
- Prolongation, disruption and delay: £73 m
- Costs arising from one failed contract: £4 m
- Design development: £68 m.

The Auditor General identified a number of shortcomings in the project delivery in his September 2000 report, many of which persisted to the end of the project. In the event, the ultimate project cost was of the order of £430 m, and the building was not opened until October 2004. Such massive cost and time overruns on a public building of such high profile inevitably led to public criticism which culminated in a public inquiry conducted by Lord Fraser QC. The final report of the inquiry,[51] and the complementary Auditor General's reports[52] provide a textbook case study of the reasons why the costs of this high-profile public project costs escalated so much from the original estimates. The Australian reader of these reports has a sense of *déjà vu*, as many of the significant reasons for the time and cost overruns of the Scottish Parliament House were a reprise of issues that had surfaced in Australia decades earlier in the Sydney Opera House, and more recently (at least in respect of cost) in Australian Parliament House.

15.4.1 Contributing factors to project performance

The Auditor General and Lord Fraser identified a number of factors that contributed to the cost and time overruns, the most important of which were:

- **Architect's performance**. The joint venture between architects of very different styles, and who had not previously worked together, appeared to be quite dysfunctional for a significant proportion of the time. Miralles worked in Barcelona, independently of the Scottish Architects, and insisted on being personally involved in all design issues, which inevitably involved delay and disruption.

50 Ibid 57.

51 Scotland, *A Report by the Rt Hon Lord Fraser of Carmyllie QC, The Holyrood Inquiry*, SP Paper No 205 (2004).

52 Auditor General, Scotland, *The new Scottish Parliament building An examination of the management of the Holyrood project* (2000); Audit Scotland, *Management of the Holyrood building project* (2004).

Communication issues were evident throughout the life of the joint-venture company.[53] Throughout the entire design the architect was apparently unable to meet the timetable for the provision of documentation, or to prepare designs that were within the budget that the Employer was aiming to achieve. Lord Fraser concluded that the architect's performance was below what could reasonably have been expected.[54]

- **Construction management**. Lord Fraser identified the decision to adopt construction management as

> the single factor to which most of the misfortunes that have befallen the Project can be attributed. ... I regard the decision to adopt construction management without advising Ministers of the attendant risks and the inflexible insistence on a rigid program was among the most flawed decisions in the history at the Project. It beggars belief that Ministers were not asked to approve the proposal to adopt construction management.[55]

The Auditor general also stated: "The difficulties of delivering the Holyrood building using the 'construction management' method of procurement lie at the heart of the problems that arose."[56]

- **Budget**. The so-called budget of £50 m (at 1998 price levels and exclusive of VAT and professional fees) in the design competition brief never had any basis in reality, and at the time of selection of the winning design was not set against even a tentative cost estimate. Notwithstanding that the winning architects' joint venture gave assurances that the design could be delivered within the budget, "it is difficult to see how that assertion could have been given conscientiously or taken seriously, given the embryonic state of the designs".[57]
- **Cost estimates and cost plan**. The Project Team engaged a quantity surveyor to assist in the preparation of cost estimates; however, it did not operate a genuine cost-control process. The civil servants apparently believed the majority of cost risks identified could be "managed out", and accordingly did not inform the politicians of the actual cost estimates that had been prepared.[58] Lord Fraser concluded that the senior officials did not fully understand the cost advice they were receiving,[59] perhaps a function of the fact that these officials did not have any previous experience of construction.[60] It is doubtful that either the design team or the construction manager were ever properly committed to the cost plan as a basis for containing costs.[61]

53 Scotland, *A Report by the Rt Hon Lord Fraser of Carmyllie QC, The Holyrood Inquiry*, SP Paper No 205 (2004) 105.

54 Ibid 136.

55 Ibid 86.

56 Audit Scotland, *Management of the Holyrood building project* (2004) 1.

57 Scotland, *A Report by the Rt Hon Lord Fraser of Carmyllie QC, The Holyrood Inquiry*, SP Paper No 205 (2004) 66.

58 Ibid 101–102.

59 Ibid 111.

60 Ibid 98.

61 Ibid 172–174.

- **Building brief.** Although extensive design development occurred over the period 1998–2000, the Building User Brief was not changed. This meant that at an important stage in the project, the design was not being developed in response to a clearly formulated set of user requirements. Lord Fraser found that whilst the brief conveyed strong messages about the symbolism of the building and the expected high quality, the messages in relation to programme and more significantly in relation to budget were more muted.[62]
- **Timetable.** The flow of design information required for construction failed to keep pace with the programme demanded by the Employer and proposed by the Construction Manager. The architect was largely responsible for this, which arose because of poor coordination and communication between the offices in Edinburgh and Barcelona. Lord Fraser was of the view that

> it ought to have been more completely understood by the client [Employer] that high-quality design work takes time, and that the programme itself was unrealistic given the complexities of the design, especially after Mr Brigg's report in February 2002. Bovis [the construction manager] too should have understood that. By the same token, the Architect should not have signed up to programmes which it could not honour and ought, in my view, to have been more vociferous in relation to the time needed to achieve designs which could be programmed accurately. The program was propelled by the client obsession with early completion. Irreconcilable objectives were being set. [The Scottish First Minister], the SPCB [Scottish Parliamentary Corporate Body] and later the HPG [Holyrood Progress Group] all wanted to maintain the character and integrity of the concept for the Parliament. What appears not to have been completely grasped, if at all, throughout the Project was that if the quality and unique complexity of the building was of overriding importance, the program and timing of completion would be affected significantly and extra cost would inevitably occur.[63]

- **Communications.** Many aspects of the lines of communication from the Project Team and the architectural joint-venture were criticised by the Auditor General and Lord Fraser as unclear and inconsistent with good practice.[64] There were a number of Project Managers and, from mid-2000 to the end of the project, there were four different Project Directors. The Project Director from July 2001 to June 2004 was an administrative civil servant with no construction background who was required to "manage the political dimension of the Project as well as earn the confidence of the professional consultants".[65]
- **Employer preferences.** The Employer placed greater emphasis on the issue of aesthetics/quality than on either cost or programme. For example, granite cladding was chosen in preference to a cheaper alternative, resulting in additional costs of £520,000 when the bids for the cladding package were already £3m over budget.[66]

62 Ibid 76.

63 Ibid 230.

64 eg Scotland, *A Report by the Rt Hon Lord Fraser of Carmyllie QC, The Holyrood Inquiry*, SP Paper No 205 (2004) 107, 164, 177, 189–192, 194, 198.

65 *A Report by the Rt Hon Lord Fraser of Carmyllie QC, The Holyrood Inquiry*, SP Paper No 205 (2004) 193.

66 Ibid 199.

As can be seen from the cost figures quoted above, the Employer did not significantly alter its requirements after 2000, and the size and layout of the building were not materially altered. The Auditor General identified that the main reasons for construction cost increases after 2000 were design development and delay in the construction process: "For this project, design development became a process of costing the developing design rather than developing the design within a cost limit."[67] The extent of design development can be gauged from the 10,000 changes that project management approved over the course of the project. There were many novel and complex features of the design, in particular the foyer roof and glazing. In some cases, complex architectural requirements involved previously untested building solutions in which the difficulties were made worse by tight tolerances and multiple complex interfaces between packages.[68] Further, the delays in producing architectural details after contracts had been let resulted in substantial increases in contract costs from the multitude of change orders and delay and disruption. As an example, the cost plan allowed a lump sum of £0.7 m for the foyer roof and glazing package for which a tender of £2 m was accepted. Ultimately the estimated costs increased to £7.4 m as a result of the extent of design development post tender, and extensions of time for delays due to other packages not completed on time and difficulties of crane access.[69]

The Auditor General was unequivocal in assigning responsibility for the programme slippage:

> The main cause of the 20 months delay to the project since September 2000 was the production of detailed design variations and the late supply of information during the construction process. There were difficulties associated with the construction of a very complex, densely developed, unusual building against very tight deadlines. In some cases trade contractors were responsible for some elements of design. Both the architects and some trade contractors did not deliver on time some critical elements of the design work.[70]

Lord Fraser apparently considered that the time required for the "design flow" was an inevitable consequence of the complexity of the design:

> In consideration of this problem, the tension among time, cost and quality is very well illustrated, in that it is plain that if the time criterion is set too tightly, it is likely to follow that the design flow will fail to meet expectations. In addition if as a result of time parameters having been set too tightly, construction cannot proceed in accordance with the programme, then there will clearly be a cost penalty, as has been the case.[71]

In hindsight, it should not be surprising that the cost and time of this project overran its budget to the extent that it did. In the real world and as discussed in Chapter 3, it is practically impossible to give equal emphasis to all three elements of time, cost and quality, and it is naive to assume that the highest quality can be achieved at a low cost in minimum time. It is clear that in the case of SPH, having selected a signature architect to deliver a landmark building, quality was paramount. In his principal conclusions, Lord Fraser aptly summed this up:

67 Audit Scotland, *Management of the Holyrood building project* (2004) 6.
68 Ibid 26.
69 Ibid 55.
70 Ibid 1.
71 *A Report by the Rt Hon Lord Fraser of Carmyllie QC, The Holyrood Inquiry*, SP Paper No 205 (2004) 228.

> Whenever there was a conflict between quality and cost, quality was preferred. Whenever there was a conflict between early completion and cost, completion was preferred without in fact any significant acceleration being achieved.[72]

15.5 Conclusion

Both APH and SPH highlight the risks and cost consequences of adopting a fast track construction management method of procuring a large complex high quality public building with tight construction deadlines. Both buildings clearly delivered the architectural and building quality expected of them, each having subsequently been awarded a number of architectural prizes. With respect to time and cost outcomes, the evidence shows that procurement of Australian Parliament House was better managed than the Scottish Parliament House. Perhaps one of the key differences between these two buildings was the Australian decision to adopt conventional structures, using existing technology. Although there were clearly issues arising from the tight timeframe for delivery of design information for construction for APH, the extent of design development for SPH was substantial and very time consuming as a consequence of the novelty and complexity of the design.

It is suggested that many of the time and cost issues that plagued the Scottish Parliament House could have been avoided or at least reduced by careful study and heeding the lessons learned from the Australian experience. The report prepared by the Parliament House Construction Authority to document its experiences provides a thorough analysis of the project and an assessment of the factors that contributed to time, cost and quality issues. In particular, the time and cost risks that arose from the use of fast track construction procurement by construction management were well identified, as were the difficulties of managing architects to procure design documents to an extremely tight programme, in circumstances where quality was paramount, and was clearly seen as such by the Employer.

No doubt managing a large and complex public building project in a political environment will never be easy, and perhaps it is impossible reconcile the conflicting demands of time, cost and quality. Nevertheless, documentation of the Australian Parliament House experience suggests that not all the same lessons had to be relearned during delivery of the Scottish Parliament House.

72 Ibid 240.

CHAPTER 16

A tale of two bridges

Issues arising from design and construct contracts[1]

16.1 Introduction

In the current enthusiasm for delivery of public infrastructure by the "new" approach of design and construct contracts, it may be overlooked that this mode of project delivery has been used for major projects in the past, notably for two high-profile Australian bridges: the Sydney Harbour Bridge and Kings Bridge in Melbourne. At that time, although the terminology was not used, the Sydney Harbour Bridge was (in addition to the Quebec Bridge (see Chapter 21)) one of the few major bridges in the world to be procured by a design and construct contract.

Both the Sydney Harbour Bridge and Kings Bridge have been the subject of many technical papers and other publications. It is instructive to consider this wealth of material to see whether the lessons of these two bridges have any relevance to project delivery of public infrastructure today by design and construct contracts.

Clearly, these bridges were designed and constructed in very different times – Sydney Harbour Bridge over 90 years ago and King Street Bridge over 60 years ago. However, many of the design and construct issues identified in these two projects are, arguably, still relevant to today's design and construct environment. The purpose of this chapter is to identify those aspects of the contract documents for these two bridges that were relevant to the design and construct aspects, both from an historical perspective, and in an endeavour to discern any issues that have relevance or interest to today's environment.

16.2 Sydney Harbour Bridge

16.2.1 History

The significance of Sydney Harbour Bridge as one of the most recognisable Australian icons, and its importance as a world-class bridge needs no emphasis. It was not only an extremely significant international achievement of engineering and construction,[2] but was apparently unique in its competitive design and tendering method of project delivery.[3]

1 This chapter is an edited version of the paper published in: Donald Charrett, "A Tale of Two Bridges: Issues Arising from Design and Construct Contracts" (2004) 17 *BDPS News* 28; (2004) 97 *Australian Construction Law Newsletter* 28. It is reproduced by permission of the Building Dispute Practitioner's Society.

2 The American Society of Civil Engineers named the Sydney Harbour Bridge an International Civil Engineering Landmark in 1988.

3 Ralph Freeman, "Discussion on Sydney Harbour Bridge" (1935) 238, *ICE Minutes of Proceedings* 402, 433.

DOI: 10.4324/9781003206897-18

This writer's material has largely been drawn from a series of technical papers published in the Institution of Civil Engineers Minutes of Proceedings published in 1935 and the ensuing discussion. The ICE Minutes include papers by the New South Wales Public Works Chief Engineer, Dr J. J. C. Bradfield,[4] who was responsible to the New South Wales Government for delivery of the bridge, Mr Ralph Freeman,[5] the Contractor's Consulting Engineer who prepared the detailed design, Messrs Pain and Roberts[6] (members of the consulting engineering firm who prepared the detailed calculations) and Messrs Freeman and Ennis (a director of the Contractor) who wrote on fabrication of steelwork and erection of the bridge.[7] These papers, and the detailed drawings accompanying them, comprise invaluable information not only on the technical engineering aspects of the design and construction of the bridge, but also provide an insight into the consequences of the design and construction delivery of the project, and even of the human interplay between the engineers who had the central roles in delivering the project.

Although proposals for linking Sydney and North Sydney date from 1815, it was not until 1900 that the Minister of Public Works called for worldwide "competitive designs and tenders" (i.e. tenders for a design and construct contract in current terminology) for a bridge from Dawes' Point to McMahon's Point, but none of the designs was regarded as satisfactory.[8] In 1903 tenders were called again, and the Advisory Board appointed by the Minister recommended acceptance of a tender by J. Stewart & Co at a total cost of £1,940,050. This was for a cantilever bridge with a main span of 411 m and anchor spans of 152 m and 177 m. By this time the government had changed, and the incoming government did not accept the Advisory Board's recommendation. One of bridges tendered was an arch of 640 m span, proposed to be erected on falsework, but the Advisory Board considered this as too risky.[9]

In 1911, Dr Bradfield, then Principal Designing Engineer in the Public Works Department, submitted a proposal to the Public Works Committee for a longer span bridge that did not obstruct shipping in the harbour. In 1912, he was appointed Engineer in Charge, Sydney Harbour Bridge and City Transit, with responsibility to the government to bring to fruition his proposals for a harbour bridge and electric railways for the city and suburbs. In 1913, the Parliamentary Standing Committee on Public Works recommended Bradfield's design of a cantilever bridge. Following a world study trip, in 1915 Dr Bradfield recommended:

> Alternative tenders to be called for local manufacture and for importation on plans and specifications fixing the essential features only, leaving the details of construction and the choice of steel to tenderers. The successful tenderer to complete the working plans to the satisfaction of the Public Works Department.[10]

---

4 John Job Carew Bradfield, "The Sydney Harbour Bridge and Approaches" (1935) 238 *ICE Minutes of Proceedings* 310.

5 Ralph Freeman, "Sydney Harbour Bridge: Design of the Structure and Foundations" (1935) 238 *ICE Minutes of Proceedings* 153.

6 J F Pain and G Roberts, "Sydney Harbour Bridge, Calculations for the Steel Superstructure" (1935) 238 *ICE Minutes of Proceedings* 256.

7 Ralph Freeman and Lawrence Ennis, "Sydney Harbour Bridge: Manufacture of the Structural Steelwork and Erection of the Bridge" (1935) 238 *ICE Minutes of Proceedings* 194.

8 John Job Carew Bradfield, "The Sydney Harbour Bridge and Approaches" (1935) 238 *ICE Minutes of Proceedings* 313.

9 Ibid.

10 Ibid 315.

The First World War delayed calling tenders, which were subsequently called on 30 September 1921. The 1921 tender called for construction of a cantilever bridge of 488 m span "on the basis of a general design and drawings (Fig 3, Plate 7), and a specification governing all aspects of the proposed contract, including the working details".[11] The tender drawing of this bridge in Dr Bradfield's paper comprises a line diagram defining spans, clearances etc., but no indication of required member sizes or types.[12]

Dr Bradfield visited the UK, United States and Europe in 1922 to interview prospective tenderers, and ascertained that there was sufficient interest in tendering on an alternative arch bridge design, similar to the shorter span Hell Gate Bridge in New York, which Dr Bradfield had seen under construction on his earlier visit. On his return to Australia, he recommended that the *Sydney Harbour Bridge Act 1922* (NSW) for construction of a cantilever bridge be amended to include an arch bridge. Dr Bradfield considered that as the bridge would be the most distinctive feature of the Sydney skyline, an aesthetic design was required and recommended a two-hinge arch bridge of 503 m span with abutment towers and pylons. This bridge was estimated to be £350,000 cheaper than a cantilever bridge, as well as having technical advantages such as greater rigidity. The *Sydney Harbour Bridge Act* was accordingly amended, and the 1921 tender specification plans withdrawn.

16.2.2 The 1923 invitation to tender

The design and construct specification was issued on 31 January 1923, with plans for a 488 m cantilever span, or for an arch bridge of 503 m span with abutment towers and pylons. Tenders closed a year later on 16 January 1924. Dr Bradfield assessed the tenders technically over a period of one month, and submitted his report on 16 February 1924. The contract was then signed five weeks later on 24 March 1924. The contract period was six years.[13] It is interesting to contrast these time periods with those that apply to current projects, in which it is not uncommon for the tender assessment and contract negotiation period to significantly exceed the tender period during which the tender design was prepared, e.g. in the case of the Melbourne City Link the two tenderers had four to five months to submit their bids, and the contract was not signed until nine months later.[14]

In the tender assessment period, Dr Bradfield and his team assessed the technical merits of a total of 20 different designs submitted by six tenderers. Fourteen of the 16 designs submitted by four tenderers were tenders that Dr Bradfield considered conformed to the conditions of the invitation to tender. Four tenders submitted by the two other tenderers did not come wholly within the scope of the *Sydney Harbour Bridge Act*.[15]

---

11 Ibid.

12 Ibid Fig 3, Plate 7.

13 Ibid 331.

14 Institution of Engineers Australia, *Journey and Arrival The story of the Melbourne City Link* (2002) 23.

15 John Job Carew Bradfield, "The Sydney Harbour Bridge and Approaches" (1935) 238 *ICE Minutes of Proceedings* 317.

The conforming tenders for an arch bridge were:

- Sir William Arrol & Co: £4,645,351
- Dorman Long & Co (three tenders): £3,499,815–£4,217,721
- McClintic Marshall Products Co: £6,053,565.[16]

Dr Bradfield had estimated that the cost of an arch bridge fabricated wholly in New South Wales was £4,339,530, with steelwork weighing 46,600 tonnes, comprising 36.7% nickel steel with the remainder carbon steel.[17] The Dorman Long tender accepted was for £4,217,721, with 50,288 tons of steel, comprising 50.9% of silicon steel with the remainder carbon steel. Mr Freeman (Dorman Long's consulting engineer responsible for the design) considered that the reduction in weight by the use of higher strength nickel steel was outweighed by the costs of material and manufacture, and accordingly opted for the use of silicon steel that had a 30% higher strength than carbon steel.[18] The proportion of fabrication of steel to be carried out in Australia was a factor in determining the successful tenderer; Dorman Long had considerable advantages over the other tenderers in this respect as it already had a fabrication workshop in Australia.

16.2.3 Tender specification

Dr Bradfield's paper notes that the specification represented his opinion of the solution for the harbour crossing, and it set out the two alternatives in general detail and no other type was allowed.[19] Nevertheless, several of the tenderers apparently thought that the specification could be interpreted broadly and submitted tenders for alternative bridge types. The Canadian Bridge Co, McClintic Marshall Products Co and the English Electric Co submitted tenders for suspension bridges, and the Goninan Bridge Corporation Ltd submitted a tender for a cantilever suspension bridge. Perhaps in an attempt to come within the terms of the invitation to tender, the McClintic Marshall Products Co called its suspension designs "inverted arches". The tenders submitted encompassed seven different types of bridge, comprising every known form of large span steel structure.

Freeman stated that the specification was interpreted by tenderers as leaving them to select the type of bridge that satisfied the requirements of the site. In what is clearly criticism of the design and construct method of project delivery, Freeman noted:

> This variety of proposals arose in consequence of the uncertainty regarding the real intention of the specification, and of the importance which might be attached to conflicting aspects of possible alternatives, and illustrates the difficulties that may arise when tenders for a great engineering project are invited without the inclusion of any design for the work to be carried out. Contractors had either to design completely and submit binding tenders for various alternative types, or to select a type by forming their own judgment of the importance of, (a) a clear headway for navigation throughout the entire span, a condition easily obtained with a cantilever bridge but impossible with an arch, (b) the improvement of the curvature of approaches

16 Ibid 319.

17 Ibid 317.

18 Ralph Freeman, "Sydney Harbour Bridge: Design of the Structure and Foundations" (1935) 238 *ICE Minutes of Proceedings* 169.

19 Dr J J C Bradfield, "Correspondence on Sydney Harbour Bridge" (1935) 238, *ICE Minutes of Proceedings* 437, 462.

> obtained with an arch design as compared with a cantilever; (c) the advisability of using either steel of a quality that could be made in Australia, or of using steel costing less, but impossible to manufacture in Australia; (d) the aesthetic value attached to pylons, structurally unnecessary, costing over £700,000. Each firm tendering, therefore, had to make its own investigation of the suitability of each type of bridge, and submitted schemes for all, in the hope that one might be accepted by the Government. On the Author's advice, Messrs Dorman, Long & Co submitted tenders for three types of bridge with seven alternative schemes, and the cost of their tender alone amounted to over £20,000.[20]

Although Freeman gave consideration to every known type of bridge, Dorman Long's tenders were confined to the specified arch and cantilever types because of technical reasons, not because Freeman considered he was confined to those two types.[21]

Dr Bradfield's paper discussed in detail the alternative designs received from the different tenderers, as well as the erection methods proposed. The erection method was fundamentally important to assessment of the risks of the different proposals, and central to maintaining the required clear navigation channel in the harbour during construction. Dr Bradfield stated that he carefully examined all tenders and recommended acceptance of Dorman Long's conforming tender for a "two hinge arch bridge with abutment towers and pylons in accordance with the official plans and specifications".[22]

Dr Bradfield clearly had firm views on the type of bridge that he wanted:

> No other type of bridge had been allowed, and, as tenders showed, no other types were as suitable. Tenderers who spent money and time on alternative types did so at their own risk, because the true solution on technical, economic and aesthetic grounds lay between these two designs.[23]

Although he considered the arch bridge to be superior to the cantilever in terms of rigidity, economy and beauty, he kept both as options for tenderers in order that there was sufficient tendering competition. It was not clear at the time of calling tenders that there would be sufficient competition for a two-hinge arch bridge, which at that time had not been used for such a large span.[24]

Dr Bradfield could not understand why there could be any uncertainty in relation to the real intention of the specification, "which was headed, 'Contract for the construction of a cantilever or an arch bridge across Sydney Harbour from Dawes' Point to Milson's Point, Sydney, New South Wales,' and in its clauses *minutely described* both alternatives"[25] (emphasis added).

16.2.4 Tender design

The Specification required tenderers to submit complete calculations in detail, including stress sheets giving primary and secondary stresses for all conditions of load during and after erection.[26]

---

20 Ralph Freeman, "Sydney Harbour Bridge: Design of the Structure and Foundations" (1935) 238 *ICE Minutes of Proceedings* 155.

21 Ibid 156.

22 John Job Carew Bradfield, "The Sydney Harbour Bridge and Approaches" (1935) 238 *ICE Minutes of Proceedings* 331.

23 Dr J J C Bradfield, "Correspondence on Sydney Harbour Bridge" (1935) 238, *ICE Minutes of Proceedings* 462.

24 Ibid 463.

25 Ibid.

26 J Jones, "Correspondence on Sydney Harbour Bridge" (1935) 238, *ICE Minutes of Proceedings* 437, 440

Freeman noted that the tender specification

> defined all the conditions to be satisfied by the bridge, but it did not include designs for either type of bridge; firms tendering were therefore obliged either to employ their own organisation to take out the necessary designs and quantities or to engage a consulting engineer to do so.[27]

Dr Bradfield apparently considered that his arch design and specification comprised *the* design of the bridge, as he described the specification and drawings in the following terms:

> There were 26 plans accompanying the specification, which contained 470 clauses; all quantities were given on the tender form except the steelwork quantities, which had to be determined by tenderers to accord with the variety of steel they proposed to use. The physical and chemical properties and the working stresses of carbon and alloy steels which were allowed to be used were set out in detail in the specification.[28]

Dr Bradfield's paper described the detailed dimensions and geometry of the arch, and the ornamental abutment towers that he considered essential to the aesthetics of the bridge. Further:

> Nothing in the nature of a 'design competition' was asked for. The only sense in which there could be anything of that nature was in respect of the class of steel to be adopted by the various tenderers, out of the completely de-limited range set out in the Specification, and he [Dr Bradfield] maintained that that was not only unavoidable but necessary in fairness to tenderers and to obtain the best final result. The tenderers, however, made a 'design competition' for themselves, against the instructions of the Specification. He was forced to the conclusion that had the Contract been for an arch bridge only, and full working drawings been presented in the Specification, a variety of proposals would still have been forthcoming, according to individual ideas of the suitability of other types of bridge, or other classes of steel, and so on. As it was, a bridge conforming to the specified design in all essential particulars was accepted.[29]

Dr Bradfield's paper did not include the name of Mr Ralph Freeman in the acknowledgements, although he referred to Mr Freeman as having prepared the detailed drawings. In his discussion on the paper, Dr Oscar Faber took Dr Bradfield to task for this:

> Personally, he would understand that [preparing the detail drawings] as meaning that the whole work had been designed, and that it was left to the contractors to prepared detailed drawings of a bridge which had been sized with regard to its structural members. He did not think that was quite the case, because the determination of the sizes of all structural members was in fact left to the contractors, and there was no doubt that the contractors and their consulting engineers had to make decisions which were vital to the safety and strength of the structure ... Clause 20 of the contract made it abundantly clear that it was left to the contractors to put forward their own design, to calculate the sizes of all members and to take complete responsibility for the structure; and that work was delegated by them to Mr Freeman.[30]

Freeman considered that "there had not been another case of competitive design and tendering comparable with that of the Sydney Harbour bridge",[31] and not surprisingly, that substantial design was required during the tender period:

27 Ralph Freeman, "Sydney Harbour Bridge: Design of the Structure and Foundations" (1935) 238 *ICE Minutes of Proceedings* 154.

28 John Job Carew Bradfield, "The Sydney Harbour Bridge and Approaches" (1935) 238 *ICE Minutes of Proceedings* 316.

29 Dr J J C Bradfield, "Correspondence on Sydney Harbour Bridge" (1935) 238, *ICE Minutes of Proceedings* 463.

30 Dr Oscar Faber, "Discussion on Sydney Harbour Bridge" (1935) 238, *ICE Minutes of Proceedings* 402, 405.

31 R Freeman, "Discussion on Sydney Harbour Bridge" (1935) 238, *ICE Minutes of Proceedings* 402, 433.

> Three types of structure were designed to the extent necessary for the accurate calculation of quantities and for the submission of tenders, namely: a two hinged arch, a two hinged cantilever arch, and a cantilever …[32] Responsibility for the design, materials, quantities, construction of the bridge, and for the specification itself were imposed on the Contractors by the terms of the contract.[33]

The costs of preparing Dorman Long's tender designs, £20,000, amounted to 0.5% of the final contract price, and indicates the amount of design work that was necessary to prepare designs to the extent required for Dorman Long to prepare a fixed-price tender.

The specification stated the span of the bridge, the level and disposition of the railway tracks and loads to be carried, the loading and the clearances for navigation. It also defined the permissible physical and chemical properties of carbon and alloy steels and their permissible working stresses in detail.[34] Freeman noted that the specification did not state that Dr Bradfield's drawings were to be adopted, and he found it not possible to follow any of them. These drawings consisted of:

- An outline drawing and cross-section of an arch
- Detailed drawings of a pylon and of the piers, and
- Structural arrangement of the approach spans.

Neither the specification nor the drawings made any reference to:

- Bearings
- Allocation of stresses at the crown between chords, and
- Disposition of lateral and sway bracing.[35]

It is submitted that any designer would recognise that, although the specification was no doubt very detailed, Dr Bradfield's arch design was only conceptual, and provided insufficient detail required for pricing purposes. Tenderers therefore had to prepare a tender design for each different concept for which a tender was to be submitted, in order to have sufficient details of members to price the fabrication and erection. In the days before computers, the manual calculations for a two-pin arch structure subject to various erection and working load conditions were particularly lengthy and arduous, as indicated in the paper on the calculations for Sydney Harbour Bridge by Messrs Pain and Roberts.[36] Given that each tenderer had to prepare its own individual designs taking into account, inter alia, proposed erection methods, economical choice of member and steel type and available material and fabrication facilities, it seems to this writer that considerable design effort was required to determine steelwork quantities and steel types, and the tenders did involve a design competition. Further, the absence of a detailed design and the choices of bridge

32 Ralph Freeman, "Sydney Harbour Bridge: Design of the Structure and Foundations" (1935) 238 *ICE Minutes of Proceedings* 156.

33 Ibid 160.

34 John Job Carew Bradfield, "The Sydney Harbour Bridge and Approaches" (1935) 238 *ICE Minutes of Proceedings* 316.

35 Ralph Freeman, "Sydney Harbour Bridge: Design of the Structure and Foundations" (1935) 238 *ICE Minutes of Proceedings* 160.

36 J F Pain and G Roberts, "Sydney Harbour Bridge, Calculations for the Steel Superstructure" (1935) 238 *ICE Minutes of Proceedings*.

FIGURE 16.1 Sydney Harbour bridge

type, member configuration, steel type and erection method available to the designers seemed to be intended to promote such competition to obtain the benefits of competitive tendering.

16.2.5 Dorman Long's tender design

Freeman discussed a number of differences between the Bradfield concept design shown on the invitation to tender drawings and specification, and the successful tender design prepared by him as consulting engineer for Dorman Long. These included:

- Even number of bracing panels between the arch chords (28, not the 27 shown on Dr Bradfield's concept drawings)
- A reduction from four to two main girders in the approach spans
- Allowable working stresses of the sandstone rock for the arch abutment were reduced from the specified 31 to 13 tons per square feet, and
- The arch foundations were founded 25 feet into the sandstone rock, instead of the five feet permitted by the specification.

The first two of these changes resulted in savings of £25,000[37] and £150,000[38] respectively, whereas the lower foundation stresses and deeper foundations cost an additional £40,000.[39] Whilst Dr Bradfield did not accept that the change to the bracing actually resulted in the

37 Ralph Freeman, "Sydney Harbour Bridge: Design of the Structure and Foundations" (1935) 238 *ICE Minutes of Proceedings* 163.

38 Ibid 188.

39 Ibid 190.

FIGURE 16.2 The pin bearing for one of the arches

saving claimed by Freeman, such design changes must have been permissible under the specification, as they were incorporated into the contractual design.

Freeman noted that the extra cost of his decision to reduce the allowable foundation stresses and sink the foundations lower into rock than required by the tender specification risked losing the contract.[40] He wrote of the relationship with his Contractor client in the following terms:

> Although he was acting as an engineer on behalf of the contractors, it was due to them to say that his position was quite as unfettered as if he had been an engineer acting independently for a client responsible for payment – perhaps more so. He could not speak too highly of the anxiety shown by Messrs. Dorman, Long and Company throughout the whole period of construction, to do nothing but the best work, altogether regardless of what it cost. That attitude never varied, even during the period of the fearful depression in Australia which struck them a blow so severe as almost to remove the possibility of a profit.[41]

Figure 16.2 shows a pin bearing taking the thrust of an arch into the foundation, 25 feet into sandstone. The foundation designed by Freeman was based on design parameters more conservative than permitted by Bradfield's specification (and consequently £40,000 more expensive), a graphic example of the final design cost risk assumed by design and construct contractors discussed in Chapter 9.

Freeman identified a number of other design changes that he considered were economically justified and could have been incorporated into the final design:

40 Ibid.

41 R Freeman, "Discussion on Sydney Harbour Bridge" (1935) 238 *ICE Minutes of Proceedings* 402, 428.

- Increasing the maximum compressive stress to 85% of the tensile stress, instead of the 75% specified (> £200,000 saving)[42]
- Elimination of the "aesthetic" pylons that had no structural function (£750,000 saving)[43]
- Reduction of the size of butt joint covers of compression members, resulting in a 20% weight saving of the main trusses (at least £250,000 saving).[44]

One of the alternative tenders submitted by Dorman Long did not include the "aesthetic" pylons but, as this was not accepted, clearly the Government Employer considered that the aesthetic benefit was outweighed by the possible cost saving of £717,906[45] (no doubt influenced by Dr Bradfield's strong recommendation that these pylons were essential to the appearance of the arch bridge). Moreover, Dr Bradfield insisted that the pylons needed to be faced with granite, despite the fact that this involved considerably more expense (approximately £240,000). He justified this on the grounds that only a "strong imperishable" natural product like granite would "humanise the landscape in simplicity, strength and sincerity".

16.2.6 Final design cost risk

One of the risks of great financial significance to a Contractor entering a design and construct contract is the final design cost risk (see Chapter 9) – that is, the possibility that after contract award when the Contractor is committed to a fixed price, preparation of the final design results in a facility whose costs are substantially different to those indicated by the concept design and on which the tender price was determined.

As with many risks, final design cost risk has a positive and negative aspect. If, by refined design or improved fabrication or erection techniques, the final design costs less to construct than allowed for in the tender concept design that formed the basis for the Contractor's fixed price then, subject to the terms of the Contract, the Contractor will improve its profit margin. Conversely, if the final design costs more to construct than the tender design priced, the Contractor's profit margin will generally be reduced or negative. The possibility of improved profit margin on a design and construct contract is frequently a driver of close interaction between constructor and designer at final design stage in an attempt to identify a more economical design that still satisfies all of the mandatory contractual requirements.

The issue of what design changes between tender and final design are permissible under the contract lies at the heart of many disputes in connection with design and construct contracts. The Employer aims to define its requirements comprehensively in the contract, particularly under the technical requirements defined in the scope of works. It usually spends considerable time in the technical assessment of the submitted tenders, and endeavours to remove any ambiguities in the submitted tenders before any tender is

---

42 Ralph Freeman, "Sydney Harbour Bridge: Design of the Structure and Foundations" (1935) 238 *ICE Minutes of Proceedings* 172.

43 Ibid 191.

44 Ibid 183.

45 Dorman Long's A1 tender for a two-hinged arch bridge was the same as the successful A3 tender, but without the abutment pylons (Bradfield, above n 356, 319).

accepted. The concept design drawings prepared by the Contractor and submitted with the tender then typically form part of the design and construct Contract.

However, by their nature, the concept design drawings cannot be used as working drawings. Time and cost limitations inherent in preparing a tender design means that the tender design is not complete or fully detailed. The Contractor takes the risk that, in completing the design, the cost of the previously undesigned items or any changes necessary to make the concept design comply with the contract requirements will not exceed the contingency provided for the financial consequences of such design development (i.e. the final design cost risk).[46] Conversely, final design also gives the designer and Contractor the opportunity to examine whether permissible refinements might lead to significant cost savings to the benefit of the Contractor. In the case of Sydney Harbour Bridge, Dr Bradfield recognised that the tender design calculations were only preliminary, and the final design calculations for the main arch could only be performed after the contract was awarded and the approach spans and abutment details had been settled.[47]

In an interesting discussion on the reasons why there was such a wide range of tender prices for a variety of bridge types for Sydney Harbour Bridge, Dr Steinman noted that the English Electric Co had added 100% to the Consulting Engineer's estimate of cost to allow for profit and contingencies, including no doubt, any final design cost risk.[48]

In view of the considerable design effort that clearly went into preparation of Dorman Long's tender design for the Sydney Harbour Bridge, it is instructive to examine the changes that did occur between tender and final design. Freeman noted that the essential features of the bridge as actually constructed differed very little from those proposed in the tender. The principal modifications made were:

- The pylons were redesigned by the prominent English architectural firm, Sir John Burnet and Partners
- The level of the bearings was altered to improve the clearance required for traffic
- The bearings were redesigned
- The angles for the heavy members were increased from 10" x 10" to 12" x 12"
- Carbon steel was used for some bracing members instead of silicon steel.[49]

16.2.7 Contract details

The contract apparently used a schedule of rates for payment for the steel,[50] but only up to 5% in excess of the tender quantities. Any steel quantities in excess of that limit were

46 This was aptly summed up by one of the authors of correspondence on the papers in the *ICE Minutes of Proceedings*: "Any tenderer who stopped his calculations at what seemed to him a reasonable point, necessarily had to protect his pocket by allowing what he estimated, from his past experience, would be ample additional weight to cover secondary stresses not yet calculated." (J Jones, "Correspondence on Sydney Harbour Bridge" (1935) 238, *ICE Minutes of Proceedings* 441).

47 John Job Carew Bradfield, "The Sydney Harbour Bridge and Approaches" (1935) 238 *ICE Minutes of Proceedings* 332.

48 Dr J J C Bradfield, "Correspondence on Sydney Harbour Bridge" (1935) 238 *ICE Minutes of Proceedings* 454.

49 Ralph Freeman, "Sydney Harbour Bridge: Design of the Structure and Foundations" (1935) 238 *ICE Minutes of Proceedings* 160.

50 Dr J J C Bradfield, "Correspondence on Sydney Harbour Bridge" (1935) 238 *ICE Minutes of Proceedings* 466.

at the Contractor's cost.[51] With such a contract, clearly there was no incentive for the Contractor to introduce any design changes post-contract award that would have resulted in a lower quantity of steel, since any weight savings would presumably be to the benefit of the Employer. Thus, having won the contract, it is not surprising that Dorman Long did not propose design changes such as the increase in maximum compressive stresses that Freeman considered would have saved in excess of £200,000.[52]

The contract provided for progress payments of fixed percentages of the price at the following milestones:

- Non-fabricated steel on delivery 5/16
- Completely fabricated steel delivered to bridge site 5/16
- Members erected between panel points and partially riveted 2/16
- Complete interaction with the exception of painting 3/16
- Completion of contract 1/16

The contract provided for deduction of a percentage from each progress payment to form a retention fund amounting to £250,000 (6% of the contract price). Increases in wages subsequent to the date of tender were a variation, and the amount paid for this increase over the contract period was £500,000.[53]

To the contract period of six years, Dr Bradfield granted extensions of time of one year and nine months for strikes and the Government's delay in making some of the land available. A further extension of time of six months was granted as a consequence of the legislated reduction of working hours from 48 to 44 hours per week.[54]

One of the contributors to the discussion of Freeman's paper indicated that Dorman Long had made a loss of £270,000 resulting from variations in the rate of exchange, and suggested that a target profit of 20% would not have been unreasonable.[55] Ennis confirmed that the finished unit costs were almost exactly as estimated for the tender and that Dorman Long's loss on the contract was due to the unfavourable exchange position, certain State legislation subsequent to the date of the contract, and general world depression.[56] A specific effect of the prevailing economic conditions at the end of the contract was that the residual value of certain erection equipment was significantly less than had been allowed for when preparing the tender. Ennis noted that Contractors never succeeded in achieving a profit of 20% when there was competitive tendering. He noted "but for the losses mentioned the margin of profit allowed for in the estimate would have been realised".[57]

Freeman confirmed that the estimates of weight and cost prepared during tender were borne out by the actual cost of the work, and the losses arose from exchange rate variations and lower residual value of plant and equipment than assumed. There were no unforeseen

51 J Jones, "Correspondence on Sydney Harbour Bridge" (1935) 238 *ICE Minutes of Proceedings* 441.

52 Ralph Freeman, "Sydney Harbour Bridge: Design of the Structure and Foundations" (1935) 238 *ICE Minutes of Proceedings* 172.

53 Ibid 159.

54 John Job Carew Bradfield, "The Sydney Harbour Bridge and Approaches" (1935) 238 *ICE Minutes of Proceedings* 331.

55 I C Barling, "Discussion on Sydney Harbour Bridge" (1935) 238 *ICE Minutes of Proceedings* 402, 334.

56 L Ennis, "Correspondence on Sydney Harbour Bridge" (1935) 238 *ICE Minutes of Proceedings* 437, 461.

57 Ibid.

events during execution of the work that caused additional cost other than those arising from economic conditions that were outside the Contractor's control.[58] The completed cost of the bridge (excluding wage variations) was £4,217,721[59] only £21,118 (0.5%) more than the tender price. The final steel weight was 51,404 tons, 1,117 tons (2.2%) more than tendered weight.[60]

16.2.8 Final design

As Chief Engineer, Dr Bradfield maintained a close check on progress of the detailed design. The contract provided that no materials should be ordered or fabricated until he had approved and signed plans, stress sheets and other documents. He noted that:

> the working drawings were all approved after revisions had been made for the Author's requirements. In no case was there any delay involved in the examination and approval, sufficient to hold up the ordering of material, placing it in the shops, and carrying out all the erection operations.[61]

It is interesting to note Dr Bradfield's choice of words in relation to the preparation of the detailed design. For example:

> the technical work which had to be submitted by the contractors was performed by the Consulting Engineers Sir Douglas Fox and Partners in conjunction with Mr C.G. Imbault; the senior partner of Sir Douglas Fox and Partners being Mr Ralph Freeman, M.Inst.C.E.[62]

Freeman stated his position forcefully on the design of the bridge the following terms:

> In conclusion, he would make one observation in justice to himself, to the contractors for the bridge, and to those who worked with them. Dr Bradfield's business was to see that Sydney was provided with a good bridge at a minimum cost, and he was justly entitled to all the credit due to him if those objects had been attained. To secure them had been his lifetime's work, and only those who had been there could realise the magnitude of the task which he undertook and his claims on the gratitude of his countrymen. One part of that work, however, was building of the structure and foundations of the bridge which now spanned Sydney Harbour, and Dr Bradfield's paper hardly did full justice to those who carried out the duty imposed on them in unmistakable language in the contract, which, as he had stated on p. 160, made the contractors entirely responsible for satisfactory design and construction of the bridge. Every drawing for the works was made by the contractors, and throughout the entire execution of the work neither Dr Bradfield nor any member of his staff directed or inspired any process of design or erection.[63]

16.2.9 The design controversy

The extracts above on the design of the bridge culminated a long-running and very public dispute between Dr Bradfield and Mr Freeman as to who was the "designer" of the

58 R Freeman, "Correspondence on Sydney Harbour Bridge" (1935) 238 *ICE Minutes of Proceedings* 437, 459.

59 John Job Carew Bradfield, "The Sydney Harbour Bridge and Approaches" (1935) 238 *ICE Minutes of Proceedings* 399.

60 Ibid 400.

61 Ibid 334.

62 Ibid.

63 R Freeman, "Discussion on Sydney Harbour Bridge" (1935) 238 *ICE Minutes of Proceedings* 402, 434.

bridge. Long before the advent of legislation on moral rights protecting a person's right to be acknowledged as responsible for a structure, both Dr Bradfield and Mr Freeman publicly claimed to be *the* designer of the Sydney Harbour Bridge. Both parties had their protagonists: Freeman had the support of the Sydney Morning Herald that acknowledged him as the designer in a series of articles, on the grounds that he had prepared most of the drawings from which the bridge was built.[64] Dr Bradfield had the support of the Public Works Department and the Minister for Public Works, who considered that the contract required that Dorman Long had to assume responsibility for the design as builders and not as designers.[65]

The issue became so serious that Dorman Long threatened to sue the Government if a plaque was placed on the bridge naming Dr Bradfield as the designer. In the event, the plaques ultimately put on the north and south pylons of the bridge probably accurately sums up the real position:

SYDNEY HARBOUR BRIDGE

THE BRIDGE WAS CONSTRUCTED FOR AND THE APPROACHES BY THE PUBLIC WORKS DEPARTMENT OF NEW SOUTH WALES.

THE GENERAL DESIGN AND SPECIFICATION WERE PREPARED AND THE WHOLE SUPERVISED ON BEHALF OF THE GOVERNMENT OF NEW SOUTH WALES BY J.J.C. BRADFIELD, D.SC(ENG), M.E., M.INST.C.E., M.I.E.AUST., CHIEF ENGINEER.

CONTRACTORS FOR THE DESIGN AND CONSTRUCTION OF THE MAIN STRUCTURE, DORMAN, LONG AND CO., LTD, MIDDLESBROUGH ENGLAND.

LAWRENCE ENNIS O.B.E., DIRECTOR OF CONSTRUCTION FOR THE CONTRACTORS.

RALPH FREEMAN M.INST.C.E., M.AM.SOC.C.E., CONSULTING AND DESIGNING ENGINEER FOR THE CONTRACTORS.

SIR JOHN BURNET & PARTNERS ARCHITECTS FOR THE CONTRACTORS.

THE HONOURABLE M.A. DAVIDSON, M.L.A., C.W. MITCHELL,

MINISTER FOR PUBLIC WORKS DIRECTOR OF PUBLIC WORKS.

The controversy between Dr Bradfield and Mr Freeman was never resolved, as the above extracts from the papers published in 1935 in the ICE Minutes of Proceedings show.

In the present-day context, it is hard to see that Dr Bradfield's claim to be the sole designer would be consistent with the contractual provisions in the design and construct contract that endeavoured to unequivocally place legal liability for all aspects of the design on the Contractor. On the other hand, perhaps the legislated protection of moral rights in the *Copyright Act 1968* (Cth) would protect Dr Bradfield's right to be publicly acknowledged as the "author" of the concept design, who conceived the form and essential features of the arch bridge, including the 503 m span and height above the water that was intrinsic to its functionality.

64 Peter Spearritt, *The Sydney Harbour Bridge* (1982) 46.

65 Richard Raxworthy, *The Unreasonable Man The life and works of JJC Bradfield* (1989) 99.

16.2.10 Criticisms of design and construct for Sydney Harbour Bridge

In correspondence on the ICE papers on Sydney Harbour Bridge, the very eminent American bridge engineer Dr Steinman articulated the following criticism of the design and construct mode of delivery:

> it was regrettable that the determination of type and design for the Sydney Harbour Bridge was left to a bidding competition, in which the individual tenderers were required to prepare their own designs as a basis for their bids. Such procedure involved heavy economic waste, owing to duplication of effort and expense. In the present instance, over £100,000 was expended by the various bidders preparing their multiplicity of alternative designs and tenders, without any resultant saving to the Government. Moreover, it was difficult to make a fair comparison of the resulting tenders, since the various quotations referred to designs that were not strictly comparable. In addition, the uncertainty as to many governing conditions prevented close figuring in preparing the tenders. Such bidding design competitions should be discountenanced by the engineering profession, and the approved procedure of retaining the best possible professional talent and advice in working out the most effective design for the given location, and calling for tenders on that completely developed official design, should be maintained.[66]

In discussing the papers, F. S. Snow was "astounded at the tremendous cost of tendering as disclosed in Mr Freeman's paper". He noted:

> it might be assumed that altogether something like £100,000 was spent by tenderers in doing no useful work. ... It was a serious loss to the country that so much time and money was wasted in preparation of tenders of that nature, which resulted in price cutting and enabled the client to get something more for his money than he was entitled to, though in the majority of cases he was perfectly willing to pay for it.[67]

The figure of £100,000 "wasted" on tendering needs to put in context. Following his overseas trip in 1914, Dr Bradfield reported on the "inefficient method adopted with the official design for the Quebec Bridge, in which two and half years work at a cost of £100,000 was wasted on useless drawings". He considered that the procedure of outline and not working drawings adopted for the Memphis Bridge over the Mississippi River was preferable, as it left the competing tenderers free to vary the details and type of steel to suit themselves.[68] The design and construct contract may well have saved the New South Wales Government £100,000 preparing working drawings, but this amount was spent collectively by tenderers in preparing their tenders. Given that the costs of unsuccessful tendering ultimately have to be paid for from the proceeds of successful contracts, it is debatable whether there was any net saving on documentation costs. However, the Contractor's "wasted" £100,000 appears to have been the Government's gain, through not having to pay that amount directly for the documentation.

Considering the concept design prepared by Dr Bradfield, it seems clear that his judgment on the mode of delivery for the project was correct. His design used different steel types and had a different steel weight to the design prepared by Freeman for Dorman Long, who were driven by the commercial imperative of preparing an economical design, specifically tailored to its own circumstances, to win the contract. Further, Dorman

---

66 Dr D B Steinman, "Correspondence on Sydney Harbour Bridge" (1935) 238 *ICE Minutes of Proceedings* 437, 452.

67 F S Snow, "Discussion on Sydney Harbour Bridge" (1935) 238 *ICE Minutes of Proceedings* 402, 426.

68 Richard Raxworthy, *The Unreasonable Man The life and works of JJC Bradfield* (1989) 99.

Long's contract price was £121,809 cheaper than Dr Bradfield's estimate, notwithstanding the additional 3,688 tons of steel in Freeman's design.[69] Had Dorman Long tendered on construction only of Dr Bradfield's design, it is possible that either the price would have been higher to build the less efficient (for Dorman Long) Bradfield design, or Bradfield's design and drawings would have had to be scrapped and replaced by the ultimate Freeman design.

An alternative view of the "design competition" was put by Mr Jonathan Jones who prepared the designs for the McClintic Marshall Products Company tenders:

> His regret that the competition did not, in his judgment, give comparable data for comparisons [of different bridge types and weights] was wholly free from criticism of the tendering procedure. Other than that the specification called for more design expenditure prior to tendering than could reasonably be expected of tenderers without arrangement for compensation, the points brought out above were the inevitable result of a complex situation.[70]

16.3 Kings Bridge, Melbourne Australia (1962)

16.3.1 History

In 1954 the Victorian Public Works Committee recommended construction of a bridge crossing the Yarra at King Street. Following investigations by the Country Roads Board (**CRB**), worldwide tenders were called for design and construction of structures comprising a high level and two low level bridges on King Street and an overpass over Flinders Street.[71]

The tender documents included an outline drawing showing the grades, clearances and other limiting conditions, and a specification that detailed the design requirements (loading, permissible working stresses etc.) and the required standards of materials and workmanship. Contractors were permitted to offer a superstructure in reinforced concrete, prestressed concrete, mild steel, high tensile steel or light alloy.[72]

Tenders were called in September 1956 and closed on 29 January 1957. Tenders were received from seven different tenderers, comprising 14 different designs. On 27 May 1957 the CRB recommended acceptance of Utah Australia Limited's (**Utah**) tender for £2,374,360, and the contract between Utah and CRB was signed on 13 August 1957. It is interesting to note that whilst tenderers had four to five months to prepare tenders that included designs in sufficient detail to prepare a fixed lump sum price, the period for tender assessment and contract negotiation was six and a half months.[73]

Utah's tender was for bridges with superstructure comprising steel plate girders fabricated from high tensile steel. Design and construction took place over four years. The high-level bridge was opened to traffic on 12 April 1961, and the final certificate of completion was published in the *Government Gazette* on 18 October 1961. The design was

69 John Job Carew Bradfield, "The Sydney Harbour Bridge and Approaches" (1935) 238 *ICE Minutes of Proceedings* 317.

70 J Jones, "Correspondence on Sydney Harbour Bridge" (1935) 238 *ICE Minutes of Proceedings* 443.

71 Victoria, *Royal Commission into the Failure of Kings Bridge, Report* (1963) 8.

72 Ibid.

73 Ibid.

FIGURE 16.3 Kings bridge over the Yarra river

carried out for Utah by Kings Street Bridge Design Limited (**KSBD**), a consulting engineering company specifically created to carry out the design of the bridge.[74] (Figure 16.3)

On 10 July 1962, when a low loader and trailer of total mass 45 tons was crossing the western high-level carriageway, the bridge suddenly collapsed, sagging a distance of about 300mm. Further collapse was prevented by the concrete deck slab and concrete walls enclosing the space under the bridge.[75] The four suspended girders, approximately 100 feet long, had fractured approximately 16 feet from the southern end. Three of the girders had similar fractures at the northern end. These fractures had initiated at the toe of a transverse weld at the end detail of a flange cover plate.[76]

The Government executed Letters Patent for a Royal Commission into the collapse on 28 August 1962. The Royal Commissioners consisted of his Honour Judge Barber of the County Court, Dr J. A. L. Matheson, then Vice Chancellor of Monash University, previously Professor of Civil Engineering at Manchester University, and Professor J. N. Greenwood, a metallurgist who was Dean of the Faculty of Applied Science at the University of Melbourne.

The Royal Commission was authorised to report not only on the causes of the collapse, but also on the following Terms of Reference:

- I Whether the terms, conditions and specifications in the invitation to tender were adequate and reasonable for their purpose.
- II The tenders received and whether investigations leading to acceptance of Utah's tender were reasonable and proper and justified in the circumstances.
- III The adequacy and suitability of the design.
- IV The materials, processes and workmanship used in the construction and erection of the bridge.
- V Supervision of construction and erection.

74 Ibid.
75 Ibid 9.
76 Ibid

VI Whether there was any negligence involved in the failure.
VII Whether the construction and erection of the bridge in accordance with the tender was reasonable in the prevailing circumstances.[77]

16.3.2 Tenders

The CRB investigated delivering the project by three alternative methods:

- In-house detail design (including a bill of quantities) followed by a construction-only contract
- Design by a consulting engineer, followed by a construction-only contract
- Design and construct contract, with the CRB's role limited to providing investigation data, outline drawings and a specification.[78]

The CRB rejected in-house design because it was said to entail a year longer to complete the bridge. Design by consulting engineers was rejected on the same grounds, and also that there were insufficient local bridge designers available outside the CRB. That latter objection proved to be misconceived because a number of local consulting engineers subsequently combined to form KSBD.

16.3.3 Contract

The Royal Commission considered that the form of contract was not true design and construct:

> Usually the constructing authority sets out the nature and extent of the required structure in wide general terms, and leaves it to the contractor to create a detailed design. Doubtless, because of the desire to have competitive tenders for construction as well as for design the Board [CRB] found it necessary to prepare quite detailed design and specifications. A "design and construct" contract as usually understood is very suitable in cases where it is desired to employ the special expertise of some particular contractor, as for example where the contractor has some patented method of construction unobtainable elsewhere. On the other hand, when used in conjunction with competitive tendering, the true "design and construct" form is inappropriate, and must be modified, as in this case, to the extent where its advantages may be lost.[79]

Notwithstanding these comments, it is submitted that the lack of a detailed design prepared by the CRB, and the contractual obligation on Utah to prepare the full detailed design made this a contract that would be regarded today as true "design and construct".

The CRB Chairman advanced four perceived advantages of this type of contract:

- The system attracted the ideas of different designers
- "[W]ith the Contractor basically responsible for his own design there should be especially good harmony in supervision"

77 Ibid 3.
78 Ibid 11.
79 Ibid.

- "[A] similar procedure had been very successfully followed in the invitation of tenders for Sydney Harbour Bridge"
- If an overseas firm secured the contract some of the design work would be done overseas relieving pressure on local consulting engineers.[80]

The Royal Commission considered that none of these arguments was really compelling. In particular, the CRB's detailed specification limited the extent to which tenderers were able to exercise their ideas of design. The Royal Commission also noted the serious criticism of design and construct for Sydney Harbour Bridge by eminent members of the engineering profession, and suggested that the success of that project may have been in spite of, not because of, the design and construct form of contract.[81]

16.3.4 Criticisms of design and construct contract

Witnesses from all parties at the Royal Commission agreed that the form of contract worked well, but the view of the Royal Commission was the opposite, as they considered that the form of the contract was most unsatisfactory:

> The most serious disadvantage was undoubtedly the absence of a design engineer responsible for not only matters of design in the first place but for general supervision and control of the various aspects of the work in progress. Had a consulting engineer been employed directly by the CRB in the first instance to design the bridge and act in a supervisory capacity he would have been responsible directly to the CRB and would have exercised supervisory functions for it. This is in marked contrast to the position under the system adopted, as the designers were responsible only to the main contractor and not to the Board. Moreover, they could not be called upon to supervise the subcontractors for the Board. The contract between Utah and KSBD specifically provided that the designers would be available for consultation but would not be required to undertake any job supervision. In the result there was a complete separation of the functions of design and supervision.[82]
>
> *[citations omitted]*

16.3.5 Failure of the bridge

The Royal Commission criticised the breakdown in organisation during the construction, and the lack of communication between the Contractor and its subcontractors. In particular the designers were confined to the design and had no right to information on any fabrication problems, nor any corresponding duty to revise the design appropriately. Whilst this was consistent with the parties' legal contractual rights, "a grave lack of liaison and cooperation between them resulted".[83]

The Royal Commission made its views known on the contribution of the form of contract to the ultimate collapse in the following forthright terms:

> To a considerable extent, this [reliance on legal contractual rights] may be blamed on the parties themselves, but we feel that the disastrous effect of it, would have been at least mitigated

80 Ibid.
81 Ibid 12.
82 Ibid.
83 Ibid.

> had the CRB used a form of contract which provided for a consulting engineer responsible for overall supervision and control. ...
>
> It is our considered opinion that the CRB, while doubtless acting with the best intentions, made what turned out to be a crucial error of judgment in deciding upon the form of contract, which shaped the pattern of contractual relationships between the parties and failed to provide the necessary over-all supervision. These factors contributed to the troubles and difficulties encountered during construction and may have had a direct bearing on the failure of the bridge.[84]

The Royal Commission found that the major causes of failure were cracks at the toe of the transverse welds terminating the cover plates on the lower (tension) flanges of the girders in the span that failed. These cracks arose from problems of welding high tensile steel by a fabricator that was unfamiliar with the welding demands of this material, and the quality of steel supplied which was high in carbon, low in notch ductility and unexpectedly variable. The cracks were not discovered by either the fabricator or the CRB's inspectors.[85]

In relation to whether the form of tender had any bearing on the collapse, the Report of the Royal Commission made the following findings on Terms of Reference I:

> (a) The form of contract which was entered into, as required by the terms, conditions and specifications, called a 'design and construct' contract was in fact a modification of the contract usually so described. It was unsuitable in that it failed to provide the necessary overall supervision of the various aspects of the work and was to some degree responsible for the absence of proper coordination of the project.
>
> (b) The terms and conditions in accordance with which tenders were invited were inadequate in that the clause dealing with the assessment of tenders should have provided that one of the factors to be considered was 'the ability and competence of the tenderer to perform the contract and, in any case in which it is proposed to sub-contract a substantial part of the work, the ability and competence of the sub-contractor.'
>
> (c) The specifications and drawings were in general satisfactory and reasonable, but were unsuitable to the following extent:-
>
> (1) In the sections relating to the manufacture, testing and inspection of steel, the specifications lacked precision and contained ambiguities.
>
> (2) A number of important problems only arose because the specifications included B.S. 968:1941 steel with added clauses. It would have been much better if the CRB had set out fully the specification of the steel required without using the B.S. 968 label at all.[86]

16.3.6 Postscript

The fractured girders were replaced in the subsequent repairs. However, for political reasons, the government of the day did not want the bridge dismantled in order to replace the remaining girders, notwithstanding that the steel was of poor quality and subject to brittle fracture in cold weather. The Board of Works engineers responsible for the repairs came up with an ingenious solution. Brittle fracture in steel only occurs at low temperatures when the tension stress exceeds a certain threshold. The engineers' solution was to install prestressing cables to impart compressive stresses in the steel girders so that the steel

84 Ibid.
85 Ibid 93.
86 Ibid 94.

FIGURE 16.4 The underside of Kings Bridge girders in 2021.

would not be susceptible to brittle fracture at the lowest temperatures likely to be achieved in Melbourne. Prestressing cables were retrofitted in situ and tensioned to make Kings Bridge a prestressed steel girder bridge – the only one in the world known to this author.

Figure 16.4 shows the underside of two sets of Kings Bridge girders. The pair on the left are original girders with the retrofitted prestressing cables anchored in a concrete block. The girders on the right were installed in the 1990s and support an additional lane of the bridge. Fabricated from better quality steel not subject to brittle fracture, these girders have no prestressing cables! (Figure 16.4)

16.4 Conclusion

The two bridges discussed above had very different outcomes. By any measure, Sydney Harbour Bridge was a successful project, not only technically, but also commercially (at least on the information reported above). It is submitted that the contemporaneous criticism of the design and construct form of project delivery for that project by eminent members of the engineering profession was more a consequence of their unfamiliarity with this mode of project delivery, and the understandable resistance of a conservative profession to change established and proven procedures, than any demonstrated deficiencies in the process itself. Much of the criticism now seems quaint, given the centrality of competition in virtually every aspect of modern society, and our familiarity with design and construct as a common delivery method.

Nevertheless, it seems that some of the issues identified above for Sydney Harbour Bridge and Kings Bridge are still relevant and pertinent today:

- The importance of unambiguous language in defining the extent of design concepts that conform to the invitation to tender
- Clear, comprehensive technical specifications that define the limits of permitted design variations from the concept designs on which tenders are called and accepted
- Contract conditions that require the designer to have an ongoing meaningful role in fabrication and erection
- The value of independent, competent and thorough technical scrutiny of the design.

Clearly, the form of contract for project delivery will not, per se, govern whether the outcome will be successful or not. A "traditional" form of project delivery in which the Employer separately contracts with designers and a Contractor of the highest reputation, well established and who have demonstrated their ability to successfully undertake important projects, is not an automatic guarantee of success, as evidenced by the tragic failure of the West Gate Bridge in Melbourne[87] (see Chapter 22 below). The unquestioned success of Sydney Harbour Bridge supports the proposition that a properly structured, executed and administered design and construct contract is capable of achieving world's best practice from a technical, and perhaps even more importantly from the Employer's perspective, a safe and commercially successful project that achieves icon status internationally.

87 Victoria, *Royal Commission into the Failure of West Gate Bridge, Report* (1971).

CHAPTER 17

State of Tasmania v Leighton Contractors Pty Ltd[1]

17.1 Background

This case involved a dispute over the Contractor's obligations in constructing a new section of the Bass Highway in northern Tasmania. The Contractor, Leighton Contractors Pty Ltd, contracted to design, construct and maintain for ten years a 13.65 km section of road, including bypasses of the towns of Hagley and Westbury. The contract (**Project Deed**) was with the State of Tasmania by its department, the Department of Infrastructure, Energy and Resources (**DIER**).

The main issue in dispute was the required level of the road in front of the historic Hagley House property, listed on the Tasmanian Heritage Register – the DIER asserted that the Project Deed required that it be in cut, whereas the Contractor asserted that the road was permitted to be on fill at that location. The Contractor prepared a design and commenced to construct the road 1.24 m above natural surface level (**NSL**) before the owner of Hagley House objected that this road level was inconsistent with undertakings he had previously been given by the DIER. Alternative designs to satisfy the owner were investigated, during which construction stopped on this part of the highway. After a construction hiatus of six months, an instruction on behalf of the DIER was issued to the Contractor to design and build the road in cut 1.5 m deep opposite Hagley House (**the Direction**). The road was subsequently completed to this design, and opened to traffic seven and a half months after the DIER approved Date for Construction Completion.[2]

The State of Tasmania instituted proceedings in the Supreme Court of Tasmania seeking a number of declarations to the effect that:

- The Contractor's design of the road on 1.24 m of fill was not in accordance with the Project Deed
- The Direction did not constitute a Change as defined in the Project Deed
- The Contractor was not entitled to additional compensation because of the Direction, and
- The Contractor was not entitled to any extension of time because of the Direction.

1 This chapter is an edited version of the paper published in: Donald Charrett, "State of Tasmania v Leighton Contractors Pty Ltd [No 3] [2004] TASSC 132" (2005) 102 *Australian Construction Law Newsletter* 36.

2 [217], [287] (All paragraph references in square brackets in this chapter refer to *State of Tasmania v Leighton Contractors Pty Ltd (No 3)* [2004] TASSC 132.)

DOI: 10.4324/9781003206897-19

The Contractor counterclaimed, seeking compensation and an extension of time for the additional work arising from the Direction. The Contractor also attacked the basis of the liquidated damages of $1.8 m that had been withheld by the DIER as a penalty and therefore unenforceable. In addition, the Contractor counterclaimed for various items it claimed were Changes under the Project Deed.

The proceeding in respect of liability only was heard by His Honour Chief Justice Cox over a total of 80 sitting days between April and October 2004. His comprehensive judgment of 152 pages provides a general description of the works and the early history of the bypass project, details the voluminous documentation that constituted the Project Deed, and the way in which the specific environmental and planning requirements were incorporated into the contract. His Honour described the tender process and construed the contract, in particular the constraints imposed on the design by the environmental documents incorporated in the Project Deed, to conclude that a complying design required that the road be built in cut opposite Hagley House.

The outcome on the required level of the road was the result of a careful construction of the requirements of the environmental documents that were formally incorporated into the Project Deed, particularly the cultural heritage requirements and, as such, was very specific to the detailed provisions of this purpose-written contract. Notwithstanding that it is so specific, the judgment has wider interest for anyone involved in design and construct contracts because of its detailed consideration of the contractual effect of the interaction of a complex set of technical and environmental documents. Some Contractors and designers may be surprised by Cox CJ's conclusion on the status of the tender design incorporated into the Project Deed, and the way in which non-specific environmental objectives ultimately had such a controlling influence on the design required to comply with the Project Deed.

Cox CJ determined that the rate of liquidated damages provided for in the contract was not a genuine pre-estimate of the likely damage to the State as a consequence of the late opening of the bypass, and was therefore a penalty that was unenforceable. The State appealed against this part of the judgment, and the appeal was upheld by the Full Court.[3] No other aspects of the case were appealed, and accordingly the findings of Cox CJ discussed below have not been overturned.

17.2 Early history of the bypass project[4]

His Honour detailed the planning for realignment of the Bass Highway that had been undertaken since the mid-1990s within the context of obtaining the necessary Federal Government funding. Four possible route options were investigated and put out for public comment. Detailed investigations were carried out on two routes, including preliminary survey work, geotechnical investigations and assessment of environmental, cultural heritage, noise and social and other impacts. Preliminary design concepts were documented for each route. Evaluation of the options was reported in two volumes of the Development Proposal and Environmental Management Plan (**DPEMP**), one for the Hagley bypass (**Hagley DPEMP**) and one for the Westbury bypass (**Westbury DPEMP**).

3 *State of Tasmania v Leighton Contractors Pty Ltd* [2005] TASSC 133.

4 [19]–[60].

The project approval process involved the Federal/State Environmental and Federal Heritage approval process and the State Planning and Heritage approval process. The DPEMP documents were central to those approval processes and were endorsed by the approvals of both the Federal and State authorities. Heritage issues were very much at the forefront, as Works Applications were required to alter or disturb sites of heritage significance included on the Tasmanian Heritage Register. Works Applications were granted for Hagley Mill and the property known as Woodside.

The Hagley DPEMP described and detailed the two routes under consideration, and outlined the various impacts that each of those routes would have on the environmental and cultural values of the area. Considerable attention was devoted to minimising the impact of the road on the historical listed Hagley Mill complex. Concept designs had been prepared by Maunsell Pty Ltd for each route, and these were described in general terms. The description of the Railway Route (the route that was ultimately adopted) included a general description of the road being depressed below ground level in the general vicinity of Hagley House, and reference to minimising the visual impact of key locations, including heritage areas, resulting in a depressed highway where possible. Appendix D showed the Maunsell concept design for the Railway Route on layout plans in 700 m sections along the Hagley Bypass, and these plans indicate that the road was in cut in the vicinity of Hagley House, although they do not indicate the depth of cut.

The Hagley DPEMP noted that Hagley House, Hagley Mill and immediate surrounds and Hagley Mill Cultural Landscape are on the Register of the National Estate, and are major historic landscapes that have cultural significance. Under visual and landscape effects, the Hagley DPEMP stated that "the new highway will be depressed by approximately 4 metres", and "the new highway will not be directly visible from Hagley House due to the depression of the road". In specific commentary on the Hagley Mill Cultural Landscape, it further stated: "At Hagley House, the road will be in a depression. The road surface will not be seen from the house and the historic visual links between the house, Church and school will be maintained."

Notwithstanding these various descriptive references, and the Maunsell concept drawings that show the road to be in cut in the vicinity of Hagley House, "The plans do not, however, give any detail as to the depth of the cut nor do they, or indeed any other parts of the DPEMP, contain any engineering information from which the depth of the cut could be calculated with precision."[5]

17.3 The tender process[6]

An Invitation to Tender (**ITT**) was issued to the selected tenderers which stated that, inter alia, "The Tenderer must base its Tender on investigating, designing, constructing and maintaining the Project in accordance with the Environmental Documents and the environmental requirements contained in the Project Deed." The Environmental Documents were included in the ITT as part of the proposed Project Deed.

The ITT included concept design drawings prepared by the Employer (**Principal**), which were the same as those attached to the Mersey Valley Council (**MVC**) permits for

5 [60].
6 [68]–[78].

the section of road in the vicinity of Hagley House. Other information provided to the tenderers included geotechnical and contamination reports. The DIER conducted a pre-tender meeting that included a site inspection of the project. At that meeting, no specific reference was made to Hagley House, or to any necessary amenity being provided in respect of that property. The importance of environmental and cultural heritage issues on the project was emphasised at the pre-tender meeting.

The tender submitted by the Contractor included drawings of the design it had prepared (**Concept Design Drawings**), and a description of its design under various headings. The road in front of Hagley House was shown in cut, 0.795 m below NSL. The road level opposite Hagley Mill, approximately 400 m to the west of Hagley House, was at a level of 149 m AHD, a level specified by the Scope of Works and Technical Criteria (**SOW&TC**) as amended by the DIER during the tender process. This amended level of the road opposite Hagley Mill was arguably inconsistent with the statement in the DPEMP that the road level was to be approximately 1–2 m below ground level "in the vicinity of the Mill". However, Cox CJ did not consider this significant, having regard to the imprecision implied by the words used to describe the location of the road.

One of the Contractor's staff reviewed the proposed Project Deed, and in an internal memorandum noted that the terms were particularly complex and in some cases unreasonable. He noted in particular his opinion that it was unreasonable to consider that a tenderer would not rely on the Information Documents, and that the Environmental Documents may have subjective and/or unreasonable requirements.

17.4 Project Deed[7]

The Contract was a design, construct and maintain contract (**DCM Contract**). It provided for the Contractor to design the highway, subject to the parameters set by the Project Deed, to construct it according to the design it evolved and which was duly verified and not rejected by the Principal's Representative, and to maintain it for a period of ten years after the Date of Construction Completion.[8] The Contract entered into consisted of the voluminous documentation comprehensively described as the Project Deed.[9]

The functions of Principal's Representative under the Project Deed were divided and performed by three persons – one from the DIER and two from Pitt and Sherry, consulting engineers. The Principal's Representative was authorised under the Project Deed to issue instructions on behalf of the Principal (DIER), and was the person the Contractor communicated with in relation to the Project Deed. The Principal's Representative's functions included, inter alia:

- Commenting on the proposed design documentation at the 15% and 85% design stages, as well as the "for construction" design.
- Directing the Contractor to change Design Documentation which was in accordance with the requirements of the Deed, as verified by the Design Verifier or the

7 [80]–[103].
8 [69].
9 [79].

Design Verifier Durability, such direction to constitute a Change to be valued in accordance with clause 7 of the Project Deed.

- Nomination of any other design component of the Project Works not specifically referred to in the Project Deed to be verified by the Design Verifier.
- Consulting with the Contractor and commenting on the submitted Design Documentation if it chose to do so.
- Rejection of any Design Documentation submitted to it that was not in accordance with the requirements of the Project Deed. Such rejection notice was to state the reasons why the Principal's Representative considered the relevant Design Documentation was not in accordance with the requirements of the Project Deed.
- Monitoring the performance of the Contractor.
- Issue of Change Price requests to the Contractor in connection with changes the Principal was considering.
- Giving directions to the Contractor in respect of work which was not compliant with the Project Deed.[10]
- The capacity to agree to construction proceeding, notwithstanding that the design documentation was non-compliant in the sense of being contrary to a specific constraint or deficient in that some documentation had not been provided.[11]

Significantly, the Principal and the Principal's Representative were protected by the following clause of Volume 1 of the Project Deed:

> 1.20 Unlimited Discretion
>
> (a) Subject to any contrary express provisions of this Deed (including in clause 10.1(i)), there will be no procedural or substantive limitation upon the manner in which the Principal or the Principal's Representative may exercise any discretion, power or entitlement conferred by this Deed.
>
> (b) Without limiting clause 1.20(a), neither the Principal nor the Principal's Representative will be under any obligation to exercise any such discretion, power or entitlement in good faith or reasonably or as required by any other legal doctrine which in any way limits the express words used in the provision of this Deed conferring the discretion, power or entitlement.[12]

The Project Deed included terms and conditions, SOW&TC and the Hagley and Westbury DPEMPs. In the event of any inconsistency between the various documents comprising the Project Deed, the order of precedence of the documents was defined as follows:

(a) The Project Deed excluding the schedules and exhibits
(b) The schedules
(c) The Scope of Works and Technical Criteria excluding appendices
(d) SOW&TC appendices provided by the Principal (appendices P1 to P23)

10 [163].
11 [201].
12 [255].

(e) Hagley DPEMP and Westbury DPEMP (together **Environmental Documents**), Principal's Insurance and overall design and construct program, and
(f) SOW&TC appendices provided by the Contractor (appendices T1 to T23).

It is interesting to note that the Appendices, including Appendix T1 which consisted of the Contractor's Concept Design Drawings, was lowest in the order of precedence, and of lower precedence than the Environmental Documents.

The following specific provisions of the Project Deed were of relevance to the dispute:

- The Deed was expressed to be an entire contract.
- The Contractor could not rely on information provided prior to entering the Deed; the "Information Documents" provided by the DIER did not form part of the Deed, and the Principal was rendered immune from suit in respect of them.
- The Contractor was specifically required to comply with the environmental requirements contained in the Environmental Documents.
- The Contractor's obligation to comply with all relevant law applied to compliance with the relevant Planning Permits and Environmental Protection Notices.
- The Contractor was required to notify DIER of any actual or potential breach or non-compliance with the Environmental Documents or any Law.
- The Contractor's particular design obligations included not only the requirement to design the Project Works, but also to give specific warranties, including that it had checked the SOW&TC and it was fit for the purpose of the other warranties, and the completed Project Works would satisfy the requirements of the Project Deed.
- The Contractor warranted that the other warranties were unaffected by design work carried out by others prior to entry into the Deed.
- The detailed provision on preparation of design documentation provided that the Principal's Representative was to have the opportunity to attend design meetings and comment on and monitor the design performance of the Contractor, specifically at the 15% and 85% stages. If the Principal's Representative directed a change to design documentation in accordance with the Deed, such direction would constitute a Change to be valued in accordance with the Deed provisions.
- Defined design components, including geometric, drainage, earthworks, subgrade and pavement design, were to be verified by the Design Verifier who was required to submit a defined "Schedule 12" verification.
- Final design documentation to be submitted for the various elements was to include a final design report and a durability assessment report, and the Contractor was not to commence construction for a period of 14 days from that submission. The Contractor was not to amend any Design Documentation which had been submitted to and not rejected by the Principal's Representative, without resubmission in accordance with the defined procedures.
- The Contractor was not to use for construction purposes any Design Documentation that had not been verified by the Design Verifier and submitted and reviewed by the Principal's Representative.
- The Contractor was to engage the Design Verifier and Design Verifier Durability and ensure that they would act honestly, fairly and independently of the Contractor. The Design Verifier and Design Verifier Durability were required to

execute a deed of covenant in which they acknowledged that in performing their services they would owe a duty of care to the Principal, and that the Principal would be relying on their skill and judgment.

- In the event of a discrepancy between verified and submitted design documentation, the Project Deed requirements prevail.
- The Contractor was required to construct the highway according to the design it had evolved, and which was duly verified by the Design Verifier and not rejected by the Principal's Representative.
- Changes to the Design Documentation, which were verified and conformed to the Project Deed requirements, could be directed by the Principal's Representative. These would be carried out and valued in accordance with procedures detailed in clause 7 of the Project Deed.
- The Contractor was required to notify the Principal's Representative within seven days if a Direction by the Principal's Representative (other than a Change Order) constituted a Change.

17.5 Scope of works and technical requirements[13]

The SOW&TC was a detailed document with 22 appendices. Cox CJ highlighted the following clauses as relevant to the dispute:

- Fundamental obligations.
- Delivery objectives and strategy.
- Nature and extent of Contractor's activities.
- Environmental.
- Landscaping and aesthetics.
- General (project plans to include Construction Environmental Management Plan and landscape plan).
- Construction Environmental Management Plan.
- General design requirements (including general design constraints).
- Final design report.
- Horizontal and vertical alignments.
- Road layout adjoining Hagley Mill.
- Noise mitigation measures.
- Clearance of overhead structures.
- Water management.
- Landscaping and aesthetics.
- General landscape and heritage issues.
- Landscape and cultural heritage design.

17.6 Value management workshop

Soon after the Project Deed was signed, the Contractor conducted a value management workshop, which was attended by a representative of the DIER (Principal), and the

13 [102]–[105].

Principal's Representative, as well as some of the Contractor's designers. At that workshop, the Contractor's road designer discussed a table of fundamental grading controls that were mandatory requirements that had to be met by an acceptable design. The designer's evidence was that he considered this list of grade controls to be complete and the basis of the various designs developed during the final design phase.

Cox CJ however did not consider that the attendees representing the Principal would

> necessarily have understood the discussion to invite the nomination of any other grading control, including that at Hagley House (if that were perceived by them to be mandated by the contract) and consideration of the question whether it could be varied as the design evolved. If the aim of the meeting was to reduce the Contractor's costs, it was really up to the Contractor to nominate all mandated grade lines including those required to be cut but in respect of which no specific dimensions of cut were laid down. There was no reason for the representatives of the Principal to raise the matter at all.[14]

17.7 The 15% design and its review[15]

The 15% design submitted by the Contractor showed the road in front of Hagley House to be on fill, 0.85 m above NSL. This was different from the Contractor's Concept Design submitted with the tender (and incorporated into the Project Deed as Appendix T1 to the SOW&TC), which showed the road to be 0.795 m in cut at this location.[16]

Although Cox CJ observed that the change in vertical and horizontal alignment was not specifically drawn to the Principal's attention, he was nevertheless satisfied that it was motivated by sound engineering reasons to get the road out of the groundwater at the earliest possible opportunity. These sound engineering reasons related to construction as well as maintenance, and included problems of batter stability and groundwater seepage into batters.

The Project Principal's Representative sent a letter to the Contractor with detailed comments on many aspects of the design, of which Cox CJ commented: "I think it is no exaggeration to say that the reviewers had been through the drawings with a fine-tooth comb and had indicated the view in many cases that changes ought to be made rather than merely making comments." His Honour noted that the reviewers, all agents of the State, must have been conscious that the 15% design showed the road in the vicinity of Hagley House to be on fill, and not in cut as the tender design had depicted. Cox CJ summarised the review of the 15% design as follows:

> The Review by the Principal and the Principal's Representative of the 15% Design made no protest at, nor critical comment about, the fact that the road at Hagley House was shown to be on fill. There was no suggestion that there was any lack of compliance with the Deed.[17]

17.8 The 85% design and its review[18]

This later iteration of the design as submitted to the Principal's Representative showed the road in the vicinity of Hagley House to be on fill of greater depth than shown on

14 [105].
15 [108]–[119].
16 [76].
17 [119].
18 [120]–[121].

the 15% drawings, being approximately 1.2 m opposite Hagley House. In the response by the Principal's Representative, no comment was made about the vertical alignment at Hagley House. Under cross-examination, the Principal conceded that the Contractor was told there were no issues of significance in connection with the 85% Review, and that the Contractor's response to four outstanding issues identified by the Principal's Representative constituted a complete response to them.

17.9 Final design submissions[19]

The Contractor submitted the final design documentation to the Principal's Representative in a number of numbered submissions. These submissions sought to obtain approval of the elements of the highway (structures and sections of road) consistent with the Contractor's construction schedule. The Contractor obtained the Principal's Representative's agreement to issue Schedule 12s with conditions attached. These conditional certifications by the Design Verifier were required as a consequence of certain aspects of the design that were incomplete at the time the Contractor wished to commence construction.

The Contractor submitted packages of design for the civil works comprising all elements of the road documentation to the Design Verifier in four stages: A, B, C, and D. The Design Verifier issued a conditional Schedule 12 for design package C (which subsumed all elements of the earlier packages A and B) prior to the Contractor's commencement of construction of the road in the vicinity of Hagley House. This highway design package C was subsequently subsumed by the later conditional Schedule 12 for design package D. None of the Design Verifier's comments on the Schedule 12 for packages C and D related to the relevant alignment of the road. Both these packages showed the road alignment on fill opposite Hagley House. The Design Verifier gave evidence that he did "not regard the change from the road being in cut in front of Hagley House in the Tender Concept Design to being on fill in the 'for construction' drawings as being significant".

17.10 Landowner's complaint about road level[20]

Shortly after the Contractor had commenced construction of the road opposite Hagley House, the owner of Hagley House complained to an officer of the DIER (**C.**) that the road alignment opposite his property was on fill, and not in cut as he had been led to believe by a previous officer of the DIER. Cox CJ found that this complaint resulted in C., in his role as the Principal, becoming aware for the first time (and in spite of his previous close scrutiny of the 15%, 85% and 100% design submissions) that the final design was on fill opposite Hagley House, which he regarded as inconsistent with the Environmental Documents. His Honour also found that, as the Principal, C. was acutely conscious of the environmental constraints which the Commonwealth authority had imposed before committing Federal funding to the project, and that he had placed considerable emphasis on the environmental sensitivity of the project at the pre-tender meeting with prospective tenderers.

19 [122]–[139].
20 [129]–[163].

Although the owner's complaint clearly related to the amenity of his own property, Cox CJ described the response of C. as follows:

> I find that when he discovered that a departmental officer had previously given [the owner] the undertaking [that the road would be in cut in the vicinity of Hagley House] he formed the view that the undertaking must be honoured and was initially unsure whether Leighton could be blamed for the elevation of the road when the Design Documentation which had been reviewed by the Principal's Representative and by himself clearly showed it to be on fill. He could see the potential for considerable embarrassment should the issue not be resolved quickly, for there could be political repercussions if the undertaking was not honoured and the Heritage Authorities might intervene claiming a failure to enforce the relatively imprecise provisions of the DPEMP designed to preserve heritage values. His claim that he would have been content for Leighton to seek and obtain approval from the Council and these authorities for the new design was likewise unconvincing. Had such approval been obtained it would not have solved the [owner's] problem and in any event would have been likely to take so long to procure that completion of the highway would have been delayed an unacceptable period of time. What remained uppermost in [C.]'s thoughts throughout this crisis was ensuring that [the owner] was placated with a redesign which also satisfied the environmental authorities. His initial willingness to pay for the lowering of the road was soon replaced with the determination to find some basis for laying the blame at Leighton's door.[21]

Within two weeks of the owner's call to C., the Tasmanian Heritage Commission (**THC**) and the MVC were aware that the road at Hagley House was on fill. The THC indicated concern and intimated the possibility of putting a statutory stop work order on the project. The Principal's Representative wrote to the Contractor one week after the owner had complained, and requested the Contractor to look at alternative vertical alignments of 1 m, 2 m and 3 m in cut. The Contractor's response was to stop construction of that section of the road in the vicinity of Hagley House, and to investigate the alternative road alignments in cut as requested by the Principal's Representative.

Over the six months from the owner's complaint to C. to the Principal's Representative's Direction to the Contractor to build the road in cut 1.5 m below NSL at Hagley House, numerous letters were sent by the Principal's Representative and the Contractor, discussing various design proposals, costings and contractual issues related to the reconstruction of the road on fill. The Contractor's position was that the costs of the reconstruction and delay were the responsibility of the State. The Principal's Representative's position was that it was the responsibility of the Contractor, on the basis that the Contractor's design did not satisfy the requirements of the Project Deed and the Contractor was in breach of contract (although this allegation was later withdrawn). The initial view of C. was that the Principal was willing to pay for lowering the road, and an early letter from the Principal's Representative to the Contractor suggested that the Principal and the Contractor share the cost, and invited the Contractor to submit a claim for extra work. A period of three months from the owner's complaint to C. elapsed before the Principal's Representative positively asserted to the Contractor that its design was noncompliant. Nearly a further three months elapsed before the Principal's Representative issued a formal direction.

21 [142].

17.11 Road design as directed[22]

Following a site meeting attended by C., the Principal's Representative, the Contractor, representatives of the THC and MVC and the owner, a possible design was suggested by the Principal's Representative: highway nominally 1 m in cut opposite Hagley House with a 1.7 m earth mound and landscaping screening 2 m high on top of the earth mound.

The THC, whose interest was the impact of the road on the cultural heritage of the area, considered that a road alignment 1 m in cut with a 1.2 m high earth mound would be a satisfactory solution. Cox CJ found that the heritage requirements of the road could be achieved by this design and that the THC neither could nor would have taken any action if that design had been implemented.

C. was apparently not satisfied with the design 1 m in cut, and suggested depressing the road a further 500 mm to counter the reduced mound height from the 1.7 m initially suggested to the 1.2 m acceptable to the THC. The Contractor's designers prepared a design on this basis which was submitted to the relevant landowners and authorities, who "signed off" on it. The Principal's Representative issued a formal direction to design and construct the highway in accordance with the agreed design, some six months after the owner's complaint had drawn attention to the issue.

The Contractor had consistently taken the view that its design on fill that it had commenced to construct was compliant with the Project Deed, and that any direction to change it constituted a compensable Change under the Project Deed. Its request for compensation for the costs of the changes directed was rejected by the Principal's Representative.

17.12 Was the Contractor's in-fill design compliant?[23]

Cox CJ considered in detail the question as to whether, properly construed, the Project Deed required that the road be in cut in the vicinity of Hagley House. He analysed the various references in the Project Deed, including the references in the SOW&TC and the DPEMP that alluded to the vertical alignment of the road in the vicinity of Hagley House. Whilst none of these mentioned a specific depth of cut (which was conceded by the State), his Honour found a number of provisions that made it clear that the concept of depressing the road near Hagley House as a means of minimising impact was to be incorporated into the design of the road.

His Honour summarised his conclusions on this issue as follows:

> An on fill construction not being in accordance with the mandated cut design contemplated by the DPEMP, Leighton's construction of the highway at Hagley House 1.239 metres on fill constituted a breach of the Planning Permit, D368/98, a condition of which was that works were to be carried out in accordance with the DPEMP. It is unnecessary therefore to consider whether the development was 'generally in accordance with' the plans attached to the permit. Mr Westerway, the Town Planner with the MVC who issued the permit, did not regard the vertical alignment as of significant concern, but the elevation or depression of sections of a major road passing over so sensitive a heritage area as the Hagley landscape should have been of significance to him and for the reasons already given, his view that the Management Requirements and Commitments contained in section 24 of the DPEMP were the only significant ones for Town Planning purposes, was erroneous. Though the depth of cut was not

22 [168]–[177].
23 [178]–[193].

> specified in the DPEMP and no longitudinal sections were attached to the permit, the plans, when considered in the context of the strategies outlined in the DPEMP (i.e., those not confined to section 24 thereof), mandated something other than an on fill design. One of a height of 1.239 metres above NSL represented, in my view, a substantial departure from the drawings and produced a situation in which it could not be said that the constructed road was generally in accordance with those drawings. The design was non-compliant with the permit.[24]

His Honour also found that the Contractor's on fill design was not properly verified, and accordingly the Principal's Representative's Direction did not constitute a compensable Change.

17.13 Consequences of noncompliance[25]

After consideration of the relevant Project Deed clauses and the relevant circumstances, Cox CJ concluded that the Contractor's noncompliance on fill design was not in fact rejected by the Principal's Representative prior to the start of construction. Sometime after the owner had complained, the Contractor was being asked not just to prepare a compliant design that satisfied the relevant authorities, but one which predominantly would satisfy the owner's amenity. As this was beyond the Contractor's contractual obligations, his Honour concluded that, to the extent that the Direction required the Contractor, in order to satisfy the owner, to construct a design which involved any greater cost than that of an otherwise compliant design, it constituted a compensable Change.

The Contractor submitted that it should at least be compensated for the additional cost of constructing the road in cut to the level at which it was ultimately built as compared with its concept tender design in cut of 0.795 m which it said must have been compliant. In a significant part of the judgment that will give future design and construct Contractors considerable food for thought, Cox CJ stated:

> I do not accept that such a degree of cut was necessarily compliant. The tender concept was just that – a concept. Other factors had to be taken into consideration such as the general heritage and cultural requirements of the contract and neither the acceptance of the tender by the Principal nor the requirement that the ultimate vertical alignment not vary significantly from the tender concept design automatically conferred compliant status on that degree of cut, nor fixed that level as the only level of cut which would be compliant. It was submitted that the State had led no evidence that the tender design was not in accordance with the Project Deed, but Mr Corney's [THC expert witness] evidence, which I accept, indicates that he regarded a depth of cut of 1 metre as necessary to satisfy the heritage requirements of the Deed (see par 171 (supra)).[26]

Contractors and designers involved in design and construct contracts should note that his Honour reached this conclusion not from any specific detailed engineering criteria in the SOW&TC, but after a careful analysis of the descriptive criteria in the Environmental Documents, and the design obligations that they entailed. Sections 2–22 of the Hagley DPEMP were largely descriptive of the proposal for the road, the problems associated with it, and measures for minimising adverse impacts, while Sections 23 and 24 contained detailed instructions or requirements, first in respect of the Hagley Mill complex itself and,

24 [185].
25 [202]–[211].
26 [208].

second, in respect of the actual construction and operation phases of the plan.[27] His Honour however considered that the obligations imposed by the DPEMP in respect of road design were not confined to the requirements and commitments specified in Section 24, which contained the constraints that had to be incorporated into the Construction Environmental Management Plan. As noted above, although the Contractor's Concept Design was incorporated into the Project Deed, its precedence was lower than that of the DPEMP.

It is also interesting to note that his Honour reached his conclusion on the acceptable depth of cut on the basis of the evidence of only one expert. The other heritage experts called by the State did not nominate any particular level of cut at Hagley House as an appropriate minimum. The Contractor's heritage expert considered that a cut of 300 mm would have been sufficient.

His Honour concluded his judgment on the claim on the road alignment that the Contractor was entitled to be paid the difference in cost between construction of the road at a depth of 1.5 m and the compliant 1 m. It was not however entitled to the cost of placing the road on fill or for removing the fill once the Direction was received.

17.14 Delay[28]

In view of his finding that the Direction to lower the road to 1.5 m in cut was more than the Principal's Representative could legitimately require the Contractor to do without compensation for the additional cost, Cox CJ found that the Contractor was entitled to an extension of time to the Date for Practical Completion. Clause 9.4(a) of Volume 1 of the Project Deed provided that if the Contractor was prevented from achieving Construction Completion by the Date for Construction Completion by an Excusable Cause of Delay, it was entitled to an extension of time. The Direction was a Change the subject of a Direction by the Principal's Representative and was therefore an Excusable Cause of Delay in accordance with Clause 1.1 of Volume 1 of the Project Deed.

The State submitted that the judge should have taken into account any other concurrent cause of delay in determining what was a reasonable time in these circumstances. His Honour however noted:

> If, irrespective of the state of progress of the works, the time necessary to carry out the work which was the subject of the Direction will be greater than the time remaining until the Date For Construction Completion, then the Contractor would, prima facie, be entitled to an extension of time even if all other work is hopelessly behind schedule and could not possibly be finished before the Date For Construction Completion.[29]

As the Contractor's arguments on the delay to the works was based on the time taken to change the level of the road from 1.24 m on fill to the directed 1.5 m in cut, there was no evidence available to his Honour that enabled him to determine what time delay was actually caused by the additional 0.5 m of cut from the complying 1.0 m in cut to the directed 1.5 m in cut.

This issue was further complicated by a lack of evidence on the specific changes that might have been necessary as a consequence of the differences between a design for 1 m in

27 [36].
28 [213]–[232].
29 [230].

cut and one for 1.5 m in cut. His Honour noted that the Contractor's tender design for 0.8 m cut was only preliminary, and it was therefore not clear whether even that design could have been made to work without a drainage blanket, as was included in the final (1.5 m in cut) design. In this situation, his Honour left the issues of the number of days delay and the number of days for which the Contractor was entitled to delay costs to the subsequent part of the trial dealing with quantum.

17.15 The independence of the Principal's Representative

The Contractor pleaded that the Principal's Representative did not act independently as required by the Project Deed, nor reasonably and fairly. Clause 10.1(i) of Volume 1 of the Project Deed required that, in exercising certain defined functions only, the Principal's Representative was to act independently of the State and the Contractor. Cox CJ acknowledged that implied terms may be found in a number of cases for a Principal's Representative to act reasonably, honestly and fairly and in good faith, and that the Principal shall not interfere with its Representative in carrying out its functions. However, he noted that it was an express term of this contract that the Principal's Representative had unlimited discretions and powers. As detailed above, the express terms of Clause 1.20 of Volume 1 of the Project Deed provided that, subject to acting independently as required by Clause 10.1(i), neither the Principal nor the Principal's Representative was required to exercise any discretion, power or entitlement in good faith or reasonably, or as required by any other legal doctrine which in any way limited the express words used.

His Honour considered that, irrespective of whether the Principal's Representative acted independently as required by Clause 10.1(i), or reasonably and fairly, his decision in not accepting that there was an Excusable Cause of Delay and determining the Extension of Time required by the Direction was flawed. He noted without elaboration that in those circumstances it was common ground that it was up to the Court to determine the issue. That is, notwithstanding the unlimited discretion provided by Clause 1.20, it was apparently not argued that the Project Deed provided for the decision of the Principal's Representative to be binding and conclusive and unable to be reviewed by the court. On the evidence, his Honour accepted that the Principal's Representative acted independently, reasonably and fairly in relation to the deductions he considered arose under the Project Deed, although his decision was in error.[30]

17.16 Summary

The essential issue from which the dispute arose was the level at which the road was contractually required be built in the vicinity of Hagley House. The judgment was that the Contractor was required to build the road at a depth of 1m in cut opposite Hagley House to satisfy the environmental criteria set out in the DPEMP, and thereby incorporated into the Project Deed. This requirement, according to Cox CJ, arose because the horizontal and vertical alignments of the road had to be such that they complied with all the requirements of the Project Deed.

The 1 m cut requirement was in spite of:

30 [324]–[327].

- The three heritage experts called by the State did not give any evidence of the acceptable depth of cut, the expert called by the Contractor considered that a shallow cutting of up to 300 mm maximum depth was sufficient to protect cultural heritage values, and only one, the heritage expert from the THC, considered that 1 m depth of cut was the minimum acceptable value.[31]
- The tender design showing the road 0.8 m in cut opposite Hagley House, which design was incorporated into the Project Deed in Appendix T1.
- The requirement that the final design not vary significantly from the tender design.[32]
- The documents comprising the Project Deed did not give any details as to the required depth of cut, nor did they contain any engineering information from which the depth of cut could be explicitly determined.[33]
- The review and absence of comment on the vertical alignment by the Principal's Representative at 15% design, 85% design and for construction drawings which all showed the road on fill opposite Hagley House.
- The DIER's acceptance of an amendment to the SOW&TC that permitted the road at Hagley Mill to be built in only 0.73 m of cut, which was in conflict with the DPEMP requirement of 1–2 m below ground level in the vicinity of the Mill.[34]
- The provisions in the DPEMP designed to protect heritage values were "relatively imprecise".[35]
- The MVC Town Planner who issued the Planning Permit did not regard as of significant concern the vertical alignment of the road in the vicinity of Hagley House.[36]
- The Design Verifier did not regard as significant the change in road design from the Concept Design Drawings (0.8 m in cut) to being on 1.24 m of fill in the "for construction" drawings.[37]

Clearly, the outcome in this case depended on construction of the terms of a Project Deed which contained a complex series of interacting documents. The complexity of this task of construction is illustrated by the number of pages of his Honour's judgment that were necessary to detail the relevant paragraphs and explain their meaning in the context of the contract as a whole. Considering the importance that environmental considerations have in any major project today, this case is a salutary reminder of the onerous and complex task undertaken by civil engineering contractors undertaking design and construct projects in accordance with purpose-written contract documents.

31 [209]–[210].
32 [208].
33 [60].
34 [77].
35 [142].
36 [185].
37 [137].

CHAPTER 18

The Canterbury earthquakes I[1]

18.1 Introduction

The Canterbury earthquakes – a human tragedy in which 185 people lost their lives and severe damage was caused to the built environment – occurred near to and within the city of Christchurch, New Zealand in 2010 and 2011. Eighteen people died in one building (**PGC**) and 115 in another (**CTV**). A further 42 people died from the failure of other buildings and many more were injured. A further 10 people lost their lives for reasons not related to building failure, including rock falls.

The New Zealand government subsequently implemented a Royal Commission, the terms of reference for which required recommendations to be made on:

- Measures necessary or desirable to prevent or minimise the failure of buildings due to earthquakes likely to occur during the lifetime of those buildings
- The cost of those measures, and
- The adequacy of legal and best practice requirements for building design, construction and maintenance related to managing the risks of building failures caused by earthquakes.

This chapter endeavours to highlight what the author considers are the most important issues and lessons learnt from the Royal Commission Report (**Report**) that are of interest to construction lawyers around the world. Given the breadth and depth of the issues covered in the Report, this chapter can only touch the surface in the space available here.

The Report is, however, an invaluable resource for those interested in the causes of earthquakes, their impact on the built environment, the design of structures to resist earthquakes, and how the prevailing legal and regulatory framework of building regulations intersects with the protection of human life in a location known to be susceptible to earthquakes. Moreover, the Report discusses a number of issues of considerable interest to construction lawyers, of which the building design standards in relation to the risk of structural failure, the engineer's duty to warn of known hazardous structures, and the liability of volunteers wishing to assist in post-earthquake recovery are merely a sample.

1 This article was first published in *Construction Law International*, Vol 8 No 2, June 2013, and is reproduced by kind permission of the International Bar Association, London, UK. © International Bar Association.

 DOI: 10.4324/9781003206897-20

The following chapter looks at several other aspects of the Report that may be of interest to engineers and readers with a technical bent. These further issues include some of the technical facets of the earthquakes, and earthquake loads on buildings.

For readers interested in reading the Report in greater detail, it is available on the internet[2] and in hardcopy.

18.2 The Royal Commission Report

The comprehensive final report of the Royal Commission comprises seven volumes and was released late in 2012. The Commissioners were a New Zealand High Court judge and two engineers. The Report is self-contained and includes detailed background material on the seismicity of the Canterbury area, earthquakes, structural design and codes for earthquake resistant design, and the legal and regulatory environment in the Canterbury area.

As an investigation into the causes of loss of life and property, the Royal Commission, unlike in litigation, was not concerned with any legal liability. The Commission thus investigated all aspects it considered relevant to its enquiry, subject of course to the terms of reference set by the government. These terms of reference required the Commissioners to investigate the performance of a reasonably representative sample of buildings in the Christchurch central business district, including four nominated buildings that collapsed totally or partially. In the event, the Royal Commission investigated all buildings that caused a fatality, all except five of which were located within the CBD.

The Royal Commission made a total of 189 recommendations, the majority of which related to the engineering aspects of earthquake-resistant building design. Seventy-five recommendations were made on roles and responsibilities in relation to building management after earthquakes, the regulatory framework for buildings and the training and education of civil engineers and organisation of the civil engineering profession.

18.3 Expert evidence in the Royal Commission

Much of the evidence before the Royal Commission was of a highly technical nature, involving structural design at the cutting edge of the worldwide practice of earthquake engineering. The procedures for submission and testing of expert evidence adopted by the Commission represented a comprehensive application of what would generally be regarded as world's best practice in the common law world. The Commission considered expert evidence put before it by interested parties and commissioned its own expert evidence on a number of issues.

The Commission used at least three "best practice" techniques for critically assessing the expert evidence put before it. The first of these was peer review – the engagement of international experts to independently review and comment on reports prepared by the foremost experts in New Zealand. The second technique was to orchestrate a conference of experts who had addressed a common issue, chaired by an independent facilitator. The experts' conference prepared a joint report identifying areas of agreement and disagreement. The third technique was to have expert evidence presented orally to the Commission in a "hot tub" – all experts giving evidence on a particular issue appearing

2 http://canterbury.royalcommission.govt.nz (accessed 14 April 2021).

before the Commission simultaneously and subject to questioning by the Commissioners and the other experts.

Interestingly, the Commission used a further technique for expert evidence that is not available to judges in litigation or arbitrators in arbitration. On a number of issues, the Commission used its own expertise to carry out independent analyses to determine for itself the cause of failure of some buildings. This was done in cases where the Commission apparently did not agree with the findings of the expert reports and reviews submitted to it.

This approach was clearly within the terms of reference that enabled the Commission to "conduct, where appropriate, your own research". It was made possible through the appointment of highly qualified engineer Commissioners who had the experience and ability to carry out detailed analyses using state of the art analytical tools and assumptions. Such a "hands-on" approach by the tribunal may be possible in an expert determination, and is certainly provided for in many Dispute Board procedures for determining disputes, such as the FIDIC rainbow suite of contracts.

18.4 Legal and statutory requirements

An important aspect of the Royal Commission's terms of reference was the requirement to enquire into "the adequacy of the current legal and best practice requirements for the design, construction, and maintenance of buildings in central business districts in New Zealand to address the known risk of earthquakes". Volume 7 of the Report addresses this in sections covering building management after earthquakes, roles and responsibilities in the building control framework, training and education of civil engineers and organisation of the civil engineering profession, and the roles of the regional authorities in the management of earthquake risk.

Whilst some of this material is particular to the New Zealand situation, a number of the issues addressed are of much wider interest. One of these is the extent to which the regulation of "social" issues of importance to the community – in particular, the preservation of heritage listed buildings – may be in conflict with the fundamental requirement of ensuring public safety. A number of heritage listed buildings required demolition after the September 2010 earthquake to ensure public safety, as they could not be economically repaired. In the Commission's view, the regulatory environment, which required a time-consuming process to obtain the requisite approvals, did not appropriately provide for the more immediate needs of protecting the safety of the public. Its recommendation 111 was that: "Life safety should be the overarching objective of building management after earthquakes as communities both respond to and recover from the disaster."

It is sobering to realise that a number of fatalities in the February 2011 earthquake were caused by the collapse of "red-carded" buildings that had been vacated and barricaded, but not demolished after the September 2010 earthquake. Unfortunately, the extent of the barricades was inadequate to protect passers-by from the total collapse of the buildings.

Another issue of general interest is the extent to which the regulation of buildings provides adequate protection to the public from the collapse of buildings from a foreseeable earthquake event. Even before the Canterbury earthquakes, it was well known that unreinforced masonry structures perform poorly in earthquakes and can suffer sudden catastrophic collapse. Chapter 7 discusses a number of aspects of structural design that are important in determining a building's resistance to earthquakes including limit state design (Section 7.6) and structural robustness (Section 7.7), which includes redundancy and ductility. Under the prevailing regulatory environment in New Zealand, there is no obligation to carry out any form of building strengthening to resist earthquakes, unless there is change of use and a consequent obligation to obtain a building permit.

Even in such a situation, the extent of strengthening required is only to bring the building up to 34% of the current earthquake load standard. It is generally not possible to build any significant ductility into an unreinforced masonry structure. Accordingly, such structures have little capacity to deform and may fail catastrophically in an earthquake of a magnitude considerably less than the current "design" earthquake.

Ultimately, the community must balance the conflicting requirements of an acceptable level of public safety mandated by statute and regulation, with the high costs of replacing legacy buildings that cannot be economically upgraded to meet modern standards. As the number of fatalities of passers-by in the February 2011 earthquake demonstrated, the performance of buildings in earthquakes is not just a matter for building owners and the occupants they are responsible for; it has much wider implications for the public at large.

18.5 Design standards and risk

New Zealand has had standards for the design of buildings and structures to resist earthquakes since 1935. The design loads and criteria for earthquake resistance have changed and evolved considerably over the years, including through the introduction of requirements for ductility and capacity design in the 1970s. The most recent design standard is NZS1170.5: 2004 "Earthquake Actions Standard", containing 153 pages of standard and commentary.

Prior to the 1960s, there was little knowledge of the principles for designing structures to resist the horizontal (and vertical) forces generated by earthquakes. The modern approach to earthquake-resistant design is to build ductility into the structure – a capability to undergo repeated deformation whilst dissipating substantial energy through the deformations of the structure. The majority of buildings constructed before the war were constructed of unreinforced masonry. Many buildings of this type, even those strengthened to upgrade their earthquake resistance, collapsed in the Canterbury earthquakes.

One outstanding lesson from the Report is that a building designed well to modern standards can provide life safety for its occupants, even when subjected to an earthquake of significantly greater magnitude than the "design" earthquake. That is not to say that all the Christchurch buildings ostensibly designed to modern standards survived the earthquakes. Sadly, a number did not, and the resulting collapses caused substantial loss of life. However, the Royal Commission found that in most cases there were aspects of the design, particularly in respect of ductility, that did not conform to the standards prevailing at the time they were built.

The Report highlighted a number of areas of design risk via its discussion of the behaviour of a number of buildings in the Canterbury earthquakes. Some of these are inherent in designs being prepared by fallible human beings, some are related to the prevailing state of knowledge (or lack of it) and others are related to the procedures adopted for procurement of design, checking and certification. Substantial earthquakes, when they impact a major city, provide a load test that will result in many design risks materialising.

In addition to the two major modern buildings that failed with substantial loss of life, there were other buildings that were so severely damaged that they were subsequently demolished. The Royal Commission's investigation of these buildings drew attention to the following design risks.

Although a building may have been designed by a reputable and competent engineer, and certified by the building authority, that is no absolute guarantee that the prevailing design standards were complied with. The Royal Commission identified several such shortcomings in designs that apparently complied with the required standards at the time they were designed. As is demonstrated by the sophistication of the analyses that the Royal Commission itself carried out for some of these buildings, design of complex buildings to resist earthquakes requires a high level of engineering expertise, and detecting non-conformance with design standards is an expensive and time-consuming exercise. In the absence of a testing event such as an earthquake that results in structural damage, or a change of occupancy, there may be no reason for a building owner to check a building's adequacy to the prevailing standards. There is, therefore, a potential risk that a building may have unknown inbuilt design weaknesses that render it unable to withstand a design earthquake.

Every earthquake that results in the failure of modern buildings adds to the knowledge of the behaviour of buildings under earthquake loads, and how to design them to preclude complete collapse. Inevitably, design standards evolve to include the lessons learnt and the results of further research. The collapse of the PGC building in Christchurch clearly illustrates the evolution of design standards. The expert panel noted that the building structure was in accordance with the design requirements when it was designed in 1963, both in terms of strength and details. However, assessed against the current code for new buildings it was only compliant to a 30–40% level with the new building standard. It collapsed because the shaking in the February earthquake was several times more intense than the capacity of the structure to resist it, and the connections between members were not designed to take the distortions that occurred.

Design risk can be reduced by careful attention to providing alternative load paths in the structure, referred to as "redundancy" by structural engineers. For example, the Hotel Grand Chancellor suffered complete failure of a major load-bearing wall during the February earthquake. Although that failure came close to causing a catastrophic collapse of the 27-storey building, there was sufficient redundancy and resilience within the overall structure to redistribute load from the failing element and to halt the collapse.

No doubt there are a number of actions that can be taken to reduce design risk in relation to any building. One of the simplest, and in this author's view one of the most cost-effective, is an independent review of a building design, carried out by a competent engineer experienced in earthquake design. The Royal Commission noted that there tends to be insufficient external peer review by independent, experienced structural engineers, and made a number of recommendations in relation to certification of building design. This included the requirement to prepare a "Structural Design Features Report" to describe the key elements of the design. It recommended that the relevant Ministry should develop criteria for determining whether a structure is complex and, for structures determined to be complex, a "Recognised Structural Engineer" should be required to certify the structural integrity of the design. A Recognised Structural Engineer would be a chartered professional engineer, with specialised competence in the field of structural engineering and well experienced in the design of complex structures.

18.6 Duty to warn

The Report highlighted some problem areas where engineers need to communicate the results of their investigations and their findings to other, non-technical people. In some cases, the language used by engineers in reports does not convey the same message to lay people as it does to technical people. In other cases, the engineer needs to clearly articulate the assumptions behind and the limitations of the analyses carried out. Perhaps most important (and perhaps also the most difficult) is the requirement to explain the inherent risks notwithstanding the engineering assessment. For example, an unreinforced masonry building still has a significant risk of failure in an earthquake, even if it has been upgraded to the required 34% standard of current earthquake loads.

Another important area identified by the Royal Commission is the obligations that an engineer might have in circumstances where they know that a building has a serious design deficiency and is unlikely to withstand a design level earthquake. An engineer who has been commissioned to carry out investigations that reveal such a deficiency will usually have confidentiality obligations to their client. Further, the engineer will rarely be in a position to insist that remedial work be carried out immediately, or in extreme circumstances require the evacuation of the building. Nevertheless, the community has an overarching interest in such information being properly communicated to appropriate authorities which can ensure that the relevant action is taken.

Chartered professional engineers in New Zealand are regulated by statute and, to be so registered, an engineer must agree to be bound by the ethical rules prescribed in the Act. The ethical rules contain a number of provisions that, inter alia, oblige the engineer to take reasonable steps to safeguard health and safety, to inform others of the consequences of not following advice, and not disclose confidential information.

The Royal Commission did not consider there was any material weakness in the code of ethics but recommended that it should be clarified in respect of:

- Defining that the test for taking action was ensuring public health and safety
- In a perceived conflict between two or more clauses, the question as to which clause should apply in the circumstances should be a carefully considered matter of judgement
- There should be clarity as to the point at which an obligation of a reviewing engineer to report a structure that has been identified to present a risk to health and safety is extinguished, and where the accountability for addressing the matter and rectifying any weaknesses rests.

A further recommendation was that the code of ethics should be amended to provide for an obligation to advise the relevant territorial authority and the Institution of Professional Engineers New Zealand in circumstances where a structural weakness has been discovered that gives rise to a risk to health and safety.

Engineers would no doubt appreciate some statutory clarity being provided to their duty to warn of known hazardous circumstances. More importantly, however, public safety will be enhanced if the wider dissemination of such information results in speedier rectification or other measures to protect life safety. Perhaps the most important lesson of all to be learned from the Report is its emphasis on life safety being the guiding principle that should lie behind all aspects of design, certification, construction and management of buildings before and after earthquakes.

18.7 Conclusion

Arising from the tragedy of the Canterbury earthquakes, the Royal Commission and its Report offers tremendous insights to the international construction community and its lawyers. In this author's view, the Report will be studied for years to come by lawyers, engineers and other industry professionals for the clarity of its exposition, and for the lessons that can be learned to avoid such a large loss of life in future, inevitable, earthquakes.

CHAPTER 19

The Canterbury earthquakes II[1]

19.1 Introduction

The previous chapter discussed some of the issues of interest to construction lawyers in the Royal Commission Report on the Canterbury earthquakes. This brief chapter looks at several other aspects of the Report that may be of interest to engineers and readers with a technical bent. These further issues include some of the technical facets of the earthquakes, and earthquake loads on buildings. Also, two aspects of the engineers' work before and after earthquakes: the assessment of existing buildings to modern standards of earthquake resistance, and safety assessment of buildings after earthquakes. These are both issues of considerable importance to the public who rely on the professionalism of engineers to ensure that infrastructure is safe.

19.2 Details of the Royal Commission Report

The Royal Commission Report contains invaluable technical details on the current "state of the art" of earthquake engineering, as well as a summary of the current New Zealand legal and regulatory background on the regulation of building approvals. Volume 1 contains the recommendations made in Volumes 1–3, and includes background material on seismicity, the seismic design of buildings and soils and foundations. Volume 2 covers the performance of Christchurch CBD buildings. Volume 3 discusses the engineering technologies available to reduce earthquake damage to buildings. Volume 4 reviews the issue of existing buildings in New Zealand that are likely to perform poorly in earthquakes. It outlines the building standards, legislation and policies in New Zealand, and reviews the characteristics of unreinforced masonry buildings, which form a significant proportion of earlier buildings and lack the capacity to resist seismic actions when compared to more recent structures of steel and reinforced concrete.

In Volume 5 the Royal Commission makes a number of recommendations for changes to the legislation, policies and practices to prevent or minimise the failure of buildings in earthquakes and on the legal and best practice requirements for the management of buildings after earthquakes and for the design of new buildings. This volume also sets out the Commission's approach to the Inquiry and describes the way in which it managed the thousands of documents it received and the reporting structure it followed.

1 This is an edited version of the paper published in: Donald Charrett, "The Canterbury earthquakes – lessons for construction lawyers" (2013) 25(1) *Australian Construction Law Bulletin* 2.

DOI: 10.4324/9781003206897-21

Volume 6 details a comprehensive investigation of the collapse of the CTV building, and identifies those previous design, certification and construction errors and failures of process that doomed the building. Volume 7 addresses the adequacy of the current legal and best practice requirements for the design, construction and maintenance of buildings.

The Royal Commission made a total of 189 recommendations. These include 29 detailed recommendations in respect of site investigations, ground improvement and foundation design. Thirty-four recommendations were made on changes in the design of buildings for earthquake resistance, including changes in the way that seismic design is undertaken and changes to structural Standards. Volume 4 contains 36 recommendations on treating the earthquake risk of existing buildings. A total of 75 recommendations were made in Volume 7 on roles and responsibilities in relation to building management after earthquakes, the regulatory framework for buildings and the training and education of civil engineers and organisation of the civil engineering profession.

19.3 The earthquakes

The sequence, location and magnitude of the earthquakes considered by the Royal Commission were significant in the resulting loss of life. A magnitude 7.1 earthquake occurred at 4:35 am on 4 September 2010, a magnitude 4.9 after-shock at 10:30 am on 26 December 2010 (a public holiday), a magnitude 6.3 after-shock at 12:51 pm on 22 February 2011 (a working day), and a magnitude 6.3 after-shock on 13 June 2011.

These details of the earthquakes underline the random nature of earthquake risk. The time of an earthquake's occurrence may have a considerable influence on the incidence of death and injury. The original magnitude 7.1 earthquake in the early morning did not cause any casualties, whereas the February 2011 magnitude 6.3 "after-shock" in the middle of a working day resulted in 185 fatalities. The exact location of an earthquake's epicentre determines its damaging effect on property – the February after-shock caused more property damage than the September 2011 higher magnitude earthquake because the epicentre in February was much closer to the Christchurch CBD.

Although New Zealand is an in an area known to be susceptible to earthquakes and has a well-developed "state of the art" earthquake design code, the magnitude of the Canterbury earthquakes was unexpected. They resulted from previously unknown faults that had not ruptured for more than 8,000 years and have resulted in a reassessment of the seismicity of the area.

19.4 Earthquake loads on buildings

Subject to some qualifications, the shaking in the September earthquake was comparable to that anticipated for a design 500-year return period earthquake for Christchurch. Thus, the earthquake resulted in loads on Christchurch CBD buildings that was approximately equivalent to the current design load specified in the New Zealand Earthquake Code[2] for buildings of "normal" importance. The accepted risk level implicit in this Earthquake

2 Standards New Zealand, NZS 1170.5:2004. Structural Design Actions, Part 5: Earthquake actions – New Zealand.

Code is based on an earthquake with a "return period" of 500 years. That is, an earthquake of this magnitude would be expected at least once in 500 years. Put another way, a 500-year return period is approximately equivalent to a 10% chance of being exceeded during a building life of 50 years.

However, the February 2011 after-shock subjected Christchurch CBD buildings to loads greater than the current "design level". The loads generated exceeded those from a 1 in 2,500-year return period, the design earthquake for structures with important post-disaster functions, which are designed for higher earthquake loads than "normal" structures.

All structures are designed for earthquake loads arising from an earthquake of a certain magnitude. As a natural, random phenomenon, there can be no guarantee that a structure may not be subjected to an earthquake of a higher magnitude during its life. That is, there is a certain probability (perhaps unquantifiable) that the structure may be subjected to earthquake loads greater than it is designed for. In the case of some building types (particularly older unreinforced masonry buildings), loading significantly more than their design load capacity is likely to result in complete failure.

The magnitude of the earthquakes in relation to the prevailing New Zealand design standards is summed up in the Royal Commission statement: "The Canterbury earthquakes have tested CBD buildings in excess of their ultimate limit state."[3]

Reassuringly, the Commission concluded that current Standards were adequate for the design of buildings in New Zealand:

> We have concluded that confidence is justified in the current processes by which earthquake risk in New Zealand is assessed and translated into the provisions of the relevant Standards used for the purposes of building design. We are satisfied that there is no need to change the existing process for setting the "z" value that plays a crucial role in the design of buildings for earthquake resistance. For reasons addressed in Volume 2, we conclude that the construction costs do not appear to increase significantly with increases in the seismic design factor of the magnitude that has occurred (or may be contemplated) in Christchurch. Further, it would not be sensible, in our opinion, to conclude that the performance of buildings in the February earthquake demonstrates a need for wholesale change.[4]

However, the Commission concluded that the regulatory framework for new buildings could be improved:

> Through the course of our Inquiry, we identified some systemic issues relating to the regulatory framework for buildings, such as misunderstanding of the framework, a complex and confusing suite of regulatory documents, and quality assurance issues. These issues relate to the design and construction of complex, new buildings.
>
> Quality assurance is vital in the structural design of complex buildings. Quality assurance occurs at a number of levels throughout the design and construction of such buildings. The currently large number of building consent authorities results in inconsistent application requirements and consent decisions around the country, and varying levels of capability within these authorities.[5]

3 NZ, *Canterbury Earthquakes Royal Commission, Final Report* (2012) Vol 2, 8.

4 NZ, *Canterbury Earthquakes Royal Commission, Final Report* (2012) Vol 1, 6.

5 NZ, Canterbury Earthquakes Royal Commission, Final Report *Canterbury Earthquakes Royal Commission, Final Report* (2012) Vol 5, 13f.

19.5 Safety assessments of buildings after the earthquakes

The Government declared a state of emergency after the September earthquake, and the initial assessment of the safety of buildings was carried out under a legislated framework. Before buildings were put back into service, they were subject to a visual inspection and posted with a green, yellow or red card. Buildings in imminent danger of collapse and unsafe to enter were red carded, and those buildings which required remedial work before normal use were yellow carded. A green card permitted normal use of the building, but owners were encouraged to obtain a more detailed assessment by a qualified engineer.

The Royal Commission was generally complimentary about this process of the rapid assessment of buildings to enable an immediate return to normality to the extent prudent. A number of experienced engineers assisted in the rapid assessment on a voluntary basis. Under the declared state of emergency, they were indemnified against liability arising from their assessment.

No state of emergency was declared after the December after-shock and, not surprisingly, engineers were reluctant to volunteer their services for building assessment in the absence of an indemnification against liability. This issue was one of the many on which the Royal Commission made recommendations for a change in the legislative environment, to ensure that in the future volunteers prepared to assist in the important task of recovery after a disaster are not inhibited by concerns over their liability.

19.6 Design risk

Design of buildings to resist substantial earthquakes requires a high level of engineering design skill. Inadequate understanding of the behaviour of a building when subjected to lateral earthquake loads from any direction, or failure to follow load paths through all the structural elements into the foundation, may result in under designed structural members, or connections between members that cannot transmit the required loads. These issues are particularly acute in geometrically complex buildings in which torsional behaviour can induce much larger member forces than are revealed by simple analysis.

Every earthquake that results in the failure of modern buildings adds to the knowledge of the behaviour of buildings under earthquake loads, and how to design them to preclude complete collapse. Inevitably, design standards evolve to include the lessons learnt, and the results of further research. Thus, a building designed in conformance with the standards prevailing in the 1970s or 1980s will not perform as well as a building designed in accordance with the current standards. Even though the earthquake design loads may not have increased substantially, some of the newer code provisions, such as the requirements to provide ductility or the amount of movement to be provided for, may mean the difference between a building which survives largely intact, and one in which there is major structural damage which may result in partial or complete collapse or subsequently require demolition. This "design code risk" would require a detailed engineering investigation to quantify.

Notwithstanding the very sophisticated computer programs that are available to analyse structures under earthquake loads, it still remains very difficult to properly model the complete building performance. Further, the time and expense of such analyses can rarely be economically justified for routine design of typical commercial buildings. Engineers rely on the requirements in design codes, which are typically regarded as defining the approach that should be followed by the ordinary competent engineer.[6] The process of reviewing and revising design codes takes into account the views of the various stakeholders who have an interest in designing buildings, and typically involve many compromises between reducing risk and the cost of doing so. It is suggested that the current design codes represent the community's view on the acceptable level of risk that it is prepared to pay for. As the failures that occurred in the Canterbury earthquakes have shown, there are many areas that may require further review and revision, and these will no doubt be considered in the light of the economic cost to the community.

19.7 Assessment of existing buildings to modern standards

The damage caused to many older buildings in Christchurch highlights a dilemma in determining where the balance should be struck between the risk of death and injury from the collapse of unreinforced masonry buildings in an earthquake, and the costs to the community in strengthening or demolishing them.

In circumstances where an unreinforced masonry building is required to be upgraded to improve its capacity to resist earthquakes, the current New Zealand practice is that it must be strengthened to resist only 34% of the current design load (new building standard). Whilst that increased load capacity may be able to be implemented at a reasonable cost, it is not usually possible to significantly improve the ductility of such buildings. The consequence is that an earthquake imposing significantly lower loads than the new building standard may cause collapse of a strengthened unreinforced masonry building, because it has insufficient ductility to deform and absorb energy. By contrast, a modern building with adequate ductility may still provide life safety to its occupants when subjected to significantly higher loads than it was designed for.

It is interesting to note that the New Zealand Society of Earthquake Engineers consider that 67% of new building standard is a reasonable level of strengthening to reduce the risk posed by existing buildings. The Christchurch Council proposed that this level of strengthening should apply in circumstances where it issued a notice to strengthen an earthquake-prone building under its Earthquake-Prone, Dangerous and Insanitary Buildings Policy. However, in a judicial review of this policy in the High Court of New Zealand, Panckhurst J determined that Councils can enforce compliance with the building code by issuing s 124 notices but they may not require work to achieve criteria which are higher than those specified in the building code:

> The building code governs building requirements in New Zealand. Compliance with the code is required in relation to new building work. Persons may not be required to achieve performance criteria above those prescribed in the code. … It would be anomalous if territorial authorities could as a matter of policy utilise s 124 notices to achieve a strengthening performance criteria higher than that used to define an earthquake-prone building.[7]

6 See chapter 10 for a discussion of an engineer's duty of care, and the extent to which s/he can rely on Codes of Practice.

7 *Insurance Council of NZ Incorporated v Christchurch City Council* [2013] NZHC 51 [43].

CHAPTER 20

Construction failures

Have we learned the lessons of history?[1]

20.1 Introduction

Failures of buildings or engineered facilities that involve collapse of structures or result in loss of life (referred to herein as **construction failures**) are usually scrutinised in a public inquiry such as a Royal Commission or Committee of Inquiry. This chapter reviews some past public inquiries into construction failures, and highlights the lessons that, in the writer's opinion, still have contemporaneous value in respect of contractual issues that were found to have relevance to the failure.

The theme of this chapter is that the lessons to be learned from construction failures are not confined to the technical quality of the engineering and construction, but include the contractual, organisational and managerial aspects of project execution. Unlike most construction disputes which, at their heart, are about money and who pays how much to whom, most of the public inquiries considered here had the further dimension that the construction failure resulted in significant (and sometimes substantial) loss of life. This should be a salutary reminder to construction law practitioners that the engineer's "art of directing the great sources of power in nature for the use and convenience of man"[2] in every project carries with it attendant execution risks which, if they materialise, can involve significant injury and loss of life.

The importance of studying failures is encapsulated in the following statements:

> Only rarely will we learn from our successes. Even if the failures are ones which we fondly think we would not cause, nevertheless there are likely to be similarities which should cause us to re-examine the work which we are doing.[3]

1 This chapter is an expanded, edited and updated version of the paper published in: Donald Charrett, "Construction Failures – Have We Learned the Lessons of History?" (2012) 143 *Australian Construction Law Newsletter* 40.

2 The objects of the ICE, as recited in the 1828 Royal Charter, were:

> The general advancement of mechanical science, and more particularly for promoting the acquisition of that species of knowledge which constitutes the profession of a civil engineer; being the art of directing the great sources of power in nature for the use and convenience of man, as the means of production and of traffic in states, both for external and internal trade, as applied in the construction of roads, bridges, aqueducts, canals, river navigation, and docks, for internal intercourse and exchange; and in the construction of ports, harbours, moles, breakwaters, and light-houses, and in the art of navigation by artificial power, for the purposes of commerce; and in the construction and adaptation of machinery, and in the drainage of cities and towns.

3 Peter Campbell (ed), *Learning from Construction Failures: Applied Forensic Engineering* (2001) viii.

 DOI: 10.4324/9781003206897-22

Disaster is most likely when new designs are based purely on successful precedents and the basic lessons of the past failures are ignored.[4]

20.2 The value of studying construction failures

Engineers have long recognised the value of studying past construction failures in order to learn their lessons so as to avoid such failures in the future. In 1856, the President of the Institution of Civil Engineers, Robert Stevenson observed:

> Nothing is so instructive to the younger members of the profession as the record of accidents in large works, and the means employed in repairing the damage. A faithful account of those accidents, and of the means by which the consequences were met, is really more valuable than a description of the most successful works. Older engineers have derived their most useful store of experience from the observation of those casualties which have occurred to their own and to other works, and it is most important that they should be faithfully recorded in the archives of the Institution.[5]

The significance of studying construction failures is recognised in the engineering specialty of forensic engineering, and the conferences, journals and books devoted to dissemination of the results of forensic engineering investigations.[6] The importance of studying construction failures and learning the lessons inherent in them is aptly summed up on the Institution of Structural Engineer's website:

> The concept of failure is central to understanding engineering, it has as its first and foremost objective the obviation of failure. Design, even structural design, is a human endeavour and thus is subject to error. Due to this, some designs are destined to fail. This can lead to a loss of life which itself is tragic, but a deeper unforgivable tragedy exists when the lessons of failure are understood and allowed to occur again.[7]

Determining the cause is at the heart of every inquiry or dispute about a construction failure, since it is essential to know the cause of failure before the responsibility for the failure can be allocated, and legal liability (if any) determined. The causes of failure have been classified in different ways by different authors. For example, McKaig considers that "usually buildings fail through men's ignorance, carelessness or greed".[8] A number of authors have observed that construction failures are frequently not the result of only one cause, but more frequently are the result of a combination of causes. The prevalence of the number of claims and counterclaims in individual construction disputes supports this statement.

It is suggested that the following classification of the primary causes of construction failures is conceptually useful, as it may assist in determining which party (or parties) is causally liable for the failure. Clearly this is not necessarily determinative of legal causation, although this may be apparent in certain cases. The suggested classification of the primary causes of construction failures is:

---

4 Phillip Wearne, *Collapse When Buildings Fall Down* (2000) 13.

5 Cited in Peter Campbell (ed), *Learning from Construction Failures: Applied Forensic Engineering* (2001) 4.

6 e.g. Kenneth L Carper (ed), *Forensic Engineering* (2nd edn, 2001); Peter Campbell (ed), *Learning from Construction Failures: Applied Forensic Engineering* (2001); B S Neale (ed), *Forensic engineering The investigation of failures* (2001); Robin Shepherd and J David Frost (eds), *Failures in Civil Engineering: Structural, Foundation and Geoenvironmental Case Studies* (1995); Kenneth Gibble (ed), *Management Lessons from Engineering Failures* (1986).

7 www.istructe.org/technical/db/279.asp (accessed April 2012).

8 T McKaig, *Building Failures: Case Studies in Construction and Design* (1962), 150.

- Unforeseen event caused by an "act of God" (or terrorist)
- Unforeseen failure resulting from inadequate engineering knowledge of structural behaviour or materials
- Failure to prepare an appropriate design
- Failure to construct or use materials in accordance with the design, or
- Failure to operate and maintain the facilities in accordance with appropriate requirements.

Apart from the two categories of "unforeseen" failures, the underlying reason for a particular construction failure could be inadvertence because of a failure to take reasonable care, recklessness because of a lack of concern for the possible consequences of a course of action, or wilful because of a conscious choice of a course of action, such as failure to comply with regulatory or other normative requirements. Whatever the cause behind a particular construction failure, the project procedures (including the provisions of the contract(s) and the quality assurance procedures) have not averted the failure.

Lack of the required quality in design or construction is usually a major issue in construction failures, and this is typically a "technical" issue. Failures in the form of collapse always have a "technical" cause, but the reason for that technical cause may be procedural and/or contractual. This chapter focuses on the extent to which non-technical issues contributed to the failures examined, particularly the significance of the relevant contractual provisions.

20.3 Sources of information on construction failures

The sources of publicly available material in respect of construction failures are many and varied:

- Disputes in respect of failure resulting in litigation that proceeds through a hearing to judgment produce the case law that forms one of the primary sources of construction law.
- Forensic engineering reports which focus on the causative engineering and perhaps the management aspects of construction failures. Typically, the ambit of such reports is constrained by legal proceedings (or the threat of them). Notwithstanding these limitations, there are many forensic engineering sources that provide a valuable guide on the causes of construction failures.
- Academic papers and books on the legal aspects of construction failures.
- Public inquiries into failures. These have a number of unique features that make them especially valuable. Although only conducted in respect of a small number of high-profile failures, they provide an invaluable resource that is often of far greater significance than its application to the particular failure for which it was conducted.

Construction law practitioners are familiar with the case law that results from building failures. Indeed, as a source of the common law and the expression of judicial opinion on the construction of statutes and contracts, it is often the primary resource from which construction law is derived. The results of such legal disputes in the reported cases provide a judgment on the disputed factual and legal issues strictly only applicable to the unique set of facts of the particular dispute, but are widely used as a guide to the law where the factual circumstances are sufficiently similar. In some cases, the judgments reveal an extant "mischief" which the legislature redresses by changing the relevant statute law. Such case law can provide valuable data on the causes of failures and lessons for the future and is definitive in establishing legal liability between the parties to the litigation. However, case law is limited by the scope of the relevant issues in the specific dispute and the identity of the parties, and it is only available in respect of the small number of disputes that proceed to judgment in a court.

Notwithstanding its name, the role of "forensic engineering" is not primarily to assist with the investigation of failures in connection with disputes. However, the preparation of expert evidence is an important role of forensic engineering and is recognised as such in the literature devoted to the subject. Accordingly, the various publications of forensic engineering are a valuable resource in the lessons learned from past construction failures. Forensic engineering is discussed in Chapter 31.

The reports of public inquiries into prominent construction failures have a number of features that make them a valuable (and often timeless) widely applicable resource on the factors that led to failure. The scope of such a public inquiry is usually much broader than a private dispute decided in court, since a public inquiry is intended to determine all the reasons for the failure, and to provide guidance on avoiding similar failures in the future. For this reason, the reports of such public inquiries usually contain a wealth of information and considered opinion on the causes of failures based on extensive evidence. The Royal Commission Report on the Canterbury earthquakes was one such invaluable inquiry, discussed in Section 18.2 and Section 19.2.

20.4 Public inquiries and Royal Commissions into failures

These have a number of unique features that make them an especially valuable resource for construction law. Although only conducted for a small number of high-profile failures, inquiry reports are often of far broader significance than their conclusions on the particular failure.

In contrast to the judicial inquiry a judge makes in litigation, a Royal Commission is an administrative inquiry, in which the findings are not binding on individuals. It is suggested that this and the following are some of the significant features of Royal Commissions and public inquiries that contribute substantially to the value of their reports on construction failures:

- Often chaired by a judge, retired judge or lawyer who is widely experienced in the conduct of adversarial proceedings and the relevant laws of evidence.
- The Commission may have relevant technical expertise in the form of one or more technically qualified and experienced Commissioners.
- The Terms of Reference enacted by the legislature are subject to public scrutiny and Parliamentary debate.
- The Terms of Reference can be widely drawn to enable the Commission's comprehensive consideration of the relevant issues that resulted in the failure, in contrast to the narrow focus of the parties to a dispute (who are normally only concerned with legal liability as between themselves).

- The findings in a Royal Commission Report provide a comprehensive resource of all the causes of the failure determined, typically with recommendations for remedial measures to avoid similar failures in the future.
- The public nature of such a Royal Commission Report puts pressure on the Government to implement remedial legislation of appropriate measures (or, in some cases, implement prosecutions of persons found to have breached the law).

The principles applying to the conduct of Commissions of Inquiry have been summarised by the Canadian Supreme Court as follows:

> A commission of inquiry is not a court or tribunal and has no authority to determine legal liability; it does not necessarily follow the same laws of evidence or procedure that a court or tribunal would observe. A commissioner accordingly should endeavour to avoid setting out conclusions that are couched in the specific language of criminal culpability or civil liability for the public perception may be that specific findings of criminal or civil liability have been made. A commissioner has the power to make all relevant findings of fact necessary to explain or support the recommendations, even if these findings reflect adversely upon individuals. Further, a commissioner may make findings of misconduct based on the factual findings, provided that they are necessary to fulfil the purpose of the inquiry as it is described in the terms of reference. In addition, a commissioner may make a finding that there has been a failure to comply with a certain standard of conduct, so long as it is clear that the standard is not a legally binding one such that the finding amounts to a conclusion of law pertaining to criminal or civil liability. Finally, a commissioner must ensure that there is procedural fairness in the conduct of the inquiry.[9]

The practice of holding public inquiries into construction failures has a long history in the common law world. For example, in 1876 the Ohio State legislature appointed a joint committee to investigate the causes of the failure of the iron railroad Ashtabula Bridge that failed after 11 years in service (resulting in over 80 fatalities), in parallel with a coroner's jury, which appointed an engineer to investigate the causes of collapse. The bridge failed under the load of a train during a winter snow storm. The joint committee concluded that the cause of the disaster was fatigue failure in an iron casting that had not been detected because of inadequate inspection. This failure bolstered the call for standard bridge specifications and highlighted the unreliability of iron castings (which were explicitly prohibited in specifications ten years later).[10]

The United States has formalised investigations of building failures by enactment of the *National Construction Safety Team Act 2002* (USA). The stated purpose of the *Act* is

> to provide for the establishment of investigative teams to assess building performance and emergency response and evacuation procedures in the wake of any building failure that has resulted in substantial loss of life or that posed the potential for substantial loss of life.

The National Institute of Standards and Technology (**NIST**), part of the US Department of Commerce, has implemented the Disaster and Failure Studies Program to establish teams to "assess building and infrastructure performance and emergency response and evacuation procedures in the wake of disaster and failure events that have resulted in

9 *Canada (Attorney General) v Canada (Commission of Inquiry on the Blood System* [1997] 3 SCR 440.

10 Robin Shepherd and J David Frost (eds), *Failures in Civil Engineering: Structural, Foundation and Geoenvironmental Case Studies* (1995) 33.

substantial loss of life or posed significant potential of substantial loss of life".[11] These investigating teams are modelled after those of the National Transportation Safety Board (**NTSB**) for investigating transportation accidents.[12] In addition to establishing the likely technical causes responsible for damage or failure and the technical aspects of evacuation and emergency procedures, the objectives of NIST's investigations also include determining the procedures and practices that were used in the design, construction, operation and maintenance of buildings and infrastructure, and recommending improvements to standards, Codes and practices based on its study findings.[13] The NIST has published study reports on blast and impact events (including the World Trade Center terrorist attack in 2001[14]), construction and in-service failures, earthquakes, fires, and windstorms and coastal inundation.[15]

The following case studies derived from the reports of public inquiries are presented to illustrate the way in which they have revealed shortcomings in contracts, procedures and practices in the implementation of construction projects that have been contributing causes of failure.

20.5 Failures contributed to by inadequate engineering knowledge

One of the significant outcomes of some public inquiries into collapses has been to highlight the causative effect of inadequate engineering knowledge, and in many cases has led to advances in the art and science of engineering. The following are some examples of construction failures that highlighted the inadequate "state-of-the-art" knowledge of the time and which led to advances in engineering:

- Quebec Bridge, Canada (1907): one cantilever arm collapsed during construction, caused by the buckling of compression members. Subsequent large-scale experiments and studies provided a scientific basis for the design of large compression members[16] (see Chapter 21).
- Tacoma Narrows Bridge, Washington USA (1940): the suspension bridge failed from the effects of severe torsional oscillation caused by a 68km/h wind after only three months service. Incompetence or neglect was not the cause of the failure, but aerodynamic forces that were not understood at the time by structural engineers.[17] Subsequent large-span bridge design involves testing in a wind tunnel to ensure that such resonance under design wind speeds will not occur.

11 https://www.nist.gov/topics/disaster-failure-studies/about-disaster-and-failure-studies-program (accessed 14 April 2021).

12 Rudolf Kapustin, 'Transportation Disaster Investigation' in Kenneth L Carper, *Forensic Engineering* (2nd edn, 2001) 159–222.

13 https://www.nist.gov/topics/disaster-failure-studies/about-disaster-and-failure-studies-program (accessed 14 April 2021).

14 https://www.nist.gov/topics/disaster-failure-studies/world-trade-center-disaster-study (accessed 14 April 2021).

15 https://www.nist.gov/topics/disaster-failure-studies/studies-hazard-types (accessed 14 April 2021).

16 David B Steinman and Sara Ruth Watson, *Bridges and their builders* (1957) 308.

17 Robin Shepherd and J David Frost (eds), *Failures in Civil Engineering: Structural, Foundation and Geoenvironmental Case Studies* (1995) 40–41.

- AMC warehouse, Ohio USA (1955): a long-span concrete-framed warehouse collapsed under the dead load of the frame and roof 18 months after casting. The design conformed to Codes current at the time, leading to more conservative shear provisions in the American Concrete Institute Code.[18]
- Ronan Point apartments, London (1968): a 22-storey apartment building suffered a partial collapse after a gas explosion. The failure highlighted the need for structures, particularly those built from large prefabricated concrete panels, to be designed with alternate load paths to avert progressive collapse (see Section 20.8).
- West Gate Bridge, Melbourne (1970): a steel box girder bridge over the Yarra collapsed during construction, contemporaneously with the collapse of a steel box girder bridge at Milford Haven in Wales. These failures highlighted deficiencies in the knowledge of the behaviour of such structures, prompting research that resulted in the "Merrison Rules" which provide a sound theoretical and empirical basis for design (see Chapter 22).
- Antelope Valley Interchange, California (1971): during an earthquake, a section of a well-constructed overpass jumped out of its seats and caused failure of the supporting column. This failure resulted in significant changes in bridge design criteria for adequate resistance to earthquakes.[19]
- San Francisco Oakland Bay Bridge, California (1989): a 15 m span of this cantilever truss bridge failed during the 1989 Loma Prieta magnitude 6.9 earthquake, when it was subjected to more than twice the horizontal accelerations it was designed for in the 1930s. Subsequent re-analysis and risk assessment of major bridges in California resulted in a multi-billion-dollar programme of strengthening and replacement, including complete replacement of the cantilever truss spans of the San Francisco Oakland Bay bridge.[20]

Failures arising solely from a lack of engineering knowledge are probably very rare, as there are generally other factors contributing to failure, such as a failure to take reasonable care, or breach of contractual obligations. In the examples above, the reports of the public inquiries identified factors other than a lack of engineering knowledge that contributed to the failures of Quebec Bridge, Ronan Point apartments and West Gate Bridge.

It should be apparent that inadequate engineering knowledge may not avoid liability for a designer in a construction dispute arising from a collapse. An assertion that a collapse was the result of the inadequate state of engineering knowledge would not provide an adequate basis of defence for the design engineer in the many modern contracts that impose an explicit fit for purpose obligation on the designer. Such a design must be fit for purpose irrespective of the state of engineering knowledge.[21] Nor, it is suggested, would

18 Ibid 61.

19 Ibid 49–50.

20 Caltrans Seismic Advisory Board, "The Race to Seismic Safety Protecting California's Transportation System" (2003) 1–4 www.dot.ca.gov/RaceToSeismicSafetyfinal.pdf (accessed 28 August 2009).

21 See Chapter 8 for a discussion of the *MT Højgaard a/s v E.ON Climate and Renewables UK Robin Rigg East Ltd* case in which the design and construct contractor was found liable for the financial consequences of the failure of the connections of wind turbine towers that were designed in accordance with the prevailing international Standard.

a technical construction failure defence necessarily be effective for the designer who prepared the design for a contractor in a design and construct contract.[22]

20.6 Monitoring of constructed facilities

A number of reports into collapses highlight the importance of monitoring and inspection of a constructed facility. The following examples illustrate collapses that occurred due to inadequate attention to monitoring and inspection:

- Vajont 275 m high double curvature concrete dam, Italy (1963): this dam failed when a massive landslide into the reservoir caused the dam to be overtopped by a wave of water estimated to be 245 m high. The potential for a landslide was known, and monitoring of the ground movement was implemented, but it failed to warn of the rate of ultimate ground movement or avert the catastrophe.[23]
- Point Pleasant bridge, Ohio USA (1967): an I-bar suspension bridge failed under traffic load after 39 years in service. The failure of one defective I-bar caused the collapse. This failure led to a national policy for bridge inspections enacted by the US Congress.[24]
- Mianus River Bridge, Connecticut USA (1983): a steel plate girder bridge collapsed under traffic load after 25 years' service. An inquiry concluded that lack of maintenance and inadequate inspection were the main causes of collapse. Many subsequent repairs and retrofits were initiated to provide increased redundancy in other bridges.[25]

Forensic engineering of the technical aspects of damage to and collapse of structures is an important aspect of earthquake engineering. The performance of engineered facilities in every significant earthquake, particularly in North America, are carefully analysed to determine lessons for the future, which are incorporated into building Codes. Notwithstanding the requirements for earthquake design that have long been recognised, each earthquake seems to highlight new, previously unrecognised problems of past engineering design, and results in revision to the previously accepted "state-of-the-art".[26] Recent earthquakes have highlighted the need to retrofit existing structures to meet revised earthquake Codes.[27] For example, the 1971 San Fernando magnitude 6.6 earthquake established the need to retrofit the Antelope Valley interchange to bring the bridge strength to modern standards, but the retrofitting had not been implemented before the 1994 Northridge magnitude 6.7 earthquake. The unretrofitted structure suffered the predicted damage, highlighting the risks of procrastination in rectifying known deficiencies.[28] NIST has published reports on

22 *Independent Broadcasting Authority v EMI Electronics Ltd* (1980) 14 BLR 9.

23 Robin Shepherd and J David Frost (eds), *Failures in Civil Engineering: Structural, Foundation and Geoenvironmental Case Studies* (1995) 14.

24 Ibid 47.

25 Ibid 52.

26 See Chapter 19 for a discussion of some of the technical issues on design to resist earthquakes.

27 Caltrans Seismic Advisory Board, "The Race to Seismic Safety Protecting California's Transportation System" (2003) www.dot.ca.gov/RaceToSeismicSafetyfinal.pdf (accessed 28 August 2009).

28 Robin Shepherd and J David Frost (eds), *Failures in Civil Engineering: Structural, Foundation and Geoenvironmental Case Studies* (1995) 49–50.

a number of earthquakes: Kocaeli, Turkey 1999, Kobe, Japan 1995, Northridge, California 1994, Loma Prieta, California 1989, Mexico City, Mexico 1985 and Miyagi, Japan 1978.[29]

20.7 R101 airship

20.7.1 Design, construction and testing

In the 1920s, the British government investigated the potential of large airships for long-distance transportation. It decided to build two airships, the R100 and the R101, substantially larger than any previous airships as "test beds" for design, construction and operation over transcontinental routes, particularly to the tropics. The two airships were designed and built in competition to the same contract specifications: R100 was built by Vickers Ltd, a private company, whilst R101 was built by the Air Ministry, a government department.[30]

The dimensions of the original design of the R101 comprised a length of 223 m, and a diameter of 40 m. The volume of gas was approximately 140,000 cubic metres, intended to have a gross lift of 150 tons. By comparison, the later Hindenburg, the largest airship ever built, was 245 m long, 41 m in diameter and with a capacity of 200,000 m^3.

Unfortunately, the R101 crashed during a storm in France on its maiden voyage to India, with the loss of 48 lives, including the designers. A public inquiry into this disaster lasting for 13 days was held in October and November 1930 at the Institution of Civil Engineers in London. The report of this inquiry[31] provides a detailed record of the relevant background of the design, construction and testing of R101 and the conditions leading to its untimely end. This report is the resource for the following factual matters.

Another source of material on the failure of R101 is Nevil Shute's book *Slide Rule*. Nevil Shute was an aeronautical engineer who was appointed as Chief Calculator for the R100. *Slide Rule* contains many trenchant comments about the adverse impacts arising from the competition between the R100 and R101 teams, some of which Shute asserts impacted on the ultimate tragedy. The contract for the design and construction of R100 was let for a fixed price. Not surprisingly for an experimental project for which there was no prior experience, the contractor made a loss. Shute notes that subsequently, more equitable contracts were let for experimental aircraft.[32]

The loss of R101 does not appear to be primarily a failure of the quality of the engineering itself. Nor does the failure appear to have been caused by inappropriate cost-cutting. The report of the inquiry was fulsome in its praise of the engineering designs and investigations for R101. Airship development in England before the R100 and R101 was based on extrapolation from previous airship designs, without any real understanding of the forces likely to be encountered during flight. The assumption had previously been that a factor of safety of four on static loads would provide adequate allowance for the aerodynamic forces. Prior to design of the R101, a series of aerodynamic experiments were carried out over a two-year period at the National Physical Laboratory in which whole forms were tested for drag, lateral forces, yawing moments and damping coefficients. This resulted in

29 https://www.nist.gov/topics/disaster-failure-studies/studies-hazard-types (accessed 14 April 2021).

30 Nevil Shute, *Slide Rule The Autobiography of an Engineer* (William Heinemann 1954) 57.

31 HMSO, *Report of the R101 Inquiry* (1931).

32 Nevil Shute, *Slide Rule The Autobiography of an Engineer* (William Heinemann, 1954) 66.

a differently proportioned airship to those built previously: the length/diameter ratio was 5.5:1 as originally designed, not as "fine" as previous airships. This resulted in a very low drag resistance. Aerodynamic tests were also carried out to determine the most efficient shape and size of the fins.

The structure of the R101 consisted of a series of 16-sided ring-shaped transverse frames, joined together by 15 continuous longitudinal girders that resisted the longitudinal bending moments. Shear resistance was provided by a system of diagonal wires in the panels between the triangular cross-section transverse and longitudinal frames. It was important for the structure to be as light as possible, and to allow for repair or replacement of members. The structural members were machined in a factory and delivered fully assembled to the airfield, where they were attached together by bolting into the complete structure. Shute writes of the complexity of hand calculations for each of the transverse frames, which required laborious mathematical computations by two persons using a slide rule for a period of two or three months to obtain a satisfactory and true solution to the forces and deflections. If initial estimates of which bracing wires were in tension were not confirmed by the calculations, the whole calculations had to be repeated for a different set of assumptions.[33] Such calculations today are routinely carried out by computers in a matter of minutes.

This method of fabrication required extensive calculations to determine component lengths, and very accurate machining: tolerances of 0.4 mm in 3.35 m long girders and 0.8 mm in 6.7 m long girders (1 in 8,800). Such tolerances are somewhat more stringent to those that civil engineers are normally used to! Substantial mechanical testing of structural members was carried out to verify the validity of the stress calculations – approximately 100 girders were tested to destruction. The Report of the Inquiry stated in respect of the engineering of R101:

> The care taken in this preliminary experimental work is beyond all praise ... It is probably no exaggeration to say that never before in the history of structural engineering has so much care been taken to explore the strength of a structure before it was used, and to check the stress calculations by actual measurement.[34]

The initial design and investigations took over two years, and erection took another two years. Trials commenced in October 1929. An elaborate series of functioning tests were planned, covering engines, fuel consumption, gas valves and gas bags, controls, instruments and many other matters. The written reports of these tests "evinced the greatest thoroughness of care in every department".[35] During the six-week period of the initial tests, R101 flew for over 70 hours, including an endurance flight lasting 30 hours. The test flights were made in good weather and did not include any full speed trials. These trials revealed that the airship was overweight.

R101 was designed to be operated by engines burning heavy oil, instead of the more volatile petrol, in order to minimise the risk of fire. This required production of a new type of diesel engine, considerably heavier than a petrol engine delivering the same power. The consequence of the overweight powerplant (plus other weight "growth" above that assumed in the design, particularly in the weight of the main structure) was that, as originally completed, the R101 only had a useful lift of 35 tons instead of the specified 60 tons.

33 Nevil Shute, *Slide Rule The Autobiography of an Engineer* (William Heinemann, 1954) 76–78.
34 Ibid 27.
35 Ibid 50.

The useful lift had to allow for the weight of crew, passengers, stores, water and fuel, and therefore had to be increased. This required some redesign to increase the lift. During the period 29 June–1 October 1930, the R101 was lengthened by cutting the airship in two to insert additional structure and gas bags, adding an extra bay in the middle. After these modifications R101 was 237 m long, with a capacity of 156,000 cubic metres, and had a useful lift of 49.3 tons.

One of the consequences of the redesign and modifications to the airship was that there was ultimately insufficient time to carry out all the airworthiness trials that had been planned before the official maiden voyage to India. The enlarged R101 only had one trial flight of 16 hours in calm weather before departing for India on 4 October. The date of that maiden voyage had been fixed months previously to take the Secretary of State for Air, Lord Thomson, to India and back to England in time for an imperial conference. Although the Inquiry Report stated that no undue political pressure was put on those responsible for arranging the maiden flight, it is hard to avoid the conclusion that the desire to maintain the schedule for the flight inappropriately outweighed the requirement to carry out the planned comprehensive series of airworthiness trial flights. Those airworthiness trial flights were to have included a 48-hour endurance flight (which was a contract requirement for the sister ship, R100, built by a private company), as well as flights in bad weather.

20.7.2 Inquiry into crash

The Inquiry, whilst praising the "policy of cautious experiment" in the early stages of design, noted that:

> in the later stages, when it became important to avoid further postponement and the flight to India became urgent, there was a tendency to rely on limited experiment instead of tests under all conditions. The program of trials as at first submitted to Major Scott by the Captain of the R101 was far from being completed as originally intended, and ... the R101 started for India before she could be regarded as having emerged successfully from all the exhaustive tests proper to an experimental stage.[36]

In the event, fewer than three hours after leaving England, R101 crashed into a hill in France in bad weather. The Inquiry found that the airship had lost a significant quantity of gas, but was unable to find a definitive cause of that loss. The weather was exceptionally bad, and may have contributed to a specific misfortune such as ripping of part of the outer envelope. Whatever was the cause, there can be no doubt that the "fast tracking" of the departure dates and dispensing with the planned airworthiness trials was a substantial causal element in the tragedy. Then, as now, "fast tracking" usually means starting before all the necessary preparatory work has been completed.

20.8 Ronan Point apartments, London UK (1968)

20.8.1 The failure and the Inquiry

Ronan Point was a 22-storey tower block of flats in east London that suffered a collapse of one corner of the building following a gas explosion in May 1968. The explosion occurred

36 Ibid 22.

early in the morning when most of the demolished rooms were unoccupied; however, four people were killed.(Figure 20.1)

The structure was typical of many high-rise system-built buildings erected in England in the 1960s. The building was constructed from factory prefabricated wall, floor and stairway concrete panels, cast off-site and bolted together on-site. This new method of construction was intended to overcome the shortage of skilled building labour, which was constraining the construction of badly needed housing. The system of load-bearing walls used at Ronan Point was developed in Denmark for low-rise buildings up to six floors but was applied virtually without change to multi-storey buildings in England, apparently without further development or design. Neither the building regulations nor the existing UK Codes of Practice specifically contemplated construction of such load-bearing multi-storey buildings.

The day after the collapse, the Minister of Housing and Local Government appointed a panel (comprising a QC and two engineers) to conduct a public inquiry into the collapse (**Inquiry**), under provisions of the *Local Government Act*. Fewer than three months after it was appointed the Inquiry reported to the Minister its concern about the possibility

FIGURE 20.1 Ronan Point tower on 16 May 1968 after the gas explosion. Derek Voller / Ronan Point collapse, Canning Town / CC BY-SA 2.0

of progressive collapse in buildings designed similarly to Ronan Point. The final report, issued five months after the collapse, detailed the immediate causes of the failure, but perhaps more importantly analysed the deficiencies in the design and made recommendations in respect of the assessment of existing buildings as well as for the design of future buildings.[37] The Inquiry led to the government implementing measures to avoid similar collapses, including a requirement for buildings with reticulated gas to be able to resist an explosive pressure of 5psi. Existing buildings had to be able to resist 2.5psi, provided the gas supply was disconnected.

20.8.2 Progressive collapse

Perhaps the most important aspect of the Inquiry findings (and the reason that Ronan Point is still remembered by structural engineers)[38] was a finding of the importance of guarding against progressive collapse:

> The extent of the collapse subsequent to the explosion was inherent in the design of the building. The collapse has exposed a weakness in the design. It is a weakness against which it never occurred to the designers of this building that they should guard. They designed a building which they considered safe for all normal uses; they did not take into account the abnormal. They never addressed their minds to the question of what would happen if for any reason one or more of the load bearing members should fail. … The designers of Ronan Point were not alone in the attitude they adopted; it is significant that we have not been referred to any English publication which has drawn attention to the need to think of tall system buildings as civil engineering structures requiring alternate paths to support the load in the event of the failure of a load bearing member. It appears to us that there has been a blind spot among many of those concerned with this type of construction and it would be wrong to place the blame for the failure to appreciate the risk of progressive collapse upon the shoulders of the designers of this building alone. They fell victims, along with others, to the belief that if the building complied with existing building regulations and Codes of Practice it must be deemed to be safe. Experience has shown otherwise.[39]

In the years since the collapse of Ronan Point, the importance of design to avoid progressive collapse has been re-emphasised by terrorist attacks that have resulted in the collapse of major buildings such as the World Trade Center[40] and the Federal Building in Oklahoma. In the Oklahoma Federal Building, whilst only 4% of the building was destroyed by the bomb blast, a further 38% was subsequently destroyed by progressive collapse.[41]

The Inquiry concluded that there was no evidence that the design of Ronan Point did not broadly comply with the byelaws and Codes of Practice.[42] However, in subsequent litigation against the designers and constructors, the judge and the Court of Appeal found

37 Great Britain, Ministry of Housing and Local Government, *Collapse of Flats at Ronan Point, Canning Town* (1968).

38 e.g. see "The Ronan Point legacy 50 years on" https://www.newcivilengineer.com/latest/insight-the-ronan-point-legacy-50-years-on-16-05-2018/ (accessed 20 April 2021).

39 Ibid 4.

40 https://www.nist.gov/topics/disaster-failure-studies/world-trade-center-disaster-study (accessed 14 April 2021).

41 www.bfrl.nist.gov/861/861pubs/collapse/workshop/5.WorkshopSlides(Murrah%20Bldg).pdf (accessed April 2012).

42 Great Britain, Ministry of Housing and Local Government, *Collapse of Flats at Ronan Point, Canning Town* (1968) 39.

that the design failed to comply with the relevant Codes of Practice because there was insufficient reinforcing steel at the joints to tie the various units together positively, and the failure to follow those Codes had thus resulted in a breach of the building byelaws. The designers were found not to have been liable in negligence, but because of the failure to comply with the byelaws, the contractor was liable for the costs of rectification as a consequence of its breach of contract.[43] It is significant that it was the weakness of these non-complying joints that caused the building to have inadequate resistance to progressive collapse. Thus, although the cause of the collapse was, arguably, inadequate engineering knowledge, it was also contributed to by failure to comply with the contract and normative requirements.

The Inquiry stated that it had painstakingly investigated the standards of both workmanship and supervision. Although it identified two cases in which it found that the workmanship fell below the desired standard, it stated: "in general the standards of workmanship and supervision are satisfactory, and it must be emphatically stated that no deficiency in either workmanship or supervision contributed to or was in any way responsible for, this disaster." The two cases of unsatisfactory workmanship were related to the design, and concerned the external wall joint to the floor, and tie plates intended to tie the wall panels and floors together. The inquiry found that the design wind pressures used, although complying with the current Code of Practice, were substantially less than could be expected during the 60-year life of the building. It found that Ronan Point

> has little or no margin of strength if a speed of 105 m.p.h. is reached. We think also that parts of the structure, particularly at the lower H.2 joints in the flank walls, might develop undesirable deformations under the repeated action of less extreme high winds.

20.8.3 The aftermath

Notwithstanding the strengthening of the building that was carried out in response to the findings of the inquiry, there were continuing concerns over the building's structural integrity, which eventually led to its demolition in 1986. It was dismantled floor by floor so that the joints could be studied. The architect responsible for investigations during this demolition commented: "I knew we were going to find bad workmanship – what surprised me was the sheer scale of it. Not a single joint was correct." "Fixing straps were unattached: levelling nuts were not wound down, causing a significant loading to be transmitted via the bolts: panels were placed on bolts instead of mortar. But the biggest shock of all was the crucial H-2 load bearing joints between floor and wall panels. Some of the joints had less than 50% of the mortar specified."[44]

The finding of such poor workmanship in Ronan Point resulted in many of the remaining tower blocks constructed using the same system being demolished in the 1980s and 1990s. Despite the availability of Building Research Station reports on the assessment of such buildings, some councils apparently did not assess the integrity of all buildings they were responsible for. In 1999, it was found that over 300 such buildings in Birmingham did not meet the 5 psi pressure criterion, and still had a piped gas supply. It has been

43 *London Borough of Newham v Taylor Woodrow-Anglian* (1982) 19 BLR 111.
44 Phillip Wearne, *Collapse: When Buildings Fall Down* (2000) 154.

queried whether the large panel-system buildings owned by the London Borough of Southwark have adequate strength to resist a 5 psi explosion.[45] A team that investigated the Packington Estate in Islington in 2004 warned that it was in real danger of progressive collapse, because appropriate strengthening work was never carried out. The floor slabs had inadequate strength to resist 2.5 psi and, despite replacement of all gas cookers, some residents were still using gas canisters for cooking.[46]

20.8.4 Robustness

Since Ronan Point, the UK and other Building Codes have explicitly addressed the technical need for "robustness" of structures, i.e. their fundamental property of resistance to disproportionate (progressive) damage. The UK has had a progressive collapse standard since 1968.[47] However, robustness of structures has been a matter of ongoing concern to the Standing Committee on Structural Safety (**SCOSS**), which considers the regulatory and contractual framework within which decisions on robustness are made to be "somewhat unsatisfactory". In a paper delivered to a workshop on robustness held in 2005, SCOSS noted that its concern extended beyond just the physical means of achieving adequate robustness in the design, construction and operation, but included procurement matters. These contractual issues which SCOSS consider relevant are:

- Competency of those organisations procured.
- "Best value" tendering.
- Clear lines of responsibility and authority.
- Clear reporting protocols.
- Adequate information for planning and pricing the construction phase.
- Adequate specification.
- Inclusion of adequate monitoring procedures (avoidance of self-certification approaches).[48]

In addition to relevant factors in procurement, design and construction of a building, SCOSS identifies the importance of subsequent maintenance in ensuring the continuance of robustness, since alteration or refurbishment works have the potential for disturbing it. It is noted that although the *Construction (Design and Management) Regulations 1994* (UK) require a "health and safety file" to be created, this is focused on personal risk rather than risk to the structure and, although legally required, may not even exist. SCOSS suggests that a building "logbook" would be worthwhile, but this currently has no legal status or universal acceptance.[49]

45 http://en.wikipedia.org/wiki/Ronan_Point (accessed 14 April 2021).

46 www.bdonline.co.uk/story.asp?sectioncode=426&storycode=3035038&c=1 (accessed 15 June 2016).

47 Standards to Avoid Progressive Collapse – Large Panel Construction.

48 Standing Committee on Structural Safety, 'A Risk Managed Framework for Ensuring Robustness' (2006) SC/06/28 www.scoss.org.uk/publications/rtf/Risk_Framework_paper.pdf (accessed April 2012).

49 Ibid 5.

20.9 Hartford Civic Centre, Connecticut, USA (1978)

The roof of the completed Hartford Civic Centre in Connecticut collapsed under snow load, fortunately whilst it was unoccupied. An innovative and very light design was used for the roof, the analysis of which was checked by computer. However, the roof was particularly susceptible to buckling failure because of light and slender members and poor detailing of the as constructed member connections, and the computer analysis was unable to detect this mode of failure. In addition to the design errors that included underestimation of the dead load by 20%, there were construction errors that further increased the slenderness of members to well beyond Code limits.

There were warning signs of excessive deflections during construction (actual deflections were twice those that had been computed), but the designers, confident of their design, dismissed these concerns. This problem was compounded by the Construction Manager who refused to employ a structural engineer to perform field inspections. He did not accept that the designer, who understood the structure being built, would be best able to recognise problems before they reached catastrophic proportions.

The collapse of the Hartford City Centre is a salutary object lesson in overreliance on the output of computer programs:

> This failure has been appropriately referred to as a 'computer aided catastrophe'. It illustrates the false sense of security offered by the multitude of data generated by computer analysis. It serves as a lesson that computer software is a tool, and not a substitute, for sound engineering experience and judgment. Relying on computer analysis only for the analysis of increasingly complex structures, where the reasonableness and thoroughness of the analysis cannot be ascertained, invites failure.[50]

As discussed in Section 14.4, this highlights the enduring application of the maxim of the Arup engineers who designed the structure of the Sydney Opera House: "if you don't know the order of magnitude of the answer, don't use the computer".

20.10 Hyatt Regency Hotel Walkways, Kansas City, USA (1981)

In 1981, after a year in service, the walkways in the atrium of the Hyatt Regency hotel in Kansas City collapsed when they were packed with spectators watching a dance competition on the floor below. One hundred and fourteen people died, and over 200 were injured. The National Bureau of Standards (now NIST) carried out an investigation into this collapse.[51] The original design for the walkways' hanging supports was found to be capable of carrying only 60% of the required load under the relevant building Code, and only just able to support the dead load. A detail change to the connections of the hanging rods to the support beams made by the steel fabricator during construction doubled the load on the supporting fourth floor walkways, making failure inevitable under full load. The significance of this change was not picked up by the designers.

---

50 Robin Shepherd and J David Frost (eds), *Failures in Civil Engineering: Structural, Foundation and Geoenvironmental Case Studies* (1995) 67.

51 USA National Bureau of Standards, *Investigation of the Kansas City Hyatt Regency Walkways Collapse* (1982) NBS Building Science Series 143 https://nvlpubs.nist.gov/nistpubs/Legacy/BSS/nbsbuildingscience143.pdf (accessed 14 April 2021).

The investigators of the collapse concluded that the basic problem was a lack of communication between the designers and the steel fabricators. In particular, the sketch drawings prepared by the designers were taken as final drawings by the fabricators. The designers accepted the fabricator's detail change (which was implemented to overcome an impractical detail) without carrying out basic calculations, which would have revealed the doubling of load on the fourth-floor support beams. Shepherd lists the following non-technical lessons learned from this tragedy:

> Clearly, there is a need for all parties to understand their responsibilities and to perform their assignments competently. The structural engineer's responsibility for overall structural integrity, including the performance of the connections, was firmly established in this case. This failure also lends credibility to the practices of project peer review and constructability review.[52]

The designers were convicted of gross negligence, misconduct and unprofessional conduct, and lost their engineer's licences. At least $140 million was paid out to victims and their families in compensation.

20.11 L'Ambience Plaza Building, Connecticut, USA (1987)

The structural frame and slabs of what was to be a 16-storey apartment building collapsed during lift slab construction, killing 28 construction workers. An investigation into the failure was conducted by the Centre for Building Technology for the Occupational Health and Safety Administration (**OSHA**). Several technical factors in the design and construction were identified as contributing to this catastrophe. In addition, it was considered that the convoluted and fragmented project delivery system also contributed, as responsibility for ultimate structural safety was confused by unclear relationships among the engineer of record, the lift slab contractor and the designer of the shear heads.[53] One significant outcome of this failure was a change in the law relating to the method of construction known as the "lift slab" technique.[54]

It is interesting to note that alternative dispute resolution was used to resolve all pending litigation following the collapse within 20 months of the disaster, a process that involved five judicial bodies, more than 44 plaintiffs, approximately 40 potential defendants, several government agencies, and nearly 200 attorneys.[55] The settlement techniques used in resolving these disputes are discussed by Schwarzer and others.[56] One result of the somewhat controversial early settlement was that the various theories on causes of the failure were discussed thoroughly in the engineering literature sooner than is typically the case.[57]

52 Robin Shepherd and J David Frost (eds), *Failures in Civil Engineering: Structural, Foundation and Geoenvironmental Case Studies* (1995) 75.

53 Robin Shepherd and J David Frost (eds), *Failures in Civil Engineering: Structural, Foundation and Geoenvironmental Case Studies* (1995) 79.

54 www.thehistorychannel.co.uk/site/tv_guide/full_details/Technology/programme_2440.php (accessed April 2012).

55 http://library.findlaw.com/1995/Jun/1/126578.html (accessed 15 June 2016).

56 William W Schwarzer, Nancy E Weiss and Alan Hirsch, "Judicial Federalism in Action: Coordination of Litigation in State and Federal Courts" (1992) 78 Va L Rev 1689, 1715–1720.

57 At least seven papers were published in the American Society of Civil Engineers' Journal of Constructed Facilities between 1988 and 1992.

20.12 Burnaby Supermarket Parking Deck, British Colombia, Canada (1988)

Part of a rooftop parking deck of a one-storey regional community centre collapsed on opening day. The Government appointed a Commissioner to investigate the failure, and his report detailed the probable technical cause of the collapse and also reviewed the many procedural deficiencies that allowed a design deficiency to cause failure.[58] The numerous contributing procedural and contractual problems identified included:

- Competitive bidding for design services.
- Unclear assignment of responsibilities.
- Inadequate involvement of designers during the construction phase.
- Poorly monitored changes during construction.
- Incomplete peer review.
- Inadequate professional liability insurance.

The Commissioner's report contained 19 recommendations to avoid similar failures in future, including:

- Independent project peer review funded by increased permit fees.
- Special examinations for structural engineers and mandatory professional liability insurance.
- The development of a manual that would clarify the responsibility of all parties in the construction process.
- A minimum fee schedule for design services.[59]

Similar recommendations on the desirability of independent peer review have been made in response to other failures. For example, the collapse of a hotel building in Singapore in 1986 resulting in 33 deaths, led to a legislative requirement for all building works to be reviewed by an "accredited checker". The efficacy of this approach to preventing avoidable failures was, however, put in question by the collapse of the roof of a building under construction in 1999, killing seven workers. The engineer and accredited checker were fined the maximum for their breaches of the legislation.[60]

20.13 De la Concorde Overpass, Quebec, Canada (2006)

The inquiry in Canada into the collapse of the De la Concorde overpass illustrates the principles behind, and the public benefits that can come from an inquiry established to determine the truth and to make recommendations to avoid a repetition of future failures. The De la Concorde overpass was a prestressed concrete bridge over Autoroute 19 in the

58 Government of British Columbia, Victoria BC Canada, *Commission of Inquiry, Station Square Development* (1988).

59 Robin Shepherd and J David Frost (eds), *Failures in Civil Engineering: Structural, Foundation and Geoenvironmental Case Studies* (1995) 81.

60 Dr Anne Magdaline Netto and Dr Alice Christudason, "Who Pays?: Culpability of experts for building failures in Singapore", in BS Neale (ed), *Forensic engineering the investigation of failures Proceedings of the second international conference on forensic engineering organised by ICE, London, UK, 12–13 November 2001* (2001) 127–132.

province of Quebec, built in the early 1970s, and designed and constructed generally in accordance with the standards prevailing at that time. In 2006 a span collapsed under light traffic load, killing five people. The Government of Quebec established a Commission of Inquiry, comprising an attorney as President, and two engineers as Commissioners. The Commission conducted its inquiry in accordance with the principles defined by the Canadian Supreme Court.[61] The Commission concluded that, whilst there were a number of defects and shortcomings, both technical and procedural, none of those by itself would have caused the collapse, which resulted from a chain of causes.[62]

The technical reason for failure of the overpass was a shear failure in a reinforced concrete cantilever slab, the concrete of which had deteriorated over the years. The reinforcement design satisfied the Code requirements at the time, but would not do so now, nor would the detailing of the reinforcement be regarded as satisfactory today. The weakness of the detail was due to errors in placement of the reinforcement (a quality-control failure during construction), and low-quality concrete that was not suitable to resist freeze-thaw cycles (arising from ambiguity in the specification). There were further contributing causes that the thick slab was not watertight (the specified waterproof membrane had apparently not been installed either originally or during subsequent refurbishment), and refurbishment work in 1992 caused damage that was not evaluated. In respect of procedural failures, the Commission identified the following:

- Failure of the consulting engineer for not fulfilling its contractual obligation to exercise full-time supervision of the construction of the overpass, and thereby not preventing the faulty installation of the reinforcement that resulted in the structure not complying with the drawings and specifications
- Failure of the Contractor to meet its legal contractual obligations
- Failure of the principal subcontractor to adequately control the quality of the work and thereby incorrectly install the reinforcement
- The Ministry responsible did not rigorously and effectively use all the means at its disposal to properly evaluate the condition of the overpass despite numerous signs of deterioration and did not maintain adequate records for the guidance of inspectors and maintenance workers.[63]

The Commission recommended that the Government review the legal framework for the design, construction and construction supervision of all new structures and for major rehabilitation work along the following lines:

- Use a transparent process for selecting consulting engineers based on competency and past performance, with cost only considered for those firms meeting the competence criteria.
- Validation of the concept, drawings and calculations of structural designs by a responsible engineer.

61 Quebec Canada, *Commission of Inquiry into the Collapse of a Portion of the De la Concorde Overpass, Report* (2007) Introduction of the Commissioners www.cevc.gouv.qc.ca/UserFiles/File/Rapport/report_eng.pdf (accessed April 2012).

62 Ibid 5.

63 Ibid 8.

- Prequalification of contractors on the basis of their ability for the type of structure to be built, with cost only considered for contractors meeting the competence criteria.
- When awarding contracts for consulting engineering or construction, ensure that the key personnel on which prequalification was based will be available for the duration of the work.
- Subcontracting requirements be identified in bids, and contractors required to produce a work quality control plan for their own and subcontract work.
- On completion, an engineer certify that the structure was built in accordance with drawings and specifications and all the documents associated with the work and structure be assembled and kept during the entire life of the structure to assist with inspection and maintenance programmes.
- Owners of structures evaluate the performance of consulting engineering firms and contractors on completion of a project, and the evaluations be kept on record.[64]

The Commission made far-reaching recommendations not only on the organisation and responsibilities of the Ministry, but also on the investment needed by the Province of Quebec to rehabilitate its bridges to a satisfactory standard, comparable with other provinces and the USA. The Commission considered that annual investment of $500 million would be required for each of the next ten years to bring the percentage of bridges in good condition from the 2005 level of slightly more than 50% to an acceptable 80%.[65]

20.14 Conclusion

The details of the failures discussed above, and as revealed by the reports of the public inquiries that ensued, highlight many issues relevant to the contracts and the execution of those contracts. In each case the direct "technical" causes of failure were accompanied by contractual and project execution deficiencies that did not prevent or detect the onset of disaster before it was too late. No doubt all the disasters discussed above had their genesis in human failings, generally and perhaps invariably in a combination of individual failures. Whilst no contract or procedure can prevent human error, it is suggested that clearly expressed agreements in which people are expected to function in known, logical and acceptable ways are at least a good starting point.

In some cases discussed above, the lessons have apparently been well learned because of the remedial measures subsequently implemented to avoid a repetition of the same type of failure. However, it is submitted that some of the causes of past failures revealed by public inquiries are still operative today, and reconsideration of such lessons from the past may assist in avoiding future failures from similar causes. The importance of history was stated long ago by Cicero: "History is the witness that testifies to the passing of time; it illumines reality, vitalises memory, provides guidance in daily life and brings us tidings of antiquity."[66] Has the importance of history really changed in the last 2,000 years?

64 Ibid 10, 11.
65 Ibid 13.
66 Cicero (106BC–43BC), *Pro Publio Sestio.*

CHAPTER 21

Lessons from failures – Quebec Bridge[1]

21.1 Introduction

Collapses of buildings or structures invariably attract considerable public attention, particularly if death or injury results. Government response to significant failures often takes the form of a public inquiry such as a Royal Commission. The terms of reference of such a public inquiry typically includes not only determining the causes of the failure, but also recommendations on avoiding similar failures in the future. The reports of public inquiries are therefore much wider in scope than any report of the litigation between disputing parties involved in a failure, and form a valuable repository of lessons to be learned and guidance for improved practice in the future.

This chapter reviews the Royal Commission Report into the first collapse of the Quebec Bridge during its construction. This failure occurred over 100 years ago and, in addition to its historical interest, the Royal Commission Report details the lessons learned that are timeless and still relevant today. Although the failure of the Quebec Bridge had a predominantly "technical" cause in respect of inadequacies in the quality of design and/or construction, the focus of this chapter is on the contractual and procedural aspects of project execution (particularly time, cost and scope of work), and the extent to which they may have been contributing factors to the collapse. The deaths resulting from this and other failures are a salutary reminder that failure to implement the appropriate contractual procedures and execute the works in compliance with the requirements of a construction contract can have much more serious consequences than a dispute over which party is liable to pay damages.

The Quebec Bridge is known for the two separate failures that occurred during construction, the first in 1907 and the second in 1916, with the tragic death of 86 workers. The day after the first collapse, the Canadian government implemented a Royal Commission, empowering it to make immediate investigations into the cause of the collapse of the bridge, and all matters incidental to it. The Commission was chaired by a practising civil engineer, the other two commissioners being another practising civil engineer and the Professor of Engineering at Toronto University. The report itself is a very succinct five pages, but is supported by 19 detailed appendices and 37 drawings covering all the relevant contractual and technical issues.[2] The Quebec Bridge Royal Commission Report

1 This chapter is an edited version of the published paper Donald Charrett, "Lessons from Failures – Quebec Bridge" (2008) 119 *Australian Construction Law Newsletter* 14.

2 Canada, *Royal Commission Quebec Bridge Inquiry, Report* (1908).

 DOI: 10.4324/9781003206897-23

has been studied by generations of engineers for its engineering lessons because of its high standards of honesty, clarity and professional competence, and is "something of a classic of its kind".[3]

21.2 Procurement of the Quebec Bridge Canada

The Quebec Bridge is a steel bridge of cantilever construction, the main span of 548m being the longest of this bridge type ever built. It was procured by the Quebec Bridge and Railway Company (**QBRC**), a company specifically incorporated in 1887 to build and operate a railway bridge across the St Lawrence River. The Government passed various Acts authorising construction of a bridge, subject to approval, as well as the ability to charge tolls (also subject to approval). For a period of 13 years the company was unable to raise the necessary finance, until the Government granted a subsidy of $1m, subject to completion within a specified time. The province of Quebec and the city of Quebec also made grants totalling $550,000. The company's finances were only assured when in 1903 the Government guaranteed the bonds of the company and enabled it to redeem its outstanding stock.

The company called lump sum design and construct tenders for main and anchor spans on minimal documentation in September 1898, with a six-month tender period. The tender documents included a clearance diagram and specifications for a cantilever bridge with a main span of 488m (1,600 feet). Four companies submitted tenders for a cantilever bridge and three for a suspension bridge. Mr Theodore Cooper, an eminent American consulting bridge engineer, was appointed to report on the tenders, and to act as the company's consulting engineer to review and approve the Contractor's designs. Mr Cooper reported that the tenders for a cantilever bridge from the Keystone company and the Phoenix Bridge Company (**Phoenix**) were acceptable designs, and reported favourably on the tender of Phoenix as the "best and cheapest". However, he advised that further site investigation was necessary before letting a contract, and there should be provision for changing the specification in any contract that was entered into. Phoenix was not at that stage prepared to enter into a contract because of QBRC's weak financial state.

Once favourable legislation was in prospect, QBRC awarded the contract for the anchor and cantilever spans to Phoenix by a brief agreement in April 1900. Phoenix executed the agreement on the understanding that it was not to become operative until the necessary legislation was enacted and satisfactory financial arrangements for payment had been made; however it did agree to proceed with the design and drawings once formal approval of the government engineers had been obtained. The agreement was extended to include the approach spans in December 1900. The agreement provided, not for a lump sum as tendered, but for the supply and erection of steel at a price per pound, based on the tender price adjusted for changes in the base price of steel. This was apparently the result of Phoenix' tender qualification that its lump sum price was subject to modification for changes in specifications or any other changes "made by the company's engineer in the size, depths and locations of the piers and their caissons". Many such changes were made, and arose mainly from the insufficiency of the original plans and the preliminary work done by the QBRC.

3 A Pugsley, *The Safety of Structures* (1963) 140.

After further site investigations and borings, Cooper recommended that the span be increased to 548m (1,800 feet), which he considered would be quicker to erect and involve fewer risks. He also advised that certain modifications be made to the specifications, to reduce the cost impact of the span increase. These included an increase in allowable stresses in the steel, significantly above those in common use at the time. The Commission considered that this increase in stresses was "in harmony with the most advanced practice at that time, and due more to an instinct of wise investment than to any endeavour to simply cheapen the structure".[4] Whilst the government engineers had to give their approval to these changes, it appears they had full confidence in Cooper and did not make any changes to his specification proposals, or interfere with his technical control at any time. Some of that confidence may have been misplaced through a misunderstanding that Cooper would be engaged continuously on the work during construction.[5] As noted below, Cooper did not have any responsibility for the critical erection phase. The Commission however considered that the decision to rely on the advice of Cooper was in accordance with the best knowledge of the time and "the most competent engineers would have endorsed the concentration of responsibility upon the most experienced and able man".[6] The revised specifications were not officially approved until the middle of 1903, at which time Phoenix conditionally agreed to the contract.

21.3 Criticism of design and construct procurement

The Commission was somewhat critical of the whole process of procurement on a design and construct basis:

> each bridge company was asked to spend several thousand dollars in the preparation of plans, and that in return was given an opportunity to bid for a contract to be let by a company of weak financial standing. The result was that although the magnitude of the work placed it outside the limits of established practice, most of the tenders submitted were made from immature studies based upon insufficient data. The evidence shows that the Phoenix Bridge Company gave more time and attention to the competition than any other tenderer, but the error afterwards made by it in assuming the weight of the structure for final designs shows how faulty the estimate accompanying its original tender was. We consider that the procedure adopted in calling for tenders was not satisfactory in view of the magnitude of the work, and was not calculated to produce the most efficient results.[7]

The Commission criticised the QBRC calling tenders on a general specification that required Contractors to prepare plans and designs which were not fully developed, clearly preferring the traditional route of tendering for construction of a fully developed design:

> Considering all the conditions pertaining to the undertaking the adoption of this method was not in the best interests of the work. [QBRC] was known not to have the capital necessary to immediately proceed with construction, and the preparation of complete preliminary plans would involve a large outlay. The evidence and documents show that the preliminary plans submitted with the tenders were incomplete; this was as might have been expected, as the several contractors who tendered for the work had little assurance that they would get any return for their expenditure of time and money.

4 Canada, *Royal Commission Quebec Bridge Inquiry, Report* (1908) 38.
5 Ibid 42.
6 Ibid 48.
7 Ibid 35.

> Specifications as a rule consist of two distinct portions, one of which relates to design and the other to fabrication, material and execution. In the case of the Quebec bridge, the difficulty of preparing an adequate specification for design was very great. It would have been better to have entrusted the preparation of plans and specifications to engineers independent of any contracting or manufacturing company, whose previous experience qualified them to handle the work. This course would have avoided duplication of designs involving expensive plans and would have prevented the letting of a contract on incomplete plans formed upon erroneous data; the engineers would have made a proper and sufficient study of the whole project, and in due time competitive tenders upon their plans would have been secured, thus enabling all contractors to tender on a common basis.[8]

21.4 The contract

The final contract document consisting of 16 Articles of Agreement was executed in June 1903. By today's standards this was a remarkably brief document for such a major project. Phoenix agreed to:

> construct, deliver and erect in the most substantial and workmanlike manner, to the satisfaction and acceptance of [Cooper] and the engineer of [QBRC], and in accordance with the general plans and specifications hereto attached, and made a part of this agreement, the metal superstructure, railings, screens and guard rails, also the timber for tracks and highway floors of the bridge over the St Lawrence River, near Quebec, consisting of one central span of eighteen hundred feet and two side or anchor spans of five hundred feet each.

The contract provided for withholding 10% from progress payments until $100,000 had been withheld, together with a guarantee bond of $100,000 to constitute a fund as a guarantee for the faithful performance of the work under the agreement. As further security for proper performance by Phoenix, all the plant and equipment was the property of QBRC until completion of the works. There was no requirement for insurance, but Phoenix was required to restore at its own cost all or any part of the work damaged or destroyed before its acceptance. Any variation not only required written authorisation by the engineer, but also approval of the QBRC Board of Directors!

Phoenix provisionally accepted the contract, subject to additional terms it proposed in a separate letter. These provided a condition precedent that the necessary legislation had to be in place, as did satisfactory arrangements for payment. Phoenix stated that it did not guarantee completion by the specified date, nor would it accept responsibility for any delay damages. However, it did agree to pay $5,000 per month in liquidated damages if the work was not completed by 31 December 1908. In February 1904 Phoenix advised that the conditions precedent were satisfied, and no further changes were made to the contractual arrangements. The Commission stated that there was nothing in the various contracts and agreements between QBRC and Phoenix that had a direct connection with the cause of the collapse.[9] Nor was there any inappropriate action by the Government, which maintained all its dealings exclusively with QBRC, which in turn was the only one who dealt with Phoenix.

---

8 Ibid 141.
9 Ibid 21.

21.5 Cost issues

Notwithstanding the financial difficulties of QBRC and the view that design and construct was not the best method of procurement, the Commission did not consider that undue pressure on costs had any bearing on the ultimate failure. Cooper, although he did not overlook costs, made his recommendations for technical reasons, and stated that he was "left absolutely unhampered in any manner in his report as to which he should consider the best plan and the best bridge".[10] It is also apparent that letting the contract on a fixed price per pound of steel provided no incentive to the Contractor to reduce the steel weight. The specification decisions which were made on design loading and to allow higher stresses than normal were made by Cooper, no doubt with the objective of achieving the best economy he believed was consistent with safe practice. The Commission, and an engineer engaged by QBRC after the collapse to review the design, considered that was an error of judgment, and did not take advantage of the improved financial situation arising from the Government's decision to guarantee QBRC's securities.[11]

Notwithstanding the Commission's view that undue pressure on costs did not have any bearing on the failure, it is difficult to avoid the conclusion that cost-cutting in respect of the engagement of the consulting engineer had an adverse impact on the level of scrutiny that the Contractor's design was subject to. The Commission made the following trenchant comments about the consequences of the inadequate remuneration Cooper was paid for his services. Although made 100 years ago, these comments have a timeless quality to them:

> Mr Cooper assumed a position of great responsibility, and agreed to accept an inadequate salary for his services. No provision was made by the Quebec Bridge Company for staff to assist him, nor is there any evidence to show that he asked for the appointment of such a staff. He endeavoured to maintain the necessary assistants out of his own salary, which was itself too small for his personal services, and he did a great deal of detail work which could have been satisfactorily done by a junior. The result of this was that he had no time to investigate the soundness of data and theories which were being used in the designing, and consequently allowed fundamental errors to pass by him unchallenged. The detection and correction of these fundamental errors is the distinctive duty of the consulting engineer, and we are compelled to recognize that in undertaking to do his work without sufficient staff or sufficient remuneration both he and his employers are to blame, but it lay with himself to demand that these matters be remedied.[12]

21.6 Engineering

At the time of his engagement as consulting engineer to QBRC, Cooper was nearly 70 and in infirm health. Cooper was the engineer who approved all the designs emanating from Phoenix, and the chief engineer of QBRC (Hoare) was responsible for all other technical decisions. Cooper was only concerned with the bridge in its final constructed configuration, and had no involvement with the engineering for erection. He disclaimed any responsibility for inspection in the shop or in the field, and made no site inspections during

10 Ibid 38.
11 Ibid 150.
12 Ibid 50.

construction. Although he assumed many of the duties of the chief engineer, he was not authorised to act in this capacity: his directions were advisory and not imperative.

There were warning signs of significant deformations in major structural members shortly before the collapse; however, there was no engineer with the appropriate experience, knowledge and ability in charge of the site in a position to take decisive action. This lack of clarity in the engineering decision-making in QBRC was the subject of criticism by the Commission:

> The impression left with us is that throughout the work Mr Cooper was in the position of a man forced in the interests of the work to take responsibility which did not fully belong to his position, and which he was not authorised to take, and that he avoided the assumption of authority whenever possible.[13]

The reliance on Cooper was in fact a significant factor in the ultimate failure:

> His professional standing was so high that his appointment left no further anxiety about the outcome in the minds of all most closely concerned. As the event proved, his connection with the work produced in general a false feeling of security. His approval of any plan was considered by everyone to be final, and he has accepted absolute responsibility for the two great engineering changes that were made during the progress of the work – the lengthening of the main span and the changes in the specification and the adopted unit stresses.[14]

The Government was keen on the bridge opening in 1908, which the Commission considered was one factor that led to Phoenix hurrying the work of design and manufacture and resulting in errors, although not the errors which resulted in the collapse. Phoenix made a significant error in not recalculating the dead weight of the bridge when it commenced the final design in 1903, after the three-year hiatus since its tender was accepted. Both QBRC and Phoenix overlooked this necessity in the rush to complete the final design, with the result that the bridge members would have been considerably overstressed after completion: "This error was sufficient to have condemned the bridge had it not fallen owing to other causes."[15] As noted by the Commission, this error could have been detected had the time between 1900 and 1903 been used to prepare the design. The significance of the finding that the bridge would have been overstressed in service had it not collapsed during construction should not be overlooked. As with the much later West Gate Bridge in Melbourne, the tragic collapse during construction averted completion of a bridge that would not have been safe in service.

Cooper did not carry out any independent check on the dead load, and was not aware of the error until February 1906. At this time, the anchor arm, tower and two panels of the cantilever arm were fabricated, and six panels of the anchor arm were in place. He permitted the work to proceed, believing that the increase in stresses from 7 to 10% were still within the limit of safety. The dead loads assumed in design were in fact too low by 18% for the suspended span, 20% for the cantilever arm and 30% for the anchor arm. The use of the preliminary and incorrect values for dead weight in the final design was in breach of the contract, as the specification required that "The dead weight used for calculating stresses must not be less than the actual weight of structure when completed."[16] The

13 Ibid 75.
14 Ibid 49.
15 Ibid 37.
16 Ibid 57.

significance of this error was compounded by the high allowable stresses permitted by Cooper, and the fact that the dead load stresses constituted approximately two-thirds of the stress in the main members. The Commission subsequently determined that the error in the design load stresses in the main chords resulting from the incorrect dead load was 10%.[17]

The Commission carried out its own studies and tests on the strength of latticed compression members of the type used in the bottom chords of the anchor am, and concluded that:

> the bridge fell because the latticing of the lower chords in the main pier was too weak to carry the stresses to which it was subjected; … We conclude from our tests that owing to the weakness of the latticing, the chords were dangerously weak in the body for the duty they would be called upon to do. We have no evidence to show that they would have actually failed under working conditions had they been axially loaded and not subject to transverse stresses arising from weak end details and loose connections. … The Phoenix Bridge Company showed indifferent engineering ability in the design of the joints, and did not recognize the great care with which these should be treated in the field.[18]

The Commission looked at the designs of a number of other long span bridges, and compared them with the Quebec Bridge:

> Consideration of the difference in the designs on drawings Nos. 34, 35 and 36, all of which have been prepared under the direction of engineers of recognized ability and high professional standing, shows that there is as yet no established system designed for large compression members. The individual judgment of the engineer is the determining factor, and this may prove to be erroneous as it did in the case of the Quebec Bridge.[19]

The design of the latticed compression members did not breach any provisions of the specification; however, the design could have been checked by testing:

> The main criticism that can be made of the designers was that they had the means of checking their theories by use of the testing machine and that they did not do nor did they thoroughly study the possibilities of lattice formulas.[20]

Pugsley has noted that the engineering significance of this failure was that it drew attention to the lack of knowledge on the behaviour of built-up compression members. Although considerable theoretical work on the design of large compression members was carried out after the Quebec Bridge, testing of major compression members was prudently carried out for the Sydney Harbour Bridge.[21]

The materials used satisfied the requirements of the specification, and the standard of Phoenix's detailing, shop work and erection was generally excellent. There were some minor fabrication errors at joints that may have contributed to the collapse, but the real issue for the Commission was a design that called for an accuracy beyond the working limits of good shop practice. The Commission criticised the judgment of some of the Phoenix senior staff, and unequivocally laid the blame for the collapse to the mistakes and errors of its designer, Szlapka. Although widely experienced in bridge design, he

17 Ibid 109.
18 Ibid 92.
19 Ibid 140.
20 Ibid 150.
21 A Pugsley, *The Safety of Structures* (1963) 141.

had limited knowledge of transportation and erection, and had no responsibility for the engineering for erection. Szlapka had the confidence of Cooper, and, according to the Commission, carried out his design work with care and energy.[22]

21.7 Erection

Although the Commission considered that the Phoenix erection staff was efficient, well trained and experienced, it did not have an experienced engineer on site responsible for erection:

> the Phoenix Bridge Company erred in judgment and showed a failure to appreciate the magnitude and difficulties of the work it had undertaken when it did not provide as part of this organisation an engineer of erection who, by virtue of technical training and long experience of large bridge work, was fitted to take complete local control of erection. In this they followed usual practice, which, however, was not applicable to this particular work.[23]

The Commission was critical of the inadequate staffing of QBRC, which comprised the chief engineer, two erection inspectors and four mill and shop inspectors, which it did not regard as either efficient or well organised:

> The staff was too small; and it is our opinion that the Quebec Bridge Company would have shown better judgment had it employed a larger staff under the direction of an independent man of wide technical knowledge and who would have been sufficiently forceful to hold his own against the contractors.[24]

It did not consider that Hoare was technically competent to fulfil the role of chief engineer and direct the work on site, a fact known to the directors of QBRC:

> While we can only consider this as a mistake on the part of the Quebec Bridge and Railway Company, yet we regret to say that such appointments are by no means uncommon, and it must be recognized that in many cases good executive ability is valued more highly or considered of more importance than special professional knowledge.[25]

The lack of a suitably experienced Phoenix erection engineer or QBRC engineer on site became a critical issue during erection of the suspended span when many of the joints were not fully riveted, and major compression members suffered from joint gaps and increasing lateral deflections that gave prior warning of substantial structural distress. The Phoenix erection personnel were unaware of the impending danger, and it was only drawn to Cooper's attention by the QBRC erection inspector when it was too late. The QBRC inspector (a qualified but inexperienced engineer) was so concerned with the deformations during erection that he travelled to New York to meet Cooper the day before the collapse. After Cooper was appraised of the situation, he sent a telegram to site warning that all personnel must leave the bridge; however, the telegram arrived too late.

Figure 21.1 shows the cantilever span on 27 August 1904, the day before the collapse.

---

22 Canada, *Royal Commission Quebec Bridge Inquiry, Report* (1908) 52.

23 Ibid 53.

24 Ibid 51.

25 Ibid 49.

FIGURE 21.1 The cantilever span of the Quebec bridge on 27 August 1907. FE Cudworth/Library and Archives Canada/PA-029229.

Figure 21.2 shows the steelwork in the river after the collapse, looking from the Quebec side of the river. Figure 21.3 shows the unbroken chain of eye-bars of the top chord after the collapse.

21.8 The Commission's conclusions

In the view of the Commission, and an engineer engaged by QBRC after the collapse to review the design, the failure was caused by an error of engineering judgment on the part of both the Contractor's design engineer and Cooper. The Commission's concise conclusions are worth repeating in full:

(a) The collapse of the Quebec Bridge resulted from the failure of the lower chords in the anchor arm near the main pier. The failure of these chords was due to their defective design.

(b) The stresses that caused the failure were not due to abnormal weather conditions or accident, but were such as might be expected in the regular course of erection.

(c) The design of the chords that failed was made by Mr. P. L. Szlapka, the designing engineer of the Phoenix Bridge Company.

(d) This design was examined and officially approved by Mr. Theodore Cooper, consulting engineer of the Quebec Bridge and Railway Company.

FIGURE 21.2 The collapsed span in the river. Canada. Dept. of Mines and Resources / Library and Archives Canada / PA-020614.

(e) The failure cannot be attributed directly to any cause other than errors in judgment on the part of these two engineers.
(f) These errors of judgment cannot be attributed either to lack of common professional knowledge, to neglect of duty, or to a desire to economize. The ability of the two engineers was tried in one of the most difficult professional problems of the day and proved to be insufficient for the task.
(g) We do not consider that the specifications for the work were satisfactory or sufficient, the unit stresses in particular being higher than any established by past practice. The specifications were accepted without protest by all interested.
(h) A grave error was made in assuming the dead load for the calculations at too low a value and not afterwards revising this assumption. This error was of sufficient magnitude to have required the condemnation of the bridge, even if the details of the lower chords had been of sufficient strength, because, if the bridge had been completed as designed, the actual stresses would have been considerably greater than those permitted by the

FIGURE 21.3 The collapsed steelwork showing an unbroken chain of eye-bars. Photograph courtesy of Public Archives of Canada

specifications. This erroneous assumption was made by Mr Szlapka and accepted by Mr. Cooper, and tended to hasten the disaster.

(i) We do not believe that the fall of the bridge could have been prevented by any action that might have been taken after 27 August 1907. Any effort to brace or take down the structure would have been impracticable owing to the manifest risk of human life involved.

(j) The loss of life on 29 August 1907, might have been prevented by the exercise of better judgment on the part of those in responsible charge of the work for the Quebec Bridge and Railway Company and for the Phoenix Bridge Company.

(k) The failure on the part of the Quebec Bridge and Railway Company to appoint an experienced bridge engineer to the position of chief engineer was a mistake. This resulted in a loose-and inefficient supervision of all parts of the work on the part of the Quebec Bridge and Railway Company.

(l) The work done by the Phoenix Bridge Company in making the detail drawings and in planning and carrying out the erection, and by the Phoenix Iron Company in fabricating the material was good, and the steel used was of good quality. The serious defects were fundamental errors in design.

(m) No one connected with the general designing fully appreciated the magnitude of the work nor the insufficiency of the data upon which they were depending. The special experimental studies and investigations that were required to confirm the judgment of the designers were not made.

(n) The professional knowledge of the present day concerning the action of steel columns under load is not sufficient to enable engineers to economically design such structures as the Quebec bridge. A bridge of the adopted span that will unquestionably be safe can be built, but in the present state of professional knowledge a considerably larger amount of metal would have to be used than might be required if our knowledge were more exact.

(o) The professional record of Mr. Cooper was such that his selection for the authoritative position that he occupied was warranted, and the complete confidence that was placed in his judgment by the officials of the Dominion government, the Quebec Bridge and Railway Company and the Phoenix Bridge Company was deserved.[26]

The Commission's comment on the "considerably larger amount of metal" that would have to be used for satisfactory design was confirmed by the redesigned bridge, which contained two and a half times the amount of steel as the original design. It is worth noting that although the Commission determined that the direct cause of the collapse was a consequence of engineering errors of judgment, it criticised a number of contractual and procedural aspects as having some significance, specifically (g), (h), (j), (k), (m) and (n) above.

21.9 Lessons from Quebec Bridge

Based on the issues highlighted above, the following are some of the contractual and project execution lessons relevant to major engineering projects to be learned from the Report of the Royal Commission, and which are still relevant today:

- The difficulties and time involved in raising finance for a project should not prevent sufficient time allowance for the preparation of initial studies, the design, tender documentation or for the execution of the works.
- Unquestioning reliance on the skill and experience of an individual engineer may be misplaced without adequate peer review.
- An Employer requires adequately qualified and experienced technical staff with the appropriate authority for both the design and erection phases, even if it procures its project via a design and construct contract.
- The engineering design of a major project should be reviewed by an independent engineer, without reference to the designer's calculations.
- The scope of the engineer's engagement should include responsibility for both design and erection, with compensation commensurate with the proper execution of that scope.
- An Employer with limited financial resources may be subject to cost pressures that result in inappropriate engineering decisions.

---

26 Ibid 9–10.

- The construction Contractor needs to have an appropriately qualified and experienced erection engineer on site with an understanding of the design and full authority for the erection.
- Appropriate allowances should be made for the additional risks inherent in unusual structures or structures of a scale not attempted before, and this may require testing of components.

21.10 Conclusion

Engineering failures inevitably have serious, sometimes grave, consequences, but each of them contains lessons to be learned if similar failures and inevitable disputes are to be avoided in the future. The report discussed above contains valuable information, not only historical and technical, but also in respect of contractual and project execution issues that had an influence on the failure of the Quebec Bridge. Although the failure was over 100 years ago, the lessons to be learned are timeless. The lessons from this and other past failures are still relevant and worth repeating, as today's generation of engineers may not be familiar with the reasons for them, or the resources available in public reports. It is a salutary reminder of the importance of history, that lessons learned and heeded from the contractual issues of scope, time, cost and quality in the execution of projects that failed in the past may assist in preventing failures (and disputes) in the future.

CHAPTER 22

Lessons from failures – West Gate Bridge[1]

22.1 Introduction

Collapses of buildings or structures almost inevitably generate disputes between the project participants. In addition, there is usually a substantial public interest dimension in such failures, particularly if death or injury results. Government response to significant failures is sometimes swift, and often takes the form of a public inquiry, sometimes a Royal Commission. The terms of reference of such public inquiries typically include determining the causes of the failure, and recommendations to avoid similar failures in the future. The reports of these inquiries are therefore much wider in scope than any report of the litigation between disputing parties involved in the failure and form a valuable repository of lessons to be learned and guidance for improved practice in the future.

This chapter reviews the reports of several public inquiries into high-profile failures of steel box girder bridges in the 1970s. It is suggested that, although these relate to failures that occurred some time ago, in addition to their historical interest, the reports contain timeless information that is still relevant today. If these lessons from the past are not heeded and learned, then perhaps today's generation of engineers will unwittingly repeat them. Although the failures discussed here had a predominantly "technical" cause in respect of inadequacies in the quality of design and/or construction, the focus of the chapter is on the contractual and procedural aspects of project execution (particularly time, cost and scope of work), and the extent to which they were contributing factors to the collapse. The deaths resulting from these failures are a salutary reminder that failure to implement the appropriate contractual procedures and execute the works in compliance with the requirements of the contract can have much more serious consequences than a dispute over which party is liable to pay damages.

22.2 West Gate Bridge, Melbourne, Australia (1971)

22.2.1 Overview

The West Gate Bridge was procured under a forerunner of a modern PPP Partnership. In the late 1950s the Government had inadequate funds to finance a new bridge and, accordingly, a private enterprise group initiated the project, with the cooperation of the

1 This chapter is an edited version of the paper published in: Donald Charrett, "Lessons from Failures – West Gate Bridge" (2008) 30 *BDPS News* 4; (2008) 120 *Australian Construction Law Newsletter* 28. The BDPS paper is reproduced by permission of the Building Dispute Practitioner's Society.

DOI: 10.4324/9781003206897-24

Government. The Lower Yarra Crossing Authority (**the Authority**), a private company limited by guarantee, was vested with various powers by the *Lower Yarra Crossing Authority Act 1965* (Vic). Those powers enabled it to make regulations, borrow money to finance the river crossing, acquire land and raise tolls so that the bridge would be paid for by its users. It was intended that the bridge would become the property of the crown when all loans had been repaid.[2]

The bridge comprises 12 concrete spans on the east side and nine concrete spans on the west side, with five steel box girder spans crossing the Yarra River, the central three spans being cable stayed. Following the unfortunate experience of the failure in service of Kings Bridge, and the Royal Commission's criticism of its procurement via a design and construct contract,[3] the procurement of West Gate Bridge by the Authority was conventional: eminent consulting engineers with long experience in the design of large bridges were engaged directly by the Authority to prepare the designs and supervise construction, and contracts were let for the construction in accordance with the engineers' designs.

On 15 October 1970, the 112m span on the western side of the Yarra known as span 10–11 collapsed suddenly during construction, resulting in the death of 35 workers. The Coroner immediately constituted a five-man expert technical committee to observe and record facts on site. The evidence collected by that committee was invaluable to the Coroner and the Royal Commission, which was announced the day after the collapse. Letters Patent dated 21 October 1970 appointed Justice Barber of the Supreme Court, an Australian Professor of civil engineering and a distinguished English bridge engineer as Commissioners. A preliminary hearing was held on 20 October 1970, followed by 80 sitting days between 5 November 1970 and 15 June 1971. It heard evidence from 52 witnesses and considered 319 exhibits. The Royal Commission was charged with enquiring into and reporting on the circumstances surrounding and the cause or causes direct and indirect of the failure of steel span 10–11, and whether any aspect of the design of the steel span was inadequate or undesirable.[4] The Report dated 14 July 1971 is the source of the following observations.

22.2.2 Construction contracts for West Gate Bridge

The original contract for fabrication and erection of the steel box girder spans of the bridge (**Contract S**) was based on a considerably amended Australian Standard General Conditions of Contract for Civil Engineering Works, with a number of other documents incorporated. The Commission criticised the drafting of the contract, particularly the vice of incorporating documents that purported to impose liability on persons not parties to the contract. It quoted as an example of such an inappropriately incorporated document in the construction contract, the minutes of a meeting between representatives of the consulting engineers and the Contractor:

> Contract S included a provision for an exchange of design information as follows:- 'To ensure that erection calculations will be in accordance with the engineer's design criteria – notably the end conditions under full load FF&P [the consulting engineer for the steel spans] will

2 Victoria, *West Gate Bridge Royal Commission, Report of Royal Commission into the failure of Westgate Bridge* (1971) 11.

3 See Section 16.3.

4 Victoria, *West Gate Bridge Royal Commission, Report of Royal Commission into the failure of Westgate Bridge* (1971) 3.

> supply to Werkspoor [the parent of Contract S contractor] a set of bridge design calculations'. Despite repeated requests from WFC [Contract S contractor], FF&P resolutely refused to hand over any calculations.[5]

The Royal Commission noted:

> As this matter was of major importance to WSC, its inclusion, merely by way of an incorporated document, can only be regarded as slipshod drafting. We make no comment on other similar instances, save to observe that contracts for works of the magnitude of this project, merit rather more careful consideration.[6]

In view of the significance of the calculations (or the lack of them) in the collapse, this was a major contractual deficiency.

Construction under Contract S commenced in April 1968, with a projected completion date of December 1970. However, the Contractor fell seriously behind its programme such that by February 1970 the Authority issued a "show cause" notice under the Contract. The Contractor issued a counter notice, and a settlement was reached in which WSC retained the work of fabrication and subassemblies of the steel boxes, with all the other work of completion and erection to be carried out by John Holland (Constructions) Pty Ltd (**JHC**) under a new contract (**Contract E**). JHC also constructed the foundations and concrete spans under separate contracts.

Contract E was a "cost plus" labour management contract in which JHC was responsible for the physical task of erecting the steel work, but had no responsibility for engineering decisions relating to final or erection stresses in the bridge. This contract had an exclusion clause which held JHC harmless in contract or tort for any failure to construct and complete the works or for any defects, unless caused by gross negligence. The Royal Commission considered the implications of the provisions of Contract E, and whether it had any bearing on the collapse. It noted that the unusual contractual arrangements with JHC, and its relative inexperience in large steel bridge work, put more responsibility on the consulting engineer (FF&P) and made its task more onerous, without changing its legal liability (which remained the skill, care and diligence contemplated by the common law and expressed in the provisions of the consultants' agreement).[7]

The Commission considered that this contractual arrangement was a contributing factor in the collapse:

> There can be no doubt that the problem created by the limitation on the responsibility and liability of JHC and the increased responsibility of FF&P became a major cause of serious trouble and difficulty. The failure clearly to define the roles of the FF&P staff and JHC engineers led to a confusion that was disastrous.[8]

Furthermore, the Commission noted that this situation could easily have been avoided by contractual means:

> All this confusion and difficulty could and should have been quite easily avoided, had the increased responsibility of FF&P been clearly defined in the first place. It is the greatest pity that nobody seems to have thought of the desirability of amending the contract between the

5 Ibid 41.
6 Ibid 15.
7 Ibid 80–83.
8 Ibid 82.

joint consultants and the Authority, contemporaneously with the execution of Contract E, in such a way as to define the consultant's responsibility.[9]

22.2.3 Cost and time issues

It is notable that cost factors were not identified as having any bearing on the collapse, as the Authority placed no particular financial limits on the cost: "There was certainly no pressure by the Authority to achieve cheese-paring economies, particularly if by so doing any risk to the safety of the structure was involved."[10] However, the same cannot be said of time pressures, and the Commission criticised the Authority in the following terms:

> Fundamental to the whole sorry situation was a constant sense of urgency and pressure to complete the construction within specified times. No one can blame the Authority for a desire to keep its contractors up to schedule. The financial consequences of any delay was serious to an organisation working on borrowed capital – and a degree of pressure to reach completion on time is understandable and even praiseworthy. Nevertheless, the determination to keep the work moving at all costs was so extreme as to engender an atmosphere in which speed was the all-important consideration. In a number of instances the burning desire for speed resulted in quick, ill considered decisions which brought about trouble, difficulty and delay, whereas time spent in careful thought, and the adoption of what appeared to be the slower method of procedure would have, in the long run, meant an earlier, and happier result. We are satisfied that this climate of urgency and pressure tended to lower morale, and in fact directly caused some of the more serious errors of judgment upon which we have had occasion to comment.[11]

22.2.4 Erection

The method of erection proposed in the tender by the original steelwork Contractor, using two half spans, jacked into position and joined along the longitudinal centreline, had not been used anywhere else in the world under similar conditions to West Gate Bridge.[12] The consulting engineer not only neglected or refused to hand over calculations that were vital for the Contractor in assessing its erection method,[13] but it rarely replied to correspondence requesting technical information or, if it responded, it often did not provide the information requested.[14]

The unusual method of erection created a number of difficulties that the Commission found were significant contributing factors to the collapse. In particular, the two half spans, when erected, had a significant difference in camber (of the order of 100mm) which had to be eliminated before they could be spliced together. JHC used kentledge (seven 8-ton blocks of concrete) on the upper flange of the span as a means of correcting the difference in camber. This kentledge caused a buckle in the upper flange in the vicinity of the 4–5 splice at mid-span. In an attempt to eliminate this buckle, about 30 bolts were removed from a transverse splice in the upper flange of span 10–11 at the 4–5 splice. The

9 Ibid 82.
10 Ibid 84.
11 Ibid 85.
12 Ibid 16.
13 Ibid 41.
14 Ibid 50.

Commission found that the removal of these bolts was the immediate precipitating cause of the collapse.

The diagrams in Figure 22.1 illustrate jacking a half span, the two half spans being joined on top of the piers, and the collapse resulting from the buckle at mid span.

Notwithstanding this immediate cause, the Commission was very critical of the quality of the design carried out by FF&P, and considered that it was a significant factor in the collapse:

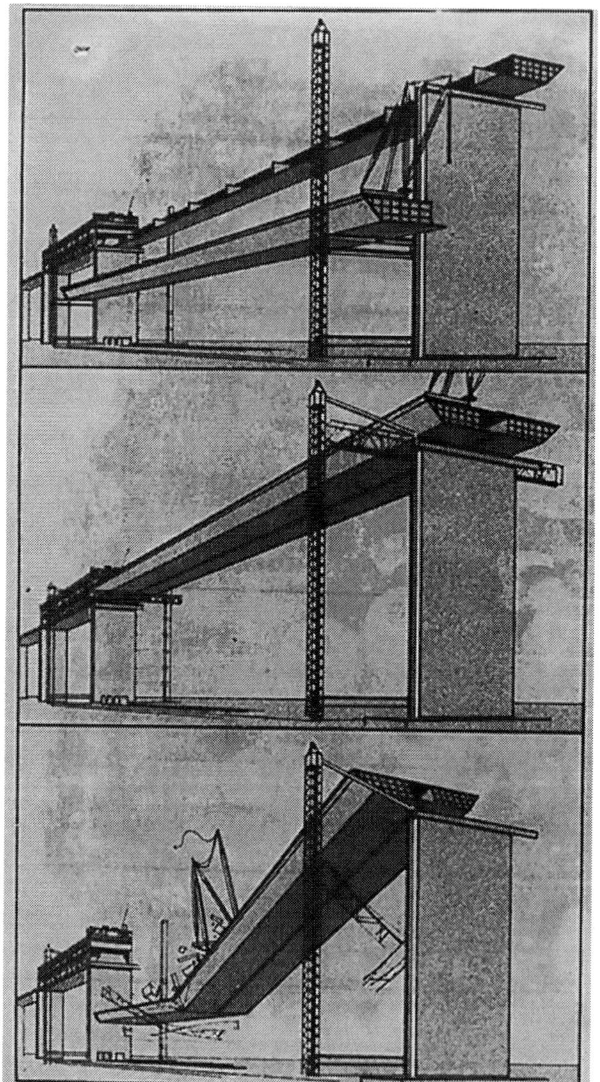

FIGURE 22.1 Diagram of the method of erection and subsequent collapse. PROV VPRS 24/P3 Inquest Deposition Files, unit 120 Sketch of the Westgate Bridge collapse from the inquest files

> Finally, as an overriding circumstance within which the above sequence [of immediate events leading to the collapse] was carried out, the factor of safety for many of the approved erection conditions was already too low, so that the abnormal actions of adding kentledge and undoing bolts reduced the narrow margin even further, and in the latter case left no margin at all.[15]

22.2.5 Design

The technical issues associated with the quality of the design and their contribution to the collapse were canvassed in detail in the Report of the Royal Commission, and these are generally outside the scope of this chapter. However, there were several general engineering issues related to the contractual arrangements that may be relevant to other large engineering and building projects. The most significant of these was the consulting engineer's responsibility for checking the erection calculations made by the Contractor. FF&P adopted the practice of British consulting engineers designing major bridges and left the analysis of erection stresses to the successful tenderer. The Commission noted that this practice meant that the consulting engineer is primarily concerned with the safety and efficiency of the bridge in service; however "he must have some regard to the limits imposed by erection problems", and "there must be at least one practical method by which the bridge can be erected".[16] Whilst in theory the Contractor can ascertain what extra strengthening may be required to meet the stresses imposed by its erection scheme, to do so they would have to understand just how the structure was designed. As discussed above, although Contract S stated that FF&P would provide WSC with the design calculations, this provision was not enforceable by WSC against FF&P (which was not a party to Contract S).

In early 1970, concerns had been expressed as to the sufficiency of the design, and the Authority requested FF&P to check its design calculations. However little progress had been made on this check by 2 June 1970, when the Milford Haven Bridge in Wales collapsed during cantilever construction of a span. In view of its similar design to West Gate, and the fact that FF&P were the designers of both bridges, the Authority requested an independent check of the design of West Gate. This "independent" design check was commissioned by the joint consulting engineers (FF&P and Maunsell), who appointed the associated firm of G Maunsell and Partners in London to carry out the work.

Although the final report of the "independent" check was not received until after the collapse, an interim report in September 1970 drew attention to the overstressing which was likely to occur in some of the member splices, and other areas where some overstressing was probable. After the Milford Haven collapse, FF&P found that high stresses in the West Gate Bridge were likely at a number of places, which led to its recommendation for a substantial programme of strengthening, requiring an additional 160 tons of steel.[17] The Commission agreed that this stiffening was vitally necessary, but did not accept that it was sufficient to make the structure safe: "We assert that the basic cause of the tragedy at West Gate was the design inadequacies which led to the safety margins being much too low, and certainly lower than the specified values."[18]

15 Ibid 105.
16 Ibid 40.
17 Ibid 26, 27.
18 Ibid 66.

In respect of the execution of the design, the Commission stated:

> We find that FF&P approached the design of West Gate Bridge in a disorganised and unsystematic manner and without any real guidance being given to the engineers doing the work by senior men such as Roberts or Brown. The calculations contain a great many errors of arithmetic and engineering principle and these have gone unchallenged until this Commission. It is doubtful if FF&P had any effective internal checking system. They certainly failed to give any adequate check to WSC's calculations although apparently prepared to approve them. … It is for all these reasons that we have formed the conclusion set out in Section 1.1.1. that the primary cause of the collapse of the West Gate Bridge was that "FF&P failed altogether to give a proper and careful regard to the process of structural design".[19]

In contrast to the maxim of the engineers who designed the Sydney Opera House on the use of computers for design,[20] the senior partner of FF&P was reported as saying "There is nothing wrong with the design, it was done by computer."[21] Those computer calculations were never made available to the Royal Commission.

It is to be hoped that this clear message conveyed by the Commission in respect of the quality of the design process has been absorbed, and that similar comments could not now be made in respect of a design office with certified quality procedures to ISO 9000. However, one might question whether the fundamental lessons arising from the quality of the design of West Gate have been learned in England, when a paper published on the Institution of Structural Engineers website substantially ignores any deficiency in the design and states in relation to the collapse of the West Gate Bridge:

> The causes of this were much more complex [than the cause of the collapse of the Milford Haven bridge] and were primarily those of adoption of a previously untried and inadequately checked method of erection and failures of site organization and communications between principal parties. These led to release of bolts in the top flange to permit alignment, to an extent that the flanges buckled.[22]

Considering the Royal Commission's unequivocal statement that the basic cause of the collapse was "the design inadequacies which led to the safety margins being much too low", the statement that the cause was primarily related to the erection method is somewhat surprising. It is even more so when written by a member of the Merrison Committee that accepted the Royal Commission's findings (see below).

22.2.6 Redesign

Following the West Gate collapse the subsequent redesign resulted in a significantly different structural form to the original design. The Australian engineering team assembled by the Authority redesigned the steel spans by eliminating the weight of the concrete deck and transformed the top flange of the boxes into a stiffened "orthotropic deck", in which the 50 mm bitumen road-wearing surface was laid directly on the steel top flange of the

19 Ibid 67.

20 "If you don't know the order of magnitude of the answer, don't use the computer." See Section 14.5.

21 Presentation by Professor Paul Grundy, 'The Collapse of the West Gate Bridge' (2010) Monash University.

22 A R Flint, "Steel Box Girder Bridges" (2001) www.istructe.org/technical/db/index.asp?page=281&bhcp=1 (accessed June 2010).

FIGURE 22.2 Reconstruction of the West Gate Bridge in 1976

box girders. Span 13–14 was heavily reinforced in situ. The reconstructed bridge was opened in 1978.

Figure 22.2 shows the construction of the redesigned bridge in 1976. A conventional method of erection was used. Boxes the complete width of the bridge were fabricated on the ground and lifted into position by cranes positioned at each end of the partially erected spans, before being bolted to the previously assembled section. Temporary steel columns supported the cantilevered sections of the span before the permanent cable stays were installed.

22.2.7 Subsequent strengthening and upgrading

The redesigned and constructed bridge had four traffic lanes in each direction. As the major road artery to the west of Melbourne, by 2006 it was carrying up to 160,000 vehicles per day. Inspections of the bridge revealed fatigue cracks in 1990 and 2004. The annual maintenance budget in 2003 was in excess of AUD2 million.[23] In order to address the maintenance issues and increase the load capacity of the bridge, a strengthening project was undertaken as part of a major upgrade of the M1 freeway between 2008 and 2011. The objectives of the upgrade were threefold: to strengthen the bridge to modern bridge design standards, to increase the traffic capacity of the bridge from four lanes to five in the peak direction, and to improve safety by installation of suicide prevention barriers and upgraded traffic barriers. The strengthening project was delivered firstly by a design alliance and subsequently by a delivery alliance for the detailed design and construction

23 Presentation by Professor Paul Grundy, "The Collapse of the West Gate Bridge" (2010) Monash University.

phase. The delivery West Gate Strengthening Alliance comprised VicRoads (the government road authority), John Holland as principal contractor, an Australian consulting engineer, and a UK consulting engineer renowned for their expertise in steel bridges.[24]

The AUD400 million upgrading and strengthening of both concrete and steel spans was completed within the agreed contract period of 36 months. During that period, the bridge was only closed completely for two nights, remaining open to the operational traffic capacity of 160,000 vehicles per day at all other times. Strengthening of the steel spans involved the addition of 1,600 tonnes of steel in over 100,000 plates and the installation of 400,000 additional or replacement bolts. Logistics for this work was a major exercise, with over 700 workers and 200 staff involved. Access to the inside of the steel boxes had to be substantially improved by the installation of hatchways in the underside of two of the steel girders and enlarging the access holes through the transverse diaphragms. Work on the outside of the steel box girders was enabled by eight suspended platforms, which had to be relocated 106 times. There were no as-built drawings of the bridge, and each additional plate had to be custom made to fit. The installation work inside the steel boxes was complicated by the use of red lead paint in the initial fabrication, requiring stringent health and safety protocols.[25]

The West Gate Strengthening Project was a finalist for the 2012 Australian Construction Achievement Award.

Figures 22.3, 22.4, 22.5, 22.6, and 22.7 show some details of the strengthening and upgrading work.

22.3 Milford Haven Bridge, Wales, UK (1970)

22.3.1 Committee of Inquiry

In June 1970, a span of the Milford Haven steel box girder bridge (now known as the Cleddau Bridge) under construction, collapsed during the erection of a pre-assembled deck section. In December 1970, a technical Committee of Inquiry was appointed by the UK Government to investigate the collapse of the Milford Haven and West Gate Bridges. The Committee's terms of reference were to consider whether it was necessary to reconsider the design and method of erection of box girder bridges about to be erected in the UK, to draw up technical guidelines for bridge engineers, to advise on any special matters affecting contract procedures and to recommend further research and development. This five-man committee, chaired by Dr Merrison, the Vice Chancellor of the University of Bristol, included two consulting engineers, the Professor of Civil Engineering of the University of Manchester and a director of a major steel fabricator/contractor.

The Committee concluded that the collapse of the Milford Haven Bridge was caused by the inadequacy of the design of a vertical pier support diaphragm, which failed in compression over the column. The lessons from Milford Haven primarily concerned the inadequacy of the design methods used for the permanent design and checking the safety

24 West Gate Strengthening Alliance, "The West Gate Strengthening Project" (2012) Submission for the 2012 Australian Construction Achievement Award.

25 Ibid.

FIGURE 22.3 Access scaffolding providing access to new hatchway

FIGURE 22.4 New access hatchway in underside of box girder

FIGURE 22.5 Additional stiffening bolted inside box girder

FIGURE 22.6 The underside of the box girder showing the additional supports to the cantilevered edge of the deck

FIGURE 22.7 A section of the cable stayed box girder showing the new safety screen

during erection. The Interim Report of the Committee[26] included comprehensive design and workmanship rules for the stress analysis and design of steel box girder bridges that were later confirmed in the Final Report after further research had been implemented.[27] The interim recommendations on checking the design of steel box girder bridges were applied to 51 highway bridges in service in England in June 1971, and 37 bridges not yet in service. Thirty-two of the in-service bridges and 28 of the unopened bridges were found to need strengthening. The amount of strengthening steel added to these bridges ranged from negligible amounts up to 12.5%, apart from two "exceptional cases" (undefined, but presumably requiring more than 12.5% additional strengthening steel).[28] The writer understands that the "Merrison Rules" are still used today in the design and checking of steel box girder bridges.

The Committee's Interim Report was published before the Royal Commission into the West Gate Bridge published its report and, accordingly, its recommendations were made in the absence of the detailed technical and contractual commentary contained in the Royal Commission Report. In its Final Report, the Committee not only accepted the Royal Commission's assessment of events which led up to the collapse of the West Gate

26 Great Britain, Department of the Environment, Committee on Steel Box Girder Bridges, *Inquiry into the Basis of Design and Method of Erection of Steel-Box Girder Bridges: Interim Report* (1971).

27 Great Britain, Department of the Environment, Committee on Steel Box Girder Bridges, *Inquiry into the Basis of Design and Method of Erection of Steel-Box Girder Bridges: Report of the Committee* (1973).

28 Ibid 5.

Bridge, but drew considerable support from it in its recommendations on contractual and procedural aspects:

> While there were also fundamental defects in the erection procedure and permanent design of the West Gate Bridge, we regard the failures of site organisation and of communication between the principal parties – Client, Engineers and Contractors – as of more general significance in this case. There are lessons to be learned from practically every page of the Royal Commission's Report and we recommend all those connected in any way with bridge construction to study it in detail, as we have done. Those who read the Report will see that the recommendations on contractual procedures made in the next chapter are much influenced by the events at the River Yarra and by the Royal Commission's comments on them. In Chapter 3 we aim to suggest procedural principles which we think should prevent situations like that on the West Gate Bridge project from arising at all.[29]

22.3.2 Contractual recommendations

The conclusions of the Committee's Interim and Final Reports included wide-ranging proposals for contractual procedures. These included clarifications of the allocation of responsibility between the engineer and the Contractor, the independent checking of designs and erection methods, vetting of the engineer's resources and of the engineer's and the Contractor's site personnel, and appropriate handling of competitive tendering. Appendix B to the Interim Report made specific recommendations on contractual procedures, and the majority of these were confirmed in the Final Report. Whilst these recommendations were made over 40 years ago and were specific to design and construction of major steel box girder bridges under the conventional procurement route of a consulting engineer engaged directly by the Employer, it is suggested that they are still applicable today to any major building or construction works. The Committee's final recommendations on contractual procedures were as follows (citations omitted):

- (i) Four essential elements in procedures for constructing major steel box-girder bridges are:-
  - (a) an independent check of the Engineer's permanent design;
  - (b) an independent check of the method of erection and design of temporary works adopted by the Contractor;
  - (c) the clear allocation of responsibility between the Engineer and the Contractor; and
  - (d) provision by the Engineer and the Contractor of adequately qualified supervisory staff on site with their tasks and functions clearly defined.
- (ii) The Client [Employer] must assure himself that the Engineer will have resources appropriate to the project.
- (iii) A certified independent check should be carried out to establish that the permanent design complies with the relevant parts of the Design Rules and is in all respects an adequate one. A differential approach to checking according to the size and complexity of structures would be appropriate.
- (iv) Adherence to tolerances and fabrication procedures assumed in the design and systematic checking of fabrication accuracy and distortions during construction are essential;

29 Ibid 4–5.

suppliers should take care to mark materials correctly; fabricators should maintain this identification until after assembly.

(v) Competitive tendering, handled appropriately, should lead to good construction.

(vi) Provided Clause 4 of the I. C. E. Conditions of Contract is properly enforced, there is no objection to sub-contracting major parts of steel box-girder bridge works.

(vii) A clear division of responsibilities between Engineer and Contractor is vitally important; contracts between the parties in a major bridge undertaking should reflect their practical engineering relationship.

(viii) A certified independent check of the erection method should be performed by engineers other than the design Engineer, who should nevertheless be given full details of the erection method and have a right of veto over it.

(ix) The Contractor should submit to the Engineer for his approval a construction programme specifying time scale.

(x) The independent checks of the permanent design and of the erection method should be complete by the time work starts and the erection of the relevant part of the superstructure starts respectively; the Client and the Engineer should allow the Contractor sufficient time to prepare himself for the start of work and should be prepared to consider a revision of his programme in the event of slippage.

(xi) The Engineer should carefully watch the progress of construction to ensure compliance with the agreed erection method; he should scrutinise the Contractor's site staff and where necessary exercise his powers under the contract.

(xii) The Client should satisfy himself as to the adequacy of the Engineer's site representatives; the functions and tasks of the Engineer's site representatives should be defined in writing.

(xiii) Those devising the erection scheme should pay careful attention to the safety implications of proposed sequences of operations; discussions with the Factory Inspectorate about safety precautions at an early stage of planning are to be encouraged.

In the period between publication of the Committee's Interim and Final Reports, the Department of the Environment issued a circular giving effect to seven of the recommendations made by the Merrison Committee. Three of the Committee's final recommendations were not implemented by the Department ((vi), (xi) and (xii) above). It is noted that each of these three recommendations (in relation to subcontracting, monitoring of construction by the Engineer and adequate site Engineer representatives) can readily be implemented under most forms of contract provided there is the will to do so, and the scope of work has been defined appropriately.

22.4 Amendments to ICE Conditions of Contract

One of the standard form contracts in use for procurement of bridges in the UK in the early 1970s was the Fourth Edition of the ICE Conditions of Contract (1953). The form made provision in clause 14 for the Contractor to supply to the Engineer information on the erection methods "if required", but with no provision in respect of the time for compliance.

The Committee recommended to the Joint Contracts Committee responsible for the ICE Conditions of Contract that clause 14 be amended to make it mandatory for the Contractor to submit a programme to the Engineer, and details and calculations of any alterations or modifications to the permanent works involved in construction or erection so that the engineer can assure itself that the completed permanent structure will not be impaired in any way. The Fifth Edition of the ICE Conditions of Contract issued in 1973 contained provisions along these lines, although the Engineer must request information pertaining to the methods of construction.

The Seventh Edition (1999) formalised the requirements for exchange and approval of information even further, and defined the role of the Engineer, including a requirement for the Engineer to provide

> such design criteria relevant to the Permanent Works or any Temporary Works design supplied by the Engineer as may be necessary to enable the Contractor to comply with sub-clauses (6) [methods of construction] and (7) [Engineer's consent] of this Clause.

It appears that these provisions are consistent with the Committee's recommendation that "contracts between the parties in a major bridge undertaking should reflect their practical engineering relationship" (vii above).

22.5 Engineer's and Contractor's responsibilities

The Interim Report of the Merrison Committee recommended that the Engineer should have responsibility for "examining Contractor's proposals and details and the checking of the adequacy, stability and safety, of the proposed methods of construction and temporary works", without relieving the Contractor of any of its responsibilities under the contract.[30] However, in the Final Report the Committee revised its view on this issue and considered that the best procedure was to require the Contractor to obtain a certificate from completely independent engineers to the effect that the erection proposals had been checked and found adequate. This change of view was consistent with the Committee's strongly expressed opinion on the appropriate division of responsibility between Engineer and Contractor:

> IT IS VITALLY IMPORTANT THAT THE ENGINEER AND THE CONTRACTOR, ONCE EMBARKED ON THE CONSTRUCTION OF A BRIDGE, SHOULD UNDERSTAND EXACTLY THE NATURE OF THEIR SEPARATE RESPONSIBILITIES. The basic division of responsibility will be the same in the case of large steel box girder bridges as it is in civil engineering works generally. The Engineer's primary responsibility is for the permanent design of the structure, while the Contractor's is for the construction and completion of the works in such a way that the permanent design is properly realised. The Engineer, as originator of the permanent design and the chief authority on it, has a duty to the Client to assure himself that the Contractor's erection proposals and the implementation of those proposals will not result in any impairment of the permanent works. The responsibility for the execution of the works, including all temporary works, remains with the Contractor. We feel it is worth pointing out at this stage that in this report we are concerned, not with the legal responsibilities and liabilities, but with procedures to ensure that steel box girder bridges are safe while under construction and in service. Nevertheless, in any major bridge undertaking, it will be a pre-requisite of success that the legal forms of the contracts between the Client and the other parties should reflect precisely the practical engineering responsibilities and how they are divided between the parties.[31]

30 Great Britain, Department of the Environment, Committee on Steel Box Girder Bridges, *Inquiry into the Basis of Design and Method of Erection of Steel-Box Girder Bridges: Interim Report* (1971) 20.

31 Great Britain, Department of the Environment, Committee on Steel Box Girder Bridges, *Inquiry into the Basis of Design and Method of Erection of Steel-Box Girder Bridges: Report of the Committee* (1973) 10–11.

In the 50 years since the Committee succinctly summarised the separate roles of the Engineer and the Contractor in this way, there have been many changes in contractual terms relating to the traditional form of construct-only contracts, including a significant reduction in the power of the Engineer (as discussed in Chapter 2). However, it is suggested that in relation to the Engineer's technical responsibility for delivery of a project to satisfy the Employer's requirements, the Committee's statement is still applicable today, and is ignored at the peril of all project participants.

22.6 Time

In respect of the programming of the works, the Merrison Committee commented on the adverse impact that undue haste in commencing and carrying out the work can have, and made the following recommendation:

> We consider that, in the case of major civil engineering undertakings, such as large steel box-girder bridges, it is particularly important in the interests both of safety and economy that the Client and the Engineer allow the Contractor sufficient time after the contract has been let to prepare for the start of work, and that they should not unduly pressurise him during the construction period itself. The Client should be prepared to accept that there may be sound reasons for modifying the Contractor's original program and the Engineer for his part should not hesitate to advise the revision of the programme if he judges that the Contractor can no longer keep to it without risk of mistakes occurring.[32]

It is suggested that this recommendation may not find favour in today's contracting environment, in which the driving principle is often to start work at the earliest available opportunity (frequently before the design is completed under fast track arrangements), and to execute the work under very tight time constraints under threat of substantial liquidated damages. However, the Committee's clear warning of the importance of allowing sufficient time for preparation and execution of the works should not be ignored, irrespective of the prevailing contractual climate.

22.7 Lessons from West Gate Bridge

Based on the issues highlighted above, the following are some of the contractual and project execution lessons relevant to major engineering projects to be learned from the Report of the Royal Commission and the Merrison Committee Reports:

- The contract terms should clearly define the responsibilities of the Engineer and the Contractor in a way that is contractually achievable.
- A labour management contract with limited liability imposes a heavier responsibility than normal on other project participants.
- Inappropriate time pressures from a desire to keep the work progressing may provide insufficient time for properly considered decisions that can lead to errors of judgment.
- The execution of the design should be organised and systematically and adequately checked.

32 Ibid 14.

- Both the permanent design and the design of the temporary works and erection methods should be checked by an engineer independent of the designer.
- The Employer should vet the Engineer's available resources and ensure they are appropriate to the design task.
- The Employer should vet the Engineer's and Contractor's site personnel and ensure they are appropriate to the demands of the erection.

22.8 Conclusion

Although the West Gate Bridge collapse occurred over 50 years ago, the lessons identified in the Royal Commission and Merrison Reports are still relevant in today's contracting environment but may have been forgotten in the intervening generation. An eminent well-qualified and experienced consulting engineer was appointed in the traditional way to design and supervise construction, and yet the confidence placed in it turned out to have been misplaced, and to have inhibited critical assessment of its decisions. The scope of the engagement of the engineer was not appropriate to the demands placed on it. Time pressures resulted in insufficient time to properly consider various issues, leading to errors of judgment that contributed to the collapse that occurred.

Many of these issues had surfaced in 1908 in the Royal Commission Report into the collapse of the Quebec Bridge during construction[33] (see Chapter 21). Notwithstanding that this Royal Commission Report has been regarded by generations of engineers as a classic because of its high standards of honesty, clarity and professional competence,[34] it is apparent that many of the lessons learned had been forgotten by the time of procurement of West Gate, particularly the importance of engineering of the erection, and the need for independent review of designs.

33 Canada, *Royal Commission Quebec Bridge Inquiry, Report* (1908).

34 A Pugsley, *The Safety of Structures* (1963) 140.

CHAPTER 23

Is conventional insurance for construction projects fit for purpose?[1]

23.1 Introduction

Large construction projects generally involve significant complexity in their procurement – in their technical challenges, and in the interaction and interfaces between the different organisations involved in design and construction. These issues (and others) are manifest in the inherent risks of construction, which range from the physical challenges of the site and the prevailing environment, the technical and organisational challenges of each party involved in design and construction completing their work to the required quality in the specified time, to completion of the works for the specified cost. The rights and obligations between the parties involved in design and construction are regulated by contracts that assign liability if the risk events occur.

Insurance is a widely used risk management tool to transfer or offset specific risks to a third party, the Insurer, that a contracting party is liable for. Some insurance is mandated by legislation, some by contract. The aim of such insurance is to provide a third-party fund that will pay for the financial consequences arising from the occurrence of risk events, to assure project completion or rectification of defects without financial detriment to the contracting parties (or owners). In an ideal world, if an insured risk event occurs, the relevant insurance company would make prompt payment, and thereby promote successful contract completion or rectification of defects and avoid disputes about financial liability.

In practice, for a variety of reasons, insurance does not always fulfil this ideal function. Instead of preventing disputes between the contracting parties as to who is liable for the financial consequences of a risk event, in many situations the insurance itself provokes or complicates disputes. This may be the consequence of, e.g. different insurance policies covering different risks, debate over the cause of a risk event, or a dispute over which party is contractually responsible for the scope of particular insurance policies. Insurance companies themselves may instigate litigation to recover the costs they have paid out.

This chapter is in five substantive parts. Section 23.2 discusses why insurance is important for construction contracts. Section 23.3 reviews the current insurance landscape for construction projects in Victoria, with particular reference to the different types of

1 This chapter is an edited and updated version of a paper Commended for the Society of Construction Law Australia Brooking Prize 2018. The paper was first published by Thomson Reuters in Dr Donald E Charrett, 'Is Conventional Insurance for Construction Projects Fit for Purpose?' (2018) 34 *Building and Construction Law* 253. For all subscription inquiries please phone, from Australia: 1300 304 195, from Overseas: +61 2 8587 7980 or online at legal.thomsonreuters.com.au/search. The official PDF version of this article can also be purchased separately from Thomson Reuters.

 DOI: 10.4324/9781003206897-25

insurance to cover design and construction risks. The following section identifies a number of problems that arise from the conventional approach to insurance for construction projects, with the consequence that it does not always respond appropriately. Section 23.5 reviews different approaches to project insurance used in a large project and a civil law jurisdiction. Section 23.6 outlines the benefits that could flow from adopting these different approaches to make insurance more fit for the purpose for which it is intended – to provide a fund from a source external to the contracting parties to assist successful completion of a project and rectification of defects.

Due to the breadth of this topic and space limitations, the chapter focuses on the Victorian position, with particular emphasis on insurance for domestic building.

23.2 Why insurance is important for construction contracts

Construction of major projects is an expensive business. It involves the input of considerable intellectual effort, the procurement of large quantities of materials, and the organisation and integration of the work of many skilled tradesmen of different disciplines. As has been stated by many commentators, cash flow is the lifeblood of the construction industry. That cash flow is significant for even the largest construction companies; it is vital for the commercial survival of many of the smaller organisations involved in the construction industry, such as trade subcontractors or design professionals, many of which have negligible tangible assets on their balance sheets. Thus, in many situations, insurance may be the only significant financial resource available to pay for damage or defective works.

Governments have recognised the risks arising from the potential impecuniosity of organisations involved in design and construction by mandating minimum levels of insurance in certain situations. For example, pursuant to the *Building Act 1993* (Vic), certain registered building practitioners (building surveyors, building inspectors, engineers, draftspersons and quantity surveyors) must maintain Professional Indemnity (PI) insurance of not less than $1 million for any one claim and in the aggregate for all claims during any one period of insurance, plus $500,000 in respect of defence costs.[2] Registered builders undertaking domestic building work worth more than $16,000 are required to take out domestic building insurance that will cover costs up to $300,000 to fix structural defects for six years, and non-structural defects for two years.[3]

The importance of insurance to protect the interests of contracting parties is recognised by the mandatory provisions for insurance in standard form construction contracts. For example, clause 19 of the FIDIC Conditions of Contract for Plant and Design Build (Second Edition 2017) (Yellow Book) requires the Contractor who constructs the project to provide insurances for the contract Works, Goods,[4] liability for breach of professional duty (PI insurance), injury to persons and damage to property (public liability), injury to employees (workers compensation) and other insurances required by laws and by local practice. Such insurance has obvious benefits for the Employer who procures the project, who may pay for insurance policies itself at the expense of the Contractor if the Contractor fails to take out the contractually required insurance.

2 Victoria, *Government Gazette*, G22, 29 May 2014, 1018.
3 Victoria, *Government Gazette*, G22, 29 May 2014, 1014.
4 Contractor's Equipment, Materials, Plant and Temporary Works (all FIDIC defined terms).

As the list of contractually required insurance under the FIDIC Yellow Book demonstrates, insurance may provide compensation for a risk event that occurs as a result of accident or natural events that were not "caused" by either contracting party, for example extreme weather events or a fire that results in property damage. Insurance may also provide compensation for a risk event "caused" by the fault of a contracting party, for example negligence in the preparation of the design of a project. The cost of rectifying the consequences of such risk events materialising may exceed the financial resources of the party which bears the contractual liability. For example, a fire which destroys a virtually completed building may entail expenditure for demolition and rebuilding that exceeds the original contract price. The financial consequences of errors in design are particularly acute for design organisations, as the construction costs are usually many multiples of the design costs.[5] Reconstruction of defective designs may therefore cost substantially more than the fees paid for design.

Insurance therefore protects the financial interests of the party which bears the contractual liability for a risk event (typically the Contractor), whether it is accidental or fault-based, by providing compensation for an event that is not included in the contract price. Insurance also protects the interests of the Employer by providing a fund to pay for events that will not have been allowed for in the contract price and which may otherwise imperil the financial stability of the Contractor and its ability to complete the project or rectify defects. The existence of insurance (and the ability of an Employer to access that insurance) is all the more important in circumstances where the Contractor is insolvent.

The ability of insurance to provide compensation in any given circumstance will depend, inter alia, on the identity of the insured parties, the scope of the insurance cover, and whether the particular event comes within the scope of that cover. Each of these issues has been a fruitful source of litigation between Insurers and insureds. This highlights the importance of Contractors (and Employers) ensuring that the scope of their insurance policies provide appropriate cover for their contractual liabilities for the duration of those liabilities, as well as satisfying any legislative requirements for mandatory insurance.

23.3 The insurance landscape for construction contracts

As noted above, a Contractor or designer has a real interest in the efficacy of an insurance policy to protect its financial interests. A construction contract typically has provisions requiring the Contractor to indemnify the Employer in respect of the financial consequences of specified risks materialising, in addition to the requirement to take out insurance against specified risks. It is important to note that the obligation to effect insurance does not necessarily limit the contracting parties' obligations or responsibilities under the indemnities in the construction contract. Whether an insurance clause has the effect of satisfying the liability under an indemnity clause depends on the proper construction of the contract terms, construed as a whole. If the construction contract expressly refers to the insurance contract, the effect of both contracts taken together must be considered.[6]

5 See Section 5.2.3 above for a discussion of the 1:10:100 "rule".

6 *Bovis Lend Lease v Saillard Fuller & Partners* [1983] 3 All ER 35, [1984] QB 127.

The contractual provision for insurance may, properly construed, be that it limits the Contractor's liability,[7] or it may be that it is limited to providing a fund of money to pay for damages in the event that the Contractor is unable to satisfy an obligation to pay damages.[8] Which of these applies in a particular circumstance may have significant financial consequences in the event that the necessary insurance has not been implemented or is inadequate to meet the indemnified liabilities.

As noted above, the FIDIC Yellow Book identifies five specific types of insurance that are typically required for a design and construct contract: Works, Goods, PI, public liability and workers' compensation. The focus of this chapter is on the insurance to protect the interests of the contracting parties arising from design or construction, and accordingly, workers' compensation insurance, insurance for the replacement value of Goods lost or destroyed and public liability insurance will not be considered further here.

Works insurance and PI insurance include features of particular importance to the contracting parties in construction contracts. In simplistic and general terms, Works insurance covers certain construction risks, and PI insurance covers certain design risks. The distinction between these two types of insurance is significant because design and construction (the implementation of the design) are usually carried out by different legal entities, even where the construction contract itself is a design and construct contract.

The essential features of these two different types of insurance are as follows.

23.3.1 PI insurance

PI Insurance (known in the USA more descriptively as Errors and Omissions or Malpractice insurance) is a contract between a professional (insured) and Insurer, in which the Insurer indemnifies the insured for claims against it by a client or person affected by the professional's activity (a third party).[9] A contract of PI Insurance entered into in Australia is subject to the relevant provisions of the *Insurance Contracts Act 1984* (Cth), which imposes a statutory overlay upon the common law.

The Insurer can provide the contracted for indemnity in the event of a claim by a third party on the insured in the following ways:

- Inducing the third party to "forbear" in its claim against the insured
- Paying the third party directly, or
- Recompensing the insured for the loss suffered.[10]

---

7 Examples of cases in which the Court found that the contractual provisions for insurance satisfied the contractual provisions for liability under the indemnity clause include: *Mark Rowlands Ltd v Berni Inns Ltd* [1986] 1 QB 211; *James Archdale & Co Ltd v Comservices Ltd* [1954] 1 WLR 459; *Scottish Special Housing Association v Wimpey Construction UK Ltd* [1986] 1 WLR 995 (HL); *Co-operative Retail Services Ltd v Taylor Young Partnership* [2002] 1 WLR 1419; *Scottish & Newcastle plc v GD Construction (St Albans) Ltd* [2003] BLR 131.

8 Examples in which the Court found that the indemnity provisions were enforceable against the Contractor, notwithstanding the requirement for joint names insurance include: *Surrey Heath Borough Council v Lovell Construction Ltd* (1990) 48 BLR 108; *Dorset County Council v Southern Felt Roofing Company Ltd* (1990) 48 BLR 96; *London Borough of Barking and Dagenham v Stamford Asphalt Company Ltd* (1997) 82 BLR 25; *Casson v Ostley PJ Ltd* [2001] EWCA Civ 1013; [2003] BLR 147; *Bovis Lend Lease v Saillard Fuller & Partners* (2001) 77 Con LR 134.

9 Ian Enright, *Professional Indemnity Insurance Law* (Sweet & Maxwell, 1st edn, 1996) 80.

10 Ibid, 126.

Whilst a claim by a third party is the event that triggers the indemnity, any amount paid by the Insurer in response to that claim is a contractual right of the insured under the provisions of the PI policy. Although it is the third party's loss that provides the reason for any insurance payment, under common law, the third party has no entitlement to any payment direct from the Insurer. Thus, even where the PI Insurance appears to have been entered into so that a third party does not suffer a loss in the event of the insured event occurring, a third party has no right of payment by the Insurer, nor, in the absence of specific contractual or statutory arrangements, to any preferential entitlement to the insurance moneys.

PI insurance is relevant to construction projects in which a professional (designer) prepares the design to be implemented by the Contractor. In a construct only contract (such as the FIDIC Conditions of Contract for Construction (Red Book)), the designer is contracted to the Employer. In a design and construct contract (such as the Yellow Book), the designer is (typically) a professional firm contracted to the Contractor.

The indemnity provided by a PI insurance policy is for liability arising from breach of professional duty, including a failure to take reasonable care (negligence) and misrepresentation. In Australia, PI insurance policies usually also include liability for misleading or deceptive conduct in breach of the *Australian Consumer Law*. An Insurer therefore only assumes liability under a PI insurance policy where there is some "fault" or culpability on the part of the designer.

PI insurance policies in Australia generally do not provide indemnification for breach of contractual obligations in the absence of a breach of professional duty. Thus, in the absence of negligence, a typical PI insurance policy will not indemnify a designer for preparing a design that does not satisfy a contractual term that it be fit for purpose.

PI insurance is typically procured by a design firm annually for a specified limit. Coverage is usually based on a "claims made and notified" basis, i.e. the indemnity is confined to a claim arising from notification of the event or circumstances made during the policy year, and not when the design was prepared, or the event occurred.

In many situations, the only significant funds available to satisfy an award of damages arising from defective design are the proceeds of a PI insurance policy. The existence and cover provided by PI insurance are therefore of real interest to an Employer; it may not be financially viable to instigate litigation against a designer in the absence of insurance cover to satisfy any liability. However, in litigation against a design professional, the existence and details of the policy may not be referred to because they are not normally relevant to the issues in the case. Outside of the special conditions provided for in certain legislation,[11] the common law position is that a third party generally has no interest in a policy of PI insurance between a professional and his/her Insurer. This means, that except in special circumstances, a plaintiff generally has no right to access the proceeds of a defendant's PI insurance policy, or to discovery of the details or even the existence of the policy.[12]

11 NSW, ACT and the NT have statutes that enable a third party to enforce a charge against insurance monies that are payable in limited situations including bankrupt, insolvent, missing or dead insured defendants: *Law Reform (Miscellaneous Provisions) Act 1946* (NSW); *Law Reform (Miscellaneous Provisions) Act 1955* (ACT) ss 25–28; *Law Reform (Miscellaneous Provisions) Act* (NT) ss 26–29.

12 Dr Donald E Charrett, 'Professional Indemnity Insurance – Do third parties have an interest?' (2003) 14 *Insurance Law Journal* 77.

23.3.2 Works insurance

Works insurance for construction projects is typically procured under the terms of a Contractor's All Risks (**CAR**) insurance policy. This type of insurance covers the risk of physical loss of or damage to the works, and for liabilities arising in the course of the works. Liability under such an insurance policy arises in respect of the occurrence of an insured event, and not on the basis of notification of circumstances, as is the case with PI insurance. The specific cover under a particular CAR insurance policy depends on the actual wording of the insuring clause, and in particular on the exclusions and extensions to the general wording of the insuring clause. These depend on the scope of insurance offered by the relevant insurance company. CAR insurance for a project may note the Employer and subcontractors and designers are named insured, in addition to the Contractor. The entities named in the policy as insureds can generally take the benefit of the insurance.

The following example is an extract from a current CAR policy provided by the City of Gold Coast Insurance Co Ltd:[13]

The Policy Schedule provides that the following are named Insured:

(1) Principal Council of the City of Gold Coast including subsidiary companies for their respective rights and interests
(2) All contractors and/or subcontractors and/or manufacturers and/or suppliers in any tier
(3) Professional Consultants to Insured (1) and (2) engaged solely to provide professional services for a fee.

Insuring clause:

> Except as hereinafter excluded the Insurers will pay to or indemnify the INSURED under this Policy against DAMAGE to the PROPERTY INSURED howsoever caused occurring during the PERIOD OF INSURANCE. [Capitalised words are defined terms in the policy.]

Notable exclusions include the following:

- Costs rendered necessary by defects of material workmanship design plan or specification
- Penalties and/or consequential pecuniary loss
- Contractor's plant, tools and temporary buildings.

This example illustrates two heads of potential Contractor's liability that are typically not covered by a CAR insurance policy: defects due to design errors, and defects of material or workmanship. The first of these may be insured under a PI policy, whereas the second is generally uninsurable under a CAR policy.

This example CAR policy provides a succinct definition of the distinction between damage and a defect as follows:

> any portion of the PROPERTY INSURED shall not be regarded as damaged solely by virtue of the existence of any defect of material workmanship design plan or specification.[14]

13 Contractors All Risks Insurance Policy Wording http://www.goldcoast.qld.gov.au/documents/bf/contract-works.pdf (accessed 14 April 2021).

14 Ibid, 6.

In general, a CAR insurance policy provides indemnity against damage to the insured property whether as a result of accident or negligence, but not against defects in the insured property that result from culpable errors of design or faulty material or workmanship. However, domestic building insurance in Victoria is required to provide cover for faulty material or workmanship in certain circumstances. Such insurance is a particular form of works insurance.

23.3.3 Domestic building insurance – Victoria

Pursuant to ss 135, 137A and 137D of the *Building Act 1993* (Vic), the Minister for Planning made an Order specifying the insurance that a builder is required to be covered by in order to carry out or manage or arrange the carrying out of domestic building work on a domestic building contract.[15]

Insurance is required if the contract price for the domestic building work is more than $16,000. The insurance policy must indemnify the building owner in respect of loss or damage resulting from non-completion of the domestic building work, and in respect of loss or damage resulting from or any of the following events:

- Domestic building work that is defective
- A breach of any warranty implied in the domestic building contract by s8 of the *Domestic Building Contracts Act 1995*
- A failure to maintain a standard or quality of building work specified in the domestic building contract
- Conduct by the builder in connection with the domestic building contract that contravenes a provision of the *Australian Consumer Law*.

Importantly, the insurance policy may provide that these indemnities only apply if the builder dies, becomes insolvent or disappears. Insurance is not mandated for a limit of liability in excess of $300,000, and the policy may limit claims for non-completion to an amount of not more than 20% of the contract price.

The requirements for such domestic building insurance are for the protection of the interests of the building owner, as the insurance cover must extend to each person who becomes entitled to the benefit of any of the warranties under the *Domestic Building Contracts Act*, and to the owner for the time being of the building or land in respect of which the domestic building work was carried out. The policy must provide the required indemnities in relation to non-structural defects in respect of loss or damage for a period of two years after the completion date of the domestic building work, and in respect of or other loss or damage for a period of six years after the completion date of the domestic building work.

Significantly, however, a builder is exempt from the requirement to take out domestic building insurance for the construction of a multi-storey residential building.[16] Considering the issues that have arisen from the installation of non-compliant cladding on multi-storey

15 Victoria, *Government Gazette*, S98, 23 May 2003, amended by Victoria, *Government Gazette*, G22, 29 May 2014, 1014.

16 *Building (Interim) Regulations 2005* (Vic) s 1808.

apartments (discussed further below), this is a substantial deficiency that is proving problematic for many building owners.

23.4 Problems with the conventional approach to insurance

The traditional implementation of separate PI and CAR insurance for Australian construction contracts suffers from a number of problems that may result in the absence of insurance cover that was intended to protect the interests of the contracting parties. Some of these problems are illustrated in the following example arising from the use of non-compliant cladding on buildings in Victoria.

Following the fire at the Lacrosse Apartments in Melbourne in 2014 and the tragic fire at the Grenfell building in London in 2017, the Victorian Government implemented a Cladding Task Force to investigate the extent of non-compliant external wall cladding on buildings in Victoria, and to make recommendations to protect the public and restore confidence in the fire safety of buildings. In its Interim Report, the Task Force found that systems failures have led to major safety risks and widespread non-compliant use of combustible cladding in Victoria.[17] The Task Force made a number of priority recommendations, including audits to determine the extent of the problem, exploration of options for low-cost financing to allow owners' corporations to fund works, and that consideration be given to introducing compulsory warranty insurance for residential multi-unit developments and insurance by commercial builders.[18]

These recommendations highlight the fact that the contractual arrangements for construction of residential buildings may not have provided the owners with a legal mechanism to obtain financial redress from the parties responsible for non-compliant cladding. A building owner, on becoming aware of non-compliant cladding (assumed to be within ten years from completion of the building), would normally seek to recover rectification costs from the entity or entities that were causally responsible. Confining attention to those involved in the design and construction, the causally responsible entity could be one or more of: the architect who designed the building, the building surveyor that certified that the building complied with the *Australian Building Code*, the fire engineer who certified that the cladding complied with the fire regulations, the Contractor who constructed the building, the subcontractor who installed the cladding, or the company that supplied the cladding material.

The relevant professionals (architect and/or fire engineer) may be able to avoid liability for many reasons, including:

- The building owner may not have a cause of action against the professional, e.g. lack of privity of contract, or no contractual obligation to prepare a fit for purpose design
- Notification of the non-compliance was made after a contractual cut-off date for liability
- The specified design was fully compliant, and the Contractor/subcontractor installed unspecified non-compliant cladding, or the supplier supplied non-compliant material in breach of its contractual obligations.

17 Victoria, *Victorian Cladding Task Force Interim Report*, November 2017, 4.
18 Ibid, 6.

If the owners successfully sued the architect, the building surveyor or the fire engineer, there may be insufficient funds to satisfy the judgment for any of the following reasons:

- The legal entity that carried out the professional services may no longer exist years after the design was prepared, or may no longer have appropriate PI insurance
- The professional may not have notified the Insurer of a claim or circumstances at the appropriate time or at all
- The limit of liability under the PI insurance may be inadequate to cover the rectification costs, either because of the limited amount of insurance cover or because the professional's liability is capped under a Professional Standards Scheme[19]
- The professional may have insufficient financial resources to cover any shortfall not covered by insurance.

Prima facie, non-compliant cladding is a breach of the statutory implied warranties in s 8 of the *Domestic Building Contracts Act 1995* (Vic), potentially rendering the Contractor liable for rectification costs. However, there may be insufficient funds to satisfy any judgment against the Contractor for any of the following reasons:

- The Contractor may not have taken out insurance
- The Contractor's insurance may not cover defective work arising from the use of non-compliant materials
- The limit of any applicable insurance may be insufficient to cover the rectification costs
- Notification of the non-compliance may have been made after the operative period of insurance
- The Contractor may have insufficient financial resources to cover any shortfall not covered by insurance.

This example highlights some of the reasons why the traditional implementation of PI insurance for breaches of professional duty and CAR insurance for Contractor's risks may not be effective in providing a fund to compensate an owner for the rectification costs arising from defective work. Further, the application of proportionate liability between concurrent wrongdoers is a driver of a multiplicity of defendants and substantial litigation costs.[20]

The issue of determining whether a defect arises from design, or the implementation of the design (construction), can lead to substantial litigation costs arising from a number of

19 In the litigation arising from the Lacrosse Building fire, the architect, building surveyor and fire engineer were each found liable in negligence to the builder for amounts in excess of the amount of PI insurance mandated by law. *Owners Corporation No 1 of PS613436T v LU Simon Builders Pty Ltd (Building and Property)* [2019] VCAT 286 [7].

20 Liability for the costs arising from the cladding fire at the Lacrosse Building in Melbourne was determined in *Owners Corporation No 1 of PS613436T v LU Simon Pty Ltd* [2019] VCAT 286. Woodward J determined that the architect, the building surveyor and the fire engineer failed to exercise reasonable skill and care and determined their proportionate liability to the builder as 25%, 33% and 39% respectively of the damages of $5.75 m plus further costs to be determined (of a claimed amount of $6.8 m).

defendants, the requirement for expert evidence and technical complexities. Importantly, the issue of whether a defect derives from design or construction may be very significant in whether or not there is any insurance covering the liability.

For the reasons outlined above, from the perspective of an owner or Employer seeking to recover damages arising from defective design, PI insurance has many drawbacks. In addition, as a third party, the Employer or an owner does not have an interest in the insurance, and therefore cannot take action to recover from the insurance company directly.[21]

The common requirements for CAR Insurance to be in joint names and to satisfy specified contractual conditions, including production of the insurance policies, generally mean that the Employer is adequately informed of its rights and, properly advised, is in a position to take action when appropriate. However, CAR insurance is generally confined to damage and not defects, and accordingly does not usually cover defective work arising from poor workmanship or faulty materials.

23.5 Different approaches to project insurance

The following two examples illustrate how non-traditional approaches to project insurance (at least from a common law perspective) can provide benefits, including greater certainty of the availability of an insurance fund for an appropriate period and significantly reduced costs of dispute resolution.

23.5.1 Heathrow Terminal 5

In procuring Heathrow Terminal 5 (**T5**), BAA plc (now called Heathrow Airport Holdings) adopted an innovative approach to procurement, recognising that it held all the risk all the time. As part of its innovative approach, it took out an insurance program to address major or catastrophic risks on a project-wide basis covering the whole supply chain. This required considerable discussion and negotiation with Insurers who were initially reluctant to adopt a new and non-traditional approach.

The project insurance included CAR, third-party liability and project PI. The PI insurance policy covered about 50% of the value of T5, with a maximum £500 million for any single item. It was the first of this kind of insurance that allowed for "collective negligence" and paid out on a no-fault basis.

In the event, following the discovery of a manufacturing fault during erection of the cabin for the new air traffic control tower, an insurance claim was made for "collective professional negligence". The insurance company paid out on this claim without blame being apportioned for the problems, and without any legal action being taken.[22]

21 This issue is discussed in more detail in: Dr Donald E Charrett, 'Professional Indemnity Insurance – Do third parties have an interest?' (2003) 14 *Insurance Law Journal* 77.

22 Sharon Doherty, *Heathrow's Terminal 5: History in the Making* (2008) at 242. The procurement of T5 is discussed in Philip Loots & Donald Charrett, *Practical Guide to Engineering and Construction Contracts* (CCH, 2009) 354–358.

23.5.2 Decennial liability insurance

France and a number of other civil law countries[23] implement "decennial liability" (***garantie décennale*** in French): strict liability imposed by law on construction contractors and design professionals for the total or partial collapse of buildings they designed and/or built, or for the occurrence of latent structural defects which imperil the safety or stability of such buildings, for a period of ten years after their approved completion and handover.[24]

The French *Civil Code* provides for decennial liability in the following terms:

> **Art. 1792**
> Any builder of a work is liable as of right, towards the building owner or purchaser, for damages, even resulting from a defect of the ground, which imperil the strength of the building or which, affecting it in one of its constituent parts or one of its elements of equipment, render it unsuitable for its purposes.
>
> Such liability does not take place where the builder proves that the damages were occasioned by an extraneous event.
>
> **Art. 1792-1**
> Are deemed builders of the work:
>
> 1 Any architect, contractor, technician or other person bound to the building owner by a contract of hire of work;
> 2 Any person who sells, after completion, a work which he built or had built;
> 3 Any person who, although acting in the capacity of agent for the building owner, performs duties similar to those of a hirer out of work.

France has given real force to decennial liability by mandating compulsory insurance in the French *Insurance Code*:

> **Article L241-1**
> Any natural person or legal entity whose decennial responsibility may be incurred on the basis of the presumption provided for in Articles 1792 and following of the Civil Code must be covered by an insurance policy.
>
> Upon the commencement of the building work, he/it must be able to prove that he/she has underwritten an insurance contract that covers his/its liability.
>
> Notwithstanding any clause to the contrary, any insurance contract underwritten by virtue of this Article shall be deemed to contain a clause ensuring that the cover shall be maintained for the term of the decennial responsibility imposed on the person who is submitted to the compulsory insurance.

As can be seen, Art 1792 of the French *Civil Code* includes liability for "damages" that render a building unsuitable for its purposes. Arguably, this is sufficiently broad to include liability for, e.g. the defect of non-compliant cladding that presents a fire danger to the occupants. Accordingly, it is submitted that in France the owner of a building with non-compliant cladding could have access to insurance to pay for the rectification costs of making the building suitable for its purposes for a period of ten years after acceptance of the Works.

23 Hök identifies 27 countries that have implemented decennial liability: Sebastian Hök, 'The Civil Law decennial (decennal) liability' http://www.dr-hoek.de/EN/beitrag.asp?t=Decennal-liability-under-FIDIC (accessed 14 April 2021).

24 Sebastian Hök, 'The Civil Law decennial (decennal) liability' http://www.dr-hoek.de/EN/beitrag.asp?t=Decennal-liability-under-FIDIC (accessed 14 April 2021).

23.6 A different approach to insurance of projects

Some of the drawbacks of the current system of separate PI and CAR insurance to cover defective building work could be eliminated or ameliorated if decennial liability and compulsory insurance was adopted in legislation along the lines of the French model.

A single insurance policy covering both design and construction, based on strict and joint and several liability, would radically simplify the process of compensating owners or Employers for defective building work that resulted in a deficiency in strength or fitness for purpose. It could:

- Avoid the time and expense of determining whether a defect was the result of design or construction
- Eliminate the uninsured gap that frequently occurs in Australia in respect of a Contractor's breach of contract in respect of defective workmanship or material
- Provide an adequate fund to pay for rectification of defects, whether the result of design or construction
- Enable an owner or Employer to claim rectification costs directly from an insurance company, rather than instigating litigation against the designer and/or Contractor
- Ensure that the fund was available for the ten-year period of liability.[25]

In the Australian context, this is a radical proposal that is at odds with some of the developments in respect of building contract insurance in Victoria over the last 20 years, including proportionate liability and exempting the builders of multi-storey apartments from compulsory insurance. It would no doubt be opposed by Insurers and builders on the basis of significant cost. However, as highlighted by the non-conforming cladding fiasco, a solution needs to be found to fund the substantial costs of remediating defective buildings. As noted above, the issue of compulsory insurance for builders of multi-storey apartments is under review by the Victorian Cladding Task Force, and this could perhaps be considered alongside a revision of the liability regime.

The implementation of project PI insurance for "collective professional negligence" on the Heathrow T5 model for large projects is a less radical proposal but would still offer significant benefits over the current annual PI insurance taken out by each professional practice. It could:

- Ensure that an insurance fund was available for the duration of liability on a project
- Substantially reduce the cost of disputes by not requiring proof of "fault"
- Enable the Employer to have direct access to insurance funds.

This proposal does not require any legislation, as it could be adopted on an *ad hoc* basis under the contracts for any project. It is only likely to be practical for large projects, due to the time and complexity of negotiating a non-traditional form of insurance. The biggest challenge is likely to come from the traditionally conservative insurance industry, which

25 *Building Act 1993* (Vic) s 134.

is not currently geared to provide this type of insurance. BAA's experience on Heathrow T5 was that it required considerable discussion and negotiation with Insurers; however, the insurance was ultimately made available on this new basis.

23.7 Conclusion

This chapter considered the importance of insurance in the context of construction projects. It reviewed three types of insurance for projects that are conventionally used in Victoria: PI insurance to cover liabilities arising from breach of professional duty (generally relevant to design), Contractor's All Risks insurance for physical loss of or damage to the works (but generally excluding defective workmanship or materials), and domestic building insurance that provides limited cover for defects under some circumstances (but is not required for multi-storey apartments where arguably it is most needed).

Some of the drawbacks of the conventional separate PI insurance and CAR insurance have been identified: increased costs in determining whether a defect was the result of design or construction, the potential for PI insurance to be unavailable when needed or inadequate in value, the inability of an owner or Employer to access the proceeds of a PI insurance policy directly and the lack of insurance for defects in construction (except for domestic buildings in limited circumstances).

Two non-conventional approaches to insurance of projects were reviewed: the project no-fault collective professional indemnity insurance for T5, and the mandatory insurance for decennial liabilities arising under French law. It was suggested that either of these models could achieve significant benefits over the conventional insurance model, including reduced costs and more certainty that an adequate insurance fund would be available for the required period of potential liability.

As illustrated by the identified problems of funding remediation of non-compliant cladding in Victoria, the conventional approach to insurance is not always fit for the purpose of providing an adequate fund to cover the cost of rectifying defects in design and/or construction. Perhaps it is time to consider unconventional approaches that have been used elsewhere.

PART 3

AVOIDANCE AND RESOLUTION OF DISPUTES

CHAPTER 24

The avoidance of disputes by Contractors in design and construct contracts[1]

24.1 Introduction

Courts uphold the doctrine of freedom of contract – the ability to enter into a binding agreement to do anything (other than matters that are contrary to public policy or statute law or are illegal). One important consequence is that the parties will be held to the specific bargain they have made, irrespective of whether it is fair, reasonable or is consistent with common practice or "normal" contracts of that type.

As a general principle, if the terms are clear and unambiguous, the parties will be held to the actual words in the contract. Surrounding circumstances, prior conduct and reference to common practice will be irrelevant.

Furthermore, it should be assumed that the other party to the contract will strictly apply the contract terms in accordance with their plain and ordinary meaning, irrespective of whether that appears unfair, harsh, unjust or not in accordance with the norms of the industry. This applies particularly in the case of a "bespoke" contract that has been specifically written by lawyers acting in the interests of one party, as considerable attention will have been focused on drafting contract terms that advance that party's interests.

In order to avoid subsequent disputes, it is essential to understand the legal effect of the proposed terms for a contract so as to prepare the tender, and to understand the risks and formulate the appropriate strategies for managing those risks, before the contract has been entered into. Once a contract has been executed, both parties are bound by its terms unless and until they agree to change those terms. Clearly, there is little scope to change the terms of a contract unless both parties believe it is in their interest to do so. Accordingly, it is imperative to ensure that the contract terms are satisfactory *before* it is executed.

After execution of a contract, both parties are bound by its terms, and these must therefore form the guidelines for successful management of the contract, and execution of the work. This chapter presents some suggestions that may assist design and construct contractors to avoid the type of contractual disputes that can result from pre- as well as post-contractual issues arising.

1 This chapter is an edited and updated version of: Donald Charrett, "The Avoidance of Disputes by Contractors in Design and Construct Contracts", first published in [2008] *International Construction Law Review* 427, published by Informa Law, London.

 DOI: 10.4324/9781003206897-27

24.2 Preparation of tender

It is trite to state that understanding the scope of work required by the contract is fundamental to preparing the cost and time estimates that will be incorporated in the tender. Further, that scope (and that of the final product) is conditioned by the quality required under the Contract.

The importance of careful preparation of the Contractor's programme that is submitted as part of the tender and that may form part of the Contract cannot be overemphasised. It will no doubt be a central element in preparing the tender price. It may also have pervasive effects on the Contractor's obligations under the Contract, as many construction contracts include the Contractor's programme as a contract document, and require the Contractor to follow that programme. The time schedule needs to be commensurate with the resource and capacity availability, and to allow a realistic time for execution of all the activities, as well as to provide for some contingency.[2]

24.3 Contract terms

Careful assessment of the proposed contract terms and their impact on scope, time, quality, cost and risk is just as important as the careful preparation of the tender itself. In the common case of a "bespoke" as opposed to a standard form contract (perhaps with modifications), the importance and time required for this assessment should not be underestimated.

Each party to a construction contract has different and perhaps irreconcilable views of what are the desirable conditions of contract, which might be along the following lines:

- Employer: conditions that deliver a complete project of the highest quality for the lowest contract price, in the shortest time with as many known risks and all unforeseen risks the responsibility of the Contractor.
- Contractor: conditions that unambiguously define the required scope and quality of the work for a defined price (as high as possible) to be completed within a time that is sufficient to carry out the work with normal resources and allowing for all possible contingencies, with as many known risks and all unforeseen risks the responsibility of the Employer.

"Nonstandard" contract terms (in the sense of altering the "normal" balanced risk allocation in standard form contracts) in either standard form contracts or bespoke contracts are usually put forward by one party to alter the risk allocation to be more favourable to it. As Employers generally put forward proposed conditions of contract with the tender documents, it is likely that nonstandard terms in these contracts will involve the Contractor in accepting more risk than normal.

Faced with an apparently onerous nonstandard contract term in the tender documents, a Contractor can adopt one of the following approaches:

2 See Philip Loots and Donald Charrett, "Reconsidering Project Procurement Criteria and Procedures for Major Infrastructure Projects" [2017] 1 *International Construction Law Review* 70, where the authors suggest that the use of "price" as the determining factor in construction procurement decisions is wrong, and that it should at least be replaced with a resourced schedule as the dominant parameter in bid evaluation.

a Qualify its tender, and negotiate a more satisfactory term
b Accept the term as proposed, and price the additional risk accepted by the Contractor as part of the tender price, or
c Accept the term as proposed without pricing any additional risk, and hope that the risk will not materialise.

Each of these approaches carries with it its own risks, and the choice of which approach to take for each onerous contract term requires a careful commercial assessment taking into account the current company and industry circumstances. In a competitive tendering environment, either (a) or (b) may make a tender uncompetitive because other contractors may accept the risks in the nonstandard term, or not price it properly or at all. The risk in (c) is obvious: if the risk materialises, the cost of dealing with it has to be absorbed by the Contractor in circumstances where there is no budget for it.

The time and cost involved in fully assessing the impact of nonstandard contract terms is considerable, as is the difficulty of negotiating less onerous terms with an Employer who is trying to achieve a contract with one-sided risk allocation. The allocation of risks to the Contractor may be dictated by the financiers providing loan funds for the project, for whom certainty of price is more important than the magnitude of the price itself. Such financiers accept that there is a cost in the Contractor accepting more risks than "normal", but it is vitally important for them in determining the viability of a project and minimising their risks that the entire funding be in place from the outset. Accordingly, from the financiers' perspective, the contract price needs to be fixed to the maximum extent possible at the time of execution of the contract, and this may involve the Contractor in accepting risks that in other contracts are borne by the Employer.

There are some contracts that a Contractor would be ill advised to enter into. A project in which major execution problems become contractual disputes will almost certainly not be successful in terms of financial performance. Given the many and varied risks that Contractors undertake in design and construct contracts, the losses on individual contracts can be very substantial, if risk that has not been adequately priced subsequently materialises. An illustration of the extent of cost overruns that can occur if the Contractor has underestimated the extent of work required to complete the work under a design and construct contract is highlighted in *Davy Offshore Ltd v Emerald Field Contracting Ltd.*[3] This case involved a contract for a floating production facility, a moored floating storage unit and subsea work for oil production in the North Sea. In a contract with a contract price of £127m, the Contractor's cost of completing the work was in excess of £200m. The Contractor was unable to recover this overrun, as it had "undertaken a design responsibility to do whatever is needed to achieve certification and completion of the facilities".[4]

Given the potential for large losses, even a substantial contractor could risk insolvency as a consequence of disastrous performance on one major design and construct contract. Accordingly, it is important for a Contractor to set the risk/cost boundaries to define the point beyond which a contract is unacceptable and will not be entered into. Amongst other things, this requires awareness of contract terms that are unacceptable irrespective

3 (1992) 55 BLR 22.
4 Ibid 33.

of price, and undesirable contract terms for which the additional risk can and should be priced.

The high transaction costs associated with nonstandard contract terms provide a compelling argument in favour of a standard contract form which is widely known and understood within the industry, e.g. Australian Standard AS4902 General Conditions of Contract for Design and Construct, NEC4 Engineering and Construction Contract, or the FIDIC Conditions of Contract for Plant and Design-Build (Yellow Book). It will frequently prove to be impossible to dissuade an Employer from using a bespoke contract for which it has already paid a substantial amount in legal fees, and which is perceived to "protect" and advance the Employer's interests. However, a tenderer could propose use of a standard contract form as a cost-effective alternative, if the price of the project/contract specific risks built into the tender price for a bespoke contract are substantial.

It should also be borne in mind that at certain times the prevailing economic conditions are more favourable to Contractors, and at other times are more favourable to Employers. Prior to the global financial crisis in 2007–2008, the boom in resource projects resulted in significant resource constraints in the ability of Australian Contractors to execute all the available work within the timeframe desired by Employers. There were also projects in which, because of the specialised nature of the work, the number of competent and available Contractors was very limited. When these factors were operative, tenderers had more ability to negotiate acceptable contract terms than when economic conditions limited the number of projects being bid, thereby favouring the Employer.

The importance of investing in good advice, including legal input on the contract terms, during the tender process should not be underestimated. An inappropriate contract will expose every shortcoming in a Contractor's project execution and will likely lead to the project contingency being exhausted (or worse).

24.3.1 Scope

It is obvious that a Contractor prepares its tender price on its perception of the scope of the work required by the proposed contract. It is equally obvious that the Employer will (almost invariably) insist on the Contractor carrying out all the work that the Employer believes is required by the Contract.

The scope (and quality) of the works required by the Employer should therefore be stated clearly and unambiguously in the Contract. To the extent that the Employer's documents do not do this, it is important that the Contractor qualify its tender accordingly to define exactly what will be provided for the tender price. Any resistance by the Employer to incorporate such a qualification should be viewed with suspicion, as it may indicate that the Employer is expecting more than the Contractor has priced and allowed for. A reasonable Employer should not have any problem with clarification of any ambiguous specification of the scope of work, as this will assist in avoiding future disputes.

Any changes to scope agreed during tender negotiations need to be incorporated into the contract documents before execution. There are likely to be adverse financial consequences of either not believing that the Employer will insist on performance of the contract scope to the letter, or failing to amend the contract to reflect the basis on which the tender price was prepared.

24.3.2 Time

Given the financial penalties of liquidated damages payable by the Contractor for not achieving completion of the works by the contractually specified date, the Contractor needs the maximum flexibility possible to make up time lost through its own culpability. That is, if the Contractor has float in its programme, it should be able to absorb that float at any stage of execution of the project works to make up for time it has lost, i.e. it should "own the float".

In some contracts, the Contractor is not entitled to an EOT for a delaying event for which the Employer is responsible, if there is any contingency or "terminal float" in the Contractor's programme. Such a contract term, commonly referred to as one in which the Employer "owns the float" is, in this writer's view, very one-sided, and could hardly be termed balanced risk allocation. If the Contractor is taking the financial risk of not completing the works by the specified date, in fairness it should also obtain the benefit of contingency in its programme. If the Employer owns the float, it can prevent the Contractor from being awarded an EOT for delay caused by the Employer early in the project, leaving no contingency for the Contractor's later culpable delays that do not qualify for an EOT. Accordingly, it is suggested that a Contractor should not accept contract terms in which the Employer "owns the float", unless a significant and realistic allowance in the price is made for the risk that qualifying causes of delay may not result in an EOT.

The terms relating to time in standard contract forms such as AS4902 General Conditions of Contract for Design and Construct or the FIDIC Yellow Book are worth referring to as balanced and accepted in the industry. Such terms have obligations on both the Contractor and the Engineer. They protect the Employer's legitimate interest in being made aware of a claim in a timely fashion, and ensuring that an EOT is only granted for qualifying events that are on the Contractor's critical path.

24.3.3 Quality

The comments above on the need for the Contract to unambiguously define the scope of work apply equally to the required quality of the work. The Contractor's perception of the required quality will be an important factor in preparation of the tender price, and the Employer will (almost invariably) insist on achievement of the level of quality it perceives is required by the Contract.

It is obvious that the basis on which the tender price is prepared needs to be consistent with the technical specifications and overriding design obligations. To the extent that the specified quality in the proposed contract documents is not clear, the Contractor should qualify its tender to be consistent with the quality it assumed in preparation of the tender. Furthermore, any changes to quality agreed during tender negotiations should be incorporated into the contract documents before execution. Drafting of wording to relax specifications should be careful and thorough to reflect exactly what has been agreed.

24.3.4 Cost

In a competitive tendering situation, a tenderer has to come up with the optimum design solution to win the tender, and this puts considerable pressure on it to have a "lean and mean" tender design. However, there is always a significant risk that the preliminary and incomplete design prepared for tender purposes may not reflect the full cost of final construction. The conventional wisdom is that "risk" or "contingency" should be allowed in the tenderer's price for the almost inevitable "design growth" during the detailed design phase. There may however be opportunities to realise savings during the detailed design phase when more engineering rigour can be applied, and some of the "risk" might be designed out. It should be noted that the cost savings that a Contractor is able to generate from its own efficiencies, including design innovations that do not involve any departure from either the specifications or any other aspect of the contract, normally do not entitle the Employer to any reduction in the contract price. That is, provided the design documents submitted by the Contractor comply with the requirements of the Contract, the Employer is not entitled to any reduction in the contract price for the design and construction of those facilities by the Contractor adopting a more economical final design than proposed in the tender. Such a cost saving for the Contractor is the obverse of the cost risk it accepts under the Contract to construct a fully compliant design.

If provisions in the Contract are proposed to share cost savings with the Employer, these will need to be carefully vetted to ensure that they will achieve the desired objective, and cannot be circumvented by the Employer using other provisions of the Contract. Whilst most Contracts will contain a provision enabling the Employer to issue a variation, such a provision needs to be carefully considered in relation to the operation of any cost-saving clause. In particular, a prudent provision in the Contract would be that once the Contractor has proposed a "cost-saving initiative", the Contract should provide an express mechanism that prevents the Engineer or Employer from initiating a variation to capture all the benefit for itself. It is suggested that the concept of seeking cost savings for an Employer is inconsistent with a hard money lump sum contract, where the Contractor essentially bears the performance risk. Costs savings are perhaps best left to alliance and similar risk-sharing arrangements.

Proposed cost-savings provisions should not dilute the normal contractual right of the Contractor to prepare the most cost-effective design it can produce by the exercise of its engineering skill, provided this is consistent with the requirements of the Contract.

24.3.5 Risk

It should be apparent from the suggestions above that the legal effect of any nonstandard contract terms should be fully assessed to understand changes in the "normal" risk allocation. This may require a very careful analysis of the proposed contractual terms, perhaps in comparison with a standard contract form, to determine the likely effect, and the extent to which it transfers risk to the Contractor. It is trite to observe that the addition or deletion of a few words from a standard form can completely change the meaning of an expression, hence the need to assess the actual meaning carefully.

24.4 The Engineer

It is a fact of life and is accepted in standard form contracts (e.g. FIDIC Conditions of Contract for Plant and Design-Build and AS4902 General Conditions of Contract for Design and Construct) that the Engineer (Superintendent) is the agent of the Employer and/or acts for the Employer in many situations. However, this is not inconsistent with a contractual requirement that the Engineer act fairly and in accordance with the Contract when exercising his/her certifying role and functions. Given the importance of the role of the Engineer, it is suggested that the Contractor should strive to ensure that the Contract requires the person fulfilling the role to act fairly when exercising his/her certifying role and functions.

AS4902 defines a simple requirement to achieve this: "The Principal [Employer] shall ensure that at all times there is a Superintendent [Engineer], and that the Superintendent fulfils all aspects of the role and functions reasonably and in good faith." Such a contractual provision should (at least in theory) avoid the potential conflict between the agency and certification roles that may occur when the Contract states that the Engineer (Superintendent) will act as the agent of the Employer (and not as an independent certifier, assessor or valuer) in discharging each of the functions of the Engineer under the Contract.

If the Contractor is unable to negotiate a contract term that requires the Engineer to act reasonably and fairly in fulfilling his/her certification role under the Contract, one must ask why is the Employer not prepared to accept such a provision? If the Contractor is not able to rely on a fair assessment of its contractual entitlements, the merits of accepting such a contract must be questioned. Further, it may be appropriate for the Contractor to insist on being given a copy of the Engineer's contract of engagement. The Contractor could then satisfy itself that the engineer's contractual duties to the Employer do not conflict with the defined role of the Engineer under the construction Contract.

It is likely that the Contractor will not necessarily agree with all the Engineer's certifications, and there will be genuine differences of opinion as to the correct contractual approach. This is all the more likely if the construction Contract does not require the Engineer to act reasonably and fairly in his/her certification role. Recognising this almost inevitable conflict, the Contractor should ensure that in this situation the Contract provides for an appropriate early dispute resolution process to resolve disputes on the Engineer's certifications.

24.5 Contractual provisions for dispute resolution

Given the technical and legal complexities and the divergences between the interests of the parties in any major design and construct project, conflict and dispute at some level is perhaps almost inevitable. The Contract can provide for proactive processes that have the aim of avoiding disputes, such as the use of Dispute Boards. However, recognising that, with the best will in the world when the Contract is signed, disputes may still occur, the Contract should provide for a sophisticated and graduated dispute resolution process. One of the challenges facing the Contractor in reviewing the dispute resolution processes provided for in any contract is to ensure that its legal rights are adequately protected, without letting any conflict and dispute adversely impact on successful execution of the project, or damage the relationship with the Employer unnecessarily.

It is suggested that the Contractor's and the Employer's interests would be served by a provision in the Contract for a streamlined and speedy process for the resolution of disputes that is independent of the contracting parties. One option for this would be an independent Adjudicator who could consider submissions from both parties on a disputed matter, and come to a speedy determination without the formality of a hearing or the preparation of lengthy documentation. If both parties accepted the Adjudicator's determination, it could become binding after, say 28 days, and that would be the end of the matter. If either party wished to challenge the determination, it could give notice within 28 days that it intended to implement the formal dispute resolution procedures provided for in the Contract. However, to ensure that the parties were not further distracted from execution of the project by the significant work necessary to prepare for arbitration or litigation, the Adjudicator's determination could be made binding on both parties until practical completion. This is the adjudication procedure in Option W1 of the NEC ECC.

The use of adjudication to provide a speedy and at least provisional resolution of a dispute on any issue under the Contract is an extension of the statutory adjudication provided for in respect of payment claims under the various Australian Acts for security of payment in respect of "construction work" that is not an oil and gas or mining project. It is similar to the wider use of statutory adjudication for all construction contract disputes undertaken under the provisions of the *Housing Grants, Construction and Regeneration Act 1996* (UK). Anecdotal evidence indicates that this *Act* has had a significant impact in reducing the number of disputes that have progressed to litigation in the courts. Such adjudication technically only provides a provisional resolution of the dispute, pending a proper determination of the rights of the parties under the formal process of arbitration or litigation. However, it appears that in many cases the parties are prepared to accept the Adjudicator's finding as an independent, albeit limited, judgment on the merits of the dispute between the parties, in effect a "mini trial". The limitations of such an adjudication arising from the constraints on time and volume of documentation, in many cases appear to be outweighed by the value of the speed with which a determination is made, the low cost, and the ability of the parties to put the dispute behind them and get on with the project.

On a major project, the concept of independent adjudication can be taken a step further by the appointment of a standing **Dispute Adjudication Board (DAB)**, a panel of suitably qualified and experienced independent persons appointed at the start of a Contract to assist the parties avoid disputes and, if necessary, provide a determination of a dispute referred to it.

The 2017 Editions of the FIDIC construction contracts[5] provide for a **Dispute Avoidance/Adjudication Board (DAAB)**, a new name given to a standing DAB. A DAAB is appointed at the time of contract execution, and comprises one or three independent and widely experienced and respected members who become familiar with the project from its inception by reviewing progress and project documentation. The DAAB is available to adjudicate on disputes at any time during the project. The experience of the use of DABs on major projects around the world has been that they are very successful in assisting the parties to avoid disputes, and even in the minority of projects in which disputes occur, from preventing these from becoming "full-blown" arbitration or litigation.[6] This success probably depends in part on the stature of the members of the DAB, who need to be widely respected professionals with considerable experience in similar projects. It probably also has the worthwhile effect of filtering ill-thought-out or unprepared claims, as neither party

5 Conditions of Contract for Construction (Red Book); Conditions of Contract for Plant and Design-Build (Yellow Book); Conditions of Contract for EPC/Turnkey Projects (Silver Book).

6 Graeme Peck and Peer Dalland, "The Benefits of Dispute Resolution Boards for Issue Management of Medium to Large Construction Projects" (2007) Vol 26 No 1 *the arbitrator & mediator* 13, 23.

would wish to have a claim rejected by the DAB as without substance. Dispute Boards are discussed in more detail in Chapter 26.

In addition to the provisional resolution of disputes through the use of adjudication or DABs, the Contract terms in relation to the ultimate resolution of disputes need to be carefully thought through. Whilst arbitration is widely used in relation to resolution of construction contract disputes, it is suggested that, unless it can offer some substantive advantages over litigation (such as the appointment of an appropriately qualified person with expertise in the subject matter, or confidentiality), there is no compelling reason why it should be preferred. In recent years the courts have been more focused on delivering just, speedy and economical dispute resolution, and have specialised building and construction lists in which experienced judges manage the interlocutory steps, and sometimes take innovative actions to expedite the litigation process.[7]

Some of the advantages that arbitration has traditionally had over litigation include confidentiality of the proceedings, an Arbitrator chosen by the parties, some party control of the way in which the proceedings are conducted and the potential to limit or exclude appeal rights. Agreement between the parties on the form of arbitration that is incorporated in a construction contract can be a compelling argument in favour of arbitration, particularly if the procedures lead to significant savings in time and cost. The experience of the "stop clock" arbitration in the Anaconda arbitration in Australia demonstrated that a final result can be achieved years earlier than if the full litigation route, including appeals, is followed.[8] It is difficult to assess whether and to what extent a shorter overall time period to resolve a dispute results in lower legal costs, because the legal team may be significantly larger in a "stop clock" arbitration to ensure that adequate preparation has been carried out in the available time. However, the shorter elapsed time is of itself a significant advantage, as it limits the disruption caused by the dispute to a shorter time period, and makes it more likely that evidence can be obtained from witnesses before memories have completely faded. It also means that company accounts do not need to carry forward contingent liabilities for as long as might occur with long-running litigation.

Accordingly, it is suggested that if arbitration is to be used as the ultimate method of dispute resolution, the contract terms should provide for a limited time "stop clock" arbitration, with the Arbitrator to be selected from a limited list of suitable candidates.

Consideration should also be given to limiting the ambit of discovery in any arbitration, since discovery of the large numbers of documents produced during execution of a major construction contract may be a substantial component of the overall expense of conducting an arbitration. The vast majority of discovered documents are not usually significant to the outcome, and it is rare to find the "smoking gun". The writer suggests that discovery according to the "train of enquiry" principles laid down long ago in the *Peruvian Guano* case[9] usually leads to discovery of voluminous documents in a construction case, and would rarely, if ever, be cost effective.

7 e.g. the procedures available to the TEC List in the Supreme Court of Victoria: http://assets.justice.vic.gov.au//supreme/resources/11cb5d7a-fb56-4c8d-93ce-73e0dc57c2d9/practice%2bnote%2b2%2bof%2b2009%2b-%2btec%2blist.pdf (accessed 14 April 2021).

8 Peter Wood, 'Anaconda v Fluor: a Case Study' (2005) Vol 24 No 1 *the arbitrator & mediator* 61.

9 *Compagnie Financiere Commerciale Du Pacifique v Peruvian Guano* (1882) 11 QBD 55 at 63 per Brett LJ.

24.6 Contract negotiations

The only time that acceptable contract terms can generally be negotiated is before the Contract is entered into, at the stage where both parties may have compelling reasons to finalise the Contract: the Employer wants the project to commence so that it can be completed at the earliest opportunity, and the Contractor (usually) wants the work. The contract negotiations thus represent an extremely important phase of the project in which a successful outcome lays the foundations on which a successful project can be built. Conversely if the contract negotiations do not result in acceptable conditions of contract, it is very likely that subsequent problems during project execution will result in disputes.

The following suggestions in relation to contract negotiations may prove to be difficult to implement in practice, but there may be adverse consequences in ignoring them:

- Be aware of which contract terms are "non-negotiable" because they involve unacceptable risk allocation to the Contractor, e.g. unlimited liability.
- Be prepared to walk away from the project if acceptable contract conditions cannot be negotiated – ultimately no contract is preferable to a contract which is doomed from the start.
- Recognise the negotiating advantages that the Contractor may have in respect of quality, time and cost because of its personnel, resources or project history.
- Recognise situations in which the Contractor has "leverage" e.g. where there is no or no credible alternative tenderer, or the prevailing economic circumstances are "Contractor friendly" because the construction industry is overheated.
- If the proposed contract terms in the tender documents are too onerous, consider not submitting a bid unless more acceptable terms are accepted.

Prohibitions on misleading or deceptive conduct under the *Australian Consumer Law* (previously the *Trade Practices Act 1974* (Cth)) in Australia condition the limits of acceptable negotiating conduct by both sides prior to entering into a contract. If the statutory requirements are breached it may afford a wronged party a subsequent remedy; however, the factual and evidentiary hurdles may be difficult to overcome. Furthermore, this is normally only available when the project has "failed" in some way, whereas the emphasis should always be on trying to ensure that the negotiated contract conditions are conducive to a successful project.

24.7 Contract management

The key to successful contract management by the Contractor is to thoroughly understand the requirements of the Contract, and ensure that it fulfils its formal and substantive contractual obligations. For example, it is almost invariably important that the Contract time limits for submission of notices are complied with.

It would usually be helpful to prepare a contract management manual, to assist the Contractor's personnel in understanding the Contract and ensuring that its notices and other communications such as invoices are consistent and comply with the requirements of the Contract as regards form and timing, and are supported by appropriate backup documentation. One of the substantial advantages of standard form contracts is that such contract management manuals already exist in whole or in part, e.g. Administration manual for AS 4000–1997, General conditions of Contract HB 140–2000 and the FIDIC Contracts Guide (2000).

It is suggested that a focus on making and pursuing difficult or unsubstantiated claims, can be counterproductive, as it tends to colour the perception of all claims submitted. It may be appropriate to implement a procedure for "vetting" and approving the submission of claims that might be referred to as "extra contractual", i.e. not ordinary variations that can easily be dealt with under the variation provisions of the Contract. Such prior vetting and approval could be carried out by a high-level committee comprising appropriate senior personnel, including in-house legal counsel. This would ensure all senior management personnel are represented and can have input into the content of the claim, and understand its impact on on-going business relationships. Such a committee could test the substance and veracity of claims and ensure in management reporting that the prospects of marginal claims were not overstated. It would not mean that the Contractor would not submit a marginal claim, but if it did it would be based on a realistic view of the prospects of the claim and its possible consequences.

If the Contractor considers that the Engineer's formal response to an issue is unsatisfactory, it may be appropriate to have a face-to-face meeting in an endeavour to find common ground. Such a face-to-face meeting promotes good communications, the absence of which is often a significant factor in conflict that ultimately degenerates into a full-blown dispute. If such a meeting is not appropriate or is ineffective, serious consideration should be given to invoking the dispute resolution provisions of the Contract at an early stage. This strategy is likely to be particularly effective if the Contract provides for disputes to be resolved on a provisional basis by an Adjudicator or DAB. It is suggested that early, even if provisional, resolution of disputes may act as a circuit breaker, and enable the parties to proceed with execution of the project without excessive distraction of senior personnel from their primary tasks.

If the number or extent of disputes requiring attention becomes significant, it may be worth mobilising a separate disputes team so that claims can be properly prepared, and project personnel are not diverted from execution of the project itself or become involved in avoidable confrontation with the Employer. A separate disputes team that is not associated with execution of the project might also act as a primary filter to weed out hopeless claims without substance. If such a Contractor team is not convinced that there is sufficient evidence to support a claim, it is probably a strong indication that the claim lacks substance and should not be put to the Employer.

24.8 Management of project execution

It is obvious to state that any failure by the Contractor to fulfil its obligations under the Contract may lead to a dispute. However, statement of this obvious fact serves to emphasise the fundamental importance of the Contractor managing its substantive and formal contractual obligations in accordance with the requirements of the Contract. The following are some of the project management issues that may be problematic:

- Sufficient resources need to be available from the start of the project so that there is no unnecessary and avoidable slippage in the programme.

- Realistic and credible "as built" programmes should be maintained that are consistent with actual progress, and can form the basis of accurate reporting to the Contractor management and to the Employer as required by the Contract.
- All work needs to be completed to the quality required by the Contract.
- Design documents should be submitted to the Employer as required by the Contract.

It is critical that appropriate resources be devoted to developing and maintaining a comprehensive and contractually compliant programme against which progress can be measured. A properly prepared programme that is regularly updated during the course of the project to reflect actual progress and realistic projections of remaining work will be an invaluable project management tool in achieving timely performance of completion of the works under the Contract, and reporting progress to the Employer. If there are disputes with respect to time, such a programme provides cogent and compelling evidence of what actually happened on the project, a task that is very difficult to do retrospectively. Courts or an Arbitrator will be more persuaded by contemporaneous documents than those prepared after the fact. Furthermore, accurate, contemporaneous documentation that comprehensively demonstrates the Contractor's entitlements may well dissuade the Employer from initiating a dispute.

Good documentation is an essential aspect of proper project management. It is important for proper administration of the Contract, particularly records of any work done that may be outside the contractual scope and that may form the basis of a variation claim – these include time sheets, and records of material procurement and equipment hire. There may also be formal contractual obligations in respect of documentation deliverables.

The other reason for the importance of good documentation is that it is invaluable for disputes that have to be resolved through the formal processes provided for in the Contract. The explanatory notes accompanying the FIDIC contracts is apt and applicable to every contract:

> The importance of good record-keeping cannot be over-emphasised. The resolution of disputes frequently rests on the adequacy of contemporaneous records. If a Party declines to agree matters for record purposes, on the spurious ground that agreement of facts indicates an admission of liability, the DAB or arbitrator(s) may decide to rely upon the other Party's unchallenged contemporaneous records.[10]

Managers responsible for projects need to be familiar with the relevant conditions of the Contract, and the formal obligations it places on them. Engineers need to be familiar with the relevant technical documents incorporated in the Contract, and must know the extent of the contractual scope of work and the required quality, as well as the contractual dates that must be met. This is particularly the case in respect of a bespoke contract, which may place more onerous obligations in respect of scope, time, cost or quality than is normal in the construction industry for similar projects.

10 International Federation of Consulting Engineers (FIDIC), *The FIDIC Contracts Guide* (2000) 302.

24.9 Resolution of disputes

The focus of contract and project management will be to try and avoid disputes but, despite the Contractor's best endeavours, disputes may occur that require resolution in the manner provided for in the Contract. As with any other aspect of execution of a project, proper management of the dispute resolution process is important to ensure that it is undertaken efficiently and effectively, and remains focused on achieving the appropriate outcome for the Contractor.

The most appropriate personnel resources for such a dispute resolution team will depend on the stage of the project at which it is required. For dispute resolution by an Adjudicator or DAB during the course of the project, a separate team as discussed above may be appropriate. Such a team will need to draw on the resources of the project execution team; however, the resultant disruption should be minimised.

If the final dispute resolution process such as arbitration or litigation is required after the project has reached practical completion, the most effective dispute resolution team will include some senior team members who were involved in the project management and execution. This will provide continuity, and ensure that the corporate memory in respect of the project is available for planning and executing the steps to be taken in the dispute resolution. In addition, the dispute resolution team will need access to all the senior key personnel on the project whose work was relevant to the subject matter of the dispute, in order to prepare witness statements and brief experts. For a major dispute, the time involvement of the key relevant personnel is likely to be significant, dependent of course on the extent of evidence required. Making such personnel available after the conclusion of a project may be challenging because of their importance on other projects, or because they are no longer employed by the Contractor. However, the failure to present key evidence from an important witness can only harm a party's case. As a minimum, it is suggested that a workshop and debrief with lawyers present before the project team is demobilised and/or relocated, is essential on every project where a dispute exists or is likely.

It is suggested that there may be value in workshops comprising senior Contractor personnel and independent experts. These workshops can review the claims and the evidence, and formulate an opinion on how or whether claims should be prosecuted or defended. The value of this process is that it will enable the Contractor to take a pragmatic view on the strength of each element of its case, and to concentrate its resources on those aspects in which it has the best chance of success. Such workshops should be implemented at the earliest opportunity, and the workshop recommendations used to plan the Contractor's conduct of the dispute resolution process. It is important that this process is supervised or managed by the Contractor's in-house and external lawyers in order to ensure an appropriate framework is developed, efforts are focussed appropriately and to maintain legal privilege in the materials produced.

24.10 Conclusion

There are many challenges for a Contractor in successfully executing a design and construct contract without dispute. These start with careful preparation of the tender, not only the time and cost estimates on which the tender price is based, but assessment of the risks inherent in the proposed contract terms. Bespoke contracts in particular may require a Contractor to assume unacceptable or unmanageable risks. Negotiation of appropriate contract terms in respect of scope, time, quality and cost, as well as the role of the Engineer is the foundation from which the successful outcome of a project can be managed. Speedy and interim resolution of disputes that do occur, by an Adjudicator or a DAB, may be effective in enabling the parties to get on with the project without compromising their legal rights. Finally, some suggestions have been made to assist the efficient resolution of disputes that do ultimately result in arbitration or litigation.

CHAPTER 25

Cost-effective resolution of construction disputes[1]

25.1 Introduction

Corporate counsel are well aware of the cost and time involved in litigation or arbitration of commercial disputes. For some types of disputes, there is no realistic alternative, such as where a binding court precedent is required to assist in the resolution of a large number of similar disputes. However: "The rule of law does not require that the entire apparatus of the judicial system be brought to bear upon all disputes, or even upon all disputes about legal rights and obligations."[2] Many disputes are settled on a commercial basis by the disputing parties themselves, or with the assistance of an independent third-party facilitator such as a mediator. The commercial settlement of a dispute in this way may be driven more by the parties' desire to preserve relationships, or their relative bargaining positions, rather than their legal or contractual rights.

There are various methods of alternative dispute resolution that are intermediate between the commercial "non-legal" methods such as mediation, and the full-blown (and time-consuming and expensive) formal "legal" methods of arbitration and litigation. This chapter reviews three "evaluative" methods: adjudication, expert determination, and Dispute Boards, all widely used in construction disputes. These evaluative ADR methods are equally applicable to other forms of commercial disputes. Each of these ADR methods seeks to provide the parties with a determination of their rights according to the contract and the law, prepared by an independent and impartial third party with relevant legal and technical skills, and based on the facts.

This chapter looks at the features of adjudication, expert determination and Dispute Boards, their advantages over litigation or arbitration, and the types of disputes they are suited to. The important role of Dispute Boards in dispute avoidance is also discussed.

25.2 Adjudication

Adjudication can be defined as "a method of dispute resolution in which an independent adjudicator resolves the dispute by providing a provisionally binding determination of the

1 This chapter is an edited and updated version of the paper published in: Donald Charrett, 'Cost Effective Resolution of Construction Disputes' (2015) 9.33 *International In-house Counsel Journal* 1. It is reproduced by kind permission of the publishers of *International In-house Counsel Journal*.

2 Gleeson CJ, 'Courts and the Rule of Law' (2001) Speech in the Rule of Law Series at Melbourne University, 7 November 2001 https://www.hcourt.gov.au/assets/publications/speeches/former-justices/gleesoncj/cj_ruleoflaw.htm (accessed 15 April 2021).

 DOI: 10.4324/9781003206897-28

parties' contractual rights following an impartial assessment of the parties' submissions and other evidence".[3] In principle at least, parties can agree on adjudication of any contractual dispute and enter into a contract to implement the agreed procedure (**contractual adjudication**).

A number of common law jurisdictions have implemented adjudication in a statutory form for construction disputes, as a speedy and economical alternative to litigation for provisional resolution of disputes (**statutory adjudication**). The UK was the first jurisdiction to implement adjudication in statutory form in the *Housing Grants, Construction and Regeneration Act* 1996 (***HGCRA***). Parties to a construction contract (as defined in the *Act*) are given a unilateral right to refer a dispute arising under the contract to adjudication. The contracting parties can define their own adjudication process, provided that it satisfies the mandatory provisions of the *Act*. Although the outcome of such an adjudication is provisional, and the disputed legal rights can be finally determined by arbitration or litigation, in a large majority of cases the parties are prepared to accept the outcome as final. This has led to a substantial reduction of cases heard by the Technology and Construction Court, and adjudication has become the principal method of dispute resolution in construction contracts in England.[4]

Statutory adjudication for certain types of construction disputes has been enacted in a number of other common law jurisdictions: New Zealand, Australia, Singapore, Isle of Man, Malaysia, Ireland and Ontario. Australia, Singapore, Malaysia, Ireland and Ontario have taken a narrower approach to the scope of statutory adjudication, and have confined it to disputes over payment, in an endeavour to maintain contractor and subcontractor cash flow, "the lifeblood of construction". The differences between these *Acts*, and their advantages and disadvantages are beyond the scope of this chapter. However, they are all based on an **Adjudicator** assessing the factual and legal submissions of the parties, and providing a provisional determination of the parties' legal rights in respect of the dispute referred to him or her within a very limited time frame. The Adjudicator's decision is not a final determination of the parties' legal rights; their right to litigation or arbitration is preserved. However, notwithstanding the "rough and ready" nature of the time-constrained Adjudicator's assessment, for many parties it apparently provides an acceptable outcome.

The mandatory statutory adjudication regime in a particular jurisdiction may therefore significantly limit the parties' options in respect of devising their own contractual adjudication regime, if their construction contract comes within the ambit of the relevant *Act*. Whilst a party's resort to statutory adjudication is optional, it is also a legal right that cannot be contracted out of. Accordingly, any alternative contractual adjudication that was in conflict with the relevant statutory adjudication *Act* would not be enforceable, if a party chose to file a statutory adjudication claim.

The NEC ECC contracts provide that disputes are referred to and decided by an Adjudicator appointed by the Parties under the NEC Adjudicator's Contract. The Adjudicator's decision is binding on the Parties. If either Party is dissatisfied with the Adjudicator's decision, it may notify the other party within four weeks that it intends to refer the dispute to the tribunal (arbitration or litigation). Referral of a dispute to an Adjudicator is a condition precedent to referring a dispute to arbitration or litigation.

3 Philip Loots and Donald Charrett, *Practical Guide to Engineering and Construction Contracts* (2009) 362.
4 Cyril Chern, *The Law of Construction Disputes* (1st edn, 2010) 343.

Contractual adjudication procedures are in Option W1, and statutory adjudication procedures under the *HGCRA* are in Option W2.

The advantages of contractual adjudication include the short time frame and limited costs involved in obtaining an independent neutral's evaluation of the parties' contractual rights. The parties have control over the process, including selection of the Adjudicator. The Adjudicator's decision is provisionally binding, i.e. the parties are contractually bound to comply with it, unless and until it is overturned by mutual agreement or (finally binding) arbitration or litigation. The provisionally binding resolution of a dispute by adjudication, even if ultimately disputed, enables the parties to deal with issues in a timely fashion when the evidence and memories are fresh.

The disadvantages of adjudication mainly stem from the limited time and scope of the process. The short time period allowed for may be insufficient for a complex legal and factual dispute that requires careful consideration of a large number of documents and other evidence.

25.3 Expert determination

Expert determination can be defined as "a method of dispute resolution in which an independent impartial Expert is engaged by the disputing parties to determine those disputed questions of fact and/or law in the reference defined by the parties".[5]

Expert determination is purely a creature of contract, the procedural rules and enforceability being those defined in the relevant Contract. Thus, parties can agree to a finally binding expert determination from which there is no appeal, a provisionally binding expert determination that only becomes final if neither party issues a notice of dissatisfaction within a defined period of time, or a non-binding expert determination. A non-binding expert determination provides the parties with a reasoned assessment of the facts and the law in dispute, prepared by an independent and impartial Expert; such a determination may provide the parties with an appropriate basis for reaching a negotiated resolution of their dispute.

The parties need to be careful in preparing the procedural rules for conducting a binding expert determination, to ensure that their agreement is not void for uncertainty, or for ousting the jurisdiction of the court. However, there is ample case law to demonstrate that the courts will uphold an expert determination conducted by an **Expert** in conformance with a properly drawn-up expert determination agreement and keep the parties to their bargain of resolving their dispute by expert determination.[6]

The advantages of expert determination stem from the independence and skills of the Expert. A non-binding determination provides the parties with a "reality check" on the dispute and may dissuade them from proceeding to expensive litigation or arbitration. A binding determination resolves the defined issues in contention by means of an assessment of the relevant facts and law by an independent third-party Neutral. The Expert can rely on her/his personal expertise on the issues in dispute and is not confined to the evidence submitted by the parties. The time and cost of an expert determination are usually substantially less than for the more formal procedures of arbitration or litigation.

5 Philip Loots and Donald Charrett, *Practical Guide to Engineering and Construction Contracts* (2009) 368.
6 e.g. *Shoalhaven City Council v Firedam Civil Engineering Pty Ltd* [2011] HCA 38.

The major disadvantage of non-binding expert determination is that it may not conclude the dispute between the parties if they are unable to subsequently negotiate a settlement. Binding expert determination suffers from the disadvantage that there may be no avenue to appeal a determination that is plainly wrong because it is based on errors of fact or a misapprehension of the law (a disadvantage it shares with arbitration). As an Expert normally acts inquisitorially and does not hear evidence, a determination may not be based on all the available evidence. A court will not enforce an expert determination if it finds that the Expert exceeded his/her jurisdiction by not making a determination in accordance with the contract.[7]

25.4 Dispute Boards

A **Dispute Board (DB)** can be defined as:

> a panel of one or three suitably qualified and experienced independent persons appointed under the contract to be available to confer with the parties to assist in the avoidance of disputes or if necessary to provide a determination on a dispute referred to it.[8]

This is the definition of a "standing" Dispute Board, typically appointed at the commencement of a Contract, becoming familiar with the Contract and the project, and meeting regularly with the parties to facilitate resolution of issues before they mature into formal disputes. Such a Dispute Board is able to provide a reasoned decision on a formal dispute in a limited time and at low cost because it is already "up to speed" with the issues.

By contrast, an *ad hoc* Dispute Board is only established after a dispute has arisen and acts essentially as an Adjudicator or Expert to provide a reasoned decision of the dispute referred to it. Since an *ad hoc* Dispute Board is only appointed to determine the specific dispute, it cannot assist the parties to avoid disputes in the way that a standing Dispute Board can. There is little to distinguish an *ad hoc* Dispute Board from contractual adjudication or expert determination; the use of the term "Dispute Board" in this chapter will be confined to a standing Dispute Board.

There are several variants of Dispute Boards. A **Dispute Resolution Board** or a **Dispute Review Board (DRB)** provides a non-binding decision on a dispute referred to it; the DRB decision will only be binding if the parties agree that they will adopt it. This is the preferred Dispute Board model in the United States. A Dispute Adjudication Board (DAB) or a Dispute Avoidance/Adjudication Board (DAAB) provides a provisionally binding decision on a dispute referred to it; if neither party issues a notice of dissatisfaction within a defined time, the decision becomes final and binding. If either party issues a notice of dissatisfaction, the decision is binding unless and until it is later overturned by agreement or arbitration or litigation. A DAB/DAAB is the Dispute Board model adopted by FIDIC in its widely used construction contracts (commonly referred to as the **rainbow suite**).[9]

---

7 Ibid [27].

8 Philip Loots and Donald Charrett, *Practical Guide to Engineering and Construction Contracts* (2009) 367.

9 FIDIC Conditions of Contract for Construction for Building and Engineering Works Designed by the Employer (1st edn, 1999; 2nd edn, 2017) (Red Book); FIDIC Conditions of Contract for Plant and Design-Build for Electrical and Mechanical Plant and for Building and Engineering Works, designed by the Contractor (1st edn, 1999; 2nd edn, 2017) (Yellow Book); FIDIC Conditions of Contract for EPC/Turnkey Projects (1st edn, 1999; 2nd edn, 2017) (Silver Book).

In their dispute resolution role, Dispute Boards have features in common with adjudication and expert determination, and the respective advantages and disadvantages discussed above also apply to Dispute Boards.

In assessing the full role of a standing Dispute Board, the major perceived disadvantage is the cost. Whilst the cost of a Dispute Board is typically a small percentage of the overall contract cost, in absolute terms the cost of three senior and experienced people with the appropriate expertise along with their associated travel costs may appear to be substantial. In this writer's view, these costs can be well justified as "insurance", given the track record of projects with Dispute Boards having very few disputes.

25.5 The features of evaluative methods of ADR

The evaluative methods of ADR outlined above have a number of common features. Leaving aside statutory adjudication, each of these three methods is defined by the terms of the relevant contract. They all involve one or more independent and impartial third party Neutrals to produce a reasoned decision on a dispute, based on an assessment of the relevant facts in light of the Contract and the applicable law. The parties are free to select the Neutral based on her/his expertise in the relevant technical area and the law, and the parties are free to define the procedural rules that the Neutral is required to follow.

Every dispute is different, and it is arguable that the "best" method of dispute resolution for a specific dispute should ideally be selected as appropriate to the features of that dispute, after it has arisen (see Chapter 30). However, that utopian view assumes that parties in dispute will agree on the procedure for resolving their dispute at a time when they may be disinclined to agree to anything. The usual situation is that, at the time that they enter into the Contract, the parties agree to the form of ADR to be adopted in the event of a dispute, even though the nature of any dispute is unknown at that stage. The application of ADR, its enforceability under the Contract, and the procedural rules to be adopted are therefore frequently included in the original Contract.

Implementation of one of the evaluative methods of ADR typically requires the following three documents:

- An agreement by the contracting parties to adopt a specific form of ADR in the event of, or on the occurrence of, a dispute, and the contractual consequences of the decision of the independent Neutral (**ADR clause**)
- Procedural rules for conduct of the ADR method (which will typically be incorporated in the parties' ADR clause, at least by reference), and
- A tripartite agreement between the contracting parties and the independent ADR Neutral that incorporates the procedural rules.

Unless the parties have agreed to the identity of the independent Neutral, their agreement to adopt a specific evaluative method of ADR will usually need to provide for the method of appointment of the independent Neutral in the event that they cannot agree. The selection of the most appropriate Neutral to adjudicate a particular dispute is perhaps the parties' most important decision. In addition to independence and impartiality, the Neutral may require specific technical skills to fully understand the issues in dispute and will also usually require sufficient legal expertise to construe and apply the relevant terms of the Contract (and the tripartite agreement).

Many institutions perform the role of a nominating authority for the independent neutral, in the event that the parties cannot agree. For example, in the UK the Royal Institute of British Architects and the Royal Institution of Chartered Surveyors are nominating authorities for Adjudicators under the *HGCRA*, in Australia the Resolution Institute will nominate an expert, and internationally FIDIC will nominate Dispute Board members from the President's list of approved Adjudicators.

Standard forms of procedural rules for evaluative methods of ADR are available from many sources. In England and Wales, the Secretary of State has made regulations that are the default rules if a construction contract does not satisfy the adjudication requirements of s 108(1)–(4) of the *HGCRA*.[10] In Australia, the Resolution Institute has published expert determination rules.[11] FIDIC includes the procedural rules for Dispute Boards in its rainbow suite of contracts. Procedural rules for Dispute Boards are also published by the Chartered Institute of Arbitrators,[12] and the Dispute Resolution Board Foundation.[13]

The International Chamber of Commerce (**ICC**) publishes a document that contains all of the three procedural requirements for implementation of a Dispute Board – an ADR clause, procedural rules and a tripartite agreement.[14] The ICC rules are unique in that they provide for three different types of Dispute Board – a DAB, a DRB, and a combined Dispute Board (**CDB**) that is primarily a DRB but can be a DAB if the parties choose.

The parties are always free to prepare their own bespoke version of an evaluative method of ADR appropriate to their specific dispute, accompanied by the appropriate ADR clause, procedural rules and the tripartite agreement. Such bespoke agreements need careful drafting to ensure that they are workable, comprehensive and enforceable. Standard agreements such as those identified above may provide useful guidance in the preparation of bespoke agreements.

25.6 Advantages of evaluative methods of ADR over litigation or arbitration

The advantages of evaluative methods of ADR over litigation and arbitration can be summed up in two words – speed and cost.

The applicable procedural rules may have explicit times within which the Neutral's decision must be delivered, e.g. an adjudication under the *HGCRA* must be completed within 28 days after the date of the referral notice (subject to limited extension by agreement), and a Dispute Board decision under one of the FIDIC rainbow suite contracts must be delivered within 84 days of the date of referral to the DAB/DAAB.

In the case of a bespoke agreement for an evaluative form of ADR, the parties will generally be concerned to obtain a decision in the shortest reasonable time, and will engage the Neutral accordingly.

10 *Scheme for Construction Contracts (England and Wales) Regulations 1998.*

11 https://www.resolution.institute/documents/item/1845 (accessed 15 April 2021).

12 The Chartered Institute of Arbitrators, *Dispute Board Rules* (2014) https://www.ciarb.org/media/3934/ciarb-dispute-board-rules.pdf (accessed 15 April 2021).

13 Dispute Resolution Board Foundation, *Dispute Board Manual* 2019) https://drbf.mclms.net/en/package/3545/course/7648/view (accessed 15 April 2021).

14 International Chamber of Commerce, *Dispute Board Rules* (2015) https://iccwbo.org/dispute-resolution-services/dispute-boards/rules/ (accessed 15 April 2021).

The ability to obtain a decision on resolution of a dispute in a short period of time is itself important. On many long-running projects such as construction projects, resolving disputes as they occur materially assists in maintaining working relationships between the parties. It is far preferable to deferring all disputes to the end of the project to be resolved in what may be a large arbitration or litigation when memories have faded and key witnesses may not be available.

Speedy resolution of a dispute also has the collateral benefit that it materially assists in minimising the costs. It is trite to observe that the more formal the procedures are to be complied with, the more time will be required to comply with them, and this will almost inevitably incur significant cost.

Most procedural rules for evaluative forms of ADR provide the Neutral with the power to determine in detail the procedures to be used, subject to any specified requirements in the procedural rules. The following is typical of this type of provision: "The Expert shall adopt procedures suitable to the circumstances of the particular case, avoiding unnecessary delay and expense, so as to provide an expeditious cost-effective and fair means of determining the Dispute."[15]

This power enables the Neutral to consider the real needs of what is required to determine the specific dispute, considering such things as the availability and extent of existing documentation, the necessity for further lay evidence, expert reports, the form of legal submissions, whether the dispute can be decided on the documents alone or whether a hearing is necessary. This flexibility to tailor the procedures to the needs of the specific dispute is in contrast to the formal procedures of litigation and (to a lesser extent) arbitration, both of which are subject to the constraints of the applicable legislation.

The Neutral's key role in determining the expeditious and cost-effective procedures to be adopted emphasises the importance of selecting the appropriate individual as Neutral – he/she needs to be fully conversant with the range of appropriate techniques for parties to present their evidence and submissions in the most efficient ways that afford them the required degree of procedural fairness.

25.7 The types of disputes most suited to evaluative methods of ADR

Because adjudication is normally carried out within a very limited time frame, it is particularly suitable for disputes in which the disputed issues are confined in scope. Complex disputes involving many separate issues, large volumes of documentation or complex legal issues may not be appropriate for adjudication. The parties must be prepared to accept that the Adjudicator's determination may be "rough and ready" because of the limited time available, and that the determination will be provisionally binding and must be complied with.

Expert determination is particularly suitable in disputes in which there are complex technical issues, the questions of law are straightforward, and both parties have confidence in the Expert's skill and ability to determine the issues fairly and justly. The parties will usually have control over the timing and can ensure that the Expert has sufficient time to consider the issues properly. It can be very suitable for the final determination of relatively low value disputes that would not justify the expense of litigation or arbitration.

15 Resolution Institute, *Expert Determination Rules* (2015) Rule 5.3.

A DAB/DAAB required to give a decision on a formal dispute essentially undertakes a role akin to adjudication or expert determination, and the remarks above about the types of disputes suitable for these methods of ADR are apposite. A standing Dispute Board required to make a determination of a formal dispute enters that role already prepared with detailed knowledge of the Contract, the project, the parties and the issues. It is therefore able to address the issues in a complex dispute within a short time period, as it is already "up to speed".

25.8 How a Dispute Board assists parties in avoiding disputes

Whilst the ability of a Dispute Board to provide a reasoned decision for a complex dispute within a limited period of time is important, its role in assisting parties to avoid disputes may be even more important. The experience of Dispute Boards around the world has been that many of them have not been required to give a decision on a single formal dispute, as the parties, aided by the Dispute Board, have been able to avoid disputes. Recent Dispute Boards appointed for government infrastructure projects in New South Wales are called "Dispute Avoidance Boards", as the avoidance of disputes is seen as their primary role. FIDIC has adopted the term "Dispute Avoidance/Adjudication Board" in the Second Edition of the Red, Yellow and Silver Books to emphasise its role in dispute avoidance.

Many authors have written on the reasons why Dispute Boards have been effective in assisting contracting parties to avoid disputes. In this writer's view, the primary reason is that the implementation and operation of a Dispute Board on a project requires the parties to effectively communicate with each other and the Dispute Board on a regular basis. There is a useful discipline in regular Dispute Board meetings, attended not only by those personnel at the "coalface" of the project, but also by senior executives of the contracting parties who have management oversight of the Contract. Routine Dispute Board meetings are typically held "without prejudice", to encourage free and frank discussion of issues in a forum that does not impact on legal or contractual rights. Senior management hear issues from the "other side", which may be at odds with information provided by their own personnel. The parties will generally prepare for a Dispute Board meeting, on the basis that they do not wish to appear unrehearsed by the Dispute Board.

The following is a succinct statement by a very experienced Dispute Board member of how a Dispute Board assists the parties to avoid disputes:

> Its very existence (its 'long shadow') minimises the outbreak of disputes and fosters cooperation between the parties, often providing the impetus for amicable settlements. The damaging 'duel of the egos' is avoided. Claims and defences are more carefully prepared and more credible as there is a natural desire not to appear foolish before the Dispute Board, or be seen as unhelpful or exaggerating. The parties thus undertake their reality check before embarking on the referral. Fewer spurious claims are advanced and fewer meritorious claims are rejected. Dealing is more open and the procedural posturing, so common in arbitration or litigation, is rarely evident.
>
> Parties are less inclined to send acrimonious correspondence that can damage relationships. They are aware, possibly subconsciously, of the Dispute Board's reaction to such exchanges. The parties' approaches are thus tempered by their perception of the Dispute Board's view of their behaviour. Attitudes remain positive, not adversarial.[16]

16 Cyril Chern, *The Law of Construction Disputes* (1st edn, 2010) 370.

CHAPTER 26

Dispute Boards and construction contracts[1]

26.1 What is a Dispute Board?

In the context of construction contracts, a Dispute Board (DB) comprises a board of one or three persons, independent of the contracting parties, engaged to perform an overview role of the execution of the project and the Contract. Its primary function is to assist the parties to avoid disputes if possible or, if avoidance is not possible, to assist them to a speedy, cost-effective and acceptable resolution of disputes, and avoid the need for arbitration or litigation. The Dispute Resolution Board Foundation (**DRBF**) defines a DB as follows:

> A Dispute Board (DB) is a board of impartial professionals formed at the beginning of the project to follow construction progress, encourage dispute avoidance, and assist in the resolution of disputes for the duration of the project.[2]

The members of a Dispute Board need to be relevantly experienced in the type of project under construction, and have a thorough understanding of contractual issues. They need to be respected for their experience and expertise, and they must be impartial. Both contracting parties must agree on membership of the DB.

The usual selection process for a Dispute Board on projects with a value greater than $30 m is for the Employer to nominate one member, and the Contractor to nominate a second member. Notwithstanding their nomination by a party, each of those members must be independent of both contracting parties. Each party has the right of reasonable objection over the other party's selection. The Chair is usually nominated by the party nominees, and then agreed to by the parties.

The most effective Dispute Boards are organised at the start of the Contract, and before construction begins. The Board is provided with the contract documents, plans and specifications, and is provided with regular progress reports during the course of the project. Thus, the Board members become and remain familiar with the Contract, the project and the participants from the beginning, and have an up-to-date knowledge of all the relevant issues which might impact on potential disputes.

The Dispute Board meets on regular site visits with representatives of the Employer and Contractor together, and is briefed on progress and potential problems. The Board also

1 This chapter is an edited and updated version of the paper published in: Donald Charrett, 'Dispute Boards and Construction Contracts' (2010) 132 *Australian Construction Law Newsletter* 19; (2010) 7 *Buildlaw* 37.

2 https://www.drb.org (accessed 15 April 2021).

DOI: 10.4324/9781003206897-29

carries out an inspection of the works on each of its site visits, and thus obtains first-hand knowledge of the site and the project.

The aim of the Board's site meetings is to facilitate communication with the contracting parties, and encourage resolution of contentious issues at the job level, before they become actual disputes. With the acquiescence of both parties, it is able to provide an informal advisory opinion on a potential dispute.

Either party has the right to refer a dispute to the Dispute Board. Following such a referral, the Board will hold a hearing, question witnesses, consider submissions and then provide a reasoned determination of the dispute, all within a defined limited time. The contractual effect of the Board's determination depends on whether the Dispute Board is a so-called Dispute Resolution (or Review) Board (DRB) or a Dispute Adjudication Board (DAB).

The determination of a DRB (the US model) is a recommendation to the parties of the DRB's considered opinion as to the appropriate resolution of the dispute. The DRB's recommendation has no contractual effect, unless the parties agree to implement it. However, notwithstanding the lack of a binding contractual effect of the DRB's recommendation, it is generally very persuasive because of the stature of the Board members, and the structured, fair and independent process by which they came to their reasoned decision. The Dispute Resolution Board Foundation recommends this model, and its track record of success supports its efficacy as an effective method of dispute resolution.

By contrast, the determination of a DAB (the European model) is a decision that is contractually binding on the parties unless and until it is overturned by agreement or in accordance with the contractual requirements for final determination of disputes (arbitration or litigation). There is a defined limited period of time after the DAB's decision within which either party may give notice of dissatisfaction with the DAB's decision. In the absence of such notice, the DAB's decision is finally binding on the parties. Even if one of the parties gives formal notice of dissatisfaction, the final resolution of the dispute by arbitration or litigation is usually deferred until the end of the project; in the meantime, the DAB's decision is binding on the parties.

The Dispute Resolution Board Foundation website provides a comprehensive database on projects around the world which have used DRBs, identifying the Contractor and Employer, contract value, and the numbers of disputes heard, settled or referred to other dispute resolution procedures.[3] As of 2021, the database listed 2,813 projects started from 1975 to 2017, with a total contract value of USD277.5 b. Of the 3,249 disputes heard, 80.9% had been settled, and only 14.7% had been referred to binding dispute resolution procedures.

26.2 Contractual requirements

Dispute Boards have been used with a variety of different forms of construction contract:

- Construct only
- Design and construct (**D&C**)
- D&C, with early contractor involvement (**ECI**)

3 https://www.disputeboard.org (accessed 15 April 2021).

- Design, construct and maintain (**DCM**)
- Design, construct, operate and maintain (**DCOM**)
- Semi or hybrid alliances.

The formal requirements for implementation of a Dispute Board comprise the following three contractual documents:

- **Dispute Board clause** in the construction contract between Employer and Contractor
- **Procedural rules** defining the operations of the DB, and
- **Tripartite agreement(s)** between Employer, Contractor and DB Members, incorporating the procedural rules.

26.2.1 Standard form contracts with a DB clause

A number of Standard Form contracts contain a DB clause, including:

- International Federation of Consulting Engineers (FIDIC)[4]
- ConsensusDocs (USA)[5]
- California Department of Transportation (Caltrans).

The FIDIC Conditions of Contract for Construction (Red Book) (First Edition, 1999) contains contractual clauses on the DB as follows.

Sub-clause 20.2 [Appointment of the DAB] provides that disputes are to be adjudicated by a DAB in accordance with sub-clause 20.4 [Obtaining DAB's Decision]. The parties jointly appoint a DAB by the date stated in the Appendix to Tender. Sub-clause 20.2 covers the following:

- The DAB comprises 1 or 3 members (default 3).
- Appointment process for a 3-person DAB.
- Selection from a list of potential members in the Contract.
- Tripartite Agreement(s) to incorporate by reference the General Conditions of Dispute Adjudication Agreement [Appendix].
- Remuneration of DB member(s).
- A matter can be referred to DB for opinion only if parties agree.
- Appointment of a replacement DB member.
- Termination of a DB member's appointment by mutual agreement of parties.

Sub-clause 20.3 details the process to be followed if the Parties fail to agree the DAB. Sub-clause 20.4 [Obtaining the DAB's Decision] provides that if any kind of dispute arises between the Parties in connection with, or arising out of, the Contract or the execution

4 FIDIC Conditions of Contract for Construction (1st edn, 1999; 2nd edn, 2017); FIDIC Conditions of Contract for Plant and Design – Build (1st edn, 1999; 2nd edn, 2017); FIDIC Conditions of Contract for EPC/ Turnkey Projects (1st edn, 1999; 2nd edn, 2017); FIDIC Conditions of Contract for Construction MDB Harmonised Edition for Building and Engineering Works Designed by the Employer (MDB Harmonised Edition 2010).

5 200 Standard Agreement (LS) (lump sum); 300 Tri-Party Agreement for collaborative project delivery; 410 Design – Build Agreement (GMP) (guaranteed maximum price).

of the Works, either Party may refer the dispute in writing to the DAB for its decision. Disputes may relate to any certificate, determination, instruction, opinion or valuation of the Engineer. Sub-clause 20.4 covers the following:

- Time of receipt for a 3-person DAB.
- Parties are to make available information, site access and facilities requested by DAB.
- DAB members are not acting as Arbitrators.
- DAB is to give a reasoned decision within 84 days.
- The DAB's decision is binding on both parties unless and until it is revised in an amicable settlement or arbitral award.
- Either Party may give notice of dissatisfaction (with reasons) of the DAB's decision within 28 days of receiving the decision.
- Notice of dissatisfaction is a condition precedent to a party's entitlement to commence arbitration.
- The DAB's decision is final and binding unless notice of dissatisfaction is given within 28 days.

26.2.2 Standard contract clauses for a DB

The International Chamber of Commerce (**ICC**) recommends a DAB clause for use in construction contracts in which the parties agree to establish a Dispute Adjudication Board (DAB) comprising one or three members appointed under the contract or appointed pursuant to the Rules, to operate in accordance with the DB Rules of the ICC. The clause includes:

- All disputes are to be submitted to the DAB in the first instance.
- The DAB shall issue a decision in accordance with the Rules.
- If a party fails to comply with a DAB decision, the other party may refer the failure to arbitration.
- If either party expresses dissatisfaction with a DAB decision, the dispute shall be finally settled by ICC arbitration.
- If there is no DAB decision, the dispute shall be finally settled by ICC arbitration.[6]

26.2.3 Procedural rules and operation of a DB

The procedural rules fulfil the dual purpose of formalising the operation of the DB as between the contracting parties and defining the operational procedures that the Board members are required to follow. As such, the procedural rules are usually incorporated not only as part of the construction contract, but as part of the DB members' tripartite agreements with the parties.

DB members must become and remain familiar with all aspects of the project by reading regular site reports, carrying out site inspections, and meeting with Employer and Contractor representatives, three or four times per year. This is an essential part of the function of Board members, and is a necessary preparation for informed engagement by

6 https://iccwbo.org/dispute-resolution-services/dispute-boards/standard-clauses/ (accessed 15 April 2021).

DB members in the project. These aspects of the DB members' role should be incorporated in the procedural rules.

The procedural rules for operation of a DB also need to provide for two different modes of activity undertaken by the Dispute Board. Each mode of operation has different requirements and makes different demands on the Board:

- Dispute avoidance, and
- Dispute resolution, if a dispute cannot be avoided.

26.2.4 Dispute avoidance

In "dispute avoidance mode", the Board's role is fulfilled by a flexible, informal format for meetings and communications. At their regular "without prejudice" meetings with the DB, the parties provide detailed reports on:

- Status of the project
- Actual and potential delays
- Variations
- Claims
- Potential issues of concern, and
- Future opportunities.

It is highly recommended that Senior Executives of the contracting parties attend all meetings. This ensures not only that they are aware of progress of the project and potential issues before they become disputes, but the Senior Executives can play a proactive role in interactions with the Dispute Board, and assist in maintaining a focus on the "big picture".

As part of its dispute avoidance role, the DB can provide an advisory opinion on a potential dispute, if both parties agree to refer it to the DB. The DB members are ideally placed to provide such an opinion, acting as experts, as they are already fully conversant with the Contract, the project and the issues. Such an advisory opinion can be produced speedily, with a minimum of formality, and does not bind the DB if the dispute is subsequently formally referred to it for a decision.

Although there may be significant documentation produced in connection with DB meetings, discussions and advisory opinions, all reports and communications produced during the DB's dispute avoidance activities are "without prejudice". This facilitates free and frank exchange between all parties, and ensures that neither contracting party will ultimately be disadvantaged by its position taken or documents produced without detailed consideration.

The process engaged in by the DB during its dispute avoidance activities has some similarities with mediation/non-binding expert determination:

- The DB's role includes promoting communication and assisting the parties to avoid entrenched positions
- The DB facilitates the parties to achieve their own resolution of contentious issues

- A "best for project" outcome is sought, i.e. "win-win" for both parties
- An advisory opinion of the DB does not prejudice the parties' contractual rights to initiate a formal dispute to be determined by the DB in accordance with the provisions of the Contract
- The parties themselves decide whether or not to implement any outcome proposed by the DB.

26.2.5 Dispute resolution

However, if, despite the DB's best efforts, a dispute between the parties cannot be avoided, the DB acts in "dispute resolution mode", where either party formally refers a dispute to it. Unlike the dispute advisory role where each contracting party must agree to refer a dispute to the DB for its opinion, both parties have the contractual right to refer a dispute to the DB independently.

In its resolution of a dispute formally referred to it, the DB acts somewhat more formally than in its dispute avoidance mode, to ensure that the parties are afforded procedural fairness. The process is commenced by the parties submitting details of their case with supporting documentation to the DB, which may convene a hearing at which evidence is adduced, and witnesses can be questioned by the DB.

Within a defined limited period of time, the DB produces a written decision on the dispute with detailed reasons. The submissions made to the DB and its decision can be used subsequently as evidence in litigation or arbitration if the DB's decision does not ultimately resolve the dispute.

The process engaged in by the DB during its dispute resolution activities has some similarities with expert determination/adjudication:

- There is a certain defined formality to proceedings
- The parties are afforded procedural fairness, in that they have a fair opportunity to present their case, rebut the case of their opponent and have a decision on the dispute handed down by fair, disinterested and impartial adjudicators
- Resolution of the dispute is based on the legal requirements of the Contract
- The DB's decision is in writing with detailed reasons
- Implementation of the DB's decision is carried out in accordance with the provisions of the Contract
- A party can seek enforcement of a binding DB decision as a contractual agreement through the Court.

The DB process of dispute resolution avoids the potential conflicts that can occur if an Arbitrator acts as a Mediator but is ultimately unsuccessful in avoiding an arbitration hearing. In the case of a DB decision, it is only finally binding if the parties accept it (DRB), or do not seek final resolution of their legal rights by arbitration or litigation (DAB). Thus, any "contamination" of the DB by its prior knowledge of the "without prejudice" discussions and communications during the dispute avoidance process does not prejudice the parties' contractual rights to have their dispute ultimately resolved by a Judge or Arbitrator, independent of the DB.

It should be apparent that there is only a distinction between a DRB and a DAB at the stage of implementation of a formal DB decision on a dispute:

- DRB: the DB's decision only becomes binding if both contracting parties agree to accept it
- DAB: the DB's decision is binding unless and until it is overturned by agreement or subsequent arbitration or litigation, consequent on one of the contracting parties serving a formal notice of dissatisfaction within the limited time provided for in the Contract. Such a DAB decision is referred to as provisionally binding.

26.2.6 Standard procedural rules

Procedural rules for the conduct of DB proceedings are issued by the following organisations:

- FIDIC[7]
- International Chamber of Commerce[8]
- American Arbitration Association[9]
- Dispute Resolution Board Foundation.[10]

The FIDIC Procedural Rules for a DAAB[11] cover the following issues:

- Informal assistance.
- Meetings with the parties and site visits.
- Timing and agenda of site visits.
- Attendance and organisation of site visits.
- Copies of documents furnished to the DAAB.
- Powers of the DAAB.
- Procedure for a dispute referred to the DAAB.
- Hearing of a dispute at the DAAB's option.
- Ambit of the DAAB's procedural powers for a hearing.
- Defined procedural powers of the DAAB in deciding a dispute.
- The process for the DAAB making its decision.
- Decision procedure in the event of a DAAB member's termination.
- Procedure for an objection and challenge to a DAAB member by a party.

Chapter 28 contains further details of the operation of a DAAB under the 2017 FIDIC rainbow suite.

---

7 Annex DAB/DAAB Procedural Rules, FIDIC rainbow suite of contracts.

8 https://iccwbo.org/dispute-resolution-services/dispute-boards/rules/ (accessed 15 April 2021).

9 https://www.adr.org/sites/default/files/document_repository/Construction_DRB_Operating_Procedures.pdf (accessed 15 April 2021).

10 DRBF, 'Dispute Review Board Specification' (2021) https://www.disputeboard.org (accessed 15 April 2021).

11 Annex Procedural Rules, FIDIC rainbow suite of contracts (2nd edn, 2017).

26.2.7 Tripartite agreements for a DB

As the Dispute Board members are not parties to the construction contract between the Employer and Contractor, it is necessary for each of the DB members to enter into a contract for their services. It is important that the members' independence of both contracting parties and its equal obligations to both are reflected in the contractual arrangements for the services of every DB member. Accordingly, it is appropriate for each DB member to enter into a contract jointly with the Employer and Contractor – a tripartite agreement.

As with other agreements for professional services in connection with dispute resolution by a third-party neutral, the tripartite agreement should define the scope of work for the DB member, his/her responsibilities, the duration of services, compensation and reimbursement for services, and legal relations. The tripartite agreement almost invariably will require that the DB member maintains confidentiality about the operations of the DB. Payment of the DB members invoices should be authorised by both contract parties, or separately paid in equal shares.

As with Adjudicators and Arbitrators, it is appropriate that a DB member have quasi-judicial immunity for anything s/he does in good faith in connection with the DB process. If the tripartite agreement did not provide such immunity for a DB member, it would suggest that the parties may hold her/him personally or professionally liable for his/her efforts to resolve the parties' disputes.

These principles are generally incorporated in tripartite agreements for DBs published by the following organisations:

- FIDIC[12]
- ICC[13]
- Dispute Resolution Board Foundation.[14]

26.3 Cost of Dispute Boards

The conventional wisdom in respect of three-person Dispute Boards is that they are more suited to large projects, say in excess of $50 m. Certainly, the not insignificant cost of engaging a team of three experienced Board members to provide ongoing regular services throughout the life of a project is a disincentive to implementation of a DB on lower cost projects.

This can, however, be mitigated by implementing a one-person DB for lower cost projects, as is now common in Australia. It is interesting to note that with the increasing use of DBs by major US Employers such as the California Department of Transportation, a higher proportion of DBs are now implemented on lower cost projects. The database on the DRBF website shows both the increasing number of DBs worldwide in recent years,

12 FIDIC rainbow suite of contracts (2nd edn, 2017) 'Dispute Avoidance/Adjudication Agreement' and 'General Conditions of Dispute Avoidance/Adjudication Agreement'.

13 ICC, "Model Dispute Board Member Agreement" https://iccwbo.org/dispute-resolution-services/dispute-boards/model-dispute-board-member-agreement/ (accessed 15 April 2021).

14 DRBF, "Dispute Review Board Agreement" (2021) https://www.disputeboard.org (accessed 15 April 2021).

and the higher proportion of those projects in the USD10–20 m and USD20–40 m contract price ranges.[15]

The known and predictable costs (or the perceived costs) of DBs frequently appear to be a stumbling block to their implementation.

The direct costs of DBs (i.e. the "external" costs of the DB over and above the costs of personnel involved in the project) usually comprise the following:

- A retainer for each member of the DB, typically 1–2 times their daily fee
- A daily fee per DB member for site meetings and dispute determinations, and
- Travel time and expenses.

In addition to these direct costs, there are indirect costs of the contract parties' employees' time in preparing for and participating in DB meetings. Arguably, many of these costs would be incurred in any event, in planning, project managing or negotiating issues with counterparts in the other contracting party's organisation.

Clearly, implementation of a DB involves a real and significant cost that is not present directly in contracts that do not use a DB. However, to put it in context, that cost is usually less (often considerably) than 0.25% of the final contract price. It is suggested that, in view of the track record of DBs as effective dispute avoidance mechanisms, this cost should be viewed as an "insurance cost" paid to dramatically reduce the risk of a serious and costly dispute.

We are all familiar with the concept of insurance: we pay a fixed known amount each year to protect us from the (potentially large) costs of a known risk materialising. We know that, statistically, there is a relatively low probability of the risk event occurring, but that, if it does occur, the costs are likely to be very high. We understand that paying the known amount of an insurance policy will protect us from the indeterminate and potentially financially crippling costs that could occur if the risk event occurred. Usually, we are thankful in each year if the risk event did not occur, and that we did not have to make a claim on our insurance policy. Most of us would not consider that the amount we paid for the insurance policy was a waste of money because the risk event did not occur. Typically, we regard the insurance costs as part of the cost of doing business, as this enables greater certainty in planning and budgeting our activities (and projects).

It is suggested that the same approach should be taken to the cost of implementation of DBs in construction projects, and that it is fallacious to suggest that a particular DB was a waste of money because "it never had to do anything", i.e. it never had to resolve a dispute. In the writer's view, it is those projects with a DB that did not have a dispute that provide the greatest justification for the decision to implement a DB, and to pay the "insurance cost" of maintaining the DB's ongoing involvement during the life of the project.

If a DB is effective in avoiding disputes in a major project, its cost is likely to be good value for money "insurance". This can be demonstrated as follows by considering the entire population of construction contracts. It has been suggested that in almost 10% of construction projects in Australia, between 8% and 10% of the total project cost is legal

15 https://www.disputeboard.org (accessed 15 April 2021).

cost, and 50% of all legal cost is expended in connection with disputes.[16] Using the methodology commonly used in pricing contract risks at the tender stage, the cost of the risk of disputes in a construction contract could therefore be calculated as follows:

> 10% (probability of a dispute) × 8% (legal costs of 10% of projects) × 50% (proportion of legal costs typically expended in a dispute) = 0.4% × project cost.

That is, without considering any other factors, the risk cost of a dispute on a "typical" construction contract is at least 0.4% of the project cost.

However, as with any risk event, a dispute may occur, or it may not. If a dispute does not occur, there will be no legal costs incurred in relation to it. If a dispute does occur, the legal costs may range from negligible to 8–10% of the project cost (and sometimes significantly more). In that event, the statistical risk cost of 0.4% of project cost for disputes becomes meaningless, and is likely to be a substantial underestimate of the actual costs.

In the light of these considerations, the costs of implementing a DB which has the effect of avoiding disputes makes economic sense from an "insurance" perspective. Paying an amount of, say, 0.15% of the project cost for a DB as "insurance" makes economic sense if it eliminates the need for, on average, the risk cost of 0.4% of the project cost for disputes. It makes even more sense in those terms if it reduces to a minimal level the not insignificant risks of legal costs ultimately exceeding 10% of the project price.

The DRBF 2019 Dispute Board Manual contains a very helpful chapter on the costs of Dispute Boards detailing DB cost components, types of DB fee structures and typical fee structures and rates in a number of jurisdictions: USA, Australia, NZ and the Pacific Islands, Latin America and for FIDIC contracts. A general method of estimating DB fees is given with examples, and recommendations are made for payment arrangements.[17]

26.4 Dispute Boards in Australia

To the knowledge of the Dispute Resolution Board Australasia Inc. (Region 3 of the DRBF) (**DRBA**), in the period 1987–2020 there were 101 contracts in Australia which implemented a DB in one form or another, with an approximate value of AUD57 b. Details of these contracts and their DBs are in a table on the DRBA website.[18] The range of contract values (excluding inflation) has been from AUD22 m to over AUD8 b.

The DB concept can be and has been used with virtually any form of standard or bespoke contract in Australia. Since 2006 the following contract types have had DBs:

- Design and construct
- Construct only
- Design, construct (operate) and maintain
- Maintenance
- Management contract.

16 Peter Chapman, 'Dispute Boards for Major Infrastructure Projects' (Paper presented at Seminar on The Use of Dispute Boards in Australia, Queensland, 30 November 2006).

17 DRBF, *Dispute Board Manual A Guide to Best Practices and Procedures* (2019) Chapter 11 https://drbf.memberclicks.net/dispute-board-manual (accessed 15 April 2021).

18 https://www.drbf.org.au/projects-members/australia (accessed 15 April 2021).

Anecdotal evidence is that the majority of DBs in Australia have not been required to formally determine any disputes. Of those disputes formally referred to a DB, all were resolved within the DB process, and none required ultimate litigation or arbitration. Further, the contract values of these projects generally remained within the Employer's budget.

26.5 Benefits of DBs

It is suggested that DBs have the following dispute-prevention benefits:

- Tend to promote bilateral agreement.
- Facilitate positive relations between the contracting parties.
- Facilitate open communications.
- Facilitate trust and cooperation.
- Minimise aggregation of claims until late in or at the conclusion of the project.
- Minimise contractual posturing.
- Encourage identification, evaluation and dealing with claims in a prompt, business-like manner.
- Focus on early identification and analysis, and prompt resolution of issues which could fester into disputes.

It is suggested that DBs have the following dispute-resolution benefits:

- A high-resolution rate for disputes referred to them.
- An impartial forum in which each contracting party can present its case and "have its day in court".
- An informal and rational basis for resolution of a dispute that can provide political cover for personnel in the contracting parties.
- Parties are normally predisposed to DB proceedings, because of their familiarity with the process, its informality and their respect for the DB members.
- DBs reduce transactional costs, both legal fees and consulting fees.
- DBs reduce lost productivity time by enabling dispute resolution in "real time".
- DBs produce better informed decisions in minimum time because of their intimate familiarity with the contract, the project and the participants. And
- Tenderers may submit lower bids because of a lower bid premium for the risk of disputes.

26.6 Reasons for the high success rate of DBs

DBs provide an impartial, informed, rational mechanism for resolving issues quickly. DB members have knowledge and experience with:

- The relevant design and construction issues
- Interpretation and application of contract documents
- The general process of resolving disputes, and
- A track record with the specific project at-hand.

Both parties are favourably disposed to accept the DRB's recommendations or not dispute the DAB's determinations since the parties themselves have selected and approved the particular Board members, and have confidence in and respect them.

The parties themselves select or approve all the DB members, and have confidence in their skills and experience as facilitators and dispute resolvers.

The DB process is cost effective when compared with formal arbitration and litigation, especially with respect to time.

Disputed matters can frequently be scheduled, heard, recommended and resolved within the time it may take to select an arbitration panel or file a statement of claim in court.

Issues are heard by the DB just after an impasse is reached whilst the facts and circumstances are still fresh in the minds of the participants. Thus, better informed resolutions are possible since eyewitnesses are still available, and the DB can actually see the problem and its impacts, if any, in the field.

DB hearings are held in real time and transactional costs are thereby minimised.

Expensive and time-consuming legal and consultant expenses are reduced if not eliminated.

Importantly to the Employer and Contractor, internal management time and associated costs are greatly reduced or done away with.

CHAPTER 27

The commercial value of Dispute Boards under FIDIC contracts[1]

27.1 Introduction

The FIDIC rainbow suite contracts[2] are the most widely used international construction contracts, particularly in eastern Europe, the Middle East and Africa. Since 1999, these contracts have provided for the appointment of a Dispute Adjudication Board (DAB)[3]/Dispute Board (DB)[4]/Dispute Avoidance/Adjudication Board (DAAB)[5] that can adjudicate disputes more speedily and economically than arbitration.[6] This innovation removed the Engineer's[7] role as initial dispute adjudicator, and thereby addressed the perceived lack of independence of the Engineer, appointed by the Employer.[8] Notwithstanding the detailed process of dispute resolution in the modern FIDIC contracts, there has been some doubt as to their efficacy, particularly following several judgments in Singapore. Recent judgments, reviewed in this chapter, have provided welcome clarity on the mandatory requirement for a DB decision, and its enforceability.

The commercial value of DBs is potentially far greater than that arising from their role as adjudicators of formal disputes. A standing DB, implemented at the start of a project and meeting regularly with the contracting parties during the design and construction

1 This chapter is an edited and updated version of the paper published in: Donald Charrett, 'The Commercial Value of Dispute Boards under FIDIC Contracts' (2015) 1.3 *Turkish Commercial Law Review* 205. It is reproduced by kind permission of Turkish Commercial Law Review.

2 FIDIC Conditions of Contract for Construction for Building and Engineering Works Designed by the Employer (1st edn, 1999)/(2nd edn, 2017) (Red Book); FIDIC Conditions of Contract for Construction MDB Harmonised Edition for Building and Engineering Works Designed by the Employer (MDB Harmonised Edition 2010) (Pink Book); FIDIC Conditions of Contract for Plant and Design-Build for Electrical and Mechanical Plant and for Building and Engineering Works, designed by the Contractor (1st edn, 1999)/(2nd edn, 2017) (Yellow Book); FIDIC Conditions of Contract for EPC/Turnkey Projects (1st edn, 1999)/(2nd edn, 2017) (Silver Book).

3 1999 1st edns of the Red, Yellow and Silver Books.

4 Pink Book.

5 2017 2nd edns of the Red, Yellow and Silver Books.

6 The term DB used in this chapter includes a DAB (1st edns of the rainbow suite), and a DAAB (2nd edns of the rainbow suite).

7 The Engineer is a defined term under the Red, Pink and Yellow Books, and is the person who administers the Contract on behalf of the Employer. The definition in sub-clause 1.1.2.4 of the 1st edns is:

> "Engineer" means the person appointed by the Employer to act as the Engineer for the purposes of the Contract and named in the Appendix to Tender [Red & Yellow Books]/Contract Data [Pink Book], or other person appointed from time to time by the Employer and notified to the Contractor under Sub-Clause 3.4.

8 In this chapter, capitalised terms not otherwise defined in this book are as defined in the FIDIC rainbow suite of contracts.

 DOI: 10.4324/9781003206897-30

phases, is able to assist them to avoid disputes. The procedural rules for a standing DB in the FIDIC 1999 Red Book and Pink Book enable it to advise the Parties on an informal "without prejudice" basis on potential issues in an endeavour to promote a "best for project" agreed solution, by providing a non-binding advisory opinion. This role of assisting the parties to avoid disputes has been considerably strengthened in the 2017 editions of the rainbow suite by providing for a standing Dispute Avoidance/Adjudication Board for all three books, with enhanced procedural rules to promote dispute avoidance.

The track record of standing DBs around the world is that they are very effective in helping the parties avoid formal disputes; however, if disputes eventuate, in adjudicating an outcome according to the contract and the law in a timely and cost-effective manner.

This chapter looks briefly at the costs of DBs, often advanced as the reason they are not implemented under FIDIC contracts. These costs are reviewed in the light of the significant risk cost of disputes and this writer concludes that the "insurance" cost provides clear commercial value to the parties in an international construction contract.

27.2 Dispute Boards under FIDIC contracts

In the FIDIC contracts, a DB consists of one or three suitably qualified persons, appointed by agreement of the contracting parties in accordance with sub-clause 20.2 (1999 editions) or sub-clause 21.1 (2017 editions) of the General Conditions in each of the rainbow suite contracts. The members of the DB are required to be independent of the Parties, and to have no financial interest in the Parties or the Engineer. Each DB member enters into a tripartite agreement with the Employer and Contractor that contains stringent obligations on the member to be, and be seen to be, independent and impartial.[9]

The 1999 first editions of the rainbow suite contracts provide for two types of DB – a standing DB in the 1999 Red Book and 2010 Pink Book, and an *ad hoc* DB in the 1999 Yellow Book and 1999 Silver Book. The fundamental difference between them arises from the date of the appointment of their members. In a standing DB, the members are to be appointed by a specified date, which is 28 days after the Commencement Date.[10] By contrast, an *ad hoc* DB under the 1999 Yellow Book or 1999 Silver Book is to be appointed within 28 days "after a Party gives notice to the other Party of its intention to refer a dispute to the DAB".[11] Both standing and *ad hoc* DBs are appointed to adjudicate a dispute (of any kind whatsoever) arising between the Parties "in connection with, or arising out of, the Contract or the execution of the Works, including any dispute as to any certificate, determination, instruction, opinion or valuation of the Engineer" (Silver Book: Employer).[12]

The General Conditions in each of the 1999 Red, Yellow and Silver Books and the 2010 Pink Book contains an Appendix "General Conditions of Dispute Adjudication Agreement", to which is attached an Annex that contains procedural rules on the operation of the DB. The Red Book and the Pink Book contain the following nine rules:

9 General Conditions of Dispute Adjudication Agreement – Red, Yellow and Silver Books; General Conditions of Dispute Agreement – Pink Book.

10 Appendix to Tender (1999 Red Book); Particular Conditions – Part A: Contract Data (2010 Pink Book).

11 1999 Silver Book, sub-clause 20.2; 1999 Yellow Book, sub-clause 20.2.

12 1999 Silver Book, sub-clause 20.4; 1999 Yellow Book, sub-clause 20.4.

1. Intervals between DB site visits
2. Timing and agenda of site visits
3. Attendance and organisation of site visits
4. Copies of documents furnished to DB
5. Procedure for dispute referred to DB
6. Hearing of a dispute at DB's option
7. Ambit of DB procedural powers for hearing
8. Defined procedural powers of DB in deciding a dispute
9. Process for DB making its decision.

The first three of these rules relate to the DB's "standing" role, in which it is required to become and remain familiar with the Contract and the Works, including by regular site visits (typically at 3–4-month intervals). The remaining six rules relate to the DB's role as Adjudicator of a formal dispute and these rules (numbered 4–9 above) also comprise the procedural rules for a DB under the 1999 Yellow and 1999 Silver Books.

A standing DB is in a unique position to assist the parties to avoid disputes: it comprises one or three experienced members independent of the parties, familiar with the Contract, the Works, the personnel and the technical and contractual issues that typically arise during the execution of construction projects. By holding "without prejudice" meetings with the parties, a standing DB can facilitate resolution of issues on a "best for project" basis that is acceptable to the parties. The DB will employ mediation type skills in such a role, and the parties are free to agree to a "non-legal" solution. Many DBs function exclusively in this "dispute avoidance" mode and are never called on to adjudicate a formal dispute.

Clearly, an *ad hoc* DB that is only implemented after a formal dispute has arisen is unable to act in dispute avoidance mode and is confined to adjudication of a dispute in accordance with the Contract and the law. FIDIC has recognised the importance of the DB's role in dispute avoidance in the 2017 second editions of the Red, Yellow and Silver Books. The DAAB Procedural Rules in those books comprise the following rules:

1. Objectives
2. Avoidance of disputes
3. Meetings and site visits
4. Communications and documentation
5. Powers of the DAAB
6. Disputes
7. Hearings
8. The DAAB's decision
9. In the event of termination of the DAA Agreement
10. Objection procedure (against a DAAB Member)
11. Challenge procedure (if a DAAB Member objected to does not withdraw)

The DB adjudication process detailed in the FIDIC contracts provides for a much speedier and more economical dispute resolution process than arbitration. The DB is required to give its decision, with reasons, within 84 days after a dispute has been referred to it. That decision is binding and both parties must give effect to it. However, it may be a "rough and ready" process due to insufficient time to review in depth all of the relevant documents, engage expert witnesses etc. The independence, experience and expertise of the

DB members, and their reasoned decision, may produce an outcome that will be accepted by the Parties. If neither Party serves a notice of dissatisfaction within 28 days after the DB has handed down its decision, that decision becomes final.

Provided that the DB is not constituted by the Engineer, this adjudication process in large measure addresses one of the major contractor criticisms of the traditional role of the Engineer, by removing his/her dispute resolution function.[13] In earlier editions of FIDIC contracts, the Engineer not only certified the Contractor's entitlements under the Contract, but also in the first instance adjudicated on any disputes arising from his own certifications. When coupled with the fact that the Engineer was engaged by the Employer, and acted as his agent in many functions under the Contract, it is not surprising that the impartiality of the Engineer as adjudicator of disputes arising from his own determinations has long been questioned.[14] Absent a DB to adjudicate on disputes over the Engineer's certification, the Contractor's only remedy was (and is) to embark on lengthy and costly arbitration.

One of the important features of a DB is that it can provide an independent, reasoned and economical resolution of a dispute arising from an Engineer's determination in a reasonably short time frame. Given the long execution time of many major construction projects, it is in both parties' interests to resolve contentious issues as they arise (at least provisionally), and focus on progressing the Works, rather than preparing for a long and detailed arbitration.

Notwithstanding the DB's reasoning in its binding decision, a party may not be satisfied that the decision is correct. In this case, the dissatisfied party may issue a notice of dissatisfaction (**NOD**) within 28 days of the DB decision, with a view to the issue being finally decided by arbitration. Such arbitration may be deferred until after completion of the Works, although it need not be.

The parties have, what is in effect, a "cooling off" period of 56 days after the NOD has been issued (28 days under the 2017 second editions), during which they "shall attempt to settle the dispute amicably before the commencement of arbitration". There is no contractual requirement for the form of such amicable settlement and, even if it has not been attempted, arbitration may still be commenced after the 56- or 28-day period. This writer considers that the "cooling-off" period is a worthwhile pause before the commencement of a (frequently) long and expensive arbitration: the parties have the benefit of the DB's reasoned decision that provides an independent view of the legal merits of each party's position – a useful starting point for any commercial negotiation. It is worth noting that the decisions of DBs in the United States (referred to as Dispute Resolution Boards) are generally advisory and not binding; nevertheless, in a large majority of cases the parties negotiate an acceptable resolution without resorting to arbitration or litigation.

13 The Guidance for the Preparation of Particular Conditions in the 1999 Red and Yellow Books suggest that, as an alternative to independent member(s) of the Dispute Board, the Engineer could be the sole member of the Dispute Board and make the pre-arbitral decisions that have traditionally been part of the Engineer's role in common-law countries. For the reasons given above, this writer does not consider this to be consonant with the modern approach to the Engineer's role, who should not be seen to be a witness and judge in his own cause.

14 "We have no reason to hope that he will approach the question without being grievously fettered and grievously embarrassed by the fact that he has already decided, and that his professional character is involved in upholding the decision." *Nuttall v Manchester Corporation*, (1899) *Hudson's Building Contracts* (4th edn, 1892) Vol. II 203 per Mathew J.

The FIDIC provisions on the DB, therefore, do not compromise the parties' right to a final and binding resolution of their dispute that is enforceable in most jurisdictions. The Red, Yellow and Silver Books provide for international arbitration under the rules of the International Chamber of Commerce, thus (usually) ensuring that the arbitral decision is enforceable in any country that is a signatory to the *New York Convention.* The arbitration is a hearing *de novo* and the parties are not limited to the evidence or arguments previously put before the DB or to the reasons for dissatisfaction given in the NOD. The DB decision is admissible in evidence, although clearly the arbitral tribunal is not bound by it or its reasoning.

27.3 Is a Dispute Board decision a pre-requisite to referring a dispute to arbitration?

27.3.1 Relevant provisions in the FIDIC contracts

Notwithstanding that the 1999 Red Book and the 2010 Pink Book provide for a standing DB and the 1999 Yellow and 1999 Silver Books for an *ad hoc* DB, the following extracts from clause 20 are worded identically in the 1999 Red, Yellow and Silver Books, and with minor changes in the wording, to the same effect in the Pink Book.

Sub-clause 20.2 in the 1999 Red, Yellow and Silver Books provides that: "*Disputes shall be adjudicated by a DAB* in accordance with subclause 20.4 [Obtaining Dispute Adjudication Board's Decision]" (emphasis added). Sub-clause 20.4 in the 1999 Red, Yellow and Silver Books provides that:

> If a dispute (of any kind whatsoever) arises between the Parties in connection with, or arising out of, the Contract or the execution of the Works, ... *either party may refer the dispute* in writing to the DAB for its decision ... *The decision shall be binding on both Parties* who shall promptly give effect to it unless and until it shall be revised in an amicable settlement or an arbitral award as described below. ... If either Party is dissatisfied with the DAB's decision, then either Party may, within 28 days after receiving the decision, give notice of its dissatisfaction. ... neither Party shall be entitled to commence arbitration of a dispute unless a notice of dissatisfaction has been given in accordance with this subclause. If the DAB has given its decision as to the matter in dispute to both Parties, and no notice of dissatisfaction has been given by either Party within 28 days after it received the DAB's decision, *then the decision shall become final and binding upon both Parties.*
>
> *[emphasis added]*

Sub-clause 20.6 in the 1999 Red, Yellow and Silver Books provides that: "Unless settled amicably, any dispute in respect of which the DAB's decision (if any) has not become final and binding shall be finally settled by international arbitration." Sub-clause 20.8 in the 1999 Red, Yellow and Silver Books provides that:

> If a dispute arises between the Parties in connection with, or arising out of, the Contract or the execution of the Works and *there is no DAB in place*, whether by reason of the expiry of the DAB's appointment or otherwise:
>
> (a) subclause 20.4 [Obtaining Dispute Adjudication Board's Decision] and subclause 20.5 [Amicable Settlement] shall not apply, and
> (b) *the dispute may be referred directly to arbitration* under subclause 20.6 [Arbitration].
>
> *[emphasis added]*

Sub-clauses 21.1, 21.4, 21.6 and 21.8 in the 2017 second editions of the Red, Yellow and Silver Books contain wording to similar effect as the above clauses, albeit that there are some additional procedural steps, and a more prescriptive procedure in respect of obtaining the DAAB's decision. The remainder of this chapter refers to the provisions of the 1999 first editions. Chapter 28 discusses the changes between the 1999 and 2017 FIDIC contracts relating to DBs.

Whilst sub-clause 20.4 requires a DB decision on a dispute and a Notice of Dissatisfaction with that decision within 28 days as a prerequisite to referring the dispute to arbitration, sub-clause 20.8 contemplates referring a dispute directly to arbitration where there is no DB in place. In view of the combination of mandatory and permissive text in the above extracts ("shall" and "may"), this divergence raises the question as to whether a party can bypass the DB process and refer a dispute directly to arbitration if it does not cooperate in the appointment of a DB.

27.3.2 Case law

In *Doosan Babcock Ltd v Comercializadora de Equipos y Materiales Mabe*,[15] the Contractor sought an injunction in connection with an arbitration to prevent the Employer from having recourse to the performance securities. No DAB had been appointed under the FIDIC Contract, and Edwards-Stewart J concluded, without analysis, that sub-clause 20.8 applied: "By clause 20.8, if no DAB has been appointed, the dispute can be referred directly to arbitration. That is the position here."[16]

This issue was subsequently addressed in detail by Edwards-Stewart J in the case of *Peterborough City Council v Enterprise Managed Services Ltd*.[17] In the context of an amended FIDIC Silver Book Contract, he determined that the parties were required to obtain a DAB decision on their dispute before it could be referred to a final determination in court (the standard FIDIC General Conditions had been amended by the substitution of arbitration with litigation in sub-clause 20.8). The decision was made in the particular circumstances of an amended Silver Book Contract and the judge's reasoning was influenced by the fact that an *ad hoc*, not a standing, DAB was to be appointed.

The issue was also addressed in the Supreme Court of Switzerland, following an arbitral tribunal's partial award that it had jurisdiction to hear a dispute notwithstanding that a DAB had not been appointed.[18] The Employer sought to have the partial award set aside on the grounds of lack of jurisdiction, arguing that DAB proceedings must be completed before arbitration could be initiated. The court construed the dispute resolution provisions in the FIDIC contract as a whole under Swiss law, looking beyond the literal meaning of the contract to seek to establish the parties' real and common intention. The Court determined that submitting a dispute to a DAB is a mandatory requirement, rather than an option. It considered that "shall" in sub-clause 20.2 is directory, and "may" in sub-clause 20.4 simply means that it is open to either party to initiate DAB proceedings. In respect of the provision in sub-clause 20.8 that a dispute may be referred directly to arbitration if "there is no DAB in place", the Court considered that this cannot refer to the

15 [2013] EWHC 3010 (TCC).
16 Ibid [2].
17 [2014] EWHC 3193 (TCC).
18 *A. SA v B. SA* [2014] Swiss Federal Supreme Court 4A_124/2014.

situation where there is no DAB in place when a dispute arises, inevitably the case when the Contract provides for an *ad hoc* DAB.

Notwithstanding that the Court found that referral of a dispute to a DAB was a pre-condition to arbitration, it accepted that there are exceptions to this requirement, arising from sub-clause 20.8 and the general principle of good faith, to be assessed on a case-by-case basis. The circumstances of this case included that the attempt to constitute an *ad hoc* DAB had only begun after completion of the Works, the DAB was not operational 15 months after the initial referral of the dispute, and the party's failure to sign the DAB agreement meant that the DAB was not "in place" within the meaning of sub-clause 20.8. Accordingly, the Court concluded that the fact that there was no DAB decision was not fatal, and it rejected the Employer's challenge to the arbitral tribunal's jurisdiction.

This decision was based on Swiss civil law that entails a more subjective approach to construction of contract terms than under the common law. Nevertheless, it is suggested that the court's reasoning would generally be applicable under the objective approach to construction of contract terms in common law jurisdictions also. This observation supports the view that, in many aspects of construction law, civil law and common law, courts will arrive at a similar conclusion, albeit via different routes[19] (see Chapter 35).

A number of recently reported ICC arbitration cases also generally conclude that it is mandatory to refer disputes to a DB prior to arbitration.[20]

27.4 A Dispute Board decision is (provisionally) binding

27.4.1 Relevant provisions in the FIDIC contracts

As noted above, sub-clause 20.4 contains the following provisions in relation to the enforceability of a DAB decision:

> The decision shall be binding on both Parties who shall promptly give effect to it unless and until it shall be revised in an amicable settlement or an arbitral award as described below. … If the DAB has given its decision as to the matter in dispute to both Parties, and no notice of dissatisfaction has been given by either Party within 28 days after it received the DAB's decision, then the decision shall become final and binding upon both Parties.

Taken in isolation of other provisions of clause 20, the above extracts state unequivocally that a DAB decision is *binding*; if no notice of dissatisfaction is given within 28 days, it becomes *final and binding*. If notice of dissatisfaction is given within 28 days, the decision remains binding, but it is *provisionally binding*, i.e. it is binding "unless and until it shall be revised in an amicable settlement or an arbitral award".

If a Party fails to comply with a binding DAB decision, sub-clause 20.7 provides that the other Party can refer that noncompliance directly to arbitration. However, the situation in respect of a Party's failure to comply with a provisionally binding DAB decision is not so clear from the provisions of clause 20, demonstrated by the long saga of litigation between PT Perusahaan Gas Negara (Persero) TBK and CRW Joint Operation in the Singapore High Court and the Singapore Court of Appeal between 2010 and 2015.

19 Donald Charrett, "A Common Law of Construction Contracts – or Vive la Différence?" (2012) 29(1) *International Construction Law Review* 23.

20 ICC Cases 14431, 16155, 16262 and 16765, reported in 1 *ICC Dispute Resolution Bulletin* (2015).

27.4.2 PT Perusahaan Gas Negara (Persero) TBK (PGN) and CRW joint operation (CRW)

PGN is a public-listed State-owned company established under the laws of the Republic of Indonesia. **CRW** is a tripartite joint operation established under the laws of the Republic of Indonesia, comprising three Indonesian contractor companies.

PGN entered into a contract with CRW to design, procure, install, test and pre-commission a gas pipeline project in Indonesia (the **PGN Contract**). The PGN Contract adopted the General Conditions of the 1999 FIDIC Red Book.

27.4.3 2008 DAB

A dispute arose between the Parties regarding 13 different Variation proposals issued by CRW to PGN. The dispute was referred to a DAB pursuant to sub-clause 20.4. The DAB issued a decision in favour of CRW for the sum of USD17.3 m.

27.4.4 2009 arbitration

PGN issued a NOD alleging the amount awarded by the DAB was excessive and refused to pay CRW the adjudicated amount. CRW filed a request for arbitration pursuant to sub-clause 20.6 with the ICC. The seat of the arbitration was Singapore.

CRW referred to arbitration not the underlying dispute that formed the basis of the DAB decision (the first dispute), but rather the issue of whether PGN was obliged to comply with the DAB decision and pay the sum of USD17.3 m (the second dispute). CRW sought a declaration that PGN had an immediate obligation to pay the adjudicated sum, in order to give prompt effect to the DAB's provisionally binding decision.

The arbitral tribunal issued a final award in favour of CRW, entitling CRW to immediate payment of the sum of US$17.3 m. In reaching this conclusion, the arbitral tribunal found that PGN was not entitled in the arbitration to request the arbitral tribunal to open up, review and revise the DAB's decision as it had not submitted a counterclaim in the arbitration.

27.4.5 2010 Singapore High Court

CRW sought to enforce the final award in Singapore and an order of court giving effect to CRW's application was made (the enforcement order). PGN filed a separate application in the Singapore High Court to have the enforcement order and final award set aside.

In *PT Perusahaan Gas Negara (Persero) TBK v CRW Joint Operation*,[21] the Singapore High Court set aside the final award under the *Singapore International Arbitration Act* (***IAA***)[22] on the basis that:

21 [2010] SGHC 202.
22 Cap 143A.

- The majority members of the tribunal had issued a final award on the second dispute even though that dispute had not been referred to the DAB in accordance with the provisions set out in the Contract.
- Even if the second dispute was referable to arbitration, the Contract did not entitle the arbitral tribunal to make the DAB's decision final without first hearing the parties on the merits of the decision.

27.4.6 2011 Singapore Court of Appeal

In *CRW Joint Operation v PT Perusahaan Gas Negara (Persero) TBK*,[23] the Singapore Court of Appeal upheld the High Court decision to set aside the final award issued by the majority members of the arbitral tribunal under the *IAA*. The Court of Appeal held that the scope of the arbitral tribunal's jurisdiction was defined by sub-clause 20.6 of the PGN Contract and the terms of reference of the arbitration.

The Court of Appeal dismissed CRW's application on the basis that the majority members of the arbitral tribunal had exceeded their jurisdiction and breached the rules of natural justice by failing to review the merits of the DAB's decision and afford PGN the opportunity to defend its position.

The Court of Appeal held that it was plain that a reference to arbitration under sub-clause 20.6 of the Contract in respect of a "binding but non final DAB decision" is clearly in the form of a rehearing so that the entirety of the parties' disputes can be resolved afresh and, therefore, the majority members had not issued their final award in accordance with sub-clause 20.6 of the Contract. The Court of Appeal noted that whilst the DAB's decision was enforceable under a partial award, the subject matter of the DAB decision was required to be opened up, reviewed and revised by the arbitral tribunal in the *same arbitration* in accordance with sub-clause 20.6 of the 1999 Red Book.

The Court of Appeal noted the majority members of the tribunal should have made an interim award in favour of CRW for the amount assessed by the DAB and then proceeded to hear the parties' substantive dispute afresh before making a final award. Accordingly, the Court of Appeal held that the final award was not issued in accordance with sub-clause 20.6 of the PGN Contract.

27.4.7 2011 arbitration

CRW commenced a second arbitration, following the guidance provided by the Court of Appeal. CRW placed both the first dispute and the second dispute before the tribunal.

The tribunal issued an "interim or partial" award compelling compliance with the DAB's 2008 decision. The tribunal decided unanimously that the DAB decision was binding, even though PGN had issued a NOD. The majority of the tribunal determined that CRW was entitled to enforce the DAB decision by way of an interim award which was made, ordering PGN to "promptly pay" CRW "pending the final resolution of the parties' dispute raised in these proceedings".

23 [2011] SGCA 33.

27.4.8 2013 Singapore High Court

PGN refused to pay CRW the amount of the interim award. CRW sought and obtained an enforcement order from the Singapore High Court. PGN filed a summons to set aside the enforcement order.

In *PT Perusahaan Gas Negara (Persero) TBK v CRW Joint Venture Operation*,[24] the Court considered the provisions of the DAB and the arbitration provisions in the Contract in detail (sub-clauses 20.4–20.7 of the Red Book), which were largely unamended from the Red Book standard.

The Court considered whether the first dispute and the second dispute were in fact one dispute or two. If there were two disputes, the effect would be that the second dispute and the first dispute would be decided in separate proceedings. This would mean that it would be necessary for every dispute that was to be referred to arbitration to be preceded by a DAB decision in respect of that dispute. The result would be that once an Employer serves a notice of dissatisfaction, the Contractor would have to refer the second dispute to the DAB before it could proceed to arbitration, resulting in a never-ending loop. Clearly, such a result would conflict with the accepted intention of the Contract to implement the DAB's decision pending final resolution of the issues, thereby preserving the cash flow of the Contractor.

By contrast, in the "one dispute" approach, the reference to "dispute" in the DAB clause is intended to mean only a "first dispute", rather than a dispute about the dispute-resolution regime. It follows that the failure to pay the amount determined as due by the DAB can be considered to be an aspect of the first dispute and does not in itself need to be referred to the DAB for a decision before it is arbitrated.

The Court accepted the "one dispute" approach. The Court noted that this was the approach adopted by CRW in the 2011 arbitration.

The Court took the view that the award, although expressed as "Interim", was final and binding on its subject matter and, therefore, compliant with the *IAA*. The subject matter of the award was the right to be paid immediately (i.e. the second dispute), not the DAB's 2008 decision (i.e. the first dispute). The Court noted that the award was not provisional in the sense that it would not be "varied", "amended" or "revoked" at a future stage. If the final decision on the first dispute was that a different (or no) sum was payable by PGN, then the appropriate accounting exercise would be set out in the final award on the first dispute. The Court dismissed PGN's application to set aside the Interim award.

27.4.9 2015 Singapore Court of Appeal

In May 2015, the majority of the Singapore Court of Appeal dismissed PGN's appeal.[25]

PGN's appeal was based on two arguments:

1. The 2011 Interim award is inconsistent with s 19B of the *IAA* because it is an award that only has interim finality.

24 [2014] SGHC 146.

25 *PT Perusahaan Gas Negara (Persero) TBK v CRW Joint Operation* [2015] SGCA 30.

2. The effect of clause 20.4 of the PGN Contract is that the DAB decision ceases to be binding as soon as the arbitral tribunal makes any award on the parties' underlying dispute.

The Court of Appeal comprehensively dismissed all of PGN's submissions on its two arguments, based on a careful construction of the relevant contractual terms. The Court of Appeal dismissed PGN's first argument because it failed to appreciate the distinct contractual obligation of sub-clause 20.4 for the parties to comply promptly with a DAB decision. That obligation applies irrespective of whether or not the DAB decision is subsequently revised or opened up. It also applies whether or not the arbitral tribunal eventually concludes that the receiving party is entitled to a different amount from that awarded by the DAB:

> Without derogating from the obligation of the parties to immediately implement and give effect to the DAB's decision, an arbitral tribunal may, usually at a significantly later point in time (and only if the parties fail to settle their differences over the DAB's decision), open up and revise the DAB's decision. In doing so, the arbitral tribunal would be considering a conceptually distinct question, namely, the state of the final accounts between the parties.[26]

The issuance of a NOD does not and cannot displace the binding nature of a DAB decision or the parties' concomitant obligation to promptly give effect to and implement it. The non-issuance of a NOD within 28 days means that the DAB decision becomes *final* as well as binding and an arbitral tribunal does not have jurisdiction to consider the merits of the decision. The Court of Appeal determined that it was unnecessary to refer a dispute over the "binding" effect of this DAB decision back to the DAB to enable it to be referred to an arbitral tribunal.

The key to the Court of Appeal's reasoning was as follows:

- There was an inherent premise embedded in the DAB's decision that the adjudicated sum (i.e. the sum that the DAB determined was payable) was payable *forthwith*.
- If, for any reason, the DAB had intended that its decision ordering payment should only take effect later, it would have had to make this explicit.
- "The point, in essence, is that dissatisfaction expressed in an NOD already inherently extends to the requirement that payment of the adjudicated amount be made forthwith, and there is nothing further to be referred back to the DAB."[27]
- "Given the purpose and context of the DAB scheme, it would not be commercially sensible to interpret cl 20 as requiring the receiving party to satisfy the conditions precedent in cll 20.4 and 20.5 before it can refer a dispute over the paying party's non-compliance with a binding but non-final DAB decision to arbitration."[28]

Importantly, in respect of the following issues, the Court of Appeal respectfully disagreed with the 2011 Court of Appeal decision:

26 Ibid [54].
27 Ibid [66].
28 Ibid.

- There is no requirement that all differences between the parties must be settled in a single arbitration. It is possible to refer the dispute over the paying party's failure to promptly pay the adjudicated sum to a separate arbitration.
- PGN's submissions on the merits of the DAB decision were not a defence to the claim for immediate payment of the adjudicated amount.
- The 2009 arbitral tribunal was correct to limit its final award to giving prompt effect to the DAB decision and to decline to review the merits of that decision.

27.4.10 Conclusions on enforcing a provisionally binding DAB decision

The 2015 Singapore Court of Appeal judgment is an important outcome for the application of the 1999 FIDIC DAB and arbitral processes. The carefully reasoned majority judgment confirms various academic writings on the intention behind the FIDIC DAB provisions and provides clarity on issues that have vexed arbitral tribunals, such as the ability to render a final award on payment pursuant to a provisionally binding DAB decision.[29]

A DAB decision must be complied with promptly, even if a NOD is submitted and a party wishes to dispute the merits of the decision. The failure to promptly pay an amount in a DAB decision can be referred to an arbitral tribunal as a single issue, whether or not a NOD has been issued. The failure to pay an adjudicated amount does not have to be referred back to the DAB as a precondition to arbitration.

FIDIC issued a *Guidance Memorandum to Users of the 1999 Conditions of Contract* dated 1 April 2013 with revisions to the standard form wording in clauses 14 and 20 of the 1999 editions. This was intended to enable the failure to pay any decision of the DAB, whether (provisionally) binding or final and binding, to be referred to arbitration for summary or other expedited relief as appropriate. Whilst the latest Court of Appeal decision indicates that the existing wording achieves the same effect, use of the proposed revised wording would put the issue beyond doubt.

The dissenting 2015 Court of Appeal judgment and the 2011 Court of Appeal judgment may still provide arguments against enforceability in other jurisdictions if the existing wording is not amended.

In the 2017 Second Editions of the Red, Yellow and Silver Books, FIDIC has attempted to put this issue beyond doubt with the following wording:

> 21.7 Failure to Comply with DAAB's Decision
>
> In the event that a Party fails to comply with any decision of the DAAB, whether binding or final and binding, then the other Party may, without prejudice to any other rights it may have, refer the failure itself directly to arbitration under Sub-Clause 21.6 [*Arbitration*] in which case Sub-Clause 21.4 [*Obtaining DAAB's Decision*] and Sub-Clause 21.5 [*Amicable Settlement*] shall not apply to this reference. The arbitral tribunal (constituted under Sub-Clause 21.6 [*Arbitration*]) shall have the power, by way of summary or other expedited procedure, to order, whether by an interim or provisional measure or an award (as may be appropriate under applicable law or otherwise), the enforcement of that decision.
>
> In the case of a binding but not final decision of the DAAB, such interim or provisional measure or award shall be subject to the express reservation that the rights of the Parties as to the merits of the Dispute are reserved until they are resolved by an award.

29 e.g. in ICC Case 16119, the tribunal held that it could not issue a final award ordering payment of the sums ordered in the (binding but non-final) decision of the DAB, although it recognised it could issue a final partial award declaring the binding force of the DAB's decision ((2015) 1 *ICC Dispute Resolution Bulletin* 70).

Any interim or provisional measure or award enforcing a decision of the DAAB which has not been complied with, whether such decision is binding or final and binding, may also include an order or award of damages or other relief.

27.5 Costs of Dispute Boards

The direct costs of standing DBs include a daily fee per member for site meetings and dispute determinations, travel time and expenses. Standing DB members are also frequently paid a monthly retainer for those months in which there is no DB meeting, as remuneration for keeping up to date with progress of the Works by reading site minutes, monthly reports etc. A monthly retainer is also recompense for being available to conduct dispute determinations at short notice, and for constraining the member's employment in any other role by either the Employer or the Contractor for the duration of the project.

There are also indirect costs for the Parties in employee time in preparing for and participating in DB meetings.

These costs may appear to be large in absolute terms in a major project that runs for a number of years. The daily fee rates for experienced DB members with the necessary technical and legal expertise and experience will be significant, and such members frequently have to travel internationally for DB meetings. However, when put in the context of the hundreds of millions of dollars of a major international construction contract, the cost of a DB is usually considerably less than 0.15% of the final contract price.

In this writer's view, the costs of a standing DB make commercial sense as "insurance" against the risk costs of significant disputes. The experience of projects with DBs around the world is that only a small proportion have disputes that are not resolved by the DB process and require arbitration or litigation for final resolution. Over the last 30 or so years in Australia, there have been over 100 projects with DBs, typically major infrastructure projects. Many of these DBs have not had any formal disputes to adjudicate on, as their dispute-avoidance role has been very effective. In the small number of disputes adjudicated by DBs, none have gone on to arbitration or litigation.

The "insurance" value of DBs can be demonstrated by the following metrics:

- In 10% of projects, 8–10% of the total project cost is legal cost.[30]
- 50% of the legal cost is expended in connection with disputes.

Thus, the risk cost of disputes on any construction contract (legal fees only) is 10% × 8% × 50% = 0.4% of project cost.

As noted above, the typical DB cost is usually less than 0.15% of the contract cost. Based on the track record of DBs being overwhelmingly effective at avoiding disputes, or containing the costs of dispute resolution within the costs of the DB itself, the 0.15% "insurance" cost of a DB is significantly less than the 0.4% risk cost of disputes if there is no DB.

Put another way, without a DB there is a 10% chance that the legal costs of disputes will amount to 4–5% of the project cost.

30 Peter Chapman, "Dispute Boards for Major Infrastructure Projects", paper presented at the Seminar on the Use of Dispute Boards in Australia (Queensland, 30 November 2006).

If there is insufficient project funding for a three-member standing DB, the parties could contemplate a single member for smaller projects. Although an *ad hoc* DB cannot perform the important role of assisting the parties in avoiding disputes, such a Board is preferable to no DB at all, as it provides a mechanism for dispute resolution that is substantially quicker and cheaper than the alternatives of litigation or arbitration.

In this writer's view, it does not make commercial sense to remove the DB provisions from a FIDIC contract. Whilst it may appear to avoid cost, it introduces (perhaps significantly greater) costs in other areas: tender prices may be higher because of the Contractor's perception of increased costs in pursuing claims and resolving disputes, and there is a significantly greater risk of major and expensive disputes.

CHAPTER 28

FIDIC Conditions of Contract New Edition 2017 and Dispute Boards[1]

28.1 FIDIC contracts

FIDIC, the International Federation of Consulting Engineers (Fédération Internationale des Ingénieurs-Conseils) publishes the most widely used contracts for international construction projects. They are commonly referred to as the "rainbow suite" because of the different colours of their covers. The most commonly used contracts in the rainbow suite are the:

- Red Book: Conditions of Contract for Construction
- Yellow Book: Conditions of Contract for Plant and Design Build
- Silver Book: Conditions of Contract for EPC/Turnkey Projects.

Other forms of contract in the FIDIC suite of contracts include the Green Book (Short Form of Contract), the Gold Book (Design, Build and Operate), the Pink Book (MDB Harmonised version of the Red Book) and the White Book (Client–Consultant Agreement).

The earliest edition of the Red Book was published in 1957; this was followed by later editions published in 1969, 1977 and 1987. Editions of the Yellow Book were published in 1963, 1980 and 1987. FIDIC responded to the increasing popularity of projects being procured on a design and build or turnkey basis in 1995 by publishing the Conditions of Contract for Design/Build and Turnkey (Orange Book). An Orange Book contract was administered by the "Employer's Representative", who unlike the Engineer[2] administering a Red Book or a Yellow Book contract was not required to be impartial in certifying the Contractor's entitlements. In the absence of an "impartial" Engineer, a Dispute Adjudication Board was introduced to determine disputes between the Parties.

A supplement was published for the Red Book 4th edition in 1996 which gave an option for an independent Dispute Adjudication Board, able to give a decision on disputes. This avoided the perception that the Engineer who administered the Contract and was employed by the Employer may not act independently in determining disputes, particularly in circumstances where the dispute was over a decision made by the Engineer.

1 This chapter is an edited version of the author's paper "FIDIC Conditions of Contract Second Edition 2017 and Dispute Boards" presented at the DRBF conference in Yogyakarta Indonesia on 21 August 2018,

2 Capitalised terms not defined in this chapter are defined in the 2017 Second Edition Red Book, Yellow Book and Silver Book.

DOI: 10.4324/9781003206897-31

Updates of the Red, Yellow and Orange Books were published in 1999, identified as the first editions of the Red, Yellow and Silver Books. The aim of these major revisions was to standardise the terminology, make the documents as user-friendly as possible, and solve the problem of the Engineer not being seen as acting impartially while he/she was employed and paid by the Employer. Each of the 1999 editions provides for a Dispute Adjudication Board to decide on disputes submitted to it.

This chapter presents a brief overview of the provisions on Dispute Boards in the 2017 FIDIC second editions of the Red, Yellow and Silver Books.

28.2 Overview of the 2017 Dispute Board provisions

The structure of the 2017 and 1999 editions are generally the same; however, the 2017 editions are more prescriptive and provide more detailed contract management provisions. One result of this is that the 2017 editions are more than 50% longer than the 1999 editions[3] and also have more time bars.

28.2.1 Claims and Disputes

Claims and Disputes have now been separated into two separate clauses in the 2017 editions. In the 1999 editions, Clause 20 was titled Claim, Disputes and Arbitration. Clause 20 is now Employer's and Contractor's Claims, and Clause 21 is Disputes and Arbitration. These Clauses have been split to emphasise that Claims do not necessarily lead to Disputes (discussed further below). Claims are specifically defined as "a request or assertion by one Party to the other Party for any entitlement or relief under any Clause of these Conditions or otherwise in connection with, or arising out of, the Contract or the execution of the Works", whereas Disputes are defined as a situation where a claim made by one Party is rejected by the other Party and the first Party does not acquiesce to that rejection.

28.2.2 Terminology – DAB/DAAB

Dispute Boards are an integral part of both the 1999 and 2017 editions, although the terminology is somewhat different. In the 1999 editions the Dispute Board was called a Dispute Adjudication Board (DAB), whereas in the 2017 editions it is called a Dispute Avoidance/Adjudication Board (DAAB). The name change is more than cosmetic, as it reflects the two important functions of the Dispute Board – assistance in the avoidance of disputes and adjudication of disputes that were not avoided.

28.2.3 Standing Dispute Board

The other substantive difference is that in the 1999 Yellow and Silver Books the DAB was an *ad hoc* Dispute Board, whereas the DAABs in each of the 2017 editions are standing Dispute Boards. A standing Dispute Board is established at the start of a project, and its

3 For example, the General Conditions in the 1999 Yellow Book comprise 75 pages, whereas the General Conditions in the 2017 Yellow Book comprise 131 pages.

TABLE 28.1 FIDIC rainbow suite provisions on DAB/DAAB

1999 Red, Yellow & Silver Books	*2017 Red, Yellow & Silver Books*
20.2 Appointment of the DAB	21.1 Constitution of the DAAB
20.3 Failure to Agree DAB	21.2 Failure to Appoint DAAB Member(s)
	21.3 Avoidance of Disputes
20.4 Obtaining DAB's Decision	21.4 Obtaining DAAB's Decision
20.5 Amicable Settlement	21.5 Amicable Settlement
20.6 Arbitration	21.6 Arbitration
20.7 Failure to Comply with DAB's Decision	21.7 Failure to Comply with DAAB's Decision
20.8 Expiry of DAB's Appointment	21.8 No DAAB in Place

members become and remain familiar with the Parties, the Contract and the progress of the Works by regular visits and reading regular project reports. Because of its familiarity with the project and the issues, a standing Dispute Board can play an important role in assisting the Parties to avoid disputes. By contrast, an *ad hoc* Dispute Board is only established to adjudicate a dispute after it has arisen. In these circumstances, it is unable to play any significant role in dispute avoidance.

28.2.4 Sub-clauses relating to the resolution of disputes

28.2.5 Establishment of Dispute Board

Sub-clause 21.1 provides for either a one-person or a three-person DAAB as stated in the Contract Data. The default option is for a three-person DAAB. The members are selected from the names listed in the Contract Data. For a three-person Board, each Party selects one member for the agreement of the other Party and the Parties consult both these members to agree the third member who is appointed to act as chairperson. The Parties agree on the remuneration of each DAAB member when agreeing the terms of the DAAB agreement. A member's appointment can be terminated by mutual agreement of the Parties, but not by either Party acting alone. The sub-clause contains provisions on the replacement of a member and the expiry of the DAAB's term – either on the date of discharge of the Contract or 28 days after it has given its decision on all Disputes (sub-clause 21.1).

Sub-clause 21.2 contains provisions to deal with the following situations:

- If the Parties cannot agree on the appointment of a sole member
- If a Party fails to select a member
- If a Party fails to agree a member selected by the other Party
- The Parties fail to agree the appointment of a replacement member
- One Party refuses or fails to sign a DAAB Agreement.

Each of these provisions has a specific time limit. In the event that any of these situations prevent the timely constitution of the DAAB, either or both Parties can request the appointing entity or official named in the Contract Data to appoint the member(s) of the DAAB.

The appointment is final and conclusive, and thereafter the Parties and the member(s) so appointed shall be deemed to have signed and be bound by a DAAB Agreement.

The comprehensive provisions of sub-clause 21.2 are designed to ensure that neither Party can thwart the process of setting up the DAAB in a timely fashion and thereby prevent it from fulfilling its obligations during the course of the Works.

28.2.6 Dispute avoidance

Table 28.1 identifies a specific sub-clause dealing with the avoidance of disputes in the 2017 editions (sub-clause 21.3), emphasising the explicit role that the DAAB has in dispute avoidance. Although the DAAB's role in dispute avoidance is emphasised by sub-clause 21.3, it existed in the 1999 Red Book within sub-clause 20.2 [Appointment of the Dispute Adjudication Board]:

> If at any time the Parties so agree, they may jointly refer a matter to the DAB for it to give its opinion. Neither Party shall consult the DAB on any matter without the agreement of the other Party.

Sub-clause 21.3 of the 2017 Books is more detailed in prescribing the DAAB's dispute avoidance role:

> If the Parties so agree, they may jointly request (in writing, with a copy to the Engineer) the DAAB to provide assistance and/or informally discuss and attempt to resolve any issue or disagreement that may have arisen between them during the performance of the Contract. If the DAAB becomes aware of an issue or disagreement, it may invite the Parties to make such a joint request.
>
> Such joint request may be made at any time, except during the period that the Engineer is carrying out his/her duties under Sub-Clause 3.7 [*Agreement or Determination*] on the matter at issue or in disagreement unless the Parties agree otherwise.
>
> Such informal assistance may take place during any meeting, Site visit or otherwise. However, unless the Parties agree otherwise, both Parties shall be present at such discussions. The Parties are not bound to act on any advice given during such informal meetings, and the DAAB shall not be bound in any future Dispute resolution process or decision by any views or advice given during the informal assistance process, whether provided orally or in writing.

These further details of how the DAAB can assist the Parties informally are no doubt very useful in providing more detailed guidance than in the 1999 Red Book. However, note that a DAB under the 1999 Red Book can perform the same dispute avoidance functions that are detailed in the 2017 Red Book.

28.2.7 DAAB's decision on a dispute

If a dispute cannot be avoided, sub-clause 21.4 details the process of obtaining the DAAB's decision on a Dispute formally referred to it. These detailed provisions cover the following:

- Reference of a Dispute to the DAAB
- The Parties' obligations after the reference
- The DAAB's decision
- Dissatisfaction with the DAAB's decision.

There are certain formalities involved in the formal reference of a Dispute to the DAAB. If the subject matter of the Dispute involves a determination made by the Engineer under sub-clause 3.7 (Red Book and Yellow Book) or the Employer's Representative under sub-clause 3.5 (Silver Book), it can only be referred to the DAAB within 42 days of giving or receiving a Notice of Dissatisfaction (NOD) with the determination. The Parties' obligations after the reference include providing necessary assistance to the DAAB and continuing to perform their obligations in accordance with the Contract. The DAAB is required to complete and give its decision within 84 days after receiving the reference, unless another period is agreed by the Parties. The decision must be reasoned and in writing; however, the DAAB does not act as an arbitrator.

The DAAB's decision on a Dispute is *binding* on both Parties who must give immediate effect to it, including payment of any amount by one Party to the other Party. The DAAB has the discretion to require the payee to provide an appropriate security if there are reasonable grounds to believe that it will be unable to repay the amount in the event that the decision is reversed in subsequent arbitration. The DAAB is not obliged to hand down its decision until all its outstanding invoices have been paid.

If either Party is dissatisfied with a DAAB decision (or any part of it) it may give a NOD to the other Party within 28 days after receiving the DAAB's decision. If the DAAB fails to give its decision within the agreed period, either Party may issue a NOD within 28 days after the end of the period. If no NOD is issued within the 28 days, the DAAB's decision is *final and binding*.

Neither Party is entitled to commence arbitration of a Dispute unless a NOD in respect of that Dispute has been given in accordance with sub-clause 21.4.4. There is a 28-day period after the issue of a NOD for amicable settlement (sub-clause 21.5). No particular process is mandated for amicable settlement, and even if no attempt at amicable settlement is made, either Party can commence arbitration on or after 28 days after the day on which the NOD was given.

28.2.8 Arbitration following NOD

The provisions for arbitration in sub-clause 21.6 are more detailed than in the 1999 editions. Arbitration is by one or three arbitrators under the Rules of Arbitration of the International Chamber of Commerce. In an award dealing with costs of the arbitration, the arbitrator(s) may take into account the extent to which a Party failed to cooperate in constituting the DAAB. The Parties are not limited to the evidence or arguments they previously put before the DAAB. Any amount awarded by the arbitrator(s) is immediately due and payable without any further certification or Notice .

Sub-clause 21.7 provides the following detailed provision for failure to comply with the DAAB's decision:

> In the event that a Party fails to comply with any decision of the DAAB, whether binding or final and binding, then the other Party may, without prejudice to any other rights it may have, refer the failure itself directly to arbitration under Sub-Clause 21.6 [*Arbitration*] in which case Sub-Clause 21.4 [*Obtaining DAAB's Decision*] and Sub-Clause 21.5 [*Amicable Settlement*] shall not apply to this reference. The arbitral tribunal (constituted under Sub-Clause 21.6 [*Arbitration*]) shall have the power, by way of summary or other expedited procedure, to

> order, whether by an interim or provisional measure or an award (as may be appropriate under applicable law or otherwise), the enforcement of that decision.
>
> In the case of a binding but not final decision of the DAAB, such interim or provisional measure or award shall be subject to the express reservation that the rights of the Parties as to the merits of the Dispute are reserved until they are resolved by an award.
>
> Any interim or provisional measure or award enforcing a decision of the DAAB which has not been complied with, whether such decision is binding or final and binding, may also include an order or award of damages or other relief.

This detailed provision addresses the issue that previously arose under sub-clause 20.7 of the 1999 Red Book in the long-running saga of litigation between PT Perusahaan Gas Negara (Persero) TBK and CRW Joint Operation in the Singapore High Court and Singapore Court of Appeal between 2010 and 2015. The issue that was not clear from the provisions of clause 20 in the 1999 Red Book was the consequences of a Party's failure to comply with a binding DAB decision that was not final and binding.[4] The new provisions of sub-clause 21.7 make it clear that a Party can seek an arbitration award confined to the other Party's failure to comply with a DAAB decision; that interim or provisional measure or award will not deal with the merits of the Dispute determined by the DAAB. A final award dealing with the merits of the Dispute may overturn the DAAB decision.

Sub-clause 21.8 provides that if there is no DAAB in place or no DAAB is being constituted, whether by reason of the expiry of the DAAB's appointment or otherwise, the dispute may be referred directly to arbitration under sub-clause 21.6 and sub-clause 21.5 [Amicable Settlement] shall not apply. It appears from this sub-clause that a dispute can be referred directly to arbitration if the Parties have agreed not to engage the contractual machinery to constitute a DAAB. However, there are reported judgements in England and Switzerland and reported arbitration cases that conclude that under the equivalent clause in the 1999 rainbow suite, it is generally mandatory to refer disputes to a Dispute Board prior to arbitration.[5]

28.3 Dispute Avoidance/Adjudication Agreement

Each member of the DAAB must enter into a tripartite agreement between the Employer, the Contractor and the DAAB member. A pro forma DAA Agreement is at the back of each of the 2017 Books. The conditions of the DAA Agreement comprise

- Clause 21 [Disputes and Arbitration] of the Conditions of Contract, and any other provisions of the Contract that are applicable to the DAAB's Activities
- The General Conditions of Dispute Avoidance/Adjudication Agreement.

4 See Section 27.4 above for a detailed discussion of the binding nature of a DAB decision under FIDIC contracts and the PGN and CRW litigation on this issue.

5 See Section 27.3.2 above for a discussion of these cases.

TABLE 28.2 FIDIC rainbow suite General Conditions for DA/DAA Agreement

1999 Red Book *General Conditions of Dispute Adjudication Agreement (4 pages)*	*2017 Red, Yellow & Silver Books* *General Conditions of Dispute Avoidance/ Adjudication Agreement (9 pages)*
1. Definitions	1. Definitions
2. General Provisions	2. General Provisions
3. Warranties	3. Warranties
	4. Independence and Impartiality
4. General Obligations of the Member	5. General obligations of the DAAB Member
5. General Obligations of the Employer and the Contractor	6. General Obligations of the Parties
	7. Confidentiality
	8. The Parties' undertaking and indemnity
6. Payment	9. Fees and Expenses
7. Termination	10. Resignation and Termination
8. Default of the Member	11. Challenge
9. Disputes	12. Disputes under the DAA Agreement

28.3.1 General Conditions of the Dispute Avoidance/Adjudication Agreement

The considerably more prescriptive nature of the 2017 General Conditions of the DAA Agreement is highlighted by its nine pages in comparison with only four pages in the 1999 General Conditions.

28.3.2 Member's independence and impartiality

Sub-clause 4 of the General Conditions of the DAA Agreement prescribes seven specific matters that the DAAB member must comply with to assure the Parties of his/her independence and impartiality. Under the 1999 DA General Conditions a member's independence and impartiality were succinctly stated in sub-clause 4:

> The Member warrants and agrees that he/she is and shall be impartial and independent of the Employer, the Contractor and the Engineer. The Member shall promptly disclose, to each of them and to the Other Members (if any), any fact or circumstance which might appear inconsistent with his/her warranty and agreement of impartiality and independence.

28.3.3 DAAB fees

Sub-clause 9 (2017 editions) provides that DAAB fees comprise:

- A monthly fee as payment in full for being available on 28 days' notice for all meetings, Site visits and hearings, becoming and remaining knowledgeable about the Contract and the Works and all office and overhead expenses.
- A daily fee for each day or part of a day for travel time (maximum of two days in each direction), attending meetings and making Site visits, giving Informal Assistance, preparing for and attending hearings and preparing decisions.

If the Parties and a DAAB Member fail to agree the amount of the monthly or daily fee, either may require the appointing entity named in the Contract Data to set the fee.[6]

28.3.4 Challenge to a DAAB member

Sub-clause 11 is a new provision that entitles either Party or a DAAB member to object to a DAAB member on the grounds of alleged lack of independence or impartiality or otherwise. Rule 10 Objection Procedure and Rule 11 Challenge Procedure of the DAAB Procedural Rules define the procedure to be adopted in the event of a challenge. If the challenge is successful, the DAAB member's appointment is terminated with immediate effect, and any DAAB decision made after the challenge was referred becomes void and ineffective.

Any dispute arising out of or in connection with the DAA Agreement or the breach, termination or invalidity thereof shall be finally settled by arbitration by a single arbitrator under the ICC Rules of Arbitration using the Expedited Procedure Rules (sub-clause 12).

28.4 DAAB Procedural Rules

28.4.1 Contents of Rules

The DAAB Rules are defined in sub-clause 1.4 of the DAA General Conditions to mean the document entitled DAAB Procedural Rules published by FIDIC which are annexed to, and form part of, the General Conditions of DAA Agreement. The DAAB Procedural Rules comprise the following:

1. Objectives
2. Avoidance of Disputes
3. Meetings and Site Visits
4. Communications and Documentation
5. Powers of the DAAB
6. Disputes
7. Hearings
8. The DAAB's Decision
9. In the event of Termination of DAA Agreement
10. Objection Procedure
11. Challenge Procedure

The 1999 Red Book contains nine Procedural Rules on one and a half pages. The very detailed Procedural Rules in the 2017 Books contain 35 sub-clauses on six and a half pages.

The objectives of these Rules are defined in rule 1.1 as:

(a) to facilitate the avoidance of Disputes that might otherwise arise between the Parties; and

6 See DRBF, *Dispute Board Manual* (DRBF, 2019) 89-90 for a discussion of typical fee structures and rates for FIDIC contracts.

(b) to achieve the expeditious, efficient and cost-effective resolution of any Dispute that arises between the Parties.

28.4.2 Avoidance of disputes

Rule 2.1 specifies the following for avoidance of disputes:

> Where Sub-Clause 21.3 [*Avoidance of Disputes*] of the Conditions of Contract applies, the DAAB (in the case of a three-member DAAB, all three DAAB Members acting together) may give Informal Assistance during discussions at any meeting with the Parties (whether face-to-face or by telephone or by video conference) or at any Site visit or by an informal written note to the Parties.

Informal Assistance means the DAAB's assistance and informal discussions requested jointly by the Parties under sub-clause 21.3 [Avoidance of Disputes] of the Conditions of Contract.

Rule 3, Meetings and Site Visits, requires face to face meetings with the Parties and/or visits to the Site at regular intervals and/or at the written request of either Party. These are to be at intervals of not less than 70 days nor more than 140 days (except as required to conduct a hearing). Site visits can also be made at the written request of either Party at times of critical construction events.

28.4.3 Powers of the DAAB

Rule 5 provides that the DAAB has the power to:

- Establish the procedures for Site visits, Informal Assistance and decisions on Disputes
- Decide on its own jurisdiction and the scope of any Dispute referred to it
- Appoint experts with the agreement of the Parties
- Decide if there will be one or more hearings
- Conduct meetings with the Parties and/or any hearing as it sees fit, without being bound by any rules or procedures other than those in the Contract and the Rules
- Make use of its own specialist knowledge.

28.4.4 Resolution of disputes

Rule 6.2 specifies the following for the resolution of Disputes:

> The DAAB shall act fairly and impartially between the Parties and, taking due regard of the period under Sub-Clause 21.4.3 [*The DAAB's decision*] of the Conditions of Contract and other relevant circumstances, the DAAB shall:
>
> (a) give each Party a reasonable opportunity (consistent with the expedited nature of the DAAB proceeding) of putting forward its case and responding to the other Party's case; and
> (b) adopt a procedure in coming to its decision that is suitable to the Dispute, avoiding unnecessary delay and/or expense.

In respect of hearings, the DAAB has powers under rule 7.1 to:

- Decide on the date and place for any hearing and its duration
- Request written documentation and arguments
- Adopt an inquisitorial procedure
- Request the production of documents and/or submissions from the Parties
- Request the attendance of persons that it considers may assist
- Refuse admission to any persons other than representatives of the Employer, the Contractor and the Engineer
- Proceed in the absence of any Party who received adequate notice of the hearing

28.4.5 Correction of errors in a DAAB decision

Rule 8 addresses a lacuna in the 1999 DAB Procedural Rules providing for the correction of inadvertent slips or errors:

- If the DAAB finds a typographical, clerical or arithmetical error in its decision, it may advise the Parties of the error and issue an addendum within 14 days after giving its decision.
- If a Party finds a typographical, clerical or arithmetical error in the decision, it may request the DAAB to correct the error in writing within 14 days after the decision has been received.
- If a Party considers that a decision contains an ambiguity, it may request clarification within 14 days of receiving the decision, and the DAAB shall respond within 14 days of receiving the request with sole discretion to decline the request or correct the decision by issuing an addendum.

28.5 Claims

The most important tool for dispute avoidance is maintaining clear lines of communication between the contracting Parties. The genesis of many disputes is in the submission and rejection of Claims. As the 2017 Books make clear in the Definitions, a Claim is not the same thing as a Dispute:

> '**Claim**' means a request or assertion by one Party to the other Party for an entitlement or relief under any Clause of these Conditions or otherwise in connection with, or arising out of, the Contract or the execution of the Works.
>
> '**Dispute**' means any situation where:
>
> (a) one Party makes a claim against the other Party (which may be a Claim, as defined in these Conditions, or a matter to be determined by the Engineer under these Conditions, or otherwise);
> (b) the other Party (or the Engineer under Sub-Clause 3.7.2 [Engineer's Determination]) rejects the claim in whole or in part; and
> (c) the first Party does not acquiesce (by giving a NOD under Sub-Clause 3.7.5 [Dissatisfaction with Engineer's determination] or otherwise),

> provided however that a failure by the other Party (or the Engineer) to oppose or respond to the claim, in whole or in part, may constitute a rejection if, in the circumstances, the DAAB or the arbitrator(s), as the case may be, deem it reasonable for it to do so.

Some Employers appear to regard Claims as somehow illegitimate or tantamount to a dispute. However, the Contractor has a contractual right to assert a legitimate Claim in accordance with the provisions of the Contract, and it should be treated accordingly:

> Claims should not be regarded as either inevitable or unpalatable, and complying with claims procedures should not be regarded as being an aggressive act. Major projects give rise to major risks, which have to be dealt with if they occur. Whilst the Parties might prefer everything to remain unchanged, they should not instinctively seek to attribute blame if circumstances arise or events occur which give rise to an adjustment of the Contract Price. In these events, the claims procedures are specified so as to provide the degree of formality considered necessary for the proper administration of a building or engineering project. Complying with these procedures and maintaining a cooperative approach to the determination of all adjustments should enhance the likelihood of achieving a successful project.[7]

Thus, one of the techniques to avoid a Claim becoming a Dispute starts with clear communication of a Claim to the other Party: the factual basis of the Claim, including supporting documents where appropriate, and the legal basis that supports the entitlement. If the Claim is rejected, the basis for rejection of the Claim should be clearly communicated, including any additional or different facts (including documents), and the legal basis that supports the rejection.

28.6 Techniques for dispute avoidance under FIDIC contracts

In this writer's view, management of project execution in accordance with the requirements of the Contract will materially assist in dispute avoidance. This involves, amongst other things:

- The Contractor committing sufficient resources to carry out the contractual scope of work within the Time for Completion.
- Realistic and credible "as built" programmes that reflect what has actually occurred as well as what is actually planned for the future.
- Work completed to the contractually required quality.
- Design documents submitted to the Employer in accordance with the requirements of the Contract.
- Maintaining and managing comprehensive documentation from the start of the Tender through the execution of the project to ensure that the best evidence is available to support/defend a Claim.
- Familiarity with the Contract conditions.

The following are some of the dispute avoidance techniques that can be adopted by a proactive DAAB / DAB:

7 The FIDIC Contracts Guide (2000), 88, 89.

- Ensure that all DAAB/DAB meetings with the Parties are "without prejudice" (except hearings in connection with a Dispute). This ensures that anything said by a Party in a meeting cannot be used to the detriment of that Party if the issue subsequently becomes a Dispute.
- Encourage open communication between the Parties at the DAAB/DAB meetings.
- Ensure that senior off-site personnel from both the Employer and the Contractor are present at every DAAB/DAB meeting. This ensures that senior personnel hear the other side of every issue, not just the view of their own personnel.
- Ask probing questions, particularly if it appears that the Parties are not addressing the right technical or legal issues.
- If it appears that the Parties cannot agree on an issue, e.g. a Variation, request each of them to prepare a brief position paper prior to the next DAAB/DAB meeting. A position paper should state the relevant facts, refer to appropriate documents and articulate the Party's position in respect of the issue, and its opinion of the correct contractual position.
- If the position papers and subsequent negotiation between the Parties do not resolve the issue, they will provide the background for the DAAB/DAB to give further Informal Assistance.
- If the Parties request the DAAB/DAB to give a written (informal) opinion, the DAAB/DAB should provide a "without prejudice" opinion, referring to the relevant facts and providing brief reasons for the conclusions it comes to. The DAAB/DAB should carefully consider whether a written opinion is necessary or appropriate in the circumstances. The Parties are not bound to accept an informal opinion, and nor is the DAAB/DAB bound by it if a dispute ensues.
- The DAAB/DAB should bear in mind that, unlike a DAAB/DAB decision, the recommendation of an informal opinion does not need to be confined to strict contractual rights, but may suggest an extra-contractual 'best for project solution' that the Parties could agree to.

The skills and techniques of a DAAB/DAB in "dispute avoidance mode" are the skills and techniques of a mediator or conciliator. The DAAB/DAB's objective is to assist the Parties to communicate and find a commercial solution that is acceptable to them. It can materially assist by asking questions and making suggestions from its own experience of other projects, and its knowledge of the Contract, the Works and the Parties it has gained from its regular Site visits and reading the Contract communications.

CHAPTER 29

Construction disputes after COVID-19 – jaw-jaw or war-war?[1]

29.1 Introduction

The rapid spread of COVID-19 in early 2020 transformed economic life around the world. Many construction projects saw massive impacts ranging from complete shutdown in some countries to stringent new work health and safety regulations required as a consequence of "social distancing". Virtually every project was subject to delayed performance and increased costs. There will inevitably be many disputes as to which contracting party is to bear the time and cost risks that eventuated. In this environment, the availability and suitability of appropriate methods for resolution of international construction law disputes will undoubtedly receive increased scrutiny.

The disruption caused by COVID-19 emphasised the extent to which the economies of the world are interconnected. Construction projects are a significant and important element of international trade, responsible for essential infrastructure, transfer of skills and technology and substantial employment. As with domestic construction projects, disputes are not unusual. However, an international contractor will generally be reluctant to submit disputes to the domestic courts of the country where the project is situated. This may be due to a perception of a bias by domestic courts (particularly where the Employer is a government entity), or because of unfamiliarity with local law. For similar reasons, the parties may have agreed to the governing law of the contract being that of a jurisdiction different to that of the site location.

Until a few years ago, there was only one (almost) universally accepted method of dispute resolution suitable for international construction law disputes: international arbitration subject to the *New York Convention* which entered into force in 1959. However, the formation of international courts in Dubai (2011) and Singapore (2015) now provides an alternative method of judicially determining legal rights. Since 2019, there is the further option of international mediation subject to the *Singapore Convention*. Dispute Boards provide a further alternative means of resolving disputes that is gaining international traction from the widespread use of FIDIC contracts and the support of multilateral development banks such as the World Bank.

Whilst the types of construction disputes arising as a consequence of the impact of COVID-19 will mostly be well-recognised, the sheer scale of the economic fallout is an

1 This chapter is an edited and updated version of a paper commended for the 2020 Society of Construction Law Australia Brooking Prize that was subsequently published in (2020) 193 *Australian Construction Law Newsletter* 6.

DOI: 10.4324/9781003206897-32

order of magnitude greater than that experienced by the current generation. Employers and Contractors will be keen for projects to be restarted and completed expeditiously but may be subject to severe cash flow and other constraints arising from COVID-19. As many commentators have observed, the world will not be the same after the pandemic, and it is suggested that contracting parties will need to carefully consider the most appropriate method of resolving any disputes in this new world.

This chapter discusses the challenges of using different methods of dispute resolution for international construction disputes in the post-COVID-19 environment. Protagonists have the choice of "jaw-jaw" methods involving discussion, negotiation and compromise (such as mediation) or "war-war" adversarial methods in which an independent Neutral will determine legal rights in a winner takes all process, typically arbitration.[2]

29.2 Disputes arising from the impact of COVID-19

As discussed in Chapter 12, governments around the world responded in a variety of ways to slow and halt the spread of COVID-19, particularly by restricting the congregation of people by means of "social distancing" and prohibiting many types of economic activity. In addition to legal constraints on activities, some individuals took their own precautions against infection, such as not turning up for work even where it was not prohibited. The combination of legislated and voluntary restrictions had a significant impact on the normal operation of construction sites and their supply chains, inevitably leading to increased costs and delays.

The legal profession responded rapidly to the impacts on construction projects by identifying the issues that are likely to arise from the additional costs and delays. Many firms provided webinars and other guidance, emphasising the importance of following the requirements of the Contract in matters such as health and safety obligations, mitigating the impacts of COVID-19 to the extent possible, the timely submission of claims and the requirement to maintain proper contemporaneous records. FIDIC published a Guidance Memorandum for users of its standard form contracts, outlining several possible scenarios and relevant contract likely responses.[3] These scenarios include the impact of substantially enhanced health and safety precautions on operating construction sites, construction sites prevented from operating due to government regulations, and slow decision-making by the Engineer or the Employer's Representative.[4]

Many of the claims that will arise will be of the types generally familiar to construction practitioners, such as *force majeure* under the Contract or under the law, changes in laws or delays arising from circumstances beyond the Contractor's control. However, it is suggested that the scale and number of claims will be significant, as will be the impact of the economic environment after "normal" work has resumed. It should be borne in mind that a claim is not a dispute per se. A claim is an assertion of an entitlement to a legal right in connection with or arising out of the Contract or the execution of the Works, whereas

2 Harold MacMillan, British Prime Minister, 1894–1986 noted that "jaw-jaw is better than war-war" https://www.greatest-quotations.com/search/search.html (accessed 24 May 2020).

3 FIDIC COVID-19 Guidance Memorandum to Users of FIDIC Standard Forms of Works Contract, April 2020. https://fidic.org/sites/default/files/COVID%2019%20Guidance%20Memorandum%20-%20PDF.pdf (accessed 23 May 2020).

4 These scenarios are outlined in Section 12.8.

a dispute only arises from the rejection of a claim where the rejection is not accepted. As discussed in Section 28.5, the 2017 editions of the FIDIC rainbow suite emphasise this clear distinction between claims and disputes by splitting clause 20 in the 1999 editions on claims and disputes into two separate clauses in the 2017 editions. The first opportunity that contracting parties have to avoid disputes is to negotiate an appropriate commercial outcome for properly articulated claims.

The construction industry in Australia was (mostly) allowed to keep operating during the pandemic, but the required social distancing and enhanced health and safety measures will inevitably have resulted in increased costs and delays. The entire construction industry was shut down for a period in a number of other countries. Many contracts will not recognise the impacts of COVID-19 as an Employer's risk event, leaving Contractors with liability for the costs, and perhaps even for the delays.

International construction is a very competitive, high-risk industry worldwide, yet operates on very low margins: McKinsey states that the construction industry has bottom-quartile profit margins, with an average profit margin of only 4.4% over sales.[5] The international construction industry depends for its existence on reliable cash flow, but is subject to significant performance risks of time and quality. History is replete with the examples of major contractors forced into liquidation as a consequence of unbudgeted project risks eventuating. It would be unsurprising if the costs and delays consequent on COVID-19 threatened the viability of some international contractors or prevented their resumption of work. The financial impact of COVID-19 may also threaten the financial viability of some Employers.

Parties considering their options for avoiding or resolving disputes will need to keep these considerations in mind. Insisting on legal contractual rights in a dispute might ultimately be a pyrrhic victory if the counterparty has inadequate financial resources to continue in operation. Parties in dispute will need to focus even more than usual on what their real interests in the outcome are, in a very different commercial environment. To quote the business-performance guru Stephen Covey: "we all need to start with the end in mind". In many cases, the most appropriate end to have in mind will be what is best for the project. Avoiding disputes would undoubtedly be beneficial for any construction project.

In an ideal world, the best method of avoiding disputes or resolving the inevitable disputes that will arise would be pragmatic commercial negotiation between representatives of the contracting parties with authority to settle. In the real world this will not happen in many cases, and an independent Neutral (or Neutrals) will be required to either assist the parties to come to a negotiated commercial settlement or to determine their legal rights in a way in which they can be enforced.

Dispute resolution procedures that are suitable for construction disputes are Dispute Boards, mediation, expert determination, adjudication, arbitration or litigation. This chapter focusses on Dispute Boards, mediation and arbitration, all of which are frequently used for construction disputes.[6]

5 McKinsey Global Institute, 'Reinventing construction: a route to higher productivity' (February 2017) 10 https://www.mckinsey.com/~/media/McKinsey/Business%20Functions/Operations/Our%20Insights/Reinventing%20construction%20through%20a%20productivity%20revolution/MGI-Reinventing-construction-A-route-to-higher-productivity-Full-report.pdf (accessed 31 March 2021).

6 'International Arbitration Survey – Driving Efficiency in International Construction Disputes' (Queen Mary University of London, November 2019) 9.

29.3 Dispute Boards

As discussed in Chapter 26, Dispute boards (DBs) are now a well-established means of assisting contracting parties to avoid disputes, or if disputes cannot be avoided, of determining legal and contractual rights in an expeditious and cost-effective way. The primary focus of DBs has shifted from their initial dispute resolution role to that of dispute avoidance. The Dispute Board Manual recently published by the Dispute Resolution Board Foundation (DRBF) devotes a chapter to dispute avoidance and management.[7] The 2017 editions of the FIDIC contracts include specific provisions on the avoidance of disputes and renamed the previous Dispute Adjudication Board (DAB) the Dispute Avoidance/Adjudication Board (DAAB) to reflect the importance of the dispute avoidance role.[8]

The dispute avoidance role of a DB is best provided by a standing DB, i.e. one appointed at the start of the project which meets regularly with the contracting parties during its progress. FIDIC recognised the value of dispute avoidance by replacing the *ad hoc* DAB in the 1999 editions of the Yellow and Silver Books with a standing DAAB in the 2017 editions. A DB can assist parties to avoid disputes in its "without prejudice" discussions and advice during a regular site visit or, if requested by the parties, can issue an advisory opinion. Such an advisory opinion may assist the parties to negotiate a commercial settlement in the knowledge that the DB's opinion is probably a good indicator of its likely decision if it were required to decide the dispute formally.

The dispute avoidance and resolution roles of a standing DB are well suited to dealing with COVID-19 disputes. The DB is familiar with the parties, the project and the Contract, and as a respected third-party Neutral is well placed to advise the parties on a best for project resolution of an issue before it becomes a dispute or providing a "black letter law" determination of a formal dispute. The DB can thus function effectively as a mediator in assisting the parties to avoid disputes, or as an adjudicator in deciding on the parties' legal rights. Dispute avoidance under FIDIC contracts is discussed in Section 28.6.

29.4 Mediation

The advantages of mediation to achieve a commercial settlement of a construction dispute are well established and well known. Mediation is reported to resolve a high percentage of disputes, and in consequence, mediation is a condition precedent to obtaining a court hearing date in many jurisdictions. Of relevance to the resolution of COVID-19 construction disputes, mediation requires limited preparation, can be implemented without delay, takes limited time and is considerably cheaper than alternatives that determine the parties' legal rights. Most importantly the mediated outcome of a dispute does not have to be confined to the parties' legal rights – as a negotiated settlement agreed by the parties, it can involve commercial compromises and other outcomes not achievable within the four walls of the relevant contract.

Mediation lacks certainty as a method of dispute resolution as it depends on the contracting parties' agreement to a proposed settlement. Nevertheless, in many cases the

7 Graham Easton & Ann Russo (lead editors), *Dispute Board Manual A Guide to Best Practices and Procedures* (DRBF, 2019) https://www.drb.org/publications-data/library/ (accessed 23 May 2019).

8 *Conditions of Contract for Construction*, (FIDIC, 2nd edn, 2017) (Red Book); *Conditions of Contract for Plant and Design-Build*, (FIDIC, 2nd edn, 2017) (Yellow Book); *Conditions of Contract for EPC/Turnkey Projects*, (FIDIC, 2nd edn, 2017) (Silver Book).

"jaw-jaw" in a mediation results in the disposition of a dispute between parties without them having to resort to the "war-war" inherent in adversarial proceedings such as arbitration or litigation.

The commercial settlement achieved in a mediation does not come cost-free. Although mediation is generally touted as "win-win", it generally involves compromise by all sides as the price for a speedy and cost-effective process. For example, one party may accept a lower settlement sum than it expected to achieve in legal adversarial proceedings, whilst the other party may make a payment in circumstances where it considered it had a good defence. The flexibility inherent in a mediated settlement is one of mediation's most powerful features as it can make provision for non-contractual obligations that have real value. The wins for both parties are the avoidance of costly, time-consuming adversarial proceedings that would otherwise distract senior personnel from the normal running of their business, and the preservation of working relationships.

Mediated settlements are usually documented in the form of a binding agreement (often drawn up by lawyers) that the parties expect will be adhered to. In the event that one party does not comply with the terms of the settlement agreement, the other party will seek to enforce it through the courts, as it would if a party did not comply with the terms of an arbitral award. That would not normally be problematic if enforcement of a domestic agreement was sought within the jurisdiction. However, the situation may be very different for enforcement of a settlement agreement where the agreement involves parties from different countries and/or where enforcement is sought in a third country. There are many reasons for potential difficulties of enforcement of a contract in jurisdictions with a different legal environment, such as differences in contract law, court congestion or corruption, perceptions of home country bias or a lack of comity between courts. These issues may be compounded where enforcement is sought in a third country.

The potential problems of enforcement of international arbitral awards were resolved by the implementation of the *New York 1958 Convention on the Recognition and Enforcement of Arbitral Awards* (***New York Convention***), the efficacy of which made international arbitration the only practical avenue of dispute resolution for international commercial contracts until the recent advent of International Courts. However, there is now an equivalent to the *New York Convention* for mediation: the *United Nations 2019 Convention on International Settlement Agreements Resulting from Mediation* known as the *Singapore Convention on Mediation* (***Singapore Convention***). The *Singapore Convention* establishes a harmonised legal framework for the right to invoke settlement agreements as well as for their enforcement. It has been signed by 52 countries including the United States and China and has already entered into force in six countries (Belarus, Ecuador, Fiji, Qatar, Singapore and Saudi Arabia). The United Nations Commission on International Trade Law (**UNCITRAL**) prepared the *Singapore Convention* and summarises its value and importance in the following words:

> The Convention is an instrument for the facilitation of international trade and the promotion of mediation as an alternative and effective method of resolving trade disputes. Being a binding international instrument, it is expected to bring certainty and stability to the international framework on mediation, thereby contributing to the Sustainable Development Goals (SDG), mainly the SDG 16 [*peace, justice and strong institutions*].[9]

9 https://uncitral.un.org/en/texts/mediation/conventions/international_settlement_agreements (accessed 23 May 2020).

The *Singapore Convention* applies to international written settlement agreements of commercial disputes resulting from mediation, which is defined as:

> A process, irrespective of the expression used or the basis upon which the process is carried out, whereby parties attempt to reach an amicable settlement of their dispute with the assistance of a third person or third persons ('the mediator') lacking the authority to impose a solution upon the parties to the dispute.[10]

The *Singapore Convention* has many similarities with the *New York Convention*, and also some modern additions. For example, a settlement agreement "in writing" can be in electronic form and a regional economic organisation can participate on behalf of its constituent States. Article 5 states limited grounds on which a competent authority "may" refuse to grant relief, including legal impediments, procedural irregularities in the settlement agreement or the mediator's breach of relevant standards of conduct. In parallel with the *New York Convention*, enforcement can be refused where granting relief would be contrary to public policy.

The *Singapore Convention* has the potential to elevate mediation as a viable method to resolve international construction disputes in much less time and for much less cost than arbitration. At the present time that potential is limited by the *Singapore Convention* only being in force in six countries. It applies to settlement agreements concluded after the date when the *Convention* enters into force, so other signatory States still have the opportunity of bringing it into force to cope with the inevitable disputes arising from COVID-19.

29.5 International arbitration

In the event that disputing parties to an international construction contract cannot agree to "jaw-jaw" methods of dispute resolution, the usual "war-war" method of choice is arbitration. Arbitration has many features that make it well suited to the resolution of intractable international construction disputes. The recent Queen Mary College survey of international construction disputes found the following top ten reasons why parties chose international construction arbitration over litigation:

- Avoiding legal systems/national courts.
- Ability to select arbitrators.
- Confidentiality and privacy.
- Avoiding local political pressure/intimidation.
- Enforceability of award.
- Ability to select technical (non-legal) arbitrators.
- Speed.
- Ability to appoint party experts.
- Neutrality.
- Flexibility.[11]

10 Art 2.3 *Singapore Convention*.

11 'International Arbitration Survey – Driving Efficiency in International Construction Disputes', (Queen Mary University of London, November 2019) 24.

A significant advantage of international arbitration is the widespread acceptance of the *New York Convention.* It is in force in 163 States – the majority of the 193 member States of the United Nations. The *New York Convention* ensures that a properly constituted arbitral award will be recognised and enforced in most countries of the world. The grounds for refusing enforcement are very limited, perhaps the most widely used being where the arbitral award is contrary to public policy where enforcement is sought.

Governments around the world have responded to the economic impact of COVID-19 by passing laws that have provided substantial restrictions to freedom of contract. It is suggested that these laws will provide fruitful grounds to argue for the application of the public policy exception to enforcement.

29.6 Jaw-jaw or war-war?

29.6.1 Construction disputes post-COVID-19

To provide some context for discussing the appropriate resolution of construction disputes arising from the impact of COVID-19, the following discussion is confined to an international construction contract based on the General Conditions of the 1999 or 2017 FIDIC rainbow suite. The 1999 Yellow and Silver Books provide for an *ad hoc* Dispute Adjudication Board, the 1999 Red Book provides for a standing Dispute Adjudication Board and the 2017 editions of all three books provide for a standing Dispute Avoidance/Adjudication Board. It is assumed that the Contractor has submitted a claim to the Engineer (Red and Yellow Books) or the Employer's Representative (Silver Book) for delay and/or additional payment based on circumstances arising out of the COVID-19 pandemic.

The extent to which governments injected money into their economies in an endeavour to preserve as many jobs and businesses as possible highlights the fragility of the environment for resumption of normal project work. Many businesses, both Employers and Contractors, will have significant cash flow problems. Due to the different times the pandemic impacted different countries there may be ongoing availability issues with the supply chain or with obtaining labour. Governments and multilateral development banks may be fast-tracking new infrastructure projects to revive hard-hit economies, leading to increased competition for resources. Or the costs of dealing with the pandemic may adversely impact the progress of existing projects. The cliché that cash flow is the lifeblood of the construction industry will be truer than ever.

The intense interest that was shown in structuring claims arising from the impact of COVID-19 from the early days of the pandemic is, in this writer's view (and confirmed by anecdotal evidence), a harbinger of a greater number of disputes than normal. Employers and Contractors will want to know who is to bear the liability for delay and increased cost; in some cases, the resolution of these issues may mean the difference between a going concern and insolvency. It is suggested that in the post-COVID-19 environment, parties will be more concerned than ever to resolve their disputes with celerity and with certainty so that projects can proceed with the minimum of disruption. If there is a significant increase in the number of disputes to be resolved quickly, this will put considerable pressure on the existing facilities for dispute resolution. As has been shown by many surveys of consumers of dispute resolution services, arbitration is often considered to be too time-consuming and costly. If the usual proportion of an increased number of disputes proceed to arbitration, some of them will inevitably take a considerable time to resolve. For some protagonists, that time may be fatal.

What can be done to speed the process up? Our experiences during the pandemic have demonstrated that much commercial life can be conducted remotely via appropriate communication technology. For instance, the courts in Australia have generally been able to proceed with the conduct of commercial trials without the physical presence of counsel, witnesses and experts in the courtroom. Arbitral institutions have provided detailed guidance on the conduct of "virtual" arbitrations. For example, the American Arbitration Association/International Centre for Dispute Resolution have published 'Model Order and Procedures for a Virtual Hearing via Videoconference'.[12] With our new-found skills in remote working, there is every reason to expect that resolution of construction disputes can proceed even in a world with social distancing and travel bans. Conferences, DB meetings and hearings, mediations and arbitrations can generally be conducted using one of a number of widely available platforms based on internet communication. There is significant potential for this new method of working to result in significant efficiencies and flexibility and consequent cost savings by not requiring the parties, their counsel, witnesses and independent neutrals to travel to an international destination. No doubt there will still be some hearings that will need to be conducted face to face, but recent experience has shown these to be in the minority.

29.6.2 Dispute avoidance

Under a FIDIC contract the Engineer/Employer's Representative (**Contract Administrator**) is required to consult with each party in an endeavour to reach agreement on a claim, and only if agreement is not achieved does the Contract Administrator make a fair determination in accordance with the Contract. Whilst the Contract Administrator is required to make a determination strictly in accordance with the provisions of the Contract, the same constraints do not apply to the parties. Irrespective of strict legal rights, a commercial negotiation to determine a fair resolution of a claim may be able to achieve a resumption of normal work as soon as possible in a way that the parties can live with. This would have the further benefit of avoiding a dispute and all the uncertainty, time and cost entailed.

Contracts that have a standing Dispute Board are in the best position to deal with claims and disputes in the most expeditious and cost-effective manner. The DB is familiar with the project, the parties and the Contract and can operate in both "jaw-jaw" and "war-war" mode. Before issues have crystallised into disputes, a standing DB can provide informal advice in its regular "without prejudice" meetings to provide the parties with a way forward. Even if an issue has crystallised into a dispute, a standing DB can, on the request of the parties or at the suggestion of the DB, issue an advisory opinion before the parties resort to the "war-war" of a dispute formally referred to the DB for a decision.

An *ad hoc* DB is only appointed after a dispute has crystallised and therefore cannot assist the parties in dispute avoidance to the extent possible with a standing DB. For this reason, both the DRBF and FIDIC strongly recommend the appointment of a standing

12 https://go.adr.org/rs/294-SFS-516/images/AAA270_AAA-ICDR%20Model%20Order%20and%20Procedures%20for%20a%20Virtual%20Hearing%20via%20Videoconference.pdf (accessed 26 May 2020),

DB. Nevertheless, with the agreement of the parties, an *ad hoc* DB could still provide an advisory opinion for the parties' consideration prior to embarking on making a decision on a formal dispute.

The legal restrictions and the factual circumstances of the impact of COVID-19 on the parties' performance will be key parameters of a dispute. In addition, the prevailing economic climate as it impacts on the parties may be of overwhelming importance in determining whether a resolution based on legal and contractual rights is feasible, or whether a negotiated commercial solution is necessary to enable the project to proceed. This is not a unique situation, but the scale and extent of disruption to economic life as a consequence of COVID-19 brings these issues into sharp focus in assessing the most appropriate form of dispute resolution.

The parties' agreement to resolve a dispute by accepting the DB's advisory opinion would normally be documented and signed by the parties. Notwithstanding voluntarily entering into such a settlement agreement, there is no guarantee that it will be adhered to. The recent Queen Mary survey on international construction disputes found that only 28% of the respondents reported frequent compliance with pre-arbitral decisions, 31% reported compliance "half of the time" and 41% experienced parties not voluntarily complying.[13] The enforceability of a settlement agreement is therefore a significant issue for a dispute resolution process other than arbitration. This is the issue that the *Singapore Convention* was designed to address and could provide the required enforcement certainty in those limited jurisdictions where it is in force. It is suggested that a settlement agreement signed in response to a DB advisory opinion would come within the definition of mediation in the *Singapore Convention*, provided the appropriate formalities in Art 4 were complied with, in particular evidence that the DB acted as "mediator".

29.6.3 Adjudication

Whilst the decision of a DB must be based on legal rights under the Contract and the law, this form of "war-war" does not involve the heavy artillery required for arbitration. The DB process involves a war of limited scope; it is limited in time and may not involve a hearing or the involvement of lawyers or external experts. A standing DB is already familiar with the Contract and the issues and requires far less information and preparation from the parties to understand the dispute than an arbitral panel would. It is suggested that as the parties typically have an established relationship with and respect for the DB, a DB decision does not involve the extent of adversarialism and destruction of commercial relationships that often occurs with arbitration. This is supported by the recent Queen Mary survey which found that a decision by a standing DB was more likely to be complied with than that of an *ad hoc* DB, especially if the standing DB was appointed at the outset of the works.[14]

A DB decision under a FIDIC contract is immediately binding on the parties and is final unless a Notice of Dissatisfaction is served within 28 days of the decision. Nevertheless, as the long-running saga of the *PT Perusahaan Gas Negara (PGN) (Persero) TBK v CRW Joint Venture Operation* cases in Singapore between 2010 and 2015 (discussed in Section 27.4),

13 "International Arbitration Survey – Driving Efficiency in International Construction Disputes" (Queen Mary University of London, November 2019) 18.

14 "International Arbitration Survey – Driving Efficiency in International Construction Disputes", (Queen Mary University of London, November 2019) 19.

demonstrated, enforcing a binding DB decision under the 1999 editions may be problematic. FIDIC endeavoured to resolve this issue in the 2017 editions by a comprehensive re-wording of the clause on failure to comply with the DAAB's decision; this provides for an expedited arbitral award on enforcement of the decision without prejudice to the final disposition of the underlying dispute.

A DB decision or an arbitral award is a matter of contract, and its enforcement is ultimately an issue for a court in the jurisdiction where enforcement is sought. However, unlike arbitration, a DB decision does not have the same international recognition or support from legislation (with a few notable exceptions, such as in Indonesia).[15] The enforcement of a binding DB decision by a court will therefore be subject to local law. The following are examples of jurisdictions where direct enforcement of a DB decision by a court may be problematic:

- Brazil – A DAAB may not have the power to issue a final and binding decision.
- Czech Republic – A DAAB decision may not be binding unless it is an *ad hoc* arbitration.
- Italy – The obligation to accept a DAB decision as binding requires approval in writing.
- Peru – FIDIC DAAB clauses need to be reviewed for conformity with legislation.
- Switzerland – A DAAB decision is not directly enforceable.
- UAE – An arbitration award is required for a DAAB decision to be enforceable.[16]

29.6.4 Mediation

In the majority of cases, a DB decision is probably a good indicator of the likely result of an arbitration.[17] Once the parties are in possession of the DB decision, they are well placed to make a critical choice: accept it and comply with it, negotiate a commercial settlement or mobilise for arbitration.

FIDIC contracts provide for the parties to attempt amicable settlement after a DB decision that is subject to a Notice of Dissatisfaction. No process is specified, but mediation would be an obvious choice if the parties are inclined to further "jaw-jaw" after their limited scope "war-war". As the US experience with non-binding DRB decisions has shown, a reasoned decision on the merits prepared by a knowledgeable and respected DB can often assist the parties to reach a negotiated commercial solution.

Mediation after receipt of a DB decision should involve little preparation or cost; the parties have already considered and articulated their position for the DB, and they have the DB's view of the legal outcome and their reasons for it. However, the essence of amicable settlement is a compromise of legal rights; each party accepts something different to its preferred outcome in order to resolve the dispute and move forward without the further time and cost commitments of preparing for arbitration.

15 *Government Regulation No 22 of 2020, Implementation Regulations of Law No 2 of 2017* Articles 93 – 96.

16 Donald Charrett (ed), *The International Application of FIDIC Contracts A Practical Guide* (Informa Law from Routledge, 2020).

17 The 2019 Queen Mary survey found that only 25% of respondents considered that an international construction award infrequently reached the same conclusion as in pre-arbitral dispute resolution.

As noted in Section 29.4 , there may be difficulties in enforcing a mediated settlement agreement in many of the jurisdictions where the *Singapore Convention* does not apply.

29.6.5 Arbitration

Notwithstanding the time, cost and other benefits of pre-arbitral methods of dispute resolution, inevitably some disputes will require the detailed scrutiny and finality of arbitration. In some cases, this will be because of the complexity or importance of the issues, or because of the value of the dispute. In some jurisdictions, an arbitral award will be essential to ensure finality.

The efficacy of a DB adjudication depends on whether it is accepted and complied with by the parties, or there is an effective enforcement mechanism through the courts. As illustrated by the above examples, in some jurisdictions, an arbitral award may be a necessary precondition to enforcement in court. Thus, for some intractable disputes and some jurisdictions the most efficient method of dispute resolution may be expedited arbitration without the precursor of a DB decision. However, if the parties choose this route, it would be appropriate to amend the FIDIC General Conditions to ensure that a DB decision is not subsequently found to be a condition precedent to arbitration.[18]

Irrespective of the reasons for arbitration, the parties will be concerned with ensuring the most efficient and cost-effective process, particularly in an environment where there is likely to be an increased number of disputes. This is an issue which was considered in detail by the 2019 Queen Mary survey. Respondents were asked, inter alia, to identify factors that make international construction arbitration inefficient, what due process elements they would be prepared to forego to save time and money and what aspects of arbitral procedure offer the greatest potential to improve efficiency. Some of these issues are within the control of the arbitral panel, such as limits on submissions and oral arguments, and some are within the control of the parties, such as party tactics, unclear expert evidence and defective arbitration provisions. That survey provides a valuable checklist of issues that parties should take account of before embarking on an international arbitration or selecting an arbitrator. Substantial efficiencies can be achieved by refining procedures in known ways to suit the needs of the dispute and by the arbitral panel exercising more control.

29.7 Conclusion

COVID-19 had a considerable impact on construction projects around the world. It stopped or delayed progress, impacted supply chains, required new health and safety measures on construction sites, prevented site attendance and resulted in substantial increased costs. These impacts will inevitably result in claims for cost and delay in a changed environment where the contracting parties are subject to considerable economic pressures. Such claims are not illegitimate per se, nor do they necessarily imply a dispute. Construction contracts

18 In *Peterborough City Council v Enterprise Managed Services Ltd* [2014] EWHC 3193 (TCC) Edwards-Stewart J determined that under a modified Silver Book contract the parties were required to obtain a decision on their dispute before it could be finally determined in court. Similarly, the Supreme Court of Switzerland determined that submitting a dispute to a DAB is a mandatory precondition to arbitration in *A. SA v B. SA* [2014] Swiss Federal Supreme Court 4A_124/2014. See Section 27.3.2 above.

usually provide a detailed procedure for the submission and assessment of claims, often with strict time limits. Procedures such as those in the FIDIC contracts provide a first opportunity for avoiding disputes by enabling parties to agree on an outcome that is acceptable to them.

Contracts that provide for standing DBs provide a further opportunity for parties to avoid disputes by using the DB's expertise, for example by the use of advisory opinions. The successful track record of DBs in dispute avoidance, particularly in Australia, demonstrates the efficacy of this process. Even in contracts that do not provide for a standing DB, the parties can subsequently agree on the appointment of an *ad hoc* DB that may be able to assist parties to avoid a dispute.

Not all disputes arising from the impact of COVID-19 can or will be avoided. In the prevailing economic environment and where there may be considerable demand for experienced third-party Neutrals, there will be more need than ever for effective and efficient means of dispute resolution. Disputing parties will need to be pragmatic in assessing achievable negotiated outcomes where possible or utilising a method of dispute resolution that will result in a final and enforceable outcome as expeditiously as possible.

Whilst no one size will fit all, in this writer's view, a DB process as provided for in the FIDIC contracts will be suitable for many disputes arising out of the impact of COVID-19 – it provides for a third-party Neutral who can assist the parties to avoid disputes, or make a decision on the merits of a dispute in a limited time. The parties can use a DB decision to negotiate a commercial settlement with the assistance of a mediator or embark on arbitration with the background of the DB's decision and reasons. If arbitration is unavoidable the parties have the opportunity of tailoring an efficient procedure appropriate to the needs of the dispute.

In dealing with disputes in the aftermath of COVID-19, this writer considers that parties should exhaust their "jaw-jaw" methods of dispute resolution before resorting to "war-war". A party may find that winning the battle of an arbitration may ultimately result in losing the war for the project.

CHAPTER 30

The "best" method of resolution of construction disputes – elusive or illusory?[1]

30.1 Introduction

The argument about what is the "best" method of resolution of construction disputes has been a topic of discussion at construction law conferences, if perhaps somewhat tongue-in-cheek. For example, at the Second International Construction Law Conference in London in 2008, there was a debate entitled "Arbitration – is it the best form of dispute resolution?"

At the IBA Vancouver conference in 2010, the International Construction Projects Committee ran a session entitled "Construction dispute resolution – is it broken or can it be fixed?" The questions posed in the publicity for that session are typical of the search for the "best" dispute resolution method:

- Is twenty-first century arbitration too much like litigation?
- Is it failing to deliver cost effective and timely decisions?
- Should arbitration be more like adjudication?
- Should tribunals have more inquisitorial powers?
- Is disclosure necessary in every arbitration?
- Should Arbitrators be able to direct what evidence is heard?
- Who owns the process and who should own it: the clients, lawyers, the Arbitrator or the institutions?
- Is there a way forward?

Such issues are not confined to construction disputes. A conference in Ireland, "Alternatives to Litigation in a Civil Society"[2] discussed "some of the most pressing issues in current international dispute resolution", including whether viable arbitration and mediation regimes are a critical component of a modern justice system, and how do States, investors and NGOs bring about a change in the culture of justice.

The "best" method of resolution of construction disputes is arguably the avoidance of disputes. Considerable attention has recently been given to techniques for avoiding differences between the contracting parties from becoming disputes that need resolution.

1 This chapter is an edited and updated version of the paper: Donald Charrett, "The 'best' method of resolution of construction disputes – elusive or illusory?", first published in (2008) *International Construction Law Review* 88, published by Informa Law, London.

2 International Centre for Dispute Resolution, American Arbitration Association and Trinity College Dublin School of Law, 11 October 2011.

 DOI: 10.4324/9781003206897-33

Alliancing, in which the parties agree to "no disputes", and Dispute Boards (discussed in Chapters 25–28) are two such techniques that have proved effective in many projects. The emphasis on communication and risk management in modern standard form contracts such as the New Engineering Contract and the FIDIC rainbow suite are also aimed at reducing the potential for disputes to occur. However, such dispute avoidance techniques do not come cost free – there are recurring criticisms that the costs of alliancing, Dispute Boards and the use of NEC contracts are higher than those incurred in more "traditional" contracting. It is suggested that such criticisms rarely consider the real cost of the more frequent disputes that occur in traditional contracting, or that higher up-front investment in dispute avoidance may be "insurance" money well spent.

However, despite the parties' efforts at avoidance, construction disputes continue to occur, and require resolution. To use the well-worn legal cliché, the "best" method of resolution of such disputes "depends".

First, it depends on what criteria are appropriate to determine what is the "best" method. This chapter is based on the premise that, consistent with various civil procedure and arbitration rules, the objective of dispute resolution (**DR**) is to find a just solution in a timely manner with a minimum of expense. However, a "just, quick and cheap" method is almost certainly an oxymoron, as no method can deliver the most just outcome in the shortest time at the least expense. In what follows, the time, cost and "justice" (or quality of outcome) of a DR method will be referred to as its elements.

Second, a given dispute has a specific scope, involves specific parties, and occurs at a particular place and time. Since by definition disputing parties have different interests and different views of the relevant facts (alternative facts?) and/or the application of the law to the facts, there will often be different subjective and perhaps irreconcilable views of what criteria determine the "best" method of DR. For example, a plaintiff usually seeks a speedy resolution of a dispute, whereas a defendant may have commercial reasons to delay, so as to defer the time when damages are payable.

Third, each DR method has a unique combination of features that may all have a bearing on what each party perceives as the "best" method for the particular dispute. This chapter discusses these features, and notes that some of them may assume overwhelming importance in specific situations or for individual parties.

The chapter suggests some criteria that may make the search for the "best" method of DR for a particular dispute not illusory, and hopefully a little less elusive. It is implicit in the following that the analysis must ultimately be in the context of a specific and unique dispute, and not a generalised class of disputes. In each dispute, the disputants will view the relevant factors from their own subjective viewpoint. Accordingly, it is submitted that there is no objective "best" method in the abstract, even for a generalised class of disputes.

The thesis of this chapter is that the "best" method of resolution of a particular dispute from an individual disputant's perspective is typically the one that achieves the appropriate proportionality between the competing demands of the time and cost of the process, and the "justice" it delivers. In practice, this generally involves the selection of a DR method that gives the highest priority to the most important element(s), and balances the remaining element(s) accordingly, whilst giving necessary weight to the desired features of the process.

The overarching importance of providing for appropriate dispute resolution processes in a construction contract is emphasised by the following:

> An ordered efficient dispute resolution mechanism leading to an enforceable award or judgment by the adjudicator, is an essential underpinning of commerce. Disputes arising from commercial bargains are unavoidable. They are part of the activity of commerce itself. Parties therefore often deal with the possibility of their occurrence in advance by the terms of their bargain.[3]

30.2 Categories and methods of DR

The *methods* of DR considered here include all forms of ADR (however defined), as well as arbitration and litigation.

There are many methods of dispute resolution in current use, with generally understood terminology such as mediation, expert determination or adjudication. There are however, no universally accepted definitions that specify the exact characteristics of each method. For example, the way in which mediation is practised in one country may be different to the way it is practised in others; the same may well apply between mediators with different "styles" within one country. Furthermore, the nature and extent of the features that are inherent in any method of dispute resolution mean that there is a virtually continuous spectrum of alternatives, and one method may overlap with another because of certain common characteristics. For the purposes of this chapter, the exact definitions of different methods of dispute resolution are unimportant, although there is value in noting the different characteristics of some broad "families" or categories of dispute resolution methods.

It is suggested that the methods of dispute resolution in common use can be conveniently classified into the following broad categories, each of which has certain distinctive features:

- Negotiation
- Facilitation
- Evaluation
- Determination.

The distinctive feature of negotiation is that it involves the disputing parties only, and does not require a third party. With the right approach, negotiation is often successful:

> [H]onest business people who approach a dispute about an existing contract will often be able to settle it. This requires an honest and genuine attempt to resolve differences by discussion and, if thought to be reasonable and appropriate, by compromise, in the context of showing a faithfulness and fidelity to the existing bargain.[4]

Facilitation is a category of ADR in which an independent third-party (**Neutral**) endeavours to facilitate the parties' own resolution of their dispute, but does not impose a solution on them. It includes ADR methods such as mediation, conciliation and non-binding expert determination. In both negotiation and facilitation methods, the parties' resolution of their dispute is typically on a commercial basis rather than on the basis of strict

3 *Comandate Marine Corporation v Pan Australia Shipping Pty Ltd* [2006] FCAFC 192, 157 FCR 45, 95 [102] per Allsop JA.

4 *United Group Rail Services Ltd v Rail Corporation New South Wales* [2009] NSWCA 177, [70] per Allsop JA.

legal rights. It is also commonly accepted that the commercial outcomes that often result from negotiation or facilitation are the ones most likely to preserve business relationships, rather than the more formal evaluation and determination categories that determine the parties' legal rights according to their contract and the law.

Evaluation includes ADR methods such as early neutral evaluation, mini-trial and adjudication (both statutory and contractual). The distinctive feature of evaluation methods is that a Neutral evaluates the parties' rights in the dispute and (generally) provides a reasoned decision of how the dispute should be resolved according to the parties' legal rights under the relevant contract and otherwise according to law. The Neutral's decision is provisionally binding on the parties whether they agree with it or not, and may become finally binding unless the decision is disputed in accordance with a defined procedure.

Determination includes binding expert determination, arbitration and litigation; in these DR methods, a Neutral assesses the facts and the law in relation to a specific dispute, and provides a reasoned determination on how the dispute is to be resolved according to the parties' legal rights. Determination methods of DR can be distinguished from evaluation methods in that, subject to limited rights of appeal (if any), a binding expert determination, arbitral award or litigation judgment is final and binding on the parties.

It should be noted that similar procedures may be used in different methods. For example, a Dispute Board meeting with the parties before any dispute has arisen will function in a facilitation role in an endeavour to avoid disputes; however, it must act in an evaluation role once a formal dispute has been referred to it.

The terminology adopted in this chapter distinguishes between categories of DR (negotiation, facilitation, evaluation and determination), methods of DR (mediation, adjudication, arbitration etc.), and the procedures under which a DR method is conducted.

30.3 Hierarchy of DR categories

It is suggested that these four categories of DR methods comprise a gradation of both increasing time and cost and increasing formality. The term "formality" is used somewhat loosely to include issues such as the role of the Neutral and the rules/procedures within which s/he must operate, options available for possible outcomes, the extent to which the parties must be afforded natural justice, the nature and conduct of any hearing, the rules in relation to evidence, the extent to which a resolution of the dispute is binding, and the availability of further dispute resolution methods if either party is unhappy with the outcome.

To a large extent, the time and cost of a DR method go hand in hand – the longer a given method takes, generally the more it will cost when compared with methods that can be completed in a shorter time. One of the drivers for the modern approaches to expedite arbitration or litigation is a clear recognition that one of the most significant cost factors is the overall time taken for the process, and Arbitrators and Judges make strenuous efforts to shorten it.

These different categories are frequently used in a hierarchy of DR methods in progressive attempts to resolve a dispute, presumably on the basis that those methods lower in the hierarchy (such as negotiation), if successful, will resolve the dispute in a shorter time and at less cost than those higher up the hierarchy (such as arbitration). The 2017 FIDIC Red Book provides a practical example of the use of such a hierarchy:

- The Contractor submits a claim if he/she considers that he/she is entitled to any extension of the Time for Completion and/or any additional payment.[5] The Engineer is then required to consult with each Party and encourage discussion between the Parties in an endeavour to reach agreement,[6] and thereby seek to avoid a dispute over the claim. Only if the parties do not agree on the claim is the Engineer required to make a determination of the extension of time and/or any additional payment the Contractor is entitled to.
- The parties appoint a Dispute Avoidance/Adjudication Board (DAAB) at the outset of the project, which conducts regular site visits to enable the DAAB to become and remain acquainted with the progress of the Works and of any actual or potential problems or claims.[7] The Parties "may jointly request (in writing, with a copy to the Engineer) the DAAB to provide assistance and/or informally discuss and attempt to resolve any issue or disagreement that may have arisen between them during the performance of the Contract".[8] In this role, the DAAB would provide a non-binding expert determination (facilitation) of a potential or actual dispute.
- Either party may refer a dispute to the DAAB for its decision.[9] The DAAB is required to give its reasoned decision on the dispute in a limited time (84 days), and in accordance with the pre-defined procedural rules which require the DAAB to act fairly and impartially as between the Employer and Contractor, giving each of them a reasonable opportunity of putting their case and responding to the other's case, and adopt procedures suitable to the dispute avoiding unnecessary delay or expense.[10] The DAAB may conduct a hearing on the dispute.[11] This contractual adjudication (evaluation) is evidently intended to afford the parties procedural fairness, and the limited time frame is possible because of the DAAB's familiarity with the contract and the project.
- The DAAB's decision is provisionally binding on the parties and becomes final and binding if neither of the parties submits a Notice of Dissatisfaction within 28 days. If such a notice is served, then "both Parties shall attempt to settle the Dispute amicably before the commencement of arbitration".[12] The procedure for attempting amicable settlement is not defined, but clearly could include, inter alia, negotiation and/or mediation (facilitation).
- If attempts at amicable settlement do not resolve the dispute within 28 days, or if no such attempts are made, the dispute shall be finally settled by international arbitration (determination) under the Rules of Arbitration of the International Chamber of Commerce.[13]

5 FIDIC Conditions of Contract for Construction for Building and Engineering Works Designed by the Employer (2nd edn, 2017), sub-clause 20.2.

6 Ibid sub-clause 3.7.1.

7 Ibid Annex DAAB Procedural Rules 3.1.

8 Ibid sub-clause 21.3.

9 Ibid sub-clause 21.4.

10 Ibid Annex Procedural Rules 6.2.

11 Ibid Annex Procedural Rules 7.

12 Ibid sub-clause 21.5.

13 Ibid sub-clauses 21.6–21.8.

Thus, whilst the adjudication prepared in accordance with the 2017 FIDIC Red Book procedures is initially an "evaluation", it becomes a final and binding "determination" if neither party issues a Notice of Dissatisfaction. If a Notice of Dissatisfaction is issued, the parties are encouraged (by means of the 28-day delay in commencing arbitration) to resolve their dispute by amicable methods (negotiation or facilitation) before embarking on the time and expense of arbitration. If attempts at amicable settlement do not resolve the dispute, the parties are left to the final and binding determination of a formal arbitration.

30.4 The proportionality between time, cost and quality

It is implicit in this approach to DR categories that there is an increase in the time and cost of resolving a dispute as the parties move up the hierarchy. The value of adopting such hierarchical methods is that the time and expense of resolving a dispute is confined to the extent required to achieve an outcome accepted by all parties.

It is suggested that, along with increasing time, cost and formality as one moves up the hierarchy, there is also increasing "quality" or "justice" in the outcome. "Justice" in this sense is that there is a greater likelihood that the dispute will be decided correctly in accordance with the parties' legal rights. Thus, whilst the required outcome of an adjudication of a dispute under the FIDIC DAB procedures, or under the *Housing Grants, Construction and Regeneration Act 1996* (UK) is a decision in accordance with the parties' legal rights, the limited time available (and consequently limited cost) means that the result may not be of the "quality" that could be achieved by a more "formal" method such as arbitration or litigation. That is, the trade-off in adjudication is that a resolution is achieved in less time and at lower cost than arbitration or litigation, but at the risk that the outcome may not be legally correct. This is not a criticism of adjudication, but an observation that the limited time and cost of the method may not permit the more comprehensive investigation of the facts and the law relevant to the dispute that would take place in arbitration or litigation (and which may be required to determine the most "just" outcome).

It is suggested that the undoubted success of "quick and cheap" methods of DR is a reflection of the importance that parties place on the time and cost elements of a DR method, whilst recognising that they may not necessarily produce the most "just" outcome. Parties to an *HGCRA* or security of payment adjudication are aware that an incorrect evaluation, although provisionally binding, can be overturned in arbitration or litigation. The fact that so few adjudicated disputes are subsequently so determined is evidence that, to a substantial extent, parties are prepared to accept the "rough justice" of an adjudication.[14] It appears that, in the majority of cases, the parties accept that the justice they receive from the adjudication is appropriately proportionate to the time and cost of the process. As in construction projects, the required "quality" of a DR method may ultimately be governed by what the parties are prepared to pay for.

The concerns of constraining the cost and time required for DR is manifest not only in the emergence and development of new methods, but also in a continuing focus on

14 Robert Fenwick Elliott, "Building and Construction Industry Adjudication – the UK Experience" https://feg.com.au/papers-articles/building-and-construction-industry-adjudication-the-uk-experience/ (accessed 15 April 2021).

reducing the time and cost of arbitration (e.g. by limited time arbitration)[15] and litigation (e.g. by significant constraints on disclosure).[16]

It is submitted that as no method of DR can deliver in equal measure, the mutually incompatible aims of a just, quick and cheap outcome, one of the most significant differentiators of dispute resolution methods is in their different emphasis on the three essential elements of time, cost and quality. Every method achieves some proportionality between the demands of time and cost on the one hand, and "justice" on the other; the fundamental distinction between methods is in where the balance between "justice", and time and cost is struck.

The acceptable proportionality between the time and cost of a DR method and the "justice" it delivers is not immutable. For example, until recently the High Court in Australia considered that the requirements of justice meant that a litigant could not be prevented from litigating a fairly arguable case, even if that resulted in significant delay and additional cost: "Justice is the paramount consideration in determining an application such as the one in question [seeking leave to amend pleadings]."[17] In a more recent decision however, the High Court held that the just resolution of a dispute was not to be determined without considering the time and costs of the process:

> An application for leave to amend a pleading should not be approached on the basis that a party is entitled to raise an arguable claim, subject to payment of costs by way of compensation. ... limits will be placed upon their ability to effect changes to their pleadings, particularly if litigation is advanced. That is why, in seeking the just resolution of the dispute, reference is made to parties having a sufficient opportunity to identify the issues they seek to agitate.[18]

The reference in this judgment to a sufficient opportunity was a reference to rule 21(1) of the *Court Procedures Rules 2006* (ACT), which in common with other modern *Civil Procedure Rules*[19] and *Arbitration Acts*[20] stated an overarching purpose: "The purpose of this chapter, and the other provisions of these rules in their application to civil proceedings, is to facilitate the just resolution of the real issues in civil proceedings with minimum delay and expense." The acceptance of the need for proportionality in the costs of attaining justice in litigation in NSW is recognised in modern *Civil Procedure Rules*, e.g. s 60 of the *Civil Procedure Act 2005* (NSW):

> In any proceedings, the practice and procedure of the court should be implemented with the object of resolving the issues between the parties in such a way that the cost to the parties is proportionate to the importance and complexity of the subject matter in dispute.

On the premise that the fundamental objective of DR is to find a just solution in a timely manner with a minimum of expense, it is suggested that the theoretically "best" method

15 e.g. The Expedited Procedure Rules in the ICC Arbitration Rules https://iccwbo.org/dispute-resolution-services/arbitration/rules-of-arbitration/ (accessed 15 April 2021).

16 e.g. Lord Justice Rupert Jackson, *Review of Civil Litigation Costs: Final Report* (2010).

17 *Queensland v JL Holdings Pty Ltd* [1997] HCA 1; (1997) 189 CLR 146; (1997) 141 ALR 353; (1997) 71 ALJR 294.

18 *Aon Risk Services Australia Ltd v Australian National University* [2009] HCA 27 per Gummow, Hayne, Crennan, Kiefel and Bell JJ.

19 R 1.1 Civil Procedure Rules 1998 (UK); R 5 Uniform Civil Procedure Rules 1999 (Qld); s 56 Civil Procedure Act 2005 (NSW); s 7 Civil Procedure Act 2010 (Vic).

20 S 1C Commercial Arbitration Act (2010) NSW; s 1 Arbitration Act 1996 (UK); s 3(1) Arbitration Ordinance Cap 609 (HK).

of DR is the one that gives the most "just" outcome for the cost and within the time that the parties are prepared to accept.

30.5 Significant features of DR methods appropriate to construction disputes

Within any category of DR there are a number of methods that each have distinct features. In a specific dispute, there may be particular features of such importance as to effectively determine which DR method within a given category is "best". Further, certain DR methods are statutorily mandated (e.g. adjudication of disputes under the *HGCRA* in the UK or certain cost disputes in Australia, New Zealand, Singapore, Isle of Man, Malaysia, Ireland and Ontario under the relevant *Security of Payment Acts*), or prohibited (e.g. contractual commitment to arbitration of domestic building disputes in a number of Australian jurisdictions). Where such statutes apply, to the extent that they cannot be contracted out of, their requirements will prevail over normal party autonomy. Such legislative abrogation of the freedom of contract principle is generally justified as intended to protect weaker parties in construction projects, e.g. home owners and subcontractors.

The following are some of the important features of DR methods that need to be evaluated in the context of the suitability of a particular method to a specific dispute:

- Time and cost.
- Is a Neutral required to assist the parties?
- Party selection of Neutral: subject to agreement of the parties, or determined by a third party?
- Role of the Neutral: facilitation, evaluation or determination?
- Party and/or Neutral control over the DR proceedings: flexible subject to party agreement or limited by specific rules?
- Predefined procedures: none, broad guidelines or specific rules (e.g. Rules of Court)?
- Privacy and confidentiality of the proceedings: private and confidential, or open to the public?
- Finality and enforceability: determined by agreement of the parties, provisionally binding or finally binding?
- Possible outcome: non-contractual resolution that addresses other aspects of the parties' relationship, or legal rights according to law?
- Use/acceptance: well-known and widely accepted method, or bespoke and innovative?
- Hearing: do the parties have the right to be heard by the Neutral, or can the Neutral make a decision on the papers?
- Natural justice: are the parties to be afforded natural justice?
- Statutory requirements: are there statutory requirements mandating or prohibiting specific methods or procedures and, if so, to what extent can they be contracted out of?

Any disputing party is likely to have preferences for desirable features and may even be able to rank them in order of importance. Further, a party may have specific requirements that make one or more of the above features of overwhelming importance. Some typical examples of such cases in which the importance attaching to a particular feature may well dictate the only acceptable method of DR are as follows.

- Many construction disputes involve a complicated intersection of the facts and the law, in a contractual environment in which there may be a number of participants with potential liability. In some such cases, the time and costs of any formal method of DR, even facilitative methods, may be out of proportion to the amount in dispute. In these cases, the only commercially feasible method of DR may be negotiation.
- In a situation where preserving commercial relationships is paramount, the ability to achieve a "win-win" non-contractual outcome indicates that a facilitative method may be most suitable. Arguably the "win-win" outcomes so promoted by the protagonists of facilitation methods such as mediation come at the expense of the "just" resolution of the dispute according to the parties' legal rights. Such an outcome negotiated to preserve the parties' commercial relationship may result from one or both parties surrendering part of their legal entitlements.
- A commercial organisation may have a strong legitimate interest in maintaining confidentiality in the existence of a dispute. Whilst this is generally not problematic for negotiation, facilitation or evaluation methods (which are based on agreements between the parties and usually contain confidentiality provisions), it may make litigation unacceptable as a final and binding method, because of the public interest in open court proceedings. In these circumstances, binding expert determination or arbitration may be the only acceptable alternatives.
- Some organisations, such as insurance companies, are "repeat players" in DR in that the nature of their business inevitably generates a number of disputes with common characteristics. Such organisations have an interest in being able to resolve disputes with certainty, strictly in accordance with the law. If there is any uncertainty in the law on a particular issue that continually recurs, it is in the interest of a repeat player to have the law settled by litigation in a court of law, in order to establish a binding legal precedent. This wider interest in the resolution of a particular dispute may mean that negotiation, facilitation and evaluation methods are unsuitable. Nothing less than the time and cost of litigation will achieve the desired outcome of a legally binding precedent that can subsequently be used to resolve similar disputes in the future (probably by DR methods lower in the hierarchy).

30.6 Communication

Negotiation between contracting parties to resolve a dispute is always theoretically possible under the principle of freedom of contract. Whether or not there are formal requirements for negotiation built in to the contractually specified DR mechanism, the parties are always free to negotiate and agree to something different to that provided for in their original Contract, e.g. an extension of time that the Contractor is not contractually entitled to. The potential difficulty with negotiation, or any other form of DR not contractually specified, is that, by the time a dispute formally crystallises, communications between the parties may have broken down to the point that the parties are unwilling to agree to anything.

A further communication issue may arise once the disputing parties' lawyers are driving a dispute. The natural adversarialism of the DR methods the lawyers are familiar and comfortable with, and their professional (and commercial?) interest in achieving their client's strict legal entitlements, may be more prominent than ongoing negotiations to preserve the parties' future commercial relationship.

It is trite to observe that inadequate or lack of communication between disputing parties is often one of the root causes of disputes that arise. Unless appropriate communication in relation to a dispute can be established and/or maintained, neither negotiation nor facilitation methods are likely to be effective in resolving a dispute, since these methods are based on the parties finding their own resolution. The more "formal" methods of evaluation and determination are not predicated on party agreement, but explicitly include default provisions that apply in the absence of party agreement, e.g. the method of appointing an Arbitrator in the event that the parties cannot agree.

30.7 When should DR methods be selected?

Perhaps in an ideal world, all construction disputes would be resolved by negotiation, thereby preserving the parties' autonomy at the least expense and resolving their dispute in the quickest time. However, whilst such negotiation would achieve a commercial outcome, it is unlikely to always achieve a "just" outcome because of factors such as an imbalance of power between the parties. The involvement of a Neutral, perhaps technically qualified, in some role becomes essential if parties cannot resolve their dispute by negotiation.

Each of the DR methods within any category has its strengths and weaknesses, and may be more or less suitable for a particular dispute.[21] The "best" DR method should ideally be selected as appropriate to the features of the particular dispute. The difficulty with this approach is that the features of a dispute are only known when the parties are already in dispute, at which time they may be disinclined to agree to anything. In the absence of any agreement on methods of DR, a party seeking a remedy is left to its legal rights, i.e. litigation in the courts, or such other tribunal as is specified in any relevant legislation.

Hence, as a threshold issue, there is a need for parties to agree to the use of any alternative method(s) of DR to litigation, whether these are negotiation, facilitation, evaluation or arbitration as the final and binding method of determination. Many standard form contracts include a hierarchy of DR methods culminating in arbitration or litigation. There are obvious practical advantages in the parties defining alternative DR methods in the original Contract, which is negotiated before work starts when both parties have an obvious incentive to reach agreement. However, such prior agreement may commit the parties to use DR methods that, in the event, are not the most suitable for the particular dispute that ultimately transpires.

21 For a discussion of the pros and cons of different methods of DR of construction disputes, see: Philip Loots and Donald Charrett, *Construction Contracts for Infrastructure Contracts* (Informa Law from Routledge, 2022) Chapter 28.

A more flexible alternative approach, which can be incorporated in the Contract, is to leave selection of the most appropriate DR method(s) for a particular dispute to be determined by the parties with the assistance of a Neutral. This is the approach taken in the International Chamber of Commerce ADR Rules. These Rules are based on the appointment of a Neutral who assists the parties in determining the most appropriate ADR technique for the particular dispute, from the various alternatives of mediation, neutral evaluation, mini trial, any other settlement technique, or any combination of techniques. In the absence of agreement to use another ADR technique, mediation will be used. These ICC ADR Rules need to be supplemented by an arbitration agreement, if the final and binding determination of a dispute is not to be litigation.

The ICC ADR Rules give effect to party autonomy, to the extent that the parties agree. The Neutral's role can therefore be more or less proactive, depending on the parties' requirements. In neutral evaluation or mini trial for example, the technical and/or legal expertise of the Neutral can be drawn on in recommending a settlement or making a determination. The parties' autonomy extends to the procedures to be adopted for the chosen form of ADR, as these are not specified in the Rules. Thus, the parties could agree to the use of any appropriate institutional rules, or a "bespoke" set of procedural rules agreed to by the parties or proposed by the Neutral.

As institutional rules, the ICC ADR Rules provide for the administration of the procedure by the ICC. This has the advantage of a default mechanism for the nomination of the Neutral in the event that the parties cannot agree, and the quality control procedures inherent in the ICC process. Disadvantages include the additional costs, and perhaps time, involved in an ICC administered ADR procedure.

30.8 "Final and binding" determination

The majority of disputes are settled by a DR method in one of the categories of negotiation, facilitation or evaluation. To successfully resolve a dispute, each of these methods requires party acceptance of the outcome – of a negotiated settlement, a non-binding expert determination, an adjudication etc. Accordingly, none of the methods in these categories guarantee a successful outcome that will be acceptable to all disputing parties. There is thus always the possible need for a method of determination that will provide a final and binding resolution of a dispute, irrespective of whether the parties agree with it or not.

At the top of the DR hierarchy are those methods of determination that do not depend on party agreement of the outcome: binding expert determination, arbitration and litigation. Each of these methods decide the parties' rights according to law and are subject to no or limited rights of appeal. The procedures of arbitration and litigation afford the parties natural justice or procedural fairness, and are likely to remain the most widely used ultimate methods of DR. The distinctions between arbitration and litigation define features that may be determinative of which is the "best" for a given dispute.

30.8.1 Arbitration

In arbitration, but not in litigation, the parties have significant autonomy to agree on the conduct of the DR process. Importantly this includes the identity of the Neutral(s), the timetable and the procedures to be adopted. Further, arbitration can be truly international,[22] whereas litigation is conducted in courts subject to the procedural laws of a single jurisdiction.

A corollary of the parties' autonomy in the conduct of arbitration is that they can maintain confidentiality of the proceedings. This is generally not available in litigation because of the overarching public interest in the open administration of justice.

The above distinguishing features of arbitration identify a number of possible reasons why arbitration may be the "best" DR method for a particular construction dispute:

- Confidentiality of proceedings may be of overwhelming importance, particularly for large multinational companies that want to keep the existence of disputes and their ultimate outcome confidential because of commercial considerations.
- Party choice of Neutral(s) may be very important where there are complex technical issues that need particular expertise for a proper understanding of the issues in dispute.
- The outcome of "international" disputes may need to be enforced in several jurisdictions, or there may be a perception that the local courts may favour the "home team".

There are only limited circumstances in which a party unhappy with an arbitration award may have it overturned or not enforced by a court. Notwithstanding the parties' original acceptance of arbitration as the final and binding resolution of their dispute, the courts have ultimate jurisdiction to determine whether the due process of arbitration and the law was followed. This is not to say that litigation is a normal avenue of appeal from arbitration; courts in most jurisdictions around the world recognise the parties' freedom of contract to agree on arbitration as their final and binding method of DR. This is particularly so in those jurisdictions that have accepted the *New York Convention* or whose arbitration laws are based on the *UNCITRAL Model Law*, or similar principles.

30.8.2 Litigation

The High Court of Australia has expressed the courts' unique role in DR as follows: "The 'unique and essential function' of the judicial branch is the quelling of controversies by the ascertainment of the facts and the application of the law. Once a controversy has been quelled, it is not to be relitigated."[23]

In their function as the ultimate arbiter of legal disputes, courts occupy a unique position in the DR universe. Litigation in the courts has a number of characteristics that may make it the "best" DR method for a particular dispute. Some of these characteristics that may be significant for resolution of a construction dispute include:

- The final "quelling of controversies": once litigation (including any appeals) has been concluded, there are no other DR avenues available.

22 See Chapter 36 for a discussion of international arbitration subject to the UNIDROIT Principles, a set of legal principles independent of any particular jurisdiction.

23 *D'Orta-Ekenaike v Victoria Legal Aid* [2005] HCA 12 per Gleeson CJ, Gummow, Hayne and Heydon JJ.

- Court judgments state (or restate) the law, including both the authoritative construction of statutes and the common law.
- Court proceedings are generally public, and judgments are in the public domain and are widely known and discussed in the academic literature.
- The appeal process generally ensures that the final outcome is not dependent on the (perhaps idiosyncratic) views of a single judge.

Thus, in the quest for a "final and binding" resolution of a dispute, litigation could be preferable if the arbitration process adopted was readily susceptible to challenge in the courts. One of the modern responses to make arbitration a genuine alternative to litigation has been change in *Arbitration Acts* to substantially narrow the grounds on which an award can be appealed.[24]

30.9 Conclusion

In the third decade of the twenty-first century, there is a veritable smorgasbord of DR techniques. Each of them has its protagonists who sell (oversell?) its benefits and virtues, sometimes with the implicit message that a particular technique is the "best" method of dispute resolution.

For a specific dispute, one method may well be the "best" from a particular disputant's subjective perspective. It is suggested that other things being equal, it will generally be chosen to achieve the most appropriate proportionality of speed, economy and justice for the specific circumstances that the individual disputant judges to be efficacious. However, particular features required, such as confidentiality, the ability to choose an appropriate technically qualified Neutral, or the requirement for a legally binding precedent, may in fact determine the "best" method of DR. To the extent that disputing parties may have very different perspectives, the search for the "best" method for a particular dispute may be elusive.

It is suggested that the ultimate selection of the "best" method for a particular dispute should ideally be selected after the parameters of the dispute are known, if necessary, with the assistance of a Neutral. This proposal is, however, subject to the caveat that, if the parties propose to use arbitration as their final and binding method of DR, the arbitration agreement should be entered into at the time of the original Contract.

The fundamental thesis of this chapter is that there is no one "best" method of dispute resolution, either for a particular type of dispute, or from a particular protagonist's point of view. To that extent, the search for the "best" method is illusory.

24 e.g. *Commercial Arbitration Act 2010* (NSW); *Arbitration Ordinance* (Cap. 609) (HK).

PART 4

FORENSIC ENGINEERS AND EXPERT WITNESSES

CHAPTER 31

The engagement of forensic engineers[1]

Dr Donald Charrett & Professor Andrew Potts

31.1 Introduction

Commercial enterprises may need the assistance of forensic engineers for a variety of purposes. This chapter is intended to provide guidance for corporate counsel (and others) that have to engage the services of a forensic engineer. Faced with such a need for the first time, corporate counsel may be bewildered by the range of expertise available and may not be clear on the most appropriate procedures for finding and engaging the most appropriate forensic engineer for the task in hand.

The chapter suggests a procedure for finding, engaging and managing a forensic engineer who is appropriately qualified, and who will deliver value for money with appropriate predictability and accountability.

31.2 What is forensic engineering?

As used in this book, the term **forensic engineering** is:

> [T]he application of the art and science of engineering in the jurisprudence system, requiring the services of appropriately qualified [and experienced] professional engineers. Forensic engineering may include investigation of the physical causes of accidents and other sources of claims and litigation, preparation of engineering reports, testimony at hearings and trials in administrative or judicial proceedings, and the rendition of advisory opinions to assist the resolution of disputes affecting life or property.[2]

A **forensic engineer** (an engineer that practises forensic engineering) may also be required to give evidence to a tribunal as to the cause and reasonable options for replacement or repair.

Thus, forensic engineering may be confined to giving technical advice to counsel for "internal" purposes of an organisation, such as a technical review of the adequacy of a facility as part of pre-purchase due diligence, or it may be required for "external" purposes, such as expert evidence in a trial or arbitration that will determine the legal liability for defects or failures.

1 This chapter is an edited and updated version of the paper published in: Donald Charrett and Andrew Potts, "What corporate counsel need to know about engaging forensic engineers" (2012) 5(19) *International In-house Counsel Journal* 1. It is reproduced by kind permission of the publishers of *International In-house Counsel Journal*.

2 Peter Campbell (ed), *Learning from Construction Failures: Applied Forensic Engineering* (2001) 2.

 DOI: 10.4324/9781003206897-35

As noted below, it is important for corporate counsel to clearly understand the role they wish the forensic engineer to undertake, as this will have a considerable influence on the way the engineer is briefed and how s/he reports.

31.3 "Clean" and "dirty" experts

Corporate counsel should understand before briefing a forensic engineer whether s/he is required to act as an independent expert (often referred to as a "**clean expert**") or an expert consultant (often referred to as a "**dirty expert**"). The terms "clean expert" and "dirty expert" relate to whether or not the expert is seen as a member of the legal "team". Which type of expert role is required of the forensic engineer will determine how the forensic engineer is instructed, what documents s/he is provided with, what investigations s/he may conduct and what type of report the forensic engineer is instructed to prepare. It is therefore critically important that corporate counsel define in the brief to the forensic engineer whether s/he is engaged as an expert required to maintain independence from the legal team, or as an expert consultant to assist the legal team.

The appropriateness of engaging a forensic engineer as a "clean expert" or a "dirty expert" can only be assessed in the light of the relevant facts at the time. If the forensic engineer is specifically engaged to provide expert evidence in litigation or arbitration, it is clear that the forensic engineer must not be provided with any documents, e.g. on the client's case theory, that could jeopardise his/her independence.

Conversely, if it is not known whether or not litigation or arbitration might ensue, it may be appropriate to engage an expert consultant who can assist the legal team in whatever manner is appropriate and to the fullest extent possible, recognising that an independent expert may have to be engaged at a later time. This may often be the case at the early stages of an investigation that corporate counsel is required to undertake, before the legal dimensions of the issue are known, or whether litigation may ensue. In such cases, corporate counsel would be well advised to obtain the services of a "dirty expert" who can participate in determining the legal course to follow subsequently. Such an expert may ultimately be a valuable resource in selecting and briefing a "clean expert" when required.

There is a possible third type of role that an expert may be required to fulfil: an independent party who determines disputes between parties in an expert determination, acting as an Expert,[3] but not as an Arbitrator. An Expert role would not normally be regarded as within the remit of a forensic engineer and is not considered in this chapter.

31.4 Selecting the most appropriate forensic engineer

31.4.1 Defining the scope

The first step in the engagement of a forensic engineer is for corporate counsel to clearly define the task that the engineer is required for, i.e. the scope of the forensic engineer's services. It is frequently the case that the full extent of the forensic engineer's role is not clear at the outset. However, the initial task should be defined with some precision, e.g.:

3 See Section 25.3 for a discussion of expert determination.

- Investigate a failed facility and provide a report to corporate counsel on the technical causes of failure, to enable counsel to report to management on the legal consequences for the organisation, or
- Review pleadings and evidence in litigation or arbitration and prepare an expert witness statement for use in the proceedings.

Defining the scope with precision is fundamental to selecting the most appropriate forensic engineer, because it is the scope that determines the threshold issue of the skills required. Of course, the scope may evolve over time: corporate counsel may not understand the full ramifications of the issue at the outset, or have insufficient knowledge of the technical requirements, or the forensic engineer's investigations may need to go in a different direction to that initially anticipated.

Part of the scope of the forensic engineer may be to define the full scope of services required, after an initial investigation of the facts and the issues. Nevertheless, the initial scope should be defined as clearly as possible, particularly what are the "deliverables": those outputs of the forensic engineer's intellectual property provided to the client, e.g. a report on the causes of failure, or a presentation to senior management as to the recommended further investigations necessary.

31.4.2 Engineers and forensic engineers

Selecting the most appropriate forensic engineer is no different in principle to the process of selecting the most appropriate engineer for any design or construction task. Many organisations regularly engage consulting engineers for a variety of design and construction tasks and have well-established procedures for procuring the most appropriate engineer for the task in hand. Contracts for design services are discussed in Chapter 6. The difference between the engagement of a designer and a forensic engineer is that the "client" for the forensic engineer will be a lawyer, who may not be familiar with the engineer's discipline, but needs the engineer's technical expertise to assist in the resolution of (usually) a legal issue.

There are many branches of engineering, and many subspecialties within each of those branches. Whilst there is no universally accepted classification of the main branches of engineering, the main branches of civilian engineering (as opposed to military engineering) would probably be generally agreed to be: civil engineering, mechanical engineering, electrical engineering and chemical engineering. There are also many other specialised disciplines which are recognised as unique areas of engineering expertise, e.g.: petroleum engineer, mining engineer, materials engineer, aeronautical engineer.

Civil engineering includes structural engineering, geotechnical engineering, environmental engineering, traffic engineering, hydraulic engineering, hydrologic engineering, as well as "classical" civil engineering comprising engineering of roads, dams, tunnels, canals, harbour works and other infrastructure. Mechanical engineering involves mechanical equipment of all kinds and includes various sub-specialties such as air conditioning. Electrical engineering includes power engineering, electronics and instrumentation. Chemical engineering includes process engineering and metallurgy.

Specialisation within every branch of engineering has reached the point where the traditional "branches" are no longer very useful descriptors of the skills that any individual engineer has. If a corporate counsel requires a forensic engineer to investigate the failure of a piece of machinery, he may require the services of a structural engineer (a species of civil engineer) and/or a mechanical engineer, depending on the ultimate cause of the failure. Whatever the basic discipline of such a forensic engineer s/he will need to have sufficient expertise to recognise the possible causes of failure, and knowledge of the appropriate analytical tools to use in theoretical investigations to confirm a failure hypothesis. S/he will also need to know the limits of her/his expertise, to be able to advise when another expert is required.

Engineering of a project of any size requires the input of a team of engineers. Any modern project will inevitably require the skills of different types of engineers as outlined above. For example, even in a traditional civil engineering project such as a bridge, other discipline engineers will be involved: electrical engineers for the lighting and any electrical services, traffic engineers for planning traffic management during construction and in final service, electronics and software engineers for any electronic tolling system, materials engineers to specify the materials required to fulfil the specified durability requirements, mechanical engineers to design maintenance platforms required to inspect and maintain the bridge during its life, etc.

31.4.3 Quality management of engineering

In addition to the different engineering discipline teams involved in any engineering project of any size, each individual engineering discipline will involve a team of engineers to provide independent checking and quality assurance of the final product. In many developed countries, it is now virtually mandatory for the engineering of any significant facility to be carried out by an organisation that has an accredited quality management system **(QMS)**, usually certified to an international standard such as ISO 9000. Such a QMS requires documentation of the processes that the organisation will follow in producing its deliverables, and the certification is based on audits that provide objective evidence that these procedures are being followed.

An integral part of any QMS in engineering practice is the element of checking, particularly where there are complex engineering calculations and/or modelling using advanced analytical software. Such work requires the input of a team, indeed the checking requirement cannot be achieved without more than one individual. Often an engineering firm has specialists in analysis, who work alongside subject matter experts, whereby their combined efforts are integral to deliver the design. Similarly, when undertaking forensic engineering investigations, particularly those involving complex engineering calculations and analyses, for the client to have any degree of confidence in the findings, there should be a requirement to demonstrate that the work has been done by an appropriately qualified and experienced team, in accordance with an accredited QMS, involving formal checking of the work.

The engagement of a single named "expert" as a forensic engineer, no matter how eminent or experienced, does not of itself guarantee that a correctly derived finding will be delivered.[4] Indeed, without checking it may be just as prone to individual error as the engineering

4 See Section 21.6 for a discussion of the consequences of misplaced reliance on the expertise of a very eminent and experienced engineer to check the calculations of the design and construct Contractor for the Quebec bridge.

that is the subject of the investigation. This does not suggest that the forensic engineering team should not be led by a "lead expert" who may also present, represent and defend the work in court if required. However, in the modern world of engineering practice, it is considered to be "bad practice" to engage engineers who deliver work of a critical nature if they do not operate a recognised QMS. This applies equally to the work of forensic engineers (which may be relied upon in court), which should also be subject to formal checking along each stage of its production. Why should an individual expert be considered to be above good engineering practice and not as prone to human error as other engineers?

31.4.4 Matching scope with required expertise

It should be clear from this that the most appropriate forensic engineer for a particular brief will have specialised expertise and experience in the specific scope of work for which they are to be engaged. Whilst no two engineering problems are identical, previous proven experience in the same type of work is usually of great importance. Further, if the forensic engineering may lead to a requirement to give written and oral testimony, previous experience in preparing expert evidence is of great benefit.

For those experts who have a particular subject matter expertise, the giving of an expert opinion based on evidence put before them (e.g. specimens, data records etc.) can often be provided without the need to undertake complex calculations and/or analyses. Often practising academics, researchers or senior level consultants in a narrow field of expertise are well placed to provide an expert opinion as a sole practitioner. However, where the opinion relies upon detailed and complex engineering calculations and/or analyses, academics and sole practitioners typically do not have the technical resources and quality management systems and procedures to deliver work that would meet "expected good practice". Legal counsel are often not aware of the significant differences in engineering practice, and the associated resources, procedures and systems required to provide quality assured engineering design calculations and analyses. In the writers' view, where complex engineering calculations and analyses are central to the expert opinion being provided, the engagement of sole practitioner experts is not good engineering practice and invites the possibility of flawed opinions. This is because the opinions of a sole practitioner have not been subject to necessary checking, nor rigorous team questioning in their formulation (particularly in terms of modelling assumptions adopted).

The sources of information available to a corporate counsel seeking a forensic engineer with experience and expertise in a particular narrowly defined area are many and varied. If the counsel's organisation has its own engineering expertise, this is usually a good place to start. Professional organisations such as the Association of Consulting Engineers (UK) or the local member organisation of Fédération Internationale des Ingénieurs-Conseils (FIDIC) should be able to provide the names of consulting engineers with suitable expertise. Legal colleagues, including corporate counsel, solicitors and barristers may have had recent experience with forensic engineers. There are also commercial organisations that maintain databases of experts on the internet that may include appropriate forensic engineers.[5]

5 e.g. https://www.jspubs.com/search/index.htm#! (accessed 16 April 2021) contains 60 entries under "forensic engineer"; www.experts.com/ (accessed 16 April 2021) contains 83 entries under "forensic engineer".

However, the source of expertise for any such databases of experts should be understood and used appropriately. Some of these databases comprise mainly or solely academics or researchers who offer themselves as sole experts for forensic engineering and litigation. Many of the bodies which provide the databases of experts tend to be "clubs" in nature, and are thus run as closed shops with restricted access. The qualifications of the gate-keepers and the criteria they use to assess who should or should not be on their registers is often opaque and does not guarantee genuine current expertise. Selecting an expert by carrying out an internet search is fraught with risk: overblown claims of expertise cannot be critically assessed from the information presented even when read by those with expertise in the area.

Whilst the individuals on academic databases are usually well credentialed, with large lists of seemingly relevant publications related to the particular subject matter expertise, they often lack genuine experience in the practical implementation of the technology in the "real world". Without in any way criticising the intellectual output of modern engineering academics, it should be noted that current career pathways promote those who remain within the university system. The emphasis is on the output of a large quantity of papers each year, without necessarily encouraging, rewarding or recognising the benefit that engineers gain from participation in industry and/or having spent a significant part of their career in industry (as was certainly the case in the past). Academics, though expert in aspects of technology, do not always bring a worldly perspective as to how a practising engineer would or should in the "real world" use the expertise the academic may have, or have access to from their research. As such it is rare for an academic to be in a credible position to give an informed opinion as to what a "peer practitioner" would or should have done in a practical situation, what assumptions should have been employed and analytical tools used, etc., as they often have little or no recent current industry practice on they could base such an opinion.

From our experience, we tend to find that there are few engineers with genuine skills and expertise in forensic investigations, and those that do have such expertise tend to work in the "space" of remedial engineering, upgrade and life extension, working on legacy systems or structures, or in the application or adaptation of new technology into industry. Those involved in conventional detailed design or construction tend to be driven by Codes of Practice and the economics of projects that demand using proven off-the-shelf solutions or approaches, which are well established in practice and do not rely upon niche expertise for application. As such, these engineers, though competent and well-experienced practitioners, do not necessarily make experts, and do not normally employ a forensic engineering approach in their day-to-day practice.

31.4.5 Where does one find experts?

A genuine expert with current expertise will, as a general rule still be in practice. If retired, they will rarely be "put out to pasture", without ongoing links to a firm still working in the "space". Large project engineering firms tend to have an aversion to their engineers being involved in forensic engineering work in which their personnel may end up as an expert in litigation; this ties up valuable resources in an often demanding and unpredictable mode, and may be viewed as detrimental to the firm's existing business relationships (e.g. making adverse observations on existing or potential clients, or competitors who may do the same to them).

Further, such large project engineering firms tend to be focussed on engineering well covered by Codes and/or with low technical risk, and thus not working in the expert "space". As such, we have found that forensic engineering skills and experts suitable for forensic engineering and litigation work are mostly found in small to medium-sized consulting engineering firms. Often these firms attract engineers with post-graduate and/or research backgrounds, who have been motivated to grow subject matter expertise throughout their practising career, which small to medium sized firms will often accommodate and encourage, as it melds well with their client-base and practice. Such firms will often know who in the industry do and do not have genuine expertise, as they come across these players both in business and in their professional reading, conferences etc.

Ideally, the search for forensic engineers with the experience and expertise appropriate to the defined task scope will identify several potentially suitable candidates. The task then becomes the selection of the "best" from the alternatives.

31.4.6 Time, cost or quality of services?

The forensic engineer ultimately engaged will have to reconcile the conflicting demands of satisfying the scope of the brief in terms of time, cost and quality:

- Performing the required scope of work within the required time frame – perhaps under considerable constraints from court set deadlines
- Maintaining the cost of the investigations within a defined budget or not-to-exceed fee
- Providing the services to the required quality.

It is trite to observe that in any forensic engineering brief (or any other intellectual endeavour), it is not possible to have the highest quality delivered in the shortest time at the lowest cost. Inevitably there is a trade-off between the demands of completing the scope to the appropriate quality within the required time frame at an acceptable cost. In selecting the most appropriate forensic engineer, corporate counsel will have to make their own value judgment on where the appropriate balance lies. By way of example, the most experienced and expert forensic engineer (who could be expected to deliver the highest quality) may cost significantly more than the other contenders or may not be able to provide the deliverables within the required time frame because of other commitments.

If corporate counsel seeks proposals from more than one forensic engineer, it is recommended that these be based on the same scope of work. In addition to seeking information on the time, cost and quality of the services to be offered, corporate counsel may also wish to seek details of regular reporting to enable monitoring on the fees and progress of the work. In this context, the primary determinant of the quality that can be expected will be the identity of the individual(s) who are going to perform the work. Typically, the skills and experience that will be required will only be available in very senior individuals with years of experience. Such individuals inevitably have a high charge rate, particularly in circumstances where they are required to commit significant periods of time for court appearances.

It is suggested that, typically, a forensic engineer should be selected on the basis that s/he can provide the required quality, and their conditions of engagement should be tailored to ensure that the services are delivered within the required time and budget.

31.5 Briefing a forensic engineer

31.5.1 Who should formally engage the forensic engineer?

In most situations, it will be desirable for the forensic engineer's services to attract legal professional privilege to the maximum extent possible. In many cases, particularly if litigation is contemplated, it will be very important.

The common law test for legal professional privilege in many jurisdictions is whether a communication is made, or a document is prepared, for the dominant purpose of a lawyer providing legal advice or legal services. Ultimately it is a question of fact as to whether the communications of a forensic engineer were prepared for the dominant purpose of a lawyer providing legal advice or legal services. However, corporate counsel can preserve legal professional privilege to the maximum extent possible by ensuring that the forensic engineer is properly engaged, and the brief is carefully worded to ensure that the dominant purpose is for legal advice.

Corporate counsel should thus be aware of the appropriate entity that should engage the forensic engineer. Clearly the engagement should come from a legal practitioner, and not some other part of an organisation, such as the engineering department. In many situations, there may be a real doubt as to whether the engagement of a forensic engineer by corporate counsel would in fact preserve legal professional privilege; many courts view corporate counsel's non-legal activities as having the effect of waiving legal privilege. If considered necessary to preserve privilege, corporate counsel may need to have the forensic engineer formally engaged by, and reporting to, an outside law firm, particularly if litigation is contemplated.

Where a forensic engineer is engaged by an outside law firm as a "clean expert" on behalf of the end client, the writers strongly recommend that the formal engagement of the forensic engineer be by that law firm, and not by the end client. The writers have observed an emerging trend where the law firm, whilst instructing the experts, are not engaging the experts, but instead having the experts directly retained by their clients. The reasoning for such an arrangement is apparently to reduce the costs for the client, by avoiding the "mark-up" that the law firm would normally put on the experts' fees. It is clearly not avoiding any fees associated with management of the expert by the law firm; this interface remains, as the client is not involved in instructing the expert. It may be a moot point as to whether or not legal privilege of the expert's work is preserved by such a contractual arrangement.

However, in the writers' view, this is not an appropriate basis for retaining the expert. Indeed, it sets up and promotes a situation where the client may refuse to pay the expert's fees if they are more than they had been led to expect by the law firm. This can occur in situations where, although the law firm is instructing the expert and managing that interface, it has no direct contractual responsibility to pay the fees of the expert, even if such fees were increased based on their instructions. In our view, it is not ethically appropriate, nor constructive to the provision of an untainted expert opinion, if the expert has been required to argue for payment of its fees with the client, where it had no direct contact with that client when responding to the instructions of the law firm. This practice of engaging experts should be avoided.

Proper management of the forensic engineer's brief, along the lines outlined below, should avoid any surprises on the engineer's fees. If the scope is changed or increased, there should be a reporting mechanism that will provide early warning of the time and cost consequences of the changes that will facilitate proper management of those changes by the instructing law firm or corporate counsel.

31.5.2 Technical briefing of a forensic engineer

Corporate counsel should also be conscious of the potential for conflicts of interest to occur where their organisation's own engineers (often those involved in the original design, and sometimes themselves culpable in the failure) are the ones who liaise with the legal counsel in both recommending the experts to be engaged and in preparing the brief for experts. In some cases, particularly where they are genuine experts in their own right, this can be very beneficial in avoiding the engagement of weak or inappropriate experts (even pseudo-experts). Further, such an expert engineer may also provide a well-targeted (and well-supported by key data etc.) starting point for the experts to begin their investigations.

However, in the writers' experience, that situation tends to be the exception to the rule. In most instances, we have found the client's engineers originally involved in the project to have been dispersed to the wind, as project teams come and go, staff move on; sometimes companies (or at least their engineering/technical teams) are no longer in existence. When some part of the engineering team remains, it is often the case that they are generalists without the requisite skillsets to provide useful and insightful input to forensic investigations or litigation, or they are too narrowly focussed in their subject matter expertise, and unable to provide useful input beyond the bounds of their day-to-day operational duties. Where they were involved in the design/manufacturing/constructional failure, they tend to be very defensive in their dealings with experts. They may be in a state of denial, which does not assist in divulging the full extent of the circumstances involved, nor in identifying what expertise is required, or the scope of the forensic investigation required to provide a sound defence.

We consider it is usually better to engage a "dirty expert" up front to review the lay of the land, and to advise on the likely technical lines of attack that may eventuate and the soundest lines of defence that could be relied upon. This may in turn identify the required independent expert(s) and briefs they should embark upon. Further to the above noted points on the use of academics as experts, our experience is that engaging academics as "dirty experts" can be detrimental to the case if they are not skilled in litigation, and are without genuine and current industry practice.

31.5.3 The forensic engineer's brief

Regardless of the entity that formally engages the forensic engineer, it is suggested that the brief should contain requirements as follows. For simplicity, it is assumed in what follows that corporate counsel will brief the forensic engineer, even though that may not be the actual situation in some cases.

The importance of clearly defining the scope of the forensic engineer's services at the outset has already been emphasised. In addition to scope definition, the brief should also contain:

- The agreed basis of fees to be charged, including any cap or budget limit.
- The time in which the work has to be completed, or the time by which individual milestone activities are to be achieved.
- The deliverables to be provided by the forensic engineer at each stage.
- Any required regular reporting on progress and/or fees.
- A requirement that any change in assumptions or scope is to be communicated immediately to corporate counsel.
- Clear details of who to, and how, reporting on the substance of the forensic engineer's findings is to be done.

These items are required to provide the tools that corporate counsel need to manage the forensic engineer's brief discussed in the next section. As discussed above, in many cases it is not possible to fully define the brief at the outset. However, a properly prepared brief will recognise that changes may occur, and provide a framework for managing those changes so that there are no surprises.

An important part of the brief will be the information provided, on which the forensic engineer will base his/her advice and opinions, often supplemented by the engineer's own observations. The two prime requirements of this information are that it be comprehensive, and original. As with other aspects of the brief, corporate counsel may need assistance, perhaps from the forensic engineer, in determining what available information is required for comprehensiveness. In the writers' experience, the best solution may be to give the forensic engineer access to the original filed information and enable him/her to determine what available information is required. This is particularly the case in relation to discovered documents. The schedules of documents required to comply with court rules on discovery would rarely be adequate for the forensic engineer. A better solution is to allow the forensic engineer to make his/her own inspection of the original documents; based on his/her knowledge of the documentation of similar projects; s/he will generally be able to find the key documents expeditiously – perhaps even the "smoking gun".

The requirement to provide the forensic engineer with original documents is fundamental to maintaining his/her independence, and ability to give appropriate advice. One of the writers has experience of a brief in which the forensic engineer was engaged to act as an expert witness in court proceedings. Briefing materials included operational records that were fundamental to the analyses to be carried out by the forensic engineer. The material provided at first instance had, however, been "pre-processed" by the client organisation, perhaps in a misguided effort to save the expense of the forensic engineer carrying out the preliminary analysis of the data. The forensic engineer advised that s/he would be unable to sign the required undertaking to the court on independence unless the original data was provided. The original data was provided shortly thereafter!

31.6 Managing a forensic engineer's brief

In managing a forensic engineer's brief, corporate counsel will have expectations of the forensic engineer that have (hopefully) been defined in the brief. Corporate counsel can reasonably expect the forensic engineer to comply with the brief requirements, and report formally or informally as required, that those requirements are being met.

Given the importance of clear communications, not only in maintaining control, but also in preserving legal professional privilege to the maximum extent possible, it is highly desirable that the formal reporting process defined in the brief be adhered to at all times, both by corporate counsel as well as by the forensic engineer. The forensic engineer may have interfaces with a number of other people in the client organisation, such as lay witnesses who may need to provide factual material on which the forensic engineer bases her/his work. Nevertheless, any reporting on the forensic engineer's findings should be confined to the approved formal reporting process.

It may be desirable to emphasise to the forensic engineer that, notwithstanding the intention to maintain legal professional privilege, all of their material prepared in connection with the brief may ultimately be subpoenaed in court or arbitration proceedings, and they could be cross-examined on any material changes in wording, analysis or conclusions between draft reports. Any inadequately considered communications or draft reports revealed in discovery could thus detract from the credibility of the forensic engineer's ultimate findings.

It may be appropriate to point out to a forensic engineer that there is no requirement, ethical or otherwise, which compels retention of copies of his/her working documents and drafts prepared in the process of writing the final report. Ultimately, it is a matter for each individual forensic engineer as to how they manage their own records. Most experienced practitioners have their own internal practice of retaining on file (whether paper or electronic) only the documents of significance to their final analysis and make no effort to preserve any others.

Corporate counsel will be concerned to ensure that the forensic engineer's commitments to time and budget are met and can reasonably expect regular reporting to document actual against anticipated performance. Many consultants have internal management and reporting tools that can provide, on a weekly basis if necessary, reporting of actual progress against the budget and time programme. The discipline of the forensic engineer producing, and corporate counsel reviewing, such regular reports should give early warning of scope change or "creep", the anticipated budget being exceeded, or the projected time for deliverables not being met.

31.6.1 CTRs

One such management tool used by some consulting engineers is the cost, time and resources schedule (**CTR**) – a formal tool to plan, manage and report cost, time and resources on a task-by-task basis. The principle behind CTRs is the ability to subdivide any project into smaller tasks and, if necessary, sub-tasks that can be individually planned and resourced.

For each sub-task CTR, the following can be defined or estimated:

Scope:

- What work is required to complete the sub-task
- Client input required
- Consultant input required
- Consultant deliverable to client.

Time:

- Start date
- End date.

Resources:

- For each category of staff: estimated number of hours
- Other resources: software, consumables, communications, travel and subsistence, subcontracted services and products.

Cost:

- For each category of staff: estimated cost
- Total cost for all staff.

The total time, cost and resources for a specific task is determined by aggregating all the relevant sub-task CTRs. Similarly, the total time, cost and resources for the entire assignment is determined by aggregating all the task CTRs. By breaking down an assignment into "bite-sized chunks", a project of any size or complexity can be understood, and realistically planned and managed against tangible criteria: delivering a defined scope of work, based on known inputs and outputs, from anticipated resources and within a specific time frame. Variants of this technique for planning large projects have been used for many years; the increasing demands on performance by consultants has formalised the process such that it is now in common use, particularly in certain industries such as oil and gas.

The value of CTRs, properly used in managing performance, is that in defining what is to be done, it highlights departures from the original assumptions. These departures may be at the input level, e.g. the client may not have provided the required data by the defined start date of a sub-task, or the output level, e.g. the consultant may not have provided the agreed deliverable by the end date stated. It also provides a formal mechanism for dealing with a change in scope: e.g. if a new deliverable is required, a new CTR will need to be prepared, or an existing CTR amended. In either case, there is a basis for assessing the time, cost and resource impact of the scope change.

Whilst the client may gain great benefit from the forensic engineer's use of CTRs in planning, managing and reporting, corporate counsel should be careful not to intrude into the consultant's internal management processes. Where CTRs are used, what corporate counsel need, and should expect, is high level reporting on progress based on the consultant's analysis of the CTRs. Corporate counsel do not need, and should not expect, to be provided with the CTRs prepared by the consultant for its own internal purposes.

31.7 Conclusions

This chapter has made proposals on the selection, appointment and management of forensic engineers. They are intended to assist corporate counsel in finding the most appropriate engineer for the task in hand, ensure that the brief is properly prepared, and that the work is then managed in accordance with the brief.

The work of forensic engineers is frequently of great economic importance to corporate counsel's enterprise. It may relate to determining the organisation's liability for damages, the extent to which damages can be recovered from others, or the organisation's liability to penalties under statute. Accordingly, it is suggested that the primary focus in engaging a forensic engineer should be to find the engineer with the most appropriate experience and expertise directly related to the task for which they are engaged. In the case of forensic engineers who may be required to give expert evidence in court or an arbitration hearing, previous court experience, and a demonstrated ability to communicate complex technical issues clearly, are important attributes.

The starting point for the brief is a clear definition of the scope of the work required of the forensic engineer. In preparing the forensic engineer's brief, corporate counsel needs to be mindful whether s/he is to be engaged as a "clean" or a "dirty" expert. If the expert is required to be an independent expert, the material provided to him/her should be appropriately limited. Although it may not be possible to retain legal professional privilege over the forensic engineer's communications, the possibility of this will be maximised by formal engagement of the forensic engineer by a legal practitioner, and a careful wording of the brief so that the dominant purpose is to assist with the provision of legal advice. The brief should also recognise the possibility or likelihood that the scope may change after preliminary investigations have been carried out, and require regular reporting of progress.

Corporate counsel can endeavour to avoid surprises by requiring the forensic engineer to comply with the regular reporting requirements in the brief, both in relation to progress of the work, and the financial performance in relation to any budget. Many engineers will have internal management tools for such purposes, based on the use of CTRs or something similar. Such regular reporting should flag potential issues in relation to the timing of the deliverables, performance against the budget, or whether the scope needs to be revised for changes that have occurred because of changed instructions or changed circumstances.

However, corporate counsel should avoid engaging a forensic engineer who is a "hired gun":

> Many experts are willing for a generous (and sometimes for a modest) fee to bend their science in the direction from which their fee is coming. The constraints that the market in consultant services for lawyers places on this sort of behaviour are weak … The judicial constraints on tendentious expert testimony are inherently weak because judges (and even more so juries …) lack training or experience in the relevant fields of expert knowledge.[6]

6 *Indianapolis Colts Inc v Metropolitan Baltimore Football Club Ltd Partnership* [1994] USCA7 949, 34 F 3d 410 at 415 (7th Cir 1994) per Judge Posner.

CHAPTER 32

Guidelines for experts[1]

32.1 Introduction

As discussed in the previous chapter, lawyers frequently engage forensic engineers to provide expert evidence in connection with actual or contemplated litigation or arbitration. This chapter is confined to guidance for a "clean expert" in preparing expert reports and giving evidence in arbitration or litigation.

Expert evidence is an exception to the evidentiary rule that a witness cannot give evidence of their opinion: "If a person has specialised knowledge based on the person's training, study or experience, the opinion rule does not apply to evidence of an opinion of that person that is wholly or substantially based on that knowledge."[2] An expert or **expert witness** is a witness that gives evidence of his or her opinion based on his/her specialised knowledge acquired from training, study or experience. The terms are used interchangeably in this book.

Many disputes over design or construction involve complex technical issues that must be explained to a Judge or Arbitrator by a person with the requisite "expert" knowledge. An expert must have the appropriate training, study or experience, and must have the ability to articulate their opinions in a manner that is persuasive to and understandable by lay persons. An expert must also comply with a number of formalities for their evidence to be admissible. The detailed rules for expert evidence in several common law jurisdictions are discussed in Chapter 34.

But most importantly, an expert must be seen to be independent, and not appear to be an advocate for the party they are representing. Expert evidence is not uncritically accepted, as Judges have long been sceptical of "hired guns":

> [F]or generations judges have complained about the partiality of expert opinion witnesses. In 1843 Lord Campbell, in 1873 Sir George Jessel MR, and in 1963 Walsh J lamented their "bias". Indeed many litigation lawyers can doubtless recall instances of experts who say one thing in one case and a contradictory thing in another, each time to the supposed advantage of the party paying them. In 1849 Lord Cottenham LC and in 1876 Sir George Jessel MR drew attention to the skewed manner in which experts are selected, as each side rummages through a group of experts until the most favourable one is found.[3]

1 This chapter is an edited and updated version of an extract from an article by PJ Murphy, L Duthie, B Bielert and D Charrett titled "Australian Legal Guidelines for Forensic Engineering Experts". It was first published by Engineers Australia in the *Australian Journal of Structural Engineering* (2010), V11, No1, pp11–22, and is reproduced here with permission.

2 *Evidence Act 2008* (Vic), s 79(1).

3 *Dasreef Pty Ltd v Hawchar* [2011] HCA 21, [56] per Heydon J.

DOI: 10.4324/9781003206897-36

The costs of expert evidence in technically complex litigation or arbitration can be substantial, and modern courts and arbitral tribunals have implemented a number of techniques in an endeavour to limit the costs and ensure that expert evidence is admissible and cogent. Amongst these modern techniques are:

- Expert reports as an expert's evidence-in-chief
- Expert conferences prior to a hearing
- Concurrent evidence in a hearing in which all experts opining on an issue give their evidence in the same session.

This chapter discusses these techniques and provides some guidance to assist experts in preparing expert evidence and presenting it in court or an arbitration hearing. Experts should present their evidence in a way that avoids Heydon J's criticisms:

> The tendency of experts to dominate proceedings creates numerous other perils for the integrity of the trial process. One is that experts, who ex hypothesi know much more about their fields of expertise than judges and juries do, and who know of that vast disparity, will take over the conduct of cases and exert excessive influence over their outcomes. Another is that experts, no doubt contemptuous, often justifiably, of the ignorance of the lawyers, will appoint themselves as advocates for the party calling them. Another is that experts render their evidence less than useful by giving it in a form conventional in their discipline but not conforming to the rules of evidence. Another is the tendency of experts to drift into giving the courts reasons why they should accept or reject the evidence of lay witnesses on matters of primary fact.[4]

32.2 Expert reports

Irrespective of the nature of evidence to be given during a hearing, and indeed even if a hearing does not take place, an expert will invariably be required to provide a written report.

Such a report is required to fulfil one or more of the following objectives:

- To inform the client of the expert's opinion on the causes of an incident or event
- To inform the client's lawyers of issues which will be central to the finding of causal and legal liability for the event and its consequences
- To provide a basis for negotiations with representatives of the opposing party
- To provide an expert opinion which can be used as evidence in the legal proceedings and any hearing
- To critically analyse the reports of an opposing party's expert with a view to identifying any matters upon which the expert disagrees, and to explain the reasons for that disagreement.

To fulfil these disparate aims, more than one report may be required as the case evolves.

4 *Dasreef Pty Ltd v Hawchar* [2011] HCA 21, [58] per Heydon J.

32.3 Expert reports for the purposes of litigation

One of the most often overlooked but critical elements of an expert report is that it must set out clearly, either in the body of the report and/or by way of annexing a detailed curriculum vitae, the expert's qualifications. This is a threshold issue; if an expert is not found to have sufficient qualifications and expertise to express an opinion on a particular topic then his/her evidence will not be admitted. Alternatively, if the expert's qualifications and expertise are not as relevant or as strong as those of the opposing expert, then the tribunal may adjust the weight that it gives to that expert's evidence.

32.3.1 The brief

The dispute resolution process is managed by lawyers, who should define the brief for an expert at each stage of the engagement. A properly prepared brief will define and document in sufficient detail the factual and documentary material on which the expert is to base his/her report, and the specific questions which the expert is to answer (with detailed reasons).

An expert should not proceed with preparation of a report without a clear written brief. Furthermore, the expert should ensure that the report addresses only those issues raised and that it does not go beyond answering the questions posed in the brief.

It may be that the answers to the questions posed in the brief are not sufficient to determine the issues on which expert evidence is required, or they may lead to further questions which need to be answered. This may require modification of the brief, and further opinion evidence from the expert; however, it is preferable that the expert evidence evolves in this way rather than the expert providing extraneous material in a draft report, or answers to questions that were not asked.

32.3.2 The expert's opinion

It is essential that the expert's report reflects the opinion of the expert. The expert must not place himself or herself in a position where it can be subsequently alleged that the opinion is in fact not wholly that of the expert. Expert reports have been rejected in whole or in part by courts based on a perception that the expert's opinion has been unduly influenced by the legal team, with a consequent loss of independence on the part of the expert. All contact with the expert should be made through the lawyers in a formal way. In no circumstances should the independent expert liaise directly with the client or hold informal discussions with them without the lawyers being present. It must be kept in mind that all communications with an independent expert could be required to be disclosed during the hearing, and so caution must be exercised at all times in this regard.

Counsel of perfection would therefore be for the expert to prepare and issue their report in isolation, without discussing the contents with, or providing any drafts to, the lawyers. However, this approach fails to acknowledge the real and practical benefits that the expert (and the tribunal) can obtain by a careful, limited and proper interface with the lawyers in the course of preparation of the expert's report.

32.3.3 Expert's interface with lawyers

The first area of potential benefit is in feedback on the form of the expert's report. Especially in the case of an overseas expert not experienced in common law litigation, or a local expert providing an expert's report for the first time, receiving appropriate comment on the report can be invaluable. Questions frequently arise such as:

- To what extent, if at all, should the expert provide drafts of his/her report to the legal team?
- How should the expert deal with any comments on the draft report?
- Are there any circumstances in which an expert should change the report based on comments from the legal team?

If done properly, feedback on a report can avoid significant cost and expense by the expert presenting a report to the court which is not readily understood and will either require preparation of a supplementary report to better explain the expert's opinion, or considerable time in the witness box by the expert to explain his or her opinions and the basis for them.

An independent expert cannot and should not receive any comments from the legal team as to any matter involving the substance of the expert's opinions. However, there are several areas where the legal team may be able to assist the experts with the form of the report. For example:

- The legal team can advise on the legal admissibility of the contents of the report, e.g. opinions expressed on matters outside the expert's expertise (such as legal conclusions).
- The legal team can assist with the clarity, completeness and structure of the expert's reasoning. The legal team can suggest how further data is necessary, data could be better presented, where reference is required to professional literature and where the analysis needs to be rephrased (for example to assist a Judge or Arbitrator who has no scientific or engineering expertise).
- The legal team can assist by identifying any weaknesses in the logic and analysis of the report that an opposing expert may try and capitalise on.

The overarching requirement is however that the report must be (and be seen to be) drafted by the expert, and not by the legal team, and that the legal team should not interfere in any way in the views or opinions expressed by the expert.

32.3.4 Expert's files and documents

Experts should be aware that some parties in litigation or arbitration routinely subpoena the opposing expert's own files and documents, and then seek to cross-examine the expert on any material changes in wording, analysis or conclusions during the various phases of preparation of their report. There is no requirement, ethical or otherwise, which compels an expert to retain copies of his/her working documents and drafts prepared in the process of writing the final report submitted to the tribunal. Ultimately, it is a matter for each individual expert as to how they manage their own records – most experienced experts have their own internal practice of retaining on file (whether paper or electronic) only the documents of significance to their final analysis and make no effort to preserve any others.

32.3.5 Factual and opinion evidence

The expert should be clear in his/her own mind, and in the report, of the difference between factual evidence and opinion evidence. An expert's factual evidence is that based on the application of his/her own physical senses, i.e. what the expert personally saw, heard, smelt, felt etc. The expert's factual evidence should be clearly identified in the report, and in a different section to and preceding any opinion evidence.

The expert should also clearly identify any factual evidence provided by others on which s/he relies. The identification should not only state what "facts" are relied on, but also the source of those "facts", e.g. specific documents, or lay witness statements. Any such evidence must be proved by others, and, if it is not, the assumed "facts" will not be taken to be "facts" by the tribunal (Judge(s) or Arbitrator(s)). Witnesses for another party may give contradictory evidence, and their version of events may be regarded by the tribunal as more likely, and hence accepted as "facts".

Thus, although an expert's opinion may be "correctly" arrived at using well-established "science", if the factual basis on which it is based is not accepted as "facts" by the tribunal, the expert's opinion may have no validity. For this reason, it is essential that all the facts on which the expert's opinion is based are clearly articulated, and their importance as a basis for the opinion highlighted. The lawyers preparing the client's case can then ensure that the necessary factual evidence is given by others.

32.3.6 Contents of expert report

In summary, an expert's report should contain the following:

- Details of the expert's training, study and experience, sufficient to qualify him/her as an expert to give an opinion on the questions posed in the brief
- The brief which commissioned the expert to prepare the report
- The Court Rules or Guidelines with which the report complies, and explicit acknowledgement that those Rules have been complied with
- Any factual evidence of the expert's own observations etc.
- Any other assumed "facts" on which the expert's opinion is based, and the source of these assumed "facts"
- The scientific or technical basis on which the expert's opinion is based, and
- The expert's opinion on the questions/issues raised in her/his brief.

The recommended content of an expert report is discussed in more detail in Section 34.4.

32.3.7 Expert's report in reply

It is usual practice for an expert to be given an "opposing" expert's report, and to be asked to prepare a report in reply. As with the expert's original report, the lawyer's brief should clearly define what the expert is required to cover in the report in reply.

The issues may include some of:

- Common ground between expert opinions
- Differences between factual bases for opinions
- Differences between experts' opinions
- Whether the "opposing" expert is appropriately qualified and experienced to express the opinions he/she has expressed.

For technical and legal reasons, it may be unnecessary for an expert to address certain aspects (or even the whole of) an "opposing" expert report, and the expert should go no further in their reply than requested to do so.

32.4 Expert reports for the purposes of arbitration

Arbitration rules generally do not have any stipulations concerning how an expert is to give evidence to an arbitral tribunal.

The parties to an arbitration could choose to adopt the International Bar Association's Rules on the Taking of Evidence in International Arbitration, rules which include mechanisms for the presentation of expert evidence. These evidentiary rules, however, deal more with the form of any expert report than higher concepts of duties owed by the expert witness.

What Arbitrators will do, however, when assessing the weight of evidence given by a party-appointed expert is to take into account the perceived degree of independence of that expert. This means that party appointed experts do need to persuade the arbitral tribunal that their evidence is independent.

What should experts do to meet the required standard of independence? The Court Rules governing expert evidence represent a useful benchmark, being themselves based on case law dealing with the conduct of experts. Party-appointed experts in arbitrations would be well advised to generally follow the Court Rules in order to establish their independence to the satisfaction of the arbitral tribunal. Court Rules for expert evidence are discussed in Chapter 34.

Of particular importance are the obligations owed to the arbitral tribunal by the expert – to be objective, unbiased and not partisan – which stands side by side with the duties of the expert to the party which has appointed him or her.

32.5 Expert's obligations and duties in relation to a hearing

If a dispute progresses to the stage that a court or arbitration hearing is anticipated, the expert will encounter more involvement and participation by the barristers engaged by the client. During a hearing, it is the barrister's responsibility to present the case to the tribunal, with the support and assistance of the lawyers and experts.

32.5.1 Experts' conferences

An **experts' conference** (or **conclave**) is a pre-hearing meeting of experts, usually without lawyers, at which the experts attempt to find common ground in their respective opinions, in order to narrow their differences, and thereby reduce the extent of issues which require evidence at the hearing. An experts' conference may be chaired by an independent facilitator, or the experts may be left to their own devices.

Before the conference, it is highly desirable that the experts are provided with a set of questions for them to answer. Questions are often prepared by agreement between the parties' lawyers. The difficulty and time required to achieve this should not be underestimated, since each lawyer will have independent views on what are the key issues in their client's case. However, without such an agenda, the experts' conference may not achieve anything of value, particularly if the experts' reports have addressed different questions.

If the experts' conference is to be chaired by an experienced independent facilitator who is familiar with the pleadings, the expert reports and the legal issues in the case, the facilitator may be the best person to formulate the questions to be answered in the expert conference.

Given that there may be disagreement as to key factual evidence, the questions must be carefully structured to ensure that all experts answer them from the same factual basis. It may be that questions need to be separately answered for more than one alternative factual basis. It is therefore imperative that those aspects of the factual evidence relevant to the experts' opinions are identified as agreed or stated in the alternative as contended for by the parties.

In this writer's view, either the presence of an independent facilitator, or a prepared list of questions to be answered by the experts, is an essential precondition for an experts' conference to be worthwhile.

The discussions between the experts (and the facilitator if there is one) in the conference are "without prejudice" and cannot be subsequently used as evidence in the hearing. This is to ensure that the conference discussions can be robust, and there is no disincentive to a free and frank exchange of views and exploration of alternatives by the experts.

The "deliverable" of an experts' conference is a joint report, with the experts' answers to the questions posed to them. Where they agree on an answer to a specific question, the report may require little elucidation. However, where the experts disagree, the joint report should document each expert's reasons for holding the opinion to which they adhere. The joint report is not "without prejudice" and subsequently becomes evidence in the hearing.

32.5.2 Preparations prior to a hearing

The most persuasive expert evidence given orally in a hearing will be expressed confidently, articulately and clearly, in terms the Judge/Arbitrator will understand. This requires that the expert be completely familiar with his/her own expert report(s), and the factual assumptions and the scientific/technical basis on which their opinions are based. It should be noted that there is often a long delay between the preparation of the written report and giving oral evidence, so the expert must set aside time prior to the hearing to refresh his/her recollection of their report. As oral evidence in a hearing may be largely confined to cross-examination, it is equally important for an expert to be completely familiar with all "opposing" expert reports, and the extent of and reasons for any disagreement with the opinions of any other experts.

It is apparent that the best preparation for an expert prior to a hearing is to reread their own report(s), as well as those of the "opposing" experts. Oral evidence in a hearing is normally expected to be just that; if an expert wishes to refresh her/his memory by referring to their notes or report(s), permission should be sought from the Judge/Arbitrator. The less this is required, the more compelling the oral evidence – another reason why complete familiarity with the material is so important.

Experts should not lose sight of the fact that tribunal hearings are formal processes, in which the opposing parties may have large amounts of money and their reputation at stake. It is therefore important for an expert to ensure that his/her appearance and demeanour are appropriate to portray them as mature, experienced professionals who understand the gravity of the proceedings. Thus, formal business attire and an upright attentive posture in the witness box will give an initial favourable opinion of the expert's professionalism and will increase the likelihood that their opinion will be accepted by the Judge/Arbitrator.

The nature of tribunal hearings is such that it may not be possible to specify exactly the day and time the expert is required to give his/her evidence. The expert will therefore need to advise their instructing lawyers beforehand whether there are any conflicting engagements that could prevent the expert from giving evidence when called. Once an expert has been given the potential firm dates and time windows for their evidence, it is essential to ensure that these are kept free of conflicting appointments. It seriously detracts from an expert's professional image if s/he does not appear at the designated time or expects to be able to leave the hearing for another appointment before his/her evidence has been completed.

It would be improper for a lawyer or barrister to "coach" an expert in the evidence that s/he will give, where "coaching" refers to suggestions as to what an expert should say in response to certain questions. However, it is not improper for a lawyer to help an expert by advising the types of questions that may be asked in examination-in-chief and cross-examination. For example, the Victorian Bar Rules provide that a barrister may test in conference the version of evidence to be given by an expert, including drawing the expert's attention to inconsistencies or other difficulties with his/her evidence, but must not coach or encourage the expert to give evidence different from which the expert believes to be true.

It is usually helpful for an expert to be instructed on the general court environment and etiquette, and on the difference between examination-in-chief and cross-examination, and given advice on how to answer questions in a way that will assist in making their evidence more compelling, e.g.:

- Listen carefully to the question
- Ask for the question to be rephrased if it is not understood
- Answer only the question asked
- Do not volunteer information
- Do not argue with or question the barrister.

Careful preparation along the above lines will give an expert more confidence in giving his/her evidence. This will significantly enhance the likelihood that the Judge/Arbitrator will be persuaded by the expert's evidence.

32.5.3 Hearing protocols

The "traditional" protocol for giving evidence in a tribunal hearing is that the plaintiff presents its evidence first, usually all the lay evidence followed by all the expert evidence. This is followed by the defendant presenting all its evidence, usually lay evidence followed by the expert evidence. These "traditional" protocols are now frequently changed, particularly in regard to expert evidence which may be presented concurrently for the plaintiff and defendant. This is discussed further below. Other changes in order may be made in specific situations, e.g. to accommodate the time that an expert is available to give evidence.

There is, however, one traditional "protocol" that is adhered to, irrespective of the order and manner in which expert evidence is given. This is the requirement that, whilst an expert is being cross-examined, s/he must not communicate with their instructing lawyer or barrister for the expert's client until cross-examination has been completed (except in accordance with the terms of an agreement with the opposing party's legal advisors). Thus, if an expert's cross-examination is adjourned for lunch or overnight, the expert must not communicate with their client's lawyer, barrister or any other expert engaged by the client. Sometimes the Judge/Arbitrator will give an appropriate warning before an adjournment. However, even in the absence of such a warning, it is important that this protocol is strictly observed to ensure that there can be no suggestion of "coaching" or "interference".

Another area in which experts should seek instructions from their instructing lawyer, is whether it is appropriate or required for them to sit in the hearing to hear other witnesses give evidence, before they are called. The modern approach in some tribunals is for all experts to give their evidence in the presence of each other, in what is colloquially referred to as a "hot tub" (see below). Even in the absence of a hot tub, in some jurisdictions it is expected that experts will hear the evidence of the other experts. However, in other situations, it may be necessary to seek leave from the tribunal for an expert to hear the evidence of other experts before they have given their own evidence. There are no hard-and-fast rules, so an expert should discuss this with their instructing lawyer before the hearing.

32.5.4 The nature of evidence in a hearing

The evidence-in-chief of an expert is their "story", i.e. what they saw, heard, smelt, felt etc., and the opinions they formed and the basis for those opinions.

Traditionally, evidence-in-chief was taken by the client's barrister asking questions of the expert in the hearing (oral examination). These questions must be "open" and not leading, i.e. the barrister cannot state a proposition which s/he asks the witness to agree to or not. Non-leading questions require the witness to tell his/her own story in their own words, e.g. "when you went to the site on [date], what did you do?"

It is now also common for evidence-in-chief to be expressed in the expert report(s); this evidence may be adduced by the examining barrister asking whether:

- The report was written by the expert
- The expert wishes to make any corrections
- The expert honestly holds the opinions expressed.

Subject to any corrections advised by the expert, the report(s) may then be signed by the expert and tendered as evidence-in-chief by the client's barrister. Different protocols for the adoption of expert's reports as evidence-in-chief may apply in different jurisdictions or tribunals, or even between different lists in a specific court. An expert should consult with their instructing lawyer to ascertain the protocol that will apply to them.

If there are further matters not included in the expert's report that the client's barrister wishes to bring out in evidence, there may be some oral examination-in-chief.

By contrast, cross-examination by the "opposing" barrister would usually be entirely in the form of leading questions. Good cross-examination consists of a series of questions, each stating a simple proposition which only requires a yes or no answer (and which may be in a form to invite a yes answer). Individually, the answers to the questions may seem innocuous, and it may not be obvious to the expert where they are leading, but collectively they "ring fence" a major issue, for which the last question "closes the gate" to elicit the concession the cross-examiner is seeking.

Notwithstanding the desire of the cross-examining barrister to confine an expert witness to yes/no answers, an expert should not hesitate to put forward any qualification or explanation which s/he feels is necessary to properly explain the answer to the question asked.

Provided the expert is not perceived as merely being argumentative, a Judge/Arbitrator would normally allow an expert significant latitude in responding to cross-examination. Unless the client's barrister objects to a question, and the Judge/Arbitrator upholds the objection, an expert will normally be expected to answer all questions put to him/her in cross-examination.

Re-examination occurs when the court takes further evidence-in-chief by the client's barrister, after cross-examination has been completed. Re-examination is normally only permitted to bring out further evidence-in-chief in relation to issues raised in cross-examination. The same rules apply to re-examination as to evidence-in-chief, i.e. no leading questions.

32.5.5 Expert evidence in a "hot tub"

An Australian innovation in expert evidence is a concurrent evidence session, sometimes referred to as a "**hot tub**". This process changes the traditional order of evidence (plaintiff's evidence followed by defendant's evidence), and requires the experts giving evidence on the same issues to do so in a concurrent session. The process is only feasible if all the experts have submitted expert reports, and typically expert reports in reply. "Hot tubbing" has been adopted for expert evidence in other common law jurisdictions, e.g. Singapore.

In such a "hot tub", each expert may make a statement or give a brief presentation. The Judge/Arbitrator may then ask questions of the experts. The experts themselves may have the opportunity of asking the other experts questions, before the barristers carry out their cross-examination of "opposing" experts.

The intention of such concurrent evidence is to enable the experts' opinions on given issues to be readily compared and contrasted; this is not so easy to do if there has been a significant lapse of time between the evidence of opposing experts.

The concept of experts asking each other questions seems fine in theory but may not be so effective in practice if experts attempt to cross-examine other experts. It would be preferable if expert's questions of other experts were confined to "open" questions, seeking an explanation for differences of opinion or of the scientific/technical basis on which opinions are based. Cross-examination is a skill which few experts are likely to have.

Furthermore, attempts to cross-examine by an expert may give the impression that the expert is acting as an advocate for his/her client's case.

32.6 Expert evidence in fast track arbitration

Fast track arbitration is a process of arbitration in which strict time limits are placed on each phase of the process, in an endeavour to achieve a speedy and economical resolution of the dispute. In particular, the hearing time is generally limited, and typically each party has an equal amount of time to present its case. An essential feature of fast track arbitration is that the hearing time is insufficient to allow for comprehensive oral evidence on all issues that may be relevant to the dispute. Expert evidence in fast track arbitration is likely to include a number of the procedures discussed above, such as:

- Preparation of detailed expert reports and expert reports in reply
- One or more experts' conferences
- Joint report(s) of experts
- Adoption of expert reports as evidence-in-chief
- Little or no oral examination-in-chief
- Concurrent evidence in the hearing.

The key issue that experts in a fast track arbitration should be aware of is the short and (perhaps) inflexible time frame for the whole arbitration process. This includes tight deadlines for submission of expert reports – these must be met if the expert's evidence is to be accepted.

A contracted time frame might also have the consequence that the client's barrister does not turn his/her mind to the expert's evidence at the time the expert's report is served. When the barrister does turn his/her mind to the expert's evidence, it may be shortly before the hearing; this may place significant obligations on the expert for conferences with the barrister at short notice.

Such demands are not confined to fast track arbitration – an expert should be aware that preparing an expert report and giving evidence in any hearing may require the expert to comply with shorter time frames than s/he considers desirable, and in a way that may adversely impact other commitments of the expert.

CHAPTER 33

Getting the most out of expert witnesses[1]

33.1 When to brief an expert

The appropriate time to brief an expert in pending or actual litigation or arbitration will depend on a number of issues arising from the dispute. It also depends on what role the expert is required to fulfil – expert witness ("clean expert") or technical expert member of the legal team ("dirty expert"). The distinction between these roles is fundamental; it must be clearly understood by the legal team, and it must be made clear in the brief to the expert.

An expert witness's primary duty is to the court, not to the party who briefed them. There are strict ethical duties imposed by the court on an expert witness, breach of which may render the expert's evidence nugatory. The most important of these is that the expert witness is not an advocate for the party briefing them. The brief to an expert witness, and any discussions with him/her, must be carefully prepared to ensure that the expert is not party to the "case theory" and the expert evidence is not tainted. An expert witness is sometimes colloquially referred to as a "clean expert".

By contrast, a technical expert member of the legal team is briefed to provide technical advice so that the legal team is in possession of the technical details necessary to prepare the best case for the client in the circumstances. A technical member of the legal team (referred to colloquially as a "dirty expert") is engaged to advocate for the client's interests and will be a party to all the relevant aspects of the case theory.

It can be seen from the distinction between these two roles that it could be problematic to engage one person to fill both roles. Once an expert has been engaged as a "dirty expert", s/he is in possession of material that could be seen to influence the nature of the expert's opinion. Nevertheless, it may be possible to engage one person to act in both roles, but the legal team needs to be very clear in all its communications as to which role the communication refers to.

The nature of the dispute resolution proceedings is also relevant to the issue of whether an expert is engaged as a "clean expert" or a "dirty expert". Whilst a "clean expert" is needed for court or arbitration proceedings, in a mediation the client's interests may be better served by a "dirty expert" who can advocate the client's case from a knowledge of the technical issues.

1 This chapter is an edited and updated version of the paper published in: Donald Charrett, "Getting the most out of expert witnesses: lessons from the Victorian Bushfires" (2015) 161 *Australian Construction Law Newsletter* 6.

 DOI: 10.4324/9781003206897-37

The starting point for determining when to brief an expert is the extent to which the legal team needs technical assistance to adequately plan the litigation/arbitration steps. Most (potential) disputes that require expert opinion involve at least a perception of a "failure" of some sort. It may be a technical failure such as collapse of a structure, or it may be a failure of a professional to exercise due skill and care. If the legal team is unable to determine from the facts whether there has been a failure or not, it may be appropriate to brief an expert at an early stage to provide an expert opinion on whether there has been a failure and, if so, who appears from the evidence to be responsible for the failure.

Another factor that may indicate engaging an expert early in the process is if the legal team needs assistance to determine what factual evidence needs to be collected on which an expert opinion can be expressed. Failure of physical facilities will usually require an expert to make inspections and provide guidance on collection of evidence, further testing etc. at the earliest possible stage.

Early briefing of an expert (even a "clean expert") enables the expert to assist the legal team to determine the appropriate staging of the assembly of expert evidence. In a significant dispute, the expert's brief is likely to be undertaken in a number of stages, the exact extent and timing of which will evolve as the case progresses.

There may be budgetary considerations in determining the timing of the expert's engagement. The earlier and the more involved the expert is, the greater the expert's costs will be, particularly if the expert prepares a number of drafts of a report before it is finalised. If the legal team is able to assemble the necessary factual evidence (or provide factual assumptions that can be proved) and prepare a brief that is focused on the essential issues, it may be appropriate to brief an expert at a later stage.

Of course, the exigencies of the litigation/arbitration may ultimately control the timing at which an expert must be briefed. The legal team will be alert to complying with the timetable for submission of expert evidence set by the court/tribunal, and will need to have at least preliminary discussions with potential experts to understand their availability and the time required for the necessary investigations and report writing.

In summary, the legal team will have to weigh a number of factors in determining when to brief an expert. Other things being equal, in this writer's view, the earlier the right expert is engaged, the better prepared the legal team will be. The first challenge in engaging the right expert may well be in determining what expertise is needed, so that the right individual can be identified. It may be that the legal team will need a "dirty expert" to assist in this process before a "clean expert" can be identified. See Section 31.5 for suggestions on briefing an appropriate forensic engineer.

Establishing what expertise is needed also requires a careful consideration of what are the real issues that need expert evidence. In many situations, expert evidence is obtained (at great expense) for issues that are not important for resolution of the key issues that will be determinative in the dispute. The legal team needs to carefully assess what are the real issues on which the dispute hinges, and then establish (perhaps with the assistance of an expert) what evidence (expert or lay) is required, before briefing an expert.

33.2 Ethical considerations

The engagement of an expert involves ethical questions for the legal team, as well as for the expert.

The legal team should be well aware that their duty to the court takes precedence over the duty to their client. In respect of litigation in Victoria, there is a specific duty in relation to litigation articulated in s 7 of the *Civil Procedure Act 2010* (Vic): "to facilitate the just, efficient, timely and cost-effective resolution of the real issues in dispute".

Members of the legal team, solicitors and barristers, are usually also members of their relevant professional body such as the Law Society and the Bar. Each of these professional bodies have ethical rules that articulate detailed provisions governing the conduct of their members, including the taking of evidence. Such rules supplement the duties to the court and apply equally to their members' conduct in relation to arbitration.

The provisions of the *Civil Procedure Act 2010* (Vic) provide statutory force to specific ethical obligations of all the participants in the court process – parties, the legal team and expert witnesses.[2] These obligations are in addition to the common law and statutory obligations to the court and take precedence over other obligations such as contractual duties,[3] or the instructions or wishes of the client.[4]

The overarching obligations of the *Civil Procedure Act 2010* (Vic) include the obligation to act honestly,[5] not to make frivolous or vexatious claims, or claims that are an abuse of process or do not have a proper basis,[6] not to take unnecessary steps in the litigation,[7] cooperate with the other parties and the court,[8] and not to engage in misleading or deceptive conduct.[9] The overarching obligations also include the requirement to use reasonable endeavours to: resolve the dispute by agreement,[10] narrow the issues in dispute,[11] ensure the costs are reasonable and proportionate,[12] act promptly and minimise delay,[13] and to disclose the existence of documents.[14] There are also obligations not to disclose information or documents obtained in the litigation.[15]

These overarching obligations of the *Civil Procedure Act 2010* (Vic) are in addition to the specific obligations on expert witnesses imposed by Order 44 of the *Supreme Court (General Civil Procedure) Rules 2005* (Vic). The specific obligations in Order 44 are considered below.

An expert witness, being a member of a profession, may also be subject to the ethical rules of that profession. For example, engineers who are members of the Institution of Engineers Australia are bound by its Code of Ethics.[16] It is suggested that the requirements of that Code of Ethics are entirely consistent with the overarching obligations of the *Civil Procedure Act 2010* (Vic), including to:

2 s 10.
3 s 12.
4 s 13.
5 s 17.
6 s 18.
7 s 19.
8 s 20.
9 s 21.
10 s 22.
11 s 23.
12 s 24.
13 s 25.
14 s 26.
15 s 27.
16 https://www.engineersaustralia.org.au/ethics (accessed 16 April 2021).

- Act on the basis of a well-informed conscience.
- Be honest and trustworthy.
- Maintain and develop knowledge and skills.
- Represent areas of competence objectively.
- Act on the basis of adequate knowledge.
- Uphold the reputation and trustworthiness of the practice of engineering.
- Communicate honestly and effectively, taking into account the reliance of others on engineering expertise.

33.3 Dealing with adverse opinions

The legal team may be faced with expert opinions that are contrary to or raise doubts about the case theory. Whilst in adversarial litigation or arbitration it is to be expected that expert evidence from the other side will not support one's own case, the legal team may also receive adverse opinions from an expert it has briefed.

It is suggested that the adverse expert opinion should be reviewed in the light of the following factors, whether the adverse opinion emanates from an expert briefed on behalf of the client, or an expert briefed by an opposing party. The answers from this assessment should provide guidance as to how to deal with the adverse opinion.

Does the brief provide all the relevant reference documents? An expert's brief should include all the documents relevant to the issues in dispute, and an expert's assistance might be required to identify all the potentially relevant documents.

Does the brief ask the right questions? The expert's answers to the questions asked may suggest that different or further questions should be asked. In preparing a brief to an expert on behalf of the client it may be appropriate to provide the expert the opportunity to consider the questions before the brief is finalised. In relation to opposing experts, there may be an opportunity to pose the "right" questions for an experts' conference, if one is held before evidence is adduced. Of course, cross-examination will always provide an opportunity of asking the "right" questions of an opposing expert, which may need to be provided by an expert briefed on behalf of the client.

The expert's qualifications and experience should be assessed to determine whether s/he is qualified express their opinion on the specific issues. It is a fundamental requirement of the *Evidence Act 2008* (Vic) that a witness can only give opinion evidence if the opinion is based on their study, training or experience, and where the opinion is wholly or substantially based on that knowledge.[17] In order for an expert's opinion to be persuasive to a court or arbitral tribunal, it is important to be able to demonstrate that nexus.

The facts on which the expert's opinion was expressed should be determined:

- Was it based on the expert's own observations?
- Was it based on an assumption provided in the brief?
- Are there alternative "facts"?

17 s 79.

Ultimately, an expert's opinion will have little if any evidentiary weight if the "facts" on which it is based are not proved. Many of the "facts" on which an expert's opinion is based will have to be proved by other (lay) witnesses.

Is the expert's technical opinion soundly based on generally accepted technology in the specialist field? There may be more than one theoretical basis for a particular failure hypothesis, but an opinion based on a theory that does not have respectable support in the relevant professional community is not likely to be persuasive.

Is the opinion based on the expert's own experience? This will need to be adequately explained in the expert's report and consistent with the expert's CV. Evidence sought to be adduced from an expert that goes beyond that expert's experience as revealed in the CV may be objectionable and subject to exclusion.[18]

Has the expert considered the opinions in the opposing expert reports? Opposing opinions need to be addressed and the differences explained as precisely as possible, e.g. different factual basis or different theoretical basis.

Has the expert complied with the requirements of Order 44 (or equivalent)? Compliance with these requirements is mandatory, and any failure to do so renders the opinions expressed liable to rejection.

Is the expert a "gun for hire"? That is, does the expert have a reputation for giving evidence (always supportive of its client's case) on a wide range of issues that suggest the person purports to be an "expert" in many fields. Internet searches and discussions with colleagues can be of great assistance in identifying such individuals. Prior to engaging an expert, the legal team will normally need to carry out its own due diligence to avoid the engagement of such a person.

The issues identified above should provide guidance in preparing cross-examination of an opposing expert. The aim of such cross-examination will be to cast doubt on the opinions expressed because they are not soundly based or adequately justified, or, in some cases, to discredit the witness so that their evidence will be excluded or given little weight.

In respect of a witness briefed on behalf of the client, if the above issues do not reveal any flaws in the opinion, the legal team may need to seek a second opinion or review its case theory. In considering the consequences of an adverse opinion, the legal team needs to keep in mind its obligation not to put forward a claim without a proper basis.[19]

33.4 Court rules

The following sections briefly discuss the Court Rules applicable to expert evidence in Victoria and the Federal Court of Australia. Details of the requirements in all Australian States and Territories are provided in Chapter 34.

Order 44 of the *Supreme Court (General Civil Procedure) Rules 2005* (Vic) contains detailed requirements in respect of expert evidence to be adduced in court. Although not mandatory in arbitral proceedings, these rules (or their equivalent) are often also applied in arbitrations because they are perceived to define the norms that experts should comply with for their evidence to be relevant and persuasive. Experts would be well advised to

18 e.g. see *Matthews v SPI Electricity & Ors (Ruling No 39)* [2014] VSC 109, in which Forrest J declined to permit an expert to provide a supplementary report on issues that went significantly beyond his experience as revealed in his CV already in evidence. See Section 33.6.15.

19 *Civil Procedure Act 2010* (Vic) s 18.

comply with the requirements of Order 44 (or its equivalent) in arbitral proceedings in any event, as such compliance removes any grounds for rejection of the evidence on the grounds of admissibility.

A party briefing an expert is required to provide the expert with a copy of the Expert Witness Code of Conduct in Form 44A. A copy of the expert's report must be served on the other parties not later than 30 days before the trial.

Rule 44.03 specifies information that must be included in an expert report. This includes the details required to demonstrate that the evidence satisfies the requirements of s 79 of the *Evidence Act 2008* (Vic):

- Identification of the expert and details of their qualifications
- The facts, matters and assumptions on which the opinion is based
- The reasons for the opinion
- Details of any examinations, tests or other investigations on which the opinion is based.

In addition, rule 44.03 requires the following "ethical" obligations to be acknowledged in an expert's report:

- That the expert has read the Code of conduct and agrees to abide by it.
- That a particular question, issue or matter falls outside the expert's field of expertise (if applicable).
- A declaration –
  - That the expert has made all the enquiries which the expert believes are desirable and appropriate.
  - That no matters of significance which the expert regards as relevant have, to the knowledge of the expert, been withheld from the Court.
  - Any qualification of an opinion expressed in the report without which the report is or may be incomplete or inaccurate.
- Whether an opinion expressed in the report is not a concluded opinion because of insufficient research or insufficient data or for any other reason.

Rule 44.03 also contains requirements in respect of service of supplementary reports, including supplementary reports produced when an expert has altered his/her opinion.

The Supreme Court Expert Witness Code of Conduct in Form 44A provides succinct (1½ pages) instructions to experts as to their overarching obligations to the court, as well as providing specific instructions as to the formal requirements of their expert report(s) (as detailed in rule 44.03(2)). The Code imposes a specific obligation on an expert to prepare a supplementary report in the event that s/he changes her/his mind.[20]

The Code states that an expert may be required by the court to confer with other experts and produce a joint report stating matters agreed and, in respect of matters not agreed, reasons for the experts' disagreement.[21] Importantly, the legal team are precluded from influencing the outcome of such an experts' conference:

20 [4].

21 [5].

> Each expert witness shall exercise his or her independent judgment in relation to every conference in which the expert participates pursuant to a direction of the Court and in relation to each report thereafter provided, and shall not act on any instruction or request to withhold or avoid agreement.[22]

Practice Note GPN-EXPT of the Federal Court provides guidelines for expert witnesses giving evidence in the Federal Court. Pursuant to rule 23.12 of the *Federal Court Rules 2011* (Cth) a party must give a copy of these guidelines to any witness it proposes to retain for the purpose of preparing a report or giving evidence in a proceeding as to an opinion held by the witness that is wholly or substantially based on the specialised knowledge of the witness.

The Federal Court guidelines cover the same issues and overarching requirements as in the Victorian Supreme Court Form 44A. Subject to minor formal issues, an expert who complies with the requirements of one of these documents will also comply with the requirements of the other.

The consequences of not complying with the requirements of Order 44 or its equivalent are well illustrated in the English case of *SPE International Ltd v Professional Preparation Contractors (UK) Ltd*.[23] In that case nearly everything that could possibly go wrong with expert evidence did go wrong. The judge rejected the evidence as inadmissible because the "expert" had breached all his obligations to the court and had not complied with the fundamental requirements of giving independent expert evidence based on relevant qualifications, training and experience.

33.5 How lawyers can work effectively with experts

An important aspect of the expert's role is to educate the legal team in the "technical" issues in the case, so that they understand how those technical issues impact on the "legal" issues of causation, obligations and breach of obligations.

An important aspect of the legal team's role is to educate the expert on the "legal" issues in the case, so that the expert's report and evidence is appropriately structured and articulated to address those issues. Also, to assist the expert to prepare her/his report to be most persuasive to the court or tribunal in respect of the key issues.

The legal team working with an expert for the first time will need to assess the expert's familiarity with the court/arbitration process. An expert who has never given evidence in court before will need more instruction and explanation than an experienced expert witness.

The starting point for working effectively with an expert is to provide him/her with a clear brief that defines the scope of the investigation to be carried out, the required "deliverables", and the time by which the "deliverables" are to be provided. The brief will need to include the background of the matter, the facts and assumptions on which the expert is being asked to rely, a list of all the documents provided to the expert and the questions the expert is asked to address.

In many situations, the expert's ultimate brief will evolve over time, subject to the requirements of the case and the results of the expert's investigations. A balance will be

22 [6].
23 [2002] EWHC 881 (Ch).

required in providing sufficient definition of the scope of the "legal" requirements of the case and allowing sufficient input from the expert on the "technical" requirements of the case that are within his/her expertise.

However, the brief needs to ensure that, subject to compliance with the expert's obligations to the court/tribunal, the expert is confined to consideration of issues relevant to the case as identified by the legal team. It is usually helpful for the legal team to confer with the expert to discuss the content of his/her draft report before it is finalised, to ensure that it is in the appropriate format, addresses all of the issues in the brief, and does so in a way that is understandable to lay people.

Clearly, it would be improper for the legal team to provide comments on the substance of the expert's opinion. However, there are areas in which the legal team has a role in assisting the expert to prepare her/his report in the appropriate form that will have the best evidential impact. For example, the legal team can:

- Advise on the legal admissibility of the contents of the report
- Assist with clarity, completeness and structure of the expert's reasoning
- Identify any weakness in the logic and analysis in the report.

In the large class action case arising out of the 2009 Victorian bushfires referred to below, Derham AsJ made several rulings on whether documents provided to an expert attracted legal privilege. His Honour canvassed various circumstances related to the production of an expert's final report and his/her communications with the instructing solicitor. He noted that it is perfectly proper for the legal team to have such conferences, and "ordinarily the confidential briefing or instructing by a prospective litigant's lawyers of an expert to provide a report of his or her opinion to be used in the anticipated litigation attracts client legal privilege."[24]

However, the legal team must be careful that they are not perceived as putting pressure on the expert to change their mind to suit the requirements of the case theory or breach their obligations to the court/tribunal. Draft expert reports prepared as part of the process of briefing the expert are prima facie covered by legal professional privilege in Victoria (but not necessarily in other jurisdictions), however, "privilege is impliedly waived in the working papers and draft reports if there is a proper basis for concluding that they contain communications or information that was taken into account by, or influenced, the expert".[25]

Section 119(b) of the *Evidence Act 2008* (Vic) extends privilege to confidential documents, whether communicated or not, provided they were brought into existence with the requisite dominant purpose of the client being provided with professional legal services relating to legal proceedings.[26] Thus, whilst the dominant purpose of a final expert's report would, prima facie, not be privileged (as its dominant purpose would be for the purpose of being laid before the court as the expert's evidence), draft reports, and notes used in preparing a report, may be privileged,

24 *Matthews v SPI Electricity & Ors* [2013] VSC 33, [44] (per Derham AsJ).

25 *Matthews v SPI Electricity & Ors (Ruling No 10)* [2014] VSC 44, [22] (per Derham AsJ).

26 Ibid [21].

> particularly where the expert has been retained by the party's solicitors and it is expected that the party's lawyers will advise on the contents of, and settle the form of, the report. There is nothing improper in such a course. It is not inconsistent with the expert's paramount duty being the duty to the Court and not to the client retaining him or her. ... However, if they were brought into existence for the dominant purpose of the expert forming his or her opinions to be expressed in the final report, then it could be arguable that they were not made for the dominant purpose of the plaintiffs being provided with professional legal services relating to the proceedings.[27]

Derham AsJ noted that whilst it would be entirely improper for an expert to change his/her opinion because of influence from the plaintiff's advisors, an expert

> is permitted, indeed to be encouraged, to change his or her mind, if a change of mind is warranted. Experts should not be inhibited by fear of exposure of a draft from changing their minds when such change is warranted by the material then before the expert.[28]

The most important role for the legal team in assisting an expert is to ensure that the report answers the questions in the brief (and only the questions in the brief), and the expert articulates their reasoning to be intelligible to the Judge/Arbitrator. This normally involves the use of short sentences and (preferably) no jargon. If jargon is required, it must be explained in lay terms. The legal team can also ensure that the expert complies with the formal requirements for expert evidence in the relevant jurisdiction, e.g. Order 44 of the Supreme Court of Victoria.

An expert's report has far more impact on the court or tribunal if it concentrates on what is important. The legal team can assist the expert to concentrate on the determinative issues so that the expert's analysis of these issues has the greatest impact. Whilst the expert's report must demonstrate that the conclusions and opinions are based on a thorough analysis of the issues based on the facts, the detail of this may be distracting from the conclusions and may be better in an appendix to the report.

Nevertheless, in determining what should be in the report, it is important that it reveals the reasoning behind the conclusions, in a way that can be understood by the (non-technical) court or arbitral tribunal. The "black box" syndrome should be avoided, in which you cannot see inside the black box to work out how it produced the output.

An expert who has not previously given evidence in court will need the process explained; it may be appropriate for counsel in the legal team to subject the expert to cross-examination on the contents of their report so that they are prepared for the sort of questions that may be posed by the other side.

It will often assist an expert to provide them with a copy of a paper that explains the process of preparing and delivering expert evidence and gives guidance on behaviour in court.[29]

The independent expert's role is not necessarily compromised by his/her assistance to the legal team in preparing questions for cross-examination. Such cross-examination issues will be consistent with the expert's independent views as already expressed, and specifically where these are in conflict with the opposing experts' views.

27 Ibid.

28 Ibid [23].

29 e.g. PG Murphy, L Duthie, B Bielert and D Charrett, 'Australian Legal Guidelines for Forensic Engineering Experts' (2010) Vol 11 No 1 *Australian Journal of Structural Engineering* 11.

The expert's evidence is usually provided to the court or tribunal in a report (or reports) that are tendered as the expert's evidence-in-chief. Notwithstanding that it can be assumed that the court or tribunal has read the report(s), it may assist the court or tribunal's understanding for the expert to give an oral summary of the key issues and conclusions. Such a summary may be assisted by appropriate visual aids, such as explanatory diagrams, graphics, photographs, animations etc. A PowerPoint presentation may be the most effective form of presentation. Whatever the format, the expert must prepare adequately so that the evidence has the most persuasive impact.

33.6 Expert conferences and conclaves – *Matthews v SPI Electricity*

The following case notes refer to rulings made by Forrest J and other judges in a large class action case arising out of the disastrous bushfires in Victoria in 2009. The claim was brought pursuant to Part 4A of the *Supreme Court Act 1986* (Vic) by the plaintiff on behalf of group members who sustained personal injury and/or property damage, and/or economic loss as a result of the Kinglake/Kilmore East bushfire on 7 February 2009.

The representative plaintiff, on behalf of 10,000 plaintiffs with common claims, asserted that the bushfire was ignited as a result of the electricity conductor strung on what was referred to as the Valley Span falling to the ground close to pole 39. The plaintiff alleged that the conductor's failure and the consequential fire were caused by a breach of duty by the electricity distribution company (SPI) in the management, inspection and engineering of the Valley Span. Damages were claimed from the electricity distribution company, its contractor responsible for inspections of the distribution line, and from various State government parties.[30]

In this large and complex case (which ran for 209 sitting days) there were a number of technical issues that required expert evidence. In total, there were 40 expert witnesses who produced, over the course of the proceedings, 73 individual reports and 13 joint reports.

The judge hearing the proceedings, Forrest J, implemented a number of modern techniques for managing the expert evidence, including:

- Expert conferences, facilitated by an Associate Justice, in which the experts produced joint reports that addressed specific questions posed by Forrest J
- Expert evidence on specific issues was adduced in concurrent evidence sessions, a technique commonly referred to as "hot tubbing"
- The Judge appointed two engineering professors to sit with him as assessors of some of the expert evidence.

The importance, extent and complexity of the expert evidence in this case can be gauged from the fact that there were nine separate concurrent evidence sessions over a period of approximately two and a half months. One of these sessions involved ten expert engineers and took over a month. The assessors assisted the judge to understand the technical evidence adduced in this session.

30 *Matthews v SPI Electricity & Ors (Ruling No 20)* [2013] VSC 197 [11].

The judges involved in this case produced 52 published rulings that run for over 1,000 pages, covering case management, discovery, subpoenas, the *Civil Procedure Act 2012* (Vic), the *Evidence Act 2008* (Vic) and expert evidence. The Supreme Court and the Judicial College of Victoria considered that the jurisprudence produced during these proceedings will be invaluable for judges and practitioners in the future, and in 2015 published *Index to the Rulings from the Kilmore East-Kinglake Bushfire Class Action.* This document contains hyperlinks to the judgments under 34 headings as a means to navigate the wealth of information contained in those rulings.

The techniques adopted in this case to manage the expert evidence are well established in Victoria and have appropriate statutory support in the *Supreme Court (General Civil Procedure) Rules 2005* (Vic), the *Supreme Court Act 1986* (Vic), the *Civil Procedure Act 2010* (Vic) and the *Evidence Act 2008* (Vic). The following rulings made by the judges on various aspects of the process are invaluable for their articulation of the relevant principles, and their application to the complexities in this case "to facilitate the just, efficient, timely and cost-effective resolution of the real issues in dispute".[31]

33.6.1 Steps in the production and exchange of expert evidence

The ruling made by Forrest J in this judgment[32] included the common questions formulated by his Honour (the answers to which formed part of the judgment pursuant to s 33Z of the *Supreme Court Act 1986* (Vic)) that had been settled by agreement in the course of a case management conference.

The ruling also detailed the steps involved in the production and exchange of independent expert evidence, and the subsequent experts' conferences. Forrest J considered that it was appropriate for the complete expert evidence process to be completed prior to mediation, including expert conclaves. This was to promote the just, efficient, timely and cost-effective resolution of the real issues in dispute, in accordance with the objectives of the *Civil Procedure Act 2010* (Vic). By identifying the real issues in dispute in the proceeding as early as possible the prospects of success of the mediation would be enhanced.

Omitting the dates, Forrest J directed that the following steps were required in this case:

(1) The parties finalise the discovery process.
(2) The parties exchange draft questions for expert witnesses.
(3) The parties file and serve lists of questions for experts.
(4) The parties file and serve their expert reports.
(5) The parties' experts on particular issues meet in conference and prepare for the Court a joint report:
    (a) Addressing each of the questions on particular issues;
    (b) Identifying each of the matters on which they agree;
    (c) Identifying each of the matters on which they do not agree; and
    (d) Providing detailed reasons outlining the basis on which they are unable to agree on any matter relating to any of those questions on particular issues.
    (e) In respect of the conference(s) of the experts on particular issues:

31 *Civil Procedure Act 2010* (Vic) s 7.
32 *Matthews v SPI Electricity & Ors (Ruling No 4)* [2011] VSC 613.

(f) The experts' conference(s) to be private to the experts and confidential and there was to be no involvement of the parties or legal practitioners; and

(g) The experts' joint report(s) to be delivered to the parties' solicitors as soon as practicable.

(6) The parties file the experts' joint report(s).

(7) The parties file an agreed chronology of events relevant to the Plaintiff's claim.

(8) The parties file and serve a list of witnesses (excluding expert witnesses) they intend to call at the trial.

(9) Mediation of the proceeding be conducted by a mediator approved and/or appointed by the Court.

(10) The mediation to be attended by those persons who have the ultimate responsibility for deciding whether to settle the dispute and the terms of any settlement, and the lawyers who have ultimate responsibility to advise the parties in relation to the dispute and its settlement.

(11) The mediator report to the Court and to the Class Actions Coordinator on the outcome of the mediation.

Whilst the steps ordered were based on the specific features of the case, they are a useful summary of the procedures currently used in the Supreme Court of Victoria in relation to expert evidence in complex cases. The importance of adherence to the procedure, and participation by the experts in the conclaves, was emphasised by Forrest J:

> It will be necessary to hold separate conclaves of experts, given the disparate allegations of negligence, the different areas of expertise and the scope of the opinions likely to be expressed. The mechanics of this arrangement can be sorted out over the next couple of months – as long as the experts are aware that they must confer and be available to give evidence in May 2013. Whatever the timing of the conclaves, an important part of their function will be the provision of joint expert reports which will provide the basis for the concurrent evidence sessions at the trial. So that there is no misunderstanding about the importance of the conclaves, I emphasise that participation in the conclave and the production of a joint report is a pre-condition to the expert giving evidence in the trial.[33]

33.6.2 Limits to the application of Order 44 to opinion evidence

In this judgment,[34] Forrest J distinguished between three types of opinion evidence:

(1) Opinion evidence given by "independent experts" "engaged" by a party to the proceeding who calls the witness.

(2) Opinion evidence given by a witness not "engaged" by the party calling the witness.

(3) Opinion evidence given by an "internal witness" of the party calling the witness.

---

33 *Matthews v SPI Electricity Pty Ltd; SPI Electricity Pty Ltd v Utility Services Corporation Ltd (Ruling No 4)* [2011] VSC 613, [11].

34 *Matthews v SPI Electricity & Ors (Ruling No 9)* [2012] VSC 340.

"Independent experts" were required to file their reports in accordance with Order 44 of the *Supreme Court Rules* and, in particular, to ensure that their reports conform with rule 44.03. Forrest J noted:

> The rationale for r 44.03, and O 44 as a whole, is twofold. One is to ensure that each party has an adequate forewarning of the expert evidence to be led at trial. This, it is assumed, assists in pre-trial dispute resolution, as well as ensuring that trial ambushes are kept to a minimum. In recent times, expert reports provide the foundation for meetings of experts and the subsequent preparation of a joint expert report. The other basis is to ensure that expert witnesses engaged by the party for the purposes of the trial are aware of their responsibilities to the Court in preparing an independent opinion, notwithstanding the interests of the commissioning party. The aim is to eliminate, or at least reduce, the "gun for hire" approach endemic to adversarial litigation prior to the introduction of the Code.[35]

His Honour noted the general rule in Victoria that a witness expressing an opinion should comply with Order 44, but the rule did not apply to a situation in which a party seeks to lead opinion evidence from a witness in circumstances where it is either impractical, or unlikely, that the witness will consent to an engagement to provide a report under the terms of rule 44.03. Order 44 was directed to independent experts "engaged" by a party to prepare an opinion for the purpose of the trial, where engagement means an expert commissioned by a party to provide an opinion for the purpose of the relevant piece of litigation.

There may be various valid reasons why a person with relevant expertise may not be able or prepared to be "engaged" to prepare an expert report in compliance with Order 44, but whose opinion may nevertheless be of assistance to the court in determining the issues before it. In this case, there were witnesses who had been involved in investigations into the bushfires and their causes who were able to give evidence as to factual matters surrounding the fire and the allegations made by the parties. The party calling these witnesses also wished to lead opinion evidence from them.

An "internal witness" is one employed by or contracted to one of the parties and whom that party would seek, primarily, to adduce factual evidence, but also an opinion relevant to the trial issues. As with the second category, these witnesses have not been "engaged" to provide a report.

Forrest J stated that, as the latter two categories of witness were not "engaged" by any of the parties to the litigation, their evidence did not have to satisfy the requirements of Order 44. Nevertheless, in respect of any opinion evidence not satisfying rule 44.03, the other parties and the Court should be informed of the following essential matters:

(a) The witness' training, study or experience.
(b) The facts, matters and assumptions upon which the opinion is based (often this may be simply the observations made by the witness at a particular event).
(c) The substance of the opinion.
(d) The reasoning underpinning the opinion which is to be expressed.

In this case the witnesses in category 2 had previously given evidence at the Victorian Bushfires Royal Commission, and these essential matters were generally known. However,

35 *Matthews v SPI Electricity Pty Ltd & Ors; SPI Electricity Pty Ltd v Utility Services Corporation Ltd (Ruling No 9)* [2012] VSC 340, [14].

where the evidence had not yet been adduced or placed into written form, it would be necessary for the party calling that witness to provide the essential details.

Forrest J also made two other observations in relation to opinion evidence:

- Merely because a witness has expertise does not mean that his or her evidence is necessarily opinion evidence.
- A witness with appropriate expertise may give factual evidence – for instance, a doctor as to his observations during a clinical examination. Notwithstanding that the witness's expertise may be relevant to the making of the observation, it remains admissible as evidence of an observed fact.

Thus, where a witness gives evidence based upon his or her own observations and/or scientific or specialised analysis, such evidence may not amount to opinion evidence, but rather be properly characterised as a factual conclusion.

It is therefore important to distinguish whether evidence sought to be adduced from an expert is truly an opinion within the meaning of s 79 of the *Evidence Act 2008* (Vic) and rule 44.03 of the *Supreme Court Rules*, or whether it is evidence of a fact based on the expert's own observations or analyses. The following is a useful definition of opinion evidence quoted by Forrest J that makes the distinction from factual evidence clear: "Opinion evidence can be described as evidence of a conclusion, usually judgmental or debateable, reasoned from facts."[36]

33.6.3 Composition and conduct of expert conclaves[37]

This judgment[38] contains the rulings made by Forrest J in relation to the composition and conduct of the conclaves of expert witnesses. His Honour had to decide between two different proposals:

- Conclaves within four broad topics, in which there may be a larger number of experts for one party than the other, each with expertise in some aspects of the topics, or
- Specific issue-by-issue conclaves, requiring roughly 14 separate meetings, each with a smaller number of experts, all with expertise in the conclave issue.

Forrest J noted that, although the second model would require more conclaves and be challenging administratively, it was preferable for the following reasons:

(1) By having a conclave devoted to specific issues there can be no question about the expertise of the particular witnesses who author the joint report. That report would ultimately form part of the evidence at trial and any issue about the expertise of the witnesses (which may arise in a mass conclave where witnesses possess differing areas of expertise) would be avoided. The alternative model has real potential to lead to the production of a joint report where there are issues about the capacity of the authors to express the opinion contained in the report,

36 *RW Miller & Co Pty Ltd v Krupp (Australia) Pty Ltd* (1991) 34 NSWLR 129, 130 per Giles J.

37 *Matthews v SPI Electricity & Ors (Ruling No 10)* [2012] VSC 379.

38 *Matthews v SPI Electricity & Ors (Ruling No 9)* [2012] VSC 340.

as happened recently in the case of *Dura (Australia) Constructions Pty Ltd v Hue Boutique Living Pty Ltd.*[39]

(2) The expert evidence is not a "battle of numbers". The preferred model generally avoids an imbalance in the number of experts that would occur in the alternative model.
(3) The provision of joint reports dealing with specific and discrete issues would help refine the issues and has a greater prospect of leading to clearer identification of the issues that are in dispute and those that are not.
(4) There is scope to expand the conclaves if the experts think it would be of assistance – and it is legally permissible.
(5) The provision of joint reports using the preferred model would not determine the composition of the concurrent evidence sessions at trial. After the reports have been received and considered, it may be apparent that a concurrent evidence session involving experts from more than one conclave would be appropriate.
(6) "This is not a trial by expert. It is for the Court to determine the issues having regard to all the evidence whatever the source."

In addition to ruling on the form of the expert conclaves, Forrest J also made the following directions in respect of the procedural aspects of the conclaves:

- An Associate Justice will undertake the supervision and management of the conclaves. She will conduct a case conference and be available subsequently to assist with the conduct of the conclaves.
- The decision as to whether a moderator is required for a conclave is a question for the experts, and not the lawyers or the judge. If the experts require a moderator, the Associate Justice will be available to act.
- Administrative assistance should be provided to assist the experts with recording their discussions and preparing the report, unless they think it unnecessary.
- It is preferable for the experts to meet face to face. However, where experts reside interstate or overseas, they should determine the best way to conduct their conclave.
- Provision of an agenda is worthwhile to assist in keeping the experts on track. The parties should meet and endeavour to agree an agenda, failing which it can be discussed at a case conference with the Associate Justice supervising the expert conclaves.
- Although expert evidence will be determined on quality and not quantity, if one party feels disadvantaged by the numbers of experts on the other side, this can be canvassed with the Associate Justice.

33.6.4 Use of assessor v special referee

In this ruling,[40] Forrest J determined that, in view of the technical complexity of the issues at the heart of the case, he would be assisted by an "assessor", rather than referring specific technical questions to a "special referee".

39 [2012] VSC 99.
40 *Matthews v SPI Electricity & Ors (Ruling No 19)* [2013] VSC 180.

This issue arose because "the cause or causes of the failure of the conductor on the Valley Span is of critical importance in determining the legal liability of SPI to Mrs Matthews and the group members".[41] His Honour was conscious of the technical complexity of the issues that required to be determined and recognised the value of the expert evidence. However, he candidly expressed the view that he was unsure as to whether he would understand the expert evidence without assistance.[42]

His Honour noted that, without expert assistance:

> I am quite unsure as to whether I can give effect to the overarching purpose of endeavouring to resolve a civil dispute (whether by reference to s 7 of the CPA [Civil Procedure Act 2010 (Vic)] or to the common law) – to provide the parties with a just result or, to use the language of s 9(1)(a) of the CPA, to reach a "just determination" of the proceeding.[43]

Forrest J canvassed the issues in using a special referee to determine discrete issues, but determined that, in addition to the parties' opposition to such an appointment, this was not appropriate in the circumstances because:

(a) The technical cause of the failure was a critical issue in the case.
(b) It was likely that there would be issues of reliability and credibility of one or more of the expert witnesses.
(c) The questions would not be solely scientific but would involve a hybrid of legal and factual issues.
(d) Referral to a special referee would have a negative impact in terms of timing and subsequent fragmentation of the entire trial.
(e) There could be questions in relation to adoption of the referee's report arising from the calculations or reasoning in it.[44]

In determining that he required the assistance of an assessor, his Honour was convinced that "the judicial task can be better performed with such assistance and the likelihood of a fair determination enhanced".[45]

Forrest J noted that, notwithstanding the assistance of an assessor, "it must be borne firmly in mind that the decision and the exercise of the judicial power is that of the judge and the judge alone".[46]

33.6.5 Evidence of state of knowledge of relevant industry

The issue in this ruling[47] related to the admissibility of evidence as to the state of knowledge in the relevant industry.

His Honour held that "the state of knowledge, be it documentary or oral, is admissible and goes to both questions of duty and breach of duty in determining the foreseeability of the relevant risk".[48]

41 Ibid [1].
42 Ibid [14].
43 Ibid [15].
44 Ibid [23]–[28].
45 Ibid [34].
46 Ibid [35].
47 *Matthews v SPI Electricity & Ors (Ruling No 18)* [2013] VSC 185.
48 Ibid [5].

Such evidence is relevant in determining whether a defendant has or has not acted reasonably in the circumstances. However: "The primary rule is that the evidence of industry practice is not determinative – the test remains: what is a reasonable response to the identified risk in all the circumstances?"[49]

33.6.6 Supplementary expert report after expert conclaves

The issue in this ruling[50] was whether a supplementary expert report could be admitted into evidence at a late stage, after the relevant conclaves had produced their joint reports.

The basis of the objection was that it would potentially re-enliven the conclave process, be extraordinarily disruptive and contrary to the spirit of various orders that the judge had made in the course of the proceeding to date.

As with the other decisions on expert evidence, ultimately admissibility hinged on whether it was in the interests of justice to admit the evidence. His Honour noted that "At times, there is a price to be paid to ensure a fair trial – in this case I think it is relatively modest."[51]

His Honour noted the following were some of the relevant principles to be applied in determining the application, derived from *Aon Risk Services Australia Ltd v Australian National University*:[52]

(a) Whether there will be a substantial delay caused by the amendment.
(b) The extent of any wasted costs.
(c) Whether there is an irreparable element of unfair prejudice caused by the amendment.
(d) Concerns of case management arising from the stage in the proceeding when the amendment is sought.
(e) Whether the grant of the amendment will lessen public confidence in the judicial system.
(f) Whether a satisfactory explanation has been given for seeking the amendment at the stage when it is sought.[53]

Notwithstanding a number of cogent arguments against admission of the supplementary report, his Honour determined that it was in the interests of justice in the case for it to be admitted.

33.6.7 Engagement of expert to carry out further testing

This ruling[54] related to an application by the plaintiff to engage an expert to carry out further testing, at a time when the experts' evidence was six months away.

In determining that it was in the interests of justice to permit further testing, his Honour noted:

49 Ibid [8].
50 *Matthews v SPI Electricity & Ors (Ruling No 20)* [2013] VSC 197.
51 Ibid [7].
52 [2009] HCA 27; [2009] 239 CLR 175, 217.
53 Ibid [38].
54 *Matthews v SPI Electricity & Ors (Ruling No 23)* [2013] VSC 239.

> I have endeavoured throughout the pre-trial and trial stages of this case to immunise the experts from the solicitors (for all sides) so that they do not become an integral cog in a party's team and thus, even if subconsciously, fail to appreciate their obligations to the Court. That consideration, however, should not prevent a party from endeavouring to seek further evidence to fortify his or her case – if that be what the case demands. It is a legitimate forensic exercise for a solicitor to endeavour to adduce evidence which supports the case of his or her client.[55]

33.6.8 Admissibility of expert evidence

This ruling[56] was in relation to the admissibility of expert evidence. It followed the judge's *ex tempore* ruling that an opinion expressed on assumed (hypothetical) facts put to the expert by counsel was admissible.

His Honour noted the High Court's view that the court's primary task in applying the *Evidence Act 2008* (Vic) s 79 (exception to the opinion rule in s 76 for opinions based on specialised knowledge) is to determine that the opinion in question is one which relies upon the expert's specialised knowledge.

In light of the High Court's judgment, he noted that it is now arguable that the so-called "basis rule" (or "proof of assumption rule") is not now a prerequisite for the proper application of s 79. That is, an opinion may be admissible under s 79 notwithstanding a failure to identify the assumptions of fact which underpin that opinion.[57]

However, his Honour considered that there are limits beyond which the basis rule may effectively still apply:

> 11. If this line of reasoning is correct then the basis rule goes solely to the weight to be given to the opinion such that the greater the divergence from the established facts, the lesser the weight to be given to it. If that approach alone be applied in this case then the ruling I made yesterday would still stand.
> 12. However there is, I think, a qualification. There must be a point at which the divergence between the assumed facts and the established facts is so great that the opinion becomes irrelevant: that is, it does not satisfy the relevance test laid down by s 56 of the Act and is therefore inadmissible.

33.6.9 Tender of documents provided to experts

This ruling[58] related to the proposed tender of documents provided to experts for use in preparing their reports. His Honour was concerned that:

> There is the potential in this trial for a vast number of documents to be tendered which have little or no relevance to the essential reasoning and opinion of the various experts or to the real issues in dispute between the experts.[59]

---

55 Ibid [23].
56 *Matthews v SPI Electricity & Ors (Ruling No 24)* [2013] VSC 269.
57 Ibid [10].
58 *Matthews v SPI Electricity & Ors (Ruling No 29)* [2013] VSC 537.
59 Ibid [21].

His Honour reviewed the relevant provisions of the *Evidence Act 2008* (Vic) and the *Civil Procedure Act 2010* (Vic), particularly the court's powers to further the overarching purpose and obligations in civil proceedings and noted that "the mere provision of material to an expert does not make it relevant or admissible. Nor does the use of the material in the body of a report or as an annexure necessarily justify its admission."[60]

He concluded that it was inappropriate to permit the tender of any material which underpinned the opinions of witnesses called by any party (unless of course the material is already in evidence) prior to conclusion of the expert conclaves.[61]

His Honour accepted counsel's suggestion that it was desirable for the parties to exchange lists of documents and identify those that were the subject of objection but did not permit automatic tender of documents objected to. It was the court's role to impose limits on the amounts of evidentiary material adduced.[62]

He determined that, in order to minimise the extent of possible objections, the material should only be tendered at the end of the concurrent evidence session, at which point he would determine:

(a) Whether the material is admissible
(b) Whether it is sufficiently probative in the sense that it is significantly relevant to a contested part of an expert's opinion to justify its admission, and
(c) Whether, if the sole basis for its tender is that it is of significant relevance to the disputed opinion, it should be permitted only on a limited basis pursuant to s 136 of the *Evidence Act*.[63]

33.6.10 Scope of assessors' role

This ruling[64] addressed the scope of the role of the assessors appointed to assist the Court, as well as procedural aspects of the experts' concurrent evidence sessions. It was made after the factual evidence in the hearing had been concluded.

After consultation with the assessors and with the assistance of the parties, Forrest J finalised a set of questions to be put to the expert witnesses in the concurrent evidence session. The experts were requested to provide brief preliminary responses to each question (no more than one paragraph).

The questions were intended to identify the disputed matters of central importance in determining the cause(s) of the failure of the Valley Span conductor, and to be a guide to the evidence adduced in the concurrent evidence sessions. His Honour also hoped that the experts' responses would assist him in understanding the expert evidence adduced in court. However, the questions were only a guide to the anticipated evidence and did not preclude discussion of other evidence relevant to the cause of the failure of the conductor.

His Honour made an order precluding the expert witnesses of conclaves 1, 3 and 4 from communicating with the parties or the parties' solicitors in the period commencing from the time when the concurrent evidence session was scheduled to commence. After that,

60 Ibid [20].
61 Ibid [23].
62 Ibid [24], [25].
63 Ibid [30].
64 *Matthews v SPI Electricity & Ors (Ruling No 32)* [2013] VSC 630.

and subject to any further order, the experts were to be "quarantined" until the conclusion of their concurrent evidence session.

Forrest J reviewed the requirements of the relevant legislation (*Civil Procedure Act 2010, Supreme Court Act 1986*) and English, New Zealand and Federal Court authorities in determining the appropriate role for the assessors in this case:

> The primary role of the assessors is to assist the court in understanding the evidence of the experts. Applying the CPA [*Civil Procedure Act 2010*], combined with the principles of natural justice and the guidance from the cases I have referred to, I set out below the scope of the role of the assessors in this case:
>
> (a) The assessors' role is to assist the judge. The decision is that of the judge alone.
> (b) The assessors will sit with me during the concurrent evidence sessions. If they wish, they may question the experts (or counsel) in this context. Such questioning however will be limited to clarification of the evidence; that is, where they consider the evidence to be ambiguous, unclear or incomplete.
> (c) I may consult with the assessors while sitting if I find a point of evidence unclear and seek their immediate input as to an appropriate or useful inquiry to make.
> (d) I will consult with the assessors whilst in chambers on matters raised by the experts in their oral evidence and in their individual and joint reports. This may include advice as to any questions the assessors think I should ask counsel or the experts in order to determine the questions at hand.
> (e) I will seek the guidance of the assessors on technical matters upon which I lack the requisite knowledge to understand without qualified assistance. This may include "lessons" on matters fundamental to, for example in this case, fracture mechanics or vibration.
> (f) If the assessors raise a theory or opinion that has not previously been identified by the parties, I will discuss this with counsel.
> (g) The assessors may from time to time provide me with advice on matters over which there is dispute between the experts. Such advice is not binding and the determination of a particular issue rests with the judge.
> (h) I anticipate that I will consult with the experts immediately after the conclusion of the concurrent evidence session and, from time to time, while drafting the judgment. This is likely to include seeking confirmation from them that I have properly understood the meaning of the expert evidence of conclaves 1, 3 and 4. I repeat, however, that their role is confined to providing advice and ensuring that I have comprehended the evidence given. I also repeat that the decision on these issues is mine and mine alone.[65]

33.6.11 Use of a model to assist the court

This ruling[66] was made at a late stage of the trial when the plaintiff sought leave to use a scale model of the pole that failed as an aid in one of the upcoming concurrent evidence sessions. The defendant objected to the use of the model on the grounds that it had not reviewed the details, that it was unnecessary, and that there was a risk it would be used to introduce new evidence or supplementary experts' reports.

Forrest J referred to s 53 of the *Evidence Act 2008* that regulates the use of demonstrations and experiments and referred to High Court authority on the distinction between a

65 Ibid [27].
66 *Matthews v SPI Electricity & Ors (Ruling No 34)* [2014] VSC 40

view, a demonstration and a reconstruction. *Evans v R*[67] is authority for s 53 not applying to conduct in the courtroom, the consequence of which is that the common law applied in this case.[68]

Thus, the common law (as modified by other relevant legislation) and strict rules of proof apply in circumstances where a model is used to assist a court in the evaluation or understanding of expert evidence.[69]

His Honour determined that s 7 of the *Civil Procedure Act 2010* (Vic) gave him the power to allow the use of a model and that, in the circumstances, this would give effect to the overarching purpose in s 7: the just, efficient, timely and cost-effective resolution of the real issues in dispute. He noted that the use of aids to assist a court in understanding the evidence given in a trial is a long-standing practice permitted by the common law.[70]

Based on these considerations, his Honour gave leave for the use of the model, but

> its use must be strictly confined to that of an aid: the model will be permitted for the limited use of providing me with a reference point as to what the experts are speaking about when giving concurrent evidence. In particular, the parties will not be permitted to use the model to conduct any form of test or experiment and will not be permitted to rely on the model as an evidentiary base upon which to establish the sequence of events after the conductor broke.[71]

33.6.12 Exclusion of cross-examination under s 42 Evidence Act

This ruling[72] resulted from an application by the first defendant, during the course of the trial, to prevent cross-examination of an expert witness for the second defendant.

Forrest J referred to s 42 of the *Evidence Act 2008* that details the basis on which the judge can rule against the normal use of leading questions in cross-examination of a witness not called by the cross-examining party.

In ruling that the witness could be cross-examined without restriction, his Honour rejected the defendant's submissions on the following bases:[73]

(1) Rule 44.05 of the *Supreme Court Rules* creates no obstacle to cross-examination by counsel for the plaintiff.
(2) The Judge did not accept that the witness was in the plaintiff's "camp".
(3) The matters in s 42(2) of the *Evidence Act 2008* that permit disallowance of leading questions were merely matters to be taken into account, and did not require disallowance of leading questions *per se*.
(4) There was no real purpose in requiring notice of the questions to be asked, as the cross-examiner did not know what the witness would say in response to questions.
(5) There was no requirement for the witness to give evidence on a *voir dire* as to his expertise, as the judge was satisfied as to the witnesses' expertise to give evidence on the matters in issue.

67 [2007] HCA 59; (2007) 235 CLR 521.
68 *Matthews v SPI Electricity & Ors (Ruling No 34)* [2014] VSC 40, [10]–[11].
69 Ibid [11].
70 Ibid [14]–[16].
71 Ibid [20].
72 *Matthews v SPI Electricity & Ors (Ruling No 36)* [2014] VSC 82.
73 Ibid [19]–[23].

33.6.13 Further supplementary reports to address lay evidence at trial

This ruling[74] arose from an application late in the trial to permit further supplementary experts' reports to take into account lay evidence adduced at the trial that conflicted with the basis of facts assumed by the experts.

The application was opposed by the State parties on the basis that it was made too late in the trial, and that the first defendant was attempting to introduce a wholly new and unpleaded case. Further, that the first defendant should have been aware that its case would be attacked on the basis of its impracticability on the known facts, it would cause severe disruption and inconvenience, and it was a tactical decision in conflict with the spirit of previous rulings.

His Honour determined that it was in the interests of justice that the further supplementary reports be permitted and referred to the relevant principles in his previous ruling in *Matthews v SPI (Ruling No 20)*.[75] He gave the following reasons:[76]

(1) The evidence of the lay witness sought to be used as the basis of assumed facts was unique (the extent and clarity of which was acknowledged by the first defendant), and provided a firm evidentiary basis on which the experts could base their opinion. Further, it was likely that this evidence would be relied on in determining the appropriate assumptions of fact.
(2) The evidence would not result in the experts expressing opinions on a different basis to that on which they had previously based their reports, but merely on a different assumption of the facts underpinning those opinions.
(3) At some point in time, the factual basis underpinning the experts' reports would have to be addressed, either in evidence-in-chief or in cross-examination.
(4) Permitting a party to put an alternative set of assumptions of fact to an expert witness was quite common. The first defendant was not attempting to obtain a fresh opinion on new matters, merely providing a different set of assumptions to its expert.
(5) The assumptions of fact arising from the lay evidence did not fall outside the first defendant's pleaded case. "To decide this application on the basis of a divergence from SPI's pleadings would be a triumph of form over substance."[77]
(6) Any inconsistencies between the new assumptions provided to the first defendant's expert and the lay evidence was not a reason to preclude a supplementary report, as any discrepancy could be addressed by the weight afforded to the evidence.
(7) Any potential prejudice to the State parties could be adequately addressed by providing sufficient time for their expert to produce a supplementary report, and rescheduling the date of the relevant concurrent expert evidence session.

His Honour quoted Dixon J in an earlier ruling: "It is sensible and reasonable to conclude that a claim that is dependent for its success on expert evidence becomes fanciful once

74 *Matthews v SPI Electricity & Ors (Ruling No 37)* [2014] VSC 97.
75 [2013] VSC 197.
76 *Matthews v SPI Electricity & Ors (Ruling No 37)* [2014] VSC 97 [35]–[41].
77 Ibid [39].

the basis for the expert opinion that has thus far sustained it evaporates."[78] His Honour's fundamental rationale for permitting further supplementary reports in the circumstances was that: "It is clearly contrary to the interests of justice for the case to proceed to judgment with [the expert witness] operating on a set of assumptions that may prove to be inaccurate or unreliable."[79]

33.6.14 Striking out of expert evidence

This ruling[80] was in relation to the defendant's submissions that substantial parts of an expert's report should be struck out on the basis of admissibility on the following grounds:[81]

(a) The expert made findings of fact and therefore ventured outside of his expert role.
(b) The expert failed to distinguish between assumptions of fact and opinion.
(c) To the extent that the report contained opinion evidence, the expert failed to distinguish between assumptions of fact and opinion.
(d) The expert should be characterised as an advocate for the plaintiff.

The judge noted that these submissions resulted from "an exhaustive, and exhausting, over-analysis of the contents of the two [expert's] reports",[82] which analysis the judge found to be "distracting and unhelpful".[83] In assessing the defendant's submissions, the judge suggested that the proper procedure in this and most cases was to "examine the report as a whole and determine whether the reader can sensibly distinguish between assumed facts and the expression of opinion based on the witness' expertise".[84]

Forrest J emphasised that the adducing of expert evidence is regulated by the *Evidence Act 2008* (Vic), and procedural aspects are governed by the *Civil Procedure Act 2010* (Vic), and the *Supreme Court (General Civil Procedure) Rules 2005* (Vic). He referred to the High Court case of *Dasreef Pty Ltd v Hawchar*[85] for its articulation of the two criteria for evidence to be admissible under s 79(1) of the *Evidence Act 2008* (Vic):

> The first is that the witness who gives the evidence "has specialised knowledge based on the person's training, study or experience"; the second is that the opinion expressed in evidence by the witness "is wholly or substantially based on that knowledge".[86]

His Honour accepted that it was necessary for an expert report to make clear the distinction between assumption of fact and expression of opinion, so that counsel know the case they have to meet in preparing for cross-examination of the witness.[87]

78 Ibid [43].
79 Ibid [44].
80 *Matthews v SPI Electricity & Ors (Ruling No 38)* [2014] VSC 102.
81 Ibid [2].
82 Ibid [3].
83 Ibid [33].
84 Ibid.
85 (2011) 243 CLR 588.
86 (2011) 243 CLR 588, 602–603.
87 *Matthews v SPI Electricity & Ors (Ruling No 38)* [2014] VSC 102, [23].

The defendant's submissions were, in part, based on a distinction between "primary", and "secondary" findings of fact, based on reference to the case of *ASIC v Rich*.[88] Forrest J questioned the utility of that distinction and stated that "the distinction between primary (or intermediate) propositions only confuses and mystifies what is a basic requirement: identification of the assumed facts as opposed to opinion evidence".[89]

His Honour noted that "What is important is whether it is clear that the expert is referring to an assumed fact as opposed to an opinion."[90]

Ultimately his Honour concluded that, based on a close reading of the expert's reports and the source material referred to, the expert had distinguished between his findings of fact (based on the defendant's documents), and his opinions.[91]

Some of the defendant's submissions were based on a criticism of the expert's brief, in that it did not include "assumed facts" but was based on "open" questions from the instructing solicitor. In his comments on the defendant's submissions on this issue, his Honour made the following pertinent comment:

> Surely it is in the interests of justice to permit an expert to examine the materials provided free from the potentially biased or preconceived view of the facts that a party's lawyer may have when providing 'assumptions of fact'. Even if not so skewed, the assumed facts may be incomplete or inadequately set out due to a lack of expert knowledge on the part of the lawyer.[92]

In this writer' view, this is an important caveat to the lawyers instructing expert witnesses: the lawyers rarely fully understand the technical issues that the expert is briefed to opine on, and the expert should not be constrained by the lawyer's understanding of the "facts" on which the expert is briefed to opine. In this writer's experience, the facts underlying many technical issues are apparent from the documents: documents that were prepared in the normal course of execution of the project without any thought as to their ultimate evidential value in a dispute. Such documents often "speak for themselves", and are persuasive evidence of facts, uninfluenced by the exigencies of the dispute resolution process.

The report of this case supports such an approach: notwithstanding some minor issues with the expert reports that could be characterised as procedural defects, the judge was able to establish that the expert had satisfied the substantive requirements in relation to expert's reports. On a close reading of the expert reports, the judge was satisfied that the reports complied with the requirements of the relevant statutes, and distinguished between the facts derived from the documents, and the opinions derived from those documents.

33.6.15 Further expert evidence late in the trial

This ruling[93] was made in response to an application, made near the end of the trial, for one of the plaintiff's experts to be permitted to adduce further evidence.

88 (2005) 190 FLR 242.
89 *Matthews v SPI Electricity & Ors (Ruling No 38)* [2014] VSC 102, [36].
90 Ibid [37].
91 Ibid [42].
92 Ibid [43].
93 *Matthews v SPI Electricity & Ors (Ruling No 39)* [2014] VSC 109.

There were two issues in contention: (1) whether the expert had the relevant expertise to opine in his report as to what should have been seen from ground-based inspections, and (2) whether the expert should be permitted to adduce evidence as to other aspects of the asset-inspection process.

Forrest J had no difficulty in concluding that the experts' report was admissible in relation to ground-based inspections, as the opinions in it were appropriately based on his expertise as revealed in his CV.

In respect of the further evidence sought to be adduced, his Honour refused leave on the basis that it opened up new issues and had been served far too late.

In providing detailed reasons for this ruling, his Honour referred to his ruling No 38 for the rationale for the relevant provisions of the *Evidence Act 2008*;[94] also to the relevant provisions of the *Civil Procedure Act 2010* (Vic) and the *Supreme Court (General Civil Procedure Rules) 2005* for the relevant procedural aspects governing expert evidence in court.

Forrest J detailed the expert's expertise in his CV that underpinned the evidence he had given to date and highlighted the significant extensions to that expertise included in an amended CV submitted in support of his proposed further evidence. His Honour commented: "The fresh details in [the witness'] updated CV are surprising. They appear to have been inserted with the intention of demonstrating that [he] is qualified to give the additional evidence [the plaintiff] now seeks to adduce."[95]

His Honour also detailed the extent to which the subject of the proposed further evidence sought to extend the evidence in the expert's expert reports and evidence to date "extraordinarily".[96] His Honour noted that: "Apart from an oblique inference that may be drawn in respect of (a), not one of these matters was, as I will demonstrate, mentioned in the context of asset inspection in the report."[97] This was all new material that was not included in the report already served: "It extends into extraordinary detail that is not mentioned in the report and has never been canvassed with witnesses called by [the defendants]."[98]

His Honour concluded that the plaintiff would not be permitted to adduce the further expert evidence for the following reasons:

(1) An Expert would not be permitted to go outside the scope of the opinion(s) expressed in his report(s). From a reading of the expert's original CV and his instructions, it was clear that the plaintiff did not intend him to opine on the asset management practices the subject of the proposed additional evidence. The evidence was not necessary to deal with evidence adduced a year earlier, as leave could have been sought at that time.[99]

(2) The opinions sought from the expert went well beyond his engineering expertise. His Honour determined that there was no basis to conclude that the expert had the requisite "specialised knowledge".[100]

94 *Matthews v SPI Electricity & Ors (Ruling No 38)* [2014] VSC 108.
95 *Matthews v SPI Electricity & Ors (Ruling No 39)* [2014] VSC 109 [33].
96 Ibid [43].
97 Ibid [44].
98 Ibid [57].
99 Ibid [61]–[64].
100 Ibid [66].

(3) The submission raised the "spectre" that the expert "is not truly an expert on these asset inspection issues but an advocate for [the plaintiff's] case".[101]

(4) There would be significant prejudice to the defendants, as they had not had the opportunity of putting the issues to their witnesses, as required by the rule in *Browne v Dunne*.[102] Considering that the trial had been running for more than 180 days, "recalling a number of witnesses to satisfy [the plaintiff's] application would be inimical to the efficient, timely and cost-effective resolution of the dispute, as required by the [*Civil Procedure Act 2010* (Vic)]."[103]

(5) There were evidentiary matters sought to be adduced that went beyond the case as put in the plaintiff's statement of claim.[104]

In summary, his Honour determined that it would be inimical to the interests of justice to permit the plaintiff to adduce the further evidence.[105]

There are important lessons in this ruling, both for experts, and the lawyers instructing them. Both need to reflect on the fundamental principles enshrined in Order 44, based on the principle that an expert's duty is to the court, and not to their instructing party. An expert not only needs to express independent views, irrespective of the exigencies of the litigation, they need to be perceived to be independent by the court.

The instructing solicitor needs to be aware of the expert's expertise relevant to the issues in the case, and to ensure that the expert's brief encompasses all the issues on which the expert's opinion is sought. The expert needs to ensure that his/her CV comprehensively covers all of his/her experience and expertise that might be relevant to issues in the case, but also that s/he does not stray into expressing opinions outside that demonstrated expertise and experience.

The following observation by Forrest J in this case should give experts and their instructors pause for thought:

> The evidence that [the plaintiff] now seeks to adduce from [the expert] is new and breathtaking in its scope. Indeed, one could easily conclude that [the plaintiff's] lawyers have assembled the contents of the [expert's] notice after reflecting upon the evidence given in the trial to date, with the intention of plugging perceived gaps in [the plaintiff's] case.[106]

101 Ibid [67].
102 Ibid [68].
103 Ibid [69].
104 Ibid [71].
105 Ibid [73].
106 [61].

CHAPTER 34

The rules for expert evidence[1]

34.1 Introduction

In the previous chapter, the author reviewed various current issues involved in briefing experts, including the cases on expert evidence arising from the class action litigation on the Victorian bushfires. That chapter briefly discussed the rules relating to expert evidence in the Supreme Court of Victoria and the Federal Court.

As with many other aspects of the law in Australia, there are significant differences in the law and the rules for expert evidence between the different State, Territory and Commonwealth jurisdictions. Some jurisdictions now have *Uniform Evidence Acts*, whilst the common law of evidence still applies in three jurisdictions. A number of jurisdictions have explicit Codes of Conduct for expert witnesses, whilst the others do not. All jurisdictions have civil procedure rules that regulate expert evidence. The differences may mean that expert evidence that is complying in one jurisdiction may not necessarily comply with the rules in another jurisdiction.

This chapter provides a comparison of the rules relating to expert evidence in the nine jurisdictions of the State and Territory Supreme Courts and the Federal Court, as well as for Singapore and the UK. Table 34.2 below cites for each jurisdiction the specific clause references to the requirements for expert evidence in the *Civil Procedure Rules* and expert witness Codes of Conduct. This table provides details of the requirements for expert evidence under nine categories, including procedural requirements for expert reports, the required content of an expert report, procedural rules for expert conclaves, and giving expert evidence in court.

The final section of the chapter contains suggestions for the contents of an expert report that the author considers would generally satisfy the formal requirements in any common law jurisdiction, irrespective of the specific rules. Whilst this may seem to be an unnecessary counsel of perfection, this author believes there is merit in adopting a uniform approach to expert evidence that incorporates the current best practice in Australia.

34.2 Expert evidence rules

There are differences in the applicable evidence law between Australian jurisdictions. The Commonwealth, ACT, NSW, NT, Norfolk Island, Tasmania and Victoria are *Uniform*

1 This chapter is an edited and updated version of the paper published in: Donald Charrett, "The Rules for Expert Evidence in Australia" (2015) 163 *Australian Construction Law Newsletter* 24.

 DOI: 10.4324/9781003206897-38

Evidence Act jurisdictions, whereas the common law still applies in Queensland, SA and WA. The 180 sections in the *Evidence Act 2012 Cap 97* (Sin) substantially codifies the law of evidence in Singapore, whilst the common law of evidence applies in the UK.

Such differences in evidence law may be significant in the extent to which case law in one jurisdiction may not be applicable in another jurisdiction. For example, there are differences between the common law and the *Uniform Evidence Act* in the extent to which an expert's draft reports can be called for or disclosed.[2]

Each jurisdiction considered here has rules that govern the content of, and the manner of giving expert evidence. The provisions of regulation 31.17 of the *Uniform Civil Procedure Rules 2005* (NSW) are typical of the rationale for these rules:

(a) to ensure that the court has control over the giving of expert evidence;
(b) to restrict expert evidence in proceedings to that which is reasonably required to resolve the proceedings;
(c) to avoid unnecessary costs associated with parties to proceedings retaining different experts;
(d) if it is practicable to do so without compromising the interests of justice, to enable expert evidence to be given on an issue in proceedings by a single expert engaged by the parties or appointed by the court;
(e) if it is necessary to do so, to ensure a fair trial of proceedings, to allow for more than one expert (but no more than are necessary) to give evidence on an issue in the proceedings;
(f) to declare the duty of an expert witness in relation to the court and the parties to proceedings.[3]

The specific scope and content of the rules applicable to expert evidence differ significantly between jurisdictions. A number of jurisdictions also have Codes of Conduct that experts are required to adhere to. One common feature of the different rules and Codes of Conduct is that the court exercises considerable control over the form of expert evidence. This is reflective of the importance of, and the need for the court to rely on, expert opinion in many cases. Such reliance is only possible if expert reports comply with appropriate procedures for the preparation and articulation of expert evidence.

The exact content of the individual rules and Codes of Conduct relating to the superior courts in the various jurisdictions is beyond the scope of this chapter. Clearly, a legal practitioner or expert involved in the preparation and presentation of expert evidence in a particular jurisdiction must be familiar with and comply with the relevant rules. Table 34.1 summarises the location of the applicable Rules and Codes of Conduct in nine Australian superior court jurisdictions, Singapore and the UK.[4]

Legal practitioners or experts are referred to the relevant provisions of the applicable rules in the table in the Annexure for the detailed requirements applying in a particular jurisdiction. The significant differences between the rules, as well as the applicable evidence law, should be borne in mind when looking at the applicability of case law.

---

2 Dodds-Streeton J set out these distinctions in *Shea v TruEnergy Services Pty Ltd (No 5)* [2013] FCA 937.

3 There is a similar statement of purposes in s 1200 of *Court Procedures Rules 2006* (ACT).

4 The author is indebted to the Expert Subcommittee of Society of Construction Law Australia for a preview of their draft report and permission to use some of their content in this table, and Table 34.2.

TABLE 34.1 The Acts, Rules and Codes of Conduct for expert evidence

Jurisdiction and evidence law	*Evidence Act*	*Civil Procedure Rules relating to expert evidence*	*Expert Witness Code of Conduct*
Supreme Court of the Australian Capital Territory (**ACTSC**)	Uniform Evidence Act – *Evidence Act 2011* (ACT)	*Court Procedures Rules 2006* (ACT) Part 2.12 Expert evidence Rules 1200–1246	*Court Procedures Rules 2006* (ACT) Schedule 1 Expert witness Code of conduct
Federal Court of Australia (**FCA**)	Uniform Evidence Act – *Evidence Act 1995* (Cth)	*Federal Court Rules 2011* (Cth) Rule 5.04 & Part 23 Experts RR23.01–23.15	Expert Evidence Practice Note (GPN-EXPT) Annexure A
Supreme Court of New South Wales (**NSWSC**)	Uniform Evidence Act – *Evidence Act 1995* (NSW)	*Uniform Civil Procedure Rules 2005* (NSW) Rules 31.17–31.54	*Uniform Civil Procedure Rules 2005* (NSW) Schedule 7 Expert witness Code of conduct
Supreme Court of the Northern Territory (**NTSC**)	Uniform Evidence Act – *Evidence Act* (NT)	*Supreme Court Rules 1987* (NT) Regs 44.01–44.05	–
Supreme Court of Queensland (**QSC**)	Common law – *Evidence Act 1977* (Qld)	*Uniform Civil Procedure Rules 1999* (Qld) Ch 11, Part 5, Division 2 Rules 423–429S	–
Supreme Court of South Australia (**SASC**)	Common law – *Evidence Act 1929* (SA)	*Uniform Civil Rules 2020* (SA) Part 14 Expert Reports Rules 74.1–74.13	*Uniform Civil Rules 2020* (SA) Part 14 Expert Reports Division 3 Rules 74.3–74.9
Supreme Court of Tasmania (**TSC**)	Uniform Evidence Act – *Evidence Act 2001* (Tas)	*Supreme Court Rules 2000* (Tas) Part 19 Division 5 Expert opinion evidence Rules 514–517	Practice Direction No 1 of 2016
Supreme Court of Victoria (**VSC**)	Uniform Evidence Act – *Evidence Act 2008* (Vic)	*Supreme Court (General Civil Procedure) Rules 2005* (Vic) Order 44 Expert Evidence Rules 44.01–44.06	*Supreme Court (General Civil Procedure) Rules 2005* (Vic) Form 44A Expert Witness Code of Conduct
Supreme Court of Western Australia (**WASC**)	Common law – *Evidence Act 1906* (WA)	*Rules of the Supreme Court 1971* (WA) Order 36A Expert evidence Rule 1 Practice Direction 4.1.2.2 [50]–[55]	–

(*Continued*)

TABLE 34.1 Continued

Jurisdiction and evidence law	*Evidence Act*	*Civil Procedure Rules relating to expert evidence*	*Expert Witness Code of Conduct*
Supreme Court of Singapore	Codified law – *Evidence Act 2012 Cap 97* (Sin)	*Rules of Court 2014* (Sin) – Order 40A Experts of Parties	
United Kingdom	Common law – *Civil Evidence Act 1995* (UK) *Civil Evidence Act 1972* (UK) *Civil Evidence Act 1968* (UK) *Evidence Act 1938* (UK) …	*The Civil Procedure Rules 1998* (UK) – Part 35 Experts and Assessors	Practice Direction 35 – Experts and Assessors

A detailed comparison of the rules and Codes of Conduct referred to in Table 34.2 in Section 34.5 reveals that, collectively, they cover the following issues (although no set of rules or Code of Conduct covers all of the issues):

(1) General issues in relation to the rules for expert evidence
(2) Overarching obligations applying to an expert witness
(3) Procedural requirements for expert reports
(4) Required content of an expert report
(5) Procedural rules for pre-trial expert conferences or discussions
(6) Procedural rules for giving expert evidence in court
(7) Procedures for court-appointed expert or jointly appointed single expert
(8) Shadow experts/expert adviser
(9) Questions to experts

34.3 Details of specific provisions

34.3.1 General issues in relation to the rules for expert evidence

The general issues cover:

- Purposes
- Definitions
- Immunity of expert witness
- Expert report admissible as evidence of opinion
- Expert report to be tendered by rule or by leave of court
- Expert evidence-in-chief by experts' reports
- Expert witness bound by Code of Conduct
- Application of the rules to a party witness

- General court powers in relation to expert evidence
- Expert may request directions from court
- Conditional or contingency fees

Most jurisdictions require that expert evidence-in-chief is to be adduced by expert reports, in some jurisdictions only after the court has made appropriate directions.

In those jurisdictions that have an explicit expert Code of Conduct, an expert is bound by its provisions, and usually has to acknowledge in their report that s/he has read, understood and complied with the Code. The importance of this formal acknowledgement is highlighted by the provision in the ACTSC rules:

> If an expert report does not contain an acknowledgement by the expert witness who prepared the report that the expert witness has read the code of conduct and agrees to be bound by it, service of the expert report by the party who engaged the expert is not valid service.[5]

The rules in three jurisdictions specify whether the expert evidence Code/Rules apply to a party who is also qualified to act as an expert witness. The Expert Witness Code of Conduct does not apply in Victoria[6] nor do the Rules apply in Queensland;[7] however, the Rules apply to a party witness in South Australia.[8]

Rule 35.14 of *The Civil Procedure Rules 1998* (UK) provide that an expert has the right to seek directions from the court to assist him/her in carrying out their functions.

Payment of expert fees only in the event of a successful outcome is discouraged by courts on the basis that it may influence an expert's evidence. In respect of contingency fees, rule 31.22 of the *Uniform Civil Procedure Rules 2005* (NSW) provides that such fees must be disclosed:

> (1) A person who is engaged as an expert witness in relation to any proceedings must include information as to any arrangements under which:
> (a) the charging of fees or costs by the expert witness is contingent on the outcome of the proceedings, or
> (b) the payment of any fees or costs to the expert witness is to be deferred, in, or in an annexure to, any report that he or she prepares for the purposes of the proceedings.
>
> (2) If a report referred to in subrule (1) indicates the existence of any such arrangements, the court may direct disclosure of the terms of the engagement (including as to fees and costs).

This rule provides only for disclosure, the purpose being transparency by making it known that such an expert may have a financial interest in the proceeding. However, there is nothing in the *Uniform Civil Procedure Rules 2005* (NSW) that empowers a court to exclude an expert report in breach of this provision.[9]

The UK Guidance for the Instruction of Experts in Civil Claims notes that the payment of fees contingent on the outcome of a case is strongly discouraged. In *Ex parte*

5 *Court Procedures Rules 2006* (ACT) rule 1203(3).
6 *Supreme Court Rules 2005* (Vic) rule 44.02(2).
7 *Uniform Civil Procedure Rules 1999* (Qld) rule 424.
8 *Uniform Civil Rules 2020* (SA) rule 74.1.
9 *Fuller-Lyons v State of New South Wales (No 2)* [2013] NSWSC 445 [7], [8].

Factortame (No 8) [2003] QB 381 [73] the court said: "we consider that it will be a rare case indeed that the court will be prepared to consent to an expert being instructed under a contingency fee arrangement."[10]

34.3.2 Overarching obligations of an expert witness

Expert witnesses have some or all of the following explicit obligations in the majority of jurisdictions:

- An overriding duty to assist the court, irrespective of obligations to the party instructing them
- An expert witness is not an advocate for a party
- A duty to comply with court directions or cooperate with another expert witness.

Section 29 of the *Civil Procedure Act 2010* (Vic) provides that a court may sanction an expert who has contravened any overarching obligation, including immediately paying legal costs, expenses or compensation for financial loss of any other person, or not be permitted to take specified steps in the proceeding. The Guidance for the Instruction of Experts in Civil Claims issued by the Civil Justice Council in the UK notes that the court has the power to impose sanctions including that an expert's report/evidence be inadmissible, or more severe sanctions if an expert misleads the court.[11]

34.3.3 Procedural requirements for expert reports

All jurisdictions define in the Rules and/or Codes of Conduct some of the following procedural requirements:

- A party is required to give an expert witness a copy of the Code of Conduct
- Service of expert reports
- An expert is to issue a supplementary report when they have changed their opinion for any reason
- Notice to the court where an expert has changed their opinion
- Draft of expert report communicated to a party is to be retained by an expert.

In respect of the service of expert reports, the wording in the rules is significantly different between jurisdictions. The following reports are to be served:

- ACTSC: "each expert report obtained by the party in accordance with any direction made by the court".[12]
- FCA: "an expert report that complies with rule 23.13".[13]

10 Guidance for the Instruction of Experts in Civil Claims [88] https://www.judiciary.uk/wp-content/uploads/2014/08/experts-guidance-cjc-aug-2014-amended-dec-8.pdf (accessed 18 April 2021).

11 Sections 91, 92.

12 *Court Procedures Rules 2006* (ACT) rule 1240.

13 *Federal Court Rules 2011* (Cth) rule 23.11.

- NSWSC: "experts' reports".[14]
- NTSC: "a statement in accordance with subrule (2)".[15]
- QSC: a report that a party is intending to rely on.[16]
- SASC: "a copy of each expert report in the party's possession, custody or power relevant to the subject matter of the proceeding not previously served on that party (whether or not the party intends to rely on the report at the trial)"[17]
- TSC: "a report containing the evidence".[18]
- VSC: "a report by the expert", where "a party who intends at trial to adduce the evidence of a person as an expert".[19]
- WASC: "a report of an expert witness the substance of which a party intends to rely on at the trial or hearing."[20]

South Australia is thus the only jurisdiction that requires that all expert reports in a party's possession are to be served on every other party, whether or not the party intends to rely on them at trial or not.

34.3.4 Required content of an expert report

All jurisdictions define in the Rules and/or Codes of Conduct specify some of the following requirements for the content of an expert report:

- Statement that the expert has understood and complied with their duty
- Statement that the expert has made all inquiries that they believe appropriate
- Summary of the expert's qualifications and experience
- Statement that the expert's opinion is provisional when available information is insufficient or inaccurate
- Statement that a particular question or issue is outside the expert's expertise
- Statement that the opinions are genuinely held by the expert
- Acknowledgement that the opinions are based on the expert's specialised knowledge
- Report to be signed by the expert
- Details of the expert's fees or communications with the expert

NSW and South Australia have explicit provisions that require an expert to reveal certain details about their fees. In NSW, an expert must include information on any contingency fees or deferred payment schemes.[21] In SA, an expert must provide, on request, details of his/her fees, and details of any communications relevant to the preparation of their report with their instructing party/legal representative, or any other expert.[22]

---

14 *Uniform Civil Procedure Rules 2005* (NSW) rule 31.28.
15 *Supreme Court Rules* (NT) rule 44.03.
16 *Uniform Civil Procedure Rules 1999* (Qld) rule 429.
17 *Uniform Civil Rules 2020* (SA) rule 74.3(1).
18 *Supreme Court Rules 2000* (Tas) rule 516(1).
19 *Supreme Court (General Civil Procedure) Rules 2005* (Vic) rule 44.03(1).
20 *Rules of the Supreme Court 1971* (WA) rule 36A.3(4).
21 *Uniform Civil Procedure Rules 2005* (NSW) rule 31.22.
22 *Uniform Civil Rules 2020* (SA) rule 74.4.

34.3.5 Procedural rules for expert conferences

All jurisdictions have procedural rules and/or provisions in Codes of Conduct in respect of pre-trial conferences between experts, covering some or all of the following issues:

- The Court may direct a conference with another expert
- Court direction to produce a joint report setting out the opinions where experts agree and disagree and the reasons why they disagree
- Experts must endeavour to reach agreement
- An expert is not to act on any instruction to withhold or avoid agreement with other expert witnesses.

The clear aim of these provisions is to minimise the differences between expert opinions, by a structured process that addresses the facts on which expert opinions are based, as well as ensuring that experts address the same questions.

The procedures generally aim to minimise the influence of lawyers on the outcome of an experts' conference, perhaps by excluding lawyers from attending, and ensuring that the conference proceedings themselves are "without prejudice".

34.3.6 Procedural rules for giving evidence in court

Whilst the modern focus on expert evidence is on the preparation of expert reports as evidence-in-chief, oral testimony is often important to supplement or test expert evidence. Procedural rules cover some or all of the following issues:

- Complying expert report is a precondition to giving oral evidence
- Experts to consider factual evidence adduced at trial
- Cross-examination of experts can be separate or concurrent
- Expert permitted to question other experts
- Expert can give an exposition of his/her own opinion or their opinion about other experts' opinions
- How lay or expert evidence in the hearing may be given
- The scope of evidence-in-chief is restricted
- Expert must be available for cross-examination if required

In most jurisdictions, the preparation of a complying expert report is a precondition for giving oral evidence, and an expert must be available for cross-examination if required.

Courts generally have wide discretion to adopt procedures for giving expert evidence appropriate to the circumstances, such as their location in the hearing room, the order in which factual and expert evidence is given, the order of cross-examination, the ability for experts to give an exposition of their own opinion or question the opinion of other experts.

Five jurisdictions have a provision that experts can be required to confirm their opinions or otherwise after the factual evidence has been adduced.[23]

---

23 *Court Procedures Rules 2006* (ACT) rule 1211; *Federal Court Rules 2011* (Cth) rule 23.15; *Uniform Civil Procedure Rules 2005* (NSW) rule 31.35; *Supreme Court Rules* (NT) Order 44.05(2); *Supreme Court Rules 2000* (Tas) rule 516(4).

34.3.7 Procedures for court-appointed expert or jointly appointed single expert

Four jurisdictions have specific provisions in respect of the appointment of a single expert by the court or the parties:[24]

- Court procedure for appointment of its own expert witness or special referee
- Cross-examination of court-appointed expert
- Other expert's reports on question addressed by the court-appointed expert
- Joint engagement of a single expert.

Appointment of a single expert, either by the court or the parties, may result in significant cost savings over the appointment of separate experts by each party. However, it may result in genuine concerns as to its reliability in the absence of confirming opinion and may need to be tested by cross-examination.[25]

NSW specifically prohibits adducing other expert evidence on an issue if a court-appointed expert has been appointed in respect of that issue.[26]

34.3.8 Shadow experts

South Australia is unique in having provisions to regulate the involvement of shadow experts.[27]

A ***shadow expert*** is an expert who:

(a) is engaged to give advice or an opinion on or assist with the preparation or presentation of a party's case on the basis that the expert will not give evidence at the trial;
(b) has not previously provided a report on the subject of the case other than as a shadow expert; and
(c) as part of the engagement gives a certificate in the prescribed form certifying that the expert—
    (i) understands that it is not the expert's role to give evidence at trial; and
    (ii) has not previously provided a report on the subject of the case other than as a shadow expert.[28]

34.3.9 Questions to experts

Three jurisdictions provide that a party can request information and documents from another party who has provided an expert report.[29] In Singapore and the UK, with leave

24 *Federal Court Rules 2011* (Cth); *Uniform Civil Procedure Rules 2005* (NSW); *Uniform Civil Procedure Rules 1999* (Qld); *The Civil Procedure Rules 1998* (UK) rr 35.7, 35.8, 35.15.

25 *Federal Court Rules 2011* (Cth) rule 23.02(2); *Uniform Civil Procedure Rules 2005* (NSW) rule 31.51; *Uniform Civil Procedure Rules 1999* (Qld) rule 429M(1).

26 *Uniform Civil Procedure Rules 2005* (NSW) rule 31.52.

27 *Uniform Civil Rules 2020* (SA) rule 74.13.

28 Ibid.

29 *Uniform Civil Rules 2020* (SA) rule 74.4; *Rules of Court 2014* (Sin) rule 4; *The Civil Procedure Rules 1998* (UK) rule 35.6.

of the court, a party can put written questions for clarification of a report by an expert instructed by another party.

34.3.10 Consequences of noncompliance

The consequences of not complying with the requirements of the applicable Rules/Code of Conduct are well illustrated in the English case of *SPE International Ltd v Professional Preparation Contractors (UK) Ltd.*[30] In that case just about everything that could possibly go wrong with expert evidence did go wrong. The judge rejected the evidence as inadmissible because the "expert" had breached all of his obligations to the court and had not complied with the fundamental requirements of giving independent expert evidence based on relevant qualifications, training and experience. In this writer's view, a similar outcome could be expected in an Australian court or in the Singapore Supreme Court.

In another English case, Coulson J rejected the evidence of one expert witness in its entirety for a total of 12 reasons.[31] These 12 reasons are salutary reading for any expert witnesses, and those briefing them, particularly the judge's summary:

> For these reasons, therefore, I consider that [the expert witness] allowed himself to be used, whether wittingly or otherwise, by … (those with the most to gain in this litigation) to act as their mouthpiece. It was almost as if they were trying to see how much of their claim they could get past [the expert witness], and then [the expert witness for the other side], and ultimately the Court. It made a mockery of the oath which [the expert witness] had taken at the outset of his evidence, even though, as I have said, there were some extenuating circumstances.[32]

34.4 Recommendations on contents of an expert report

As outlined above, there are differences in the requirements of the Rules and expert Codes of Conduct between jurisdictions, and those specific Rules and Codes should be consulted to ensure that an expert report complies with the applicable procedural requirements and content of expert reports to be used in court proceedings.

Although not mandatory in arbitral proceedings, these Codes of Conduct/Rules (or their equivalent) are often also applied in arbitrations because they are perceived to define the norms that experts should comply with for their evidence to be relevant, persuasive and of assistance to the tribunal. Experts would be well advised to comply with such requirements in arbitral proceedings in any event, as such compliance should negate any grounds for rejection of the evidence on the grounds of admissibility. The Expert Evidence Practice Notes (**GPN-EXPT**) issued by the Chief Justice of the Federal Court in October 2016[33] are very suitable for use by Arbitrators, counsel and experts in arbitral proceedings; in addition to general guidance on expert evidence, they cover the role and duties of an expert witness, contents of an expert report, conferences of experts and concurrent expert evidence. The annexures to GPN-EXPT comprise a Harmonised Witness Code of Conduct, and Concurrent Evidence Guidelines, suitable for use in arbitral proceedings.

---

30 [2002] EWHC 881 (Ch).

31 *Van Oord UK Ltd & Anor v Allseas UK Ltd* [2015] EWHC 3074 (TCC).

32 Ibid [89].

33 www.fedcourt.gov.au/law-and-practice/practice-documents/practice-notes/gpn-expt (accessed 21 April 2021).

The following are recommendations on the substantive contents of an expert report to be used in litigation or arbitration in Australia. Whilst not all of these matters are specifically required by the Rules/Code of Conduct in any one jurisdiction, the writer believes that they represent best practice in the preparation of an expert report and should satisfy the specific requirements of any Australian jurisdiction, the requirements of s 79 of the *Uniform Evidence Acts*, or the common law requirements for expert evidence. Subject to any additional requirements arising from local legislation or rules, it is suggested they would also be suitable in other common law jurisdictions, including Singapore and the UK.

For clarity and logic, the following substantive matters should be addressed in separate and clearly labelled sections of the expert's report:

- A brief summary of a lengthy or complex report.
- The name and address of the expert and details of their qualifications, training and experience by which the expert has acquired specialised knowledge relevant to their opinions expressed in the report.
- The instructions the expert's report is responding to, including the questions they have been asked to address and the material they have been asked to consider (this may be by annexing the letter of instructions).
- Each of the material facts, matters and assumptions of fact (written or provided orally) on which the opinions are based (some of which may be detailed in the letter of instructions annexed), distinguishing facts identified by the expert and their source from assumed facts, and distinguishing objectively verifiable facts from matters of opinion.
- Details of any examinations, tests or other investigations on which the opinion is based, the name and qualifications of the persons who carried them out and supervised them.
- Details of any literature or other materials referred to such as photographs, plans, calculations, analyses, measurements, survey reports or other extrinsic matters relied on by the expert to support his/her opinions – these will need to be made available to the opposite party when the expert report is served.
- The expert's opinions on each of the questions addressed to him/her.
- The expert's reasons for each opinion expressed, and if there is a range of opinion on matters dealt with in the report, a summary of the range of opinion, and the reasons why the expert adopted a particular opinion.
- The expert's signature.

In addition to the above substantive content, the following "ethical" obligations should be acknowledged in an expert's report:

- Whether any particular question, issue or matter falls outside the expert's field of expertise (if applicable).
- Whether any opinion expressed in the report is not a concluded opinion because of insufficient research or insufficient data or for any other reason.
- Whether access to any readily ascertainable additional facts would assist the expert in reaching a more reliable conclusion.
- A declaration that:

(i) The expert has made all the enquiries which the expert believes are appropriate and necessary or desirable.
(ii) The report contains reference to all matters the expert considers significant, and no matters of significance which the expert regards as relevant have, to the knowledge of the expert, been withheld from the report.
(iii) Any qualification of an opinion expressed in the report without which the report is or may be incomplete or inaccurate.
(iv) The expert's opinions are genuinely held and are based wholly or substantially on his/her specialised knowledge.
(v) The factual matters stated in the report are, as far as the expert knows, true.
(vi) The expert has been provided with copies of and has read the relevant Rules and experts' Code of Conduct (if applicable), understands and will comply with his/her duty in accordance with those Rules/Code, and the expert's report complies with the Rules and experts' Code of Conduct (if applicable).

If an expert has altered his/her opinion as expressed in an expert report, the expert should prepare a supplementary report as soon as possible, expressing the change of opinion, supported by a statement of the relevant substantive matters as outlined above. Such a supplementary report should be communicated to the opposing party without delay.

34.5 Table of rules of expert evidence in Australian Supreme Courts

Table 34.2 lists the specific clauses for expert evidence in the Rules and Codes of Conduct (where applicable) in each Australian jurisdiction, Singapore and the UK under the headings of Sections 34.3.1–34.3.9.

TABLE 34.2 Detailed requirements for expert evidence

		ACTSC	*FCA*	*NSWSC*	*NTSC*	*QSC*	*SASC*	*TSC*	*VSC*	*WASC*	*Singapore*	*England & Wales*
	Applicable law in relation to expert evidence	Uniform Evidence Act – *Evidence Act 2011* (ACT)	Uniform Evidence Act – *Evidence Act 1995* (Cth)	Uniform Evidence Act – *Evidence Act 1995* (NSW)	Uniform Evidence Act – *Evidence Act* (NT)	Common law – *Evidence Act 1977* (Qld)	Common law – *Evidence Act 1929* (SA)	Uniform Evidence Act – *Evidence Act 2001* (Tas)	Uniform Evidence Act – *Evidence Act 2008* (Vic)	Common law – *Evidence Act 1906* (WA)	Codified law – *Evidence Act 2012* (Sin)	Common law
	Civil Procedure Rules relating to expert evidence	*Court Procedures Rules 2006* (ACT) (**R**)	*Federal Court Rules 2011* (Cth) (**R**)	*Uniform Civil Procedure Rules 2005* (NSW) (**R**)	*Supreme Court Rules 1987* (NT) (**R**)	*Uniform Civil Procedure Rules 1999* (Qld) (**R**)	*Uniform Civil Rules 2020* (SA) (**R**)	*Supreme Court Rules 2000* (Tas) (**R**)	*Supreme Court (General Civil Procedure) Rules 2005* (Vic) (**R**)	*Rules of the Supreme Court 1971* (WA) (**R**) Practice Direction 4.1.2.2 (**PD**)	*Rules of Court 2014* (Sin) (**R**)	*The Civil Procedure Rules 1998* (UK) (**R**)
	Expert witness Code of conduct Guidance for Experts	Code (**C**)	Practice Note (**PN**) Code (**C**) Concurrent Expert Evidence Guidelines (Annexure B to PN)	Code (**C**)				Code (**C**)	Code (**C**)			Practice Direction (**PD**) Guidance for the Instruction of Experts in Civil Claims (**G**)
1	**General issues in relation to rules for expert evidence**											
1.1	Purposes	R1200	PN2.2	R31.17		R423						R35.1 PD1
1.2	Definitions	RR1201, 1202		R31.18	R44.01	R425	R74.1		R44.01			R35.2
1.3	Immunity of expert witness	R1204				R429C						
1.4	Expert report admissible as evidence of opinion	R1244		R31.29(1)							R3(1)	R35.5 G5

(Continued)

TABLE 34.2 Continued

		ACTSC	*FCA*	*NSWSC*	*NTSC*	*QSC*	*SASC*	*TSC*	*VSC*	*WASC*	*Singapore*	*England & Wales*
1.5	Expert report to be tendered by rule or by leave of court			R31.19	R44.03	R427(2)	R74.3	R516	R44.03	R36A.1 PD50	R3(1)	R35.4 R35.13
1.6	Expert evidence in chief by experts' reports	R1243		R31.21	R44.03(3)	R427(1)	R74.3(2)	R515	R44.05		R3(1)	R35.5
1.7	Expert witness is bound by Code of Conduct	R1203	R23.13	R31.23				R516	C3			
1.8	Rules apply to a party witness?					NO – R424	YES – R74.1		NO – R44.02(2)			
1.9	General court powers in relation to expert evidence	R1205	RR5.04(3), 23.14, 23.15	R31.20							R1	R35.1 R35.4
1.10	Expert may request directions from court											R35.14 G28, G29
1.11	Conditional or contingency fees			R31.22								G88
2	**Overarching obligations applying to an expert witness**											
2.1	Expert witness' overriding duty to the court	C1.2	C1.1 C2	C2(1) C2(2)		R426(1)	R74.5	C2	C1 *Civil Procedure Act 2010* (Vic) ss 10–12, ss 16–27		R2	R35.3 G9
2.2	An expert witness is not an advocate for a party.	C1.2	C2	C2(3)			R74.5	C2	C1			PD2.2
2.3	Duty to comply with court direction or cooperate with another expert witness		C6	C3 C4			R74.8	C6				

2.4	Sanctions for expert witness not complying with Rules or court orders								*Civil Procedure Act 2010* (Vic) s 28			G90 G92
3	**Procedural requirements for expert reports**											
3.1	Party required to give expert witness a copy of the Code of Conduct	R1203	R23.12	R31.23(2)					R44.03(1)			
3.2	Service of expert reports	RR1240, 1241	R23.11	R31.28	R44.03	R429	R160	R516(1)	R44.03(1)			
3.3	Expert to issue a supplementary report when they have changed their opinion for any reason	R1242, C1.3(4), C1.3(5)	C4	RR31.27(4) 31.34, C5(4)		R429A	R74.11	C4	R44.03(3), C4			
3.4	Notification where expert has changed their opinion						R74.7					PD2.5 G14
3.5	Draft of expert report communicated to a party to be retained by expert											
4	**Required content of an expert report**											
4.1	Contents of expert report	C1.3(1)	R23.13(1), C3	R31.27(1), C5(1)	R44.03(2)	R428(2), R428(3)	R74.6 R74.10	C3	R44.03	PD53	R3(2)	R35.10 PD3 G48– 60
4.2	Statement that expert has understood and complied with their duty		R23.13(1), C3(b)			R428(3)	R74.10(c)	C3(b)	C3		R3(2)(h)	R35.10(2) PD3.2(9) G52

(*Continued*)

TABLE 34.2 Continued

		ACTSC	*FCA*	*NSWSC*	*NTSC*	*QSC*	*SASC*	*TSC*	*VSC*	*WASC*	*Singapore*	*England & Wales*
4.3	Statement that expert has made all inquiries that they believe appropriate		C3(i)			R428(3)	R74.10(j)	C3(i)	C3	PD53		
4.4	Summary of expert's qualifications and experience	C1.3(1)	R23.13(1), C3(c)	C5(1)	R44.03(2)	R428(2)	R74.10(d)	C3(c)	C3	PD53	R3(2)(a)	PD3.2(1) G54
4.5	Statement that opinion is provisional when available information is insufficient or inaccurate	C1.3(2) C1.3(3)	C3(j) C3(k)	R31.27(2), R31.27(3), C5(2) C5(3)			R74.10(l)	C3(j) C3(k)	C3			PD3.2(8) G5
4.6	Statement that particular question or issue outside expert's expertise		C3(f)	R31.27(1)			R74.10(g)	C3(f)				PD2.4
4.7	Statement that opinion is genuinely held					R428(3)					R3(2)(g)	PD3.3 G53
4.8	Acknowledgement that opinions are based on specialised knowledge		R23.13(1)									
4.9	Report to be signed		R23.13(1)			R428(1)	R74.9(p)	R516(1)	R44.03(4)		R3(1)	PD3.3
4.10	Details of expert's fees or communications with expert			R31.22								

5	**Procedural rules for pre-trial expert conferences or discussions**											
5.1	Court may direct conference or discussions with another expert	RR1210, 1211	R23.15	RR31.24, 31.25, 31.26, C6(1)	R44.05(2)	R429B(1)	R74.9	C6(a)	R44.06, C5	PD54	R5	R35.12 PD9 G70
5.2	Court direction to produce a joint report setting out the opinions where experts agree and disagree and the reasons why they disagree	C1.4(1)	R23.15	R31.24(1), C6(1)	R44.05(2)	R429B	R74.9	C6(b)	R44.06(1), C5	PD54 PD55	R5(3)	R35.12(1) PD9.2 G71 G79–82
5.3	Experts must endeavour to reach agreement		C7(b)	R31.24(1), CC4, 6(1)		R429B	R74.9(2)(b)	C7(b)			R5(1)(b)	R35.12(1)(b) G71
5.4	Expert is not to act on any instruction to withhold or avoid agreement with other expert witness	C1.4(2)	C7(a)	CC4, 6(2)			R74.9	C7(a)	C6			PD9.7 G77
6	**Procedural rules for giving expert evidence in court**											
6.1	Complying expert report is a precondition to giving oral evidence	R1203	R23.11	R31.23(4)	R44.03(3)	R427		R515	R44.03(1) R44.05		R3(1)	
6.2	Experts to consider factual evidence adduced at trial	R1211	R23.15	R31.35	R44.05(2)			R516(4)				
6.3	Cross-examination of experts can be separate or concurrent	R1211	R23.15	R31.35	R44.05(2)						R6	PD11.1, PD11.2 G83

(Continued)

TABLE 34.2 Continued

		ACTSC	FCA	NSWSC	NTSC	QSC	SASC	TSC	VSC	WASC	Singapore	England & Wales
6.4	Expert permitted to question other experts	R1211		R31.35							R6(3)	PD11.4(1)
6.5	Expert can give an exposition of own opinion or opinion about other experts' opinions		R23.15	R31.35	R44.05(2)			R516(4)			R6(3)	PD11.4(1)
6.6	How lay or expert evidence in hearing may be given	R1211	R23.15	R31.35	R44.05(2)			R516(4)			R6	PD11
6.7	Scope of evidence-in-chief restricted	R1243	R23.15	R31.21	R44.03(3)	R427(4)						PD1
6.8	Expert must be available for cross-examination if required	RR1245, 1246		R31.29		R427(3)						
7	**Procedures for court appointed expert or jointly appointed single expert**											
7.1	Court procedure for appointment of its own expert witness or special referee		RR5.04(3), 23.01, 23.02, 23.03(1)	RR31.46–31.54		RR429I–429P, R429S						R35.15 PD10
7.2	Cross-examination of single expert		R23.03(2)	R31.51		R429M(1)						G47
7.3	Other expert's reports on question addressed by court appointed expert		R23.04	NO – R31.52		R429N						
7.4	Joint engagement of a single expert			RR31.37 – 31.45		RR429G, 429H, 429R						R35.7, R35.8 G34– 46

8	**Shadow experts/expert advisor**			
8.1	Rules applying to the engagement of a shadow expert	R74.13		G6
8.2	Certificate by shadow expert	R74.13(1)(c)		
9	**Questions to experts**			
9.1	Party may put written questions to expert or request information	R74.4	R4	R35.6 PD6 G67–69

PART 5

INTERNATIONAL CONSTRUCTION CONTRACTS

CHAPTER 35

Lex constructionis – or my country's rules?[1]

35.1 Introduction

Contract law in all countries is based on the twin principles of freedom of contract, and ***pacta sunt servanda***.[2] However, each jurisdiction has laws that impact on contracts for construction work. Local laws apply if the governing law of the contract is in the jurisdiction, if the site of the construction work is in the jurisdiction or if the seat of dispute resolution is in the jurisdiction. This chapter explores the question of whether there are universally accepted principles of construction law, a *lex constructionis*, or whether it is trumped in every jurisdiction by local laws that differ from international norms. Three issues are discussed that support the concept of *lex constructionis* in the international practice of construction law: the use of FIDIC contracts, international commercial arbitration and the *lex mercatoria.*

The chapter concludes with a proposed list of 20 principles of *lex constructionis* that take into account the unique features of construction projects and construction contracts.

35.2 Construction contracts

Construction law is the law relating to construction projects: their design, construction, maintenance and operation. The legal mechanism for delivery of a construction project is a construction contract between Employer and Contractor. It defines their rights and obligations and allocates the risks between them. As a species of commercial contract that addresses the issues of construction projects enumerated below, international construction contracts have a number of features that make them *sui generis*. As discussed below, this author posits that, notwithstanding local laws, there are widely accepted principles of construction law that constitute a *lex constructionis*. That *lex* is a subset of *lex mercatoria* that takes account of the specific aspects of construction law that distinguishes it from commercial law in general.

There are a number of unique distinguishing features of construction law. These can be conveniently considered for a number of issues that are generally relevant to all

1 This chapter is an edited version of the paper: Dr Donald Charrett, "*Lex constructionis* – or My Country's Rules", first published in (2021) *International Construction Law Review* 61, published by Informa Law, London.

2 A Latin phrase that means that agreements are to be kept.

 DOI: 10.4324/9781003206897-40

construction projects. Under each of the following headings, a number of distinguishing features are identified.

35.2.1 Scope

The subject matter of the contract relates to construction of a unique facility which will be affixed to the land at a specific location over a specific period of time. That fixing to the land results in the constructed facility becoming part of the real property of the landowner when attached.

The required design, scope, time, cost and quality requirements of the works and the finished project are defined by extensive and complex technical documentation. The Employer (generally) has the right to increase or decrease the originally agreed scope of work by the issue of variations, and the Contractor is obliged to carry out or omit the varied work. The execution of the construction work and/or the performance of the Contract may be supervised by a person who is not a party to the Contract.

35.2.2 Risk

There are many risks in a construction project – known knowns, known unknowns and unknown unknowns. Ground conditions are never completely known, including geotechnical conditions, groundwater, contamination or heritage items. Weather conditions can have significant impact on construction activities and delay completion.

Freedom of contract may be constrained, e.g. statutory adjudication legislation that mandates payment obligations and makes some provisions illegal, such as "pay when paid" clauses. In addition, many aspects of the execution of a construction project are subject to Government laws and regulations, e.g. health and safety obligations.

There is usually a series of independent and interrelated contracts between a number of different parties, e.g. Employer/consultant, Employer/Contractor, Contractor/subcontractor, Contractor/surety, Contractor/insurer.

Construction activities are potentially dangerous to personnel and may involve heavy machinery, working at heights or working in confined spaces. Construction involves significant environmental impacts: noise, dust, smells, vibration, nuisance, water runoff, sediment and erosion. Other impacts on external stakeholders may include adverse impacts on adjacent property.

Insurance of the works is usually mandatory and is a significant risk transfer mechanism. Insolvency of parties to interrelated contracts may impact performance.

35.2.3 Time

The time for performance of a construction contract may extend over a number of years, including a period after completion of construction (and when the Employer is in possession of the site) during which the Contractor is liable to rectify defects.

There are usually significant financial consequences arising from late contract completion – the Employer cannot generate revenue from the facility until it is operational, and the Contractor is typically subject to liquidated damages for late completion.

35.2.4 Cost

The contract sum and cash flow is typically substantial: "There must be a 'cash flow' in the building trade. It is the very lifeblood of the enterprise".[3]

The Contractor is usually required to provide security for its performance.

35.2.5 Quality

A construction contract may involve the assumption of obligations that are very long term, e.g. maintenance or liability for defects arising many years after construction was completed. Construction work apparently completed in accordance with contractual requirements may contain latent defects which only manifest themselves many years after construction was completed.

35.2.6 Disputes

Disputes are common and frequently involve complex technical issues and large volumes of documents.

A number of these features impact third parties and are subject to various laws, such as environmental impact or work, health and safety regulations. Other third-party impacts are subject to legal doctrines such as tort or the law of nuisance. However, the majority of the issues listed above are matters between the contracting parties and are therefore regulated by the terms of their contract.

35.3 International contract law

International contract law is based on the two fundamental principles of freedom of contract and *pacta sunt servanda*. These principles are universal in jurisdictions subject to the rule of law, the necessary precondition for the exercise of the parties' autonomy and the enforcement of their rights and obligations.

Freedom of contract is the ability of legal persons (e.g. natural persons over 18 years of age and properly constituted companies) to enter into a binding agreement to do anything, provided it is not contrary to the law or public policy (and in some jurisdictions, morals). Freedom of contract and *pacta sunt servanda* are long-standing principles enshrined in the common law,[4] and courts have a natural bias to uphold freedom of contract and to take a narrow view of any statutory constraint.[5]

Freedom of contract is enshrined in legislation in both common law and civil law jurisdictions, such as the *Contracts Act 1950* (Malaysia) (ss 1, 10, 24), the *Contracts Act 1872* (India) (s 10), the *Civil Code* (France) (s 1102), the *Civil Code* (Philippines) (s 1306) and the *Civil Code* (Russia) (s 421).

3 *Modern Engineering (Bristol) Ltd v Gilbert Ash (Northern) Limited* [1973] 3 All ER 195 per Lord Denning MR.

4 *Printing and Numeral Registering Co v Sampson* (1875) L. R. 19 Eq. 462.

5 *Colin John Fitzgerald v F J Leonhardt Pty Ltd* (1997) 189 CLR 215 per Kirby J.

The universal application of freedom of contract is reinforced by its statement in principles that may be regarded as private codifications or restatements of international contract law (modern statements of the *lex mercatoria*): UNIDROIT Principles of International Commercial Contracts 2016 (art 1.1)[6] and the Trans-Lex Principles (IV.1.1). [7]

Freedom of contract generally enables contracting parties to select the governing law of the contract, to agree on the scope of their rights and obligations, to agree on the allocation of risks between themselves and to agree to resolve their disputes by private and confidential arbitration by an arbitrator of their choice in accordance with procedures they have chosen.

As the common law and statutory definitions of the principle make clear, the parties' freedom of contract is not unlimited, as it is subject to any statutory constraints or prohibitions on conduct that is in conflict with public policy (or morals).

Once parties have exercised their freedom to enter into a contract, they have the legal rights and obligations they have agreed to. Those rights and obligations would be illusory if the parties did not fulfil their agreement. The principle of *pacta sunt servanda* is therefore the essential obverse of the principle of freedom of contract. The universality and importance of this principle for construction law has been aptly summed up as follows:

> the principle of *pacta sunt servanda* … is universal to all legal systems. This means that the vast majority of construction disputes are fought and won or lost primarily over the wording of the contract (and alleged facts).[8]

Of course, *pacta sunt servanda* would be illusory in the absence of a mechanism to enforce the rights and obligations the parties have agreed to. In a jurisdiction subject to the rule of law, the courts will give effect to *pacta sunt servanda* by holding the parties to their bargain. If necessary, the coercive powers of the state can be called in aid to enforce a court judgment. Thus, for example, if contracting parties have agreed that any disputes will be settled by arbitration, the courts will generally stay any court proceedings commenced in breach of their agreement to arbitrate.

35.4 Statutory incursions into freedom of contract

Statutory incursions into freedom of contract are ubiquitous and increasing in both common law and civil law jurisdictions. Every statute whose subject matter is relevant to the content of a contract potentially impacts on freedom of contract by prescribing certain required conduct in particular circumstances or proscribing certain conduct in other circumstances.

The three categories of laws relevant to construction are: (1) project-related laws – subject to the jurisdiction of the site where the works are carried out; (2) contract-related laws – subject to the jurisdiction of the governing law of the contract; and (3) dispute resolution laws – subject to the law of the "seat" of the dispute resolution.

---

6 https://www.unidroit.org/english/principles/contracts/principles2016/principles2016-e.pdf (accessed 7 September 2020).

7 https://www.trans-lex.org/principles/of-transnational-law-(lex-mercatoria) (accessed 7 September 2020).

8 Robert Knutson (ed), *FIDIC An Analysis of International Construction Contracts* (Kluwer Law International, 2005) xvi.

35.4.1 Project-related laws

All applicable laws impacting on any aspect of a construction project explicitly constrain the parties' freedom of contract, particularly in how the work can be carried out and how it impacts on third parties, e.g. laws relating to labour, health and safety or the environment. Laws relating to activities, people and property at the site of a construction project will generally apply irrespective of the governing law of the contract.

The following are examples of project-related laws that constrain the parties' freedom of contract:

- Protective measures in favour of subcontractors, e.g. *Law on Subcontracting 1975* (France).
- Liability generally for the partial or total collapse of structures, e.g. *Civil Code* (France) Arts 1792–1792-6; *Civil Code* (UAE) Art 880.
- Deemed acceptance of variations by the Employer, e.g. *Civil Code* (Brazil) Art 619.
- Interim payments, e.g. *Construction Contracts Act 2013* (Ireland) s 3.
- Rules relating to property in goods, e.g. *Property Law* (China); *Personal Property Securities Act 2017* (Fiji); *Personal Property Security Act 2011* (PNG).

Although much of the construction law in common law jurisdictions has traditionally been determined by the common law, there has been increasing statutory intervention to alleviate long-standing challenges inherent in the application of classical contract theory to construction. Perhaps the greatest of these challenges has been to ensure the prompt and reliable flow of payments through the contractual chain. As far back as the 1880s, US States enacted mechanic's lien statutes to protect unpaid subcontractors, labourers and materialmen who had performed work on private property by granting them equitable interests in the improved real estate.[9] Following the Latham Report on procurement and contractual arrangements in the UK construction industry,[10] the UK enacted legislation that provided a statutory right to progress payments and for disputes to be determined provisionally by adjudication.[11] Similar legislation, restricted to adjudication of payment disputes has been implemented in all Australian States and Territories,[12] and a number of other jurisdictions.[13]

9 Philip L Bruner, 'The Historical Emergence of Construction Law' (2007) 34.1 *William Mitchell Law Review* 1, 6.

10 Sir Michael Latham, 'Constructing the Team' (July 1994) Final Report.

11 *Housing Grants, Construction and Regeneration Act 1996* (UK).

12 NSW: *Building and Construction Industry Security of Payment Act 1999*; Victoria: *Building and Construction Industry Security of Payment Act* 2002; Northern Territory: *Construction Contracts (Security of Payments) Act 2004*; West Australia: *Building and Construction Industry (Security of Payment) Act 2021*; Australian Capital Territory: *Construction Industry (Security of Payment Act) 2009*; South Australia: *Building and Construction Industry Security of Payment Act 2009*; Tasmania: *Building and Construction Industry Security of Payment Act 2009*; Queensland: *Building Industry Fairness (Security of Payment) Act 2017*.

13 New Zealand: *Construction Contracts Act 2002*; Singapore: *Building and Construction Industry Security of Payment Act 2004*; Isle of Man: *Construction Contracts Act 2004;* Malaysia: *Construction Industry Payment and Adjudication Act 2012*; Ireland: *Construction Contracts Act 2013*; Ontario: *Construction Act 1990*.

The constraints on freedom of contract from such statutory adjudication legislation is quite profound as, depending on the jurisdiction, it may provide statutory regulation of the following issues in legislation that cannot be contracted out of.

The Contractor may have a statutory entitlement to progress payments, and an automatic entitlement to payment if the payer does not respond to a payment claim. There may be no contractual defences to court enforcement of an adjudicated amount as a judgment debt. "Pay when paid" and "pay if paid" clauses are void. An unpaid party may stop work irrespective of contractual terms. Parties have the right to submit a defined type of dispute to adjudication, and the legislation defines formal adjudication procedures. There are strict time limits for adjudication, and parties may not be able to choose the adjudicator. In some jurisdictions, project bank accounts are required to provide a trust over monies payable to Contractors or subcontractors.

35.4.2 Contract-related laws

Examples of contract-related laws that constrain the parties' freedom of contract include the payment of penalties, e.g. *Civil Code* (Romania), *Conventional Penalties Act 1962* (South Africa); unfair contract conditions, e.g. *Standard Business Terms Act* (Germany), *Unfair Contract Terms Act* (UK); and bribery and corruption, e.g. *Bribery Act 2010* (UK).

Notwithstanding parties' agreement on the amount of liquidated damages payable in the event of specified breaches of contract, *Civil Code* provisions may allow subsequent adjustment, e.g. *Civil Code* (France) s 1152 and *Civil Code BGB* (Germany) s 343.

Many *Civil Codes* provide for relief from contractual stipulations if *force majeure* or hardship arising from a change in circumstances since the contract was executed prevent performance, such as the *Civil Code* (Philippines) s 1174, *Civil Code* (Indonesia) s 1245, *Civil Code* (Peru) ss 1315 and 1440, and *Civil Code* (France) s 1148.

35.4.3 Dispute resolution laws

The law applying to the conduct of dispute resolution will be that of the "seat" of the forum where the dispute resolution takes place. If the dispute is litigated in court, the law of the forum of the court will apply. If the parties have chosen arbitration, then the arbitration law at the "seat" of the arbitration will apply. In accordance with the principle of party autonomy, parties are free to choose an arbitral "seat" that is different to the jurisdiction of the governing law of the contract, or the jurisdiction of the site where the construction work is performed. In many cases, the contracting parties will choose a neutral forum for arbitration, so that neither party has any "home ground" advantage.

As noted above, statutory adjudication legislation may apply to the provisional resolution of disputes in the jurisdiction where the construction is carried out. However, this does not negate the parties' right to final resolution of a dispute by international arbitration in a neutral forum. Any party choice of an alternative method of dispute resolution is, of course, subject to any mandatory applicable law. For example, as noted below, a Dispute Board determination may not be final and binding in some jurisdictions, notwithstanding contractual agreement that it is. Some jurisdictions, e.g. some Australian States, prohibit pre-agreed arbitration of "consumer" disputes, such as those arising in domestic building contracts.

35.5 Public policy constraints on freedom of contract

Public policy is largely concerned with the potential for manifest unfairness or injustice in a given situation. Courts may disregard or refuse to give effect to contractual obligations which, whilst not directly contrary to any express or implied statutory prohibition, nevertheless contravenes "the policy of the law".

Examples of situations in which courts have refused to enforce a contractual agreement on the grounds that it is against public policy include:

- Imposing a penalty for breach of contract (*Andrews v Australia and New Zealand Banking Group Ltd* [2012] HCA 30).
- Unlawful conduct (*Gaffney v Ryan* [1995] 1 Qd R 19).
- Ousting the jurisdiction of the courts (*Brooks v Burns Philp Trustee Co Ltd* [1969] HCA 4).
- Economic duress – the application of illegitimate pressure to achieve an agreement (*DSND Subsea Ltd v Petroleum Geo Services ASA* [2000] BLR 530).
- Exclusion clauses in conflict with public policy (*Tercon Contractors Ltd v British Columbia (Transportation and Highways* [2010] SCC 4).
- Conduct prejudicial to the administration of justice (*Trendtex Trading Corporation v Credit Suisse* [1982] AC 679).
- Conduct prejudicing the impartiality of public officials (*Wilkinson v Osborne* [1915] HCA 92).
- Conduct prejudicial to national or international security (*Foster v Driscoll* [1929] 1 KB 470).
- Unreasonable restraint of trade (*Esso Petroleum Co Ltd v Harper's Garage (Stourport) Ltd* [1967] UKHL 1).

35.6 *Lex constructionis*

35.6.1 What is it?

For the purposes of this book, ***lex constructionis*** is the international law of construction in jurisdictions subject to the rule of law and which recognise the parties' freedom of contract. It is a subset of ***lex mercatoria*** (the law merchant), a long-standing legal concept that has regained prominence and importance in the modern globalised world.

The "new" *lex mercatoria* dates from 1957.[14] Its significance is encapsulated in the introductory speech at the London colloquium on 'The New Sources of the Law of International Trade with special reference to East-West Trade' in 1962:

> The evolution of an autonomous law of international trade, founded on universally accepted standards of business conduct, would be one of the most important developments of legal science in our time. It would constitute a common platform for commercial lawyers from all countries, those of planned and free-market economy, those from civil law and common law,

14 Klaus Peter Berger, *The Creeping Codification of the New Lex Mercatoria* (Wolters Kluwer The Netherlands, 2010) 1.

> and those of fully developed and developing economy, which would enable them to cooperate in the perfection of the legal mechanism of international trade.[15]

In this writer's view, by replacing "international trade" with "international construction" this statement is the lodestar for *lex constructionis.*

There are three theories of the meaning of *lex constructionis* that can be derived from the broader category of *lex mercatoria*:

(1) A "mass" of rules and principles for the law of construction, devoid of any internal consistency or systematic quality
(2) The totality of usages that are refined according to the needs of construction
(3) An independent, supranational legal system.[16]

The first of these theories, based on the universally recognised principle of party autonomy in contract law, is that *lex constructionis* supplements the well-known categories of applicable domestic law. The second theory is based on statutory or judicial acceptance of trade usages as a factual supplement to the applicable domestic law. Both of these theories limit the ultimate development and application of *lex constructionis* through the constraints of domestic law.

In this writer's view, the third theory is supported by a conjunction of modern developments that make such a supranational system possible. As discussed below, these developments comprise widely used and accepted international construction contracts, the articulation of the new *lex mercatoria* and the application of international arbitration to finally resolve disputes.

Consistent with the above definition, *lex constructionis* is comprised of the following four elements: the governing law of the contract, the contract between the parties, the law applying to the project at the site, and the law applying to the final resolution of disputes.

35.6.2 Why is it important?

Construction is an important industry in every country of the world. It is important because it generally represents a significant component of gross national product;[17] it is important because it employs many people: in professional occupations, in skilled trades, and in less skilled jobs such as labouring.[18] But perhaps most important of all, it provides the infrastructure on which modern life depends: the facilities to mine and process natural resources; transport infrastructure; energy generation and distribution infrastructure; the provision of clean water and water treatment; and the built environment.

15 Professor Clive M Schmitthoff, cited in Klaus Peter Berger, *The Creeping Codification of the New Lex Mercatoria* (Wolters Kluwer The Netherlands, 2010) 4.

16 Klaus Peter Berger, *The Creeping Codification of the New Lex Mercatoria* (Wolters Kluwer The Netherlands, 2010) 61–62.

17 For example, in Australia in 2016, revenue in the Construction industry division accounted for 13.5% of all industry revenue: https://www.bankwest.com.au/Blob/pdf/1292551628871/construction.pdf?pdf-link=docdetail (accessed 11 January 2018).

18 For example, in Australia in 2016, construction was the third biggest contributor to workforce numbers, employing 9.8% of the working population https://www.bankwest.com.au/Blob/pdf/1292551628871/construction.pdf?pdf-link=docdetail (accessed 11 January 2018).

The construction industry is of particular importance in less developed countries. It is fundamental to the achievement of the United Nations' Sustainable Development Goals,[19] to improving health and life expectancy, and advancing standards of living to reduce the gap between the living standards of developed and less-developed countries.

Construction is a very international industry. The scale of large construction projects, and the time required to construct them, provide attractive opportunities for experienced contractors to operate internationally and transfer their skills and technology to other countries.

In this writer's view, *lex constructionis* is important in providing a legal framework within which the international construction industry can thrive and prosper by promoting best practice for successful projects in which the contracting parties' legitimate expectations can be realised. It can lead to better value for money by enabling less expensive projects with fewer disputes and fewer insolvencies, and it can promote international trade and greater comity between nations.

The following examples provide some historical and other evidence of *lex constructionis*.

35.6.3 Examples of lex constructionis

35.6.3.1 Significant convergence between the common law and civil law

Increasingly, more of the law in common law countries is explicitly stated in legislation. This can take the form of a statute that codifies the common law, or alternatively, a statute that modifies an aspect of the common law inconsistent with modern society's expectations (as perceived by legislators). Statutes may also form new "social legislation" that mandates desirable community outcomes not achieved by the common law. Examples of such laws that impact construction projects include legislation for health and safety and environmental protection. Statutory adjudication laws (discussed above) are a recent example of "social legislation" aimed at promoting prompt payment and redressing contractual imbalances of power.

The courts in civil law countries are relying to a much greater extent than previously on the precedential value of court judgments on a similar issue, because the answer to a legal issue may not be found in the codes. Whilst previous civil law court judgments may not have the authority that ***stare decisis***[20] has in the common law, well-reasoned judgments of other courts can be persuasive in cases where the legal issues are the same and the facts similar. For example, in the Swiss First Civil Law Court case *A.________ SA v B.________ SA, 4A_124/2014*,[21] the court referred to previous decisions in support of its findings on the jurisdiction of an arbitral tribunal and its ability to review the factual findings of an arbitral tribunal.

19 The 17 Sustainable Development Goals build on the eight Millennium Development Goals which specifically sought by 2015: to eradicate extreme poverty and hunger; achieve universal primary education; promote gender equality and empower women; reduce child mortality; improve maternal health; combat HIV/AIDS, malaria and other diseases; ensure environmental sustainability; and develop a global partnership for development. https://www.un.org/sustainabledevelopment/blog/2015/12/sustainable-development-goals-kick-off-with-start-of-new-year/ (accessed 22 April 2021).

20 The decision stands (Latin). The common law doctrine that a court is bound to follow earlier decisions on the same law, unless they are inconsistent with a higher court decision or are wrong in law.

21 A case in which the court considered whether a DAB decision was a precondition to referring a dispute to arbitration under the 1999 FIDIC Red Book.

Further, despite the differences between legal theories, form, procedure and terminology, in many factual situations, the two systems will arrive at essentially the same substantive result. There is frequently broad agreement on what constitutes a just and equitable outcome in a given situation, despite the different potential routes to achieve it. The ability of international arbitral tribunals comprising members from different countries and legal systems to agree on an award is testament to widely held concepts of justice.

35.6.3.2 Liability for incorrect cost estimates

In 15BC Vitruvius noted in his seminal architectural books that in Ephesus an architect was liable for construction cost overruns in excess of 25% above his estimate.[22]

Two thousand years later, an architect in Australia could similarly be legally liable for cost overruns in excess of his/her estimate. An architect who was retained to plan a residence to a price specified by the client and represented that the house could be built for that price in accordance with the plans he drew up, was found to have engaged in misleading or deceptive conduct in contravention of the *Trade Practices Act 1974* (Cth) (now *Australian Consumer Law*).[23]

35.6.3.3 Contractor's liability for defective work

The oldest known written legal code, the *Code of Hammurabi* (c 1750BC), prescribed the financial consequences if a builder built a house that was defective:

> 232 If it ruin goods, he shall make compensation for all that has been ruined, and inasmuch as he did not construct properly this house which he built and it fell, he shall re-erect the house from his own means.
>
> 233 If a builder build a house for some one, even though he has not yet completed it; if then the walls seem toppling, the builder must make the walls solid from his own means.

Thus, in the event that the consequences of the defective work were confined to property damage, the builder was liable for reinstatement costs. That is still the situation today. For example, in the UK recently, the Contractor was liable for rectification costs arising from the structural failure of wind turbine towers that occurred within two years of installation. The failure occurred as a result of an unknown error in the specified design standard, in the absence of negligence.[24]

The *Code of Hammurabi* provided that the builder could be put to death for a collapse that killed someone. In the 21st century, strict occupational health and safety laws have been enacted to protect life; if defective work constructed negligently results in a death, a contractor would be liable to severe penalties under industrial manslaughter laws.[25]

22 *Vitruvius: the ten books on architecture* / translated by Morris Hicky Morgan (1960) 281.

23 *Coleman v Gordon M Jenkins & Associates Pty Ltd* (1993) 9 BCL 292.

24 *MT Højgaard a/s v E.ON Climate and Renewables UK Robin Rigg East Ltd* [2017] UKSC 59. See Chapter 8 for a discussion of this case.

25 For example, Queensland, the ACT and Victoria have industrial manslaughter laws that apply to negligent conduct causing death. Maximum penalties are up to 20 years' imprisonment and/or a fine of AUD 320,000 (USD240,000) for senior officers and AUD10 million (USD7.6 million) for body corporates.

35.7 FIDIC Contracts

Fédération Internationale des Ingénieurs-Conseils (FIDIC) (International Federation of Consulting Engineers) publishes standard form Conditions of Contract that are used in many countries and are the most widely used international construction contracts in the world. The following contracts are commonly referred to as the "rainbow suite":

- Conditions of Contract for Construction – First Edition 1999, Second Edition 2017 (Red Book).
- Conditions of Contract for Plant and Design-Build – First Edition 1999, Second Edition 2017 (Yellow Book).
- Conditions of Contract for EPC/Turnkey Projects – First Edition 1999, Second Edition 2017 (Silver Book).

FIDIC contracts are drafted by a Contracts Committee with international representation and are reviewed by friendly reviewers from many different countries and jurisdictions. They are based on a fair allocation of risks and rewards. Although they have a common law heritage, they are used in many countries, both civil law and common law jurisdictions. Because of their genesis from the common law Institution of Civil Engineers' contract, they are more detailed than typical construction contracts in civil law jurisdictions which rely on *Civil Codes* for many legal rights and obligations.

It is submitted that the detailed articulation of the contracting parties' rights and obligations in FIDIC contracts as the outcome of the drafting process is a significant contribution to *lex constructionis*. The Contracts Committee has distilled common practices in international construction contracting into a form that is broadly consistent with domestic law in many countries and is therefore widely accepted.

The extensive international input into the drafting of FIDIC General Conditions and its acceptance as an appropriate contract for international contracts is evidenced by the World Bank's implementation of the 2017 Red Book in its 2019 Standard Procurement Document.[26] The Particular Conditions of Contract in the World Bank Standard Procurement Document does not change the balanced risk/reward allocation in the General Conditions, and mainly comprises "social provisions" to provide protections for labour, local communities and the environment that may not be adequately covered by legislation is less developed countries.

Each of the printed FIDIC rainbow suite standard forms comprise General Conditions, Guidance for the Preparation of Particular Conditions, and Forms. A FIDIC contract comprises the General Conditions as published by FIDIC, as amended by Particular Conditions to comply with the governing law of the contract, and the law of the site where the works are performed.

The extent to which the FIDIC contracts contribute to *lex constructionis* may be gauged from the extent to which Particular Conditions essential for conformity with local law are required. A recently published book on the application of FIDIC contracts contains chapters on 18 jurisdictions from around the world, each written by a locally experienced

26 http://pubdocs.worldbank.org/en/865231562944956956/SPD-Request-for-Bids-WORKS-after-prequalification.docx (accessed 28 August 2020).

construction law practitioner.[27] The brief for these chapter authors included a requirement to identify what Special Provisions in the Particular Conditions were necessary for consistency with local laws in circumstances where FIDIC General Conditions are incompatible or inconsistent with the governing law of the contract, the law of the site/country or the laws of the seat of the dispute determination.

Tables 35.1, 35.2 and 35.3 identify the issues in each of the above categories that the chapter authors identified as requiring Special Provisions in the Particular Conditions for conformity with local law. It should be noted that as a consequence of freedom of contract, the jurisdictions for the governing law of the contract and the law of the seat of arbitration could be different from the law of the site for a specific construction project. The parties will, of course, have no choice as to the law of the site, as this is automatically the law of the country where construction occurs.

No Particular Conditions are necessary for the use of FIDIC contracts subject to the governing law of the common law jurisdictions of Australia,[28] Fiji,[29] Ghana,[30] Hong Kong,[31] Papua New Guinea,[32] Sri Lanka[33] or the civil law jurisdiction of Switzerland.[34]

No Particular Conditions are necessary for the use of FIDIC contracts where the site is in Australia, Czech Republic, Fiji, France, Germany, Ghana, Hong Kong, Malaysia, Papua New Guinea, Peru, South Africa, Sri Lanka, Switzerland or United Arab Emirates.

No Particular Conditions are necessary for the use of FIDIC contracts where the seat of arbitration is in Australia, China, Fiji, France, Germany, Ghana, Hong Kong, Italy, Malaysia, Papua New Guinea, Peru, Romania, South Africa, Sri Lanka, Switzerland or United Arab Emirates.

Considering the range of jurisdictions covered, there are a relatively small number of changes that need to be made to FIDIC General Conditions for their international use. In this writer's view, Tables 35.1–35.3 highlight the extent to which FIDIC contracts approach an international norm, and show support for *lex constructionis*.

35.8 International commercial arbitration

Freedom of contract allows parties to select arbitration to finally resolve disputes, rather than the courts. Arbitration is frequently preferred over litigation in court for construction disputes because of features such as confidentiality, and the exercise of party autonomy to tailor a suitable process and select a tribunal with the appropriate legal and technical skills. For international disputes, international arbitration is also preferred as it avoids any perceived home country bias in domestic courts.

The importance for *lex constructionis* of the adoption of the *1958 New York Arbitration Convention on the Recognition and Enforcement of Foreign Arbitral Awards* (*New York Convention*) by over 160 countries cannot be overstated. The *New York Convention*

27 Donald Charrett (ed), *The International Application of FIDIC Contracts A Practical Guide* (Informa Law from Routledge, Abingdon England, 2020).

28 Donald Charrett, Chapter 4.

29 Nicholas Barnes & Melvin Chand, Chapter 8.

30 Kwame Amankwah-Twum & Priscilla Tara Buckman, Chapter 11.

31 Ben Bury & Julie-Ann Pemberton, Chapter 12.

32 Joseph Barbaro, Andrew McCormack, Nick Thorne, Ryan Warokra & Kenneth Imako, Chapter 15.

33 Harsha Cabral, Malith Mendis & Chamaka Ambagahawita, Chapter 19.

34 Sam Moss, Tino Schneider & Jean-Rodolphe Fiechter, Chapter 20.

TABLE 35.1 FIDIC General Conditions are incompatible or inconsistent with governing law of the contract

Jurisdiction	*Particular Conditions*
Brazil[1]	Exclude indirect damages
	Time for notification of claims to be consistent with statutory limitations
China[2]	Subcontracting the main structure not permitted
Czech Republic[3]	Replace liquidated damages with contractual penalty
	Replace financing charges with contractual penalty or statutory interest
France[4]	Payment of subcontractors by the Employer
	Termination of the construction contract by the Employer
Germany[5]	Limitation of liability
	Define "indirect loss"
	Performance security
	Cessation of Employer's liability
Italy[6]	Acknowledgement that the contract has been completed by expert parties fully aware of the content and the implications
Malaysia[7]	Copyright
Peru[8]	Implied terms
	Time-bar clauses are illegal
	Fitness for purpose – Yellow & Silver Books
	Meaning and scope of liability for fitness for purpose
	Liquidated or delay damages must be considered *penalidades*
	Limitation period of liability
	Defects Notification Period is a timeframe of responsibility
	Contractual waiver of liability is illegal
	Definition of parties' specific liabilities and scope of work
Romania[9]	Fit for purpose obligation
	Limitation period for liability
	Bankruptcy, insolvency, liquidation
	'Unusual clauses'
	Specific requirements for public procurement contracts
South Africa[10]	Unfair or unreasonable Particular Conditions unenforceable
	Builder's lien
	Innocent or negligent representation
	Election in case of breach of clauses 8.7 & 8.8
	Termination for Contractor's default
United Arab Emirates[11]	Defects Notification Period
	No exclusion of gross negligence
	No contracting out of statutory prescription periods for bringing a claim
	Exceptional circumstances
	Termination

1 Thiago Fernandes Moreira & Caio Gabra, Chapter 5.
2 Sun Yiwen, Chapter 6.
3 Lukas Klee, Vojtech Hradecny & Anastazie Jegorova, Chapter 7.
4 David Brown & Michael Conrad, Chapter 9.
5 Götz-Sebastian Hök & Henry Stiegelmier, Chapter 10.
6 Nicola Davide Romano, Chapter13.
7 Ben Bury & Julie-Ann Pemberton, Chapter14.
8 Jaime Gray & Jonnathan Bravo, Chapter 16.
9 Cremona Cotovelea, Chapter 17.
10 Johan Beyers, Chapter 18.
11 Erin Miller Rankin & Samantha Lord Hill, Chapter 21.

TABLE 35.2 FIDIC General Conditions are incompatible or inconsistent with the laws of the site/country

Jurisdiction	*Particular Conditions*
Brazil	Defect notice period
China	Construction contract cannot materially change the bidding documents and proposals
	Defects Notification period cannot be more than 2 years
	Retention is limited to 5%
	Commencement date of Defects Notification Period
Italy	Provisions relating to bankruptcy, insolvency and liquidation.
Romania	Design
	Taking over the Works

TABLE 35.3 FIDIC General Conditions are incompatible or inconsistent with the laws of the seat of the arbitration or relevant laws on dispute determination

Jurisdiction	*Particular Conditions*
Brazil	Engineer's decision not final and binding
	Dispute Board decision not final and binding
Czech Republic	Dispute Board decision not enforceable

ensures that international arbitration is accepted in the majority of countries as a binding method of dispute resolution, so that court proceedings can be stayed to permit arbitration, and arbitral awards can be enforced in most jurisdictions.

International arbitration is well suited to the resolution of international construction disputes. International arbitral tribunals typically comprise practitioners from different jurisdictions and legal systems, and there are many international arbitrators with expertise in handling complex construction disputes and their extensive technical documentation.

International arbitration is supported by a number of international organisations. These organisations promote principles, rules and procedures that are widely accepted as international norms, independent of legal systems. The following are a few examples of such organisations, and their publications that support international arbitration practice: the United Nations Commission on International Trade Law (UNCITRAL);[35] the International Bar Association (80,000 members in 170 countries);[36] the Chartered Institute

35 UNCITRAL publishes: *Convention on the Recognition and Enforcement of Foreign Arbitral Awards 1958 – New York Convention* (165 parties); *UNCITRAL Model Law on International Commercial Arbitration 2006* (83 countries, 116 jurisdictions); *UNCITRAL Arbitration Rules*. https://uncitral.un.org/en/texts/arbitration (accessed 8 September 2020).

36 IBA publishes: Rules on Taking of Evidence in International Arbitration; Guidelines on Party Representation in International Arbitration; Guidelines on Conflicts of Interest in International Arbitration; Guidelines for Drafting International Arbitration Clauses. https://www.ibanet.org/Publications/publications_IBA_guides_and_free_materials.aspx (accessed 8 September 2020).

of Arbitrators (16,000 members in 149 countries);[37] and the International Chamber of Commerce.[38]

There are also many institutions that publish arbitration rules and administer international arbitrations, such as the ICC Court of Arbitration, the London Court of International Arbitration,[39] the Singapore International Arbitration Centre[40] and the Hong Kong International Arbitration Centre.[41] Notwithstanding the inevitable differences in rules and procedures, it is submitted that there is broad consensus on the principles of international arbitration that promote consistency of approach and just and equitable outcomes.

A considerable degree of international comity in arbitration law is evidenced by the 116 jurisdictions that have based their arbitration law on the UNCITRAL Model Law. This uniformity of arbitral law coupled with respected international organisations that administer international arbitrations is a significant contributor to *lex constructionis*.

35.9 *Lex mercatoria*

As noted above, *lex constructionis* is a subset of *lex mercatoria* which applies to the broad class of international commercial contracts. However, the concept of *lex mercatoria* is of limited practical value unless its content can be determined. Fortunately, there are at least two modern expressions of *lex mercatoria* that can be applied to international construction contracts: the UNIDROIT Principles of Commercial Contracts[42] and the TransLex Principles.[43]

There are many references discussing *lex mercatoria*, but few discussing *lex constructionis*.[44]

35.9.1 UNIDROIT Principles of Commercial Contracts[45]

35.9.1.1 What is UNIDROIT?

UNIDROIT is the International Institute for the Unification of Private Law, an independent intergovernmental organisation with its seat in Rome. It studies needs and methods for

37 Chartered Institute of Arbitrators publishes: International Arbitration Practice Guidelines; ADR Procedures in Arbitration; Consumers and Parties with Significant Differences of Resources; Multi-Party Arbitrations; CIArb Code of Professional and Ethical Conduct. https://www.ciarb.org (accessed 8 September 2020).

38 ICC publishes: ICC Rules of Arbitration; Procedure; Practice Notes; Checklists; ICC Terms of Reference; ICC procedural timetable. https://iccwbo.org/dispute-resolution-services/ (accessed 8 September 2020).

39 https://www.lcia.org (accessed 8 September 2020).

40 https://www.siac.org.sg (accessed 8 September 2020).

41 https://www.hkiac.org (accessed 8 September 2020).

42 https://www.unidroit.org/contracts#UPICC (accessed 9 September 2020).

43 https://www.trans-lex.org/principles/of-transnational-law-(lex-mercatoria) (accessed 10 September 2020).

44 A Google search on 9 September 2020 yielded the following in English: Charles Molineaux, 'Moving Towards a Construction Lex Mercatoria – A Lex Constructionis' https://www.trans-lex.org/126700/_/a-lex-constructionis-14-j-int-l-arb-1997-no-1-at-55-et-seq/; Yuliya Pshenichnaya, 'Lex constructionis as the legal source of the international construction contract' https://www.hse.ru/en/edu/vkr/206782720; CEC Jansen, 'The Case for the European Lex Constructionis' https://research.vu.nl/en/publications/the-case-for-the-european-lex-constructionis ; Novoselov Mikhail Alexandrovich, 'Application Lex Constructionis for the Regulation of International Construction Contracts in Russia' http://urvak.org/articles/bizne-vypusk-4-primenenie-lex-constructionis-v-ros/; Lukas Klee, *International Construction Law* (Wiley Blackwell, Hoboken NJ, 2nd edn, 2018) Chapter 5.

45 A more detailed discussion of the use of the UNIDROIT Principles in international construction contracts is in Chapter 36.

modernising, harmonising and co-ordinating private law, and in particular, commercial law as between states and groups of states. UNIDROIT's 63 member States are drawn from the five continents and represent a variety of different legal, economic and political systems as well as different cultural backgrounds.[46]

35.9.1.2 What are the UNIDROIT Principles?

The UNIDROIT Principles of International Commercial Contracts (**UP**) are a set of ana-tional principles that apply to the formation, validity, interpretation, performance and termination of commercial contracts.

They are considered to be a modern statement of a *lex mercatoria* for international contracts which are drafted by legal experts from many countries, common law and civil law in which the rules are not derived from any particular national law. Accordingly, the UP embody contractual principles which are, or can be, recognised by the laws of any country, whether common law or civil law.

There have been four editions of the UP: 1994 – 120 articles; 2004 – 185 articles; 2010 – 211 articles; and 2016 – 211 articles. The dynamic nature of the UP in responding to contemporary developments is evident in the addition of new chapters on set-off, assignment of rights and limitation periods in the 2004 edition, and the new chapter on plurality of obligors and obligees in the 2010 edition. The 2016 edition is not intended as a revision of the previous edition, but was altered marginally to take better account of the special needs of long-term contracts.[47]

The UP and explanatory notes on each clause are available on the UNIDROIT website.[48]

35.9.1.3 How are the UNIDROIT Principles applied?

The possible applications of the UP are aptly summed up in the Preamble:

> These Principles set forth general rules for international commercial contracts.
> They shall be applied when the parties have agreed that their contract be governed by them.
> They may be applied when the parties have agreed that their contract be governed by general principles of law, the *lex mercatoria* or the like.
> They may be applied when the parties have not chosen any law to govern their contract.
> They may be used to interpret or supplement international uniform law instruments.
> They may be used to interpret or supplement domestic law.
> They may serve as a model for national and international legislators.

The UP have been applied in these various ways by many hundreds of arbitral tribunals and courts around the world.[49]

46 https://www.unidroit.org (accessed 8 September 2020).

47 UNIDROIT, *UNIDROIT Principles of International Commercial Contracts* (UNIDROIT, Rome, 2016) vii.

48 https://www.unidroit.org/contracts#UPICC (accessed 8 September 2020).

49 http://www.unilex.info/instrument/principles (accessed 8 September 2020); IBA, *Perspectives in Practice of UNIDROIT Principles 2016* (IBA, 2019) https://www.ibanet.org/Publications/Perspectives-in-Practice-of-the-UNIDROIT-Principles-2016.aspx (accessed 9 October 2020).

35.9.1.4 What are the benefits of using the UNIDROIT Principles?

The UP are a private codification of civil law, approved by an intergovernmental institution. Although neither treaty, nor compilation of usages, nor standard terms of contract, they are in fact a manifestation of transnational law:

> The UNIDROIT Principles of International Commercial Contracts are a reliable Fonti [sic] of international commercial law in international arbitration for they 'contain in essence a restatement of those 'principes directeurs' that have enjoyed universal acceptance and, moreover, are at the heart of those most fundamental notions which have consistently been applied in arbitral practice'.[50]

The UP comprise rules "broadly recognised throughout the world and the practice of international contracts".[51]

35.9.1.5 UNIDROIT Principles on hardship and *force majeure*

The UP include provisions that provide principles applicable to situations where contractual performance as originally anticipated is adversely affected by unforeseen circumstances. These provisions are particularly relevant to the contractual issues in construction projects arising from the COVID-19 pandemic in 2020.[52]

Whilst these provisions provide adjustment mechanisms to relieve a party from the consequences of events that impose excessively onerous financial burdens, they do so within the principles of freedom of contract and *pacta sunt servanda*. In circumstances where the performance of a contract becomes more onerous for a party because of hardship,[53] it is still required to perform its obligations.[54] However, it is entitled to request renegotiation of the contract; in the event that the parties fail to reach agreement within a reasonable time, either party may resort to the court.[55] The court has the power to terminate the contract or adapt the contract with a view to restoring its equilibrium.[56]

The *force majeure* provisions excuse performance in circumstances where "the non-performance was due to an impediment beyond its control and that it could not reasonably be expected to have taken the impediment into account at the time of the conclusion of the contract or to have avoided or overcome it or its consequences".[57] Non-performance is only excused for the reasonable period in which the impediment operated and is subject to notice within a reasonable time.[58]

50 ICC Award No 9797 http://www.unilex.info/principles/case/668 (accessed 8 September 2020).

51 ICC Award No 8264 http://www.unilex.info/principles/case/658 (accessed 9 September 2020).

52 For a discussion of the application of the UNIDROIT Principles on hardship and *force majeure* to address the contractual impacts of non-performance arising from the COVID-19 pandemic, see: UNIDROIT Secretariat, 'The UNIDROIT Principles of International Commercial Contracts and the COVID-19 Health Crisis' https://www.unidroit.org/english/news/2020/200721-principles-covid19-note/note-e.pdf (accessed 7 September 2020).

53 Hardship is defined in Article 6.2.2 Definition of hardship.

54 Article 6.2.1 Contract to be observed.

55 Article 6.2.3 Effects of hardship.

56 Ibid.

57 Article 7.1.7 *Force majeure*.

58 Ibid.

A party that owes an obligation other than one to pay money is required to perform unless, inter alia, performance is impossible in law or fact, or performance or enforcement is unreasonably burdensome or expensive.[59]

These articles have been introduced, either literally or with only few modifications, in a number of national codifications, including: People's Republic of China (only *force majeure*), Russian Federation, France, Argentina, Estonia, Lithuania and Brazil.[60]

35.9.1.6 Summary

The UP represent a set of overarching principles that are appropriate to regulate an international construction contract in a manner that is fair to all parties, straightforward to apply, predictable in outcome, independent of a particular national legal system and generally consistent with the contract law and principles in any country (with some exceptions). They are discussed in more detail in Chapter 36.

35.9.2 TransLex Principles

35.9.2.1 Content

The TransLex Principles are a recent manifestation of what Klaus Berger refers to as the "creeping codification of the *lex mercatoria*". These principles are based on compilation of a list that

> reproduces all those rules and principles of the NLM [new *lex mercatoria*] as black-letter law which have been accepted in international arbitral and contract practice together with comprehensive comparative references. The list unifies the various sources that have fostered the evolution of a transnational commercial legal system into one single, open-ended set of rules and principles: reception of general principles of law, codification of international trade law by "formulating agencies", case law of international arbitral tribunals, the law-making forces of international model contract forms and general conditions of trade, and the analysis of comparative legal science. [61]

The recognition that the "new" *lex mercatoria* is constantly evolving and needs to draw on all relevant sources for its legitimacy has resulted in a different approach to UNIDROIT. The TransLex Principles take into account comparative research and the comprehensive case law of international arbitral tribunals. "[T]he most significant contribution is not the list *per se*, but the technique that gave rise to it and is meant to ensure its open-endedness and continuing evolution: the technique of Creeping Codification."[62]

A basic difference between the UNIDROIT Principles and the TransLex Principles is that the latter is not limited to the field of international commercial contract law. The TransLex

59 Article 7.2.2 Performance of non-monetary obligation.

60 UNIDROIT Secretariat, 'The UNIDROIT Principles of International Commercial Contracts and the COVID-19 Health Crisis' 4 https://www.unidroit.org/english/news/2020/200721-principles-covid19-note/note-e.pdf (accessed 7 September 2020).

61 Klaus Peter Berger, *The Creeping Codification of the New Lex Mercatoria* (Wolters Kluwer The Netherlands, 2010) 256.

62 L Yves Fortier, "The New, New *Lex Mercatoria*, or Back to the Future" (2001) 17.2 *Arbitration International* 121, 127, cited in Klaus Peter Berger, *The Creeping Codification of the New Lex Mercatoria* (Wolters Kluwer The Netherlands, 2010) 255.

> list follows the decision-making practice of international arbitration and therefore contains legal principles that are related to those fields of law which play a predominant role in international arbitral case law, such as international company law, conflict of laws, rules of evidence, the international law of expropriation and general arbitration law. [63]

The TransLex Principles are maintained in an online database, easily accessible to practitioners in any jurisdiction. The website has four sections as follows (as at 11 September 2020):

- **Principles** comprising 143 TransLex Principles in 14 chapters, 1,408 full text comparative references and 2,193 contract clauses
- **Bibliography** containing 1,025 entries on transnational law
- **Materials** comprising a collection of contemporary materials on transnational and arbitration law (86 documents)
- **Archive** comprising 62 rare historical documents on arbitration and ADR (including England's oldest surviving arbitral award from AD118).

35.9.2.2 TransLex Principles on hardship and force majeure

The TransLex Principles contain provisions on hardship[64] and *force majeure*[65] applicable to situations where contractual performance as originally anticipated is adversely affected by unforeseen circumstances. These provisions are similar to the corresponding UNIDROIT Principles. In respect of hardship,[66] there is a good faith obligation to renegotiate the contract if there is a need to adapt it to changed circumstances;[67] failing party agreement, a court can adapt the contract to the changed circumstances or terminate the contract.[68] Non-performance as a consequence of *force majeure* is excused for the period of the impediment, subject to reasonable notice. Any limitation period is suspended so as not to expire before one year after the relevant impediment has ceased to exist. [69]

As with the corresponding UP discussed above, these provisions are particularly relevant to the contractual issues in construction projects arising from the COVID-19 pandemic in 2020 by providing a mechanism for equitable changes to contractual obligations arising from circumstances outside the control of either party.

35.10 Proposed principles of *lex constructionis*

It is suggested that *lex constructionis* can promote best practice for successful projects in which the contracting parties' legitimate expectations can be realised. In this writer's view, those legitimate expectations are typically along the following lines:

63 Klaus Peter Berger, *The Creeping Codification of the New Lex Mercatoria* (Wolters Kluwer The Netherlands, 2010) 258.

64 No. IV.6.7 – Duty to renegotiate; No. IV.6.8 – (Re-) Negotiation agreement / clause (*pactum de negotiando*); No. VIII.1 – Definition [hardship]; No. VIII.2 - Legal consequences [of hardship].

65 No. VI.3 – *Force majeure*.

66 No. VIII.1 – Definition [hardship].

67 No. IV.6.7 – Duty to renegotiate.

68 No. VIII.2 – Legal consequences [of hardship].

69 No. VI.3 – *Force majeure*.

- The Employer expects completion of the project on time, for the contract price and to the agreed standard of quality, and timely and adequate communication from the Contractor of any departures from the original scope of works, the materialisation of risks and any claims.
- The Contractor expects prompt payment of all amounts due under the Contract, and the freedom to carry out the construction in accordance with the Contract without hindrance by the Employer. The Contractor also expects timely and adequate communication from the Employer of the materialisation of any risks, communication of instructions and assessment of claims.

It is submitted that the principles proposed below, if followed, would fulfil those expectations. The proposed principles have been formulated taking into account the unique features of construction projects and construction contracts discussed above, the Abrahamson principles of balanced risk allocation,[70] the FIDIC General Conditions in the rainbow suite, the FIDIC Golden Principles[71] and "social obligations" owed to third parties. They are also influenced by Charles Molyneaux's paper on this topic in which he formulated a "modest Mosaic ten" principles.[72]

One of the criticisms that could be directed to the proposed (or any) principles of *lex constructionis* is that they cannot cover all situations, nor can they necessarily be applied in their entirety in many situations. The following discussion of principles in the context of *lex mercatoria* is equally applicable to the proposed principles of *lex constructionis*:

> General principles do not necessarily have pre-set conditions for application. Instead they merely constitute "rules of optimal application" which means that they may be complied with in varying degrees. The required degree of compliance depends not only on the actual but also on the legal options open to the target group. Application of general principles therefore requires a substantial process of weighing up contradictory principles and rules. General principles are therefore always subject to a continual discussion about the effectiveness and scope.[73]
>
> *(citations omitted)*

35.10.1 Proposed principles

Overarching principles

1. *Pacta sunt servanda.*
2. *Rebus sic stantibus* – doctrines or rules relating to changed conditions.
3. The parties must act in accordance with good faith and fair dealing in construction contracts.

70 Max W Abrahamson, 'Risk Management' (1983) *International Construction Law Review* 241, 244.

71 FIDIC, *The FIDIC Golden Principles* (1st edn, 2019). For a discussion of these Principles, see Donald Charrett (ed), *The International Application of FIDIC Contracts A Practical Guide* (Informa Law from Routledge, Abingdon England, 2020) Chapter 2.

72 Charles Molineaux, 'Moving Towards a Construction Lex Mercatoria – A Lex Constructionis' (1997) 1 *JIntArb* 55.

73 Klaus Peter Berger, *The Creeping Codification of the New Lex Mercatoria* (Wolters Kluwer The Netherlands, 2010) 201.

SCOPE

4. The contract defines, in writing, the original scope of work and the known conditions at the site.
5. The Employer has the right to instruct variations consistent with the original scope of the contract, and the Contractor has the obligation to carry out all such variations.
6. Construction works must be carried out so as to protect the health and safety of workers.
7. Construction works must not adversely affect the environment or the interests of third parties.
8. Subject to any contractual requirements, the Contractor selects the methods and timing of the works.

RISK

9. Each risk is allocated to the party best able to manage and control it and the consequences if it eventuates, or to the party who will derive any benefit or suffer the least consequences if the risk eventuates.
10. A party is not allocated risks that it cannot insure for or has insufficient financial resources to bear.
11. The Contractor is responsible for the works whilst it is in possession of the site.

TIME

12. The parties have a reasonable time to perform their obligations and exercise their rights.
13. The Contractor provides the Employer with prompt and adequate notice of any unexpected conditions that affect its performance, the occurrence of any risk events and any claims.
14. The Employer provides the Contractor with prompt and adequate notice of the occurrence of any risk events that affect the Contractor, instructions and responses to claims.
15. The Contractor is liable to pay damages if it does not complete the works by the contractually agreed date.

COST

16. The Employer has adequate financial resources to complete the contract.
17. The Contractor provides security for its performance.
18. The Employer pays the Contractor its contractual entitlements promptly.

QUALITY

19. The Contractor either rectifies defects in its works or pays damages to reinstate the works to the contractually specified quality.

DISPUTES

20. Unresolved disputes are finally determined by arbitration.

35.10.2 Discussion

Space does not permit a detailed exposition of each of the above principles. Some would probably be accepted as implied terms that go without saying. Others may be more controversial.

The overarching principles are contained in statements of the *lex mercatoria*, such as the UNIDROIT Principles. In this writer's view they are important for successful execution of construction projects that frequently take place over a long time and involve changed circumstances. In particular, the requirements of honesty, fairness and reasonableness inherent in the good faith principle will necessarily be relied upon to resolve amicably (where possible) many of the expected and unexpected issues that can arise during the execution of a construction contract.

The principles on scope acknowledge the complexity of construction projects, the possibility that the scope may need to change, and that the works impact on third parties and the environment. Risks are inherent in any construction project, and their appropriate allocation is often critical to achieving a successful project.[74]

The principles on time reiterate the requirement of reasonableness and emphasise the importance of adequate and timely communication from Contractor to Employer and vice versa. Damages for late completion are appropriate to compensate the Employer for its inability to make commercial use of the constructed facility from the agreed date.

Certainty and promptness of payment are usually of great importance to the Contractor and may be critical to its solvency. The requirement for a Contractor to rectify or pay for defect rectification is merely a construction specific implementation of *pacta sunt servanda.*

The near-universal implementation of the *New York Convention*, the norms of international arbitration and the finality and enforcement of awards are the basis for arbitration to be the most appropriate method for resolving international construction disputes.

35.11 Conclusion

The impact of COVID-19 on construction projects reinforced some aspects of *lex constructionis*, specifically the legislated adjustments to working methods on construction sites to ensure worker safety. Conversely, the frequent lack of legal or contractual provisions suitable to make appropriate adjustments for unforeseen circumstances in situations such as COVID-19 indicates the need for wider application of the principles of *lex constructionis*.

The foundations of *lex constructionis* already exist: a *lex mercatoria*, international contracts that can be implemented in any jurisdiction and international arbitration of disputes in accordance with widely accepted laws and rules that results in final awards that can be enforced in most jurisdictions.

It is submitted that the 20 principles of *lex constructionis* proposed can encourage projects that provide better value for money and promote international trade and greater

74 For a discussion of the consequences of inappropriately allocating risk, see: Japan International Cooperation Agency, 'Check List for One Sided Contracts' (2011) 1. https://www.jica.go.jp/english/our_work/types_of_assistance/oda_loans/oda_op_info/guide/c8h0vm0000aoeprl-att/guide02.pdf (accessed 9 September 2020). The JICA check list is discussed in Section 4.7.3.

comity between nations whilst fulfilling the parties' legitimate expectations. As with the *lex mercatoria*, the *lex constructionis* is "not carved in stone but has always been, still is, and will always be subject to constant review, textual refinement and adaptation to new developments in international business practice."[75]

The closest approach to a *lex constructionis*, that is, as an independent, supranational legal system not subject to the vagaries of a particular jurisdiction may be achieved by:

- Use of an internationally accepted standard form of contract such as FIDIC
- UNIDROIT Principles (or TransLex Principles) as the governing law of the contract, and
- International arbitration as the final method of dispute resolution.

As discussed in more detail in the following Chapter 36, such a contract exercises the parties' freedom of contract and is de-localised to the maximum extent achievable for a construction contract. It must always be accepted that the construction of a facility at a particular location in a specific jurisdiction will be subject to laws applicable to construction projects in that jurisdiction. However, it is submitted that there is considerable international agreement on many of the overarching principles underlying laws to protect the health and safety of workers, the environment and the rights of third parties impacted by construction, and these are probably the least controversial of the proposed principles of *lex constructionis*.

75 Klaus Peter Berger, *The Creeping Codification of the New Lex Mercatoria* (Wolters Kluwer, The Netherlands, 2010) 277.

CHAPTER 36

The use of the UNIDROIT Principles in international construction contracts[1]

36.1 UNIDROIT Principles

The UNIDROIT Principles of International Commercial Contracts (**UP**) are a set of anational principles that apply to the formation, validity, interpretation, performance and termination of commercial contracts. They are intended to be a modern statement of a *lex mercatoria*[2] for international contracts in which the rules are not derived from any particular national law, but nevertheless embody contractual principles which are or can be recognised by the laws of any country, whether those laws are based on the common law or the civil law.

The International Institute for the Unification of Private Law (UNIDROIT) is an independent intergovernmental organisation with its seat in Rome. Its purpose is to study needs and methods for modernising, harmonising and coordinating private and in particular commercial law as between States and groups of States. It was set up in 1926 as an auxiliary organ of the League of Nations. It was re-established in 1940 on the basis of a multilateral agreement, the UNIDROIT Statute. Membership of UNIDROIT is restricted to States acceding to the UNIDROIT Statute. UNIDROIT's 63 member States are drawn from the five continents and represent a variety of different legal, economic and political systems as well as different cultural backgrounds.[3]

UNIDROIT first published the UP in 1994. The Second Edition of the UP was issued in 2004, the Third Edition in 2010, followed by the Fourth Edition (2016).[4] A helpful Table of Correspondence is available to cross-reference the Articles in the four editions and identify new or changed clauses or comments.[5] The 2016 UP are available to download from the UNIDROIT website in three official languages (English, French and Italian).

1 This chapter is an edited and updated version of the paper: Donald Charrett, "The Use of the UNIDROIT Principles in International Construction Contracts", first published in [2013] 30(4) *International Construction Law Review* 507, published by Informa Law, London.

2 The *lex mercatoria* has been defined as: "*Lex mercatoria* is the Latin expression for a body of trading principles used by merchants throughout Europe in the medieval. Literally, it means 'merchant law'. It evolved as a system of custom and practice, which was enforced through a system of merchant courts along the main trade routes. It functioned as the international law of commerce. It emphasized contractual freedom, alienability of property, while shunning legal technicalities and deciding cases *ex aequo et bono*." www.lawteacher.net/free-law-essays/commercial-law/the-theory-of-the-lex-mercatoria-commercial-law-essay.php (accessed 11 January 2018)

3 www.unidroit.org/about-unidroit/membership (accessed 6 January 2018).

4 UNIDROIT International Institute for the Unification of Private Law, *UNIDROIT Principles of International Commercial Contracts 2016* (4th edn, 2016) www.unidroit.org/instruments/commercial-contracts/unidroit-principles-2016 (accessed 11 January 2018).

5 Ibid xxxvii.

DOI: 10.4324/9781003206897-41

The 2010 UP are also available in the official languages of German and Spanish as well as Arabic, Chinese, Greek, Hungarian Japanese, Persian, Portuguese, Romanian, Russian, Turkish and Ukrainian.[6] In addition to the text of the 2016 UP, a version with comments is also available in English and French, in which the reasons for and application of each sub-clause is explained. Many provisions are illustrated by examples of applicable contractual situations. There is a considerable literature available on the UP, and their application to contractual issues and national legal systems.[7] Citations of court and arbitration cases in which the UP have been considered are also available by jurisdiction, and by subject. They have also usefully been tabulated by sub-clause, so that it is easy to find the treatment a particular sub-clause has been given in different jurisdictions.[8]

The UP have received limited attention by common law courts to date. As of January 2018, of the total of 236 court citations listed on the Unilex website, only 38 are for common-law countries. The greatest number of common law judicial citations is in Australia (14), followed by the United Kingdom (10). These citations comprise cases in which the UP have been referred to, either noting whether or not the relevant national law is consistent, or as additional support for legal conclusions based on other principles.

The UP have been referred to in a significant number of publicly reported international arbitrations, in which the question of the choice of law has frequently been a live issue. As of January 2018, the Unilex website listed a total of 194 international arbitration awards which have referred to the UP and noted that the real number is undoubtedly considerably more because arbitration awards are generally confidential to the parties and therefore many awards are not publicly accessible. In a similar presentation to the case law citations, the details of the publicly available arbitration awards that have referred to the UP (without any identification of the parties), are accessible by keywords, in abstract, and, in a number of cases, the full text of the judgement/award is available.[9]

The number and variety of the arbitration awards which have referred to the UP provide a range of situations in which Arbitrators have found the UP relevant to the law applying to the contract in dispute. One of the significant applications in arbitration has been to apply the UP as the governing law of the contract where the parties have not made an express choice, or to supplement or reinforce national law. This is discussed in more detail below.

The UP have evolved from a considerable amount of work by a number of skilled and experienced lawyers from many countries and from all the major legal systems. It is suggested that they represent a set of overarching principles that are appropriate to regulate an international contract in a manner that is:

- Fair to all parties
- Straightforward to apply
- Predictable in outcome
- Independent of a particular national legal system, and
- Generally consistent with the contract law and principles in any country (with some exceptions).

6 www.unidroit.org/instruments/commercial-contracts/unidroit-principles-2010 (accessed 11 January 2018).

7 www.unilex.info/dynasite.cfm?dssid=2377&dsmid=13623&x=1 (accessed 11 January 2018).

8 www.unilex.info/dynasite.cfm?dssid=2377&dsmid=14311 (accessed 11 January 2018).

9 www.unilex.info/dynasite.cfm?dssid=2377&dsmid=13620&x=1 (accessed 11 January 2018).

Although the UP have been formulated with input from common lawyers as well as civil lawyers, there is probably a closer correspondence with civil law than the common law; as discussed further below, there are some important differences between the UP and the common law in England and other common law jurisdictions.

As a set of principles, the UP may be complementary to and supportive of the specific contract which applies to a given situation, in a similar way that the common law, civil law or statute law typically applies to regulate the entry into, and execution and termination of, the contract in the given legal system. However, because the UP are transnational, they do not and cannot have the legal force of a national legal system which is based on government power. Any force that the UP have can only be derived from the parties' contractual arrangements. Furthermore, any such power the parties themselves have invested in the role of the UP will be illusory, unless that power is supported by a relevant legal system which supports the parties' freedom of contract.

The United Nations Commission on International Trade Law (UNCITRAL) endorsed the 2010 edition of the UP in the following terms:

> Expressing *its appreciation* to the International Institute for the Unification of Private Law (UNIDROIT) for transmitting to it the text of the 2010 edition of the UNIDROIT Principles of International Commercial Contracts,
>
> Taking note that the UNIDROIT Principles 2010 complement a number of international trade law instruments, including the United Nations Convention on Contracts for the International Sale of Goods,
>
> Noting that the preamble of the UNIDROIT Principles 2010 states that:
>
> 'These Principles set forth general rules for international commercial contracts,
>
> They shall be applied when the parties have agreed that their contract be governed by them,
>
> They may be applied when parties have agreed that their contract be governed by general principles of law, the *lex mercatoria* or the like,
>
> They may be applied when the parties have not chosen any law to govern their contract,
>
> They may be used to interpret or supplement international uniform law instruments,
>
> They may be used to interpret or supplement domestic law,
>
> They may serve as a model for national and international legislators,'
>
> Congratulating UNIDROIT on having made a further contribution to the facilitation of international trade by preparing general rules for international commercial contracts,
>
> Commends the use of the 2010 edition of the UNIDROIT Principles of International Commercial Contracts, as appropriate, for their intended purposes.[10]

36.2 Contents of the UP

The Preamble to the UP sets out the following Purpose of the Principles:

> These Principles set forth general rules for international commercial contracts.
>
> They shall be applied when the parties have agreed that their contract be governed by them.
>
> They may be applied when the parties have agreed that their contract be governed by general principles of law, the *lex mercatoria* or the like.

10 *Report of the United Nations Commission on International Trade Law on the work of its 45th session, 25 June–6 July 2012*, 33 https://documents-dds-ny.un.org/doc/UNDOC/GEN/V12/551/54/PDF/V1255154.pdf?OpenElement (accessed 11 January 2018).

They may be applied when the parties have not chosen any law to govern their contract.
They may be used to interpret or supplement international uniform law instruments. They may be used to interpret or supplement domestic law.
They may serve as a model for national and international legislators.[11]

The 2010 and 2016 editions of the UP consist of 211 Articles (120 Articles in the 1994 edition and 185 Articles in the 2004 edition) in the following chapters and sections:

Chapter 1 General Provisions
Chapter 2 Formation and Authority of Agents
 Section 1 Formation
 Section 2 Authority of agents (not in 1994 edition)
Chapter 3 Validity
 Section 1 General provisions
 Section 2 Grounds for avoidance
 Section 3 Illegality (not in 1994 or 2004 editions)
Chapter 4 Interpretation
Chapter 5 Content, Third Party Rights and Conditions
 Section 1 Content
 Section 2 Third party rights (not in 1994 edition)
 Section 3 Conditions (not in 1994 or 2004 editions)
Chapter 6 Performance
 Section 1 Performance in general
 Section 2 Hardship
Chapter 7 Non-performance
 Section 1 Non-performance in general
 Section 2 Right to performance
 Section 3 Termination
 Section 4 Damages
Chapter 8 Set-off (not in 1994 edition)
Chapter 9 Assignment of Rights, Transfer of Obligations, Assignment of Contracts (not in 1994 edition)
 Section 1 Assignment of rights
 Section 2 Transfer of obligations
 Section 3 Assignment of contracts
Chapter 10 Limitation Periods (not in 1994 edition)
Chapter 11 Plurality of Obligors and Obligees (not in 1994 or 2004 editions)
 Section 1 Plurality of obligors
 Section 2 Plurality of obligees

It can be seen from this list of contents that the UP contain detailed provisions on all the main elements of entry into, performance and termination of contracts. The additional Articles added in the 2004 and 2010 editions indicate an ongoing development of the scope to keep up with the requirements of modern international contracts. The 2016 edition of the UP was not intended as a revision of the previous editions; the main objective was to better take into account the special needs of long-term contracts. Accordingly, only six

11 UNIDROIT International Institute for the Unification of Private Law, *UNIDROIT Principles of International Commercial Contracts 2016* (4th edn, 2016) 1 www.unidroit.org/instruments/commercial-contracts/unidroit-principles-2016 (accessed 11 January 2018).

provisions were amended from the 2010 edition; however, a number of alterations were made to the comments.[12]

36.3 The application of the UP to international construction contracts

In contracts where the parties have expressly referred to the UP, then in accordance with the principle of freedom of contract, they will generally apply to the extent and in the manner that the parties have provided for in their contract. This statement is subject to the two important exceptions discussed below, that the parties' freedom of contract is subject to any applicable statute law and must not conflict with public policy. Thus, as one possibility, the parties may explicitly nominate the UP as the system of law to govern their contract, to the exclusion of any national law that would otherwise apply based on the application of the well-established principles of conflict of laws. Any dispute arising under such a contract could, in principle, be resolved by the award of a properly constituted arbitral tribunal sitting anywhere in the world. If, as UNIDROIT suggests, the UP are sufficiently developed as a *lex mercatoria*, an arbitral tribunal would not need to refer to any national law to determine the meaning of the contract, and the law of the contract (the *lex contractus*) would be the UP.

Interface with national law does, however, occur where:

- A dispute is litigated in court
- Support of the courts is required in the conduct of an arbitration
- An arbitration award is appealed
- Where an arbitration award needs to be enforced.

These applications of the relevant national law may involve issues relating to the entry into, execution or termination of the contract the subject of the dispute. In any such case, the court in the relevant jurisdiction may be required to enquire into the legal basis of the contract, the arbitration and/or the arbitration award, and the extent to which the UP are compatible with the local law.

It is suggested that the principle of party autonomy and freedom of contract generally accepted across all jurisdictions means that a court would uphold all the terms of the contract the parties have agreed on, except those terms which are in breach of a relevant statute, or are against public policy.

Thus, if contracting parties explicitly nominated the UP as the law governing their contract, a court would generally be expected to uphold the parties' bargain, unless the choice of the UP as the governing law or specific aspects of the UP were in breach of a relevant statute or public policy. For example, although the European Regulations on the law applicable to contractual relations (***Rome I***)[13] allows the incorporation of a non-State body of law into a contract, a European court would limit the parties' choice of governing law to a national system of law and, in the absence of the parties' choice, would apply the

12 UNIDROIT International Institute for the Unification of Private Law, *UNIDROIT Principles of International Commercial Contracts 2016* (4th edn, 2016) vii www.unidroit.org/instruments/commercial-contracts/unidroit-principles-2016 (accessed 11 January 2018).

13 *Regulation (EC) No 593/2008* of the European Parliament and of the Council of 17 June 2008 on the law applicable to contractual obligations.

conflict of laws rules in *Rome I* to determine the applicable law.[14] The extent of application of the chosen UP in these circumstances would depend on the relevant national law.

As another example, Article 869 of the Colombian *Commercial Code* states that contracts that are performed in Colombia will be governed by Colombian law; it would be expected that even if the UP were chosen by the parties, a Colombian court would limit their application to issues not addressed by Colombian law, and then only to the extent that the UP were not inconsistent with Colombian law. Public policy varies from jurisdiction to jurisdiction and is sometimes widely construed by courts so as to significantly limit the operation of contractual terms agreed by the parties.

The relevance of the UP in cases where the parties have not expressly agreed to use them as the law of their contract raises different issues. As some of the cases below show, in appropriate circumstances the UP have been used by an arbitral tribunal to fill the gap resulting from the parties' failure to nominate the system of law within which their contract operates.

As discussed below, there are a significant number of reported cases of courts and arbitral tribunals that have referred to the UP in a variety of ways. In 2011 Agro tabulated the statistics on these cases.[15] That paper enumerates the reported cases of courts and arbitral tribunals referring to the UP in the following categories:

(1) Applied as the law governing the substance of the dispute: (1) expressly chosen by the parties, and (2) applied ex-officio by the Arbitral Tribunal (55 arbitral awards, 6 court decisions).
(2) To confirm that the solution provided by the applicable domestic law is in conformity with international standards (25 court decisions, 33 arbitral awards).
(3) As a means of interpreting and supplementing domestic law (49 court decisions, 27 arbitral awards).
(4) As a means of interpreting and supplementing international uniform law instruments (11 court decisions, 24 arbitral awards).

Agro notes that, although the majority of applications of the UP in these cases are sales contracts, they also cover a great variety of other important international commercial contracts, especially service contracts, distribution contracts and licensing contracts.[16] Although there are few reported construction law cases, there is no apparent reason why the issues highlighted by the cases would not be applicable to construction law contracts in appropriate circumstances.

36.4 Case law referring to the UP

The UP have been referred to in a number of reported judgements in common law countries, in litigation based on the common law in those countries. By virtue of their nature as a set of principles that have not been formally adopted in statute, the UP cannot themselves

14 Guido Carducci, "The Impact of the EU 'Rome I' Regulation on International Litigation and Arbitration, A-National Law, Mandatory and Overriding Rules" (2011) V22 No 2 *ICC International Court of Arbitration Bulletin* 31, 36.

15 Eleonora Finazzi Agro, "The Impact of the UNIDROIT Principles in International Dispute Resolution in Figures" (2011) 3 *Uniform Law Review* 719.

16 Ibid 721.

be a source of law for a judge, except to the extent expressly adopted by the parties in their contract. However, they can be of value in establishing international contractual norms that assist judges in developing the common law towards greater international consistency.

The relatively few reported court common law cases that have referred to the UP are valuable both for identifying areas where the common law is (or is becoming) consistent with the *lex mercatoria* of the UP, and for highlighting where the common law diverges from the UP.

36.5 Good faith

The issue of whether there is a general duty of good faith in the entry into and execution of contracts differs from jurisdiction to jurisdiction in the common law world. Whereas in the United States the *Uniform Commercial Code* has enshrined in legislation the obligation of good faith in the performance of contracts,[17] good faith is not part of the common law of England. In Australia, although the High Court has not considered the issue, there is case law that indicates that there may be a general duty of good faith in the performance of some contracts. Article 1.7 (Good faith and fair dealing) of the UP has been used as support for this proposition by several judges.[18] In *United Group Rail Services v Rail Corporation of New South Wales*,[19] Allsop J found that a commitment to negotiate in good faith was enforceable, good faith was not a concept foreign to the common law and was part of the law of performance of contracts in numerous sophisticated commercial jurisdictions, and expressly referred to Art 1.7 of the UP. And in *Macquarie International Health Clinic Pty Ltd v Sydney South West Area Health Service*,[20] Allsop J found support in UP Art 1.7 as a factor confirming an increasing recognition at international level of the principle of good faith and fair dealing.

36.6 UP as support for the common law

Common law judges have also used other articles of the UP as additional support for findings as to what the common law is. For example, in *GEC Marconi Systems Pty Ltd v BHP Information Technology Pty Ltd*,[21] Finn J referred to Art [2.1.18][22] (Modification in a particular form) in relation to the parties' right to make an oral variation, and Art 6.1.4 (Order of performance) in relation to the time at which instalment payments become due and payable under an "entire contract" clause.

In *Koompahtoo Local Aboriginal Land Council v Sanpine Pty Ltd*,[23] the Australian High Court noted that a distinction between breach of essential terms and "intermediate" terms is not part of Australian law and referred to UP Arts 7.3.1 (Right to terminate the

17 §1–304. Obligation of Good Faith: "Every contract or duty within [the *Uniform Commercial Code*] imposes an obligation of good faith in its performance and enforcement."

18 *Hughes Aircraft Systems International v Airservices Australia* (1997) 146 ALR 1; *Aiton v Transfield* (2000) 16 BCL 70.

19 [2009] NSWCA 177.

20 [2010] NSWCA 268.

21 [2003] FCA 50.

22 Article numbers in square brackets are quoted as those in the 2016 edition, although the Article number originally quoted from the 1994 edition was different.

23 [2007] HCA 61.

contract) and 7.3.3 (Anticipatory non-performance), implicitly recognising that the UP and Australian law coincide on this issue.

In *Hannaford (trading as Torrens Valley Orchards) v Australian Farmlink Pty Ltd*,[24] Finn J recognised that a prior course of dealing between parties and practices and usages can provide for both the drawing of inferences as to the actual terms on which the parties have contracted, and also for the imputation of implied terms in their contract, and referred to UP Arts 1.9 (Usages and practices) and 5.1.2 (Implied obligations) in support.

The High Court of Delhi in *Sandvik Asia Pvt. Ltd v Vardhman Promoters Pvt. Ltd* had to construe the terms of a contract for the sale of real estate. In reaching its conclusion the Court referred not only to a number of Indian and English decisions and legal writings, but also to the UP, citing Art 4.4 (Reference to contract or statement as a whole) and quoting Art 4.5 (All terms to be given effect).[25]

36.7 UP articles incompatible with common law

In Chapter 4, the UP contains eight articles on the interpretation of the terms of contracts. Art 4.4 (Reference to contract or statements as a whole), Art 4.5 (All terms to be given effect), Art 4.6 (*Contra proferentem* rule) and Art 4.7 (Linguistic discrepancies) are probably consistent with most common law rules of contract construction. However, Arts 4.1 (Intention of the parties), Art 4.2 (Interpretation of statements and other conduct), Art 4.3 (Relevant circumstances) and Art 4.8 (Supplying an omitted term) allow for a greater amount of factual material to assist in interpreting the meaning of a contract, particularly in allowing for evidence of pre-contractual negotiations, earlier drafts of the contract, and each party's subjective intent than is generally applicable to many common law rules. In *Chartbrook Ltd v Persimmon Homes Ltd*,[26] Lord Hoffmann confirmed the traditional exclusionary rule of the inadmissibility of evidence of pre-contractual negotiations. Referring to UP Art 4.3 he noted that this reflects the French philosophy of contractual interpretation, which is altogether different from that of English law:

> English law, on the other hand, mixes up the ascertainment of intention with the rules of law by depersonalising the contracting parties and asking, not what their intentions actually were, but what a reasonable outside observer would have taken them to be. One cannot in my opinion simply transpose rules based on one philosophy of contractual interpretation to another, or assume that the practical effect of admitting such evidence under the English system of civil procedure will be the same as that under a Continental system.[27]

However, this issue is not without controversy, as several judges have argued in favour of a flexible application of the exclusionary rule whenever a cautious use of the pre-contract material would enable the court to arrive at a meaning of the contract that accorded with the ascertainable intention of the parties. In *Proforce Recruit Ltd v The Rugby Group Ltd*,[28] Arden LJ suggested that consideration should be given to the possibility of admitting

24 [2008] FCA 1591.
25 www.unilex.info/case.cfm?id=1242 (accessed 11 January 2018).
26 [2009] UKHL 38.
27 Ibid [39].
28 [2006] EWCA Civ 69.

evidence of pre-contractual negotiations in interpretation questions on a wider basis than the law presently permits. In her view "it may be appropriate to consider a number of international instruments applying to contracts", such as the UNIDROIT Principles which "give primacy to the common intention of the parties and on questions of interpretation requires regard to be had to all the circumstances, including the pre-contractual negotiations of the parties (Article 4.3)".

36.8 Arbitration cases referring to the UP

One of the reasons for the popularity of arbitration as a method of dispute resolution is the extent to which the parties have autonomy to set their own rules, not only in relation to the arbitration procedures, but also in relation to the law governing the substance of their dispute. In *Musawi v R.E. International (UK) Ltd*,[29] the High Court of England affirmed that s 46(1)(b) of the UK 1996 *Arbitration Act*

> allows parties the freedom to apply a set of rules or principles which do not in themselves constitute a legal system" and that "such a choice may include a non-national set of legal principles (such as the 1994 UNIDROIT Principles of International Commercial Contracts) or, more broadly, general principles of commercial law or the *lex mercatoria*.

If the parties have not made a choice of governing law in their contract, it will fall to the arbitral tribunal to determine it. Such a tribunal typically has considerable latitude in determining the applicable law under the applicable procedural arbitration rules. For example, Art 21.1 of the ICC Arbitration Rules (2021) provides:

> The parties shall be free to agree upon the rules of law to be applied by the arbitral tribunal to the merits of the dispute. In the absence of any such agreement, the arbitral tribunal shall apply the rules of law which it determines to be appropriate.

Article 53.1 UNCITRAL Arbitration Rules (2013) provides:

> The arbitral tribunal shall apply the law designated by the parties as applicable to the substance of the dispute. Failing such designation by the parties, the arbitral tribunal shall apply the law determined by the conflict of laws rules which it considers applicable.

Thus, under these (and other institutional) rules, the arbitral tribunal determines the rules of law it determines to be appropriate in the circumstances, perhaps taking into account relevant trade usages. It is generally accepted that an arbitration has no *lex fori* (the law of the country in which an action is brought), and accordingly provisions such as *Rome I* that would require a court to apply a national system of law do not apply to an arbitral tribunal.[30] An arbitral tribunal is therefore generally free to select the UP as the governing law of the contract if appropriate.

The cases discussed below illustrate the ways in which arbitral tribunals have applied the UP, including applying the UP as the governing law of the contract.

---

29 [2007] EWHC 2981 (Ch).

30 Guido Carducci, "The Impact of the EU 'Rome I' Regulation on International Litigation and Arbitration, A-National Law, Mandatory and Overriding Rules" (2011) V22 No 2 *ICC International Court of Arbitration Bulletin* 31, 36.

36.9 UP applied as the law governing the substance of the dispute

In addition to cases in which the parties themselves have expressly adopted the UP as the governing law of the contract, or supplementary to their choice of law, there are a number of reported arbitration cases in which the arbitral tribunal has applied the UP as the law governing the substance of the dispute, or supplementary to the law chosen by the parties. These cases are valuable for identifying the factors that may be relevant in determining the application of the UP in cases where the parties have not explicitly made their own choice of law.

In a dispute between a US national and the Government of the Ukraine, an International Centre for the Settlement of Disputes (**ICSID**) arbitral tribunal recorded a settlement agreement in the form of an award. The US plaintiff subsequently commenced arbitral proceedings alleging breach of the terms of settlement. The settlement agreement provided that the applicable law was to be determined by the arbitral tribunal who shall apply "(a) the law determined by the conflict of laws rules which it considers applicable and (b) such rules of international law as the Tribunal considers applicable". The arbitral tribunal found that such a choice of law clause amounted to an implied negative choice of any municipal legal system by the parties and concluded that the most appropriate approach was to submit the settlement agreement to the rules of international law and, within these, to have particular regard to the UP. In support of its decision the arbitral tribunal noted that, when negotiating their agreement, the parties had evidently given thought to the issue of applicable law, but were apparently unable to reach an agreement to apply either Ukrainian or US law. Instead, they incorporated extensive parts of the UP into the agreement, and included a clause authorising the tribunal either to select a municipal legal system or to apply the rules of law the tribunal considered appropriate. In determining the merits of the dispute, the arbitral tribunal referred to UP Arts 4.1 (Intention of the parties), 4.3 (Relevant circumstances), 2.1.17 (Merger clauses), 1.8 (Inconsistent behaviour) and 5.1.4 (Duty to achieve a specific result. Duty of best efforts).[31]

A dispute arose in a contract between parties from two Middle Eastern countries relating to high technology services to be provided by the claimant with respect to certain instances of alleged non-performance. The contract did not contain a choice of law clause but provided for resolving disputes by ICC arbitration in London with the language of the arbitration to be English. The claimant argued, based on English case law, that there had been a tacit choice of English law as the law governing the contract. The respondent argued in favour of the applicability of the law of its own country. In a partial award, the arbitral tribunal decided that the law governing the contract was the UP, if and where necessary supplemented by the otherwise applicable law as determined in accordance with Art 17.1 of the 1998 ICC Arbitration Rules (Art 21 in the 2021 ICC Arbitration Rules). The Tribunal gave the following reasons for the choice of the UP:

(1) There had been a "negative choice" as regards the laws of the claimant's and respondent's countries, and there had been no shared expectations of the parties in this respect.
(2) There was no clearly identifiable "objective" connecting factor or other conflict of laws rule.

31 www.unilex.info/case.cfm?pid=2&do=case&id=1533&step=Abstract (accessed 11 January 2018).

(3) The UP were shaped by the laws of the community of trading nations and constituted an international re-statement (and pre-statement) of modern contract law in its most authoritative form.
(4) In the meantime, they were well-known, not least due to many hundreds of publications and more than 150 documented arbitral awards and court decisions.
(5) UNCITRAL had endorsed the UP.[32]

A contract between a French company and a US company was silent as to the applicable law. The arbitral tribunal held that none of the connecting factors advocated by the parties to select the applicable law, such as the parties' domicile, the place of contracting or the place of performance of the contract, was compelling. And since the parties themselves accepted the general principles of law as a subordinate alternative, it concluded that it would be more appropriate not to apply any particular domestic law but rather follow the so-called direct method admitted under Art 17(1) of the ICC Rules of Arbitration and base its decision on general principles of law or the *lex mercatoria*. The arbitral tribunal recalled that several ICC cases have considered that the UNIDROIT Principles are the best approach to apprehend the general principles of law and determined that it would likewise have recourse in the case at hand to the UP "as a primary set of guidelines in determining international rules of law applicable to the parties' contract".[33]

36.10 Reference to UP as evidence of international trade usages

The significance of international trade usages is that some arbitration rules include them as a factor to be taken into account by the arbitral tribunal in determining the law to be applied to the merits of the dispute, e.g.:

> The arbitral tribunal shall take account of the provisions of the contract, if any, between the parties and of any relevant trade usages.[34]
>
> In all cases, the arbitral tribunal shall decide in accordance with the terms of the contract, if any, and shall take into account any usages of trade applicable to the transaction.[35]

A number of arbitral tribunals have referred to the UP as evidence of international trade usages, including the following examples.

In an arbitration in which the governing law of the contract was Lithuanian, the claimant also invoked the application of the UP and the Principles of European Contract Law as a source of trade usages. The arbitral tribunal decided that it would refer, when necessary, to "the relevant trade usages" according to Art 17 of the 1998 ICC Rules of Arbitration, and that such reference included but was not limited to the UP and the Principles of European Contract Law.[36]

In an arbitration between two Italian companies who had chosen New York law as the law governing the validity of their agreement, the arbitral tribunal concluded that the silence with respect to all other matters was an indication of the parties' intention not to

32 www.unilex.info/case.cfm?pid=2&do=case&id=1440&step=Abstract (accessed 11 January 2018).
33 www.unilex.info/case.cfm?pid=2&do=case&id=1409&step=Abstract (accessed 11 January 2018).
34 *ICC Rules of Arbitration* (2017) Art 21.2 Applicable Rules of Law.
35 *UNCITRAL Arbitration Rules* (2013) Art 35.3.
36 www.unilex.info/case.cfm?pid=2&do=case&id=695&step=Abstract (accessed 11 January 2018).

have these matters governed by a particular domestic law. The arbitral tribunal therefore decided to apply, in addition to the terms of the agreement, "the usages of international trade", having regard whenever necessary to "international public policy" and for this purpose to refer to the UNIDROIT Principles which it considered an "accurate representation, although incomplete, of the usages of international trade".[37]

In a contract for the sale of fuel oil between an English and an Italian company, the contract contained an express reference to Italian law as the law governing the contract. In view of the fact that Art 834 of the Italian *Code of Civil Procedure* requires the arbitral tribunal in an international arbitration to take into account the terms of the contract and the trade usages, the arbitral tribunal repeatedly referred to the UP, which it defined as a parameter of the principles and usages of international trade in order to prove that the solutions provided by Italian law were in conformity with international standards.[38]

36.11 Reference to UP as corroboration for a conclusion arrived at by reference to national law, or consistent with national law

The following give some examples of reported arbitration cases in which the arbitrator(s) found specific provisions of the UP to be compatible with domestic law:

- Arts 1.1 (Freedom of contract), 1.3 (Binding character of contract), 1.7 (Good faith), and 2.1.15 (Negotiations in bad faith) and New York law.[39]
- Art 1.7(1) (Good faith) and French Law.[40]
- Arts 1.7 (Good faith), 1.8 (Inconsistent behaviour), 4.1 (Intention of the parties), 4.2 (Interpretation of statements and other conduct) and 4.3 (Relevant circumstances) and Greek law.[41]
- Art (2.1.19) (Contracting under standard terms) and French Law.[42]
- Arts 3.5 (Relevant mistake), 4.1 (Intention of the parties) and 4.2 (Interpretation of statements and other conduct) and Swiss law.[43]
- Art 6.2.1 (Contract to be observed) and Dutch law.[44]
- Art 6.2.2 (Definition of hardship) and Art 6.2.3 (Effects of hardship) and French Law.[45]
- Art 7.4.1 (Right to damages) and Lebanese law.[46]
- Art 7.4.8 (Mitigation of harm) and English law.[47]
- Art 7.4.9 (Interest for failure to pay money) and Italian law.[48]

37 www.unilex.info/case.cfm?pid=2&do=case&id=680&step=Abstract (accessed 11 January 2018).
38 www.unilex.info/case.cfm?pid=2&do=case&id=631&step=Abstract (accessed 11 January 2018).
39 www.unilex.info/case.cfm?pid=2&do=case&id=644&step=Abstract (accessed 11 January 2018).
40 www.unilex.info/case.cfm?pid=2&do=case&id=973&step=Abstract (accessed 11 January 2018).
41 www.unilex.info/case.cfm?pid=2&do=case&id=699&step=Abstract (accessed 11 January 2018).
42 www.unilex.info/case.cfm?pid=2&do=case&id=662&step=Abstract (accessed 11 January 2018).
43 www.unilex.info/case.cfm?pid=2&do=case&id=642&step=Abstract (accessed 11 January 2018).
44 www.unilex.info/case.cfm?pid=2&do=case&id=630&step=Abstract (accessed 11 January 2018).
45 www.unilex.info/case.cfm?pid=2&do=case&id=1062&step=Abstract (accessed 11 January 2018).
46 www.unilex.info/case.cfm?pid=2&do=case&id=1365&step=Abstract (accessed 11 January 2018).
47 www.unilex.info/case.cfm?pid=2&do=case&id=691&step=Abstract (accessed 11 January 2018).
48 www.unilex.info/case.cfm?pid=2&do=case&id=1068&step=Abstract (accessed 11 January 2018).

In an arbitration in which the parties had chosen Mexican law as the governing law of the contract, the arbitral tribunal noted that "the UNIDROIT Principles, which are the result of a thorough comparative study, may be used to interpret [the domestic law chosen by the parties] and solve unexpected difficulties in applying [that law] to an international contract".[49]

36.12 UP referred to as supplementary to national law

When a Swiss company initiated arbitration proceedings against a Polish company alleging violation of contractual rights, the question arose as to whether the claimant, when it transferred those rights to its subsidiary, had transferred them alone or had transferred the whole contract. The applicable Polish law did not provide any specific solution on this point, and the arbitral tribunal determined to "subsidiarily apply international law instruments" such as the UP. The arbitral tribunal found the solution by interpreting the terms of the contract, and referred to the canons of interpretation laid down in the Polish *Civil Code* as well as in UP Arts 1.1 (Freedom of contract), 4.1(1) (Intention of the parties) and 4.8(2) (Supplying an omitted term), i.e. that a contract is to be interpreted and supplemented having regard to the common intention of the parties, the nature and purpose of the contract, good faith and fair dealing and reasonableness.[50]

In a contract governed by Egyptian law for the supply of equipment for an industrial plant and the supervision of the construction of the plant, an Egyptian company claimed that due to the French company defendant's faulty design and performance, the plant could not be run on schedule. The claimant initiated arbitration proceedings, claiming damages for loss of profits. In addressing the question of the quantification of the losses the arbitral tribunal referred not only to the relevant provisions in the Egyptian *Civil Code* but also to UP Arts 7.4.1 (Right to damages), 7.4.2 (Full compensation) and 7.4.3 (Certainty of harm).[51]

A German company concluded two contracts with an Indian company defendant, for the delivery and installation of industrial equipment. When the defendant declared its intention to return allegedly defective equipment, the claimant filed a request for arbitration. In interpreting the choice of law clause contained in the contract to determine that the applicable law was Swiss law, the arbitral tribunal expressly referred to UP Arts 4.1 (Intention of the parties) and 4.2 (Interpretation of statements and other conduct). In relation to the merits of the case, the arbitral tribunal pointed out that the issue of fraud and misrepresentation would not be determined differently even if Indian law were found to apply. It noted that the avoidance of a contract for wilful deception is "a common understanding of all civilised jurisprudence" and in this context referred to UP Arts [2.1.15(2)] (Negotiations in bad faith), 3.8 (Fraud) and 3.9 (Threat).[52]

In an arbitration on alleged breach of a settlement agreement governed by Italian law, the arbitral tribunal referred, in addition to the relevant provisions of the Italian *Civil Code*, to provisions contained in the *United Nations Convention on Contracts for the International Sale of Goods* (*CISG*) and the UP, defining both as "normative texts that can

49 www.unilex.info/case.cfm?pid=2&do=case&id=1423&step=Abstract (accessed 11 January 2018).
50 www.unilex.info/case.cfm?pid=2&do=case&id=1070&step=Abstract (accessed 11 January 2018).
51 www.unilex.info/case.cfm?pid=2&do=case&id=1061&step=Abstract (accessed 11 January 2018).
52 www.unilex.info/case.cfm?pid=2&do=case&id=692&step=Abstract (accessed 11 January 2018).

be considered helpful in their interpretation of all contracts of an international nature". In support of the provisions of the Italian *Civil Code* on the rules of interpretation, the arbitral tribunal referred to the corresponding rules contained in UP Arts 1.7 (Good faith and fair dealing) and 4.1–4.8 (Interpretation). And in finding that a modified acceptance amounts to a counteroffer which the original offeror may tacitly accept by not objecting to the varied terms contained in the acceptance, and by starting performance of its own obligations, the arbitral tribunal referred to UP Art [2.1.11] (Modified acceptance) as consistent with the Italian *Civil Code*.[53]

36.13 Parties to an arbitration agreed to use general principles of international law, as complementary and supplementary to the choice of national law

One case concerned two 1977 contracts for the sale and the installation of military equipment, between a US corporation and the Iranian Air Force. The contracts were duly performed until the advent of the Islamic Revolution in early 1979. The contracts' choice of law clause designated the law of Iran, but the parties eventually agreed to the complementary and supplementary application of general principles of international law. In relation to the substantive applicable law to the dispute, the arbitral tribunal held that, to the extent necessary, it would be guided by the UP as manifesting the general principles of international law. Thus, in finding that each party was entitled to unilaterally request termination of the contracts or adaptation of their terms, the arbitral tribunal expressly referred to UP Art 6.2.3 (Effects of hardship). Furthermore, in order to justify the application by analogy of a "Termination for Convenience Clause" contained in the contracts, to the termination of the contract as a result of changed circumstances, the arbitral tribunal applied UP Arts 5.1 (Express and implied obligations) and 5.2 (Implied obligations), and the "widely accepted principles therein set forth regarding implied obligations." In dealing with the consequences of the termination of the contracts, the arbitral tribunal quoted UP Art 7.3.6 (Restitution) in support of the right of either party to claim restitution of whatever it had supplied, provided that such party concurrently made restitution of whatever it had received.

However, in relation to the date from which interest was to be awarded, the arbitral tribunal declined to award interest from the time when the payment became due without any need for the aggrieved party to give notice of the default (as provided for in UP Art 7.4.9 (Interest for failure to pay money)). It concluded that

> [e]ven if a generally accepted principle of international law existed in this respect, the Tribunal would only be authorized to apply it as a complementary and supplementary rule, not as a rule in clear contradiction to an unambiguous provision of the Iranian law chosen by the Parties.[54]

53 www.unilex.info/case.cfm?pid=2&do=case&id=663&step=Abstract (accessed 11 January 2018).

54 www.unilex.info/case.cfm?pid=2&do=case&id=653&step=Abstract (accessed 11 January 2018).

36.14 To what extent do the UP cover construction law?

Construction contracts contain a number of unique features that distinguish them from other types of contracts. Those unique features of "construction law" may be covered by the terms of the construction contract itself, or by the *Civil Codes* of some jurisdictions. For example, Chapter 16 (Contracts for Construction Projects) of the Peoples' Republic of China *Contract Law* contains general construction law provisions, and PRC *Construction Law* contains detailed legal requirements for the execution of construction projects.

This raises the question as to whether the UP, as a general statement of principles of contract law, adequately address the specific requirements of construction contracts to the extent necessary for them to be the governing law of the contract.

Without attempting to define the unique characteristics of construction contracts,[55] or enumerate the specific issues that may arise in particular circumstances, the following represent some typical areas of "construction law":

- Who is liable for ground conditions?
- Can work be suspended and why?
- Extension of the time for completion.
- Can work be added or omitted?
- How are changes valued?

These typical areas of construction law are frequently covered in some detail in the General and Particular Conditions of a specific construction contract. To the extent that the Contract addresses these "construction law" areas, the role of the UP as the governing law would generally be confined to upholding the terms of the contract that the parties had agreed to. Pursuant to Art 1.1 (Freedom of contract): "The parties are free to enter into a contract and to determine its content." Further, pursuant to the principle of *pacta sunt servanda* in Art 1.3 (Binding character of contract): "A contract validly entered into is binding upon the parties. It can only be modified or terminated in accordance with its terms or by agreement or as otherwise provided in these Principles."

The primary role of the UP as the governing law of a comprehensive construction contract, such as the FIDIC Red Book, would be construction of the contract terms in accordance with Chapter 4 (Interpretation). Specifically, the UP provide in Art 4.1 (Intention of the parties):

> (1) A contract shall be interpreted according to the common intention of the parties.
> (2) If such an intention cannot be established, the contract shall be interpreted according to the meaning that reasonable persons of the same kind as the parties would give it in the same circumstances.

It is submitted that an experienced arbitral tribunal would generally have little difficulty in applying these principles of interpretation to a comprehensive construction contract, if provided with the appropriate evidence. However, if a construction contract does not

55 These are discussed in Section 35.2 above.

make provision for a construction law issue that arises (e.g. one of the five issues identified above) the UP typically only provide general principles to apply to fill the gap.

One such general principle is in Art 1.9 (Usages and practices):

> (1) The parties are bound by any usage to which they have agreed and by any practices which they have established between themselves.
> (2) The parties are bound by a usage that is widely known to and regularly observed in international trade by parties in the particular trade concerned except where the application of such a usage would be unreasonable.

Article 1.9(1) may enable the parties, by agreement during the execution of a project, to establish practices such as addition or deletion of work or extension of time for completion, that were not specifically detailed in the contract. Article 1.8 (Inconsistent behaviour) would support the consistent application of such practices: "A party cannot act inconsistently with an understanding it has caused the other party to have and upon which that other party has acted to its detriment."

In the absence of the parties' agreement to such practices, Art 1.9(2) may apply widely accepted practices of international construction law to fill gaps in the contract. Although there would inevitably be evidential hurdles to overcome to convince an arbitral tribunal as to the relevant "widely known to and regularly observed" construction law practices, it could be argued that provisions common to widely used international construction law contracts such as the FIDIC Red Book satisfied this requirement.

Another general principle from the UP that may assist in gap filling is that if the parties have not made provision for an issue, then a term can be implied pursuant to Art 4.8 (Supplying an omitted term):

> (1) Where the parties to a contract have not agreed with respect to a term which is important for a determination of their rights and duties, a term which is appropriate in the circumstances shall be supplied.
> (2) In determining what is an appropriate term regard shall be had, among other factors, to
>   (a) the intention of the parties;
>   (b) the nature and purpose of the contract;
>   (c) good faith and fair dealing;
>   (d) reasonableness.

Other provisions of the UP that may be of assistance in filling gaps in the parties' specific construction contract include:

- Art 5.1.1 (Express and implied obligations).
- Art 5.1.2 (Implied obligations).
- Art 5.1.3 (Cooperation between the parties).
- Art 5.1.4(1) (Duty to achieve a specific result).
- Art 6.1.1 (Time of performance).
- Art 6.1.11 (Costs of performance).
- Chapter 6, Section 2 (Hardship).
- Art 7.1.7 (*Force majeure*).
- Art 7.2.2 (Performance of non-monetary obligations).
- Art 7.4.13 (Agreed payment for non-performance).

The text of these articles do not provide a definitive answer to any of the "construction law" issues enumerated at the beginning of this section, in the absence of appropriate contractual provisions. At best, the UP provide some general principles that may assist an arbitral tribunal, experienced in construction law and provided with appropriate evidence, to fill gaps consistently with the parties' intentions and international construction law practice. The evidential issues involved in invoking these general principles emphasise the importance of the parties addressing the foreseeable construction law issues specifically in their contract; the advantages of applying a widely used form of contract such as FIDIC should be self-evident in comprehensiveness, wide acceptance and understanding.

There is one "construction law" issue identified above that appears to be adequately covered by the UP: that of how changes are valued. Article 5.1.7 (Price determination) provides:

> (1) Where a contract does not fix or make provision for determining the price, the parties are considered, in the absence of any indication to the contrary, to have made reference to the price generally charged at the time of the conclusion of the contract for such performance in comparable circumstances in the trade concerned, or if no such price is available, to a reasonable price.

Thus, if the contract does not provide a mechanism for valuing changes, this article provides the benchmark to assess the evidence submitted in respect of a given item of additional work.

36.15 Summary

Many arbitral awards in the Unilex database highlight the essence of the UP and the ways in which they may be used by parties to international construction contracts, illustrated by the following Arbitrator's comments:

- "The UP are a private codification of civil law, approved by an intergovernmental institution. Although neither treaty, nor compilation of usages, nor standard terms of contract, they are in fact a manifestation of transnational law, as confirmed in the Preamble stating that the Principles 'shall be applied when the parties have agreed that their contract be governed by them' and that they 'may be applied when the parties have agreed that their contract be governed by 'general principles of law', the 'lex mercatoria' or the like'".[56]
- The rules should be applied in the case at hand not only because the relevant rules of contract interpretation of Italian law do not substantially differ from them but also because the UP "represent, at least as far as [contract interpretation] is concerned, a kind of summary of the generally commonly accepted principles on interpretation developed in the Western countries and deriving from the main civil law codes and case law in the international trade."[57]
- "The UNIDROIT Principles of International Commercial Contracts are a reliable source of international commercial law in international arbitration for they

56 www.unilex.info/case.cfm?pid=2&do=case&id=1533&step=Abstract (accessed 11 January 2018).

57 www.unilex.info/case.cfm?pid=2&do=case&id=1427&step=Abstract (accessed 11 January 2018).

'contain in essence a restatement of those '*principes directeurs*' that have enjoyed universal acceptance and, moreover, are at the heart of those most fundamental notions which have consistently been applied in arbitral practice."[58]
- The UP consecrate rules "broadly recognised throughout the world and the practice of international contracts".[59]

If parties to an international construction contract wish to incorporate the international and widely accepted principles of the UP as the governing law of their contract, they would be well advised to make an explicit choice in terms. If they do not make an explicit choice of law, the UP may nevertheless be found by an arbitral tribunal to be governing law of the contract in situations where some of the following apply:

- The parties authorise the tribunal to determine the applicable law, as in Article 21.1 of the 2021 ICC Rules.
- The parties have agreed to use international law, international trade usages, general principles of commercial law or the *lex mercatoria.*
- The parties have made a "negative choice" of the laws of their own jurisdictions.
- There is no common connecting factor such as the parties' domicile, the place of contracting or the place of performance of the contract to make one of the laws of their own jurisdictions appropriate.
- There is no common intention as to the applicable law.
- There is no applicable conflict of laws rule that would determine otherwise.

An arbitral tribunal making such a decision would no doubt draw comfort from the international recognition of the UP by UNCITRAL, from the extensive literature on the UP, and from the considerable number of reported court and arbitration cases which have applied many of the provisions of the UP in a variety of circumstances and jurisdictions.

As a general "contract code" applicable to a wide range of commercial contracts, the UP do not have specific provisions to address most "construction law" issues *per se*, i.e. the issues that are unique to the nature of a construction contract. It is therefore important for the parties to agree, to the greatest extent possible, on the relevant "construction law" to be applied within the ambit of the UP. Conventionally this is done by the terms of the construction contract itself. To the extent that there are gaps in the relevant "construction law" in the construction contract, the UP incorporate a number of general principles that would guide an arbitral tribunal in determining the parties' intentions and the applicable construction law. However, these general principles do not necessarily provide a definitive answer and are not an effective substitute to the parties' prior agreement on the appropriate contract terms.

58 www.unilex.info/case.cfm?pid=2&do=case&id=668&step=Abstract (accessed 11 January 2018).
59 www.unilex.info/case.cfm?pid=2&do=case&id=658&step=Abstract (accessed 11 January 2018).

CHAPTER 37

Final comments

37.1 The construction industry

Construction is an important industry in every country of the world. It is important because it generally represents a significant component of gross national product;[1] it is important because it employs many people: in professional occupations such as engineers, architects, quantity surveyors, project managers and lawyers, in skilled trades such as carpenters, electricians and plumbers, and in less skilled jobs such as labourers.[2] But perhaps most important of all, it provides the infrastructure on which modern life depends: the facilities to mine and process the raw materials into the products of manufacture; the transport infrastructure required to distribute food and every other commodity and manufactured product to their consumers; the energy generation and distribution infrastructure without which modern life would be impossible; the provision of clean water and water treatment facilities essential for health; and the built environment necessary for shelter, manufacturing and commercial operations, and cultural and entertainment facilities.

The significance of the construction industry has been summed up as follows:

> The construction industry has historically been linked with the process of industrialisation and urbanisation, particularly since the advent of the Industrial Revolution. ... Besides its multiplier effect on other sections of the economy, a well devised reconstruction programme of building and community service infrastructure can contribute to sustainable development and protect the natural and built environments.[3]

The construction industry is of particular importance in less developed countries, as it is fundamental to improving health and life expectancy, advancing standards of living and reducing the gap between the living standards of the developed and less developed countries. Multilateral development banks (**MDBs**) have an important role in improving standards of living in less developed countries by funding the infrastructure required by modern societies. MDBs provide the essential finance to enable countries to contract with international contractors. Economic studies have shown that the mean percentage of GDP

1 Construction is one of the largest sectors of the world economy, equivalent to 13% of GDP. Annual expenditure on construction related expenditure is of the order of USD 10 trillion. McKinsey Global Institute, 'Reinventing Construction: A Route to Higher Productivity' (February 2017) 1.

2 The construction industry employs approximately 7% of the global workforce. http://oecdinsights.org/2016/08/22/global-construction-sector-corporate-responsibility/ (accessed 22 April 2021).

3 JP Lopes, RU Oliveira and MI Abreu, "The Construction Industry and the Challenge of the Millennium Development Goals" Conference on Management and Innovation for a Sustainable Built Environment MISBE 2011 https://repository.tudelft.nl/islandora/object/uuid%3A8c0f430b-045a-428a-a188-84575441c605 (accessed 11 January 2018).

DOI: 10.4324/9781003206897-42

in construction increases with increasing GDP per capita,[4] declining only for the countries with the highest GDP per capita (the 'Bon curve').

Lopes and others looked at the impact of the construction industry in achieving the United Nations' Millennium Development Goals (**MDGs**)[5] for Sub-Saharan Africa, and quoted 2009 World Bank figures that demonstrate the importance of the construction industry for less developed countries:

> the estimate for the overall cost to build, maintain and operate Africa's infrastructure is US $93 billion annually over the period 2006–2015, approximately 15% of Sub-Saharan Africa's GDP in 2006. Of this total, about two thirds are for investment and about one third operation and maintenance. In sectoral terms, about 40% is allocated to the power sector. The second-largest component is water and sanitation – a key sector for meeting the MDGs – with about 23% of the total and the third largest share of the cost is associated with transport, which is approximately 20% of the overall spending needs. In terms of regional groups, the burden of the price tag relative to the countries' GDP is markedly different across groups. For middle income countries and resource-rich countries, the amount is in the range of 10% to 13% of their respective GDPs. For low-income countries, as much as 25% of GDP would be needed, and for a particular sub-group of the latter – fragile states (war-ravaged countries), the burden would be an astonishing 37% of GDP.
>
> ...
>
> The WSS [water supply and sewerage] sector, besides its direct effect on the provision of water and sanitation services, has a pervasive effect on other social targets, namely in the prevention of disease, improvement in education and promotion of gender equality so that women save time when they begin using an improved water source. Transport fosters trade by reducing the cost of transporting goods and passengers, reduces child/maternal mortality and improves access to education services. Electricity enhances productivity, eradicates poverty by fostering economic growth and reduces child/maternal mortality.[6]

Construction is a very international industry. The scale of large construction projects, and the time required to construct them provide attractive opportunities for experienced contractors to operate internationally and transfer their skills and technology to other countries.

37.2 Construction contracts

The construction industry around the world is founded on the bedrock of contracts, and the rule of law. As noted by Lord Dyson MR: "Contracts are the cornerstone of commercial life. In principle, construction contracts are no different from any other commercial contracts."[7] The two universal aspects of contract law, irrespective of jurisdiction are: freedom of contract, and *pacta sunt servanda*.

4 Les Ruddock & Jorge Lopes, "The construction sector and economic development: the 'Bon curve'" (2006) 24 *Construction Management and Economics* 717.

5 The MDGs are the world's time-bound and quantified targets for addressing extreme poverty in is many dimensions – poverty, hunger, disease, lack of adequate shelter, and exclusion – while promoting gender equality, education, and environmental sustainability (United Nations Development Program, *UN Millennium Project 2005: Investing in Development – A Practical Guide to Achieve the Millennium Development Goals* (United Nations, New York, 2005).)

6 Ibid.

7 Lord Dyson MR, "The contribution of construction law cases to the development of the common law" (2016) 32 BCL 160.

Freedom of contract means that parties can enter into an agreement for a construction project that is specific to their needs for the particular site, and at the particular point in time. The constraints on that freedom of contract are reasonably well known: the particular statute laws relating to the site, such as protection of the environment, employment of labour, health and safety and property rights; applicable public policy; and the governing law of the contract. Lawyers clearly have an important role to play in drafting contracts that satisfy the relevant legal provisions, can be practically implemented, and in which the legal rights enshrined in them are ultimately enforceable

Pacta sunt servanda means that a party entering into a contract expects that the other contracting party will comply with the contractual obligations it has agreed to. Those contractual obligations are defined, explicitly or implicitly, in the contract. Modern construction contracts for major projects are very detailed documents, often composing a number of lever arch files (or now sometimes a number of gigabytes of data on a hard drive).

In one sense, all of the documents comprising a construction contract are "legal", as they must be construed as a whole to understand the contracting parties' rights and obligations. In a narrower sense, the "legal" documents are in the Conditions of Contract: in a FIDIC Contract in the Contract Agreement, General Conditions and the Particular Conditions for the specific requirements of a particular Contract. These "legal" documents explicitly state the parties' legal rights and obligations, and, implicitly or explicitly, the risk allocation between the parties.

The other documents comprising a modern construction contract could be viewed as "technical" documents: documents that specify the detailed requirements of the scope, and the time, cost and quality requirements of the Contractor's work. These will typically comprise some or all of: the scope of work, technical requirements in the form of drawings and specifications; environmental requirements; health and safety requirements; and other "social" issues such as community involvement and employment and training obligations. These may all be contract documents in the strict legal sense. The differences between learned judges' construction of all the terms of the contract in the *MT Højgaard a/s v E.ON Climate and Renewables UK Robin Rigg East Ltd* cases referred to in Chapter 8 emphasises that construction of the terms of a construction contract is not a trivial task.

A well-written construction contract will not only define the parties' rights and obligations in a way that is clear, unambiguous and legally enforceable, but also detail the parties' obligations in a structured way that constitutes a form of contract management manual. It is worth noting that the 2017 Second Edition of the FIDIC Red, Yellow and Silver Books are significantly longer than the 1999 First Editions, in part because they are more prescriptive in the steps involved in contract management. The following statement in the 2000 FIDIC Contracts Guide is apposite:

> Major projects give rise to major risks, which have to be dealt with if they occur. ... In these events, the claims procedures are specified so as to provide the degree of formality considered necessary for the proper administration of a building or engineering project.[8]

In this writer's view, because a construction contract is a contract management manual as well as a legal document, it is essential for engineers, and project and construction managers

8 Commentary on clause 3.5 (Determinations).

responsible for a construction project, to be familiar with the Contract for that project. Every construction contract is different: each one is specific to a particular facility to be constructed at a certain location on the earth's surface at a certain point in time. Even if the project appears to be the same as a project executed by a construction professional in the past for the same Employer at a similar location, it will not be identical: there will be differences in site conditions, there may be different statutory requirements, the Employer may have changed the Conditions of Contract, or the applicable technologies may have changed. The world does not stand still, and it is therefore imperative for a construction professional to be familiar with the requirements of the specific Contract for the current project.

The contract bedrock of construction projects outlined above also referred to the importance of the rule of law. The principle of *pacta sunt servanda* is meaningless unless there is a mechanism for the enforcement of the bargain that the parties have made in their contract by the courts or arbitration. Neither of these mechanisms is effective in the absence of the rule of law. If, through corruption, judges can be bought, the courts make a mockery of the concept of the rule of law. Apart from the corrosive effects of such corruption on a society in general, absence of the rule of law in a country will inevitably increase the risk for contractors undertaking construction work; a rational contractor will undoubtedly increase its tender price in such a country as recompense for the extra risk, if it is prepared to tender at all.

The risks arising from the lack of the rule of law in certain countries can often be substantially counteracted by the use of international arbitration as the binding method of dispute resolution in a construction contract. The efficacy of international arbitration is underpinned by the principle of freedom of contract, and the *1958 New York Convention on the Recognition and Enforcement of Foreign Arbitral Awards* (*New York Convention*). The principle of freedom of contract means that the parties can choose that their disputes will be determined by arbitration, rather than by litigation in court. With limited exceptions, courts around the world will stay court proceedings commenced in conflict with a properly written arbitration clause. And in those 168 countries that have ratified the *New York Convention*, a competent arbitration award will generally be enforceable by the court. The importance of the *New York Convention* in facilitating international construction contracts can hardly be overstated: without it, the risks of carrying out construction work in some countries would be such as to preclude many reputable international contractors from working there, or they would apply such a large risk premium as to make projects prohibitively expensive.

37.3 Successful construction projects

In this writer's experience, construction projects will be successful if:

- The parties get the contract right before it is executed
- The parties sign the contract before the work commences, and
- The parties execute the contract in accordance with its terms.

Getting the contract right involves a clearly written and unambiguous agreement that not only defines the parties' legal rights and obligations, but also defines the scope of work and the parties' expectations in respect of time, cost and quality in terms acceptable to each of them. If the parties' perceptions of these issues are not aligned because of ambiguity in the contract wording, or because a more powerful party has enforced an unequal bargain, there is a significant risk of a dispute. Lawyers and engineers both have important roles in getting the contract right: lawyers will generally be responsible for drafting the "legal" documents and engineers for drafting the "technical" documents. However, communication between the two is essential to produce a clearly written and unambiguous document that accurately and consistently defines the contract management procedures in a way that supports the subsequent contract administration.

It is important for the contracting parties to sign the contract before work commences so that their rights and obligations are clearly defined. Reducing an agreement to writing is an important discipline; without writing there may well be different perceptions of many aspects of the contractual rights and obligations. In the absence of proof of agreement on the essential terms, there may be no concluded contract, and it would be up to a court to determine any dispute. In this situation, the parties' legal rights may be very different to their assumptions.

If the executed contract properly reflects and clearly articulates the parties' expectations of their rights and obligations, it will also be an effective contract management manual. Execution of such a contract in accordance with its terms will fulfil the parties' expectations, and accordingly they would perceive it as successful. Disputes would not occur in these circumstances. Engineers typically have many roles in the execution of a construction contract, as discussed in detail in Chapter 2.

37.4 Disputes

The real world of course does not always work in this idealistic way. A contract may have ambiguities, it may not be executed, the parties may have different perceptions of their rights and obligations, or the contract may not be executed in accordance with its terms.

The importance of executing the contract in accordance with its terms is encapsulated in the following quote:

> However, if, as is too often the case, the parties ignore the contract on a day to day basis until it proves difficult to find a common understanding, sophisticated and expensive legal solutions have to be worked out and disputes will then become unavoidable.[9]

Given the complexity and scale of major construction projects and the time for their execution, it is not surprising that disputes are common. Accordingly, there is a significant risk of a dispute in any construction contract. It is therefore important for the Contract to provide for the expeditious resolution of disputes in the most efficient and cost-effective manner. In the absence of contractual provisions on dispute resolution, the parties will have to negotiate the form of dispute resolution after a dispute has arisen, or if they cannot agree an appropriate process, they will have to rely on litigation in the courts.

In this writer's view, it is appropriate to provide contractual provisions that promote dispute avoidance (such as a Dispute Board), and a hierarchy of dispute resolution provisions of increasing "formality" to enable disputes to be resolved in the minimum time and at the least cost practically achievable. Generally, the earlier that a dispute can be resolved

9 Axel-Volkmar Jaeger and Götz-Sebastian Hök, *FIDIC – A Guide for Practitioners* (2010) viii.

(even if only provisionally), the more likely it is that the parties can proceed with executing the project, and, importantly, maintain the inter-party communication that is essential for the successful completion of a project. Lack of communication is a recurring theme in many, if not most, failed projects.

Notwithstanding a cooperative working relationship between the contracting parties, contractual procedures for dispute avoidance and a tiered dispute process to resolve disputes cost effectively, some disputes are intractable, and must be finally determined in accordance with the parties' strict legal and contractual rights. The two dispute resolution methods that can provide a final and binding determination are litigation and arbitration. Litigation may be appropriate for a "domestic" dispute (i.e. between parties from the same country) where the court has expertise in the size and technical complexities of construction disputes, such as the Technology and Construction Court in the UK, or the Technology, Engineering and Construction list of the Supreme Court of Victoria.

However, for international construction contracts in which the parties are from different countries, arbitration has overwhelming advantages, not the least of which is enforcement pursuant to the *New York Convention*. The importance of arbitration as the appropriate means of resolving commercial disputes between international parties has long been recognised. For example, in 1975 the European countries, the United States and the Soviet Union, "motivated by the political will, in the interests of peoples, to improve and intensify their relations and to contribute in Europe to peace, security, justice and cooperation as well as to rapprochement among themselves and with the other States of the world",[10] enshrined the following provision on arbitration in the *Helsinki Final Act of 1975*:

> The participating States,
>
> *Considering* that the prompt and equitable settlement of disputes which may arise from commercial transactions relating to goods and services and countries for industrial cooperation would contribute to expanding and facilitating trade and cooperation,
>
> *Considering* that arbitration is an appropriate means of settling such disputes, recommend, where appropriate, to organisations, enterprises and firms in their countries, to include arbitration clauses in commercial contracts and industrial cooperation contracts, or in special agreements;
>
> recommend that the provisions on arbitration should provide for arbitration under a mutually acceptable set of arbitration rules, and permit arbitration in a third country, taking into account existing intergovernmental and other agreements in this field.[11]

37.5 Review

This book has endeavoured to highlight some of the many aspects of the application of contracts to engineering and construction contracts. The important roles that engineers and other construction professionals play was explored in Part 1. Those roles require an understanding of the management of risks including time, cost and quality, and of the particular features of design that distinguish design contracts from construction contracts. The chapters on design and fit for purpose obligations may assist construction lawyers to understand some of the issues confronting design engineers, whilst providing a salutary

10 Conference on Security and Co-Operation in Europe Final Act, Helsinki 1975, 2 www.osce.org/helsinki-final-act (accessed 19 January 2018).

11 Conference on Security and Co-Operation in Europe Final Act, Helsinki 1975, 22 www.osce.org/helsinki-final-act (accessed 19 January 2018).

warning to engineers of the importance of "getting the contract right". Engineers will be interested in the extent to which they can rely on Codes of Practice, and their potential contractual obligations on the important issue of fitness for purpose.

Part 2 looked at a number of the contractual challenges in achieving successful projects. In this author's view, there are usually many advantages in using standard form contracts, rather than bespoke contracts purpose written for a specific project. Standard form contracts are typically more "balanced" than bespoke contracts, in that they are usually founded on the Abrahamson Principles of fair and balanced risk allocation. The chapter on the impact of COVID-19 on construction projects and contracts highlighted unforeseen issues that in some countries were resolved by existing *Civil Codes*, and in others by specific legislation. There are particular challenges in achieving successful megaprojects, which have worse track records of achieving their contractual time, cost and quality goals than lower value projects. The documented performance of many megaprojects shows that the parties did not get the contract right before it was executed, frequently because of inadequate "front-end loading", i.e. inadequate time spent in adequately defining the scope, or setting unrealistically short times for project execution. As the case studies of projects illustrate, inadequate management of the risks of any of time, cost or quality can lead to "failure", and technical quality failures of civil engineering structures can lead to substantial loss of life. Whilst many risks in the execution of construction projects are insured, the chapter on insurance questioned whether the conventional insurance taken out for construction projects in common law jurisdictions is fit for purpose.

The construction industry is renowned for the frequency of disputes. There are various modern contractual approaches to encourage cooperation between the contracting parties that can materially assist in avoiding disputes or minimising the time and cost of resolving disputes that cannot be avoided. Part 3 explored some of these techniques, with particular emphasis on the operation of Dispute Boards. It is worth noting that many recommendations on the most appropriate of skills required for a Dispute Board emphasise the importance of expertise in contracts and efficient dispute resolution (a role typically filled by lawyers), as well as in the technical aspects of the design and construction (a role that typically requires experienced engineers). The time and cost impact of COVID-19 on construction projects will inevitably lead to disputes, which the writer suggests may be best resolved by "jaw-jaw" processes, rather than "war-war". The chapter on the "best" method of resolution of construction disputes concluded that although avoidance of disputes is preferred, the ultimate selection of the "best" method for a particular dispute should ideally be selected after the parameters of the dispute are known, if necessary with the assistance of a Neutral; however, there is no one "best" method of dispute resolution, either for a particular type of dispute, or from a particular protagonist's point of view.

Evaluation and determination methods of dispute resolution require an independent Neutral to consider the facts, the contract and the applicable law, and provide reasons for the decision on the parties' rights and obligations. Construction disputes typically involve the intersection of legal and complex technical issues. Given the specialisation in every branch of engineering, it is not surprising that no single dispute determiner will have the breadth of technical expertise necessary for a full understanding of the technical issues arising in a large or complex construction dispute. Accordingly, experts have an important role to play in the resolution of construction disputes, by assisting lawyers and the dispute determiners to understand complex technical issues in the light of the relevant facts. Engineers have an important role as forensic engineers to determine the causes of failures, and to act as expert witnesses in arbitration hearings or litigation. The guidance in Part 4 on the engagement of forensic engineers and expert witnesses should be of assistance to engineers and other construction professionals undertaking such roles, and to the lawyers briefing them. The chapter on the rules for expert evidence provides a snapshot of current approaches to various aspects of expert evidence, including the overarching obligations of expert witnesses, the substantive and procedural requirements for expert reports, pre-hearing conferences of experts, and concurrent evidence in a hearing. The differences in the requirements for expert evidence between Australia's nine jurisdictions, Singapore and the UK highlights the range of modern approaches to this important issue.

The final Part 5 specifically addresses two issues of international construction law. Is there a common law of construction contracts, a *lex constructionis*? Are the UNIDROIT Principles of International Commercial Contracts applicable and useful for international construction contracts? This author concludes that there is increasing convergence between construction law in different legal systems, and, importantly, there is often widespread agreement as to the just outcome in a given situation, even though the routes to get there are different. The use of an internationally accepted standard form contract such as FIDIC, international arbitration as the final method of dispute resolution, and the application of the UNIDROIT Principles or the TransLex Principles as the governing law of the contract provides perhaps the closest approach to a truly international construction contract that is not subject to the vagaries of particular jurisdictions.

This book is a collection of papers written on a variety of topics, at different times, and for a variety of audiences. As the title indicates, it explores a number of facets of the application of contracts to engineering and construction projects. If it assists engineers to better understand the role of contracts in their work and their necessary interaction with lawyers, and lawyers to be more aware of engineers' roles in the successful execution of construction projects, it will have achieved the aim of furthering the inter-disciplinary cooperation and communication that is essential to project success. The construction industry is very important to the world economy, and all citizens have an interest in a successful construction industry that provides quality and affordable infrastructure. If, in some small way, this book makes a positive contribution to the success of that industry, the author's efforts will be amply rewarded.

GLOSSARY

Term	*Meaning*	*Defined in Section*
Abrahamson Principles	Principles of fair and balanced risk allocation, articulated in Max W Abrahamson, 'Risk Management' (1983) *International Construction Law Review* 241, 244.	**¶4.7.1**
ACE	Association of Consulting Engineers (UK).	
ACTSC	Supreme Court of the Australian Capital Territory.	**¶34.2**
adjudication	A method of dispute resolution in which an independent **Adjudicatoe** resolves the dispute by providing a provisionally binding determination of the parties' contractual rights following an impartial assessment of the parties' submissions and other evidence.[a]	**¶25.2**
Adjudicator	The independent person (**Neutral**) who carries out an **adjudication**.	**¶25.2**
ADR	Alternative dispute resolution.	**¶1.4**
ADR clause	An agreement by the contracting parties to adopt a specific form of **ADR** in the event of, or on the occurrence of, a dispute, and the contractual consequences of the decision of the independent **Neutral**.	**¶25.5**
APH	Australian Parliament House in Canberra.	**¶15.1**
Architect	See **Engineer**.	**¶2.1**
AS	Australian Standard.	**¶11.3.1**
ASCE	American Society of Civil Engineers.	**¶3.6**
Authority	Lower Yarra Crossing Authority.	**¶22.2.1**
balance of representation	In the context of writing an Australian Standard, balance of representation means: "The membership of a Standards Australia Committee is formally balanced as part of the constitution of the Committee to represent the broadest possible spectrum of stakeholder interests."	**¶10.2**
BCA	Building Code of Australia.	**¶10.3**

(*Continued*)

(*Continued*)

Term	*Meaning*	*Defined in Section*
Blue-Green Book	**FIDIC** Form of Contract for Dredging and Reclamation Works – First Edition 2006, Second Edition 2016.	**¶11.3.1**
bouleversement de l'économie du contrat	Contractual equilibrium (France).	**¶12.5.5**
BWE	Bucket wheel excavator.	**¶10.8.1**
CAR	Contractor's All Risks (insurance policy).	**¶23.3.2**
CDB	Combined Dispute Board. A **Dispute Board** under the ICC Dispute Board Rules that is primarily a **DRB**, but can be a **DAB** if the parties choose.	**¶25.5**
CDM	*Construction (Design and Management) Regulations 1994* (UK).	**¶20.8.4**
CISG	*United Nations Convention on Contracts for the International Sale of Goods*. Also known as the *Vienna Convention.*	**¶36.12**
clean expert	An independent **expert** who is not a member of the legal team.	**¶31.3**
Code	See **Code of Practice**.	**¶10.2.1**
Code of Practice	"A publication describing good practice. It does not have the force of law unless quoted as having such in the relevant regulations."[b]	**¶10.2.1**
Concept Design Drawings	Drawings of the design prepared by Leighton Contractors Pty Ltd for the Bass Highway project and included in its tender submitted to the State of Tasmania.	**¶17.3**
consensus	In the context of writing an Australian Standard: "General agreement, characterised by the absence of sustained opposition to substantial issues by any important part of the concerned interests and by a process that involves seeking to take into account the views of all parties concerned and to reconcile any conflicting arguments."[c]	**¶10.2**
contract	A legally binding agreement in which each party accepts obligations in exchange for rights granted by the other party in order to achieve the contract objective.	**¶4.2**
Contract	The **construction contract** being referred to.	**¶1.1**
Contract Administrator	The **Engineer** or Employer's Representative administering a **FIDIC** contract.	**¶29.6.2**
Contract E	The work of completion and erection of the steel spans of the West Gate bridge under a "cost plus" labour management contract, not including fabrication and subassemblies of the steel boxes.	**¶22.2.2**

(*Continued*)

(*Continued*)

Term	*Meaning*	*Defined in Section*
Contract S	The original contract for fabrication and erection of the steel box girder spans of the West Gate bridge.	**¶22.2.2**
Contractor	The party to a **construction contract** (the **Contract**) who carries out the work.	**¶1.1**
construction contract	Any contract where one person (including a corporation) agrees for valuable consideration to carry out construction of a physical structure (including building or engineering works) for another.	**¶1.1**
construction failures	Failures of buildings or engineered facilities that involve collapse of structures or result in loss of life.	**¶20.1**
Construction Manager	The **Contractor** in a construction management contract who has contractual responsibility for programming and coordinating the design and construction activities.	**¶5.6**
contractual adjudication	**Adjudication** of a dispute pursuant to the parties' agreement to implement the agreed procedure in a contract.	**¶25.2**
contractual expectations	The contracting parties' expectations of their rights and obligations based on the terms of the contract, objectively determined.	**¶4.2**
COVID-19 requirements	COVID-19 specific mandatory requirements introduced by governments.	**¶12.3**
CRB	Country Roads Board (Victoria).	**¶16.3.1**
CRW	CRW Joint Operation - a tripartite joint operation established under the laws of the Republic of Indonesia, comprising three Indonesian contractor companies. One of the parties in the Singapore High Court and Singapore Court of Appeal cases between PT Perusahaan Gas Negara (Persero) TBK and CRW Joint Operation.	**¶27.4.2**
CTR	Cost, time and resources schedule, a formal tool to plan, manage and report cost, time and resources on a task by task basis in a consulting engineer's assignment.	**¶31.6.1**
CTV	Building in Christchurch that collapsed in the February 2011 earthquake, with the loss of 115 lives.	**¶18.1**
D&C	Design and construct (contract).	**¶26.2**
DAAB	A **Dispute Avoidance/Adjudication Board.**	**¶24.5**
DAB	A **Dispute Adjudication Board**.	**¶24.5**
DB	A **Dispute Board**.	**¶25.4**
DCM	Design, construct and maintain (contract).	**¶26.2**

(*Continued*)

(*Continued*)

Term	*Meaning*	*Defined in Section*
DCOM	Design, construct operate and maintain (contract).	**¶26.2**
design	All plans, drawings, sketches, instructions, and descriptions that determine the way the **Works** (or parts of it) are to be constructed. Design includes the writing or selection of specifications as well as the production of plans and drawings and any element of choice on the part of the designer, such as requirements as to materials or working methods.	**¶5.2**
design contract	A contract for the preparation of a **design** to be constructed under a **construction contract**.	**¶1.1**
design life	The **expected service life** that results from the **design** process.	**¶7.9**
design working life	"Duration of the period during which a structural element, when designed, is assumed to perform for its intended purpose with expected maintenance but without major structural repair being necessary."[d]	**¶7.9**
design parameters	The required functions, **service life** and assumptions made for the design of a **facility**.	**¶7.2**
determination	A category of **DR** in which a **Neutral** assesses the facts and the law in relation to a specific dispute and provides a reasoned determination on how the dispute is to be resolved according to the parties' legal rights. Determination methods include binding **expert determination,** arbitration and litigation.	**¶30.2**
DIER	Department of Infrastructure, Energy and Resources, Tasmania.	**¶17.1**
Direction	The instruction issued to the Contractor on behalf of the DIER to design and build the Bass Highway in cut 1.5m deep opposite Hagley House.	**¶17.1**
dirty expert	An expert consultant who is a member of the legal team.	**¶31.3**
Dispute Avoidance/ Adjudication Board	A standing **Dispute Board** appointed under a 2017 **FIDIC** Contract to assist the parties in avoiding disputes, and to provide a provisionally binding decision on a dispute referred to it; if neither party issues a notice of dissatisfaction within a defined time, the decision becomes final and binding.	**¶24.5**

(*Continued*)

(*Continued*)

Term	*Meaning*	*Defined in Section*
Dispute Adjudication Board	A **Dispute Board** that provides a provisionally binding decision on a dispute referred to it; if neither party issues a notice of dissatisfaction within a defined time, the decision becomes final and binding.	**¶24.5**
Dispute Board	A panel of one or three suitably qualified and experienced independent persons appointed under the **Contract** to be available to confer with the parties to assist in the avoidance of disputes or if necessary, to provide a determination of a dispute referred to it. A Dispute Board may be a **Dispute Avoidance/ Adjudication Board (DAAB)**, a **Dispute Adjudication Board (DAB)**, a **Dispute Review Board (DRB)** or a **Dispute Resolution Board (DRB)**.	**¶25.4**
Dispute Board clause	The clause in the **Contract** between **Employer** and **Contractor** in which they agree to use a **Dispute Board** to recommend a resolution of, or resolve a dispute between them.	**¶26.2**
Dispute Resolution Board	A **Dispute Board** that provides a non-binding decision on a dispute referred to it.	**¶25.4**
Dispute Review Board	A **Dispute Board** that provides a non-binding decision on a dispute referred to it.	**¶25.4**
DNV	Det Norske Veritas – an international accredited registrar and classification society headquartered in Norway.	**¶7.10**
DPEMP	Development Proposal and Environmental Management Plan for a new 13.65km section of the Bass Highway in northern Tasmania, bypassing the towns of Hagley and Westbury.	**¶17.2**
DR	Dispute resolution.	**¶30.1**
DRB	A **Dispute Resolution Board** or **Dispute Review Board**.	**¶25.4**
DRBA	Dispute Resolution Board Australasia Inc (Region 3 of the **DRBF**).	**¶26.4**
DRBF	Dispute Resolution Board Foundation.	**¶26.1**
ductility	Ductility or ductile behaviour of a member or connection is the ability to deform without losing strength above the point where the member or connection is unable to sustain increased load.	**¶7.7**
ECC	**NEC** Engineering and Construction Contract.	**¶2.3**
ECI	Early Contractor Involvement.	**¶26.2**
EFCA	European Federation of Engineering Consultancy Associations.	**¶5.24**

(*Continued*)

(Continued)

Term	*Meaning*	*Defined in Section*
Emerald Book	**FIDIC** Conditions of Contract for Underground Works, First Edition 2019.	**¶11.3.1**
Employer	The party to a **construction contract** (the **Contract**) for whom the work is done. Also referred to as the Principal or sometimes the Owner.	**¶1.1**
engineer	The person/entity providing one or more "engineering" (including project management) services in relation to one or more aspects of a construction project, such obligations being defined under the engineer's contract with the **Employer**.	**¶2.3**
Engineer	The person, firm, or company that administers the **Contract** as defined in the **Contract**. The term is synonymous with Architect or Superintendent as used in certain contracts.	**¶1.1**
Environmental Documents	Hagley **DPEMP** and Westbury **DPEMP** for the Bass Highway project.	**¶17.4**
EOT	Extension of time.	**¶4.7**
EPC contract	Engineer, procure and construct contract. A construction contract (also referred to as a turnkey contract) in which the **Contractor** takes total responsibility for the engineering (design), procurement and construction, and provides a fully equipped facility ready for operation (at the "turn of the key").	**¶4.11**
EPCM contract	A construction contract in which the **Contractor**, as **Construction Manager**, designs, procures and manages the construction as agent of the **Employer**.	**¶4.11**
evaluation	A category of **ADR** in which a **Neutral** evaluates the parties' rights in a dispute and (generally) provides a reasoned decision of how the dispute should be resolved according to the parties' legal rights under the relevant contract and otherwise according to law. Evaluation methods include early neutral evaluation, mini-trial and **adjudication** (both statutory and contractual).	**¶30.2**
ex aequo et bono	Latin for "according to the right and good" or "from equity and conscience". An Arbitrator authorised to act *ex aqueo et bono* has the power to dispense with strict consideration of the law and consider solely what they consider to be fair and equitable in the circumstances.	
expected service life	The **service life** expected to be achieved by a **facility**.	**¶7.8**

(Continued)

(*Continued*)

Term	*Meaning*	*Defined in Section*
Expert	The **Neutral** who conducts an **expert determination**.	**¶25.3**
expert	An **expert witness**.	
expert determination	A method of dispute resolution in which an independent impartial **expert** is engaged by the disputing parties to determine those disputed questions of fact and/or law in the reference defined by the parties.[e]	**¶25.3**
expert witness	A witness that gives evidence of his or her opinion based on his/her specialised knowledge acquired from training, study or experience.	**¶32.2**
experts' conference	A pre-hearing meeting of **experts**, usually without lawyers, at which the **experts** attempt to find common ground in their respective opinions, in order to narrow their differences, and thereby reduce the extent of issues which require evidence at the hearing.	**¶32.5.1**
E.ON	The **Employer** in *MT Højgaard a/s and E.ON Climate and Renewables UK Robin Rigg East Limited* [2014] EWHC 1088 (TCC); *MT Højgaard a/s and E.ON Climate and Renewables UK Robin Rigg East Limited* [2015] EWCA Civ 407; and *MT Højgaard a/s and E.ON Climate and Renewables UK Robin Rigg East Limited* [2017] UKSC 59.	**¶8.2**
facilitation	A category of **ADR** in which a **Neutral** endeavours to facilitate the parties' own resolution of their dispute, but does not impose a solution on them. Facilitation methods include mediation, conciliation and non-binding **expert determination**.	**¶30.2**
facility	A building, infrastructure, structures and equipment for the extraction of natural resources or the processing of natural resources into manufactured products etc.	**¶7.2**
failure	"An unacceptable difference between expected and observed performance."[f]	**¶3.5**
fast track construction	Starting construction before the **design** is complete.	**¶3.1.2**
FCA	Federal Court of Australia.	**¶34.2**
FIDIC	International Federation of Consulting Engineers (Fédération Internationale des Ingénieurs-Conseils).	**¶1.2**

(*Continued*)

(*Continued*)

Term	*Meaning*	*Defined in Section*
final design cost risk	The risk that the final "for construction" **design** will cost more to construct than the preliminary **design** that was used to price the **construction contract** tender.	**¶9.2.2**
forensic engineer	An **engineer** who practices **forensic engineering**.	**¶31.2**
forensic engineering	"The application of the art and science of engineering in the jurisprudence system, requiring the services of appropriately qualified [and experienced] professional engineers."[g]	**¶31.2**
front end loading	The period in which the scope and execution detail of a project are defined before a final investment decision is made.	**¶13.5.1**
garantie décennale	**Decennial liability** (French).	**¶23.5.2**
Gold Book	**FIDIC** Conditions of Contract for Design, Build and Operate Projects - First Edition, 2008.	**¶11.3.1**
Goonyella case	*BHP Coal Pty Ltd and Ors v O & K Orenstein & Koppel AG* [2008] QSC 141.	**¶10.8.1**
GPN-EXPT	Expert Evidence Practice Note issued by the Chief Justice of the Federal Court of Australia, dated 25 October 2016.	**¶34.4**
Green Book	**FIDIC** Short Form of Contract First Edition – First Edition 1999.	**¶11.3.1**
Hagley DPEMP	Development Proposal and Environmental Management Plan for the Bass Highway Hagley bypass.	**¶17.2**
HGCRA	*Housing Grants, Construction and Regeneration Act* 1996 (UK).	**¶25.2**
hot tub	An evidence session in a court or arbitration hearing in which the **experts** giving evidence on the same issues to do so in a concurrent session.	**¶32.5.5**
IAA	*Singapore International Arbitration Act.*	**¶27.4.5**
ICC	International Chamber of Commerce.	**¶25.5**
ICE	Institution of Civil Engineers.	**¶2.2**
IChemE	Institution of Chemical Engineers.	**¶4.12**
ICSID	International Centre for the Settlement of Disputes	**¶36.9**
imprévision	The Contractor's right to indemnification when there is a major change in economic factors existing at the time of contracting and which destroys the contractual equilibrium (France).	**¶12.5.5**
Inquiry	The panel (comprising a QC and two engineers) appointed by the Government to conduct a public inquiry into the collapse of the Ronan Point tower block.	**¶20.8.1**
IP	Intellectual property.	**¶5.2.1**

(*Continued*)

(*Continued*)

Term	*Meaning*	*Defined in Section*
ISO	International Organisation for Standardisation.	**¶10.2.2**
ITT	Invitation to Tender for the design, construction and maintenance for 10 years of a 13.65km section of the Bass Highway in northern Tasmania.	**¶17.3**
JHC	John Holland (Constructions) Pty Ltd, the second erection contractor for the West Gate bridge.	**¶22.2.2**
JICA	Japan International Cooperation Agency.	**¶4.7.3**
J101	Det Norske Veritas Standard DNV-OS-J101 Design of Offshore Wind Turbine Structures.	**¶8.2**
KSBD	Kings Street Bridge Design Limited – the design subcontractor for Kings Bridge in Melbourne.	**¶16.3.1**
lex constructionis	The international law of construction in jurisdictions subject to the rule of law and which recognise the parties' freedom of contract.	**¶35.6.1**
lex mercatoria	The law merchant. (Latin)	**¶35.6.1**
MDBs	Multilateral development banks.	**¶3.1.1**
MDGs	Millenium Development Goals.	**¶37.1**
MEAT	Most economically advantageous tender for public procurement in *European Union Directive 2014/24/EU* Article 67.	**¶5.2.4**
MT Højgaard	The **Contractor** in *MT Højgaard a/s and E.ON Climate and Renewables UK Robin Rigg East Limited* [2014] EWHC 1088 (TCC); *MT Højgaard a/s and E.ON Climate and Renewables UK Robin Rigg East Limited* [2015] EWCA Civ 407; and *MT Højgaard a/s and E.ON Climate and Renewables UK Robin Rigg East Limited* [2017] UKSC 59.	**¶8.2**
MVC	Mersey Valley Council.	**¶17.3**
NCC	National Construction Code (Australia).	**¶10.3**
NCDC	National Capital Development Commission	**¶15.3.1**
NCST	*National Construction Safety Team Act 2002* (USA).	**¶20.4**
NEC	The New Engineering Contract published by the Institution of Civil Engineers.	**¶2.2**
Neutral	An independent third-party who provides **ADR** services to disputing parties, in one of the categories of **facilitation**, **evaluation** or **determination**.	**¶30.2**
New York Convention	*United Nations 1958 New York Convention on the Recognition and Enforcement of Foreign Arbitral Awards.*	**¶29.4**

(*Continued*)

(*Continued*)

Term	*Meaning*	*Defined in Section*
NIST	National Institute of Standards and Technology (USA).	**¶20.4**
NOD	Notice of dissatisfaction issued under sub-clause 20.4 (sub-clause 21.4 of the 2017 Second Editions) of one of the **FIDIC rainbow suite** contracts.	**¶27.2**
NPWC3	National Public Works Contract 1981.	**¶2.8**
NSL	Natural surface level.	**¶17.1**
NSWSC	Supreme Court of New South Wales	**¶34.2**
NTSB	National Transportation Safety Board (USA).	**¶20.4**
NTSC	Supreme Court of the Northern Territory.	**¶34.2**
O&K	O & K Orenstein & Koppel AG.	**¶10.8.1**
OSHA	Occupational Health and Safety Administration (USA).	**¶20.11**
Owner	See **Employer**.	
pacta sunt servanda	A Latin phrase that means that agreements are to be kept.	**¶35.1**
parties	The parties to a **contract**.	**¶1.1**
personal IP	**IP** in the form of knowledge, experience and skill possessed by an individual.	**¶5.3**
PGC	Building in Christchurch that collapsed in the February 2011 earthquake, with the loss of 18 lives.	**¶18.1**
PGN	PT Perusahaan Gas Negara (Persero) TBK, a public listed State owned company established under the laws of the Republic of Indonesia. One of the parties in the Singapore High Court and Singapore Court of Appeal cases between PT Perusahaan Gas Negara (Persero) TBK and CRW Joint Operation.	**¶27.4.2**
PGN Contract	The contract between **PGN** and **CRW** to design, procure, install, test and pre-commission a gas pipeline project in Indonesia.	**¶27.4.2**
PHCA	Parliament House Construction Authority.	**¶15.1**
Phoenix	Phoenix Bridge Company, design and construct contractor for the Quebec bridge.	**¶21.2**
PI insurance	Professional Indemnity insurance.	**¶5.6.9**
Pink Book	**FIDIC** Conditions of Contract for Construction MDB Harmonised Edition for Building and Engineering Works Designed by the Employer – Version 1: 2005, Version 2: 2006, Version 3: 2010.	**¶11.3.1**
PPE	Personal protective equipment.	**¶12.2**
Principal	See **Employer**.	
procedural rules	The rules in the **Contract** and the **tripartite agreement** defining the operations of the **Dispute Board**.	**¶26.2**

(*Continued*)

(*Continued*)

Term	*Meaning*	*Defined in Section*
Project Deed	The Contract between the State of Tasmania and Leighton Contractors Pty Ltd to design, construct and maintain for 10 years a 13.65km section of road in northern Tasmania, including bypasses of the towns of Hagley and Westbury.	**¶17.1**
QA	**Quality assurance**.	**¶3.1**
QBRC	Quebec Bridge and Railway Company.	**¶21.2**
QBS	Quality Based Selection.	**¶5.2.4**
QC	Quality control.	**¶3.1**
QMS	Quality management system.	**¶31.4.3**
QSC	Supreme Court of Queensland.	**¶34.2**
quality	The attributes the client is prepared to pay for.	**¶3.1**
quality assurance	A formalised process of recording conformance with a documented set of procedures that specify the steps to be followed to achieve a **quality** product.	**¶3.1**
rainbow suite	The construction contracts published by **FIDIC**: **Red Book** **Pink Book** **Yellow Book** **Silver Book**	**¶25.4**
rebus sic stantibus	Doctrine or rules relating to changed conditions. (Latin).	**¶12.5.5.**
Red Book	**FIDIC** Conditions of Contract for Construction for Building and Engineering Works Designed by the Employer. (First Edition 1999)/(Second Edition 2017).	**¶11.3.1**
redundancy	Multiple load paths in a structure that can transmit forces to the ground.	**¶7.7**
reliability	The probability that a system will perform its intended function for a specific period of time under a given set of conditions. Reliability is also the probability that unsatisfactory performance or failure will not occur.	**¶7.5**
Report	NZ, Canterbury Earthquakes Royal Commission, *Final Report* (2012).	**¶18.1**
required service life	The **service life** desired by the owner.	**¶7.8**
Response Tracker	Coronavirus Government Response Tracker prepared by the Blavatnik School of Government at the University of Oxford.	**¶12.1**
risk	"The chance of something happening that will have an impact on objectives".[h]	**¶4.5**
risk event	An event that, if it occurs, has an impact on fulfilment of the contractual objectives.	**¶4.5**

(*Continued*)

(*Continued*)

Term	*Meaning*	*Defined in Section*
Rome I	*Regulation (EC) No 593/2008* of the European Parliament and of the Council of 17 June 2008 on the law applicable to contractual obligations.	**¶36.3**
SASC	Supreme Court of South Australia.	**¶34.2**
serviceability limit state	The limit state of a structure that corresponds to conditions beyond which specified service criteria are no longer met. These criteria are based on the intended use and may include limits on deformation, vibratory response, degradation or other physical aspects.	**¶7.6**
SCOSS	Standing Committee on Structural Safety (UK).	**¶20.8.4**
service life	The period of time that a **facility** is in functional operation.	**¶7.8**
SfIR	Scope for Improvement Reports: Blake Dawson Waldron Lawyers, *Scope for Improvement: A Survey of Pressure Points in Australian Construction and Infrastructure Projects* (2006); Blake Dawson, *Scope for Improvement 2008: A Report on Scoping Practices in Australian and Infrastructure Projects* (2008); Blake Dawson, *Scope for Improvement 2011: Project Risk — Getting the Right Balance and Outcomes* (2011); Ashurst Australia, *Scope for Improvement 2014: Project Pressure Points — Where Industry Stands* (2014).	**¶13.3**
Silver Book	**FIDIC** Conditions of Contract for EPC/Turnkey Projects (First Edition 1999)/(Second Edition 2017).	**¶10.4**
Singapore Convention	*United Nations 2019 Convention on International Settlement Agreements Resulting from Mediation*	**¶29.4**
SLS	See **serviceability limit state.**	
SOW&TC	Scope of Works and Technical Criteria for the Bass Highway project, provided to tenderers and amended during the tender period.	**¶17.3**
SPH	Scottish Parliament House in Edinburgh.	**¶15.1**
Standard	Sets "out certain tests, dimensions, tolerances and qualities for a product or process. Historically in certain areas, e.g. structures, they have set out prescribed methods for specific calculations and even prescribe permissible stresses. More recently these kinds of standards have become normative".[i]	**¶10.2.1**

(*Continued*)

(*Continued*)

Term	*Meaning*	*Defined in Section*
stare decisis	The decision stands (Latin). The common law doctrine that a court is bound to follow earlier decisions on the same law, unless they are inconsistent with a higher court decision or are wrong in law.	**¶35.6.3.1**
state of the art	The art and science that would be applied by competent and experienced practitioners involved in the relevant practice of engineering, not necessarily the science of engineering as known to academics researching at the cutting edge of known technology.	**¶7.2**
statutory adjudication	**Adjudication** of a dispute pursuant to the requirements of legislation.	**¶25.2**
Stringency Index	An index of government activity based on eight containment and closure policies adopted by governments to respond to the COVID-19 pandemic, prepared by the Blavatnik School of Government at the University of Oxford.	**¶12.1**
structural reliability index	A number quantifying the **reliability** of structural elements.	**¶7.5**
structural robustness	The ability of a structure to withstand events like explosion, fire, impact or consequences of human errors, without being damaged to an extent disproportionate to the original cause.	**¶7.7**
successful contract	A contract in which the contractual expectations are fulfilled by the actual performance of the contractual obligations, and there are no issues arising between the contracting parties that have to be resolved judicially by an independent tribunal, external to the contracting parties.	**¶4.4**
sujétions imprévues	Technical difficulties of an unforeseeable nature and of sufficient magnitude to fundamentally affect the contractor's performance (France).	**¶12.5.2**
Superintendent	See **Engineer**.	
T5	Heathrow Terminal 5.	**¶23.5.1**
THC	Tasmanian Heritage Commission.	**¶17.10**
TR	Technical Requirements.	**¶7.10**
transparency	In the context of writing an Australian Standard, transparency means: "that information on current work programs and proposals is available to all interested parties. Transparency also includes the concept of openness, participation on a non-discriminatory basis, impartiality and a balanced participation in the development process by interests that will be significantly affected by the final Standard."[j]	**¶10.1**

(*Continued*)

(*Continued*)

Term	*Meaning*	*Defined in Section*
tripartite agreement	An agreement between the **Employer**, **Contractor** and a **Dispute Board** that defines the Dispute Board's scope of work, responsibilities, the duration of services, compensation and reimbursement for services, and legal relations.	**¶26.2.7**
TSC	Supreme Court of Tasmania.	**¶34.2**
turnkey contract	See **EPC contract**.	
UKCS	UK continental shelf.	**¶11.4**
ULS	See **ultimate limit state.**	
ultimate limit state	The limit state of a structure at incipient collapse.	**¶7.6**
UNCITRAL	United Nations Commission on International Trade Law.	**¶29.4**
unforeseen final cost	Any excess cost of construction arising from materialisation of **final design cost risk**.	**¶9.2.2**
UNIDROIT	International Institute for the Unification of Private Law.	**¶35.9.1.1**
UP	UNIDROIT Principles of International Commercial Contracts.	**¶35.9.1.2**
Utah	Utah Australia Limited – design and construct contractor for Kings Bridge in Melbourne.	**¶16.3.1**
VSC	Supreme Court of Victoria.	**¶34.2**
WASC	Supreme Court of Western Australia.	**¶34.2**
Westbury DPEMP	Development Proposal and Environmental Management Plan for the Bass Highway Westbury bypass.	**¶17.2**
White Book	**FIDIC** Client/Consultant Model Services Agreement (5th ed 2017)/(4th ed 2006).	**¶5.5**
Works	The work, materials and plant which the **Contractor** is or may be required to carry out and complete or provide under the **Contract**, and includes variations, rectification of defects, temporary works and equipment.	**¶27.2**
Yellow Book	**FIDIC** Conditions of Contract for Plant and Design-Build for Electrical and Mechanical Plant and for Building and Engineering Works, designed by the Contractor (First Edition 1999)/(Second Edition 2017).	**¶10.4**

[a] Philip Loots and Donald Charrett, *Practical Guide to Engineering and Construction Contracts* (2009) 362.
[b] David Blockley, *The New Penguin Dictionary of Civil Engineering* (Penguin Books Ltd London, 2005) 88.
[c] Standards Australia: www.standards.org.au
[d] Australian Standard AS1170.0:2002 Structural design actions Part 0: General Principles.
[e] Philip Loots and Donald Charrett, *Practical Guide to Engineering and Construction Contracts* (2009) 368.
[f] G A Leonards "Investigation of Structural Failures" (1982) No GT2 (February) *Journal of the Geotechnical Engineering Division (ASCE)* 108
[g] Peter Campbell (ed), *Learning from Construction Failures: Applied Forensic Engineering* (2001) 2.
[h] AS/NZS 4360:2004 Risk Management
[i] David Blockley, *The New Penguin Dictionary of Civil Engineering* (Penguin Books Ltd London, 2005) 442.
[j] Ibid.

INDEX

Made in the USA
Monee, IL
13 September 2026

62977681R10317